Paraguay

Other Places Travel Guides
Paraguay

Romy Natalia Goldberg

Published by
OTHER PLACES PUBLISHING

First edition
Published August 2012

Paraguay
Other Places Travel Guide

Written by: Romy Natalia Goldberg
Edited by Nicole Arriaga

Cover designed by: Carla Zetina-Yglesias
Front cover photo by: Ricardo Brickman
Back cover photo of monkey and the photo of trees by: Emily Horton Reilly
Back cover photo of woman by: Junior Ortiz, courtesy of Ahecha Paraguay National Exhibit, 2009

Published by:
Other Places Publishing
www.otherplacespublishing.com

All text, illustrations and artwork copyright
© 2012 Other Places Publishing

ISBN 978-1-935850-11-3

About the Author

The daughter of a Paraguayan mother and American father (a Peace Corps Volunteer who served in Paraguay), Natalia spent most of her childhood living in and traveling throughout Latin America. As a child she often played "guide book author" with her sister, who would pretend to be a hotel owner. From an early age she visited Paraguay frequently, soaking up the country's unique traditions, marveling at the beautiful landscapes and eating plenty of *chipa*. In writing this guidebook she hopes to share the country she knows and loves with fellow travelers. Natalia writes the bilingual blog *Discovering Paraguay* (*www.discoveringparaguay.com*) and currently lives in Paraguay with her husband and twin daughters.

Este libro está dedicado a Tía Nuni, la mujer más paraguaya que conozco. ¡Nde guapa!

Acknowledgements

First and foremost, I would like to acknowledge my family, Alex Little, Robert and Carmen Goldberg, Adriana Goldberg, Sara and Art Little, Alicia Little, Mia and Sienna. Words cannot express how thankful I am for your support. I could not have done this without you.

This book would not have been possible without the help and friendship of Paraguay's Peace Corps community, in particular the members of G-25, 26, 27 and 28, who were always willing to share their homes, experiences, and *tereré* with me. Special thanks to Gariety Pruitt, Carin Paupore, Alizabeth Brady, Brigitta Mast, Adam Drolett, Fred McClelland, Anne Kenney, Mary Cinadr, Anthony Fierstos, Nathan Antonio, Travis Long, Mandy Horvath, Joan Ngo, Emily Horton, Alistair Kerlin, Kevin Pierce, Krisin Tanis, Eric Murphy, Betsy Curry, Courtney Wong, Austin Durr, Adam Poinsett Hall, Eric Morrison, Jesús del Rosario, John Robinson, Brad Vanderford, Manuel Colón, Ricardo Brickman, and to Ashley McPhee for her editing assistance.

I also owe a huge thanks to my Paraguayan friends and family for sharing their insights into Paraguay's fascinating culture: Ana María del Castillo, Oscar and Luchi Brítez, José María and Nuni Gerez, Margarita Sotelo, Enrique and Ida Rodriguez, Juan Ramón and Mercedes Fleitas Colmán. *¡Mil gracias por su apoyo y por compartir conmigo la belleza de la cultura paraguaya!*

Thanks as well to Paul Smith, Patrick Wilson, Craig Anthony Rychel, Saúl Árias, and David Donmoyer.

And to my wonderful Guaraní teacher Mariela Gonzalez, *¡Graciamante!*

QUICK REFERENCE

Since most travel throughout Paraguay is done by bus or automobile, this book has been organized around Paraguay's highway system. There is also a chapter on the Paraguay River, another transportation route. For Routes 1, 2, 3, and the Trans-Chaco Highway, directions are listed with Asunción as your starting point. Meanwhile, listings along the Paraguay River begin with travel downriver.

Prices in this book are in Paraguayan Guaranies (Gs), the national currency for Paraguay, unless specifically given in U.S. Dollars.

Currency: Guaraní

Exchange Rates at time of publication:

1 USD = Gs 4,300

1 Euro = Gs 5,657

Electricity: Paraguay accommodates 220V

Hours of operation:

Government offices tend to open from 7am to 1pm while businesses such as supermarkets and cyber cafés open from 9am to about 6pm. Many businesses break in the middle of the day for a *siesta* (this practice is more common in rural areas than in urban ones). The majority of small businesses remain closed on Sundays. As many smaller stores are connected to people's houses, it is worth ringing the doorbell if you are in need of immediate assistance or goods, even if the sign says they are closed (*cerrado*).

Climate: Tropical to Subtropical

Administrative Regions (Departments): Central, Cordillera, Paraguarí, Ñeembucú, Misiones, Itapúa, Caaguazú, Alto Paraguay, Alto Paraná, Amambay, Canindeyú, San Pedro, Concepción, Presidente Hayes, Boquerón, Caazapá, Guairá

Neighboring Countries: Argentina, Brazil, Bolivia

Capital: Asunción

Population: 6,068,000

Official Languages: Spanish and Guaraní

Area: 406,752 km^2 (157,048 mi^2) – approximately the size of California

Religion: Majority Roman Catholic

Type of Government: Republic with presidential elections held every five years.

Population makeup: mixed race (*mestizos*), immigrant colonies, indigenous (for more, see Paraguay's People on page 36)

Time zone: GMT-4 (GMT-3 during summertime daylight savings)

Calling Paraguay: Landline: 595 (country code) + local number. Cell phone: 595 + cell phone number (omitting 0 from start of the cell phone number)

Calling internationally from Paraguay: Landline: 002 + international country code. Cell phone: plus sign + international country code (on most cell phones press the * key twice to dial the plus sign)

Texting internationally: plus sign (+) and international country code

Calendar of Holidays & Festivities

January 1st: Año Nuevo (New Year's Day) *Official Holiday*

January 6th: Día de los Reyes Magos (Three Kings Day)

February 3rd: Día de San Blas (Feast of St. Blaise)

February/March (dates vary): Carnaval (Carnival)

March 1st: Día de los Héroes *Official Holiday*

March/April (dates vary): Semana Santa (Easter/Holy Week); Jueves Santo and Viernes Santo (Holy Thursday and Good Friday) *Official Holidays*

May 1st: Día del Trabajador (Labor day) *Official Holiday*

May 15th: Día de la Independencia Nacional (Independence Day) *Official Holiday*

June 12th: Paz del Chaco (End of Chaco War) *Official Holiday*

June 24th: Fiesta de San Juan (Feast of St. John)

July 30th: Día de la Amistad (Friendship Day)

August 15th: Fundación de Asunción (Founding of Asunción) *Official Holiday*

September 29th: Día de la Victoria de Boquerón (Victory of Boquerón) *Official Holiday*

December 8th: Día de la Virgen de Caacupé (Feast of Virgin of Caacupé/The Immaculate Conception) *Official Holiday*

December 25th: Navidad (Christmas Day) *Official Holiday*

(A complete calendar of events is available on the Paraguayan government's tourism website www.senatur.gov.py.)

Municipal Office Telephone Numbers

Altos 0512 230030

Areguá 0291 432410

Asunción 021 663 311/20

Atyrá 0520 20188

Ayolas 072 222 384

Bahía Negra 021 490 237 (rings in Asunción)

Bella Vista 0767 240 219

Caacupé 0511 242 382

Caaguazú 0522 42393

Caazapá 0542 232 201

Capiatá 0228 634727

Carapeguá 0532 212 234

Colonia Independencia 0548 265 477

Concepción 0331 242 212

Coronel Oviedo 0521 203 468

Emboscada 0529 20025

Encarnación 071 203 982

Filadelfia 0491 433 374/6

Fuerte Olimpo 021 452 652 (rings in Asunción)

Itá 0224 632 575

Itaguá 0294 220 358

La Colmena 0537 223 298

Luque 021 642 215

Mariscal Estigarribia 0494 247 201

Paraguarí 0531 432 204

Pilar 0786 232 218

Piribebuy 0515 212 202

San Ignacio Guasú 0782 232 218

San Juan Bautista 081 212 511

San Lorenzo 021 570 000

San Miguel 0783 248 205

Santa Rosa 0858 285 379

Santiago 0782 20244

Sapucai 0539 263 214

Tobatí 0516 262 206

Vallemí 0351 230 764

Villa Florida 083 240 216

Villarica 0541 42 225

Yaguarón 0533 232 296

Yataity del Guairá 0549 20 003

Contents

Country Map

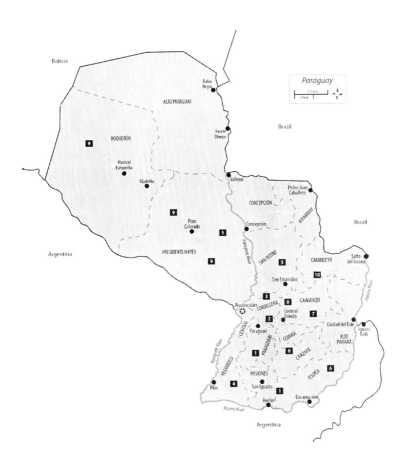

Regional Maps

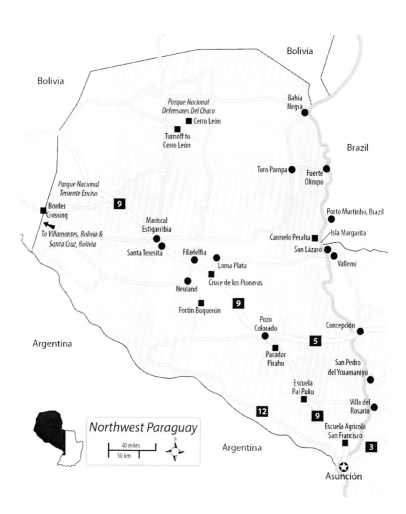

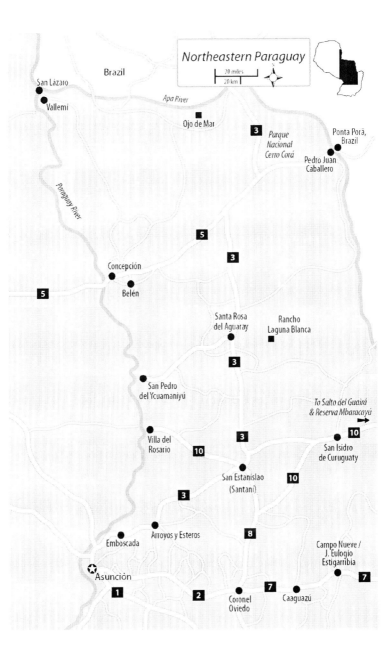

Northeastern Paraguay

20 miles
20 km

Brazil

San Lázaro

Vallemí

Apa River

Ojo de Mar

3 Parque
Nacional
Cerro Corá

Ponta Porá,
Brazil

Pedro Juan
Caballero

Paraguay River

5

Concepción

3

Belén

5

Santa Rosa
del Aguaray

Rancho
Laguna Blanca

3

San Pedro
del Ycuamandyú

To Salto del Guairá
& Reserva Mbaracayú

Villa del
Rosario

3

10

San Isidro
de Curuguaty

10

San Estanislao
(Santaní)

10

3

Emboscada

Arroyos y Esteros

8

Campo Nueve /
J. Eulogio
Estigarribia

Asunción

7

7

1

2

Coronel
Oviedo

Caaguazú

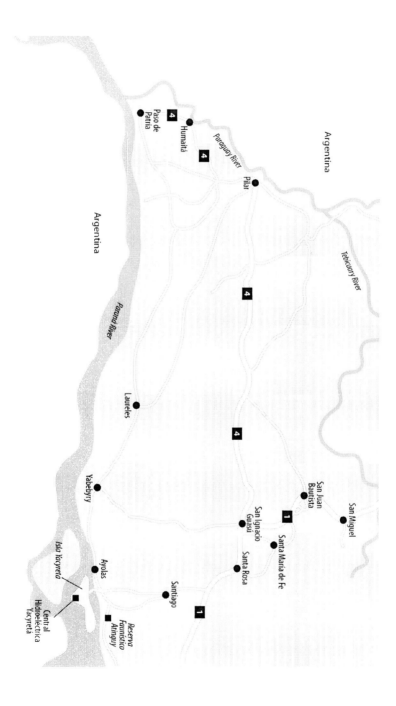

Southwest Paraguay

10 miles
20 km

N

Paraguay River

Argentina

Asunción

Capiatá
Areguá
Ypacarai Lake
Itaguá
Itá
San Bernardino
Altos
Atyra
Tobatí
Caacupé
Eusebio
Ayala
Piribebuy

Wetlands of Ypoa

Yaguarón
Eco Reserva Mbatoví
Chololó
La Quinta

Carapeguá

Quiindy

 Paraguari

Sapucai

 1

Acahay

Ybycui

Turnoff to Mbocauzú Waterfalls

La Colmena

Salto Cristal

Mbocauzú Waterfalls

Entrance to Parque Nacional Ybycui

Caapucú

Villa Florida

 1

2

2

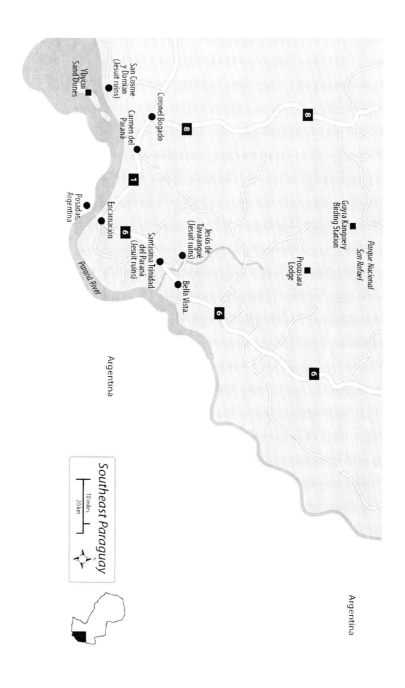

Southeast Paraguay

10 miles
20 km

Ybycuí Sand Dunes

San Cosme y Damián (Jesuit ruins)

Carmen del Paraná

Coronel Bogado

8

1

Posadas, Argentina

Encarnación

6

Santísima Trinidad del Paraná (Jesuit ruins)

Jesús de Tavarangüé (Jesuit ruins)

Bella Vista

6

Paraná River

Argentina

8

Guyra Kanguery Birding Station

Parque Nacional San Rafael

Pro Cosara Lodge

6

6

Argentina

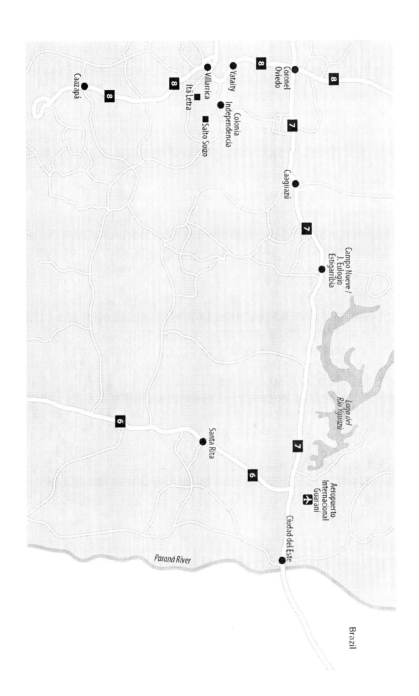

Top Paraguayan Experiences

EXPLORE THE PARAGUAYAN CHACO

A number of endangered species roam the vast expanses of the Paraguayan Chaco. Nature lovers visiting this largely uninhabited wilderness with an experienced guide will delight in spotting the region's elusive and exotic wildlife.

ENGAGE WITH ARTISANS

Paraguayan artisans keep the country's ancient traditions alive, designing delicate ñandutí lace, embossing leather crafts, and embroidering finely woven ao po'i linens. Many are happy to share their craft with foreigners, explaining the history and showing off their workshops.

VISIT THE JESUIT RUINS AND TOWNS

Established in the 17th and 18th centuries, the once vibrant Jesuit Missions are considered one of the most unique social experiments in history. Step back in time as you visit the ruins of Trinidad and Jesús (both UNESCO World Heritage sites) or the still thriving towns of San Ignacio and Santa María.

HIT THE TOWN IN ASUNCIÓN

Paraguay's capital boasts an energetic and highly affordable nightlife, even for those on tight budgets. As Paraguayans are highly social, going out is a great way to interact with locals, whether it's at a free concert or packed night club.

TAKE IN A SPORTING EVENT

From the Trans Chaco Rally to local soccer and piki-volley matches, Paraguay's passion for sports is infectious. Choose a local favorite and catch a game at the stadium or watch from a bar, surrounded by cheering locals.

MARVEL AT LARGE-SCALE WONDERS

Combine a tour of the Itaipú Hydroelectric Dam, the world's second largest, with a trip over the border to the majestic Iguazú Falls for a one-two punch of large scale spectacle.

EMBARK UPON A RIVERBOAT ADVENTURE

Riding a passenger boat up the Paraguay River is the most interesting way to access the Paraguayan Pantanal, where remote indigenous communities coexist with endangered wildlife and tourists are rare.

Introduction

Paraguay is a welcoming country, rich in history, culture, and unexploited wilderness that has much to offer the adventurous traveler. Paraguayan author Augusto Roa Bastos described his homeland as "an island surrounded by land." Isolation has marked this nation's history from the start, causing Paraguay's Spanish colonists and indigenous inhabitants to intermarry, a situation that was unique to the New World. The blending of European and indigenous languages, traditions and lifestyles has continued throughout Paraguay's history and still exists today. Since then, Paraguay has emerged from its isolation yet retains its strong, vibrant culture despite globalization efforts. Paraguayans are very friendly and inviting, eager to show off their country and culture to visitors. Its central location makes traveling through Paraguay an inexpensive and exciting addition to any South American itinerary. No matter your budget or appetite for adventure, this book will help you make the most of your time in Paraguay.

Tips for traveling in Paraguay:

Engage with locals: Visitors will find Paraguayans extremely hospitable and friendly. Most are eager to help you discover their country – they may teach you a few words in Guaraní, give you an impromptu tour or connect you with friends and family in other parts of Paraguay. Getting to know the country like a local often times makes up for the lack of tourism infrastructure.

Learn the Guaraní language: Paraguay is the only country in Latin America where the majority of the population speaks an indigenous language. Paraguayans have a soft spot for foreigners that speak even just a few words of Guaraní. Spanish and Guaraní are often intermingled, even within the same sentence. So don't be afraid to practice the Guaraní words and phrases in this book when appropriate (for more, see Languages, p38, and the Language Reference, p325).

Visit the countryside: Travelers who venture beyond Paraguay's major cities will be rewarded with beautiful landscapes and a glimpse into the country's rich rural traditions. The way of life in the *campo* or *interior* (countryside) is an important part of Paraguayan culture.

Drink *tereré*: Sitting in the shade, drinking *tereré* is one of the best ways to bond with Paraguayans. Delving into the *tereré* tradition is a good way to combat the heat and a hands-on way to experience a key aspect of Paraguayan culture (see Tereré, p87).

Be flexible: Take a cue from Paraguayans and adopt a *tranquilo pa* (no worries) attitude. Being flexible will make your time in Paraguay immensely more enjoyable.

Mind the weather: Paraguayans organize their daily routines around the weather, be it hot, cold or rainy. Tourists should emulate locals and adapt their travel plans accordingly (see When to Visit, p53).

Seek information offline: Paraguayan businesses have only recently begun to embrace the Internet. In general, you will have much better luck getting accurate information either in person or over the phone rather than online (see Staying Connected, p92).

SUGGESTED ITINERARIES

Most visitors will be comfortable with the Route 1 – Route 2 loop featuring Paraguay's most popular tourist attractions. Travelers with more time on their hands can use this as a starting point and add on other routes based on their travel plans, budget, and appetite for adventure. Unless otherwise noted, these itineraries assume travel by public transportation. Traveling by car will allow you to move at a faster pace but remember to allocate sufficient time for weather-related delays in more remote regions.

Route 1– Route 2 Loop: Ciudad del Este, Encarnación, Asunción, Guairá, & Ciudad del Este

Minimum time: 4-6 days

Start by visiting the magnificent **Iguazú Falls** either on the Argentine or Brazilian side (the former is recommended over the latter). Cross the border into **Ciudad del Este**, take advantage of low prices on items such as digital cameras and other electronics. Head to the **Itaipú Dam**, the world's second largest hydroelectric dam. On the way there, stop by the **Museo de la Tierra Guaraní and adjoining zoo** for a look at the region's fauna and cultural heritage. Head south on Route 6 to Encarnación. Along the way you can visit the **Yerba Mate Selecta factory** (mornings only) in Bella Vista and the **Jesuit Ruins of Trinidad** and **Jesús**, both UNESCO World Heritage sites. However, most (especially those riding public transportation) will find it easier to stay along Route 6 or remain in Encarnación and backtrack the following day to visit the Jesuit ruins. Nature buffs and birders can take a day or two to visit the **San Rafael Nature Reserve**, which preserves biologically rich remnants of the once expansive Atlantic Forest. This is one of the few places in Paraguay where the *guyra campana* (bell bird) can still be heard.

From Encarnación, head west along Route 1 to **San Ignacio Guasú**. The town's **Jesuit museum** and those of nearby **Santa María de Fe** and **Santa Rosa** display the decorative elements that once stood in the Jesuit missions. These attractions are the perfect complement to your visit to the even more popular Jesuit ruins. Those with a special interest in Jesuit history should stay in **Santa María de Fe**.

Continue along Route 1 towards Asunción. Adventure seekers can take a 1- or 2-day side trip to the popular and relaxing **Parque Nacional Ybycuí** and the large **Salto Cristal** waterfall hidden in a maze of sugar cane fields near the Japanese colony, **La Colmena**. Steam train buffs will enjoy a half-day side trip to the historic **Taller de Trenes** steam train workshop in Sapucai. Stop in Yaguarón to visit the **Iglesia San Buenaventura**, Paraguay's most beautiful church. Once in **Asunción** take in the city's historic sites and enjoy the affordable nightlife. Birders will enjoy crossing the **Bay of Asunción** (an important stopover for migratory birds) to bird watch in **Chaco'i**, the southernmost tip of the Paraguayan Chaco.

From Asunción, travel by bus to Colonia Independencia (those traveling by car may opt to travel on Route 1, turning off towards Villarrica at Paraguarí and stopping at the aforementioned **Taller de Trenes** in Sapucai). Explore the **waterfalls in the Ybytyruzu mountains** then head to **Villarrica** to enjoy the nightlife and pet the capybaras in the **Ykua Pyta park**. Afterwards, you can take a day trip to **Yataity** to purchase finely woven and embroidered *ao po'i* creations from local artisans. Those seeking a relaxing stay at an upscale ranch can take a side trip to **Estancia Don Emilio** before heading back to Ciudad del Este.

Additional side trips and recommendations: Travelers who wish to do this trip in reverse (Asunción, Encarnación, Ciudad del Este) can cross from Encarnación, Paraguay to Posadas, Argentina. From Posadas it is easy to travel to Puerto Iguazú and **Iguazú Falls** as well as the Jesuit Ruins of San Ignacio Miní. Day trips from Puerto Iguazú to Ciudad del Este in order to visit the **Itaipú dam** and shop for electronics are easy.

If you are traveling during Carnival season (dates vary between February and March) visit Encarnación over a weekend to enjoy the glittery *Carnavales Encarnacenas*. The **Jesuit Ruins of San Cosme y Damián** are easy to visit in a day from Encarnación. Alternatively, you might choose to stay overnight in order to visit the nearby **Ybycuí sand dunes**. Ayolas, home to the **Yacyretá hydroelectric dam**, is a good day trip from both Encarnación and San Ignacio Guasú. Those who wish to continue on to Resistencia, Argentina, can take a bus from either San Ignacio Guasú or Encarnación to the laid back town of Pilar, making sure to visit the large **Manufacturas Pilar** cotton factory before crossing the border by ferry boat.

The Golden Circuit: Asunción to Towns along Route 1 & Route 2

Minimum time: 2-3 days

There are several towns worth visiting along Routes 1 and 2, just a short distance from Asunción. However, travel between towns on public transportation can be time consuming (especially for side trips to towns off the main road). The following is a simplified itinerary with highlights of the "Golden Circuit" (see The Franciscan Route & Golden Circuit, p69). As many of these towns are known for specific attractions, whether its traditional handicrafts or religious monuments, travelers are encouraged to read about each town and create itineraries based on their interests. Travelers with time on their hands may prefer to break these up in to a series of day trips from Asunción, rather than deal with trying to hit each town in one loop. Because both Routes 1 and 2 are heavily transited national highways, trying to visit more than 2 or 3 towns per day can prove tiring even by car.

From Asunción head east along Route 1 to Yaguarón, home to the country's most beautiful and historically significant church, the **Iglesia San Buenaventura**. Continue to Paraguarí, stopping for a bite to eat at the popular *Frutería Paraguarí*. Here, a turn off winds its way over the hilly landscape past the historic town of Piribebuy and connects with Route 2. Thrill seekers can take a taxi to the **Eco Reserva Mbatoví** to enjoy the beautiful views while rappelling and doing a ropes course. Kick back and relax at the upscale *La Quinta* ranch or enjoy a quiet evening in Piribebuy. Before heading towards Route 2, visit Rosa Segovia's workshop where local artisans can demonstrate how they painstakingly weave sewing thread into traditional ponchos known as *"poncho sesenta lista."*

From Piribebuy, head on over to Caacupé where every December the town is swarmed with pilgrims who travel to the **Basílica de Caacupé** to show their devotion to the *Virgen de Caacupé,* Paraguay's national patron saint. For a scenic side trip, head to the *Casa del Monte* located high on the hillside in the town of **Atyrá**. The town is known for its leatherwork – stop by the ornate *Complejo Marianela* or the stalls in the *Peatonal Indio José* to pick up a professionally decorated thermos for *tereré* or *mate*.

San Bernardino, accessed via Ypacaraí, is a lakeside town that fills up with elites vacationing from Asunción during the summer. Head to the nearby town of **Altos** to view Lake Ypacaraí from upon high or hit San Bernardino's *discotecas* at night. Continue along Route 2 and stop at **Itaguá** where multicolored thread is woven into delicate *ñanduti* lace. Just past Itaguá, there is a turn off to Areguá. Along the way you can stop by the **Museo del Mueble** featuring a large collection of antique furniture. In Areguá visit the **Centro Cultural del Lago** or **El Cántaro** for a look at traditional **ceramic** works and then head uphill to the town church for a great view of the lake. On your return to Asunción, visit the **Museo del Barro**, Paraguay's best museum.

Additional side trips and recommendations: Travelers with an interest in Paraguay's indigenous can leave Areguá for another day (an easy day trip from Asunción) and continue along Route 2 to San Lorenzo's **Museo Guido Boggiani**. The museum presents a good overview of Paraguay's indigenous tribes and profits from the excellent selection of handicrafts in the gift shop go directly to indigenous artisans.

The Paraguayan Pantanal by River: Asunción, Concepción, & Bahía Negra
Minimum time: 2 weeks
Due to weather conditions (heat and rain) and limited transportation options, this trip is best undertaken by those with a flexible travel schedule and not recommended between the months November and March (see Traveling along the Paraguay River, p305).

From Asunción head north to Concepción. The white sandy shores along the pristine **Laguna Blanca**, off Route 3, make for an enjoyable beach getaway during the summer, though bird lovers will find the trip to be worthwhile year round. Once in Concepción, stay either in town or enjoy the scenery and home cooked meals of **Granja El Roble** in nearby Belén. A visit to **Parque Nacional Cerro Corá** overlooking Amambay's strange rock formations is a doable daytrip from Concepción, though you should get an early start.

From Concepción, take the three day trip to Bahía Negra on the Aquidaban passenger boat (departs weekly). For travelers on a budget this is a great way to enjoy the scenery of the **Paraguayan Pantanal**. Once in **Bahía Negra,** visit the nearby **indigenous community of Puerto Diana** and then head upriver to the **Tres Gigantes birding station** (it is best to make arrangements with Guyra Paraguay ahead of time). The station is named after three endangered animals found in the area: the giant anteater, giant armadillo, and giant river otter. Wildlife is abundant in this area and tourists are rare.

Travelers wishing to continue on to Bolivia can hire a motorboat to take them upriver to Puerto Busch. Upon the return trip those who wish to minimize river travel can disembark in **Fuerte Olimpo** or **Vallemí** and continue by bus to Asunción or Concepción respectively. In Fuerte Olimpo, be sure to climb to the top of the **Cerro Tres Hermanos** for an unparalleled view of the Pantanal. In Vallemí, guides can take you to recently discovered **limestone caves** as well as on a tour of Paraguay's national cement factory.

Additional side trips and recommendations: Flying to Bahía Negra and returning by boat downriver is the fastest and most comfortable way to do this trip. However, flights to Bahía Negra are often rescheduled or cancelled at the last minute due to poor weather conditions or lack of passengers. Therefore, this is only practical for travelers with flexible schedules.

Though it takes a fair bit of leg work, travelers with very flexible schedules and budgets (and a taste for adventure) can combine a trip to Bahía Negra with some nature observation in the Chaco. The best way to do so is to travel from Bahía Negra or Fuerte Olimpo to Filadelfia (if traveling from Bahía Negra to Fuerte Olimpo by boat you will have to prearrange your accommodations as the boat usually arrives past midnight). You might want to hire someone to drive you or consider taking the bus towards Asunción and getting off at the Cruce de los Pioneros crossroads where you can catch a bus to Filadelfia. Tours from Filadelfia to the remote **Parque Nacional Defensores del Chaco** or more easily accessible **Parque Nacional Teniente Enciso** should be previously arranged. It is sometimes possible to visit both with public transportation (buses to Teniente Enciso leave from Mariscal Estigarribia) but attempting this in combination with the trip to Bahía Negra is likely too complicated for most. Those who wish to continue on to Santa Cruz, Bolivia can travel from Filadelfia to Mariscal Estigarribia and catch buses there.

The Paraguayan Chaco by Land

Take the bus from Santa Cruz, Bolivia disembarking at Cruce los Pioneros in order to catch a bus to Filadelfia. From Filadelfia take a guided tour of the region's **salt lagoons**, where wildlife abounds, and historic Chaco War battleground **Fortín Boquerón**. Nature buffs should consider side trips to either **Parque Nacional Defensores del Chaco** or **Parque Nacional Teniente Enciso** as these are known habitats of jaguar and other endangered species. Both are sporadically accessible by public transportation but it is best to arrange a guided tour ahead of time. Head south to Pozo Colorado and then catch a bus to Concepción. Relax at **Granja El Roble** in Belén for 1-2 days and then head south to Asunción either by bus or on the **Cacique II passenger boat** (a full day's travel). **Parque Nacional Cerro Corá** is a doable day-trip from Concepción. Those who wish to cross in to Brazil rather than travel to Asunción can continue from the park to **Pedro Juan Caballero** and then cross over into Ponta Porã, Brazil.

> This itinerary is set up with backpackers coming from Bolivia in mind.

Paraguay in Depth

History

Paraguay's tumultuous history is one defined by isolation and conflict. A long history of strong-arm rule generated a passiveness amongst the country's citizens who, in many instances, found dictatorships to be more stable and prosperous than democratic government. Only recently has the military ceased to be the predominant player in Paraguay's political scene. Since colonial times the nation has struggled to maintain its ground against larger and more powerful neighbors. The country was limited by its isolation, lack of sea access, and a small under-educated population. This resulted in conflictive, and mostly unbalanced, relationships with neighboring Brazil and Argentina, a trend that continues to this day. Over the course of its existence, first as a Spanish colony and then as an independent nation, Paraguay's resources have slowly been chipped away by internal warfare and its corrupt regimes. Despite being the constant underdog, Paraguay has kept itself from being engulfed by its neighbors, maintaining a strong national identity and culture.

> At the time of independence, Paraguay consisted of an area of 653,500 square kilometers. Today Paraguay is 406,750 square kilometers. That's almost the size of the state of California.

PRE-COLONIAL PARAGUAY

The Guaraní natives were the most significant indigenous group to inhabit pre-Hispanic Paraguay. The Guaraní were part of a larger tribe known as the Tupí Guaraní, whose disperse population extended from the Caribbean and Northeastern tip of South America to points as far west as Brazil and as south as Uruguay. According to legend, the nomadic tribe was ruled by two brothers, Tupí and Guaraní, who parted ways after a family dispute. Tupí led his followers east to Brazil while Guaraní and his followers continued west to present day Paraguay, Bolivia, Uruguay, and Argentina. The Guaraní inhabited what is now eastern Paraguay, living as semi-nomadic hunters who also practiced subsistence agriculture. Though they did not leave any large ruins or monuments behind, many traces of their culture, from language to religious rituals, remain today.

> **Paraguay in Photos**
> For a wide variety of old photos of Paraguay check out: www.meucat.com/album.html

The Paraguayan Chaco was home to a diverse group of indigenous tribes including the Guaycurú, and Payaguá, who survived in the harsh environment by hunting, gathering, and fishing.

The lives of all of Paraguay's indigenous inhabitants changed tremendously when European explorers entered their territory in the sixteenth century.

COLONIAL PARAGUAY

The city of Asunción was founded by Spaniards Juan de Salazar and Gonzalo de Mendoza on August 15, 1537. Asunción soon became home to refugees from the colony of Buenos Aires fleeing from indigenous attacks. At first, Paraguay was considered a crucial element within Spain's colonial holdings. However, once it was understood that the country possessed no real wealth to offer the Spanish crown, the colony's purpose lost momentum.

RELATIONSHIP WITH INDIGENOUS

Paraguay's lack of easily exploited mineral wealth was a blessing for its indigenous, who were spared the wide scale annihilation that befell the original inhabitants of Spain's more prosperous colonies (such as Peru, Bolivia, and Mexico). Initially, Asunción's original Guaraní inhabitants chose to align themselves with the colonists in order to strengthen their position against the hostile Guaycurú natives of the Chaco. The Spanish took Guaraní women as their wives and concubines, kick starting what is referred to as the *mestizo* population today. The alliance between the colonists and indigenous was weak. Once European colonists gained a foothold, the region's indigenous found their way of life under constant threat.

Of those who chose to integrate with the new arrivals, many found themselves trapped in the abusive *encomienda* system, a form of legalized slavery. Put into place by the Spanish crown in 1555, this system allowed Spaniards to claim Guaraní natives as their own property. The colonists were responsible for the physical and spiritual well being of their indigenous. However, this responsibility was rarely a priority. The *encomienda* system generated several indigenous rebellions and was also met with resistance from the Jesuit Order. Indigenous living in Jesuit missions were spared the cruelties of the *encomiendas* but were stripped of their religious traditions and practices. Natives who managed to avoid both the *encomiendas* and Jesuit missions were in constant danger of being captured by Brazilian slave traders (see Missions Under Attack, p168).

Many tribes viewed the colonists as trespassing enemies. The indigenous groups of the Chaco were particularly hostile. Asunción, located across from the southern-most tip of the Chaco, was raided by the Guaycurú natives regularly, and those explorers who dared to venture up the Paraguay River soon found themselves under attack by the Payaguá tribesmen. The hostilities suffered at the hands of these bellicose tribes kept outsiders away from the Paraguayan Chaco throughout the colonial era, and into the 20th century.

MISSIONARY EFFORTS: THE FRANCISCANS & THE JESUITS

As with the rest of the New World, evangelizing natives was a key component of colonization. Two missionary groups held a strong influence in Paraguay – the Franciscan Order and the Jesuit Order. Each differed in their level of integration within the colonial system. In many ways, this determined their continued presence in the country. Possibly the most profound impact these orders had on Paraguayan culture was the conservation of the Guaraní language, which both groups endeavored to learn and preserve.

The Franciscans arrived soon after the colony's creation and founded missions throughout Eastern Paraguay. Under the direction of Franciscan priests, the missions' indigenous inhabitants produced crops such as tobacco, cotton, and *yerba mate*. Missions had workshops where natives were taught skilled crafts such as weaving, carpentry, ironworking, sewing, sculpture, and painting. The missions were well integrated within the rest of the colonial structure. This proved to be problematic for the missions' indigenous who were often forced to work for colonial *encomiendas*.

The convergence of Spanish and indigenous cultures at the hands of the Franciscans is widely credited as the genesis for modern day popular Paraguayan culture – from crafts, to language, to religious beliefs and traditions. Mission towns such as Yaguarón, Atyrá, Altos, Tobatí, and Itá remain some of Paraguay's most charming towns. In many of these towns, original buildings from the Franciscan era are still in use. Town churches still contain sculptures, pulpits, altars, and frescoes decorated in the ornate decorative style known as *"Barroco Franciscano-Guaraní"* (Franciscan-Guaraní Baroque). Town artisans still create many of the crafts that originated from the Franciscan missions.

> Fray Luis de Bolaños, founder of several Paraguayan Franciscan missions, dedicated himself to learning the Guaraní language and was subsequently one of the first Europeans to create a written form of Guaraní.

Arriving later, the Jesuits also created similar missions focusing on evangelizing and educating the indigenous. Between 1609 and 1767, the Jesuit Order established a total of thirty missions (also known as reductions) in South America, most of which were located in what are now Paraguay, Brazil, and Argentina. Each mission strove to be self sufficient, trading surpluses with other missions and selling them to the colonists. Among the most important goods produced in Paraguay's Jesuit missions were *yerba mate*, hides, cotton, and tobacco. Like the Franciscans, the Jesuits helped the Guaraní language thrive through publications written in the native language. A majority of the Jesuit order was made up of highly educated priests who praised the arts and sciences. The mission of San Cosme y Damián was a center for astrological research while that of Santa María de Fe was home to an extensive sculpture workshop. The Jesuits instructed their charges in decorative arts (such as sculpture and painting), music and instrument making, and other skilled trades.

Unlike the Franciscans, however, the Jesuits purposefully distanced themselves and their flock from the colonists. The Jesuits sought to safeguard the indigenous on their missions from the brutal conditions of the colonial *encomiendas* as well as from Brazilian slave traders known as *"bandeirantes"* (see Missions under Attack, p168). Various measures were undertaken to ensure an almost complete separation between the missions and the Spanish colonists. Missions were closed to visitors – non-natives or non-Jesuits were not allowed in without special permission. Even visiting government officials could only remain three days. The Jesuit missions generated a great deal of suspicion and jealousy amongst Paraguay's elite. Rumors of vast riches coupled with the Jesuit missions' exemption from colonial taxes provoked resentment from the upper class. In addition, colonists felt the Jesuits were depriving them of a vast source of free indigenous labor. In response to their increasing wealth, power, and their protection of indigenous populations, Spanish King Carlos III expelled the Jesuits from Spain's colonies in 1767.

The missions subsequently passed into the hands of the Franciscans but were large-ly abandoned by their indigenous populations, and eventually collapsed. In Paraguay, there are remnants of eight Jesuit missions, testaments of a once vibrant social experiment. The two largest sets of ruins, Santísima Trinidad del Paraná (p178) and Jesús de Tavarangue (p180), have been declared UNESCO World Heritage Sites, and the sculptures that adorned the missions can be seen in the churches and museums of Jesuit towns throughout the departments of Misiones and Itapúa.

Paraguay in Depth

An Uncertain Future

Upon the expulsion of their Jesuit leaders, the indigenous within the missions faced an uncertain future. While some chose to remain in the missions, now under the supervision of the Franciscans, many opted for life outside the mission. Some returned to the forest while others decided to use their learned skilled trades to get by in nearby towns.

INDEPENDENCE & THE RULE OF DR. FRANCIA

Throughout the early 1800's, one by one, Spain's colonies in Latin America declared independence. When Argentina did so in 1810, it attempted to absorb Paraguay in the process, even going so far as to send an army to invade the country. However, Paraguay resisted, determined to hang on to its own dream of independence. On the night of the May 14, 1811, Paraguay declared itself independent from Spain. Over the course of the next several years, Paraguay was ruled by the new nation's founding fathers. Slowly but surely, Dr. Gaspar Rodriguez de Francia, the most educated and politically savvy of the group, emerged as their leader. In 1814 he was declared the ruler of Paraguay and in 1816 his rule was extended for life with the official title of *dictador perpétuo* (perpetual dictator).

The National Flag

Paraguay's flag is the only one in the world with different seals on each side. On the front, there is a wreath of palms and an olive branch framing a blue circle with a yellow star. The phrase *"República del Paraguay"* encircles the wreath in yellow letters on a red background. The other side features a lion and behind it, a staff with a red Phrygian cap symbolizing liberty. Above is a semi-circular red banner with the words *"Paz y Justicia"* (Peace and Justice).

Dr. Francia's twenty-six-year rule was marked by his policy of isolation. Above all, Dr. Francia sought to solidify Paraguay's independence, protecting the young nation from Argentine and Brazilian expansionist ambitions. This was achieved through noninterventionist foreign policy and micromanagement of all aspects of life in Paraguay – political, economic, and even social. The country's borders were shut and international trade was severely restricted. Dr. Francia ruled with a heavy hand, maintaining an extensive network of spies and jailing anyone who dared to challenge him. The majority of foreigners were suspected of being spies and many were held hostage in Paraguay for indefinite periods. Though his methods were harsh, they enabled Dr. Francia to maintain peace in Paraguay at a time when instability

In order to keep Asunción's power hungry elites at bay, Dr Francia forced the upper classes into marriages with Paraguay's indigenous population. This kept the elite from consolidating power while also furthering the development of the country's *mestizo* culture.

reigned throughout the region and neighboring countries continually eyed Paraguay's vast territory. Dr. Francia died in September 1840, ending Paraguay's first, but not its last, dictatorship.

Lingering Legacies

Under Dr. Francia, Paraguayans found themselves forced to become almost completely self-sufficient. Dr. Francia assigned goods for each town to produce, from textiles to bricks. In many towns, the cottage industries that were born during that era still thrive today. Perhaps the most notable example is the creation of *ao po'i* cloth in the town of Yataity and the *poncho sesenta lista* in Piribebuy (see *Artesanías*, p43).

THE RULE OF CARLOS ANTONIO LÓPEZ

As Dr. Francia left no clear successor, the years following his death were marked with uncertainty and a series of governmental changes. In 1844, Carlos Antonio López was declared President of Paraguay. Much like his predecessor, Carlos Antonio López proved to be a tyrannical dictator. However, during López's rule, Paraguay prospered and flourished.

Carlos Antonio López capitalized on the wealth that Dr. Francia had amassed in the state coffers, opening Paraguay to international trade and investment. Turning to European experts to improve the country's infrastructure, under López's regime Paraguay saw the creation of the country's first iron foundry (La Rosada), shipyard, telegraph service, printing press, and newspaper. Perhaps most importantly, Paraguay became home to Latin America's first steam-powered railway. Many of the large and ornate buildings standing in downtown Asunción date from this period.

Under Carlos Antonio López's rule, Paraguay reached an economic highpoint. Yet despite its newfound economic prosperity, tense relations with Argentina and Brazil continued to loom like a specter over the nation's politics. Both neighbors remained eager to determine lingering boundary disputes with Paraguay to their favor. The diplomatic failings of Carlos Antonio López's successor soon drove the prosperous nation into a devastating war.

The Steam Train

The steam-powered locomotive (*tren a vapor*) represented Paraguay's biggest advance in infrastructure. The railway linked Asunción to Encarnación (a distance of 376 kilometers), stopping in numerous small towns along the way. In Encarnación, the network connected via ferry to the Argentine city of Posadas where the railway continued to Buenos Aires. The railway was built and operated by English investors until 1959 when it passed in to the hands of the Paraguayan government. The train continued to carry passengers until 1999, though its importance greatly diminished as improvements to the country's highway and public transportation system were made. Nowadays, the train is mostly defunct, leaving behind a series of dilapidated stations, isolated towns, and grass covered tracks. However, there are still ways to see and experience vestiges of this historical railroad system. The railway's central station in Asunción has been turned into a museum (see Museo Ferroviario, p125) and a train known as the "*Tren del Lago*" operates between Asunción and Areguá (see Tren del Lago, p127). In addition, the original workshop where all the trains were serviced, still stands in Sapucai (see Taller de Trenes Train Workshop and Ferrocarril Presidente Carlos Antonio López Museum, p151).

MARSICAL FRANCISCO SOLANO LÓPEZ & THE TRIPLE ALLIANCE WAR

In September 1862, Carlos Antonio López died, leaving his son Francisco Solano López (known, due to his military rank of Marshal, as "Mariscal López") as his successor. According to legend, upon his deathbed Carlos Antonio López begged his hotheaded son to rule with a pen instead of a sword. Instead, the new ruler took an aggressive stance on borders issues with Argentina, Uruguay, and Brazil. In 1864, Marsical López sided with Uruguay and declared war on Brazil. From there, a domino effect took hold. Paraguay requested permission to cross Argentine territory in order to attack Brazil. When its request was denied, Paraguay also declared war on Argentina. In an ironic twist of fate, Uruguay, under a new government installed by Brazil, joined the war against Paraguay. The three enemy states signed a secret treaty, under which each swore not to enter into separate peace negotiations with Paraguay and not to suspend fighting until the Paraguayan government was overthrown.

Waged between 1865 and 1870, the Triple Alliance War had disastrous ramifications for Paraguay. Though large, the country's army was poorly trained and equipped in comparison to the enemy's troops. The majority of fighting took place in the southern department of Ñeembucú and spread north through the department of Cordillera and into the department of Amambay. Massive casualties forced the nation's women, elderly, and even children on to the battlefields. In many instances, the makeshift troops defended their tattered nation with nothing more than simple farming equipment. Mariscal López was killed on the battlefield on March 1, 1870, bringing the war to an end. By this time, more than half the population of Paraguay had been killed by a combination of enemy fire, famine, and disease. By most accounts, the male population was reduced by 90 percent. Historians disagree on exact death tolls but no matter what numbers, the war left Paraguay a broken nation. In addition to human casualties, Paraguay lost approximately 170,000 km^2 of territory to Argentina and Brazil in the ensuing peace negotiations (see Rutherford B. Hayes, Paraguay's Favorite American President, p283), and was burdened with paying its victors significant war reparations.

The war's aftermath and the country's struggle to recover had long lasting effects on Paraguayan society. With only a fraction of the original male population remaining, the brunt of the country's rebuilding was carried out by Paraguay's women. To

---

From Tyrant to Hero

During the war Mariscal Fransisco Solano López developed a reputation for cruelty which was not limited to enemy combatants – by his order many of his own troops, government and military officials were tortured and killed. Even his own family was not spared – two of his brothers were executed and his mother and sisters tortured for suspected treason. Upon his death and the subsequent end of the war Paraguay was left in complete shambles, its citizens forced to suffer at the hands of equally cruel and rapacious victors. Visitors to Paraguay may be surprised to find Marsical López, largely responsible for the Triple Alliance war, revered as a national hero. Streets are named after him and statues in his honor abound. This is due in large part to the work of Juan Emiliano O'Leary, prominent Colorado party member and revisionist historian who, in the early 1900's successfully re-branded Mariscal López as a hero who gave everything for his country.

this day, many women remain at the forefront of the household, making economic decisions, and running cottage industries and family businesses. The crippled nation received no assistance from the victors of war. Argentine and Brazilian troops remained in Paraguay for several years enjoying the spoils of war, most of the time by force. This only worsened Paraguayans' negative feelings towards Argentina and Brazil. For many, these feelings still exist today. In order to replenish the empty state coffers, the government turned to land sales. Over 50 percent of the country was sold off to foreign landowners. This caused foreign interests to wield disproportionate power over national interests, a pattern which remains an issue in modern day Paraguay. Politically, the years following the Triple Alliance War were marked by instability and the creation of the Colorado and Liberal parties, both of which still dominate national politics today.

THE CHACO WAR

In the 1930's Paraguay became embroiled in yet another brutal conflict. This time it was with its neighbor to the north, Bolivia. The ill-defined border between the two nations was a point of contention even during the colonial era, and tensions grew in the late 1800's when Bolivia lost its Pacific Ocean access to Chile. The landlocked nation then turned its attention to the Paraguayan Chaco, seeking to regain access to the Atlantic Ocean by way of the Paraguay River. The prospect of large oil deposits in the Chaco region strained relations even further. In the 1920's the Bolivian army slowly began infiltrating on Paraguay's territory, building several forts in the Chaco. Paraguay's general instability and internal political power struggles kept the government from focusing its attention on the Bolivian incursions in the north until war was inevitable. Barely recovered from the aftermath of the Triple Alliance War, Paraguay found itself once again at war.

The Chaco War was waged between 1932 and 1935. Soldiers were subjected to

The Infamous Eliza Lynch

In 1853, President Carlos Antonio López sent his son Mariscal Fransisco Solano López on a diplomatic mission to Europe to procure arms and establish commercial agreements. While in Paris, Mariscal López met an Irish courtesan by the name of Eliza Lynch who soon became his mistress. Lured by the promise of ruling over an entire nation, Eliza Lynch agreed to accompany Mariscal López back to his homeland. "Madame Lynch" or "La Lynch," as she was known, spent much of her time struggling with the female members of Asunción's high society, each plotting and scheming ways to publicly embarrass one another. One of their most infamous confrontations was an elegant boat outing along the Paraguay River to celebrate the founding of the New Bordeaux colony. Madame Lynch's guests shunned their infuriated hostess by refusing to talk to or even make eye contact with her. In turn, she retaliated by instructing her assistants to fling the entire sumptuous luncheon spread overboard and held her ungrateful guests hostage and hungry aboard the ship for several hours. Eliza Lynch was a polemic figure in Paraguay's history, and her dramatic rags to riches story continues to capture the public's imagination. Several books on Paraguay revolve around the life of Eliza Lynch and her romance with Mariscal López (with varying degrees of liberty taken with historical accuracy). Two recent books are *"The News from Paraguay"* by Lily Tuck, and *"The Lives of Eliza Lynch"* by Michael Lillis and Ronan Fanning.

the unforgiving conditions of the northern Chaco – savage wilderness, isolation, disease, extreme weather conditions, and lack of drinking water. As in the previous war, Paraguayan troops were underequipped and poorly trained in comparison to their enemies. However, they did have some advantages; the majority of the enemy troops hailed from Bolivia's frigid Altiplano region and were therefore unaccustomed to the terrain and arid climate of the Chaco. By the time peace was declared on June 14, 1935, Paraguay had suffered casualties totaling over 30,000.

The Shadows of the War

Though they were fought long ago, the Triple Alliance War and the Chaco War are brought up frequently in regards to relations with neighboring countries. Paraguayans draw parallels between the country's underdog status during the Triple Alliance War and its current political and economic circumstances. Paraguayans argue they do not wield equal power in Mercosur, a regional trade agreement between Paraguay, Uruguay, Argentina, and Brazil. Tensions between Bolivia and Paraguay remain due to the continued search for natural resources in the Chaco. In 2010, reports of increased military activity in Bolivia revived memories of the Chaco War.

The post-war period saw the rise of the military as a deciding factor in Paraguayan politics, a trend that would continue for several decades. In 1947 the country was plunged into a six-month civil war known as the *"Revolución del '47"* during which Alfredo Stroessner, then a Lieutenant Colonel, began his rise to prominence within the military and the ruling Colorado party. In 1954, Stroessner, now a General, led a coup against President Federico Chaves and was soon thereafter elected president. At first, his rule provided the country with much-needed stability. Little did Paraguayans know their current savior would remain at the head of one of Latin America's longest running dictatorships – one marked with corruption and severe repression that would have a lasting detrimental impact on Paraguayan life.

PARAGUAY UNDER STROESSNER

The Stroessner dictatorship, also known as the *"Stronato,"* was marked by economic prosperity and rampant repression. Economically, the country benefited greatly from large-scale infrastructure projects undertaken during this period. The Itaipú hydroelectric dam, built in conjunction with Brazil, was a major economic engine providing jobs to thousands of Paraguayans. Stroessner also encouraged eastern expansion towards Brazil with the creation of a highway linking Asunción to the newly created city of Puerto Presidente Stroessner (later renamed Ciudad del Este) on the border with Brazil. This opened up a previously isolated area of the country to Paraguayan and foreign farmers who flocked to the region. Paraguayans paid a dear price for these advances. Large-scale agriculture projects encouraged under Stroessner's regime have all but destroyed the once pristine forests of Eastern Paraguay. The construction of Itaipú had a significant detrimental environmental impact as well, with the majority of flooding occurring on Paraguayan soil. In addition, many felt the Itaipú treaty, under which Paraguay was to sell its excess electricity to Brazil for a fixed rate well under market value, was unfair (see The Divisive Dam, p254).

There was little recourse for those who opposed the regime. The Colorado party dominated of all aspects of government and society and those that did not comply with the party line were virtually blacklisted from employment opportunities, and, in many cases, forced into exile. Freedom of the press was almost unheard of. Although not as high profile as the human rights abuses of the Chilean and Argentine dictatorships during that time, the Stroessner regime was almost as brutally repressive (see The Archive of Terror, p125). Anyone suspected of attempting to undermine his rule was brought in for interrogation, which often entailed both physical and psychological abuse.

Pyrague

Like rulers before him, Stroessner made extensive use of espionage to maintain power. His secret service was known as *"Pyrague"* which means "feet with hair" in Guaraní. It alludes to their ability to silently sneak up on their victims, as if they had hair on the bottom of their feet. People were encouraged to spy on their neighbors and friends. Even the most insignificant information was enough to result in someone's arrest and, in many cases, their "disappearance."

Though Stroessner was deposed in 1989, remnants of his rule still linger in modern day Paraguay. The culture of corruption, which flourished under Stroessner, remains present in both the public and private sector. Just as it was during the dictatorship, political power is used on a daily basis to secure favors, bribes, and even settle personal grudges. Despite their distrust of political figures, most Paraguayans are hesitant to challenge authority, a leftover legacy of the regime's strong-arm tactics.

PARAGUAY POST STROESSNER

Upon the fall of his regime, Stroessner was granted political asylum in Brazil where he remained until his death in 2006. Though the Stroessner era had ended, the Colorado party and the military maintained firm control of the country. Starting with General Andrés Rodriguez, the next two decades saw a slew of Colorado presidents. The 1990's saw various power struggles including threats of a military coup and even the assassination of Vice President Luis María Argaña in 1999. Throughout the following decade however, the military's political prominence slowly diminished. Institutionalized under Stroessner, corruption continued to be a serious problem with scandals regarding misappropriation of funds dogging each new government.

FERNANDO LUGO: A NEW ERA?

In April 2008, Fernando Lugo was elected as the new President of Paraguay in a historic election that ended over six decades of Colorado Party rule. A former bishop from San Pedro, Paraguay's poorest department, Lugo had very little formal political training. Though a member of the small socialist political party known as Tekojoja, Lugo was placed on the ballot at the head of a coalition which included the Liberal Party, the country's second largest. Known as the "bishop of the poor," Lugo ran on a leftist platform that emphasized assisting Paraguay's rural poor through a program of agrarian land reform. Many Paraguayans voted for Lugo in the hope to end the Colorado Party's long and corrupt rule.

As President, Lugo faced many obstacles. The alliance of political parties that helped put Lugo in to power quickly crumbled and public disputes between him and his vice president, Liberal Party member Federico Franco, became common. Met by strong opposition from the Paraguayan parliament, Lugo was largely unable to enact the land reforms he promised constituents during the election. In addition, his reputation was severely tarnished by the revelation that he had fathered several children during his tenure as a bishop.

Ultimately, Lugo's inability to form and retain strategic alliances with various political parties led to his ouster from the presidency. In June 2012, just nine months prior to the next election, an armed confrontation between police and squatters in the Canindeyú Department left seventeen dead and many more wounded. Lugo's long-time opponents seized the opportunity to blame the President and declare him unfit to govern. One week after the deadly incident Fernando Lugo was ousted from power in an impeachment trial in Paraguay's parliament lead by the Colorado Party and many of his former allies including the Liberal Party. Vice-President Federico Franco was immediately sworn in as Paraguay's next president. The next presidential elections will be held, as scheduled, in April of 2013.

Government & Politics

In accordance with the 1992 constitution, Paraguay is officially known as a presidential republic. Presidents are elected to a five-year term and cannot stand for re-election. The Congress is made up of two chambers – an eighty member *Cámara de Diputados* (Chamber of Deputies) and a forty-five member *Cámara de Senadores* (Senate). Each of Paraguay's seventeen administrative regions, known as *departamentos* (departments) is run by the regional government or *gobernación*. The departments are sub-divided in to municipalities or *municipalidades* that correspond to the region's larger towns.

Traditionally, the two most important parties have been the Liberal (Partido Liberal Radical Auténtico – PLRA) and Colorado (Asociación Nacional Republicana – ANR) parties with other parties such as UNACE, Partido Patria Querida, and Movimiento Popular Tekojoja gaining ground in the years after the Stroessner dictatorship.

Red vs. Blue
The longstanding rivalry between the Liberal and Colorado parties pops up even in seemingly apolitical settings. In a way, this rivalry plays out like those between the country's soccer clubs with each side boasting its own signature songs and colors. The official polkas for both parties ring out not only at political rallies but weddings and *quinceñeras* too. The signature color of the Liberal party is blue, while Colorado party members proudly sport red. Across the country, houses and even tombstones are painted blue or red to indicate their inhabitants' political allegiance. The only force strong enough to supersede these loyalties is the patriotic sentiment inspired by the national soccer team. During game days, everyone can be seen sporting their *albirroja* jerseys, which are white and red.

Economy

Paraguay's economy thrives on agriculture, with citizens both rich and poor literally living off the land. The majority of the country's rich elite make their living off cattle ranches and large-scale farms producing soy, sugar, cotton, and other cash crops. Paraguay's rural poor dedicate themselves to small-scale farming or labor with the poorest surviving off subsistence farming. Some of Paraguay's key agricultural exports include beef, *yerba mate*, soy, and stevia.

Campesinos

Members of Paraguay's rural farming class are known as "campesinos," derived from the word "campo," which means field or countryside. Campesinos face many obstacles such as lack of education, training and little access to credit. Most are able to grow enough food to meet basic nutritional needs on a plot of land (either owned or rented) due to the fertility of the soil. This widespread living condition is known as *mboriahu ryguatá*, which in Guaraní means "poor with a full stomach." Unfortunately, for many, urban migration has damaged this safety net.

While there is very little industry, Paraguay is making the most of its river systems with two large hydroelectric plants, Itaipú and Yacyretá, built in conjunction with Brazil and Argentina, respectively. Profits from the hydroelectric plants make up over three percent of Paraguay's GDP and are distributed throughout the national and local governments in payments known as "*royalties.*"

Paraguay has an active informal economy. Many people make a living through cottage industries. Some are middlemen while others sell their own crafts and products. Illegally trafficked goods have long given Paraguay an economic edge over its neighbors. Weak and susceptible borders allow everything from fuel to cooking oil, electronics, tobacco, meat, and poultry to easily be smuggled in to the country. It is not uncommon to see both contraband and counterfeit goods for sale on the street and in shops. Ciudad del Este, in particular, is known for its high volume of smuggled merchandise.

As a landlocked country, Paraguay has always been at the mercy of its neighbors' willingness to allow Paraguay's products to enter or pass through their territories. Paraguay's membership in Mercosur (*Mercado Común del Sur*), a free trade organization founded by Brazil, Argentina, Paraguay, and Uruguay in the 1990's, opened a large market for Paraguayan goods both to Mercosur's members and to other countries that have trade agreements with Mercosur. In addition to trade benefits, citizens of Mercosur member countries enjoy the freedom to travel, work, and study in other Mercosur member countries without many restrictions. However, within Paraguay

Emigration

The lack of jobs and opportunities for advancement in Paraguay has led Paraguayans, both working professionals and the poor, to emigrate abroad (some legally, others illegally) in search of a better life. During the 60's and 70's, Argentina was full of employment opportunities. Thousands of Paraguayans voyaged by train to Encarnación and then on to Buenos Aires in search of work. Men worked in factories or construction, while women found employment in factories as seamstresses or they worked as domestic servants. In the late 90's, Spain become a popular destination. However the property bubble collapse in 2008, put an end to the construction boom that had offered employment to newly arrived immigrants. The constant flow of working professionals emigrating abroad has created a severe brain drain in Paraguay. Aside from economic effects, this large scale emigration has other, almost intangible effects on the makeup of Paraguayan society. In rural towns it is not uncommon to see entire groups of siblings being raised by grandparents or extended family members. Children might be gathered around computers at cyber cafés, catching up with parents long distance via Skype. Those with parents working in Argentina are able to visit or be visited more frequently, while children whose parents have emigrated to Europe or North America are less fortunate.

there are always complaints that economic powerhouses Brazil and Argentina truly call the shots, especially because Mercosur's main objective to eliminate all custom duties and restrictions within Mercosur has not yet been realized.

Ka'a He'ê – Paraguay's Sweet Spot

Discovered in 1899 by Swiss botanist Moisés Bertoni (see Moisés Bertoni, p258), the stevia plant (Stevia Rebaudiana Bertoni) has recently become a significant export for Paraguay. Three hundred times sweeter than sugar, the plant lives up to its given Guaraní name "Ka'a He'ê," meaning "sweet plant." Advocates tout its natural sweetening qualities and viability as a sugar substitute for diabetics. In 2008, Coca-Cola and Pepsi announced future intentions to use ka'a he'ê to sweeten their products instead of aspartame. Paraguay is beginning to capitalize on the growing demand for ka'a he'ê worldwide with the establishment of several large-scale processing plants throughout the country. Ka'a he'ê is available commercially as both a powder and a liquid.

Education

Historically, education has never been a major priority for the Paraguayan government. Although several reforms have recently been enacted, the Paraguayan education system still faces a number of obstacles. While both primary and secondary educations are public and free, the dropout rate is still high. Many families are unable to afford the costs associated with schooling such as school supplies, uniforms and testing fees. Students are often forced to leave school in order to help support their families. Quality of education varies greatly, with many schools in rural areas chronically underserved and underfunded. The Guaraní/Spanish language dynamic (see Languages, p38) represents an additional hurdle for education. With the exception of indigenous schools, classes are officially supposed to be taught in Spanish. In rural areas, however, Guaraní is the predominant language in the classroom. Many students go through their entire schooling without learning either language fully.

Religion

Paraguay's population is predominately Roman Catholic with little division between Church and State. It is not uncommon to see religious motifs in private businesses and government offices. Religious rituals play a major role in everyday life with many community and cultural events revolving heavily around religious festivities (see Religious Holidays, p70). Despite the heavy Roman Catholic influence, missionary groups (such as Mormons and Protestants) have been making significant inroads throughout the country. However, efforts to convert Paraguay's remaining indigenous tribes (by Mennonite outreach groups and the New Tribes Mission) have been controversial.

Santeros

Sculpting saints is a tradition that was born in the Jesuit and Franciscan missions and is kept alive to this day thanks to Paraguay's deeply rooted religious beliefs (see Artesanías, p43) Most families have an imágen or a small representation of a saint (the Virgin Mary is the most popular) in their homes. Some families construct shrines for saints in their house or garden. On the patron saint's feast day or special religious holidays, people take their saint to be blessed at the local church.

Paraguay's People

MESTIZOS

The mixing of the country's indigenous inhabitants and European colonists originated during the colonial period and continued throughout Paraguay's history. It resulted in a population that is predominantly mixed-race in descent and one of the most homogeneous in all of Latin America. It is worth noting that for the majority of Paraguay's *mestizos*, the mixture between European and indigenous go so many generations back that few are able to trace their actual lineage – making them simply Paraguayans.

PARAGUAY'S INDIGENOUS POPULATION

Though the majority of Paraguayans have indigenous heritage, a distinct difference is drawn between *mestizos* and pure-blooded *indígenas* (indigenous). According to the 2002 indigenous census, Paraguay had approximately 86,500 native inhabitants with a projected population of 120,000 by 2010. Paraguay's tribes are generally divided into five distinct linguistic families: Zamuco, Mataco, Maskoy, Guaicurú, and Guaraní. In total, there are seventeen different ethnicities within these five linguistic families, with Guaraní tribes accounting for more than half of Paraguay's total indigenous population. The native makeup of Eastern Paraguay is almost solely Guaraní, while the Paraguayan Chaco is home to tribes from the remaining four linguistic families as well as a small Guaraní population. Throughout this book, various indigenous communities are described in further detail.

The Totobiegosodes

Paraguay is home to one of Latin America's last uncontacted indigenous tribes, the Totobiegosodes. Members of the Ayoreo tribe, the Totobiegosode choose to remain isolated from the modern world. Though some members of the group have emerged from the wilderness of the Northern Chaco, a small subset has chosen to remain in their natural habitat. While the land they live on is, in theory, protected, it is under constant threat from landowners who defy the law and clear it for agricultural and cattle ranching purposes. For more information about the Totobiegosodes, visit www.gat.org.py or www.survivalinternational.org/tribes/ayoreo.

Resources for Learning more about Indigenous Communities

Museums
For those interested in Paraguay's indigenous culture, the Museo Etnográfico Andres Barbero in downtown Asunción and the Museo Guido Boggiani in San Lorenzo on outskirts of Asunción provide a great look at the complex mosaic of indigenous cultures that once thrived in Paraguay.

Books
The anthropology department of the Catholic University (CEADUC) has long been the main source for scholarly work on Paraguay's indigenous tribes. Their publications are available at ServiLibro bookstores (see Bookstores, p118) and through the ServiLibro website (*www.servilibro.com.py*).

 "Los Indígenas del Paraguay" by José Zanardini and Walter Biedermann offers a particularly good overview of Paraguay's indigenous tribes with information about each tribe's history, culture, and current status in society.

As Paraguay's most marginalized population, the indigenous face many challenges. People of indigenous descent are often discriminated against, and it is not
uncommon for indigenous neighborhoods in urban areas to be kept isolated from
the rest of the community. Land ownership represents a significant obstacle for the
indigenous, as the government has forced many groups to relocate from their
ancestral lands in order to make way for agricultural business. Few tribes and
individuals possess official land titles, though some groups are pressing for the
return of traditional lands. Tribes in remote areas live under harsh conditions, with
environmental and population pressures making their traditional forms of survival
increasingly difficult to sustain. Tribes closer to urban areas face different challenges,
the foremost of which is the lack of economic opportunities available to them. Most
men serve as cheap labor to nearby *estancias* (cattle ranches), while women are
increasingly forced into prostitution for lack of alternatives. The sale of traditional
handicrafts represents a significant source of income, especially for those with access
to urban centers or connections with buyers and middlemen. Many groups rely upon
missionary groups for assistance, though this aid often comes at the cost of forced
integration and abandonment of traditional beliefs and lifestyles.

IMMIGRANTS

Paraguay is also home to an interesting mix of immigrant populations. Some are
more integrated into Paraguayan society than others. Geographic isolation has led
many to adapt quickly to Paraguay and become *paraguayizados* (paraguayanized),
drinking *tereré* and picking up Guaraní.

Mennonites Perhaps the best known of Paraguay's immigrant communities, the
Mennonites arrived to the country in the late 1920's. The first groups settled in
the Paraguayan Chaco (see The Mennonites, p292). These days, there are over
seventeen Mennonite colonies consisting of more than 28,000 people, each organized around the cooperative system, throughout Paraguay. Most communities are very closed off, maintaining a purposeful distance between themselves
and Paraguayans, even those who work alongside them.

Brazilians The majority of Brazilians in Paraguay are dedicated to agriculture.
Many large cattle ranches are both Brazilian owned and operated. In certain areas of the country, you are very likely to hear more Portuguese than Spanish, although many do make the effort to learn Guaraní in order to better communicate
with *campesino* workers. Due to their permanence in Paraguay, they are given
the nickname *Brasiguayos*.

Europeans Throughout Paraguay, there are several areas with large European
(non-Mennonite) communities such as Colonia Independencia in the Guairá
department and Caacupé, Altos, and Piribebuy in the Cordillera department.
The vast majority are retirees making the most of their European pensions. They
are drawn to Paraguay because of the tropical climate, low cost of living, and
lack of restrictions on commercial ventures. Many come with an entrepreneurial
spirit, setting up restaurants, hotels, and other forms of business catering to both
the local and expat community.

Asians There are a significant amount of Japanese, Chinese, and Korean communities throughout Paraguay. For the most part, the Japanese immigrants are
concentrated in rural areas dedicating themselves to horticulture and beekeep-

ing. The Chinese and Korean populations are more prevalent in urban areas dedicating themselves to commercial ventures.

Languages

Both Spanish and Guaraní are spoken throughout the country and used daily in varying degrees by most Paraguayans. The mixture of both languages is commonly known as *"jopará"* which, fittingly, means "mix" or "blend" in Guaraní. The balance between the two languages shifts towards Spanish in urban areas and towards Guaraní in rural areas. In both areas, there are few people who speak either no Spanish or no Guaraní whatsoever.

GUARANÍ

Guaraní is one of the few pre-colonial indigenous languages that still survives in Latin America and is still widely used throughout all levels of Paraguayan society. Perhaps what makes the use of Guaraní so unique is the varying role it plays in the lives of Paraguayans. Put ten Paraguayans in a room and each will make different use of Guaraní – some might prefer to speak Guaraní over Spanish, while others may simply accentuate their conversations with Guaraní expressions. Paraguayans are keen to point out the expressive nature of the Guaraní language, often stating that, in

---

Mennonites: Paraguay's Other Farmers

The history of the Mennonite colonies in Paraguay proves a lesson in the power of collective work to overcome obstacles. Originally hailng from various corners of the globe, Paraguay's Mennonites are all bound by the same desire for religious freedom, respect of tradition and hard work ethic. The country's first colonies were sent to the hostile Chaco where they had to struggle for survival in the harsh weather and work hard to farm crops in middle of the wilderness. Though the newer colonies of Eastern Paraguay have easier living and farming conditions, they work just as assiduously. Some colonies are very old-fashioned and closed off to outsiders while others are more modern and integrated. Entering a Mennonite colony can feel a bit like the Twilight Zone. Though you are in rural Paraguay these farmers are no *"campesinos."* In fact, they are on opposite ends of the spectrum from Paraguay's native farming class. Used to working in large cooperatives, often with overseas funding from parent colonies, the Mennonites have financial resources unavailable to most rural Paraguayans. They put these funds to use investing in technology (in the form of machinery and research) that allows farming on a large scale. Agricultural experts run experimental farms where new crops are introduced and farming methods are tested. In addition to hard work, education is a priority – almost all Mennonite children finish high school and continue on to university either in large nearby cities or overseas.

Many third generation Mennonites find themselves juggling two cultures – Paraguayan culture and that of their ancestors. They drink *tereré* (and maybe Brahma as well) and speak some Guaraní and Spanish. But most are encouraged to return to their homeland to pursue higher education, as well as to find a spouse. Though they are lauded for the economic advances they bring to the country the Mennonites are roundly criticized by Paraguayans for their lack of integration. Discrimination towards outsiders is a problem, especially towards native populations. Tourists traveling through Mennonite areas will also be given a cool reception – don't take it personally.

comparison to Spanish, romantic phrases are sweeter and criticisms are stronger in Guaraní. Many aspects of Paraguayan culture, such as humor and knowledge of nature, are embedded into the Guaraní language.

The Guaraní language managed to thrive even despite Paraguay's colonization because of two factors: the *mestizo* culture created by the integration of Guaraní women and European colonists and the missionary efforts by the Franciscans and Jesuits. Having brought along no European women the Spanish colonists took Guaraní women as their wives and mistresses. It was these women that passed the language onto the new generation of Paraguayan *mestizos*. At the same time, Franciscan and Jesuit priests found Guaraní to be an

> *"Guaraní cerrado"* or *"Guaraní eté"* is the name given to Guaraní spoken by indigenous groups. It is less influenced by Spanish and closer to the original, pre-colonial Guaraní.

essential tool for the evangelization of the indigenous population. The priests not only learned to speak the language, but also took many steps to preserve it. The Jesuits in particular, dedicated much effort to creating a written version of the language, by creating reference materials such as dictionaries and religious documents. Despite these triumphs, discrimination against Guaraní is also a part of Paraguay's history. Guaraní has historically been considered inferior to Spanish. As the official business language in Paraguay is Spanish, the upper class has often discouraged the use of Guaraní altogether. For many years, it was believed that Guaraní impeded the proper learning of Spanish, and parents were discouraged from speaking Guaraní to their young children. Only recently has this begun to change, with the declaration of Guaraní as an official language of Paraguay in 1992 and the introduction of Guaraní lessons in the national school curriculum in 1994. There is a growing tendency for Guaraní to be used, many times in a tongue-in-cheek fashion, in popular culture.

Top Guaraní Words & Phrases

There are certain Guaraní words and phrases that are ubiquitous throughout the country, even amongst predominantly Spanish-speaking Paraguayans. Many of these are actually mixtures of Spanish and Guaraní. Many can easily be thrown in to any conversation.

Ndaipori problema: No problem

E'a: An exclamation used to express indignation

Graciamante: Thank you

Tranquilo pa: It's all good (the literal translation is "everything is tranquil")

Ndaikua'ai: I don't know

Che ra'a: My friend

Jaha or *jaha katu*: Let's go

Anicehe: You don't say

Chuchi: Fancy, upscale

Amóntema: It's over or gone/forget about it (used to express defeat)

Chake: Look out

Chulina: An exclamation used to declare something cute or endearing

Culture

MUSIC & DANCE

Paraguayans are very proud of their musical heritage. During the colonial era, Guaraní and Spanish musical traditions were blended, thanks to the Jesuit priests. The musical melding that took place in the Jesuit missions resulted in a style known as Guaraní-Baroque (see Guaraní Baroque Music, p181). Nowadays, polkas and *guaranias* are the most

> For a taste of the Paraguayan harp available in the US check out *"Maiteí America: Harps of Paraguay"* by Smithsonian Folkways.

representative musical styles. Paraguayan polka, a cousin of the Argentine *chamamé*, was founded by European immigrants who reached Paraguay by the Río de la Plata. No wedding is complete without an energetic set of polkas that sends couples spinning around the dance floor at a dizzying pace. In the 1920's José Asunción Flores invented a new musical style, the *guarania*. With its slower pace and slightly melancholic tone, the *guarania* was meant to capture the spirit of Paraguayan people.

The guitar and Paraguayan harp play a prominent role in Paraguay's musical traditions. Felix Pérez Cardozo is arguably the most famous Paraguayan composer and harpist – among his best-known songs are *"Tren Lechero," "Llegada"* and his version of *"Pájaro Campana."* Agustín Pío Barrios (also known as *"Mangoré"*) is considered the master of classical guitar and composed other classics such *"Danza Paraguaya."* Modern day musicians have followed in their footsteps, keeping the classics alive while creating their own compositions. Juan Cancio Barreto (who plays a small guitar known as a *"requinto"*) and guitarists Luz María Bobadilla and Berta Rojas are among today's most celebrated musicians.

Among the younger generation, musical tastes range from traditional to modern genres. Reggaeton, salsa, and cachaka blare in *discotecas* across the country. Paraguay has a small but active reggae and heavy metal scene. National bands often use Paraguay's native language to their advantage, peppering their lyrics with Guaraní. Popular musical groups include rock bands Flou, Revolber, and Paiko, reggae/ska bands Cultura Nativa, Pipa Para Tabaco, and Ripe Banana Skins and pop bands Kchiporros and Los Verduleros.

Bringing Music to Rural Communities

Though many Paraguayans have music in their blood, proper music lessons are out of reach for much of the population. Since its founding in 2002, *Sonidos de la Tierra* has been working to help children in rural communities overcome this barrier. Local professors volunteer their time teaching music lessons and are often joined by professors from Asunción. There are workshops, music camps, and, for the extremely fortunate (and talented), scholarships to go on tour in Europe with the *Sonidos de la Tierra* orchestra. The program even includes a workshop for turning recycled materials such as oil drums and empty cans of *dulce de guayaba* into musical instruments, affordable to even the poorest students. There are frequent performances throughout the country. Watching these young children with few resources play beautiful music is enough to tug at anyone's heart strings. *Sonidos de la Tierra* is the brainchild of Luis Szarán, director of Asunción's symphony orchestra. For more information on how to support the program and/or volunteer as a music professor, visit www.sonidosdelatierra.org.py.

Songs of Protest

During the Stroessner regime, music was one of the few outlets for anti-dictatorship sentiments. As part of a movement known as the *"Nuevo Cancionero Paraguayo"* musical groups, such as Sembrador, Juglares, and Grupo Vocal Dos, conveyed the frustrations of and gave hope to an entire generation with their suggestive songs *"Canto de Esperanza"* (Song of Hope) and *"Despertar"* (Awaken).

Many *bailes folklóricos* (folkloric dances) go hand in hand with Paraguayan music. Dances such as the *galopera* are beautiful and energetic with women swirling around in brightly colored, flowing skirts, their hair decorated with flowers. The ultimate showstopper is the *baile de la botella* (bottle dance) in which women dance with glass bottles balanced upon their heads. One or two bottles are standard but expert dancers can balance upwards of ten!

LITERATURE & ARTS

Paraguay has a limited literary tradition thanks to a slew of dictatorships that discouraged education and sent the educated and artistically inclined in to exile. Augusto Roa Bastos is the country's most well known author and winner of the prestigious *Premio Cervantes* prize for Spanish language literature. Social justice is a common theme in his works, which are almost entirely set in Paraguay. Among his best known are *"Yo El Supremo"* (I The Supreme) a thinly veiled critique of the Stroessner dictatorship and *"Hijo de Hombre"* (Son of Man), both of which are available in English.

Paraguay also has a handful of internationally renowned artists. Olga Blinder is one of the founders of Paraguay's *Grupo Arte Nuevo*, which is credited with ushering in Paraguay's contemporary art movement in the 1950's. Carlos Colombino is known for his unique pieces created with a combination of woodcutting and painting. Ricardo Migliorissi produces cartoonish colorful and fantastical paintings that often have a subversive streak. Collections displaying a wide range of Paraguayan art can be found at the excellent Museo del Barro (see Asunción). In addition, the works of sculptors Herman Guggiari, Gustavo Beckelmann, and Hugo Pistilli can be seen in public spaces throughout the city. Within Asunción, theater has been a common form of artistic expression. There is also a small but growing national film movement. In 2006, *"Hamaca Paraguaya"* (Paraguayan Hammock) spoken entirely in Guaraní, won the *Un Certain Regard* award at the Cannes Film Festival. Recently, national productions such as *"Cuchillo de Palo"* and *"7 Cajas"* have been released.

HANDICRAFTS

Paraguay has a wide variety of handicraft offerings, from simple and utilitarian hammocks to the ornately decorative silver filigree jewelry. Most crafts date back to the colonial era and many of the same techniques are still used today. Many handicrafts are associated with particular regions and even specific towns where the art forms have been passed down from generation to generation. While a handful of renowned artisans are able to dedicate themselves

Many Paraguayan towns in the countryside did not receive electricity until the late 60's and early 70's. Until then, women worked on their *artesanías* by the light of candles and kerosene and gas lamps.

exclusively to their craft, most have separate day jobs. The majority of female artisans work on their crafts in between household chores.

Ñanduti

"*Ñanduti*," meaning spider web in Guaraní, is a delicate hand-made lace that is perhaps the most distinctive of Paraguay's handicrafts. Legend has it that ñanduti was originally inspired by a beautifully intricate spider web. Circular designs known as *dechados* are sewn with needle and thread onto a cloth backing, creating beautifully complex designs.

> Don't have room in your backpack for a tablecloth? Individual ñanduti *dechados* make nice appliqué patches for clothes and bags.

Some *ñanduti* are made with solid colors (usually white), and other times multiple colors are combined to create a rainbow of lace. Various *dechados* are combined together and then snipped away from the backing to form everything from elegant doilies to stunning wedding dresses. Even more delicate than regular *ñanduti* creations are those made with very fine thread, known as "*ñanduti de hilo fino*." The epicenter of *ñanduti* production is the town of Itaguá in the department of Central, which has a small, but delightful Museo del Ñanduti with exhibits featuring many of the different designs. Rare antique examples of ñanduti can also be seen at the Museo del Barro in Asunción.

Ao po'i

Equally beautiful (and more utilitarian) is *ao po'i*. The name means fine cloth and the thinly woven cotton is ideal for Paraguay's hot climate. Thread is used to both embroider and manipulate the cloth (in some places still woven by hand), creating a beautiful cut out effect. The art of *ao po'i* is used to create men's dress shirts (resembling *guayaberas*), women's dresses, and intricately decorated tablecloths. Though it is made all over the country, *ao po'i* originates from Yataity in the department of Guairá.

Drawing Inspiration from Nature

Many of Paraguay's textile crafts draw their inspiration from the natural world. In each *ñanduti dechado,* one sees a stylized version of Paraguay's flora and fauna. Passion fruit, coconut, and guava flowers are all represented as are roosters, anthills, and spiders. *Ao po'i* shirts are embroidered with stylized versions of streams, beehives, and frogs. *Encaje ju* is almost exclusively dominated by floral themes.

Artisans in Action

Asacivapa (the *Asociación de Artesanos de Asunción, Ciudades Vecinas y Afines del Paraguay*) holds weekly workshops for artisans working on *ao po'i*, *ñanduti*, and *encaje ju*. This is a good opportunity to see artisans at work and learn about all the particularities of each craft. If you are interested in trying your hand, contact Arminda Careaga (Tel: 021 554 530, 021 513 536, 0981 422 983 asacivapa@gmail.com), the association president, to be sure they have extra supplies on hand; teachers and students usually bring their own. Classes usually take place on Friday afternoons from 1pm to 5pm and cost Gs. 10,000. Classes are held at the CIAMP building next to the Municipal Office of Asunción (*Municipalidad de Asunción*), corner of General R. Benitez and Dr. Justo Preto. *From downtown Asunción and Villa Morra take Linea 56 or 12 towards San Lorenzo.*

Encaje ju

Another popular textile is *encaje ju*, a different form of hand-made lace. *Encaje ju* involves painstaking work, as the thread grid upon which designs are woven must first be tied by hand. Once completed, the grid is connected to a wooden frame and is then filled in with thread stitches creating intricate geometric flower patterns. Sometimes, *encaje ju* and *ao po'i* are used to complement each other. For example, an *ao po'i* tablecloth might have an *encaje ju* inset or border. *Encaje ju* is produced in Yataity and Carapeguá although it can also be found in other parts of the country.

Leatherwork

Even the most basic leather goods are decorated using a number of methods from painting and etching to embossing, known as *"repujado."* Leather is stretched while wet and a number of small metal stamps are employed to create ornate designs on leather goods such as thermoses, suitcases, saddles, and wallets. While most retain their natural brown color, items such as women's handbags and wallets are dyed or painted (dyed leather is preferable as painted leather fades with time). The city of Atyrá in the department of Cordillera is known for its leatherwork.

Silver Filigree

Silver filigree jewelry is another painstaking craft with beautiful results. Though the technique is not unique to Paraguay, the country's filigree artisans do add their own touch, deftly manipulating fine silver threads into the shape of typical plants and animals such as orchids and butterflies. The city of Luque is home to many silver filigree workshops. Due to their proximity to the capital, however, there is a wide selection of filigree available in Asunción as well.

Ceramics

Many towns in the departments of Central and Cordillera such as Areguá, Tobatí, and Itá specialize in ceramic work. Ceramics range from large water jugs known as *"kambuchi"* to small sculptures and are usually left unglazed.

Buying *Artesanías*

Larger stores in cities have a wide variety, while smaller storefronts in the countryside offer you the opportunity to purchase goods directly from the artisans themselves. In many instances, artisans are happy to provide demonstrations and even let you try your hand (after which you are sure to appreciate their craft even more).

Whenever possible, it is best to purchase items directly from the artisan who makes them. Though highly admired and appreciated, traditional crafts are trade that is slowly dying out in Paraguay. The pressures of modern life mean new generations are increasingly seeking salaried jobs rather than working as artisans. By supporting local artisans you enable their craft to remain a viable way to make a living and thus increase the likelihood that they will be taken up by younger generations.

Despite the amount of labor involved in their production, Paraguayan *artesanías* are generally inexpensive. This is because artisans typically price their items barely above cost. Before balking at the price of higher end *artesanías* such as *ao po'i* made of hand-spun cotton or fine gauge (*hilo fino*) ñanduti, be sure to ask the artisan how long it took to make. You'll be surprised when you learn just how little they are earning per hour.

Indigenous Handicrafts

Many of Paraguay's indigenous groups rely on handicrafts as a source of income. While in some cases the quality of crafts is decreased due to mass production, for the most part, indigenous handicrafts are unique. The Maká specialize in bags and sashes of brightly colored cotton woven into striped designs. Both the Nivaclé and Ayoreo Indians are known for their geometrically patterned satchels made from hand-dyed fibers of the *karaguatá* plant. Perhaps the most interesting of the indige-

---

Meet the Mitos

Paraguayans often make reference to a number of strange creatures roaming the country. The so-called *"mitos"* (myths) are invoked in a variety of settings. Parents often use them as a threat to scare their children into behaving. Both innocent mischief and serious crimes are sometimes attributed to the more aggressive myths. Like Aesop's fables, each *mito* has its own back-story and an implied lesson. The *mitos* are a big part of the heritage of the indigenous. Their myths have survived and evolved over time, changing to suit the beliefs of the population as it mixed with European colonists. Some myths are so deeply embedded in Paraguayan culture that they still have a place in the modern world. Among the most widespread *mitos* are:

Jasy Jatere
An elflike childish figure with blonde hair and blue eyes, the *Jasy Jateré* takes children as his prey during *siesta* time. He bewitches them with games, leading them deep into the *monte* (woods) where he eventually abandons them. Although children usually survive encounters with the *Jasy Jateré*, they may be temporarily dazed and even comatose.

Pombero
A stocky, hairy, caveman-like creature, the *Pombero* roams the countryside spooking farm animals and causing mischief. Those who dare to disrespect him can expect trouble. In Guaraní, he is known as *Karai pyhare* (man of the night). Some attempt to remain in his good graces by leaving him offerings of hand rolled cigars and *caña*, sugar cane alcohol at its least refined.

Kurupi
The *Kurupi* is a wild creature with an enormous phallus that wraps several times around his waist. He lives in the wilderness but is always on the prowl for women to impregnate.

Lobisón
The *Lobisón* is Paraguay's version of a werewolf. Popular legend has it that the seventh son of any couple is destined to become a *lobisón*. According to popular belief, the only way to prevent this is for the President of the Republic to serve as the child's godfather.

Ao Ao
A fierce, hairy creature with razor sharp claws. Should you be chased by an *Ao Ao* your only recourse is to climb a coconut tree.

Do people actually believe in *mitos?* Well, it depends on where you are and who you ask. Most Paraguayans have a distant family member or know someone who knows someone that suffered the wrath of the *Pombero*, deprived of cigars, or was gripped with fear at the howl of the *Lobisón*. In the countryside, many swear by the *mitos*. Even for non-believers there is always a small hint of doubt.

nous handicrafts are the wonderfully expressive wooden animal carvings, also created by the Nivaclé.

Because Paraguay's indigenous tend to live in remote areas, it is difficult to purchase crafts directly from the artisans themselves. Many communities rely on middlemen to sell their crafts, leaving very little profit for the actual artisan. An excellent source of indigenous crafts near Asunción is the Museo Guido Boggiani, not only due to the wide variety of offerings but also because the artisans themselves set sale prices and receive the full amount.

SPORTS

From the well-manicured fancy pitches of Asunción to the countryside fields with makeshift goal posts, *fútbol* (soccer) is undoubtedly, the most predominant sport in Paraguay. The national team inspires pride like none other. In the 2010 *"Mundial"* (World Cup), the *Albirroja* as they are known, made it to the quarterfinals, a record for the team. There are several local and regional teams, and foreigners will frequently be asked which "club" they cheer for *("de qué club sos?")*. The largest national clubs, based in Asunción, are *Olimpia* (with club colors black and white) and *Cerro Porteño* (blue and red). A match between these two clubs is referred to as a *"super clásico"* and is among the most widely anticipated. Partake in Paraguay's soccer fever by attending a match or joining locals in a bar or restaurant to watch televised matches. Both options are just as entertaining.

Volleyball and its more complex cousin piki volley are other popular sports in Paraguay. Piki volley is played on the same court as volleyball but instead of using their hands, piki volley players use their heads, chest, and feet to lob volleyball across the net. Volleyball is more popular with women while piki volley is almost an all-male sport. Volley and piki courts can be seen throughout the countryside, even in the poorest communities.

Attending a Soccer Game:

The sections behind either goal post are generally occupied by the *barra brava* – hardcore fans who often lead the entire section in chants against the other team, many times accompanied by drums and other instruments. Though the *barra brava* section is the most animated (and the cheapest), things can get a bit rowdy during heated matches. It is best not to take backpacks or thermoses to large stadiums, as they may not be allowed in for security purposes. In some cases, even belts are confiscated. It is usually easy to acquire scalped tickets near the stadiums, especially once matches have already started. Vendors will be shouting *"compro entradas"* ("I'm buying tickets") to indicate that they are, in fact, selling tickets. Most will find it more practical to buy tickets ahead of time though.

Trans Chaco Rally

The Trans-Chaco Rally is a grueling automotive rally that takes place every September in the Paraguayan Chaco. The three-day route winds its way through the Chaco's difficult terrain, destroying many cars along the way. The rally is the biggest international sporting event held in Paraguay, drawing professional drivers from all over the world. Paraguay may soon be home to yet another international automotive rally. Due to safety concerns, the Dakar Rally has been transferred to Latin American from Africa and is scheduled to include sections of the Paraguayan Chaco in its 2013 route (for more information, see The Trans Chaco Rally, p303).

ETIQUETTE

Whether it is inviting you to sit down for a *tereré* break, helping you figure out what bus to take, or refusing to let you leave without a parting gift, Paraguayans are generally very friendly. They are also very proud of their *tranquilo* (laid back) attitude towards life. Travelers with experience in other Latin American countries will find similarities in basic etiquette, though Paraguayans tend to be more religious and conservative.

Greetings

A kiss on each cheek is a standard greeting among women and between men and women. Technically, one places their cheek against someone else's and makes a kissing sound. This is also done when saying goodbye. When greeting members of the opposite sex, it is also appropriate to shake hands instead of kiss. Men generally shake hands with one other. When greeting someone in passing, most Paraguayans simply say *"adiós"* as they walk by. This is customary in the countryside but much less so in urban areas.

Punctuality

In Paraguay, tardiness is common and not considered rude. Most business meetings start between fifteen to thirty minutes late while guests for a large party typically arrive between forty-five to ninety minutes late. If you are determined to show up on time, be ready to offer to help set up if your host seems flustered at your "early" arrival. When arranging to meet with Paraguayans and expats, be sure to clarify whether you will be operating on "Paraguayan time" (*hora Paraguaya*) or not.

> *"Enseguida"* (right away) can actually mean anything from several minutes to several hours.

Communication

Paraguayans' innate desire to be friendly can translate into a reluctance to be the bearer of bad news. White lies, such as saying a broken down bus is arriving *enseguida* (right away), are par for the course but not made with bad intentions. An indirect, sugarcoated approach is often favored over blunt honesty. For example, when Paraguayans are invited to an event, they almost always confirm their attendance in order to avoid appearing rude. It is up to the host to read between the lines and decipher whose *sí* (yes) or *puede ser* (maybe) really means *no*. Foreigners should note that being very direct is considered rude and can sometimes be misinterpreted as having a confrontational attitude.

> Unless it is an emergency, avoid calling on people during *siesta* time (noon to mid-afternoon).

Paraguayans' laid-back *tranquilo* attitude extends to even the most basic transactions, which are often preceded by several minutes of friendly chit-chat. Though it can be tempting to speed things up by cutting to the chase, this can be counterproductive. You may unintentionally come across as rude or pushy. For those looking to get things accomplished in a hurry, it is best to attempt to strike a middle ground between laid back and insistent.

Personal Space & Personal Information

Paraguayans are not accustomed to the idea of personal space or "alone time." If you are participating in a volunteer program that pairs you with a host family, be aware that they may think something is wrong if you spend too much time alone. An equally underused concept is that of personal information – it is not uncommon for people to openly discuss topics which many foreigners would consider off limits such as money, personal relationships, and health issues. In addition, gossip is quite common. Especially in the countryside, long stretches of the day may be passed sitting in the shade keeping a running commentary of everything that happens and everyone that walks by. And while Paraguayans are very friendly, they are not particularly tactful. Foreigners may be shocked to hear otherwise kind hosts blithely comment that someone is fat or ugly (many times to their face). Though difficult, it is best not to take these comments to heart, as most Paraguayans do not consider this form of frankness to be rude.

Clothing

At the government and business level, attire is formal. Dress shoes are a must. In less formal occasions, people are dressed more casually, but an effort is always made to

---

Paraguayan Hand Gestures

Thumbs up – It's all Good!
Paraguayans are big fans of the "thumbs up" gesture. Many times instead of (or sometimes in addition to) giving the thumbs up, people will say *"al pelo."* This means "towards the hair," indicating that their thumb is pointing upwards.

Clapping
When in front of houses without doorbells, people make their presence known by clapping. Between one and four claps are made with hands cupped for maximum volume. Paraguayans like clapping in general – it is not uncommon to hear people break into applause during lectures, movies, and even in church. Occasionally, when a plane lands, passengers will burst into applause.

Emongarú
Emongarú is the Paraguayan version of a high five. It means "feed" in Guaraní (in this form the word is a direct order). The hand motion is meant to simulate a mother hen feeding her baby chick. The proper way to perform an *emongarú* is as follows: press all five fingers together and extend your arm with your fingers downwards. Extend your hand towards the recipient. You may choose to say *"emongarú"* as well. The recipient should then extend his or her hand in the same fashion but with fingers facing upwards. Once your fingers have touched briefly you have successfully completed an *"emongarú."* The imaginary hen has fed her chick! It is anyone's guess where this originated from, but it is a lot of fun, especially since everyone's pseudo chicken is different. Some peck at the other hand while others prefer to just touch once. There are no accompanying sound effects, although if you make one up, it'll be sure to get some laughs.

Vení Un Poco
The Paraguayan signal for "come here" is an extended arm with palm facing down and all fingers moving down into the palm (like a downward one-hand clap). Often this is accompanied with a *"chh chh"* sound through closed teeth. In Spanish, people will say *"vení un poco"* and in Guaraní they say *"ejumina."*

look tidy and presentable, even in the poorest of settings.

Foreigners working in politics or government might avoid wearing blue or red, as those colors are closely associated to the Liberal and Colorado political parties. Wearing either color will often prompt commentary from Paraguayans.

Showing Respect

As in Argentina and Uruguay, Paraguayans use the informal *"vos"* instead of *"tu"* as the second person singular pronoun. *"Usted"* is only used in situations of extreme protocol. For the most part, respect is shown to others via prefixes. People with university degrees are often referred to as *"Licenciado"* and teachers as *"Profesor"* or *"Profe,"* more informally. In more traditional homes in the countryside, it is customary for children to refer to their parents as *"Señor"* and *"Señora"* when they are responding as a sign of respect and for the eldest brother and sister to be called *"Hermano"* or *"Hermana"* by younger siblings. Elderly men are given the prefix *"Don"* and women *"Doña"* which is sometimes shortened to simply *"Ña."*
Before entering a room, it is customary to request permission to enter by saying *"permiso."* Permission is granted with an *"adelante."* When leaving a gathering it is important to say goodbye to your host and others in the room. Doing a full round of *despedidas* (goodbyes) may be time consuming, especially at large gatherings, but it is still worthwhile.

Environment

GEOGRAPHY

Paraguay is a landlocked country located in the heart of South America with Bolivia to the north, Brazil to east, and Argentina to the west and south. The majority of Paraguay's borders are formed by rivers. The Pilcomayo River, Paraná River, and a section of the Paraguay River create the border with Argentina. The Apa and Paraná Rivers create the border with Brazil. The Paraguay River, which runs north to south, bisects the country into two geologically distinct regions: Paraguay Oriental (Eastern Paraguay) and the Paraguayan Chaco.

The Guaraní Aquifer

Shared between Paraguay, Brazil, Argentina, and Uruguay, the Guaraní Aquifer is the largest fresh water aquifer in South America. It is believed to be the second largest aquifer in the world. At 1,190,000 km² it is estimated to hold approximately 45,000 cubic kilometers of water. While only six percent of the aquifer is in Paraguayan territory, the Guaraní Aquifer is one of Paraguay's most important sources of fresh water. The aquifer covers the eastern departments of Caaguazú, Alto Paraná, as well as small portions of Canindeyú, Amambay, Itapúa, Caazapá, San Pedro, Guairá, Concepción, Ñeembucú, and Misiones. Water is accessed via wells and used for both human consumption and agricultural purposes. The aquifer is replenished by rainwater along recharge zones in Caaguazú and Alto Paraná. Given that the industry in these areas is largely agricultural, the use of agro-toxins is considered a potential threat to the aquifer's water quality.

Eastern Paraguay makes up about 40 percent of the country's total area and is where 97 percent of the population lives. The region's lush forests and fertile ground make it highly preferable to the inhospitable Chaco, home to a mere three percent of the population. Most of the Chaco's population lives in or near the Mennonite colonies of the Central Chaco. Paraguay is very flat with only a few small mountain ranges scattered throughout Eastern Paraguay such as the Cordillera Ybytyruzu in the province of Guairá (the highest peak is Cerro Tres Kandu at 842 meters) and the Cordillera Amambay in the province of Amambay (the highest peak is Punta Porá at 700 meters). The department of Cordillera has smaller, gently rolling hills. At 604 meters, Cerro León is the highest point in the Chaco region, a great alluvial plane.

Paraguay is home to several distinct ecoregions. The western half of the country contains the Pantanal to the northeast, the Dry Chaco to the north, and the Humid Chaco to the south. The Dry Chaco is a semi-arid and impossibly hot region covered in thorny plants and dotted with occasional salt and fresh water lagoons, which attract the region's mostly endangered species. This is one of the few places in the world where one can encounter a wild jaguar. The Dry Chaco's savannahs are part of South America's largest ecosystem, second only to the Amazon. Further south, the landscape changes completely. The Humid Chaco floods seasonally and is blanketed with *karanda'y* palm trees and populated by birds a plenty. Making up ten percent of the country's wetlands, the Pantanal runs along the northern section of the Paraguay River. The world's largest wetland, the Pantanal, floods seasonally and is home to an astonishing array of wildlife, much of which is easily visible at the water's edge. Eastern Paraguay is home to the Cerrado ecoregion as well as the Mesopotamian Grasslands, and Atlantic Forest ecoregions. The Cerrado is a tropical savannah while the Mesopotamian Grasslands in the southern portion of the country contain both grasslands and wetlands. The Atlantic Forest is one of the most biologically rich ecoregions in the country, but unfortunately, has also suffered the most degradation.

Paraguay in Depth

Beware of the Red Dirt

The iron-rich red dirt that characterizes Eastern Paraguay is known as *"yvy pyta."* Travelers in nice clothing should beware: *yvy pyta* will dye all of your light colored belongings deep orange between washes. A common Paraguayan trick for removing red stains is to soap up the article of clothing and then let it bake in the sun for several hours.

CLIMATE

Paraguay's climate varies between tropical to subtropical (the Tropic of Capricorn cuts through Northern Paraguay). Summertime (December to February) temperatures average around 33° Celsius (91.4° Fahrenheit), though it is not uncommon for the mercury to rise above 40° Celsius (104° Fahrenheit), with temperatures climbing even higher in the Chaco region. With the exception of the dry, Northern Chaco, humidity runs high throughout the year. Winter (June to August) temperatures vary between 10° and 20° Celsius (between 50° and 68° Fahrenheit) but can drop much lower in the southern part of Paraguay.

FLORA

Paraguay has an abundance of flowering trees – each season different ones bloom, filling the landscape with bright colors. There is always a new color to enjoy – the *chivato's* orange, the *jacaranda's* lilac, the deeply saturated yellow of the *yvyrapyta*. The *lapacho* is the national tree of Paraguay and comes in three varieties: pink,

Naturaleza del Paraguay (www.familiadiarte.com) has excellent photos of Paraguay's flora and fauna with descriptions in Spanish.

yellow, and white, the latter being the rarest of the three. The *lapacho* is often referred to by its Guaraní name *"tajy."* The explosion of pink *tajy* flowers keeps many Paraguayans' spirits high during cold winter days. The mango tree, with its enormous shade-giving foliage and vast quantities of fruit, may as well be another national tree. Other important trees include several hard wood trees such as *trébol, quebracho,* and *palo santo.* In the Chaco, the *palo borracho* (drunken stick) tree is especially adapted to the dry climate, soaking up water until its thorny trunk looks bloated and ready to pop. Other flowering plants include the passion fruit plant whose strangely beautiful flower, the *mbaracuya poty,* is the national flower of Paraguay. Paraguay is also home to several species of orchids.

> Guaraní is the third most common language used in scientific names of plants, after Greek and Latin.

Palo Santo, Bullet Proof Wood

Palo Santo is perhaps Paraguay's most intriguing hard wood. The wood is one of the hardest in the world and is even said to be able to withstand bullets. It has a bluish green tint and gives off a pleasant, vaguely medicinal smell. This unmistakable scent makes *palo santo* ideal for use in *mate* and *tereré guampas* where it adds a distinct flavor to the water. U.S.-based brewery Dog Fish Head has recently released Palo Santo Marron, an ale aged in a barrel made of *palo santo.*

FAUNA

Paraguay is home to an extremely wide variety of wildlife relative to the country's small size. This is due to country's relatively small population and the presence of six distinct ecoregions. Vast and relatively uninhabited the Paraguayan Chaco, which includes the Dry Chaco, Humid Chaco, and Pantanal, boasts a number of rare and endangered species. Though Eastern Paraguay is home to the majority of the country's human population, there is great biodiversity in the Cerrado, Atlantic Forest, and Mesopotamian grasslands.

Lone, fierce predators such as jaguars and puma still roam through the Chaco and some parts of Eastern Paraguay. Both are increasingly rare as they are much sought after by poachers and are also often shot by cattle ranchers. The Chaco is also

Christmas Smells Like Coconut

Flor de coco or coconut flowers, play an important role in Paraguayan culture. In the days leading up to Christmas, the streets and markets are full of these two to three foot long fuzzy brown pods with rows of yellow seeded strands peeking out. The *flor de coco* does not look like a flower at all, rather, it looks more like an enormous ear of baby corn. These are an essential component to any nativity scene or *pecebre*. The aroma permeates the atmosphere, and most Paraguayans associate this fragrance with Christmastime. There is even a Christmas song called *"Navidad de Flor de Coco, Navidad del Paraguay."*

Like many traditions in Paraguay, the use of *flor de coco* during Christmas is the result of a mixture of Spanish and Guaraní culture. The *"mbokaja,"* as the coconut is called in Guaraní, is sacred in Guaraní culture. Legend has it that during the *Gran Diluvio* (the Great Flood), survivors fled to safety atop a very high coconut tree. Spanish missionaries later incorporated the *flor de coco* into their Christmas traditions.

home to the aptly named Chaco peccary, which looks like a small wild boar and, until 1976, was believed to be extinct. Giant river otters live exclusively in the Pantanal, making their homes by the water's edge. Large and shaggy, the bushy tailed giant anteater ambles purposefully through the underbrush. Lowland tapirs look like stocky gray/brown pigs with curiously flexible snouts and can weigh up to a quarter ton. Juvenile tapirs have striped and spotted coats and are impossibly cute. Paraguay is home to eleven species of armadillo (see Tatus of the Chaco, p302) including the large and endangered giant armadillo. South America's largest deer, the marsh deer, is found in the Pantanal as well. Its reddish brown hue tends to contrast with the surrounding vegetation. Weighing up to 140 pounds, capybaras, the world's largest rodents, are found living in waterways throughout the country. These fat bottomed rodents are often hunted for their meat. Another curious animal is the maned wolf, a long legged fox distinctive for its lopping gait and strong skunky smell. There are also five species of monkeys: the capuchin, titi, electric, howler, and night monkey. Paraguay also hosts a large reptile population, which can be seen slithering and swimming across aquatic and terrestrial habitats. The most well known and easily spotted is the *caiman* (which looks like a small crocodile), known commonly as the "yacaré." Other reptiles include various species of pit vipers and rattlesnakes. The Chaco's flat landscape and dusty roads are ideal for spotting tortoises (one species is said to be a preferred food of Ayoreo still living in voluntary isolation). Among the larger fish are the *surubí* and *dorado*, both of which are popular catches with fishermen (see Fishing, p68). Also of interest to nature lovers is Paraguay's amphibian population, which boasts some seventy-six species. Toads, known in Guaraní as "kururu," can be seen hopping throughout the countryside, each larger than the next. Locals claim that the *kururu* will squirt toxic milk into the eyes of those brave enough to approach it. There are also several species of frogs including the coralline frog with black and red mottled spots on a cream-colored body and the cartoon-

> For footage of Paraguay's wildlife, check out *Paraguay Salvaje*. This television show can be seen Saturdays at 12:30 on the LaTele channel but several videos are also available online (www.paraguay-salvaje.com and on Facebook).

> **Sneaky Crocodiles**
> "Jacare" is the Guaraní word for caiman. *Jacare* has another more mischievous meaning. In general, it can be used to imply doing something in a secretive manner, but more specifically, a *jacare* is a man who sneaks into his girlfriend or mistress' bedroom window.

Behaving like an Animal

In Guaraní, animals are commonly referenced when describing human behavior. This derives from a rural tradition of living in close proximity with nature. You can learn a lot about animals by paying attention to this peculiarity of Paraguayan culture.

Aguara: Nickname for someone who is either very intelligent or very smelly, both characteristics of the *Aguara Guazu* (Maned Wolf).

Alonsito: Nickname for a man who is helping to rear another man's offspring, a fate which often befalls the *Hornero* (Ovenbird), also known as an "Alonsito."

Pira kutu: Used to describe someone who is falling asleep, head bobbing like a fish (*pira*) on a hook (*kutu*).

ish Budgett's frog with a puffy body and small beady eyes.

Birdlife, in particular, is very abundant. With its black head, red throat and white body the *jabiru* stork, one of South America's largest birds, is easily spotted soaring through the sky in the Chaco and the Pantanal. Curiously pink flamingos and spoonbills can be seen rooting around for food in the Chaco's lagoons. Toucans are present throughout the country as well as parakeets, rheas (which look like ostriches), herons and egrets. In addition, Paraguay has several sites that are popular rest spots for migratory birds heading both north and south (see Birding, p.67).

Guyra Campana

The bell bird, known as the *"pájaro campana"* in Spanish and the *"guyra campana"* in Guaraní, is the national bird of Paraguay. Its call once rang through the Atlantic Forests of Mbaracayú and Itapúa but is now quite rare as the species is under threat of extinction due to loss of habitat. *"Pájaro Campana,"* one of Paraguay's most well known harp songs (composed by Carlos Talavera and played by Felix Pérez Cardozo on the harp), was inspired by the bell bird's distinctive call.

Paraguayan Nature Conservation Organizations

Unfortunately much of the country's flora and fauna are increasingly under threat due to the pressures of a growing population, large scale agriculture, cattle grazing, as well as poaching, and illegal logging. Paraguay has the most rapid rate of deforestation in all of South America. The resulting natural habitat destruction has pushed several animals onto the endangered species list including the giant anteater, giant armadillo, maned wolf, giant river otter, tapir, jaguar, and marsh deer. The following is a list of organizations dedicated to studying and protecting Paraguay's flora and fauna.

Guyra Paraguay: www.guyraparaguay.org

Fauna Paraguay: www.faunaparaguay.com

Fundación Moisés Bertoni: www.mbertoni.org.py

Procosara: www.procosara.org

Paraguay Silvestre: www.paraguaysilvestre.org.py

Desde El Chaco: www.desdelchaco.org.py

Alter Vida: www.altervida.org.py

A Todo Pulmón – Paraguay Respira: www.atodopulmon.org

The Basics

When to Visit

The best time to visit Paraguay is during its dry season, between May and October. Daytime temperatures are mild and pleasant with lows in the nighttime notwithstanding. Travel to remote areas is considerably easier and more comfortable than the rest of the year when temperatures soar and rain renders dirt roads impassable. Travel during the spring and summer can be unpleasant due to the extremely hot climate. Trips to the north of the country should be avoided if possible during the summer. Visitors should take appropriate measures to protect themselves from the heat, and anticipate travel delays due to rain. In addition, many smaller businesses and museums are closed for vacation during the month of January.

WEATHER & TRAVEL

Daytime Highs

Given Paraguay's intense tropical heat, shielding yourself from the sun is essential, and you will find that, on hot days, everyone's activities revolve around the temperature. Wear a hat, lightweight clothing, sunglasses, and sunscreen. Remain indoors, or at the very least, in the shade during the *siesta* hours (noon-3ish). Seek refuge inside air-conditioned malls or restaurants in urban areas and shady plazas in rural areas. Even visitors during the winter months should be prepared to deal with warm snaps.

> In the countryside water is kept cool in a ceramic jug called a *"cántaro"* in Spanish and a *"kambuchi"* in Guaraní.

Staying hydrated is fundamental, even if your physical activity is limited. Bottled water is widely available, though most Paraguayans prefer to stay hydrated with the ubiquitous ice-cold *tereré* (see *Tereré*, p87). Most plazas have at least one stand renting out all the necessary elements for a *tereré* session. Hydration packs such as a Camelpak, will come in handy, especially while on the road. Many businesses will provide free tap water on request or have a water cooler available for customers.

"Haku eterei!"

In Guaraní the word for hot is *"haku,"* pronounced "hakoo" with an emphasis on the last syllable. If you want to say "it's hot," all you need to say is *"haku!"* If it is really hot, you can say *"haku etere'i."* Exclaiming *"haku eterei!"* will elicit an affirmative *"haku eterei"* in response. However, you should take care not to say *"Che haku"* (I'm hot), as that has a different, sexual meaning. It is also probably best to refrain from saying *"Che ro'y"* (I'm cold) as the subtle difference in pronunciation between it and *"Che ro'u"* (I want to have sex) is difficult to master.

Winter Lows

Though Paraguay's winter temperatures are moderate, the humidity and general lack of insulation, even in upscale constructions, mean low temperatures are felt acutely. Often the difference in the temperature indoors and outdoors is minimal, and in some cases it can actually be colder inside. During the winters, Paraguay is hit by a cold southern front known as the *"viento sur"* causing temperatures in the south to drop to freezing cold.

Much Needed Relief

Every winter has a handful of warm days scattered throughout which offer respite from the cold. As the majority of homes do not have dryers, sunny days are ideal for doing laundry. If you need clothing washed during the winter, a sunny morning is the perfect time to seek out a local laundry lady. Make sure to specify whether clothes are dried on a clothes line or barbed wire to avoid having clean but holey clothing.

If you are planning to be in Paraguay between mid-May and mid-August, light to medium weight thermals, a jacket, and a sleeping bag should do the trick. Short term winter travelers should still come prepared with warm weather clothes, as warm snaps are common even in the dead of winter.

Rain

Heavy rains are often the cause for travel delays and cancellations. Asphalted or cobblestone roads may suffer an hour or so of flooding after a heavy rainstorm. Dirt roads, especially those of the Paraguayan Chaco, may become impassable for anything from several hours to days. Visitors to Asunción are advised to be careful during storms and to stay indoors. The city's major roads flood quickly and heavy winds can bring down tree limbs and power lines. In the countryside, life slows to a standstill during rainy days with all non-essential activities postponed until the weather improves.

Travel Documents

With the exception of Mercosur members (Uruguay, Brazil, and Argentina), all visitors traveling to Paraguay are required to carry a valid passport. As of 2012, travel visas are required for Americans, Australians, Canadians, and New Zealanders – travelers of all other nationalities should, nonetheless, double check with the Paraguayan Embassy for updated travel requirements. Visas must be obtained in advance through the Paraguayan Embassy or consulate – they are not available for purchase upon entering the country. Visa applications cost US$45 for a single entry and US$65 for a multiple entry visa – both are good for ninety continuous days within Paraguay. One-time visa extensions, good for ninety days, may be obtained at the immigration office in Asunción (see Visa Extensions and Immigration, p116) for Gs. 277,000. Tourists who wish to extend their stay in Paraguay by exiting and then re-entering the country should note an absence of more than forty-eight hours might be required in order to begin a new ninety day stay. However, the Paraguayan government is constantly changing immigration rules, so it is best to double check with the immigration office should any visa issues arise (see Visa Extensions & Immigration on page 116).

Getting There

AIRLINES

The majority of commercial flights to Paraguay arrive at the Aeropuerto Internacional Silvio Pettirossi in the capital city of Asunción. Airport tax is US $41, paid upon departure. However, some airlines include this fee in their ticket prices. Check at the airline counter to be sure you won't accidentally pay the exit tax twice.

TAM Mercosur Offers the most frequent connections to Paraguay with most flights connecting through Sao Paolo, Brazil (a planned merger between TAM and LAN is in the works). Not to be confused with Transportes Aereos Militares, a military transport plane, which operates flights within Paraguay. *Tel: 021 615 061/2, 645 444 (airport office), Corner of Mariscal López and Mayor Infante Rivarola, www.tam.com.br*

TACA TACA flights to Paraguay often involve several layovers in Central and South America. *Tel: 009 800 511 8222, Galerías Viabella corner of Avenida España and Dr. Feliciangelly, www.taca.com*

Aerosur Most Aerosur flights connect to Asunción from Santa Cruz, Bolivia. *Tel: 021 614 743/744, 021 646 125 (airport office) Corner of Senador Long and Avenida España, www.aerosur.com*

Gol Daily flights to Asunción from both Brazil and Argentina. *Tel: 021 454 772, Paseo Carmelitas, Corner of Avenida España and Malutin, www.voegol.com.br*

LAN Most flights to Asunción connect through Santiago, Chile, or Buenos Aires, Argentina. *Corner of Juan de Salazar and Washington, www.lan.com*

COPA Flights to the United States connect in Panama City, Panama. *Tel: 009 800 542 0074, Corner of Avenida Boggiani and Capitán Nudelman, Edificio Boggiani, www.copaair.com*

American Airlines Direct flights from Miami are scheduled to begin in November, 2012. *Currently, there is not an office in Asunción. www.aa.com*

Sol Del Paraguay A new national airline that flies between Asunción, Ciudad del Este, and Buenos Aires with plans to expand to Brazil, Chile, and Bolivia. *Tel: 021 224 555, Eligio Ayala 988 between EEUU and Tacuary, www.viajaconsol.com*

INTERNATIONAL BUSES

Paraguay is serviced by many international buses from neighboring countries. Varying levels of services are available. Though names vary by company, in general, *semi cama* seats recline at about a 130° angle and *cama* seats recline at about 160°. Some companies offer *ejecutivo suite* seats that recline 180°. Higher priced services also include nicer bathrooms and better and more frequent meals. Most Paraguayan bus companies require purchase in person (or with passengers' ID) and will not make advanced reservations. Peak travel times requiring advanced purchases are Christmas, New Years, Easter week, and winter school vacation (varying weeks in July). All companies have offices in Asunción's bus terminal (see Terminal de Omnibus, p114).

At border crossings, bus drivers will collect passenger IDs and give them to immigration officials. Some bus companies do not allow luggage in the passenger section until after passing immigration so make sure your travel documents and valuables are on hand. When you disembark for immigration controls, take personal possessions with you, and note the number of your bus (there are often several buses from the same company). ID's are returned as passengers re-board the bus after passing through immigration.

The Basics

Buses to/from Argentina

Buses to Argentina cross from Puerto Falcón (near Asunción) to Clorinda or from Encarnación to Posadas.

Crucero del Norte *Tel: 021 559 087, 5411 5258 5000 (Argentina), www.crucerodelnorte.com.ar*

Nuestra Señora de la Asunción *Tel: 021 289 1000, 5411 4311 7666 (Argentina), www.nsa.com.py*

La Encarnacena *Tel: 021 555 077, 021 555 862, 5411 4313 2393 (Argentina), www.laencarnacena.com.py*

Buses to/From Brazil

Buses to Brazil cross from Pedro Juan Caballero to Ponta Porã or from Ciudad del Este to Foz do Iguaçu. Less transited crossings include Salto del Guairá to Guairá in northeastern Paraguay and Bella Vista del Norte to Bela Vista in northern Paraguay.

Pluma *Tel: 021 551 758, 0800 6460300 (Brazil), www.pluma.com.br*

Catarinense *Tel: 021 551 738, 0800 470 470 (Brazil), www.catarinense-viacao.com.br*

Buses to/from Bolivia

Buses to Bolivia cross from Mayor Infante Rivarola to Villa Montes and then on to Santa Cruz, Bolivia, however it is important to note that the immigration office is located in Mariscal Estigarribia (see Crossing Into Bolivia, p300).

Stel Turismo *Tel: 021 551 647, 591 03343 388 (Bolivia)*

Yacyretá/TransSuarez (operated by Nuestra Señora de Asunción) *Tel: 021 289 1000, 551 725, 591 03343 388 (Bolivia), www.nsa.com.py*

BORDER CROSSINGS

Travelers with Mercosur IDs (Paraguay, Uruguay, Brazil, and Argentina) can cross freely between countries – as a result most public transportation crossing borders will not automatically stop at immigration controls. Even tour operators have been known to breeze past border controls. As a foreigner, it is your responsibility to make sure your passport is stamped both when entering and exiting the country – border agents will charge the official fine of Gs. 360,000 (or may ask for a bribe) if any irregularities with passport stamps are discovered. Keep in mind many immigration offices in less popular border crossings are closed for lunch and on the weekends (in many cases you will still be able to physically cross the border but won't have an official exit stamp to show for it). It is best to call ahead of time and make sure they are open. For more information about specific crossings contact the main immigration office in Asunción (see Visa Extensions & Immigration, p116).

The following is a list of official border crossings most transited by tourists. More information is provided in each respective city's section. Though there are other, smaller border crossings throughout the country, these are mostly used by locals and do not count with immigration facilities.

Puerto Falcón – Clorinda, Argentina

About an hour by bus from Asunción, this border is popular with Paraguayans looking to buy merchandise in Clorinda. All international buses stop to clear customs and immigration. There are also several mini-buses that run from the border to Asunción with stops at the bus terminal and Mercado Cuatro. *Tel: 021 499 140*

Encarnación – Posadas, Argentina
Regular city bus services operate between the bus terminals of Encarnación and Posadas. The immigration office is located at the foot of the San Roque González de Santa Cruz bridge. *Tel: 071 202 253, 071 206 286*

Pilar – Resistencia, Argentina
A ferry crosses the Paraguay River from the Port of Pilar to Puerto Colonia Cano in Argentina daily. From there, one can catch buses to the cities of Resistencia, Formosa, and Corrientes. *Tel: 086 32507*

Ciudad del Este – Foz do Iguaçu, Brazil & Puerto Iguazú, Argentina
Technically this involves going through Brazil first, though tourists without Brazilian visas can take direct buses from CDE's terminal to Puerto Iguazú's terminal that bypass Brazilian immigration. The immigration office is located at the foot of the Puente de Amistad Bridge. *Tel: 061 512 417*

Presidente Franco/Puerto Iguazú, Argentina (by ferry)
A regular ferry service is available from the Puerto Hito Tres Fronteras, a short distance from Ciudad del Este in the city of Presidente Franco, to the port of Puerto Iguazú.

Pedro Juan Caballero/Ponta Porã, Brazil
There is no official border crossing between the two cities, which are divided by one large main road. In order to get stamped out of Paraguay you must go to the immigration office at the southern end of town and then head to a separate building several blocks away in Ponta Porã to get stamped in to Brazil. *Tel: 03431 6312, 03362 72195, Naciones Unidas 144*

Mariscal Estigarribia/Mayor Infante Rivarola – Villamontes, Bolivia
The immigration office for those traveling on the Trans Chaco Highway to Bolivia is located at Mariscal Estigarribia, well before the actual border with Bolivia at Mayor Infante Rivarola. *Tel: 0494 247 315, Ruta Trans Chaco km 530*

Bahía Negra – Puerto Busch, Bolivia & Corumbá, Brazil
Carmelo Peralta is the northernmost immigration control office along the Paraguay River. However, for those traveling by boat, it is best to get your exit stamp before boarding in Concepción, as the boat will not wait for you in Carmelo Peralta. Another option for those worried about timing is to attempt to get your exit stamp in Asunción, explaining your travel situation. For more information about this crossing see Obtaining Exit-Stamps Before Continuing to Bolivia and Brazil, p310. *Tel: 0972 193143, corner of Presidente Franco and Pedro Juan Caballero.*

Capitan Carmelo Peralta – Porto Murtinho, Brazil
The Aquidaban boat drops passengers off at Isla Margarita from which you can take small water taxis across to Carmelo Peralta as well as to Porto Murtinho.

Planning Your Trip

TOURIST INFORMATION

The Secretaría Nacional de Turismo, known by the acronym Senatur, has tourist information offices in Paraguay's most popular tourist destinations including Asunción (an office downtown and a stand at the airport), Ciudad del Este, Encarnación, and

The Basics

Villa Florida. Senatur offices vary in the amount of printed materials they have available but are your best source for free maps (see Maps and GPS, p63). The Senatur website (www.senatur.gov.py) is a good source for basic information and is available in English, Spanish, Portuguese, and German. The seasonal calendar of events (*Calendario de Eventos*) is especially useful and is available as a PDF featuring details regarding festivals, holidays, and celebrations happening throughout Paraguay. Senatur has pamphlets providing listings for lodging, restaurants, and tourist attractions in each department. These can also be accessed online at the websites www.siente(department name).com (i.e.: www.sientecentral.com, www.sientealtoparana.com). The quality of information provided by Senatur officials working the visitor's centers varies greatly – some are quite knowledgeable and others merely offer you brochures. Most will answer your questions but are unlikely to volunteer additional information. It is best to be proactive and ask lots of specific questions.

There are a handful of locally available Spanish language guide books. *"La Magia de Nuestra Tierra"* published by Fundación en Alianza (www.enalianza.org.py) is very detailed covering almost every town in the country. This book may prove especially helpful to those traveling to or working in less visited areas of the country such as San Pedro, Amambay, and Canindeyú. The *"Guía Turística TACPy"* is a succinct guide book published by Paraguay's Touring and Automotive Club (*www.tacpy.com.py*). Both are written with Paraguayans (with cars) in mind. They can be found in gas stations and book stores throughout Asunción (though you may have to try more than one) as well as the Senatur office in downtown Asunción.

Many town municipal offices (*la municipalidad*) have someone in charge of tourism who can provide information on local sights and activities and can help connect you with potential lodging and guides. Ask to speak to the *"Secretario de Turismo."* They may also be able to put you in touch with Peace Corps volunteers or other foreigners living in the area. Keep in mind most municipal offices close for the day between noon and 1pm.

When calling government offices and tour operators for information, keep in mind that many offices have time limits on incoming and outgoing phone calls. Be prepared to call back in case your call is disconnected (the person on the other end may warn you with *"Se corta!"*).

MUSEUMS, CHURCHES, & OTHER SITES

Most museums offer free admission, although museums associated with a church parish may charge a small fee (usually no more than Gs. 10,000). Entrance fees are only listed when applicable. With a few notable exceptions (the majority in Asunción), museum exhibits are minimally labeled. Visitors will benefit greatly from historical information provided by guides, when available (ask whoever is in charge of tours). Non-Spanish speakers should note that most exhibit information and tours are available only in Spanish. If a member of your group speaks Spanish, guides will be happy to pace themselves to allow that person to translate for the rest of the group. If you are interested in English language tours, it is best to call ahead to inquire about arranging one, or visit the museum with a private English speaking guide.

Museums in small towns tend to house a disparate collection of historical objects donated by town residents as well as artifacts from the Triple Alliance and Chaco Wars. In some towns, the town church essentially functions as a museum, housing interesting historic religious artifacts. Most churches are open to the public during business hours. If mass is being held, consider returning later, especially if you wish to take photographs. If the church is closed, there is usually a church office nearby – ask for the *casa parroquial*. Explaining you are a tourist interested in seeing the church's artwork is usually enough for someone to let you in.

> Voltage can fluctuate wildly at times, especially during storms. Voltage regulators are recommended for sensitive electronics.

TRAVEL ESSENTIALS

✓ **First aid kit**: Most of the supplies for a first aid kit are available in pharmacies and supermarkets.

✓ **Insect repellant:** Many forms of DEET-based repellants are readily available throughout the country including spray, cream, and even repellent impregnated wristbands. Mosquito repellent spirals (*espirales*) are also popular and effective for keeping mosquitoes out of a room – Mata Iris brand carries a *palo santo* scented spiral that doesn't give off a strong chemical smell. Mosquito nets are not as easy to find but can be quite convenient as most windows don't have screens. In a pinch, tulle fabric is available at most fabric stores (*tienda de telas*) in Asunción and forms a good makeshift mosquito net.

✓ **Sun protection:** Sunscreen is essential, as the sun in Paraguay can be very strong, even during the winter months. Sunscreen is available at pharmacies and supermarkets. The selection may be limited in small towns, so it is best to stock up on higher SPFs in urban pharmacies or supermarkets. Wide brimmed hats and parasols are commonly used in the countryside, less so in urban areas (baseball hats are fine in cities though). Both are available throughout the country – straw hats (*sombrero de paja*) can easily be purchased in small stores (*almacén* or *despensa*). Sunglasses with UV ray protection are essential; those headed to the dusty Chaco will be best served by wraparound styles.

✓ **Hydration pack, water bottle, or *tereré* thermos.**

✓ **Unlocked GSM cell phone** (see Staying Connected, p92): Not necessary but will make life much easier if you plan on organizing travel yourself.

✓ **Copies of passport and other travel documents**: Keep these with you at all times in case the originals are lost or stolen.

✓ **Universal plug:** Both European (round) and American (straight) two prong outlets are used, and adapters can be purchased in supermarkets and hardware stores (*ferreterías*).

✓ **Earplugs** will make it easier to ignore movies blasting full volume on buses and mosquitoes buzzing around at night.

✓ **Rain coat or poncho.**

✓ **Light weight thermals:** Recommended for winter visitors (see When to Visit, p53).

✓ **Spanish language phrasebook:** For those with little or no Spanish background.

The Basics

Additional Items for Camping

- ✓ Duct tape

- ✓ **Leatherman or Swiss Army knife:** Chinese knockoffs are sold by many street vendors in Ciudad del Este.

- ✓ **Headlamp**

- ✓ **Dust protection for photography equipment:** Serious photographers headed to the Chaco should bring Ziploc bags or dry bags to protect their camera and lenses from the fine dust. Trash bags are an available in all supermarkets.

- ✓ **Nylon hammock:** Particularly useful, especially models with built in mosquito netting. Normal woven hammocks can be found throughout Paraguay but can be too bulky and heavy for backpacking.

- ✓ **Inflatable ground pad:** Can double as floating device in rivers and lakes.

Expensive & Hard to Find Items

- ✓ **Contact lenses and solution:** These are available only in urban pharmacies and are very expensive.

- ✓ **Binoculars:** Quality binoculars are hard to find and quite pricey. Serious wildlife aficionados will be happier bringing their own from home.

- ✓ **Lightweight backpacking gear:** While gear for car camping is available in the camping section of department stores in Asunción (see Shopping, p143), specialty gear, such as ground pads, multi-fuel camping stoves, and lightweight tents, is hard to find.

- ✓ **Professional fishing gear:** Avid fishermen should bring their own poles and lures. Though there is good fishing throughout Paraguay, high quality gear is difficult to purchase outside of cities and almost impossible to rent.

Getting Around

BY BUS

Buses (*colectivos*) are the main form of transportation in Paraguay with quality ranging from large double-decker buses that feature bathrooms, A/C, and TVs, to local commuter buses with plastic bucket seats. City buses that have been pressed into regional services do not have bathrooms onboard but often make at least one pit stop en-route. Buses can be taken from the bus terminal or flagged down along the highway, though you are less likely to get a seat this way. Most towns have specific passenger pick up points, usually by the main plaza or entrance to the town. Stops are rarely marked so you will have to ask locals where *la parada* (the bus stop) is. Purchasing a ticket ahead of time from the bus agency will save you a lot of hassle and waiting. Large towns may have dedicated agency offices, while agents in smaller towns may sell tickets out of their homes. The more popular your destination, the better (more comfortable) bus options will be available. Double-decker (*doble piso*) buses are generally preferable as they are more comfortable and often faster. *"Directo"* (direct) buses are faster, and only stop to pick up passengers a few times at key points en-route (these are listed at the beginning of each chapter). *"Removido"* services make innumerable stops and should be avoided whenever possible. Always double check with the driver to make sure the bus will pass your destination, even if it is listed on the bus' sign, as routes can sometimes change without any notice. Buses run less frequently on the weekends and are even rarer on holidays. In general, it is best not to count on the last regional or city bus of the day, especially on Sundays.

NASA and Nuestra Señora de Asunción (NSA) are the bus lines with the most routes throughout Paraguay. Bring earplugs to block out loud movies and a long-sleeved garment or blanket, as the A/C can be pretty powerful on some buses. Make sure your travel plans include leeway in case buses run late or break down.

National Bus Companies

Alborada: 021 551 612

Altos: 0512 230 097

Atyrá: 0520 20005

Beato Roque Gonzalez:
021 558 795, 071 204 850

Cardozo Hermanos: 021 555 728

Ciudad de Pilar: 021 558 393

Cometa de Amambay:
0336 273 555, 0336 273 247

Crucero del Este: 021 555 082

Empresa Canindeyú: 021 555 991

Empresa del Sur: 0786 233 083

Empresa Paraguarí: 051 432 479

Empresa Piribebuy: 0515 212 164

La Aregueña: 0513 432 182

La Concepcionera:
0351 230 446, 0331 240 813

La Encarnacena: 021 551 745

La Guaireña: 021 551 727

La Ovetense: 021 551 737

La Pilarense: 021 551 736

La Santaniana: 021 551 607

La Tobateña: 0516 262 660

La Yuteña: 021 558 774

Loma Grandense: 0516 252 495

Mariscal López: 021 551 612

Nasa-Golondrina: 021 551 731

Nuestra Señora de la Asunción: 021 551 725

Pycasu: 021 551 735

Rysa: 021 551 602

Salto Cristal: 021 555 728

San Cosmeña: 021 551 641

San Juan SRL: 021 555 728

Stel Turismo: 021 558 196

Tebicuary: 021 555 991

Tres Fronteras: 061 550 105

TTL Libertador: 0351 230 613, 0331 42320, 0331 43414

Turismo García: 061 502460

Virgen Serrana: 0516 262 660

Yacyretá: 021 294 05,
021 551 725

Ybytyruzu:
021 558 393

Chiperas

Most buses do not make more than one pit stop, but roadside *chiperas* get on frequently to sell *chipa* (p79) and *cocido* (p89) to hungry passengers. Often you can tell a *chipera* has boarded by the jangling of pocket change as passengers prepare to make their purchase.

BY CAR

Car rentals start at US$45 per day plus additional charges per kilometer and US$70 per day for unlimited mileage plans. Four wheel drive vehicles (necessary for off-roading) start at US$115 per day plus additional charges per kilometer and US$200 per day for unlimited mileage plans. The majority of rental cars have manual transmissions and run on either gasoline (*nafta*) or diesel, both of which are readily available. Expect to spend roughly US$1.40 per liter for both gasoline and diesel. Localiza (*www.localiza.com*), National (*www.national.com.py*), and Avis Rent a Car (*www.avis.com.py*) have offices in Asunción, Ciudad del Este, and Encarnación. Note most rental companies' contracts forbid you from crossing international borders.

Most towns have taxi services though the quality of the cars themselves can vary greatly. In Asunción, Ciudad del Este, and Encarnación, taxis are metered whereas in smaller towns you may have to negotiate a fixed price ahead of time. Taxi stands (*parada de taxi*) are usually located outside the town bus terminal or by the town's main or secondary plaza.

BY MOTORCYCLE

Motorcycles can be the cheapest and most efficient way to get around Paraguay. In muddy terrain they can be preferable to 4x4 vehicles. Official rentals are uncommon but if you ask around, sometimes you can find someone willing to loan you their motorcycle. As a common courtesy be sure to return it with a full tank – often this is all owners will accept as form of payment. Motorcycles are relatively inexpensive and resell quickly. New Chinese made, nationally assembled motorcycles run between US$700 to US$1,500.

Legal Requirements

Expect to encounter police checkpoints on most highways. Complying with all legal requirements will minimize the likelihood of being targeted for a bribe.

By law, foreign drivers in Paraguay must have the following documents handy:

- ✓ Driver's license from country of origin.

- ✓ Additional official ID (i.e. a passport, as in Paraguay, a driver's license is not an official form of identification.)

- ✓ Proof of entry (passport or photocopy of stamped page in passport)

- ✓ Cars from Mercosur countries must have the "Cédula Verde" paperwork, and non-Mercosur cars must have paperwork issued by Customs.

In addition drivers must:

- ✓ Keep headlights on when driving outside of urban areas.

- ✓ Have a fire extinguisher with a valid expiration date.

- ✓ Have two reflective triangles.

If you feel you are being targeted unfairly by police, make sure to report this to Senatur (*Tel: 021 494 110*) and your embassy.

TACPY

The Touring and Automotive Club of Paraguay is a good resource for information about road conditions and maps. The TACPY guidebook (available at Petrobras gas stations and the TACPY headquarters on Cerro Cora and Brazil in downtown Asunción) is geared specifically to those driving through Paraguay. *www.tacpy.com.py*

MAPS & GPS

Senatur distributes handy pocket-sized guides called "Quick Guides" for Asunción, Encarnación, Ciudad del Este, as well as a combination San Bernardino and Villa Florida guide. These include several useful maps as well as some information about upcoming events. Should Senatur offices be out of guides, the Quick Guide website (www.quickguide.com.py) has printable maps.

Large scale detailed maps of the entire country are available in Asunción at the Servicio Geográfico Militar at the intersection of Avenida Artigas and Avenida Peru (Tel: 021 205 237, Mon-Fri 7am-5pm). Touring and Automotive Club of Paraguay (TACPY) driving maps for Eastern Paraguay and the Paraguayan Chaco are available

---

Deciphering Directions & Addresses

When asking for directions keep in mind that many would rather make an educated guess and risk providing inaccurate information than provide no answer and potentially come across as unfriendly. In addition, many Paraguayans are not accustomed to using maps or giving directions using cardinal points or street names. Instead, they rely on easily (usually) visible reference points such as gas stations, sign posts, and water towers. If directions given are vague or the people giving them seem unsure, always get a second opinion – police men and taxi drivers are a good bet (For commonly used terms and questions see the Language Reference, p325).

Because house numbers are often missing or not visible, written addresses usually include reference streets. Common abbreviations for written addresses are as follows:

Esq/: *esquina*, or corner. "Alberdi esq/ Palma" is on the corner of Alberdi and Palma.

E/: *entre*, or in between. "Alberdi e/ Palma y Estrella" is on Alberdi between Palma and Estrella.

C/: *casi*, or almost. "Alberdi c/ Palma" is on Alberdi almost at the corner of Palma.

The ground floor is referred to as "*planta baja*" and the next floor up is referred to as the first floor.

Common abbreviations used in street names include:

Tte: Teniente

Mscl: Mariscal

Cnl: Coronel

Grl: General

Av: Avenida

Pte: Presidente

at most gas stations. Paraguay's cities and large towns are also now available on Google maps, though you cannot search for specific directions or addresses and street names are sometimes mislabeled.

Garmin compatible maps of Paraguay are available at www.proyectomapear.com.ar (Paraguay maps come bundled with Argentina and Chile).

BY AIR

TAM Mercosur and Sol del Paraguay airlines run flights between Ciudad del Este and Asunción. This route is the only regional commercial flight within Paraguay. The military transport airline, Transporte Aereo Militar, offers sporadic services between Asunción, Fuerte Olimpo, and Bahía Negra. Although it can be prohibitively expensive, chartering a small plane is the best option for those seeking to access remote areas of the country (i.e. the northern Chaco) by plane.

Transporte Aereo Militar *Tel: 0983 454486 (Sonia Suarez), Aeropuerto Militar, next to the Aeropuerto Internacional Silvio Petirossi*

Aero Centro, S.A. *Tel: 021 645 380/1/2, Autopista Aeropuerto Internacional No. 555 next to the Aeropuerto Internacional Silvio Petirossi, www.aerocentro.net*

BY RIVERBOAT

Three passenger boats make regular trips on the Paraguay River between Asunción, Concepción, and Bahía Negra, the northernmost town along the river. The Crucero Paraguay passenger boat is a luxury cruise for tourists, while the Aquidaban and Cacique II are passenger and cargo boats. Though crowded and uncomfortable, the latter provide adventurous travelers with a unique way to experience the river. For more information on riverboat travel see The Paraguay River, p304.

Hitchhiking
Hitchhiking is possible, though uncommon, and not recommended for single females. The signal for hitch hiking is to splay your hand and wave it back and forth parallel to the road in the direction of traffic. Hitchhikers are more likely to be picked up in rural areas than along main highways.

BACKPACKING

Those used to seeing backpackers traveling in droves throughout Latin America will be surprised to see just how few make their way to Paraguay. Nevertheless, backpacking in Paraguay is a rewarding challenge. On the one hand, foreign visitors are few and far between, and as such there are few resources tailored specifically to backpackers (such as hostels or English speakers). On the other hand, it is generally safe and locals are very friendly and helpful. Basic language skills, a flexible travel plan, and desire to engage with the locals are essential as you prepare to step off the beaten path.

Accommodation, food, and transportation are generally highly affordable, though in some cases you get what you pay for. In many cases, public transportation will get you within walking distance of your destination. Paying a local to drive you or hitch hiking are also often options for traveling those last few kilometers.

Backpackers should note that travel in rural Paraguay is not without potential dangers, most revolving around the extreme climate and bad road conditions. While some of Paraguay's more popular attractions, such as Iguazú Falls (technically just over the border in Brazil and Argentina) and the Jesuit Ruins of Trinidad, are easily visited on your own, others, such as the Chaco, are best visited with guided tours.

GUIDED TOURS

Nature observation trips in particular are best made with the help of a knowledgeable guide as remote locations can be difficult (and potentially dangerous) to reach unaccompanied. Visitors with limited time and language skills will also benefit from joining guided tours. The most popular tour packages include Iguazú Falls and Itaipú Hydroelectric Reserve, the Jesuit Ruins, and the Golden Circuit, a series of traditional small towns surrounding Asunción. Tour operators and private guides are happy to put together specialized tours, although you should expect to pay a premium for this service. With the exception of Fauna Paraguay, the following companies operate out of Asunción. One interesting result of Paraguay's nascent tourism industry is that there are a handful of trained guides who do not have steady work with established tour operators. For many, the small number of tourists means they must have other jobs in order to support themselves. Certain areas of the country have guide associations that will put together a tour upon request. The advantage of this is that you are supporting a local industry and more than likely paying less than you would for a tour originating in Asunción. However expect some extra leg-work. Guides will probably have to take time off from their regular jobs, so advanced notice is almost always necessary. Payment may be expected upfront (or at the beginning of the day) in order to cover the rental of vehicles or other necessary equipment. This option is especially recommended for Spanish speakers (guides rarely speak English) and backpackers willing to splurge to make it to sights that would be otherwise difficult to reach on public transportation.

DTP Tour Operator *Tel: 021 449 724, General Bruguez 353 almost at 25 de Mayo, www.dtp.com.py, inforeceptivo@dtp.com.py*

Intertours *Tel: 021 211 747, Avenida Perú 436 almost at Avenida España, www.intertours.com.py, www.martintravel.com.py, incoming@intertours.com.py*

Guides Specializing in Nature Observation
For guides based in the Chaco, see Chaco Tour Guides on p288.

Birding Paraguay/Guyra Paraguay Guyra Paraguay, a birding and nature conservation NGO, offers a wide variety of birding tours through their Birding Paraguay program. Tours are offered to all of Paraguay's important birding areas and include ornithological guides. In addition, Birding Paraguay can help arrange personalized private tours for birders with specific interests. *Tel: 021 229 097, Corner of Gaetano Martino and Teniente Ross, www.guyra.org.py, on Facebook, birding.paraguay@gmail.com*

Fauna Paraguay Based out of Encarnación, Paul Smith specializes in wildlife and birding tours throughout the country. He has contributed to several well-known travel guidebooks and has in-depth knowledge of Paraguay's fauna, flora, and culture. There are several good simple itineraries complete with details on species you may see in each destination on the Fauna Paraguay website. *www.faunaparaguay.com/tours.html, on Facebook, faunaparaguay@yahoo.com.ar*

The Language Barrier

Getting around Paraguay without basic Spanish is tricky but not impossible. A Spanish language phrasebook is highly recommended for travelers with limited language skills (also be sure to check out Language Reference, p325, for useful phrases). English is not widely spoken, even amongst those working in the tourism industry. When joining a tour, try to talk with guides beforehand to ensure you'll be able to communicate sufficiently. Most museums and attractions do not have English speakers on staff, but those in Asunción may be able to find an English speaking guide with sufficient advanced notice. If you speak German, consider joining a tour company that caters to German tourists such as Klassen Tours (*Tel: 021 612035, www.klassentours.com*) or Hotel Westfalenhaus/Paraguay Travel (*Tel: 021 292374, www.paraguay-travel.de*).

Visitors looking to improve their Spanish conversation skills will find the lack of English speakers beneficial, as there will be ample opportunities to practice. Most Paraguayans are eager to interact with foreigners and help them with their language skills. Do not be discouraged by the heavy presence of Guaraní in Paraguayan Spanish. Just think of it as an opportunity to learn Paraguayan slang. It is common for people to leave Paraguay and subsequently discover that words they thought were Spanish are actually Guaraní. The further into the countryside you venture, the more Guaraní speakers you will encounter (see Languages, p38). However, the majority of tourists are unlikely to venture into areas where people speak Guaraní exclusively.

> Do not let a fear of making mistakes keep you from trying to speak Spanish or Guaraní. Being able to laugh at our own language gaffes will prove to locals that you are a good sport, not to mention provide fodder for further conversation.

See Language Reference, p325, for useful phrases in Guarani and Spanish, pronunciation tips, and resources for learning either language formally.

Nature Tourism

Paraguay is home to seventeen national parks as well as a number of reserves. In addition, the bi-national entities running the Itaipú and Yacyretá hydroelectric plants operate several nature reserves, which are open to the public with prior reservations (see Itaipú Dam, Nature Reserves, p256, and Central Hidroeléctrica Yacyretá, p186). Visitors will often find they have the parks to themselves. Public transportation may not pass by the park entrance but in many cases it will get you within a short hike or taxi ride. The most popular and easily accessible parks are Parque Nacional Ybycuí (p156), 123 kilometers from Asunción, and Parque Nacional Cerro Corá (p279), along the road between Concepción and Pedro Juan Caballero.

Lodging is free at all national parks, though the quality of visitor's centers varies greatly. Some only have campsites, while others have full-fledged facilities including private rooms with air-conditioning (though a donation for fuel costs may be required in order to run generators). Plan to bring and prepare your own food; most parks do not have food options inside visitor's centers or nearby. Park rangers are knowledgeable and friendly, making the most out of scant resources and limited contact with outside world. Rangers will often be happy to take visitors on tours and patrols if you chip in (or cover) fuel costs. Many risk their lives patrolling protected areas for loggers and poachers.

Other options for coming into contact with Paraguay's nature include private reserves and ranches (*estancias*) which are often better run and include more reliable facilities for visitors. Prices vary depending on the level of comfort provided, and often reservations and payment must be made in advance to headquarter offices in Asunción. Hiring a private guide or tour operator will facilitate transportation (and access to supplies) significantly. It can also, in many cases, help you gain access to natural areas not open to the general public. Serious nature-lovers are advised to hire an experienced guide in order to make the most of their time and maximize chances of seeing wildlife.

Essential Reading

Written in both English and Spanish, Peter T. Clark's *"Guide to Paraguay's National Parks and other Protected Wild Areas"* is essential reading for anyone interested in exploring Paraguay's natural resources – especially for those who want to venture off on their own.

The Basics

BIRDING

As a birding destination, Paraguay falls under the radar, overshadowed by Latin America's more touristy areas. However, birding enthusiasts (both amateur and professional) will find the country is an extremely exciting place to visit, binoculars in hand. The country's small size and variety of ecosystems mean that even a short itinerary is likely to result in a long and varied list of sightings. Paraguay is home to over 670 species of birds and there are 57 important birding areas covering 3,325,000 hectares. Paraguay is also an important stopping point for migratory birds. Over 40 species are neotropical, and over one hundred are austral migrants. Jabiru, pink flamingoes, and spoonbills abound in the Chaco, the country's most popular birding area. The Atlantic forest is home to Paraguay's national bird, the increasingly rare bell bird (see *Guyra Campana*, p52), the harpy eagle, and several species of toucans. Another fascinating bird watching area is the Cerrado region, one of two sites in Paraguay (and three worldwide) where the White-winged Nightjar is likely to be spotted. Bird Life International has an excellent report on Paraguay's bird species available in a PDF format at www.birdlife.org.

There are only a handful of options for birders wishing to take guided birding tours. Guyra Paraguay, which is partnered with Bird Life International and the World Land Trust, is considered the national authority on birding ("guyra" means bird in Guaraní). They organize birding trips throughout the country and have two birding lodges – one in the Atlantic Forest (see Guyra Kanguery Birding Station, p183) and one in the Pantanal (see Los Tres Gigantes Field Station, p323). In addition, Guyra Paraguay has several publications including *"Guia Para la Identificación de las Aves de Paraguay,"* to date the most comprehensive field guild to Paraguay. Another excellent resource for birding trips is Fauna Paraguay, run by nature enthusiast Paul Smith. Paul leads groups throughout the country and the Fauna Paraguay website is full of extensive information about Paraguay's wildlife, including birds. Paul often works with Hugo del Castillo, another well known guide much sought after by experienced birders (see Guided Tours, p65, for more information on both organizations).

The country's lack of tourism infrastructure means birding tours do not offer the level of comfort that more established birding destinations have. Most birding tours involve stays at a combination of private nature reserves and national parks. Rooms are basic and often times dorm-style with bunk beds and shared bathrooms. Before booking a trip, double check what type of transportation will be used – comfortable vehicles with air conditioning may increase trip costs but are worthwhile expenses. Though forgoing a private tour requires more legwork, birders on a budget can enjoy Paraguay's bird life on their own. Laguna Blanca, a popular birding spot in the Cerrado ecosystem, is reachable by public transportation. Those who wish to visit the Procosara lodge, Guyra's Kanguery lodge or the Mbaracayú lodge, all in the Atlantic Forest, will be able to take public transportation most of the way and arrange for a lift for the last bit. Filadelfia, in the Chaco, can be reached by bus, and from there one can pay a local guide for a day trip to one of the nearby salt lagoons where flamingos and jabiru storks can be found. The bay of Asunción is an official important birding area and is the easiest area to access. Chaco'i, at the southern tip of the Paraguayan Chaco is another good place to bird and it's only a 20-minute water taxi ride from Asunción. Locals tend to have good knowledge of birds, and by asking around, you may be able to find someone willing to accompany you on a walk through the countryside or on a boat trip down a nearby river to point out popular species. Keep in mind however, that most Paraguayans (even official birding guides) tend to refer to birds by their Guaraní, rather than scientific, names. Nature enthusiasts should come equipped with their own binoculars if possible.

FISHING

Fishing is a popular Paraguayan past time with many national competitions taking place throughout the country. Thanks to their large size and delicious taste, long-headed *surubí* (catfish) and speckle-skinned *dorado* are prize catches known to put up quite a fight. The bounty of Paraguay's rivers includes other fish such as *pacu*, *boga*, and even piranha in certain spots.

Paraguay has yet to capitalize on the bounty of its rivers the way neighboring Argentina and Brazil have. Travelers in those countries will find many options for sport fishing tours along the Paraguay and Paraná rivers. Within Paraguay, there are few organized fishing tours per se, but hotels in popular fishing spots such as Villa Florida (along the Tebicuary River) and Ayolas (along the Paraná River) in Misiones should be able to help arrange private outings. When hiring a guide, it is important to be clear about what is covered and what isn't in the fee. In addition to the cost of the tour, you may be expected to provide fuel, bait, food and beverages, and even transportation to and from the river (some guides may have a boat but not a car). During the low season and in poorer areas, expect to spend an hour accompanying the guide to pick up supplies – do make sure that this time does not count towards your tour though.

If you are living in or visiting a rural community, going fishing with locals can be a good bonding experience – don't expect any fancy equipment though, most people fish with simple lines or nets.

Overfishing is becoming an issue in Paraguay's rivers with the population of *dorado*, in particular, declining precipitously. Fishing enthusiasts should be aware of the yearly fishing ban (*veda*) in place from November to December (and in some cases extending till January). Many local fishermen do not respect this, but it is best to abstain from fishing during this period to allow fish to reproduce.

For more information about fishing in Paraguay contact:

Federación Paraguaya de Pesca Deportiva Organizes fishing competitions and events throughout the country. *Tel: 021 447 735, 0981 405 595, Manduvirá 948 between Colón and Montevideo*

Asociación Paraguaya de Caza y Pesca Deals with both hunting and fishing. Located on the outskirts of Asunción by the port of Itá Enramada. *Tel: 021 905 556, 909 131, Avenida Perón 4280*

Cultural Tourism

THE JESUIT RUINS

The Jesuit ruins are the best-known cultural attraction in Paraguay. Over 240 years after the Jesuits were expelled from colonial Paraguay, impressive remnants of three missions stand to this day. **Santísima Trinidad del Paraná** (p178) is easily accessible from

See *Jesuit Town & Ruins* on page 147 for a more detailed explanation of each town and ruins.

Encarnación and the most visited of Paraguay's missions. It is also the most complete. There are remains of several different buildings that made up the mission. Unlike the other ruins, a significant population does not remain in or around the Trinidad mission. Eleven kilometers away in the town of Jesús are the remains of the former **Jesús de Tavarangue** mission church (p180). Further out, but worth the trip, are the remains of the **San Cosme y Damián** mission (p188), set in a picturesque town of the same name along the Paraná River. Paraguay's tourism ministry has recently focused its attention on the ruins, investing in improvements to infrastructure and creating a single ticket to cover visits to all three ruins.

While most tourists gravitate towards the ruins, it is equally worthwhile to visit Jesuit towns along Route 1 where the former mission buildings are still used by the current community. These towns have what the ruins lack – examples of decorative objects that adorned each mission. The museums of **Santa María de Fe** (p168) and **San Ignacio** (p164) house excellent collections of large sculptures crafted by Guaraní artisans working in the missions under the direction of Jesuit artists. Santa Rosa de Lima's small **Nuestra Señora de Loreto Chapel** (p170) retains its original fresco covered interior. A visit to these towns is the perfect complement to a tour of the ruins, providing tourists with a well-rounded view of the missions as they once were.

THE FRANSISCAN ROUTE & GOLDEN CIRCUIT

Lesser known, but more relevant to modern day Paraguayan culture, are the remains of Franciscan missions scattered throughout Eastern Paraguay. Unlike the Jesuits, the Franciscans were permitted to stay within colonial Paraguay and many of the original missions are now thriving towns with ornate churches and a deep-running sense of religious tradition. The crown jewel of Paraguay's Franciscan legacy is the San Buenaventura church (generally referred to as the **Iglesia de Yaguarón,** p. 149) in the town of Yaguarón. The interior of this large church is decorated in the Guaraní Baroque style marked by ornately carved wooden altar pieces, rich colors, and generous applications of gold leaf. In addition to their churches, many Franciscan towns are known for their handicraft work. **Itaguá** (p200) is the center of *ñanduti* production in Paraguay, with women throughout the town crafting brightly colored painstakingly detailed lace creations day in and day out. The displays in Museo de Ñanduti prove the sky is the limit when it comes to *ñanduti* designs, many of which are inspired by the natural world. The ceramics of **Tobatí** (p216) and **Areguá** (p202) are yet another example of the honest way in which Paraguayan artisans transform their deep connection with nature into works of art. Many Franciscan towns are part of the *Circuito de Oro* (Golden Circuit) one day tour offered by most tour operators. This tour includes visits to towns along both Route 1 and Route 2, all of which are easily accessible from Asunción. Each town is easily reached by public transportation and makes for an easy day trip from Asunción. Though they are close together, it can be difficult to get from one town to the other on public transportation. Travelers with time on their hands may prefer to break this up as a series of day trips from Asunción, rather than trying to create a single itinerary. Those who prefer to travel without a tour are advised to limit their itinerary to two towns per day (three at most) in order to allow for travel time between towns.

Religious Holidays

Paraguay remains a deeply religious country with deep-rooted traditions. Religious festivities are a visitor's best bet for experiencing Paraguay's customs and tasting traditional foods. In addition to nationally celebrated religious holidays, each region and town has its own patron saint day festivities known as *"fiestas patronales."* Even the most basic *fiestas patronales* include a religious procession followed by a town

---

Quirky Fiestas Patronales & Processions

Certain *fiestas patronales* stand out from the rest due to peculiar traditions associated with the patron saints in question, such as special costumes, ritual dances, and games. Some are so popular that they draw onlookers from all over the country. These ceremonies can be an enjoyable experience even if you are not religious and participation is a good way to bond with the locals. Some standouts include:

María Auxiliadora, Asunción – May 24th This celebration involves a *procesión náutica* (nautical procession) along the Paraguay River. The statue of the Virgen Maria Auxiliadora travels by boat from the neighborhood of Sajonia to the port of Asunción with the faithful following in colorfully decorated boats (see María Auxiliadora, p104).

San Pedro y San Pablo, Altos – June 29th Celebrated in a small section of Altos in the Cordillera Department, this festivity involves two to three days of dancing in traditional costumes made of banana leaves (see Fiesta de San Pedro y San Pablo, p209).

San Francisco Solano, Emboscada – July 24th Also known as "guaicurú ñemondé" – the faithful gather fully decked out in costumes covered head to toe with chicken and guinea hen feathers (see Fiesta Patronal San Fransisco Solano, p267).

Arete Guazú, Santa Teresita and Filadelfia (dates vary) Celebrated in Guaraní communities. Of the country's religious festivals, this is the most heavily influenced by indigenous culture (see The Arete Guazú, p295).

fair with music, special performances, traditional foods, and dancing in the evenings. These events are rarely put together with tourists in mind and therefore offer an unfiltered view of Paraguayan culture. The Senatur event calendar (available in PDF form at www.senatur.gov.py) includes detailed listings of upcoming religious festivities.

DÍA DE LA VIRGEN DE CAACUPÉ

The *Virgen de Caacupé* is not only the patron saint of the town Caacupé itself but also for the entire country as well. The saint engenders particular devotion in Paraguayans, drawing well over one million devotees to her hometown in the days leading up to December 8th. In fact, the *Día de la Virgen de Caacupé* is one of Paraguay's most important holidays. The procession to Caacupé is like something out of *"The Canterbury Tales"* – part walk-a-thon and part street-fair. The faithful arrive in droves from all over the country, mostly on foot. The extremely pious travel on their knees, others on bicycle, and, though it is becoming a rare sight, some pilgrims from the countryside make their way by ox-drawn cart. Participating in the pilgrimage to Caacupé is a unique opportunity to witness Paraguay's religious fervor at its apex (see The Pilgrimage to Caacupé, p211).

> September 21st, the first day of spring, is celebrated as the *Día de la Juventud* (Youth Day) with parades and music festivals.

The Basics

Foods of Easter Week

The celebration of Easter week (*Semana Santa*) is pretty similar to festivities in other Catholic countries. However, there is one major distinguishing factor: the food. *Semana Santa* is a chance for urban Paraguayans to return to their rural roots and savor some good ol' down home country cooking. Food is such a significant part of *Semana Santa* that, as the date draws near, there is hoarding and price gouging of main ingredients such as corn flour, eggs, and cheese.

The MVP of *Semana Santa* gastronomy is *chipa* (p79). During *Semana Santa* chipa is elevated to a new level both in terms of quantity and creativity. On the Wednesday of *Semana Santa*, families fire up the *tatakua* (wood burning brick oven) and make large quantities of *chipa*, enough to last for several days. This is due to the fact that cooking is forbidden between Thursday and Sunday morning for religious reasons. Some stick to the classic donut shape, but many choose to sculpt the dough into all types of shapes. The most common shapes are animals; from crocodiles and rabbits to birds in nests with eggs. This adorned chipa is known as *chipa yegua*. *Chipa* is then consumed throughout the weekend and distributed to friends and family as a sign of affection.

On Thursday (*Jueves Santo*), a huge meal is prepared for the entire family in commemoration of the Last Supper. It's the last time you are supposed to do any (major) cooking or eat red meat until Easter Sunday, so Paraguayans go all out. People spend Wednesday and Thursday preparing their favorite Paraguayan dishes. A popular main dish is *tallarín* (linguini noodles) with *gallina casera* (farm-raised chicken) or beef in red sauce. City folk may opt for *bacalao* (cod) instead. Desserts include *leche crema* (custard), *budín de pan* (Paraguayan style bread pudding similar to a thick flan), and *arróz con leche* (rice pudding). After Easter Sunday Mass is over, everyone gathers once more around the table to celebrate, this time usually with a large *asado* (barbeque).

CARNAVAL

While Paraguay is a devout Catholic country with deep-rooted beliefs and traditions, Paraguayans still enjoy a good party. Nowhere is this combination of traits on better display than during *carnaval* season. *Carnaval* is a blow out festival that involves revelers engaging in sinful activities before the forty days of Lent leading up to Easter week. Although this tradition has religious roots, for many *carnaval* is more about partying than anything else. In the case of Paraguay, the sins of *carnaval* mostly involve beer drinking, dancing, and ogling semi-naked girls. The largest *carnaval* celebrations take place in Encarnación

> Though Paraguay has several small pockets of indigenous communities, for the most part these have not yet begun to promote their cultural activities to tourists. This is due in large part to their remote locations and marginal status within Paraguayan society.

where an entire section of city blocks is set up as the parade route, known as the *"sambódromo."* This name comes from the Brazilian samba music that accompanies the parade, usually played by live bands and marching drum lines. For several weekends, groups of drum lines, themed floats, and costumed women representing different clubs or neighborhoods dance down the *sambódromo*. The bleachers are filled with partygoers cheering, dancing, and drinking. Groups compete for popularity with the crowds and a chance at winning the grand prize at the end of *carnaval* season. The spectacle of hundreds of women in glittery carnaval costumes resembles a Victoria's Secret fashion show on acid. *Carnaval* get-ups involve as little clothing, and as much glitter, as possible: skimpy bedazzled lingerie, high heels, a large colorfully feathered head dress, neck piece, waist piece, and an enormous back piece. *Carnaval* festivities take place on a smaller scale in cities and towns throughout the Paraguay such as Villarica, Caacupé, and Asunción.

FIESTA DE SAN JUAN

Though the official *Día de San Juan* is June 24th, San Juan festivals are held throughout the month of June. San Juan traditions involve food, religion, and playing with fire, which make the festivities popular with Paraguayans of all ages and one of the most widely celebrated holidays of the year. Many San Juan events are put on by schools and church groups who raise funds by selling traditional winter foods – hot *cocido,* warm gooey *mbeju*, and all sorts of fried treats from funnel cakes to *empanadas*. The biggest draw of the festival are traditional fire games including kicking a flaming ball (*pelota tata*), being chased by a make-believe bull with flaming horns (*toro candil*), and the dramatic main event: walking over coals (*tata ári jehasa*). Not all games involve such daring though – there are also kid-friendly games such as climbing a greased pole (*yvyra syi*) and breaking open a clay piñata (*kambuchi jejoka*). In the town of San Juan Bautista itself, the celebration also has a large rodeo aspect due to the heavy influence of cattle ranching in the Misiones department. Undoubtedly, the festival of San Juan is the highlight of Paraguayan winter.

> On the eve of *Día de los Reyes Magos* (Three Kings Day), children put out their shoes in front of the nativity scene, and in the morning find they have received presents from the three kings.

The Día del Amigo

The *Día del Amigo* (Friendship Day) is celebrated on July 30th with gift exchanges and get-togethers among friends. It is common for people to send text messages, make phone calls, and engage in other exchanges of affection with all of their friends.

Traveling & Volunteering

Volunteering is a particularly good way to get to know the culture and make a difference at the same time. Cultural exchanges and volunteer programs are possible through a variety of established international aid organizations with long track records in Paraguay such as the Peace Corps, Amigos de las Américas, American Field Service, and Rotary Club. There is no lack of Paraguayan organizations willing to take on extra help either, especially if you have decent Spanish skills. It can be a challenging to coordinate volunteering details from a distance though. You will have better luck finalizing plans in person. As with all other matters in Paraguay, having a contact within the organization can help things run smoothly. Unless the organization already has a pre-existing volunteer program, don't expect to hit the ground running. If you are on a tight schedule but would like to fit in some volunteer work, it makes more sense to work with programs that have specific scheduled short-term projects such as Habitat for Humanity.

Many people like to combine volunteering with travel. Plan to travel after having been in country for a while, rather than upon arrival. This will allow you to acclimate to the culture and make Paraguayan contacts, both of which will significantly improve your subsequent travel experiences.

VOLUNTEER ORGANIZATIONS

Fundación Paraguaya

This organization is linked to several micro-financing institutions worldwide including Kiva and Teach a Man to Fish. One of the few NGOs in Paraguay that has a system set up for receiving foreign volunteers. *Tel: 021 609-277, Manuel Blinder 5589 almost at Teniente Espinoza, www.fundacionparaguaya.org.py*

Made in Paraguay

Paraguay is a minimally industrialized country where many things are manufactured by hand instead of on assembly lines. Throughout the countryside you will find people producing everything from sugar cane honey to woven fabrics and other handicrafts on a small scale. Most people are happy to show you around their makeshift workshops and explain their craft, which in many cases has been passed down to them by their parents and grandparents.

When visiting small factories keep in mind few safety regulations are enforced. Be careful and respectful of the fact that you are a visitor. Larger factories may require advanced notice or permissions for guided tours, but many are willing to let you take an informal tour if you explain your interest. Particularly worthwhile is the Manufactura de Pilar textile factory in Pilar (see Manufactura de Pilar Factory, p192).

Un Techo Para Mi País

A Latin American NGO that coordinates groups of volunteers to build houses for impoverished families. There are several projects throughout the year. *Tel: 021 660274, 0984 607 600, Raúl Carmona 759 almost at Lillo, www.untechoparamipais.org/paraguay, on Facebook*

Habitat for Humanity

An international NGO that builds homes for the needy. *Tel: 021 299 229, 282 760, Sargento Primero Tomás Lombardo almost at Ambay, www.habitat.org.py*

Peace Corps Paraguay

Paraguay is home to one of the largest and longest running Peace Corps programs worldwide. Peace Corps volunteers live and work in communities for 27 months. *Tel: 1 800 424 8580 (United States), Chaco Boreal 162 almost at Mariscal López, www.peacecorps.gov*

Amigos de las Américas

Service based summer programs for high school and college aged youth. Volunteers live with host families in rural communities. *Tel: 1 800 231-7796 (United States), www.amigoslink.org, on Facebook*

American Field Services

A global cultural exchange program for 18 to 28-year-olds. Participants attend school and stay with host families. Many Paraguayans also go abroad through the Paraguayan chapter of AFS. *Tel: 212.807.8686, www.afs.org*

Kansas Paraguay Partners/Comité Paraguay-Kansas

Paraguay and the U.S. state of Kansas have been closely linked since they were declared sister states in 1968 though the Partners of the Americas program. Kansas natives volunteer in Paraguay and Paraguayans are able to study in Kansas state schools for reduced rates. *Tel: 021 212540, corner of Avenida. Mariscal López and Acá Carayá, www.cpk.org.py*

Rotary International

Rotary club members visit Paraguay for a variety of programs, from short-term service projects to long-term cultural exchanges. *Tel: 847-866-3000 (United States), 01789 765411 (England), www.rotary.org*

Sonidos de la Tierra

This musical outreach program is always searching for music teachers to instruct eager students throughout the Paraguayan countryside. *www.sonidosdelatierra.org.py/*

More information about volunteering in Paraguay can also be found at the *Somos Voluntarios Por Un Paraguay Mejor* Facebook group.

Money & Costs

CURRENCY

Local currency is the "Guaraní." Guaraní bills are available in denominations of Gs. 100,000 (green), Gs. 50,000 (purple and peach), Gs. 20,000 (blue), Gs. 5,000 (orange) and Gs. 2,000 (lilac and mint green).

Guaraní bills are notoriously fragile. It is common to be given bills that are weathered and patched together with tape. Even the most damaged looking bills are generally accepted, though to be on the safe side it is okay to reject any that looks particularly beat up. In 2010, the central bank began experimenting with Gs. 2,000 bills made out of plastic materials said to be both more durable and hygienic than paper bills. The central bank had announced plans to replace the Guaraní with the "Nuevo Guaraní" (the new bills would have three less zeroes) in 2011 but these plans appear to be postponed. As of 2010 copper coins and Gs. 1,000 bills are no longer accepted.

> *"Pira pire,"* which literally means "fish skin" in Guaraní, is slang for money.

Changing Money

Currency exchange offices (*casas de cambio*) in city centers often post better rates than branches in suburban and rural areas. Banks and *"financieras"* often post slightly better rates than *casas de cambio*. All of them are willing to give a better rate when dealing with larger money exchanges. Official ID is required to make a transaction. Take your passport, as drivers' licenses aren't generally accepted. Travelers should note that as of this writing, US$100 bill series CB and D are not accepted, and many money exchange offices refuse to accept bills that have been written on. Cambios Chaco is the largest national chain of money exchange offices (*www.cambioschaco.com.py*). US dollars are generally accepted throughout the tourism industry. In Ciudad del Este, where most commercial activity is geared towards foreigners, many places accept dollars, Aregentine pesos, Brazilian reals, and euros.

CREDIT CARDS & CHECKS

Paraguay runs mostly on cash, not plastic. Credit cards are accepted at large stores and higher-end hotels. Check beforehand whether credit cards are accepted at restaurants and smaller businesses, even if they have signs purporting to do so. Outside of urban areas, expect to pay for everything in cash (with the possible exception of gas stations). You can avoid carrying around large sums of money by extracting money from town bank ATMs periodically. However, it is always wise to have a backup stash on hand. Away from major cities and towns, ATMs are harder to find, therefore, you should always keep cash on hand in case of emergencies. Traveler's checks are nearly impossible to cash.

BANKS & ATMS

Large nationwide banks include Banco Itau (*www.itau.com.py*), Visión Banco (*www.visionbanco.com*), and BBVA (*www.bbvaparaguay.com*). Bank hours are 8:30am to 1:30pm, though most have 24 hour ATM machines. All ATMs charge Gs. 25,000 per transaction and have a limit of three withdrawals per day and Gs. 1,000,000 per withdrawal. Only certain ATMs dispense US dollars. Note that your home country bank may charge an additional transaction fee for foreign withdrawals.

BARGAINING

Many times, listed prices in stores accepting credit cards are for purchases made with a credit card. Make sure to ask for the price paid for transactions in cash (*el precio en efectivo*) and always ask for a discount. Prices set by store owners and private guides are rarely fixed and may vary significantly depending on the rapport you develop before addressing the issue of money. Being friendly, using Guaraní words, and making small talk could result in a lower price. This tactic is much better than asking for prices right off the bat, as being upfront can be considered rude (see Etiquette, p46).

In general, prices are not inflated, so bargaining is unlikely to grant you deep discounts. In open markets and when dealing with artisans, it is acceptable to ask for a discount, especially if you are buying multiple items or have become a regular customer. Keep in mind, however, that most goods are priced fairly, and bargaining too aggressively may leave artisans with very little profit.

La Yapa

A common bargaining tactic is to ask for a bonus or a freebie, otherwise known as a *"yapa."* It is totally normal and acceptable to ask for a *yapa* in most informal purchasing situations (i.e. with market vendors and artisans, not at malls or supermarkets). Many vendors automatically throw in a *yapa*. An artisan may give you a small keychain while a vendor at a farmer's market may add an extra piece of produce to your shopping bag.

TIPPING

While a ten percent tip for restaurants is standard, many locals do not partake in this practice. In the majority of places, tips must be paid in cash. It is a good idea to hand the tip directly to the intended recipient. People in rural areas generally do not expect a tip and may be reluctant to accept the money. If this happens, stating a specific purpose for the money such as, "This is for your child's school supplies," can make the exchange seem more like a collaboration rather than a donation.

Lodging

HOSTELS

Hostels are only just beginning to catch on in Paraguay – as of this writing there are only a handful in the country. However, family run hotels and *hospedajes* are often willing to allow travelers access to a kitchen while providing perks such as private rooms with bathrooms.

How to Take a Hot Shower

Most Paraguayan bathrooms in areas with running water have an electrical showerhead called a *"calefón."* Water is heated by an electrical element in the showerhead before being dispersed into droplets. Temperature is regulated by the water flow – more water pressure will decrease the temperature of the water and vice-versa. Tourists may find this contraption involving water and electricity alarming, especially because the electrical wiring is clearly visible in most *calefón* installations. Avoid receiving a slight shock by shutting off the *calefón's* power before making any adjustments to the showerhead. The interrupter switch for the *calefón* is usually a red and black light switch. Despite the fear-factor, *calefóns* do have one main benefit: you will never run out of hot water. If your hotel room appears to have a water heater tank rather than a *calefón*, be sure to switch it on at night in order to have hot water for a morning shower.

HOTELS

With the exception of Asunción, Ciudad del Este and Encarnación, the majority of the country's hotels are small, family run affairs. There are very few international chain hotels in Paraguay. Higher-end travelers should note that Paraguay's hotel industry does not conform to the international star ratings system. Breakfasts are usually included and consist of coffee, *cocido* (see *Mate Cocido Quemado*, p89), and toast, though establishments with Brazilian or German ownership often offer a more substantial breakfast spread. Many hotels have both rooms with air conditioning units (with heating options in the winter) and cheaper rooms with fans. These options are noted where applicable. Unless otherwise noted, all hotels listed in this book have private bathrooms and include breakfast. Charges are usually per person, not per room. Sometimes, there is a slight price difference between a double room with two twin beds (*doble*) and a double room with a queen size bed (*doble matrimonial*). It is not unusual for hotels to have triples, quadruples, and even quintuple rooms to accommodate families or groups, especially in popular vacation areas such as Colonia Independencia, Villa Florida, and Ciudad del Este.

Bedding

While most high-end hotels have spring mattresses known as a "*sommier,*" the majority of beds in low and mid-range hotels use a foam mattress known as a "*colchón.*" These can range from firm to extremely squishy. Placing a fully inflated ground pad underneath a sagging *colchón* mattress for extra support can mean the difference between a good night's sleep and an achy back (be sure to remember your ground pad upon departure). Long-term visitors, such as Peace Corps Volunteers, should consider making the upfront investment of buying a "*sommier*" style mattress – cheaper models run about Gs. 400,000 in Asunción and more in the countryside. The extra expense may be worth it, especially if you have back problems.

ALTERNATIVE HOUSING

There are a variety of websites dedicated to connecting travelers with locals. These can come especially in handy in Paraguay where having local friends and contacts can more than make up for the lack of official tourism infrastructure. They offer a good way of getting to know Paraguayans on a more social level. For many visitors, social interactions with Paraguayans in the form of *tereré* circles, visits to the countryside, and Sunday *asados* are the highlights of their time in Paraguay.

Couch Surfing Locals sign up through this website, listing what type of hosting situation they are offering – from a place for visitors to stay to simple willingness to meet up with travelers and grab a bite to eat. This is an especially good option for vegetarians who will have a better time with kitchen access. Offering to cook for your host is a good way to take your meals into your own hands. A number of Paraguayans are signed up in urban areas. In rural areas foreigners such as Peace Corps Volunteers and other aid workers predominate. Travelers should not be discouraged by the lack of Paraguayan hosts though. A foreign host can be helpful, as their time in country and language skills (Guaraní or Spanish) allow them to act as a link to, and interpreter of, Paraguayan culture. *www.couchsurfing.com*

Localyte Many Paraguayans are signed up on Localyte as willing to meet for a meal or coffee – these social encounters can be your ticket to getting linked into a network. In Paraguay everything works via word of mouth, and knowing locals will get you places and information that you would not have access to otherwise. *www.localyte.com*

ESTANCIA (RANCH) TOURISM

Visiting a working *estancia* can be a rewarding, yet often overlooked, component of a trip to Paraguay, providing visitors with a glimpse of life in rural Paraguay. There are *estancias* for every taste from upscale to bare basics – your level of involvement in the farm's daily chores depends on your interest. Though removed from urban areas, many will help arrange for private transportation from the nearest town. Most include a flexible pricing structure whereby you can choose *pensión completa* (full room and board) or pay for accommodations and food separately. Those on a budget should inquire about cooking their own food and find out how accessible the nearest town is. Some *estancias* are too remote to make buying outside food an option. Prior reservations are often necessary, and it is common for upscale *estancias* in remote areas to require guests to pay in advance to its headquarters in Asunción.

> Many *estancias* and retreat complexes offer day passes that include use of cooking facilities such as outdoor grills – (*parrillas*), covered *quinchos* with tables and chairs, as well as pools and soccer or volleyball courts. They are a great option for backpackers looking for some R&R.

Rural tourism organizations APATUR (covering all of Paraguay) and EMITUR (specializing in the Misiones department) can provide further information on specific estancias.

APATUR – Asociación Paraguaya de Turismo Rural *Tel: 021 210 550,* *www.turismorural.org.py*

Emitur – Empredimiento Misionero de Turismo *Tel: 0782 20 286, 0975 626780,* *www.emitur.com.py*

CAMPING

Outside of national parks there are few official campgrounds, and the facilities that do exist are rudimentary at best. The exception to this rule are establishments run by European immigrants in areas such as Colonia Independencia – as these cater to European guests they often include decent camping options. Throughout the country there are many establishments set up for group retreats or *retiros* (for schools and religious groups, etc) that have dorm-style rooms and options for camping as well. These offer very basic cabins with dorm rooms and access to kitchen facilities (most groups bring their own food). Furnishings rarely include more than bunk beds and bare mattresses, so expect to bring your own linens.

Small Town Paraguay – Traveling in the *Interior*

Every Paraguayan town has almost all of the following: a church and small museum, a main plaza, and a watering hole *(arroyo or balneario)*. Once these have been visited, you may find there is not much else to do but hang out. Take advantage of the downtime to stroll towards the outer edges of town and get a peek at the *campo* (country) life. Usually the roads turn from cobblestone to dirt only three to four blocks from the town center. Early morning or late afternoon are the best times for a walk, as the weather is cooler. The pace of life is slow and everything is *"tranquilo pá."* Walking along these roads, you'll see women sweeping their front patios with handmade brooms, tending to their chickens or hanging laundry, uniformed school kids skipping their way to and from school, and men with straw hats returning from the fields on horseback or ox drawn carts. As you pass, you will be greeted with an *"adiós,"* the last vowel drawn out and the "s" swallowed completely. Adopt the same relaxed attitude, reply with your own *"adiós,"* and you may find yourself drawn into conversation.

Balnearios or swimming holes are another option for camping, although these tend to attract rowdy crowds, especially on summer weekends.

EXTENDED STAY OPTIONS

Furnished apartments are rare in Paraguay, and long term visitors may find it easier to take advantage of extended stay options offered by a handful of hotels. Clasipar (*www.clasipar.paraguay.com*) is a good source for rental listings, though the rental market operates mostly through word of mouth. If you are working with a local NGO your best bet is to ask your local contact to help you find available housing.

Love Hotels
As it is common for Paraguayans to live with their extended families well into adulthood, the need for privacy has spawned a widespread by-the-hour hotel industry. These "love hotels" are referred to as "motels" and often have suggestive names such as "Motel Love Toys" and "Passion Clasp." Motels are used by people at all levels of society, and options are available for every budget.

Food

Paraguayan cuisine features hearty country cooking that is both filling and comforting. As with all other aspects of Paraguayan culture, the cuisine (known as *"tembi'u Paraguay"* in Guaraní) is a mixture of colonial Spanish and indigenous dishes with influences from newer immigrant communities popping up here and there. Corn (*choclo*) and cassava root (*mandioca*) are at the heart of most traditional Paraguayan dishes. Meat is also readily available and most often included in the main course. Though they are not heavily featured in the cuisine, the country's fertile land and tropical climate mean fruits and vegetables are always available.

Paraguayans start the day early with a simple breakfast – usually no more than *mate* or *cocido* with *galletas* (a cross between biscuits and hard tack) or *coquitos* (miniature *galletas*). Lunch is the largest meal of the day; the majority of people break from work between 11am and noon in order to return home for lunch. *Merienda*, the afternoon snack, usually consists of *cocido* or coffee along with *chipa* or pastries. Dinner is fairly light, although heavier fare is consumed when going out to restaurants. In many rural homes, meals are prepared over an open fire or baked in a brick oven known as a *"tatakua."* Gas ranges hooked up to propane tanks are the most common method of cooking in towns and cities.

Fire in the Hole
The name *tatakua* is made up of two Guaraní words: *"tata"* (fire) and *"kua"* (hole). *Tatakuas* are dome shaped brick ovens (usually about three feet in height and about four feet in diameter) with openings in front and back. Wood is burned down to embers and then pushed to the back or removed completely before dishes are placed inside, and the openings are sealed. *Tatakuas* are not just used for cooking food – many artisans have *tatakuas* that they use for firing ceramics, and *tatakuas* about ten feet in diameter are utilized to make large amounts of charcoal for commercial use.

CHIPA

The most unique and ubiquitous dish of all is *chipa*, a dry, corn flour based bread. Chipa dough is made of corn flour, cheese, eggs, starch, oil, or lard, and a tiny bit of anise. The dough starts off dry and crumbly and must be kneaded by hand until it is silky and elastic. It is then shaped into individual portions and baked on banana leaves in a *tatakua*. *Chipas* are usually baked in donut shapes, but for special occasions, such as Easter week, chipa is baked into decorative shapes (*chipa yegua*). Popular forms include doves, armadillos (*tatu*), and crocodiles (*yacaré*). At its best, chipa has a crunchy dry crust that gives way to a warm chewy, cheesy center. At its worst, it is dry and starchy.

    Chipa is consumed throughout Paraguay (though less so in the Chaco) and sold in most cases by *chiperas* (female) or *chiperos* (male), vendors who walk through neighborhoods with large baskets full of *chipa* balanced

> In Asunción alone, over one million *chipas* are consumed each day.

on their heads. Most major roads have *chipa* stands known as "*chiperías*" which employ *chiperas* dressed in short skirts, aprons, and knee-high socks. *Chiperas* hop on passing buses, selling their snacks to hungry passengers. Their ability to make it to the back of even the most crowded bus without dropping a single *chipa* from their baskets is an impressive spectacle. In urban areas, *chipa* is available in cafés (such as Ña Eustaquia and Hermanas Feliciana), and there are also *chipa* trucks specializing in selling to revelers as they exit nightclubs at dawn.

Indigenous Roots

Chipa's roots originate from Paraguay's indigenous community where it played an important role in religious ceremonies. To this day Paraguayans regularly partake in several rituals revolving around the preparation and distribution of *chipa*. *Chipa* is given out to friends and family during Easter week as well as at the end of prayer sessions known as "*rezos*" which are held during funerals and at regular intervals thereafter. On the Day of the Cross (*Kurusu Ara*), *chipa* is used as a decorative element hung from the canopy built to enshrine the cross. More information on the indigenous roots and religious significance of *chipa*, as well as *chipa* recipes, can be found in "*Alimentación y Religiosidad Paraguay: Chipa, Pan Sagrado*" by Margarita Miro Ibars.

A Chipa for Every Taste

Chipa is not a one note dish. Some of the most widely available variations of chipa include:

Chipitas or Chipa piru Chipitas are miniature versions of chipas. They're small rings of *chipa* dough about two inches in diameter. They are dry, crunchy, and highly addictive. The guaraní name, *chipa piru*, means "skinny *chipa*." If you wish to take *chipa* back to your home country, this is the best option as they keep well and can be stored in the freezer.

Chipa so'o and Chipa ryguazu These are chipas filled with beef (*so 'o*) or chicken (*ryguazu*). Often the dough itself is heavier on the corn flour than regular chipa, creating a texture that is vaguely reminiscent of a dry tamale.

Chipa asador Chipa asador is cooked over an open fire and therefore mainly consumed in the winter. The dough is similar to regular chipa but with more starch and less corn flour. It is pressed around the end of a wooden dowel or broomstick resulting in what looks like half of a giant q-tip. This is slowly turned above hot coals until the dough is cooked through, resulting in satisfyingly thin and crispy edges and a warm chewy interior.

Chipa candoi Chipa candoi is prepared with crushed peanuts and can be either sweet or salty. It is most often seen in the countryside, though it is occasionally available in urban areas as well.

SOPA PARAGUAYA

Although the word *"sopa"* means soup in Spanish, *"sopa paraguaya"* is not soup, it is cornbread. Sopa is prepared with corn flour, onions, eggs, and cheese. As with *chipa*, *sopa paraguaya* is an important element of special occasions such as birthdays and parties. Fancy variations of sopa include using natural yogurt and beating egg whites, leading to lighter, fluffier *sopa*. One must be careful in making sure that the corn flour is fresh, as old corn flour can ruin a good batch of *sopa*.

> *Sopa paraguaya* is so prevalent at weddings that asking someone *"¿Cuando vamos a comer sopa?"* (When are we going to eat sopa?) is code for "When are you getting married?"

CHIPA GUAZÚ

Though its name implies otherwise, *chipa guazú* is not one of the variations of *chipa*. Rather, it is a variation of *sopa*. Instead of corn meal, whole corn kernels are used to make this cheesy corn soufflé. Some prefer their *chipa guazú* baked until firm, while others like it crisp on top and soft and mushy on the inside.

Queso Paraguay

Paraguayan cheese, known as *"kesu Paraguay"* or *"queso Paraguay,"* is an essential ingredient in traditional Paraguayan cooking. Without cheese, *chipa* would just be a corn bagel, *sopa* would be plain old cornbread, and *mbeju* would be a starchy mess. When fresh, it is soft, white, and very bland in flavor. Fresh *kesu* is combined with either guava jam (*dulce de guayaba*) or molasses (*miel de caña*) as a dessert. It is often thrown into soups and combined with rice as well. *Kesu* goes from plain to pungent (sometimes awfully so) in a matter of days, becoming yellow, hard, and kind of greasy. In this state, it is ideal for inclusion in *chipa, sopa*, and *chipa guazú*. Most Paraguayans only eat cheese in *queso paraguay* form, as it is just about the only type of cheese available in the countryside.

MANDIOCA

Mandioca (cassava or yucca root) is a staple food of Paraguay, so much so that there is a popular saying: *"Es más paraguayo que la mandioca"* (He's more Paraguayan than mandioca). The tuber has an outer bark-like layer that is brown and papery. This is removed along with the first inner layer of the root. The remaining bright white to pale yellow interior is then boiled until soft. *Mandioca* is eaten plain alongside most meals. *Mandioca* is very filling as well as cheap and easy to grow. For the rural poor, it is a significant source of carbohydrates, and a small plot of *mandioca* can act as a nutritional safety net. One of the most popular *mandioca* based dishes is *mandi'o chyryry*, a concoction of fried mandioca, eggs, and onions.

Mandioca starch (tapioca), known as *"almidón,"* is a key ingredient in several traditional dishes. In the countryside, many families still make their own starch, an arduous and lengthy process involving grinding up the *mandioca*, allowing the starch to separate from the tuber's liquid, and spreading it out to dry in the sun. *Almidón* is the primary ingredient for *mbeju*, a traditional winter dish. Starch, cheese, lard, and eggs are combined until they form a crumbly dough, which is then pressed into an iron skillet and placed over the fire. Everything melds together to form a gooey pancake. Once is it cooled, you can pull and rip off pieces.

There Is a Day for Every Food

Certain foods are traditionally consumed on specific days. *Locro*, a hearty stew made with hominy and beef, is prepared on Mondays in order to start the week strong. Thursdays and Sundays call for special dishes such as *tallarín*. Following in the footsteps of Argentina, the 29th of every month is *ñoqui* (gnocchi or potato dumpling) day. Knocking back a shot of *carrulim* (made with caña alcohol, rue herb, and lemon) on August 1st and eating a bowl of *jopará* (a bean and beef soup) on October 1st are said to ward off bad luck.

MEATS

Paraguayans are quite carnivorous – for most, a meal based around meat is preferable to one based around vegetables. *Bifes* (steaks) and *lomitos* (thin-cut steaks) are popular as are *milanesas* (breaded fried steaks). These are sometimes accompanied by fried eggs and onions *(bife koygua* or *bife al caballo)* or topped with red sauce, ham, and cheese (*a la napolitana*). As many rural Paraguayans live on a limited diet, there are a variety of dishes designed to use all parts of the animal. *Guisos* (stews), *estofados* (ragu type sauces), and *caldos* (soups) abound. Larger portions of meat are served up during *asados* (barbeques). Generally all *asados* consist of large hunks of beef, chorizo (sausage), *morcilla* (blood sausage), and of course, *mandioca*. Sides, such as *sopa paraguaya* and rice or potato salads, are also common. In the Misiones department, *asado* is prepared *a la estaca* – cuts of meat are skewered onto large stakes placed around a large patch of burning coals.

World Records

In 2011, Paraguay became the Guinness Book of World Records holder for the world's longest hotdog at 203 meters. Paraguay also holds the record for the largest open-air barbeque, set in 2008 when over 40,000 people gathered to consume 26,715 kilos of meat.

Street Meats

It is not surprising that the majority of street food options (aside from *chipa*) revolve around meat. Every night in every town, street stands or kiosks feature the following:

Lomitos Cooked to order, *lomitos* are thin cuts of meat, grilled up, slapped between two pieces of bread, and topped with a fried egg, ham, cheese, lettuce, and tomato.

Lomito Árabe Paraguay's small Middle Eastern community has made a widespread contribution to the country's cuisine in the form of the *shwarma*, known here as a *"lomito árabe."* The most authentic *lomito árabe* stands serve *shwarma* in pita bread with optional hummus, falafel, and babaganoush. Paraguayan twists include copious amounts of mayonnaise.

Asadito *Asadito* are meat kabobs – grilled bite-sized chunks of meat on a stick. *Asaditos* are usually accompanied with a side of *mandioca*. No frills, but it gets the job done.

Empanadas These ubiquitous mini calzones are usually deep fried and filled with ground beef (*carne*), chicken (*pollo*), or ham and cheese (*jamón y queso*). *Empanadas de mandioca* have a thick dough made with *mandioca* starch. There are vegetarian options such as corn (*choclo*) or onion (*cebolla*), though these are rare outside of urban areas.

FISH

Being a landlocked country fish commands a premium, and popular fish dishes are often reserved for special occasions. With its thick white meat and few bones, surubí is the most sought after fish. Fish is usually prepared one of three ways:

Caldo de pescado A thin fish chowder with vegetables.

Milanesa de pescado Breaded and fried fillets.

Chupín A casserole baked with onions and tomatoes and topped with cheese.

VEGETARIAN OPTIONS

Despite the prevalence of animal products, Paraguay's cuisine does have several standard dishes that are vegetarian – however, most Paraguayans will do their best to provide meat to visitors. They may be surprised and amused to find out you want to eat vegetarian foods generally considered too humble to be served to foreigners. Some readily accessible vegetarian options include:

Porotos Beans (or *kumandá* in Guaraní) are often served as salad (*ensalada de porotos*), tossed with oil, hardboiled eggs, and parsley, or a soup (*caldo de porotos*). Lima beans (*porotos de manteca*) are also popular and often turned into a stew with rice and tomatoes.

Huevos Eggs are easy to come by as most rural Paraguayans have their own chickens. The chickens are fed table scraps resulting in eggs with a rich flavor and deep orange yolk (free range eggs are known as *"huevos caseros"*). Eggs can be cooked with another vegetarian staple, *mandioca*, to make *mandi'o chyryry* or eaten plain. Sunny side up eggs (*huevo frito*) are particularly delicious, perhaps because they are prepared in hot oil. If you are not picky about the "meatiness" of cooking surfaces, you can request an egg sandwich from a *lomito* stand. When requesting your *lomito "sin carne,"* be sure to specify that you don't want ham either (*"sin jamón"*).

Maní High in protein, peanuts are readily available throughout the country and make up several traditional snack and desserts (see Peanuts, p226).

Emapandas Larger *empanada* chains such as Don Vito have a variety of vegetable and cheese *empanadas* including corn (*choclo*), onion (*cebolla*), kale (*acelga*) and heart of palm (*palmito*).

Tortillas In Paraguay, *tortillas* are actually fritters and not Mexican-style corn tortillas. Batter usually includes cheese and a leafy green such as kale.

Tartas Vegetable *tartas* (quiches) are another good option, usually made with spinach, kale, or zucchini.

Arroz quesu White rice cooked with *queso Paraguay* is a popular side dish.

Tallarín Another tasty option if you are okay with simply removing meat from a dish. Though the dish is simple (thick yellow noodles with red sauce) it is Paraguay's number one comfort food.

The Basics

FRUIT

Fresh fruit is readily available in markets, and it is common for people to give away fruit from their own trees as gifts. During the summer, tree branches hang heavy with mangoes and guavas, and precarious pyramids of watermelons fill the markets. The winter months fill trees with grapefruits, oranges, and tangerines (*mandarinas*). Vendors hit the street corners of Asunción in early spring, baskets brimming with strawberries. Some of the highlights of Paraguay's tropical bounty include:

> *Bananas de oro* are miniature bananas (about three to four inches long) with thin skin that are starchier and sweeter than normal bananas (known as *"banana karape"*).

Maracuyá (Passion Fruit)

Though the *maracuyá* fruit starts out as a smooth creamy orb (first green, then yellow) it becomes ugly and wrinkled when ripening, as if puckering from the tart taste developing inside. The juicy pulp is usually blended and strained to make *maracuyá* juice, although *maracuyá* mousse and ice cream are also popular.

Guayaba (Guava)

Green on the outside and sticky, sweet, and pink on the inside, *guayaba* (guava) is perhaps the most emblematic fruit of Paraguay. When in season, they are in such abundance that many are left to fall from the trees onto the ground where they bake and sizzle in the sun, filling the air with an intoxicating and mouth watering aroma. Although sometimes eaten raw, guayaba is mostly turned into *dulce de guayaba* or guayaba jam. Guavas are boiled, blended, and passed through a sieve. The *guayaba* puree is then boiled down, along with generous amounts of sugar until it thickens and turns from light pink to a deep burgundy. This is often consumed as a dessert alongside *queso Paraguay* but is delicious on its own.

Mango

Mangoes are so abundant that most supermarkets do not even bother to stock them. Paraguayan mangoes are sweet but small and very fibrous, unlike their larger and creamier Brazilian counterparts. Mangoes are often juiced, although for the most part people eat them right off the tree. The mango tree itself plays an important role in the daily lives of rural Paraguayans. The trees can grow to an enormous size, providing

> **Naranja Jai**
> *Naranja jai* or *apepu* is a bitter orange often squeezed onto salads and used to cut the grease on grilled and fried meats.

plenty of much needed shade. All types of activities from drinking *tereré* to eating Sunday lunch with the whole family take place *mango guype* (under the mango tree).

Chirimoya (Custard Apple)

With their large bumpy green exteriors, *chirimoyas* (known as *"aratiku'i"* in Guaraní) are bizarre looking, but tasty. As *chirimoyas* ripen, the skin between the bumps turns pale yellow and begins to split. The interior is full of pointy shaped, creamy white sections that separate easily from the outer skin with a taste vaguely reminiscent of green apple.

Deadly Watermelon

Watermelon is believed to be a volatile fruit when combined with any number of foods, beverages, and activities. Paraguayans avoid eating watermelon after drinking *tereré*, beer, showering, and swimming for fear of everything from massive stomachaches to possible death. When confronted with a cool slice of watermelon on a hot day, you may find it hard to heed their warnings though.

DESSERTS

Miel Negra *Miel negra* or *miel de caña* is a dark, sweet syrup made by boiling down cane juice. Its rich deep flavor, similar to that of molasses, makes it a popular dessert when paired with cheese, bananas, or peanuts.

Queso Paraguay *Queso Paraguay*, present in almost all other dishes, is part of Paraguay's dessert offerings as well. A hunk of squeaky fresh cheese is often paired with a generous helping *of miel negra* or *dulce de guayaba*. This is best when the cheese is fresh.

Dulces Paraguayans take advantage of the overabundance of fruits by turning many into jams and sweets ranging from spreadable to solid sliceable jellies. Popular flavors include guava (*guayaba*), papaya (*mamón*), and, oddly enough, sweet potato (*batata*). These are eaten plain or paired with *queso Paraguay*.

Budín de pan Similar in taste to flan but with a more of a custardy texture, *budín de pan* is an all-time favorite dessert. Chunks of soft bread soaked in milk are blended with eggs and sugar, placed in a jello-mold pan with caramelized sugar (*almíbar*) at the bottom, and cooked in a baine marie. The result is a dish that is deep brown on top, creamy yellow on the bottom, and delicious throughout.

Andai Butternut squash, known as *"andai"* in Guaraní, is used to make two popular desserts. For *andai kambu* pieces of squash are boiled in milk along with cinnamon and cloves. It is served warm or cold. *Kiveve* is prepared by cooking pureed squash with milk, fried onions, and a bit of corn flour, resulting in a creamy squash and corn porridge.

Beverages

YERBA MATE BASED BEVERAGES

Yerba mate (*ilex paraguaiensis*) is consumed in massive quantities throughout Paraguay in a variety of forms. Visitors who have passed through Argentina and Uruguay will recognize the traditional *mate* with hot water. *Tereré, yerba* served with cold water, is unique to Paraguay. A variety of medicinal plants (*"yuyos"* in Spanish and *"poja ñana"* in Guaraní) are typically added to the water for both *mate* and *tereré*. Paraguayans also drink *mate cocido*, another hot *mate* drink vaguely reminiscent of chai.

> Though it has always been an industrialized product, there are families in the countryside that continue to harvest and process their own yerba mate.

Mate Caliente

Regardless of the season most adult Paraguayans start off the day with a few rounds of *mate caliente*. While water is heated, a recipient known as a *"guampa,"* usually made out of wood or a hollowed out gourd, is filled about two thirds of the way with loose *yerba mate* and a straw shaped metal tea strainer known as a *"bombilla"* is added. Once hot, but not boiling, water is poured into the *guampa*, and the *yerba* is allowed to

> Coffee addicts should note that Paraguayans generally get their morning caffeine buzz from mate, while coffee is often reserved for an afternoon pick me up.

steep momentarily. The water is then sipped through the *bombilla*. Once drained, the *guampa* is passed to the server (known as the *"cebador"*) who refills it and hands it to the next member of the group. Each serving is known as a *"ha."* There is usually enough water for each participant to get several *"has."* Sugar is sometimes added to the water and medicinal herbs to the *yerba* itself. During the summer months, most drink *mate caliente* around dawn and then switch to *tereré* as the heat sets in.

On cold winter days, a special treat called *"mate de coco"* is often prepared. Hot water is substituted with sweetened hot milk and *yerba* with shredded unsweetened coconut and some anise seed (this is particularly good when drunk with a *guampa*

Yerba Mate – From the Tree to the Guampa

The processed leaves of the *yerba mate* bush, related to the holly tree, have always been one of the country's top exports. Historically, Paraguayan *yerba mate* commanded a premium price in foreign ports. In the past, *yerba mate* was harvested from the wild. Large camps were set up near wild areas of *yerba* trees known as *"yerbales,"* with the entire production process taking place on site. The Jesuits pioneered the idea of cultivating the *yerba mate* bush, a practice which was largely abandoned after their expulsion and only took hold once more in modern day Paraguay. Currently, the majority of yerba mate production plants are located in the Itapúa province.

Though machinery and technology have been incorporated, very little has changed in the actual process of creating *yerba mate* since colonial times. Branches and leaves from the *yerba mate* bush are gathered and then dried. Nowadays, the drying takes place in specialized ovens, whereas before large wooden platforms were constructed for bundles of branches to hang under an indirect fire for days at a time. Once fully dried, the *yerba* is then ground to a coarse consistency before being packaged for transport to national and international markets. Historically, *yerba mate* was packaged for transport in large hides. Today, it is available in stores throughout the country in packages as small as half of a kilo to bulk bags as large as fifty kilos. Each *yerba* brand is slightly different than the next – some are bitter and strong, others are milder and come with medicinal herbs (these are referred to as *"yerba compuesta"*). Approximately 18,750 hectares of yerba are cultivated annually, resulting in over 30,000 tons of processed *yerba mate*. Pajarito, Selecta, and Campesino are the classics – bitter and strong. Kurupí, whose packaging depicts indigenous processing wild *yerba mate*, is a good bet for beginners, as is the more expensive but mild La Rubia. There is even an organic *mate* called Yerba Guayakí. The seemingly limitless variety of *yerba* brands and blends can seem daunting, but visitors will soon find a *yerba mate* to suit their tastes.

or *bombilla* made out of *palo santo*). Rich and comforting, *mate de coco* is Paraguay's answer to a cup of hot cocoa.

Tereré

Cold and refreshing, *tereré* is Paraguay's secret weapon against the heat. *Tereré* is often described as "cold *mate*," a description that fails to convey the importance of the drink in everyday life and the myriad of rituals involved in its consumption. Aside from the temperature of the water, there are other differences between *mate caliente* and *tereré*. The *guampa* is usually made of

> Thanks to endless rounds of tereré, Paraguayans boast one of the lowest levels of kidney disease in the world.

a hollowed out bull horn instead of a gourd. *Palo santo guampas* are also popular as they impart a distinct flavor to the *tereré*. Medicinal herbs or *yuyos* are added directly to the water, rather than the *yerba*. Lemon is often added to the water to make it more refreshing. Though any jug will do, it has recently become fashionable to pour ice-cold *tereré* water from a personalized leather-covered thermos. From the

The Basics

Jazzing Up Your Mate or Tereré with Yuyos

Paraguayans are firm believers in using medicinal plants on a regular basis to heal ailments and prevent illness. Nowhere is this practice seen more than in the addition of *yuyos* (or "*poja ñana*" in Guaraní) to *mate* and *tereré*. In plazas and street corners throughout Paraguay you will see *yuyo* vendors (*yuyeras*) sitting behind tables covered with a wide array of medicinal plants. They will also have a large mortar and pestle. Customers stop by, make their selection, and watch as their custom blend is mashed up to order and either handed over in a small bag or dunked directly into their waiting thermos. *Yuyos* are generally not used in *tereré* after lunch and it is almost impossible to find yuyeras in the afternoon.

Choosing from the many small bundles of roots, leaves, and flowers may seem intimidating at first but will become quite fun once you get the hang of it. Some options, such as mint (*menta*), rosemary (*romero*), sage (*santa lucía*), lemongrass (*cedrón kapi'i*), and chamomile (*manzanilla*), will be familiar, while others are a mystery waiting to be discovered. Generally, you should stick to three *yuyos* – two leafy ones and one root. *Yuyos* also fall into categories based on their effects – medicinal, refreshing, diuretic. *Yuyeras* are happy to make recommendations. Are you tired? Do you have a stomach ache? Are you hung over? Think of the *yuyera* as your personal apothecary. Each *tereré* session is a chance to experiment with different combinations of *yuyos*. Between the myriad of *yuyos* and *yerba mate* brands the possibilities are endless. No two *tererés* are the same!

Suggested combinations (note certain *yuyos* are seasonal and may not be available year round):

Perdudilla, burrito, cedron kapi'i or menta'i.

Santa lucia, parapara'i, and cedron or menta'i or burrito.

Menta'i, cedron kapi'i or cedrón en palo, and mbokaja rapo.

Yuyeras often also rent out *tereré* and *mate* equipment (*equipos*) if you don't have one of your own. For roughly Gs. 3,000 to Gs. 5,000 you will be given a *bombilla*, *guampa* with *yerba*, and either a pitcher of cold water or thermos of hot water depending on whether you are drinking *tereré* or *mate*. Wander over to the nearest bench and enjoy!

moment your lips touch the cool metal of the *bombilla* to when you feel the cold water fill your stomach, everything about *tereré* is refreshing. Even the drops of water from a leaky *termo* are a welcome respite from the heat.

Wearing Your Heart on Your Termo

Leather-covered *tereré* thermoses (*termos*) are popular throughout Paraguay from the Chaco to Caacupé. Thermoses come in a dizzying array of styles. Some are decorated in traditional artisanal styles with idyllic scenes of the Paraguayan countryside etched or pressed into the leather. Others are covered by a patchwork of brightly colored patent leather (*cuerina*). Many choose to personalize their thermos with their name, favorite soccer club, or profession.

To some, the main deterrent to drinking *tereré* is the fact that it is shared amongst several people. This is a real, though generally ignored, concern. For those who do not wish to step so far outside their comfort zone the easiest way to participate in the in the camaraderie of a *tereré* circle is to offer to *cebar* or serve the *tereré*. Traditionally this role is given to the youngest member of the circle (or the lowest on the pecking order) – they may thank you for relieving them of their duties! Ask the group for tips on how to properly *cebar*. There are rules and rituals for everything from *bombilla* placement to water pouring techniques, which everyone will enjoy explaining at length. Another way to politely decline tereré is to claim you've recently consumed milk, citrus fruits, or watermelon. All are believed to cause upset stomachs if combined with *tereré*.

> Mate cocido in tea bags is jokingly referred to as *"mate de avión"* (airplane mate).

Tereré & Mate: Do's & Don'ts

Drinking both *tereré* and *mate* are social events where certain rules of etiquette apply. Here are some do's and don't's that will help you integrate smoothly into a *tereré* or *mate* circle.

Do: Keep a steady pace. Drain the *guampa* fully in two to three sips and pass it back to whoever is *cebando* (serving). If you take too long you will be admonished *"No es un micrófono"* (it's not a microphone).

Do: Accept the *guampa* if it is handed to you out of turn. It's good luck!

Do: Say *"gracias"* when you've had your fill. But don't say it beforehand, or you will be passed over on your next *ha*.

Don't: Express concerns over hygiene or wipe the bombilla before drinking from it. If you are not comfortable sharing drinks, there are plenty of polite ways to decline.

Don't: Give up if you don't like it at first. Even when tempered with *yuyos*, yerba has an acquired taste. Work your way up by asking to be included once the *yerba* is *"más lavada"* (weaker).

Don't: Overfill your *guampa*; leave room for the *yerba* to expand as it soaks up water.

Don't: Remove the *bombilla* once it is in place.

Mate Cocido Quemado

Mate cocido quemado, usually shortened to *cocido*, is popular for breakfast and afternoon tea time (*merienda*). To make this drink, sugar is dusted over a layer of *yerba mate* and then toasted over a fire or tossed with red-hot embers. The aroma of burning sugar and *yerba mate* is intoxicating and unmistakable. Once the sugar has caramelized, the *yerba* is steeped in water, strained, and consumed either black or with milk. Many Paraguayans drink *cocido* with *galletas* (dry biscuits). The *galleta* swells up as it absorbs the *cocido*, earning this breakfast classic the nickname "*cururu*," the Guaraní word for toad. There are several brands of pre-made *mate cocido* available in both loose and tea bag form. One of the best is Abuelita PY whose labels feature a cute white-haired granny.

OTHER DRINKS

Carbonated Drinks

Soda or *gaseosa* is consumed in large quantities. In urban areas, the typical big name brands such as Coca-Cola and Pepsi are available. In rural areas, cheaper local brands such as Piri and Niko are more popular. Two flavors worth trying are *guaraná* and *pomelo* (grapefruit).

The Basics

Takuare'e

Sugar cane, "*caña de azúcar*" in Spanish, is known as "*takuare'e*" in Guaraní, which means sweet bamboo. Throughout the countryside you will see large *trapiches* or mills used for grinding sugar cane and collecting the sweet juice inside. Depending on the size of the operation, the *trapiches* are operated either by hand, by oxen, or in some cases by a small motor. The juice can then be consumed along with ice as *mosto*, made into *miel de caña*, or fermented to produce an unrefined rum known as "*caña*."

Mosto

Freshly pressed sugar cane juice, known as "*mosto*," is a popular summertime beverage. Cold, sticky and sweet, the drink is sold for Gs. 1,000 by street vendors.

ALCOHOLIC DRINKS

Beer

Paraguay has a high rate of beer consumption but a limited variety of available brands. The market is dominated by light pilsner-style beers. Though they are not particularly flavorful, beers such as Pilsen, Brahma, and Baviera are refreshing in the

---

Botellas Retornables

Although beer and soda is also sold in plastic bottles and aluminum cans, glass bottles are more prevalent for large scale sales. Large trucks carrying crates of glass bottles rumble throughout the country stopping at supermarkets, *almacenes* (small stores), and restaurants, exchanging full bottles for crates of empty ones.

This recycling system also works on a small scale. A deposit is paid for the first primordial bottle. Upon return of the empty bottle you are given a credit towards a full bottle (in supermarkets this happens at the customer service desk). Many prefer to drink soda out of glass bottles because they say it tastes better. But, if you prefer plastic, you can still participate in this eco-friendly practice by purchasing bottles that say "*retornable*" on the label.

Paraguayan heat. Most beer is sold in a three-quarter or one-liter brown glass bottles (the latter are nicknamed *ñoños*). Beer is generally cheap, with a three-quarter liter costing as little as Gs. 6,000. Artisanal beers are also available in limited quantities in specialty stores in Asunción and the non-Mennonite German colonies such as Colonia Independencia.

> At soccer games and large public events where beer sales are theoretically prohibited, beer vendors announce they have *"leche"* (milk) for sale instead.

Caña

Caña is unaged sugar cane liquor similar to rum yet sweeter. *Caña* packs a punch and is dirt cheap. All major brands offer a "Black Label" (*Etiqueta*) version that is worth the marginal price difference. Popular brands include Tres Leones, Aristócrata (known affectionately as "Ari"), and Fortín. Paraguayans like to mix *caña* with Coca Cola. In the countryside, it also consumed with *miel negra* and/or lemon.

Artisanal Liquors

Homemade liquor enthusiasts (German immigrants in particular) take advantage of the full spectrum of fruits available in Paraguay. Strawberry, passion fruit, and *guayaba* liquors, along with several other flavors, can be purchased from small roadside stands.

Wine

In the countryside, cheap boxed wines (such as Uvita) are popular but taste like alcoholic Kool-aid. Perhaps for this very reason, they are best consumed as *clericó* a wine-based fruit punch (similar to *sangria*) prepared during the holidays. Paraguayans also like to mix wine with Coca-Cola and often serve red wine chilled when it is hot out.

Paraguayan Ice

In Paraguay, most ice comes in the form of a cylindrical bar. Plastic bags are filled with water and frozen into foot-long bars. Many people sell ice out of their homes as a way to make some extra money. You will see *"Se vende hielo"* (ice for sale) signs in front of houses throughout Paraguay. The going rate is between Gs. 500 and Gs. 1,000 per bar.

What are the advantages of Paraguayan ice tubes versus ice cubes? For one, larger chunks of ice take longer to melt. One long tube broken into two chunks will keep your water cold throughout several rounds of *tereré*. Of course, having big blocks of ice isn't always convenient. Sometimes smaller pieces are required. When ice cubes are nowhere to be found, Paraguayans have fun breaking bars of ice down to smaller pieces. Here are some methods for breaking ice, depending on your mood (be sure to leave the ice encased in plastic).

Civilized method: Give the ice bar a couple of forceful taps with a hard object such as a pestle or handle of a heavy serving utensil.

Brute force method: Hold on tight and smack the bar against the edge of a sink, countertop, or table.

Anger management method: First check that no one is looking. Then hurl the ice bar at the ground with all your might. This method might not result in many useable chunks but at Gs. 500 per bar it makes for a cheap thrill.

Alcohol & Cigarettes

Drinking in public is common, though mostly amongst men (with the exception of bars and nightclubs in urban areas). In the countryside, unaccompanied women rarely drink in public. Those that do, can often send the wrong message. Smoking is not particularly common though very cheap (if you are low on funds, you can even purchase individual cigarettes from smaller stores). It is common courtesy to go to the outside section of a bar or restaurant to smoke. Locally made cigars are popular amongst rural Paraguayans, although they are more often chewed rather than smoked.

Restaurants

Most restaurants, both modest and high-end, offer affordable lunch specials (*menú del día* or *menú ejecutivo*). All you can eat Brazilian *churrasquerías* with endless streams of waiters offering up different cuts of meat are popular among locals and tourists alike. Though limited, ethnic foods can generally be found in cities as well as in immigrant colonies. German foods (baked and pickled goods as well as sausages) are especially prevalent and generally of high quality. Though the Paraguayan dishes tend to be bland, most restaurants have hot sauce (*ají picante*) to spice things up. Travelers on a budget should note that many restaurants in cities refuse to serve tap water in order to profit from bottled water.

In small town restaurants, the selection of dishes are typically limited to Paraguayan staples such as *empanadas, sopa, chipa guazú,* and *milanesas* (these types of foods are known as "*minutas*"), while cities offer a wider variety. In larger towns, the supermarket food court "pay by the kilo" buffets are popular and can be the most dependable food option. Heladería Amandau and El Heladero ice cream chains have stores selling desserts and snacks throughout the countryside.

Restaurants serve lunch roughly between 11am and 2pm, though larger, popular restaurants in the city may serve food all afternoon. Most places open for dinner between 7:30 and 8pm but don't tend to fill up until 10pm or, later on the weekends. If you need a pick-me-up between lunch and dinner, your best bet is to head to a "*confitería*" (coffee shop). These often offer a full menu in addition to snacks and pastries. Restaurants and even ice cream parlors tend to shut down between midnight and 1am. In smaller towns, many restaurants either shut down or have reduced hours during the winter (low season).

The Basics

The Best of Country Cooking

Some dishes that taste better in the countryside, thanks to the fresh ingredients and methods of cooking. Don't pass up the chance to eat the following:

Tallarín Thick yellow noodles cooked with a delicious tomato based sauce and often served with chicken, beef or pork.

Mandió chyryry Fried *mandioca* with scrambled eggs, *queso Paraguay*, and onions.

Arroz con leche Creamy and delicious when made with fresh cow's milk. Sometimes burnt sugar is added giving it a richer flavor.

Kure (pork, in all its forms) Fried (*chyryry*), *al horno*, or *tatakua* (baked in an oven or brick oven) or *asado* (grilled).

Staying Connected

CELL PHONES

Cell phone usage is becoming increasingly popular especially in remote areas of the country where landlines are still scarce. For travelers, cell phones represent the easiest method of communication.

The Paraguayan cell phone network operates on the GSM system with all phones using SIM cards (a small chip that stores cell phone data). Locally purchased SIM cards will work with foreign GSM phones as long as they are unlocked. Ask your home cell phone provider to unlock your phone before departure, or get your phone unlocked locally at a cell phone store. This usually costs between Gs. 50,000 and Gs. 100,000 depending on the phone model. Phones are easily purchased locally as well.

Tigo, Personal, and Claro are the three largest cell phone providers in Paraguay. Tigo generally has better coverage in rural areas. All cell phone numbers start with 09 and specific providers are indicated by the third digit. Tigo numbers start with 098, Personal with 097, and Claro with 099.

Both pay-as-you-go and monthly plans are available. SIM cards (also known as "*chips*") can be purchased from cell phone carrier representatives (in businesses and street-side stands) and cost between Gs 5,000 to Gs 10,000. In order to get a SIM

Text Messaging

As text messages are limited to 180 characters a slew of abbreviations are used.

The letters "h" and "e" are often dropped from the beginning of a word: *aciendo=haciendo* and *stoy = estoy*

Any time a letter sounds like a word it is used as a substitute:

Q= *Que,* C=*se,* D=*de,* T=*te*

The letter "e" is often removed if the sound of the letter preceeding it automatically makes that sound.

AC= *hace*

No is shortened to just an "N" and "Ñ" is often indicated by using a symbol such as a question mark.

X: *por* (for)

Q: *que* (what)

P: *para* (for)

XQ: porque (because)

Bs: *besos* (kisses)

TQM: *te quiero mucho* (I love you a lot)

SDQ: *si Dios quiere* (if it is God's wish)

Nts: *entonces* (so)

TB: *tambien* (also)

Example: nc q voy a acr ma?ana xq tngo sue?o. bsns.

Translated: *No se que voy a hacer mañana porque tengo sueño. Buenas Noches*

card you will have to provide official ID. Phone credit, known as *"saldo,"* is loaded onto the SIM card with phone cards or through vendors selling *"mini cargas."* As Paraguay operates on a "caller pays" system, your credit will only be used up when you make a call or send a text message. Calls range from Gs. 6 to Gs.12 per second and text messages cost between Gs. 80 and Gs. 100. Discounts apply to calls and messages within the same network. Calls from cell phones to landlines and vice versa are more expensive. Most companies also allow for texting internationally.

Because it is cheaper, many people prefer to send text messages rather than talk on the phone. However, text messages can sometimes go undelivered due to weak signals and problems with cell phones on either end. Often messages go unanswered because the recipient has no phone credit. If you need to discuss an urgent matter, it's best to make a phone call.

It is very common for people to run out of phone credit. There are two popular ways to work around the problem: *Dame saldo* and *Llamada perdida*. *Dame saldo* ("give me credit") works by allowing users to request phone credit of another cell phone user in the same network via text message. The recipient of a *dame saldo* message can then reply with the amount of *saldo* they wish to transfer. Users without credit may also communicate via *llamada perdida* (missed call) wherein

> If you are volunteering or living in a community long term, you may receive *dame saldo* requests on a regular basis – these are best ignored lest you become your community *saldo* cash cow.

users call and hang up as soon as the call registers. The recipient is then expected to return the call (and, as a result, pays for the call).

Although the price difference for calling within a network versus outside the network may be irrelevant for those passing through, the cost adds up for locals. If you are developing a network of contacts within Paraguay, you might want to consider having chips from different providers. Most people simply carry multiple cell phones, though dual chip phones are now available. It can be surprising how much of a difference having a Personal phone in an area serviced mostly by Tigo will make in your ability to communicate effectively with friends and contacts.

Phone banks known as *"cabinas telefónicas"* are the best option for travelers without cell phones. These businesses operate several phone booths from which local and international calls can be made.

INTERNET

Paraguay is only beginning to embrace an internet culture and is one of the least "wired" countries in Latin America. Personal computers are still rare outside of the upper classes, and home internet connections are not yet widespread. Most people access the internet at work (if they have office jobs) or through cyber cafés. Though many businesses do not have websites, an increasing number do have a presence online via popular social networking sites such as Facebook or Orkut. Though businesses may list an email address, responding to emails in a timely fashion is rarely a priority. For rapid responses, a phone call is always best.

> It is becoming increasingly common for main plazas in cities and larger towns to offer free Wi-Fi. As always, however, you should be careful when using fancy devices such as laptops or smart phones in public.

The Basics

Cyber cafés ("*ciber*") are common even in the countryside, though connection speeds can vary from decent to painfully slow. Most computers have Skype installed, and all have MSN messenger. If you plan to communicate via Skype, it is best to bring your own headset. Caution should be taken when using USB pen drives in cyber cafés their anti-virus software is often out of date.

> On Spanish language keyboards the @ sign is typed by hitting Alt Gr (on the right-hand side of the space bar) and the number 2 or by hitting Alt and the number 64.

All cell phone companies offer USB internet services whereby users connect to the internet through the cell phone network via a pen drive, which contains a SIM card. Both monthly and pay-as-you-go plans are available. For the latter, credit, or *saldo*, is loaded onto the chip as if it were a cell phone.

MAIL

Correo Paraguay (*www.correoparaguayo.gov.py*), the national mail service, is fairly reliable for sending and receiving letters, but not fast. Packages, unfortunately, are more susceptible to snooping and theft. Post offices are located throughout Paraguay. The weight limit for packages is twenty kilos. Postal workers must first verify the contents of all packages before shipping them. Therefore, it's best to seal the package only after it's been checked thoroughly at the post office. Unless packaging is completely unmarked, all boxes and trunks must be covered in brown paper (this can be purchased at bookstores or *librerías*). Bring your own tape as the post office rarely has enough.

Items that are time sensitive or valuable should be shipped via international courier, although you pay a premium for the peace of mind.

DHL Offices in Asunción, San Lorenzo, Caaguazú, Coronel Oviedo, Villarica, and Ciudad del Este. *www.dhl.com.py*

Photography

Photography studios such as Kodak (*www.kodak.com.py*) and Rochester (*www.rochester.com.py*) have several locations in Asunción and other parts of Paraguay. Photos can be printed directly from memory cards and other external storage devices. Discounts are offered for bulk digital prints. Processing film is becoming rare and is often pricier than digital processing.

Taking & Sharing Photos:

Though Paraguayans are usually happy to be photographed, it is best to ask permission first. In Spanish you'd say, " *¿Puedo sacar tu foto por favor?*" and in Guaraní, "*¿Ikatu anohemi la nde foto?*" Or simply say "*¿Puedo?*" or "*¿Ikatu?*" while raising or gesturing to your camera. One of the advantages of digital photography is being able to show your subject their photo instantly. In poor areas, most people rarely have the opportunity to see their photos. To ask if your subject would like to see his photo say, "*¿Quieres ver tu foto?*" in Spanish and "*¿Rehechase nde foto?*" in Guaraní. Photo processing costs are beyond the means of rural families, many of whom do not even own a camera. If you have been staying with a family or have developed a particular bond with locals, consider printing some photos (portraits in particular) as a thank you gift. If you promise to send photos at a later date be sure to make good on that promise.

Media

TELEVISION

Paraguay's first television channel, Cerro Corá, began broadcasting in 1965. Since then, a handful of local television channels have popped up, filling the airwaves with news programs, game shows, and *telenovelas* (mostly imported from Argentina, Brazil, and Mexico). Though newscasts and talk shows are ostensibly in Spanish, hosts often break into Guaraní, especially during informal segments. Most hotels offer cable TV including a few Latin American networks (such as *CNN en Español*) and movie channels. Hotels along the border with Brazil have access to Brazilian satellite TV that offers a wider variety of channels including international news networks such as CNN and BBC in English.

NEWSPAPERS

ABC Color (www.abc.com.py), La Nación (www.lanacion.com.py), and Última Hora (www.ultimahora.com.py) are printed daily. ABC Color is the most popular newspaper in Paraguay. Guaraní words are used regularly, even in headlines, especially in order to add special emphasis. All three newspapers are notorious for slanting their political coverage, each representing their own special interests. News of this nature should generally be taken with a grain of salt. Most newspapers have weekly magazines and special supplements including books on Paraguayan history, collections of Paraguayan music, and DIY courses covering everything from knitting to home repair. The *Espectáculos* section is the best place to find out about upcoming cultural events.

An interesting alternative to the large dailies is E'a, a monthly publication available at newsstands in downtown Asunción and online at www.ea.com.py.

RADIO

Radio Nacional del Paraguay (920 AM/95.1 FM, *www.radionacionaldelparaguay.com.py*) is run by the government and focuses on national events and news. Programming also includes Paraguayan folklore shows featuring music and Guaraní lessons (5pm to 7pm, weekdays). Consistently driven off the air during the Stroessner era for its anti-government broadcasts, today Radio Ñanduti (1020AM, *www.nanduti.com.py*) is an excellent source of national and international news with politically themed talk shows. The website also features several blogs and podcasts. Both stations can be streamed online.

Radio FM Concert (107.7 FM) stands out among the commercial radio stations due to its eclectic programming featuring a mix of classical, bossa nova, and traditional Paraguayan music with a few other genres thrown in for good measure. This station is an excellent source of information about upcoming cultural events in Asunción and around the country.

In the countryside, airwaves are serviced mainly by smaller community stations. The majority of these

> Reggaeton is very popular as are 80's rock and euro-pop tunes. Over the course of an hour you are likely to hear Daddy Yankee Creedence Clearwater, and Queen played on the same station.

The Basics

stations run on low-power antennas and thus have very little reach. They generally announce the latest news and upcoming community events and fill the remaining airtime with polka, *guaranias*, and a fair amount of religious programming.

WEBSITES

Though Paraguay's blogging community is still small, there are a handful of blogs worth following. Discovering Paraguay (*www.discoveringparaguay.com*) features posts on all aspects of Paraguayan culture, from food to Guaraní phrases, and is written in both English and Spanish. Camino al Paraguay (*www.alparaguay.blogspot.com*) is updated daily with a wide array of news stories and coverage of upcoming events throughout the country. Cazador de Instantes (*www.cazadordeinstantes.com*) is an excellent photoblog featuring Paraguayan festivities and traditions and Naturaleza del Paraguay (*www.familiadiarte.com*) showcases beautiful shots of Paraguay's flora and fauna.

Travelers with Special Considerations

VEGETARIANS

Paraguayan meals are heavily reliant on meat, and vegetarianism is highly uncommon. However, it is possible for flexible vegetarians to enjoy eating in Paraguay (see Vegetarian Options on page 83). Those cooking their own meals will find Paraguay's fertile land provides vegetarians with a cornucopia of fresh produce. Check out the local markets for farm-fresh fruits and vegetables. If you are in Asunción be sure to check out the Agroshopping farmer's market (see Agroshopping, p129) where a number of Asian vendors sell ready-made soy-based foods including sushi rolls. Asian markets also sell fresh tofu (*queso de soja*). Supermarkets in Mennonite communities can be a good place to stock up on peanut butter and oatmeal.

   When ordering food, vegetarians should be specific about what they can and can't eat as the Spanish word for meat, "*carne*," refers exclusively to beef. When ordering food ask whether it contains *carne de rez* (beef), *chancho* (pork), *pollo* (chicken), or *jamón* (ham). Recipes for many traditional dishes, including *chipa*, call for pig fat ("*grasa de chancho*" in Spanish and "*kure ñandy*" in Guaraní), though in urban areas, it is often replaced with vegetable oil (*aceite* or *grasa vegetal*). Being flexible about cooking surfaces and eating around meat will greatly increase a vegetarian's food options. Unfortunately, vegans will have a much harder time adjusting. Both vegetarians and vegans should bring along snacks and be prepared to eat a lot of *mandioca* (adding hot sauce will make it more interesting).

   The Unión Vegetariana del Paraguay maintains a list of vegetarian restaurants in Asunción and Ciudad del Este on their website (*www.uvpy.org/Restaurantes.html*). In the countryside, vegetarian options will be limited. Therefore, your best bet may be to seek accommodations including full room and board, specifying you are a vegetarian while making your reservation. Most lodging will be willing to let you use their kitchen to prepare your own dishes once they are aware of your special circumstance. Do not be surprised, however, if locals refuse to try your vegetarian fare. Paraguayans are notoriously unadventurous when it comes to food. Don't take it personally.

JEWISH/KOSHER TRAVELERS

Paraguay is home to a very small Jewish population, living mostly in Asunción. Generally speaking, Paraguayans are unfamiliar with Jewish beliefs and practices. If it is consistent with your practice to eat at them, there are some vegetarian restaurants in major cities. Kosher meats are available in Asunción at CO-OP, run by the Fernheim Mennonite cooperative store.

CO-OP *Tel: 021 219 5000, Avenida España 2112*

Beit Jabad Paraguay (Asunción) *Tel: 021 228-669, Juan M. Frutos Pane 378,* *www.JabadParaguay.com*

FEMALE TRAVELERS

When unaccompanied by male travel companions, foreign women, especially blondes, will receive a lot of attention from Paraguayan men. While cat calls are common (whistling or a "*ch ch ch*" sound to grab attention), for the most part, the attention is innocent. When traveling alone on long distance buses it is best to sit in an aisle seat near the front of the bus, and sit next to another female when possible. When dealing with unknown males in settings such as a bar, restaurant, or bus, friendly chit-chat, smoking, drinking, and extended eye contact may be misinterpreted as a sign of flirtation. It is best to firmly rebuff advances from the start and act cold rather than friendly. Though it is common to greet people with a double kiss on each cheek, it is perfectly acceptable for women to shake hands with men instead – it is the woman's choice whether to kiss or shake hands (though more insistent men may play dumb and used your extended hand to pull you in for a kiss). Some female travelers may wish to pretend a willing male companion is their husband. In Spanish "my husband" is "*mi esposo*" and in Guaraní it is "*che mena.*"

Tight clothing is quite common for women in Paraguay (you will see a lot of spandex, both in the city and countryside). However, clothing that reveals skin (i.e.: spaghetti straps, low cut tank tops, and short shorts) is much less common and in many cases is an invitation for unwanted attention. Revealing clothing is inappropriate and considered offensive in the Mennonite colonies and religious sites.

Tampons are not widely used in Paraguay and only available for purchase in urban areas, with the selection limited to OB brand non-applicator tampons. Female travelers considering packing their own supply of feminine hygiene products should keep in mind that non-applicator tampons and tampons with cardboard applicators are more environmentally friendly than sanitary pads and can be discarded safely in latrines.

ELDERLY & DISABLED TRAVELERS

Paraguay presents some obstacles for elderly and disabled travelers. Sidewalks in cities are often uneven and streets are full of potholes. Buses and buildings are rarely handicap-accessible. The heat can also present an issue for some travelers. However, these obstacles are not insurmountable. Most activities can be done in the early morning hours before the excessive heat sets in. Double decker buses (*doble pisos*) are generally have some seating on the lower level, are more comfortable, air-conditioned, and even have bathrooms.

LBGT TRAVELERS

The LGBT community has yet to be openly accepted in Paraguayan society, with many people preferring to remain discrete or in the closet. As a result, there are only a small number of explicitly gay friendly establishments, even in the capital. Though foreigners are less likely to feel anti-gay pressures than locals, discretion is advised, particularly in regards to public displays of affection. Especially outside of urban areas, openly gay behavior is likely to draw unwanted attention (though it will mostly be limited to stares from strangers). For updated information about gay friendly establishments and LGBT community, contact the following gay rights organizations (all in Asunción):

SOMOSGAY Tel: 021 446 258, Manduvira 367 between Chile and Alberdi, www.somosgay.org, Mon-Thu 12pm-10pm, Fri-Sat 2pm to 12am

Paragay Tel: 021 23 28 20, corner of Peru and Teodoro Mongelós, www.paragay.org

Aireana Paraguay's lesbian and women's rights advocacy group, Aireana hosts a radio show on Radio Viva 90.1FM on Thursdays from 9pm to 11pm and holds cultural events and parties in their bar La Serafina. Tel: 021 492-835, 447 976, Eligio Ayala 907 between Tacuary and Estados Unidos, www.aireana.org.py

La Lista de 108

During the Stroessner era, homosexuals were lumped into the expansive and vaguely defined category of "subversives" subject to monitoring and mistreatment. On September 1st 1959, the charred remains of radio announcer Bernardo Aranda were found in his Asunción home. As Aranda was suspected to be a homosexual, the police declared the murder a "homosexual crime of passion," and under the guise of investigating the case compiled and published a list of Asunción's known and suspected homosexuals. The men on the "*Lista de 108*" (list of 108) were subsequently rounded up, tortured, and publicly humiliated. The resulting self-censorship by Paraguay's homosexual community is evident to this day; the openly gay community remains small and marginalized. Due to the *Lista de 108*, the number 108 has been associated with the homosexual community. The number will elicit giggles or comments when it comes up in certain crowds, and the *Lista de 108* is mentioned frequently by gay rights advocacy groups.

Further Resources:

"Cuchillo de Palo" Released in 2010, *"Cuchillo de Palo"* is an award winning documentary in which filmmaker Renate Costas delves into the past of her deceased uncle, discovering he was among the 108 homosexual victims of torture and repression at the hand of the Stroessner regime. While probing into the past, the film also reveals shame and stigma that remains ingrained in many modern day Paraguayans regarding family associations with the list of 108 and homosexuality in general.

108 y un Quemado Written by Agustín Nuñez, *"108 y un Quemado"* is a play based on the Aranda murder case and subsequent anti-homosexual hysteria that swept Asunción ("*quemado,*" Spanish for burned, is also Paraguayan slang for being "outed"). The play is available in book form from Arandurā Editorial, www.arandura.pyglobal.com

Safety

For the most part, Paraguay is a safe country, but as an underdeveloped nation, both economically and in terms of infrastructure, there are still safety concerns travelers should be aware of.

PETTY CRIME

Although poverty is particularly acute in the rural areas, you are more likely to be the victim of petty crime in the cities. Steer clear of the poorer areas of Asunción, Ciudad del Este, and Encarnación where you will be clear target for theft. Always be aware of your surroundings, and avoid walking alone after dark. Watch your bags while on city buses, and keep valuables such as cell phones, cameras, and mp3 players stowed away safely in a bag in your custody. Wear your backpack in front of you, and do not keep anything valuable in your rear pants pockets.

Use common sense, and keep your guard up when in crowded areas (such as bus terminals) or touristy areas. Lock luggage when traveling to and within the country. Avoid pulling out flashy electronics in public – even basic cell phones will be a temptation and are easily pick pocketed. Keep extra photocopies of all important documents in a money belt or an extra bag (before traveling you can also scan these and email them to yourself in case you need to print them out later). Although violent crime is on the rise, criminals generally only resort to violence when encountering resistance.

NARCOTRAFFICKING & KIDNAPPINGS

Narcotraffickers operate mostly in the San Pedro, Pedro Juan Caballero, Canindeyú, and Amambay departments as well as in Ciudad del Este. These areas are considered dangerous due to rampant corruption and a weak institutional state presence. Even in these areas though, the potential danger has more to do with being in the wrong place at the wrong time rather than being targeted as a foreigner. However, travelers passing through should steer clear of any drug-related situations. The past decade has seen the rise of a small left-wing group known as the *Ejército del Pueblo Paraguayo* or EPP. The EPP has been linked to a handful of high profile kidnappings (targets have been business men and *estancia* owners) in the department of Concepción. As there is a continued effort to capture EPP members in hiding, it is best to refrain from camping in these areas.

Drug Usage

Attitudes towards recreational drug use are more conservative than in most Latin American countries. It is best not to make any reference to recreational drug use, even in larger cities where attitudes might be slightly more relaxed. Although in the countryside marijuana is sometimes chewed to alleviate tooth aches or applied topically for arthritis, most Paraguayans consider smoking marijuana to be hard drug use. This is ironic because, despite its small size, Paraguay grows more marijuana than any other country in South America. However, Paraguay's marijuana production is almost exclusively for export to neighboring Brazil and Argentina. As such, many associate drug usage directly with narco-traffickers and other criminal elements.

The Basics

CORRUPTION

Corruption is a real issue in Paraguay. Tourists are most likely to run into corruption when dealing with the police and immigration officers. Irregularities – real or invented – will prompt a request for an onsite "fine" in order to make the problem go away. Though police have the authority to issue tickets for fines, requesting that fines be paid on the spot is *illegal*. Legally, when fines are administered, they must be written up, and tickets must be paid at a legitimate office. Bribing officials *could* have you on your way faster but doing so undermines an already weak system. If you feel that police have invented a problem in order to extract a bribe the best thing to do is keep calm and collected. Police seeking bribes are likely to back down if you pull out a cell phone (especially one with a camera), ask for their name and information, and say you will call your embassy or a local Spanish speaking friend. In many cases, getting out of paying a bribe is a waiting game – if you make it clear you do not intend to pay and have time to kill, police will eventually lose patience and send you on your way.

POLITICAL INSTABILITY

Protests generally take the form of roadblocks known as "tractorazos" or marches. Most large protests are announced ahead of time in the papers and on the radio. Though violence during political protests is uncommon, it is best to steer clear of large political gatherings in case things get rowdy.

ROAD SAFETY

Pedestrians are rarely given the right of way; therefore, one needs to be cautious when crossing any road. This includes city streets, residential areas, and even country roads. If walking alongside the highway, take extra caution as buses and trucks will hug the shoulder while passing each other at full speed.

Paraguay's road conditions and aggressive drivers necessitate defensive driving. The country's highway system consists solely of two lane roads, many of which are not illuminated at night. Most intersections do not have traffic lights or stop signs. Where traffic signals and posted speed limits do exist they are often ignored by many drivers. In general, the rule of the road is "might makes right." Drivers let others know they are coming by giving a soft honk or flashing their lights. Do not mistake either of these to mean you are being given the right of way. Motorcyclists receive little respect on the road, and are often forced to ride on the shoulder. Motorcycle fatalities are one of the leading causes of death in Paraguay. Drive defensively, especially if you have never ridden a motorcycle outside of your home country. Helmet and reflective safety vest laws should be respected even though they are rarely enforced.

Be extra careful when driving through towns in rural areas. Many are bisected by the highway with small footpaths alongside for people and livestock, both of which cross freely without warning. When at all possible, avoid driving at night.

If headed to under-populated areas, be sure to have adequate supplies of fuel, food, water, medicine and a well stocked first aid kit. Be aware that in many rural areas, cell phone signals can be weak and access to hospitals or ambulances is severely limited.

Before driving across a wet dirt road, it pays to get out and inspect the road texture and its conditions. Sandy soil will absorb water and is often passable even when wet. Red clay, however, does not let water through and quickly turns to mud, often remaining impassable for days. Check any large puddles for depth before attempting to cross them. Driving conditions in the Chaco are notoriously difficult, and extreme caution is advised especially because help may be far away when needed (see Driving in the Chaco, p284).

Health

Private clinics and hospitals in urban areas offer the highest level of care. The country's top medical facilities are located in Asunción. Lab tests, consultations, and even hospital stays are affordable (though you may be expected to pay in cash at smaller facilities). Though travelers should always bring their prescription drugs, it is often possible to obtain an equivalent medication over the counter (under a different brand name). There are pharmacies throughout the country, though in remote areas pharmacies may only stock the basics. Public facilities in small towns tend to be underfunded and lack adequate medical supplies. As such, you are likely to be required to purchase or provide your own medical supplies such as gauze and syringes when seeking treatment in small town facilities.

Should you be involved in a serious accident, ask to be taken to the nearest private clinic (*clínica privada*) – depending on your location and the severity of the situation, you may be triaged and then transferred to Asunción for further treatment. Outside of major cities, emergency response units are almost non-existent and should not be counted on exclusively in case of an emergency. In certain areas, it will be faster to pay someone to drive you to the nearest medical facility.

Medical Emergencies in Remote Areas

If you suffer a medical emergency in a remote location such as the Chaco or Pantanal, hiring a private plane from a nearby *estancia* may be the fastest (and sometimes your only) option. You will be expected to pay in cash, so always keep emergency money on you at all times just in case. Even moving quickly, help may be hours away, so it is best to be prepared for any emergency by bringing a well-stocked first aid kit. A medical emergency handbook may add some weight to you pack but will be extremely valuable should you have to wait for help to arrive. Helitáctica (*Tel: 021 661 921, 0971 911 000, www.helitactica.com.py*) performs helicopter evacuations as well as search and rescue missions. However, these services can cost you thousands of dollars.

PRIVATE HEALTH INSURANCE

If you are staying in Paraguay for an extended period of time and are not covered under traveler's health insurance, acquiring private health insurance can be useful depending on your medical needs. Standard plans cover day to day medical expenses including doctor's visits, lab work, and discounts on medications. They do not, however, cover larger expenses for more complex procedures such as cardiovascular operations or dialysis treatments. If you wish to be covered in the eventuality of larger expenses, you must purchase a separate *alta complejidad* (high complexity) plan. When discussing details with sales representatives, be sure to ask whether medical care is restricted to a particular hospital or clinic and find out how extensive coverage is outside of Asunción. The two most widely used private health insurance companies based in Asunción are OAMI (*www.oami.com.py*) and Asismed (*www.asismed.com.py*).

The Basics

HEALTH CONCERNS

The Center for Disease Control recommends the following vaccines for people traveling to Paraguay: hepatitis A, hepatitis B, yellow fever, typhoid, and rabies, as well as any needed updates of routine vaccinations. Anti-malarials are also recommended for those traveling to the departments of Alto Paraná, Canindeyú, and Amambay. Dengue fever, however, is an issue throughout the country. As of yet, there are no immunizations available against dengue fever. The best prevention is to use repellant and netting to protect yourself from mosquito bites. Those who have previously had dengue fever should be extra cautious as they are at higher risk for developing hemorrhagic dengue, which can be fatal. Symptoms of dengue include fever, joint and muscle pain, severe headache, and pain behind the eyes. If you think you may have contracted dengue fever, seek medical attention immediately.

Travelers known to have allergic reactions to insect bites should take proper precautions and bring along any necessary medication. Aside from mosquitoes, wasps and sand flies (known as "*mbarigui*") are common, as are ticks in the Chaco. Another common insect is *pique*, a small flea that burrows into the skin and lays eggs. Keep your shoes on and you should be fine. A small black itchy dot, usually on the underside of your foot, is a tell-tale sign. Use a sterilized needle to pick out the flea being sure to get the egg sac as well. If you doubt your pique removing abilities, seek out a local – most rural Paraguayans will be able to assist you.

Tap water is generally safe to drink throughout Paraguay. Travelers headed to rural communities should note that while well water is safe in most areas, there is always a risk of parasites such as giardia and roundworm. To be on the safe side, avoid drinking water from a well that is close to and downhill from a latrine.

While prostitution is largely ignored by the authorities, syphilis is a significant problem and HIV/AIDS cases are on the rise. Unfortunately, there are few services and protection for this marginalized community. Though not 100% effective, it is advised that all sexual activity be protected (using condoms).

HYGIENE

Toilets in all but the fanciest hotels are unable to flush toilet paper (this can sometimes lead to overflowing trashcans). Some bathrooms charge a nominal fee for which you will receive toilet paper. It is best to go to the bathroom prepared with your own toilet paper and soap or hand sanitizer. Facilities become more basic further from urban centers. Most campgrounds have latrine-style bathrooms.

Gifts for Host Families & Friends

During your time in Paraguay, you will find that friendships with locals, long or short term, will greatly enrich your visit and help you better absorb the culture. Consider bringing along small gifts from home to show your appreciation. The following should work regardless of whether the families are in the countryside or city:

Calendars with photos of your home town.

A nice tablecloth – a very useful gift likely to be reserved for special occasions like Sunday lunches.

Reusable tote bags.

Head lamps and pocket knives – male friends in rural areas will find these especialy useful.

Asunción & Satellite Cities

Asunción is quite possibly the most laid back capital city in South America. This city of approximately 600,000 people still retains a small town feel in many areas. Amidst the dense foliage of flowering trees, the country's richest and poorest families live side by side one another. During the day Asunción's historic center is a chaotic jumble of buses, government workers, school kids, and street vendors selling everything from finely crafted handicrafts to pirated DVDs. At night and on the

> Though underdeveloped in comparison to other Latin American capital cities, Asunción's modernity stands out in great contrast to the rural nature of the rest of the country.

weekends, things quiet down as the majority of the center's daytime population returns to residential neighborhoods and satellite cities. For such a small city, Asunción has a surprisingly active cultural scene, with many plays, gallery openings, and concerts. Living up to its reputation as one of the most affordable cities in the world, nightlife offerings are varied and accessible even to those on the tightest budgets.

A City of Many Names

Upon its founding in 1537, the city was officially named "La *Muy Noble y Leal Ciudad de Nuestra Señora Santa María de la Asunción*" (The Very Noble and Loyal City of Our Lady St. Mary of the Assumption), shortened to Asunción. During the colonial period, the city earned the nickname "*Madre de Ciudades*" (Mother of Cities) because it was the departure point for expeditions that founded many cities in the Spanish empire, including Corrientes and Santa Fe in Argentina, Santa Cruz de la Sierra in Bolivia, and Santiago de Jerez and Ciudad Real in Brazil. In Guaraní, Asunción is named "*Paraguaype*" (with the "y" pronounced as a "u"), a name which many still use today.

Top Asunción Experiences

Enjoying the highly affordable nightlife.

Jostling for counter space and eating *caldo de pescado* (fish soup) at Lido Bar.

Checking out the Museo del Barro, the country's best museum.

Hearing a concert at the Teatro Municipal or one of the city's many cultural centers.

Going on a boat ride and bird watching trip across the Bay of Asunción to Chaco'i, the southernmost tip of the Paraguayan Chaco.

Enjoying the afternoon breeze and a drink at Casa Clari (within Manzana de la Riviera) with a great view of the Presidential Palace.

Seeing the cornucopia of Paraguay's produce in the bustling Mercado Cuatro or the weekly upscale "Agroshopping" farmers market.

A trip to Cerro Lambaré to see the city from upon high.

ASUNCIÓN CALENDAR OF EVENTS

Semana de Teatro (March)

The *Centro Paraguayo de Teatro* (Cepate) organizes the yearly *Semana de Teatro* (Theater Week) during which a variety of free theatrical performances are held throughout Asunción.

María Auxiliadora (May 24th)

This celebration involves a *procesión náutica* (nautical procession) where the image of the *Virgen María Auxiliadora* journeys by boat from the downtown Sajonia neighborhood along the Paraguay River and into the Bay of Asunción to arrive at Asunción's main cathedral with the faithful following in decorated boats.

Asunción Fashion Week (September & April)

About as far from rural life as you can get in Paraguay, Asunción Fashion Week is a chance to see both Paraguay's established, up-and-coming fashion designers show off their collections. *www.afw.com.py*

LGBT Film Festival (June/July)

Organized by Paraguay's gay community in conjunction with various cultural centers, the *Festival de Cine Lesbigaytrans* features movies unlikely to be shown in local movie theaters. Attendance is a chance to support this often discriminated minority group. Contact gay advocacy groups for more information (see LGBT Travelers, p98).

La Expo Feria (July)

Nicknamed "*la Expo*," this large two week fair features farm animals, business lectures, product showcases, food, games, and more. Popular with all ages, it is a good chance to experience a large county fair with Paraguayan flare (see La Expo, p143) *www.expo.org.py*

Founding of Asunción (August 15th)

The founding of Asunción is marked with celebrations throughout the city including fireworks, cultural events in front of the *Panteón de los Heroes*, a large scale Catholic mass in the cathedral as well as the nautical procession of the *Virgen María Auxiliadora* from Sajonia to downtown Asunción on the river.

Asunción's Flowering Trees

Asunción's many flowering trees, lining the main roads and filling the plazas, are one of the things that give this capital city a lush natural feel. "*Ascuncenos*" are very proud of their trees and rightfully so. Their bright colors are a visual delight. In residential areas, it is not uncommon to find large trees in the middle of the streets with neighbors steadfastly refusing their removal, or to see trees with semi-circular pruning up top to make way for power lines. Every season brings a burst of color. Lapachos (or *tajy* in Guaraní) explode with flowers throughout the winter – the pink *lapacho* blooms first followed by the yellow and the increasingly rare white *lapacho*. Spring is the season for *chivatos*, whose wide canopies burst into bright hues of orange competing for attention with the blues and lilacs of the *jacarandá* tree. During the summer, yellow flowers of the *lluvia de oro* cascade from tree branches. *Palo borrachos* with their rough, spikey exteriors show their softer side in the fall, blooming with large pink and white flowers.

Festival Mundial del Arpa (October/November)

Held in Asunción's Municipal Theater, this three-day festival features the best national harpists. It is a great chance to hear world class musicians play both Paraguayan classics and new compositions. International acts showcase other styles and traditions as well. Tickets range from Gs. 15,000 to Gs. 25,000, a real bargain considering this is a small theater and even the nosebleed section has a great view.

Festival Internacional de Cine (September/October – dates vary)

International and national films are given the spotlight with screenings in movie theaters and cultural centers throughout the city. Finalists in national film contests are also given a chance to show their work. *www.pla.net.py/cinefest*

Muestra de Cine de Asunción (dates vary)

The Municipality of Asunción and the *Asociación de Periodistas de Arte y Espectáculos del Paraguay* (APEP) organize this series of Latin American film screenings. All screenings are free and open to the public. Tel: 0981 526 922, *www.muestradeasuncionapep.blogspot.com*

Puerto Abierto (Saturday afternoons)

Started in 2011, Puerto Abierto is a free street fair held at the port of Asunción. Enjoy musical acts, art workshops, children's games, and short boat trips as the sun sets over the Bay of Asunción. *www.facebook.com/PuertoAbierto*

Resources for Asunción Events

www.asuguia.com Information on Asunción with a complete day by day event guide.

The **"*espectáculos*" section of newspapers** Most print information about upcoming events only one or two days in advance (see Newspapers, p95).

www.asunfarra.com.py Website dedicated to Asunción nightlife with listings of nightclub theme nights and concerts.

Asunción's cultural centers Their websites have extensive calendars of events (see Cultural Activities, p139).

107.7 Radio Concert FM / UniNorte's (*Universidad del Norte*) Cultural Department The *Universidad del Norte* sponsors several cultural events throughout the year.

Asunción

Indigenous in Asunción

During the colonial period most of Asunción's indigenous inhabitants were Guaraní Indians, though the city was continually under attack from the Guaycurú who lived across the bay in the Chaco. Today, the majority of indigenous seen in Asunción are not, in fact, Guaraní but Maká (belonging to the Mataco linguistic branch). The Maká played an important role during the Chaco War when they aided Russian *émigré* General Ivan Belaieff in mapping out the region. Traditionally, the Maká inhabited the province of Presidente Hayes in the central and southern Chaco, though most communities nowadays reside in the southernmost areas closest to Asunción. The Maká are well known for their presence in high-traffic tourist areas (such as Calle Palma, the airport, and bus terminal) where they sell indigenous handicrafts – both their own and those of other indigenous communities. According to the 2002 National Indigenous Census, there are approximately 1,300 Maká remaining in Paraguay.

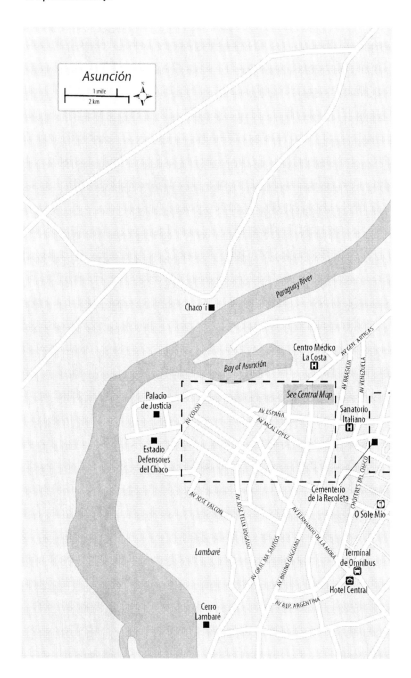

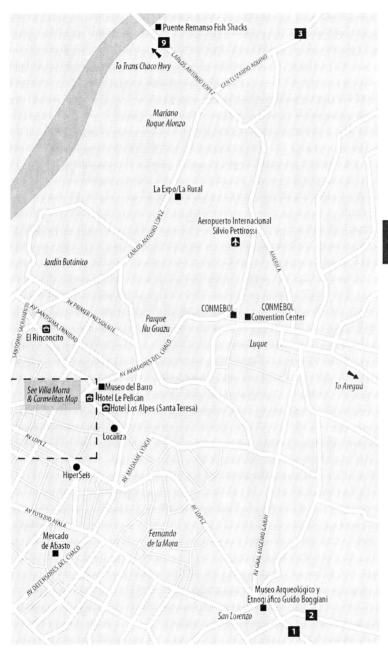

■ Puente Remanso Fish Shacks

3

9

To Trans Chaco Hwy

CARLOS ANTONIO LOPEZ

GEN ELIZARDO AGUINO

Mariano
Roque Alonzo

La Expo/La Rural ■

CARLOS ANTONIO LOPEZ

Aeropuerto Internacional
Silvio Pettirossi
✈

AMERICA

Jardín Botánico

AV PRIMER PRESIDENTE

SANTISIMO SACRAMENTO

AV SANTISIMA TRINIDAD

El Rinconcito

Parque
Ñu Guazu

CONMEBOL ■

CONMEBOL
■ Convention Center

Luque

AV AVIADORES DEL CHACO

See Villa Morra
& Carmelitas Map

■ Museo del Barro
Hotel Le Pelican
■ Hotel Los Alpes (Santa Teresa)

To Areguá

AV LOPEZ

● Localiza

AV MADAME LYNCH

● HiperSeis

AV EUSEBIO AYALA

Mercado
de Abasto

Fernando
de la Mora

AV LOPEZ

AV GRAL EUGENIO GARAY

AV DEFENSORES DEL CHACO

Museo Arqueológico y
Etnográfico Guido Boggiani ■

San Lorenzo

2

1

Asunción

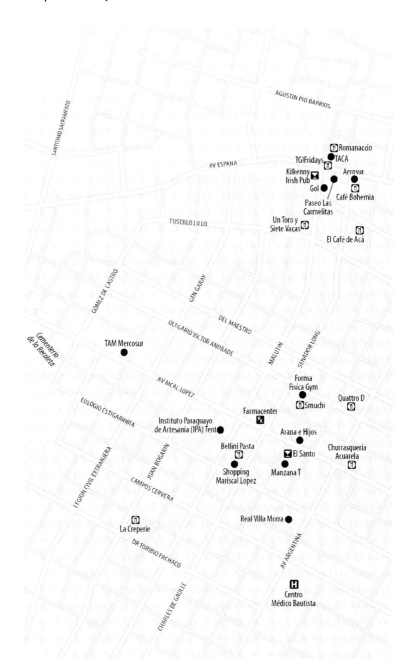

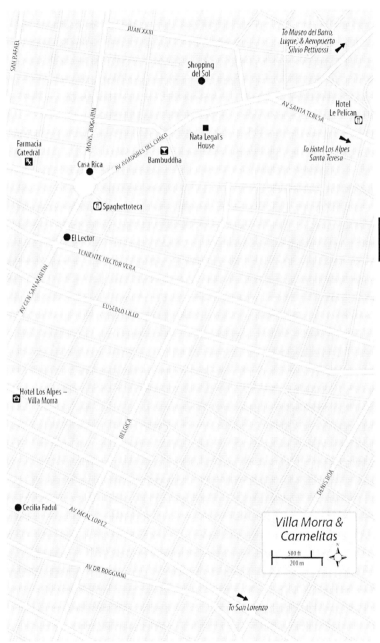

JUAN XXIII

SAN RAFAEL

To Museo del Barro,
Luque, & Aeropuerto
Silvio Pettirossi

Shopping
del Sol

AV SANTA TERESA

Hotel
Le Pelican

MONS. BOGARIN

Ñata Legal's
House

To Hotel Los Alpes
Santa Teresa

Farmacia
Catedral

AV AVIADORES DEL CHACO

Casa Rica

Bambuddha

Spaghettoteca

El Lector

TENIENTE HECTOR VERA

AV GEN SAN MARTIN

EUSEBIO LILLO

Hotel Los Alpes –
Villa Morra

BELGICA

DENIS ROA

Cecilia Fadul

AV MCAL LOPEZ

**Villa Morra &
Carmelitas**

500 ft
200 m

AV DR BOGGIANI

To San Lorenzo

Asunción

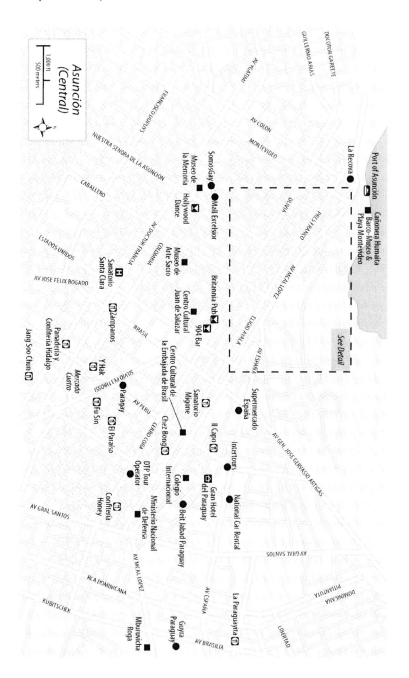

Asunción (Central)

500 meters
1,000 ft

Asunción

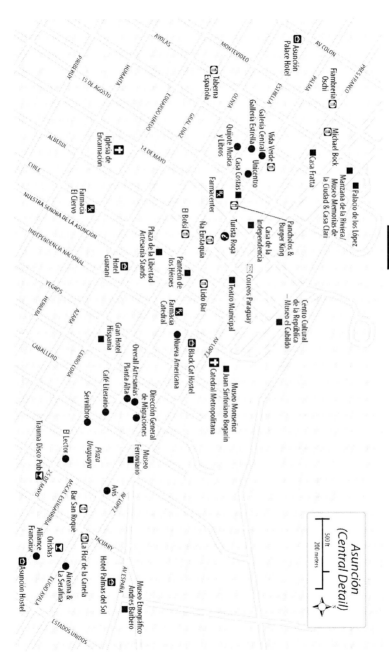

Asunción
(Central Detail)

500 ft
200 meters

Palace Hotel
Asunción

AV COLON

PBES FBANCO

AYOLAS

MONTEVIDEO

PALMA

Fiambrería
Oschi

HUMAITA

PIRIBEBUY

15 DE AGOSTO

ESTRELLA

Taberna
Española

Michael Bock

Casa Fratta

Palacio de los López

Manzana de la Riviera/
Museo Memorias de
la Ciudad & Casa Clari

OLIVA

Vida Verde

Galería Estrella
Galería Central

Unicentro

Casa Costas

EDUARDO HALDO

GRAL DIAZ

14 DE MAYO

Iglesia de
Encarnación

Quijote Música
y Libros

ALBERDI

CHILE

Farmacenter

Pancholos &
Burger King

Casa de la
Independencia

Centro Cultural
de la República
— Museo el Cabildo

NUESTRA SEÑORA DE LA ASUNCION

Farmacia
El Ciervo

El Bolsi

Ña Eustaquia

Turista Roga

INDEPENDENCIA NACIONAL

Plaza de la Libertad
Artesanía Stands

Correos Paraguay

Hotel
Guaraní

Panteón de
los Héroes

Lido Bar

Teatro Municipal

YEGROS

HERRERA

AZARA

Farmacia
Catedral

AV LOPEZ

Gran Hotel
Hispania

Nueva Americana

Black Cat Hostel

Museo Monseñor
Juan Sinfoniano Bogarin

CABALLERO

PDO COVA

CERRO COVA

Café Literario

Overall Artesanías
Planta Alta

Dirección General
de Migraciones

Catedral Metropolitana

Servilibro

Plaza
Uruguaya

Museo
Ferroviario

El Lector

AV LOPEZ

Trauma Disco Pub

25 DE MAYO

MCAL ESTIGARRIBIA

Avis

Bar San Roque

Alliance
Française

Orishas

TACUARY

La Flor de la Canela

Aireana &
La Serafina

Hotel Palmas del Sol

AV ESPAÑA

EUGIO AYALA

Museo Etnográfico
Andrés Barbero

Asunción Hostel

ESTADOS UNIDOS

NEIGHBORHOODS

Downtown (El Centro)

Built on the banks of the Bay of Asunción, the majority of the capital's government offices and historic landmarks are downtown. The *Microcentro* area is bordered by Calle Colón (northwest), Calle Estados Unidos or EEUU (southeast) Avenida Ygatimi/Avenida Dr. Rodriguez de Francia (southwest) and the Paraguay River and Avenida Mariscal López to the northeast. Though nightlife action has largely moved towards residential areas, the majority of Asunción's cultural events still take place in theaters and cultural centers downtown. (see Cultural Activities, p139).

La Costanera

Unless you are in a tall building facing northeast, it is easy to forget that downtown Asunción is built along the banks of the Paraguay River. The riverfront has traditionally been left to the city's most marginalized populations whose shanty towns (known as *"bañados"*) have few amenities and suffer increasing difficulties when the water level rises. In 2010, the city commenced a project to redevelop the river front property and create a three kilometer long boardwalk (or *"costanera"* in Spanish) from the port of Asunción to Avenida General Santos. The *Costanera* project is intended to capitalize on Asunción's prime riverfront location although it remains to be seen what will happen to the area's current inhabitants.

Recoleta/Villa Morra

Located along the main avenues of San Martín, República Argentina, and Mariscal López this area is easily accessible by buses heading both downtown and to the bus terminal. The majority of the residential area's restaurants and hotels are located in and around Shopping Mariscal López, Shopping Villa Morra, and Manzana T. Recoleta is also home to the city's historic cemetery of the same name.

Carmelitas/Shopping del Sol

The upscale restaurants and shopping areas along Avenida España (the largest being Paseo Carmelitas) are a popular hangout for Asunción's elite. Further down Avenida España is the ritzy Shopping del Sol located near the Sheraton and another hub of hotels. This area is ritzier than Villa Morra and less frequented by buses.

SATELLITE CITIES

Luque

East of Asunción and accessible primarily by Avenida Aviadores del Chaco/Avenida Silvio Petirossi, Luque is home to the large Nu Guazu recreational area, Paraguay's primary airport, the Aeropuerto Internacional Silvio Pettirossi, and the headquarters for the South American Football Association (known as the Conmebol). Luque is also the access point for the road to Areguá and Ypacaraí which connects to Route 2. Luque is well known for silver filigree work, and there are several workshops and stores selling the delicate jewelry around the town plaza.

> Luque's soccer team's mascot is a pig, which earned the city its Jopará nickname *"Kuré Luque"*(*kuré* being pig in Guaraní).

Lambaré

To the south of downtown Asunción, built in part along the banks of the Paraguay River, Lambaré is home to Cerro Lambaré and the upscale Yacht Club. It also has the dubious distinction of being nicknamed the *Ciudad del Amor* (city of love) due to the prevalence of by-the-hour motels (see Love Hotels, p79).

San Lorenzo
San Lorenzo, located to the southeast is the access point for Route 1 (heading south) and Route 2 (heading east) as well as the headquarters for the National University of Asunción (UNA). The city is home to the excellent indigenous museum, Museo Guido Boggiani.

Fernando de la Mora
Southeast of Asunción and south of San Lorenzo, Fernando de la Mora is home to one of the few small African populations in Paraguay – descendents of 400 African slaves who followed Uruguayan General José Artigas into exile in the 1820's. Every January 6th, the *"Kamba Kua"* community holds an afro-dance festival in honor of their patron saint San Baltasar (contact José Medina at 0981 131 549 for information about additional dance recitals by the group). Fernando de la Mora is also home to the Mercado de Abasto, a large, open-air market which draws farmers and buyers from all over the country.

Mariano Roque Alonzo
This satellite city is the starting point of the Trans Chaco highway and the Puente Remanso bridge crossing the Paraguay River to the Chaco – before the construction of the bridge the only way to access the Paraguayan Chaco was by ferry. This rapidly growing area is home to Shopping Mariano, Paraguay's largest mall, and the La Rural fairgrounds where the Expo is held every year (see La Expo, p143).

ARRIVING IN ASUNCIÓN

Aeropuerto Internacional Silvio Pettirossi
All international flights arrive in the Aeropuerto Internacional Silvio Pettirossi, located fifteen miles from the center of Asunción in the satellite city of Luque. This small airport has ATM machines (Itau, BBVA), a Cambios Chaco money exchange office, post and DHL office, small convenience stores, basic coffee shops, and a COPACO office for making local and international calls. The Il Capo café to the far right of the airline counters is open 24 hours and has Wi-Fi.

Quick (Helping) Hands
Bag porters at the baggage carousel are quick to act, often hoisting your bags onto carts before you have time to react. Your bags are not in any danger of disappearing though. Be sure to bring small bills for tipping – tips are expected regardless of whether you requested this service.

The airport taxi stand is located just before exiting the airport and fixed rates to a variety of Asunción locations and hotels are posted (generally between Gs.70,000 to Gs.120,000). Credit cards are accepted with a 15 percent surcharge. Fixed prices (between Gs.70,000 to Gs.90,000) are generally quoted for taxi rides to the airport from Asunción.

The Linea 30 A (*Aeropuerto*) city bus passes by the airport about once an hour from 5am to 9pm and runs to the center of town (along Aviadores del Chaco, España past the Sheraton and Shopping del Sol), and downtown along Presidente Franco until Calle Colón. The bus picks up passengers in front of the airport so there is no need to walk to the main road. Be aware, this bus is extremely full early in the morning and late at night. *Tel: 021 645 600/5, Av. Aviadores del Chaco 1690*

Terminal de Omnibus

All international and most regional buses arrive at the bus terminal located about seven kilometers away from the city center. However, very few city buses pass by the bus terminal. Phone listings for all bus companies operating out of the terminal are located on the terminal's website and listed by destination. The terminal has ATMs (BBVA), several snack shops, fast food restaurants, a cyber café, and convenience stores with basic amenities as well as souvenirs. Bathrooms are basic and cost Gs. 1,000. Ticket offices are located on the top floor, services and regional and international departures on the ground floor, and local bus departures on the bottom floor.

Metered taxis can be caught exiting the terminal on the ground floor. Cab fare to go downtown is between Gs. 30,000 and 45,000. The Linea 31 city bus picks up passengers on Avenida República Argentina, directly in front of the terminal, and continues on Mariscal López towards the center of town along Presidente Franco. Fares are Gs. 2,300 and the bus passes approximately every twenty minutes from 5am to 9:30pm. *Tel: 595 21 551740/1, corner of Avenida Fernando de la Mora and Avenida República Argentina, www.mca.gov.py/toa.htm*

Bus Shortcuts

For arriving passengers heading to the center of town it can be more convenient to get off the bus at one of the several standard stops before the terminal. Getting off at a major crossroads and continuing on in a city bus from there can save time, although it is not recommended at night. Although drivers will usually announce upcoming stops, it is best to tell them where you want to get off ahead of time. Common stops are as follows:

Route 1 and Route 2 buses: "*desvío a Luque*" in San Lorenzo. From here buses 12, 26, and 56 head downtown.

Route 3 and Trans Chaco buses: Corner of Avenida Argentina and Mariscal López. From here a number of city buses head downtown along Mariscal López (see the following Popular Bus Routes). Other popular stops for these buses are Shopping del Sol and the intersection of Avenida Argentina and Avenida España where buses head downtown along Avenida Aviadores del Chaco (in front of Shopping del Sol) and Avenida España.

CAR RENTAL

Localiza *Tel: 021 645810, offices at the airport and the corner of Avenida Santa Teresa and Austria, www.localiza.com, Mon-Fri 7am-6:30pm, Sat 8am-12pm*

Avis Rent a Car *Tel: 021 645 555, 021 446 233, 0 981 577 455, offices in the airport, Sheraton Hotel and the corner of Eligio Ayala and Antequera, near Plaza Uruguaya, www.avis.com.py, Mon-Fri 8am-6pm, Sat 8am-12pm, Sun 9am-6pm airport office only. Airport office is only open after hours with prior reservations*

National Car Rental *Tel: 021 232 990/4., corner of Avenida España and Washington, www.national.com.py*

CHANGING MONEY

Change houses or "*casas de cambio*" along Calle Palma downtown often have higher posted rates than those available in residential areas (even within the same company). Most banks will also change money (see Changing Money, p75).

Cambios Chaco *Tel: 021 445 315, Palma between Chile and Alberdi and Shopping Villa Morra, www.cambioschaco.com.py, Mon-Fri 8:15am-9pm, Sat 9am-9pm, Villa Morra Mon-Fri 8am-9pm, Sat 8:30am-9pm, Sun 10am-6pm*

Link Cambios/Brios Financiera *Tel: 021 442 145, Corner of Palma and Nuestra Señora de la Asunción and Shopping Villa Morra, www.linkcambios.com.py, Mon-Fri 8am-4:45pm*

SAFETY

Asunción is a relatively safe city with most crime limited to petty theft. Care should be taken with belongings while riding buses. At night it is best to call for a taxi if you are not close to a taxi stand. The Chacaritas shanty town borders the river downtown behind recommended tourist areas that include the Congress and the Presidential Palace. In these areas, where poverty and wealth are intertwined, you are a clear target for theft. After dark it is common to see prostitutes soliciting on street corners and in plazas downtown – men may be solicited openly.

TRANSPORTATION

City Buses

City buses are the most common method of transportation in Asunción with over fifty privately operated bus lines (*lineas*) streaming into the city from surrounding areas throughout the day. Most companies schedule their first bus to arrive in Asunción around 4am and their last bus to leave the city around 10pm with buses every twenty and forty minutes, or every hour depending on the company. Service is less

> **Linea 11**
> Taking "Linea 11" (pronounced *linea once)* is slang for walking – the joke being that the two "1's" are a pair of legs.

frequent on Sundays. As of July 2012, the standard fee for city buses is Gs. 2,300 and drivers are generally willing to break bills as big as Gs. 10,000 (although you may have to wait while they deal with other passengers first). Avoid peak hours – 6am to 8am and 5pm to 7pm if possible.

The ride is anything but smooth with drivers multitasking between picking up passengers, collecting bus fares, and swerving around traffic and potholes, all the while drinking *tereré*. The quality of buses varies greatly between companies – some buses have wooden floors and squishy bench seats while others have plastic bucket seats and a more modern feel. All bus lines are painted different colors – this can prove helpful when trying to determine whether to hail a fast moving bus. Buses stop every two blocks. In order to request a stop, pull the rope running along the ceiling or ring the bell over the back door. Caution should be taken when exiting the bus – Asunción's sidewalks are in bad condition and some drivers are reticent to come to a full stop. If you need more time to exit yell "*Momento!*" (one moment).

POPULAR BUS ROUTES

Between Villa Morra Area & Downtown (along Ave. Mariscal López)

Lineas 12, 26, 56, 30, 41, 44: Entering town, these buses run down Mariscal López, Peru, Eligio Ayala, and Presidente Franco before turning on Calle Colón. Leaving downtown they run along Olivia/Cerro Corá (note buses 12, 26, and 56 tend to be packed with university students heading to San Lorenzo from 5pm to 10pm).

Asunción

Lineas 15-1, 15-2, 28: Entering town, these run down Mariscal López, Peru, Azara, and General Díaz. Leaving downtown they run along Olivia/Cerro Corá.

Lineas 15-3 (Ñemby): This follows the same route as 15-1 and 15-2 when entering downtown but heads towards the bus terminal on the way back (see below).

Linea 31: (see below)

Between Shopping del Sol/Carmelitas & Downtown

Linea 30 A: Runs from the airport along Aviadores del Chaco (past Shopping del Sol) and then along Avenida España to Eligio Ayala, Presidente Franco, and Calle Colón.

Linea 55 TTL "El Inter": Runs along Avenida España then Avenida Sacramento and then heads downtown along Mariscal López.

Between Downtown & the Bus Terminal

Linea 31: Entering town, these run from Avenida República Argentina past the bus terminal to Mariscal López (through Villa Morra), Peru, Eligio Ayala, and Presidente Franco before turning on Calle Colón. Leaving downtown they run along Olivia/Cerro Corá.

Lineas 15-3 (Ñemby): These do not pass by the terminal on their way into downtown. Leaving downtown they run along Olivia/Cerro Corá to Avenida Fernando de la Mora past the bus terminal.

Taxis

Taxis run by the meter with a base fare of Gs. 5,000. They can be hailed off the street, picked up at a taxi stand (throughout the city), or reserved (*Tel: 021 311 080, *8294 from Personal cell phones*). When calling a cab, it is possible to request one "*con aire*" (with A/C) for no extra charge – a godsend on hot days. After 10pm, cabs increase their rates by 30 percent – this is also the case on Sundays. Don't worry about doing the math as all cabs have a printed list of the modified rates. It is sometimes possible to negotiate a fixed price for a cab ride though your success rate is often directly related to your fluency in Guaraní. The cost for a daytime trip from Shopping Villa Morra to the Plaza de los Héroes downtown is approximately Gs. 35,000.

TOURIST INFORMATION

Senatur has two tourism information offices in Asunción: one small stand at the arrivals section of the airport and the central office downtown known as "*Turista Roga*" (Tourist House). See Tourist

> For tour operators, see Guided Tours, p65.

Information, p57. *Tel: 021 494 110, 441 530, Calle Palma 468 between 14 de Mayo and Alberdi, www.senatur.gov.py, daily 7am-7pm*

VISA EXTENSIONS & IMMIGRATION

Dirección General de Migraciones For visa and residency issues. *Tel: 021 446 066, 021 492 908, 021 446 673, Corner of Caballero and Eligio Ayala, www.migraciones.gov.py, Mon-Fri 7am-1pm*

MAIL

Correos Paraguay The main post office is housed in Palacio Patri, a stately mansion built in 1904 – note the intricate ironwork on the windows and gates, write your postcards in the nice interior courtyard, and stop by the small postal museum with rotating stamp exhibits. *Tel: 021 498 112/16, Alberdi 130 between El Paraguayo Independiente, and Benjamin Constant, www.correoparaguayo.gov.py, Mon-Fri 7am-7pm, there are also post offices in Shopping Villa Morra and Shopping del Sol, the bus terminal, and the airport*

MEDICAL SERVICES

Downtown

Sanatorio Santa Clara This private clinic is the closest to Microcentro. *Tel: 021 4180 000, Avenida Rodriguez de Francia and Parapiti, www.santaclara.com.py*

Centro Médico La Costa *Tel: 021 202 800, Artigas 1500 corner of Concepción Leyes de Chávez, www.lacosta.com.py*

Sanatorio Migone *Tel: 021 498 200, Eligio Ayala 1293 on the corner of Curupayty, www.smb.com.py*

Villa Morra

Centro Médico Bautista *Tel: 021 600 171/4, Corner of República Argentina and Campos Cervera, www.drup.cmb.org.py*

Carmelitas

Sanatorio Italiano *Tel: 021 214 265, Corner of Avenida España and Zanotti Cavazzoni*

PHARMACIES

Downtown

Farmacenter *Tel: 021 497 546, 021 498 371, Estrella 526 almost at 14 de Mayo, www.farmacenter.com.py, Open 24 hrs*

Farmacia Catedral *Tel: 021 493 166/7, 021 448 805, corner of Palma and Independencia Nacional, www.farmaciacatedral.com.py, Mon-Fri 7am-10pm, Sun 8am-2pm*

Children Begging

Begging, especially by children, is unfortunately common on the streets and buses of Asunción. Small children will often board buses and hand out little cards with religious inscriptions for voluntary contributions. Cards are placed directly onto passenger's laps or crossed arms and then collected after a few minutes (if you are not comfortable with this, wave your finger when they come by). Deciding whether to contribute money to children who beg is a personal decision – though it is heartbreaking, some feel that by giving money they are encouraging children to beg on behalf of their parents or guardians, often at the expense of school attendance.

Fortunately there are other ways to contribute. Many of Asunción's supermarkets offer school aged children part-time positions as baggers. In order to be eligible for these programs, students must maintain good grades. Tipping baggers (as well as basket boys in Agroshopping) encourages a legitimate form of labor as well as school attendance. Fundación Dequeni is a non-profit organization that runs several programs aimed at combating child poverty – one easy way to participate in is by donating extra change at Super Seis supermarkets and Farmacenter pharmacies. The funds collected are used to purchase childrens' school supplies. For more information visit: www.dequeni.org.py.

Villa Morra

Farmacenter *Tel: 021 662 400, 021 611 086, Mariscal López 3683 almost at Senador Long, Open 24 hrs*

Farmacia Catedral *Tel: 021 663 696, Shopping Mariscal López in the ground floor parking lot. Mon, Wed, Thu 8am-11pm; Tue 6am-10pm; Fri-Sat 8am-12am; Sun 10am-11pm*

Carmelitas

Farmacia Catedral *Tel: 021 600 723, Corner of España and Santa Ana, Open 24 hrs*

BOOKSTORES

Downtown

Servilibro Housed in a funky looking large silver structure in Plaza Uruguaya, this Paraguayan publisher is an excellent source for books on Paraguayan history and culture. *Tel: 021 444 770, 021 451 105, Corner of 25 de Mayo and Mexico, www.servilibro.com.py, Mon-Fri 8am-5pm, Sat 8am-12pm*

El Lector *Tel: 021 491 966, 021 493 908, Corner of 25 de Mayo and Antequera, across the plaza from Servilibro in a similar silver structure, www.ellector.com.py, Mon-Fri 7am-9pm, Sat 7am-8pm, Sun 9am-5pm*

Quijote Música y Libros *Tel: 021 49 14 38, Estrella 691 almost O'Leary, Mon-Fri 9am-6pm, Sat 9am-1pm*

Carmelitas

El Lector The Carmelitas branch of El Lector includes a pleasant coffee shop and has a regular lecture series. *Tel: 021 610 639, 021 614 259, Avenida San Martín almost Austria, www.ellector.com.py, Mon-Fri 7am-9pm, Sat 7am-8pm, Sun 9am-5pm*

Quijote Música y Libros *Tel: 021 611 813, Shopping del Sol, www.quijote.com.py, Mon-Fri 9am-9:30pm, Sat 9am-10pm, Sun 11am-9:30pm*

Villa Morra

Quijote Música y Libros *Tel: 021 608 455, Shopping Mariscal López, www.quijote.com.py, Mon-Fri 9am-9:30pm, Sat 9am-10pm, Sun 11am-10pm*

Internet

Several free upscale restaurants offer Wi-Fi, as do all the shopping malls. Shopping Villa Morra, Shopping del Sol, and Shopping Mall Excelsior all have cyber cafés near their food courts.

WALKING TOURS

Asunción's Historic Center

The majority of Asunción's historic sites are located in the downtown area. Much of the colonial downtown is gone, but there are still some remaining structures that recall an era of yesteryear in Asunción. Many of these date from the rule of Carlos Antonio López when Paraguay was at its height of economic wealth.

Start at Palma and Colón. To get there by bus, take Linea 12, 26, 56 or any bus with a *"Pdte Franco/Palacio Justicia"* sign. These run down Presidente Franco and turn on left on Calle Colón – you can get off either at the corner of Presidente Franco and Colón or Colón and Estrella. Or if you're nearby, simply walk down **Calle Palma** where you will see Paraguay's street vendors in full force lining the street with stands selling delicate *ñanduti* designs, indigenous crafts, knock-off sunglasses and pirated DVDs.

Walk towards the river (downhill) along Calle Colón. To the right-hand side is "**La Recova**," a historic building now shared by the Paraguayan armada and a number of handicrafts stores (the former section is much better restored than the latter). Note the original tiled floors in most stores. This is a great place to buy a wide variety of *artesanías* and have a calmer shopping experience than at the stands in the Plaza de Democracia or along Calle Palma.

Walk towards Presidente Franco. Directly in front you will see the **Port of Asunción** and a metal sculpture by renowned artist Hermann Guggiari – take a right. For a quick snack, stop at either the Fiambrería Ochsi (short ribs, small sandwiches, and beer) on the corner of Presidente Franco and Montevideo (Mon-Fri 7:30am-11:45am & 2:30pm-7:15pm, Sat 7:30am-1pm) or German bakery Michael Bock (breads and pastries) further down Presidente Franco (number 828).

On Ayolas, take a left and head towards the river – walk alongside the Palacio de los López Presidential Palace down to the **Cañonera Humaitá Naval Museum** located in the ex-battleship, Humaitá (Mon-Fri 8am-11:30am, Sat 2pm-6pm, Sun 8am-6pm). From here you can best admire the Bay of Asunción and even see the southernmost tip of the Paraguayan Chaco to the northwest. You can also see the **Palacio de los López** (Presidential Palace) as it was meant to be seen by visitors as they entered the Bay of Asunción by riverboat. Note: *Pedestrians are not allowed along the side of the Presidential Palace that extends past Juan E. O'Leary.*

Returning along Ayolas, stop at the **Plaza de los Desaparecidos** (Plaza of the Disappeared). On the right you'll see a statue of Stroessner that has been broken apart and encased in a large cement block, representing the oppression of his dictatorship. From here, visit the **Manzana de La Rivera** on the corner of Paraguayo Independiente and Ayolas (the entrance is on Ayolas). This complex of colonial houses has been restored and is now home to Asunción's municipal cultural center which includes a nice two-story library and the **Museo de la Ciudad** whose small

---

Asunción's Street Vendors

Paraguay's informal economy is on full display in Asunción. During the early hours of the morning and in the late afternoon, men push carts with thermoses full of steaming hot and sweet *mate cocido* through the streets as *chiperas* make the rounds to government offices, baskets balanced on their heads. Warmer summer days bring *mosto* vendors with portable coolers full of ice cold, sticky, sweet sugar cane juice served in plastic or aluminum cups. All types of street food are available from hamburgers, *lomitos*, and *asaditos*, to sandwiches, donuts, and even popcorn. In shady plazas and on street corners, *yuyeros* mash custom combinations of medicinal herbs for customers renting the necessary equipment for drinking *mate* and *tereré*. Maká Indians offer indigenous handicrafts to tourists passing by. In residential areas trucks and horse drawn carts with megaphones attached wind their way through neighborhoods announcing fruits for sale.

Outside of peak hours, vendors hop on and off buses continuously, offering riders items such as candies, refreshments, fresh fruits, nail clippers, socks and toothbrushes – each of which is inexplicably hawked with a specialized intonation. "*Caramelo Halls*" throat candies and cold beverages merit a deep voice while fruit is sold at a higher pitch. Occasionally, vendors deliver elaborate, full length sales pitches for pricier products such as dictionaries and school supplies, all the while maintaining their balance as the bus lurches from stop to stop.

but well curated exhibits provide visitors information on colonial Asunción. After visiting the museum, head to Casa Clari, the center's bar, to enjoy an excellent view of the Presidential Palace (and, if you're lucky, a bit of a breeze from the river).

Exiting the Manzana de la Riviera, head left up Ayolas and take a left on Presidente Franco. A couple of houses down you'll pass the **Casa Fratta** on your right. This art nouveau style building has been both a photography studio and a pharmacy in the past and, though deteriorating, it's a great example of Asunción's many architectural gems. Remain on Presidente Franco for three more blocks until you come to the corner of 14 de Mayo. *(Alternate: If architecture is your thing, and you'd like to see one of Asunción's cool buildings in better condition, take a right on O'Leary and then continue to the left on Calle Palma past 15 de Agosto. On your right you will see the well maintained **Casa Costas** (Palma 561), built in 1915.)* Take a left on 14 de Mayo and enter the **Casa de la Independencia** (Sat 7am-6:30pm, Sun 8am-12pm) on the corner with Presidente Franco. It is from this very house, one of the few remaining colonial houses of Asunción, that the plan to declare independence from Spain was hatched. The house was restored and converted into a museum dedicated to the fathers of Paraguayan independence.

Continue down Presidente Franco and pass the **Teatro Municipal** (Municipal Theater) on the corner of Alberdi – though the box office does not open till 4:30pm you can check out the posters for upcoming events and peek inside the lobby of this handsomely restored building. You can also ask to see the theater itself which is quite nice.

If you are ready to eat, there are several good options nearby:

Classic Asunción diner, **Lido Bar** (continue on Presidente Franco till Chile and then take a right to the corner of Calle Palma), boasts some of the best *caldo de pescado* (fish soup) around and is very popular with foreigners and locals. Part of the sport of eating at Lido is hovering behind customers finishing up at the bar in order to grab their seats – worth the bother to see all the waitresses swirl past each other in their bright orange outfits. The fancier **Bolsi Bar** (head up Alberdi to the corner of Estrella) has an excellent menu of international cuisine (and air conditioning). Or if you're just in the mood for a snack, check out **Ña Eustaquia** (corner of Alberdi and Palma) for classic Paraguayan fare such as *mbeju* and *chipa ryguazu* as well as fresh juices.

Visit the **Panteón de los Héroes** directly across the street from Lido Bar. If you want to look at more handicrafts, walk to the plaza behind the Panteón and check out the *artesanía* stands. Prices are good and, although it can be a little cramped, it is safe. Now that you have your *tereré rupá* (pre-*tereré* snack) you can pay one of the plaza's *yuyeros* to rent all the requisite equipment for a *tereré* session before sallying forth. (see alternate route below.)

Head back towards the river along Nuestra Señora de la Asunción (running through the middle of the four plazas) to the large pink **Museo del Cabildo** (on the far side of the plaza Juan de Salazar) featuring exhibits of Asunción's history as well as exhibits from three other prominent museums. One should take extra precautions in this area, as it's near one of the city's poorest slums, the riverfront Chacaritas neighborhood. To the left you'll see the National Congress, its modern architecture, vaguely reminiscent of a cruise ship, standing in stark contrast to the 19th century museum. The plaza between the congress building and the Cabildo is dominated by a four ton metal tree trunk breaking through chains, sculpted by Hermann Guggiari.

Take a quick peek inside the **Catedral Metropolitana**, Asunción's main cathedral, for a look at the ornate altar piece decorated in a style known as *"Barroco Fransiscano-Guaraní."* If you are doing this tour in reverse and are interested in religious art, you can also stop by the **Museo Juan Sinforiano Bogarín** (only open till 11:30am) alongside the church.

From the cathedral walk up Independencia Nacional to Mariscal Estigarribia and take a left – the street will then "T" out into Plaza Uruguaya, a shady plaza where people relax and drink *tereré* (though it is often occupied by indigenous protesters). Take a left and head to the **Museo Ferroviario** for a look at one of the first steam trains in Latin America. The museum is housed in Asunción's now defunct central train station (Tues -Fri 9am-5pm, Sat-Sun 9am-1pm).

Those interested in Paraguay's various indigenous cultures should continue down Mariscal López (behind the museum), take a left on to Tacuary and the next right onto España to get to the **Museo Etnográfico Andres Barbero** (8am-5pm).

If it is afternoon, head back down Mariscal Estigarribia to grab a drink at the **Café Literario**, modeled after European literary cafés (open from 4:30pm onwards), or **Planta Alta** (5pm onwards), the bar/contemporary art gallery popular with Asunción's artsy crowd.

An Alternate Route

From the Panteón de Los Héroes continue up Chile (away from the river) until Haedo, and take a right. On the corner you will see **Farmacia El Ciervo**, another example of Asunción's quirky older buildings. Continue along Haedo to the **Iglesia de Encarnación** (as of 2010 undergoing restoration) on the corner of 14 de Mayo. (Mon-Fri 7am-11am and 4pm-9pm). Though less visited then Asunción's main cathedral, this church does have some nice stained glass windows.

Continue up 14 de Mayo four blocks and take a left on Jejui. Walk two more blocks and take a left onto Chile. Enter the **Museo Memorias de la Dictadura** on the left-hand side (Chile 1066, Mon-Fri 9am-4pm). Housed in what was, until the 1990's, a clandestine police holding area, this small but powerful museum details the human rights abuses of the Stroessner era.

Walking Tours Further Afield

Start at Avenida Mariscal López and Avenida Peru. To get there from downtown, take any bus with a Mariscal López sign (Lineas 12, 26, 56, 30, 41, 44), and ask to be let off once the bus turns onto Mariscal López. Depending on the bus, you may have to backtrack two to four blocks to get to Peru. While leaving downtown, be sure to take a look out the window to your left on Cerro Corá between Yegros and Iturbe (two blocks past the Plaza de la Democracia and Hotel Guaraní) for a view of the now defunct **Gran Hotel Hispania** – one of Asunción's crumbling architectural gems. If starting from Villa Morra, take any bus headed downtown along Mariscal López, and get off at the intersection with Avenida Peru.

Walk down Avenida Peru and take a right on De las Residentas, and walk to the **Gran Hotel del Paraguay** at the intersection with Padre Pucheau. Now converted into a hotel, this grand colonial manor was once owned by the infamous Madame Lynch. Ask the reception to see the ballrooms featuring elegant florid murals commissioned by Madame Lynch herself. These periodically restored murals are in extraordinary condition and are a testament to the splendor that Madame Lynch craved and created in her new tropical home.

Exit the hotel, round the corner to the right, and walk along Saubatte to Mariscal López. You will pass the Colegio Internacional where many of Asunción's wealthy families have sent their children for generations (the original building on the left of Saubatte is very interesting looking). If you are ready to eat, cross Mariscal López and go two blocks up República Francesa to **Chez Bong** for excellent Korean food.

Take a left on Mariscal López (if you stopped at Chez Bong take a right). This historic residential neighborhood was once home to Asunción's most influential families whose grand manors lined Avenida Mariscal López. Many of these historic houses are still standing – some having been taken over and restored by private companies and foreign embassies. Looking at them, you can get a sense of the grandeur of years past.

Walk to the **Ministerio Nacional de Defensa** (Ministry of National Defense) on the corner of Mariscal López and 22 de Septiembre. Out front is the *"Monumento a la Defensa Nacional"* (Monument to National Defense), an award winning sculpture by Gustavo Beckelmann. The artist was inspired by the lyrics of the song *Patria Querida*, *"Serán allá nuestros pechos las murallas"* (there our chests will be the walls). Enter the Ministry of National Defense to visit the Museo Histórico Militar (Mon-Fri 7am-1pm) which contains a large collection of paintings, photos, and other relics from Paraguay's unfortunately war-torn history.

Ready for a snack? Round the corner and walk one block farther down Mariscal López. Take a right at Vice Presidente Sánchez and walk two blocks to **Confitería Honey** (corner of 25 de Mayo and Vice Presidente Sánchez) for a deliciously rich slice of cake or an excellent *empanada*. Return to Mariscal López and catch Linea 15-1, 12, 26, 56, 28, or 31 to the **Cementerio Recoleta** cemetery (intersection of Mariscal López and Choferes del Chaco). Ask the bus driver to drop you off at *"la Recoleta."* The ride lasts approximately 15 minutes and you will pass the large white presidential residence on the right-hand side (Mariscal López and Kubitschek) known by all as **Mburuvicha Roga.** It means "The Boss' House" in Guaraní. Inside the cemetery, take a stroll around the mausoleums of the city's elite families, each decorated to their own personal tastes.

If you are interested in purchasing handicrafts, exit the cemetery through the side exit to the east (away from downtown). Walk through the residential Recoleta neighborhood down the cobblestone Quesada street for seven blocks until you reach Shopping Mariscal López. Pombero and Catedral offer nice *ao po'i* clothing options (the latter younger and more modern), and the stands in Villa Morra also have a good selection. If you'd rather buy products directly from artisans, stop by the **IPA tent** (Instituto Paraguayo de Artesanía) set up in the plaza diagonally opposite Shopping Mariscal López for a wide selection of *artesanías* that are very representative of Paraguay's handicrafts.

From here, you can continue on to one of two excellent museums – the Museo Boggiani, in San Lorenzo, dedicated to Paraguay's indigenous communities, or the larger Museo del Barro, in the Shopping del Sol neighborhood, with extensive displays of Paraguayan contemporary, indigenous, and folk art.

To get to the **Museo Boggiani** (Tue-Fri 9am-6pm, Sat 9am-12pm and 3pm-6pm) take the 56 to San Lorenzo, and ask to be let off at San Lorenzo's main plaza (approximately a 30-minute ride). Located on Coronel Bogado street, the museum is easy to miss – be on the lookout for the small sandstone sign embedded into the building's wall. Be sure to visit the museum's gift shop across the street, showcasing a large variety of indigenous crafts updated monthly.

To get to the **Museo del Barro** (Wed-Fri 3:30pm-8pm, Sat 9:30am-12pm and 2:30pm-8pm) take bus 28 past the upscale Shopping del Sol. Directly across from the mall is the former home of Alfredo Stroessner's mistress, María Estela Legal, better known as "Ñata Legal." She began her relationship with Stroessner at age 15. He was dining with her at this very house when the coup that ousted him took place. After two long blocks, get off the bus at the corner of Aviadores del Chaco and Canada (there will be a large Philip Morris building to the left). Take a right and then a left and walk half way down the block to the museum entrance.

In order to return to Villa Morra/Recoleta or downtown, cross Aviadores del Chaco and catch Linea 16 or the 28 bus. For a well-deserved break, get off at the corner of Avenida San Martin and Andrade and enjoy a heaping cone of Italian style gelato from **Quattro D**.

To return downtown, travel along Avenida España on Linea 30A (with sign "*X España*") 37C, or 44. Stop for a bite to eat or a drink at one of the many restaurants and bars along Avenida España around **Paseo Las Carmelitas**. As you continue towards downtown Asunción, you will pass the spot on España between América and Venezuela where Nicaraguan dictator, Anastasio Somoza, was assassinated by bazooka fire in broad daylight in 1981.

Calle Palma

During the 60's and 70's, before the action moved towards the residential neighborhoods of Villa Morra and Carmelitas, Calle Palma was the place to be for Asunción's elite. The street was lined with fancy storefronts and was turned into a pedestrian walkway on Sundays where people came to see and be seen. Strolling down Calle Palma in your best Sunday outfit otherwise known as going to "*palmear*" and is remembered fondly by older generations. One of the remaining vestiges of the fancy Calle Palma is Farmacia Catedral on the corner of Palma and Independencia Nacional, which retains an elegant, old-fashioned feel with its rich wood, paneled walls and counters and decoratively tiled floors.

MUSEUMS & SITES

There are several museums in Asunción, most of which offer free admission. If you are pressed for time (or limited to the city center) the Museo Cabildo is a good bet as it covers aspects of Paraguay's history and includes permanent mini exhibits from two excellent museums that are further away – the Museo del Barro (near Shopping del Sol) and Museo Guido Boggiani (in San Lorenzo).

Museo del Barro

The Museo del Barro is Paraguay's best museum. Created in the late 1970's by a group of the nation's pre-eminent artists and art scholars, the museum houses three large, well-displayed collections representing a wide range of Paraguayan art: folk art (*arte campesina*), indigenous art, and contemporary art. Visitors will walk away with a great appreciation for Paraguay's traditional arts as well as rare exposure to the country's budding contemporary art scene. Some objects from the indigenous art collection such as wooden animal carvings displaying an intimate connection with the natural world are still produced by Paraguay's indigenous. Others, such as the large ceremonial attire decorated with animal skins and feathers are from an era that has almost disappeared. Visitors who have already travelled around the countryside are sure to recognize many of the objects within the folk art collection, as it is representative of Paraguay's artisanal traditions still alive throughout the country. Especially beautiful are the antique examples of ñanduti. The Arte Urbano collection stands out the most. All of Paraguay's most important contemporary artists are represented here. Especially predominant are the large-scale works of Carlos Colombino displaying his "axilo pintura" style of painting and carving wood into three-dimensional scenes. Ricardo Migliorsi's "Carpilla Sistina" is a circus tent like installation painted with colorful and cartoonish figures vaguely reminiscent of The Yellow Submarine. The museum also has a large gift shop where scholarly publications, folk and indigenous art are available for purchase. While visiting the museum you may be lucky enough to see some of Paraguay's most famed artists in person. *Tel: 021 607 996, Calle Grabadores del Cabichui between Emeterio Miranda and Cañada, Make a right on Aviadores del Chaco just past Shopping del Sol on the corner opposite the large Marlboro building and then take a left. Buses: 30A (sign reads "X España") and 28. www.museodelbarro.com, Wed-Fri 3:30pm-8pm, Sat 9:30am-12pm, 2:30pm-8pm, Entry fee: Gs, 8,000 (although sponsoring organizations often cover the cost of admission on certain days – check museum website)*

Panteón de los Héroes

Inspired by Paris' L'Hôtel National des Invalides, the Panteón Nacional de los Héroes houses the remains of several important figures of Paraguay's history. These include Carlos Antonio López and son Mariscal Francisco Solano López (under whose direction the building was originally conceived), and Chaco War hero Mariscal José Félix Estigarribia. There are also symbolic tombs for two unknown soldiers and the child martyrs of Acosta Ñu (the battle of Acosta Ñu was fought almost entirely by children on the Paraguayan side and is considered one of the most tragic battles of the Triple Alliance War). Within the *Panteón* there is also a large shrine to the *Virgen de Nuestra Señora de la Asunción*, patron saint of the city of Asunción. Construction of the Panteón, which started in 1863, was suspended due to the Triple Alliance War and did not resume until 1936 after the Chaco War. The interior of the Panteón is airy and cool. The steps of the Panteón have become a popular spot for the masses of Asunción to gather to celebrate all manner of political and sporting victories. *Corner of Palma and Chile, Mon-Sat 6am-6pm, Sun 6am-11:30am*

Centro Cultural de la República – Museo el Cabildo

This large pink building was the seat of governmental power from 1857 to 1894. It was transformed into the National Congress before undergoing yet another transformation, when it became the government's cultural center. Permanent exhibits include three rooms with representative samplings from the collections of the Museo del Barro, Museo Guido Boggiani, and the Museo Monseñor Juan Sinforiano Bogarín. There is also an exhibit dedicated to the history of Asunción. The second floor houses a research library and two smaller exhibits dedicated to Paraguayan music and film. Guides are available from 9am to 1pm. *Tel: 021 443 095, Avenida de la República between Chile and Alberdi, http://www.cabildoccr.gov.py, Tues-Fri 9am-7pm, Sat-Sun 10am-5pm*

Museo Ferroviario

Located in Asunción's central train station, this museum houses many artifacts from the train's history (see The Steam Train, p28). On the tracks sit a dining car and fancy presidential car which can be visited as well. The building itself dates from

1861, and the upper level is home to Asunción's symphony orchestra. For a better historical context, be sure to get a guided tour. This is also where you can get information on and tickets for the Tren del Lago. *Tel: 021 447 848, Corner of Eligio Ayala and Mexico across from Plaza Uruguaya, Tue-Fri 9am-5pm, Sat-Sun 9am-1pm, Entry fee: Gs. 10,000 for foreigners, Gs. 5,000 for Paraguayans, children under seven are free.*

Plaza Uruguaya

During the day, Plaza Uruguaya is a calm spot, less frequented than the larger set of four plazas nearby. *Tereré* vendors and shoe polishers set up in the shade, and couples take a break on park benches. Plaza Uruguaya's proximity to government offices has made it the preferred camping spot for groups who come in from the countryside for protests. It can sometimes be occupied for months at a time by indigenous groups seeking to have their claims be heard. Often these groups have very limited resources and depend on donations to survive while in Asunción. Entire families can be seen living in makeshift tents made out of plastic tarps, doing laundry, cooking, cleaning, and going about their daily lives. When Plaza Uruguaya is occupied it is still generally safe to walk through during the day, but it should be avoided at night.

Museo de la Memoria

A clandestine detention facility converted into the Museo de la Memoria: Dictadura y Derechos by Dr. Martín Almada, a well-known Paraguayan human rights activists and victim of torture at the hands of Stroessner's secret police. During the Stroessner era, hundreds of people were interrogated and tortured behind this house's unassuming exterior. The museum has exhibits about Operation Condor and the Archive of Terror and the Stroessner dictatorship. It also functions as a human rights center aiding both

---

The Archive of Terror

On December 22nd of 1992, Martín Almada, a Paraguayan lawyer, former political prisoner, and human rights activist, discovered a cache of secret police documents from the Stroessner dictatorship in a police station in the Asunción satellite city of Lambaré. The archive, now known as the *"Archivo del Terror"* (Archive of Terror) contained thousands of documents detailing the imprisonment of Stroessner-era political prisoners including transcripts and recordings of torture sessions. Martín Almada's discovery shed light on the massive human rights violations that took place in Paraguay under Stroessner's dictatorship. It also confirmed the existence of Operation Condor, a coordinated effort between military dictatorships of Paraguay, Chile, Argentina, Brazil, Uruguay, and Bolivia to investigate, imprison, torture and exchange political opponents and suspected subversives during the 1970's and 1980's.

The archive is now located at the Palacio de Justicia in Asunción and is a valuable resource to those investigating and prosecuting dictatorship-era human rights violations. For more information contact Rosa Palau who is in charge of the archive. *Tel: 595-21-424212/15 ext: 2269, cdya@pj.gov.py and cdya_py@hotmail.com*

Many of the Archive of Terror documents are available online at the Centro de Documentación y Archivo Para la Defensa de los Derechos Humanos (CDyA) website, which was developed with the help of the American National Security Archive: http://www.pj.gov.py/cdya/. An English-language version of Martín Almada's book *"Paraguay: The Forgotten Jail, a Country in Exile"* is available at www.martinalmada.org/libro.html.

researchers and victims of dictatorship-era human rights violations. *Tel: 021 425 345, Chile 1066 almost at the corner of Jejui, www.martinalmada.org/museo/museo.html, Mon-Fri 9am-4pm*

Manzana de la Rivera/Museo Memorias de la Ciudad

The series of restored colonial houses that now make up Asunción's municipal cultural center are known collectively as the Manzana de la Riviera (*manzana* is the Spanish word for block, as well as apple). Included in the complex is the Museo Memorias de la Ciudad, a small museum dedicated to the history of Asunción. The museum's patio and adjoining bar offer the best view of the presidential palace in the city as well as a glimpse of the river. *Tel: 021 442 448, 021 447 683, Corner of Ayolas and El Paraguayo Independiente, www.museo.mca.gov.py/inicio.php, Mon-Fri 8am-5pm, Sat-Sun, 9am-5pm*

Casa de la Independencia

This colonial house, one of the few remaining in Asunción, was used as a secret meeting place by the forefathers of the Paraguayan independence. From here, plans were drawn up to overthrow the Spanish governor and declare independence from Spanish colonial rule. Both the original house and the adjoining alleyway (called the "*Callejón de la Independencia*") have been preserved. The museum features paintings, documents, and objects having to do with Paraguay's colonial era including the declaration of independence. The section of the house to the right contains items from daily colonial life and others pertaining to the fathers of Paraguay's independence. The section to the left of the courtyard, houses items that focus mostly on government activities. The tiled map of colonial Asunción at the entrance is also nice. *Tel: 021 493 918, Corner of 14 de Mayo and Presidente Franco, www.casadelaindependencia.org.py, Mon-Fri 7am-6:30pm, Sat 8am-12pm (call for summer hours)*

Museo Etnográfico Andres Barbero

The museum houses an extensive collection of indigenous artifacts representing all of Paraguay's indigenous tribes. The majority of the objects, from ceramics to weapons and textiles were collected during the 1900's by some of Paraguay's most pre-eminent anthropologists and ethnographers. The museum's photographic displays help bring to life the artifacts, placing them into context of the everyday life of Paraguay's native population. For those interested in researching Paraguay's rich indigenous culture further, there is also a library. *Tel: 021 441 696, Avenida España 217, www.museobarbero.org.py, Mon-Fri 8am-5pm*

Museo Arqueológico y Etnográfico Guido Boggiani

Worth the visit to San Lorenzo, this museum is a labor of love by one of Paraguay's pioneer indigenous rights activists, José Perasso. It offers a great overview of Paraguay's various indigenous tribes. The collection includes charismatic masks, stirring photographs, and a nice selection of feathered ceremonial headdresses. The museum's large gift shop (across the street) contains a large number of indigenous handicrafts with prices set by the artists themselves and proceeds are donated to the indigenous community. The museum provides indigenous groups traveling to Asunción with food and lodging (donations in the form of both food and clothing are welcome). *Tel: 021 584 717, Coronel Bogado 888 off the main plaza in San Lorenzo (the museum's sign is a lightly etched sandstone on a white wall), Tue-Fri 9am-6pm, Sat 9am-12pm, 3pm-6pm*

Museo de Arte Sacro
Housed in a fully restored historic manor, this private museum contains one hundred creatively displayed Jesuit sculptures from the 17th and 18th centuries. The museum also has a nice gift shop and library. *Corner of Manuel Dominguez and Paraguarí, Tel: 021 449 439, www.museodeartesacro.com, Tue-Sun 9am-6pm, Entry fee: Gs. 25,000*

Museo Monseñor Juan Sinforiano Bogarín
Over a thousand religious objects are on display in this museum, sandwiched between the city's main cathedral and the Catholic University. The collection once belonged to Monsignor Juan Sinforiano Bogarín, who served as Asunción's first archbishop for over fifty years. Exhibits include religious documents, sculptures from both the Franciscan and Jesuit missions, as well as other interesting objects from the colonial era. *Tel: 021 203 819, Independencia Nacional and Mariscal López, entrance is down the alleyway running alongside the Catedral Metropolitana, Mon-Sat 8am-11am, Entry fee: Gs. 2,000*

Catedral Metropolitana
Finished in 1845, Asunción's main cathedral is quite beautiful with a simple exterior and bright airy interior. The church's gold-leafed altar and pulpit are over 200 years old. The center of the altar features the *Virgen de la Asunción*, the country's patron saint. The cathedral also houses the Museo del Tesoro de la Catedral. *Tel: 021 449 512, Independencia Nacional and Mariscal López, 9am-11:30am, 6pm-8pm (museum hours 8am-11am)*

Cañonera Humaita Barco-Museo
This Italian battleship patrolled Paraguay's waters during the Chaco War and has now been converted into a naval museum. *Behind the Palacio de los López presidential palace at the end of Ayolas, Mon-Fri 8am-11:30am, 2pm-6pm, Sat-Sun 8am-6pm*

Cementerio de la Recoleta
This necropolis, located in the residential neighborhood of Recoleta, is home to mausoleums of Paraguay's elite as well as several historical figures including Eliza Lynch. The church dates from 1842. The Recoleta is actually made up of several separate cemeteries including the International Cemetery, for foreigners and their descendents, as well as the Italian Cemetery and Military Cemetery – all of which have separate entrances. *Mariscal López between Choferes del Chaco and L. Fragnaud, daily 7:30am-5pm*

Tren del Lago
The Tren del Lago is the only fully functional remnant of Paraguay's once extensive steam train network and one of the most unique experiences to be had in Asunción. This train makes two monthly trips on Sundays to and from Asunción and the charming lakeside town of Areguá. The mood is set by actors playing historic characters that help relive the glory days of the steam train. As the train makes its way through the countryside, you can see families gathered in houses along the tracks drinking *tereré* and chatting away in the shade enjoying their *tranquilo* Sunday afternoons. The train departs at 10am every other Sunday from the Estación Botánico arriving in Areguá around noon and begins the return trip at 4:30pm. *Tel: 021 447848 / 443273. Tickets can be purchased at the Estación Central in Asunción across from Plaza Uruguaya. Tickets are US$20 for foreigners (which can be paid in US dollars or Guaraníes) and Gs.30,000 for anyone with a Paraguayan ID. As of the*

Asunción

middle of 2010, train service has been suspended due to a collapsed bridge along the tracks. Service was scheduled to start in 2012 but as of yet funds have not been allocated to make the necessary repairs.

ASUNCIÓN'S MARKETS

Mercado Cuatro

This large market's epicenter is located in the middle of the city in the triangle formed by Avenida Silvio Petirossi, Avenida Dr. Francia, and Avenida Peru. From there it extends outward on all sides engulfing the surrounding streets in makeshift stalls. Everything and anything can be found in the Mercado Cuatro, from produce to electronics. The market is roughly divided by goods – wandering through you may stumble upon the *yuyo* (medicinal herbs) section -stores filled to the brim with dried plants – or the clothing section where you can purchase a myriad of cheap clothing imported from Brazil and China. Some of the market's vendors are set up in *galerías,* each containing several storefronts. Other vendors have street side stands

---

Eating in Mercado Cuatro

Mercado Cuatro is a great place to get authentic Asian food, specifically Chinese and Korean. The majority of Asian restaurants are located in the *Barrio Chino* a series of Chinese and Korean restaurants and bodegas along República Francesa. In smaller restaurants, the use of Spanish may be limited; being accompanied by a native speaker of Korean or Chinese is sure to grant you access to an extended menu. Although most Korean main courses come with meat, vegetarians will be able to enjoy the wide variety of meatless sides, known as "bahn chan," (including delicious kimchi) that accompany most dishes.

Jang Soo Chun Upon entering this hole-in-the-wall Korean barbeque, you will be asked simply *"vaca, chanco o pato"* (beef, pork or duck). Make your choice and watch the magic happen on your tabletop gas grill. *Tel: 021 223 304, Lomas Valentinas between Otazu and R. Caballero The building is mint green with a green doorway leading up stairs – the dining room is in the back. Mon-Sat 12pm-2pm, 5pm-8:30pm, Sun 5pm-8:30pm, Gs. 25,000-30,000*

Y Hak Large and centrally located, this Korean restaurant is popular with Paraguayans and Koreans alike. Menus are in both Spanish and Korean. Don't be surprised if some of your noodle dishes come with scissors to aide in serving! *Tel: 021 208 578, 1091 Peru almost at the corner of República de Colombia, 11:3am-2pm and 5:00pm-9:30pm, closed every 2nd and 4th Sunday of the month. Gs. 25,000-35,000 with the exception of sushi dishes which are pricier*

Panadería y Confitería Hidalgo This specialty Korean bakery sells green tea and blueberry ice creams, sweet red bean paste filled desserts and fresh tofu. *Tel: 021 225 263 Corner of Peru and Ana Díaz*

El Paraíso Located in a large building resembling a pagoda, this Chinese restaurant is a little removed from the market and more upscale than other options. Sweet and sour pork is sticky and delicious and tofu a la plancha is quite flavorful. *Tel: 021 206 810, 021 213 593 Herminio Jimènez 1743 almost República Francesa Gs. 25,000-35,000*

Fu Sin Everything at this popular Chinese restaurant is served family style – be ready to overeat! Spicy eggplant is a good choice for vegetarians. *Tel: 021 206 686, República. Francesa 939, Gs. 15,000-20,000*

giving many parts of the market a claustrophobic, maze-like feel. Many of Asunción's immigrant communities (Chinese, Korean, Bolivian) are heavily represented within the market, selling specialty products and food. Mercado Cuatro is best visited in the morning when it is cooler out, as opposed to the afternoon when the heat can be unbearable. Wear comfortable shoes and do not take large bags – in some places, getting by shoppers can be a tight squeeze.

Agroshopping

Held every Tuesday from 8am-8pm in the Shopping Mariscal López (see Cool Refuge, p131) parking lot, Agroshopping offers foreigners a great opportunity to experience the cornucopia of produce that Paraguay has to offer in a comfortable and manageable setting. While the quantity and variety of produce available can't match that of infinitely larger Mercado Cuatro or Mercado Abasto, Agroshopping is less overwhelming and more accessible to foreigners. In the twelve years since its inception, the market has become an Asunción tradition and meeting place for both shopping and socializing. Additionally, there are several prepared food options, including ethnic choices, which make Agroshopping a popular lunch scene. Carnivors will be happy with Chancho Rico's artisanal sausages and cold cuts, while vegetarians will enjoy the vegetarian sushi, curry, and other soy-based foods of Casa Inés. Be sure to hit up El Estadero for fresh juices and fruit salads and, nearby, La Alemana for delicious pastries. Several Asian vendors also sell vegetarian sushi and other TVP and soy based products.

Mercado de Abasto

Located just over the border between Asunción and the satellite city of Fernando de la Mora, the Mercado de Abasto is a good place for those who like to visit markets but do not want to deal with the craziness of Mercado Cuatro. The market is on its own lot, as opposed to being set up on city streets, and therefore more open and less confusing

---

Asunción on a Sunday

As many offices work half-days on Saturdays, Sundays represent the one true day of rest for many in Asunción and the call to relax is taken seriously. Sunday is a day for family gatherings, typically in the form of *asados* that start late in the day and extend into the evening. Asunción, especially the downtown area, is very quiet on Sundays. Buses run less frequently and most stores and museums are closed for the day. This can be a great time to enjoy a stroll through the city as it is much more peaceful than usual. Other Sunday activities include:

A visit to the Botanical Gardens During the week it is usually empty but on the weekends you will find many families taking advantage of the natural surroundings for picnics, drinking *tereré*, and pick up soccer games.

Take in a *partido* (soccer game) There are always matches between local soccer teams – the most popular matches are between arch rivals Olympia and Cerro Porteño. Pick a team and cheer them on at a local bar or head out to the stadium to cheer in person.

Tren del Lago Leaving every other Sunday, this train ride makes for a unique and picturesque day trip to quaint and artistic Areguá.

Antiques Market Sunday mornings in front of the La Riojana department store on the corner of Mariscal Estigarribia and Yegros.

than Mercado Cuatro. The market's vendors sell mostly produce. Should you be interested in engaging people in conversation or taking photos (always with permission), Mercado de Abasto is a good option and an easy bus ride from Asunción. On Avenida Defensores del Chaco and San José, from downtown take bus 15-3.

ACCOMMODATIONS

Given Asunción's low cost of living, lodging in the city is surprisingly high priced. This is especially so in the historic center. Lodging by the bus terminal is affordable, however expensive nighttime cab rides to and from the center will quickly offset any savings. There are several options in residential areas where the nightlife is more active – all are within short bus rides from the sites and activities of downtown.

Downtown

The Black Cat Hostel Asunción's first hostel is a welcome and affordable addition to downtown's lodging options. The three rooms have about ten bunk beds each, and there is a small courtyard with a pool and a rooftop terrace. There is Wi-Fi, and visitors without a computer, may borrow the owners' laptop. Owners are friendly and helpful. Kitchen facilities are limited to a hotplate and small fridge. *Tel: 021 449 827, 0981 986 594, Eligio Ayala 129 between Yegros and Independencia Nacional, www.hostelblackcat.com, on Facebook, Gs. 70,000 for A/C, Gs. 50,000 -60,000 for fan. Wi-Fi, kitchen access, small pool*

Hotel Palmas del Sol One of the better deals around, this clean and cheery hotel is located on the edge of the *microcentro*. The breakfast buffet is quite good. The pool and garden are a nice break from the hustle and bustle of downtown Asunción. Free pickup from the airport and transfer from the hotel to the airport costs Gs. 22,000 per person. *Tel: 021 449 485, Avenida España 202 almost at the corner with Tacuary, www.hotelpalmasdelsol.com, Single Gs. 155,000, Double Gs. 210,000, Triple Gs. 265,000, Wi-Fi, computers, TV, A/C, and mini-fridge*

Asunción Palace Hotel Built in 1843, the Palace Hotel was one of Asunción's first colonial mansions. As such, the hotel has a lot of personality – rooms have high ceilings, tiled floors, and some have balconies looking out onto busy Calle Colon. Third floor rooms offer a view of the river, and they offer a good breakfast spread. This hotel is popular among Peace Corps volunteers. Keep your exploring to the downtown/eastern side of Colon, as the area between Colon and the river is kind of sketchy. *Tel: 021 492 151, Corner of Colon and Estrella, Double: Gs, 210,000, Triple 250,000, Wi-Fi, computers, TV, A/C, and mini-fridge*

Gran Hotel del Paraguay The Gran Hotel del Paraguay used to be the private home of Madame Lynch, mistress of President Mariscal López. The stately home was witness to many of the extravagances of her life in Paraguay. Today, it is a hotel, which retains the feel and style of a grand colonial manor with nice gardens, tiled floors, and wrap around patios known as "*corredor yere.*" Perhaps the most beautiful feature is the two salons (featuring the hotel's restaurant) decorated with beautiful flowered murals commissioned by Madame Lynch herself. The hotel is located about halfway between downtown and Villa Morra and within walking distance from both of the city's main arteries Avenida España and Avenida Mariscal López. *Tel: 021 200 051/3, De la Residenta 902 and Padre Pucheau, www.granhoteldelparaguay.com.py, Double Gs, 385,000, Triple Gs. 455,000. Wi-Fi, TV, A/C, mini-fridge, pool, and tennis courts*

Asunción Hostel Another new hostel with a friendly rocker vibe. Owners are very enthusiastic, always chatting with guests. *Tel: 021 445 065, Mariscal Estigarribia 988 between EEUU and Tacuary, www.Asuncionhostel.com, www.facebook.com/AsuncionHostel, shared dorms Gs. 45,000 – 75,000 per person, Wi-Fi and kitchen access*

Jardín Botánico The city's botanical gardens are a good option for those who are on a tight budget and prefer to camp. However, facilities are very basic and the park closes at 5pm. While cheap, this is not necessarily the most practical option. *See Jardín Botánico, p140*

Villa Morra

Hotel Los Alpes – Villa Morra Located on a cobblestone street in the residential Villa Morra neighborhood, this hotel is within walking distance of Shopping Mariscal López and a very short cab ride from the ritzy Carmelitas bars and restaurants. The hotel has the feel of a large house with spacious rooms, a comfy lounge, and a medium sized, curvy pool. The breakfast buffet is good as well. Though they are not air conditioned, the dorm rooms (known by Peace Corps Volunteers as "the attic") are a good bargain for this neck of the woods. Free airport pickup is another perk that sweetens the deal. *Tel.: 021 606 286, 021 609 705, Del Maestro 1686 almost at the corner of San Martín (one block past 4D), www.hotellosalpes.com.py, Single Gs. 220,000, Double Gs. 270,000, Attic Gs. 75,000, Wi-Fi computers, TV, A/C, mini-fridge and a gym*

Hotel Suisse Funky life-sized cutouts of Swiss people welcome you to this cute home turned into a family run hotel. Tucked away in residential Villa Morra it is within walking distance of all the area's attractions. Claude, the owner is very hospitable and can help arrange all sorts of trips. He also owns another hotel, Casa Suiza, just up the street (Senador Long 389 almost Del Maestro) but Maison Suisse is nicer. *Tel: 021 600 003, Malutin 482 between Del Maestro and Bertoni, www.casasuiza.info, Single Gs.220,000, Double Gs. 280,000, Wi-Fi, computers, TV, A/C, and a pool*

Carmelitas/Shopping del Sol

Hotel Los Alpes – Santa Teresa This branch of Los Alpes offers the same homey feel as its Villa Morra counterpart. There are plants everywhere and the larger grounds have two pools for those hot summer days. Though there are no dorm-style rooms, there are apartments for long-term guests. Free pickup from the airport. *Tel: 021 607 348 / 665 345 / 606 645, Avenida. Santa Teresa 2855 between Coronel Cabrera and Dr. B. Caballero, www.hotellosalpes.com.py, Single Gs. 220,000, Double Gs. 270,000, Wi-Fi, computers, TV, A/C, mini-fridge, gym, and pools*

Cool Refuge

On a hot Asunción day, even the most stringent anti-capitalist backpackers may find themselves drawn to one of Asunción's shopping malls and with good reason. The malls offer tourists a large, air conditioned space to eat, drink, and get some respite from the glaring sun. Serving fresh cooked pastas, juicy steaks, tropical juices, and cold beers, food court offerings are good and inexpensive. In addition, the food courts are often the setting for cultural events such as art and photography exhibits or musical acts. Those looking to kill a few hours can always head to an inexpensive movie at either Shopping del Sol or Shopping Villa Morra – tickets are less than US $6 and even less for matinees and Wednesday showings (see Going to the Movies, p140).

Shopping Mariscal López *Tel: 021 611 272, Corner of Quesada and Malutín, www.mariscallopez.com.py*

Shopping Del Sol *Tel: 021 611 780, Corner of Avenida Aviadores del Chaco and Profesor Delia González, www.shoppingdelsol.com.py/*

Shopping Villa Morra *Tel: 021 605 795, Corner of Mariscal López and Malutín, www.villamorra.com.py*

Mall Excelsior *Tel: 021 443-015, Corner of Chile and Manduvirá (this is the only mall downtown), www.mallexcelsior.com*

Asunción

Hotel Le Pelican Another small hotel option two blocks from Shopping del Sol in one of the city's most exclusive neighborhoods. Early risers can stroll down the Santa Teresa walking path lined with mansions and the occasional fruit or clothing vendor. Doubles, triples and quadruples available. Most have balconies overlooking neighboring houses and palm trees. Out back, there is a small courtyard. Free transfer to the airport between 7am-8pm. *Tel: 021 625855/7, Corner of Avenida Santa Teresa and Gumercindo Sosa, www.hotellepelican.com, Single Gs. 210,000, Double Gs. 260,000, Triple Gs. 310,000, Wi-Fi, computers, TV, A/C, and mini-fridge*

El Rinconcito A set of three houses which can be rented in full or by the room, El Rinconcito is ideal for long-term visitors looking to have a personalized experience. Each house is fully furnished and equipped with all the amenities as well as a pool. Owner, Celeste, is well connected and able to organize day trips through Asunción and surrounding areas. She can also help coordinate trips in the rest of the country. *Tel: 0981-40 23 46, Espiritu Aranda 2810 and Congreso de Colombia, www.elrinconcitopy.com, Single US$50, Double US$60, Wi-Fi, TV, A/C and a pool*

Near the Terminal

Hotel Central This clean and inexpensive hotel is a good option if you have an early morning bus departure or late night arrival. If you plan to go out downtown remember that most buses stop running at 10pm. *Tel: 021 555 338, Avenida Fernando de la Mora almost at the corner of República Argentina (across the street from the bus terminal), www.hotelcentral.com.py, Double US$20, family room with queen and bunk bed US$36, Wi-Fi, TV, and A/C*

RESTAURANTS

Restaurants & Food Downtown

Lido Bar Always bustling with customers, Lido Bar offers traditional Paraguayan diner food in a 50's diner setting. *Caldo de pescado*, a chowder like soup made of *surubí* or tilapia, with a side of fresh bread. It's a longtime favorite, served almost continually to hungry customers throughout the day and night. *Chicken milanesa* is crispy and perfect and the *chipa guazú* is to die for. Servings are generally large, and the *empanadas* in particular are of gargantuan proportions. The waitress' uniforms – tight orange skirts, matching orange and white gingham vests, and pillbox hats – add to the character of this Asunción classic. *Tel: 021 444 607, Corner of Palma and Chile opposite the Panteón de los Héroes, Mon Sat 6:30am-2am, Sun 7:30am-1am, Gs 8,000-50,000*

A Crowded Place

Vying for a seat at Lido Bar's lunch counter can be a blood sport, especially if you are in a group. The trick is to find someone who looks like they are almost finished and stand directly behind them. This can involve a lot of vulture-like hovering and eye darting, but it well worth it to watch the waitresses call out orders loudly and swirl around each other in a blur of orange and white.

Zámpanos The best pizza in Asunción prepared in a cute, intimate setting. Start off with a piping hot focaccia, and move on to their delicious paper thin crusted pizza. Accompany the meal with Zámpano's homemade limoncello served ice cold. If you have room for dessert, try the deliciously rich *dulce de leche* ice cream. *Tel: 021 222 383, Brasil 1193 and the corner of Rodriguez de Francia, Wed-Sun 7pm-12am, Gs. 12,000 -50,000*

El Bolsi Another Asunción classic, Bolsi serves up Paraguayan food as well as American comfort food – burgers, chicken fingers, tuna melts, and even chocolate chip cookies. Vegetarians will be happy with the selection of salads (Ensalada Campechana with grilled vegetables and slices of fresh mozzarella cheese is a good one) and vegetable quiches or *tartas* (*tarta de zucchini* is good). Rich and creamy *mousse de mbaracuya* is an excellent dessert, as is the *waffle completo*. The air conditioning can make this place tempting even if you're not hungry, and the outdoor patio can be pleasant once Asunción's traffic has died down for the night. There is a formal dining room next to the diner with the same menu. Bolsi also delivers. *Tel: 021 491 841, Corner of Estrella and Alberdi, www.bolsi.com.py, open 24 hours Gs. 10,000-50,000*

Bar San Roque One of Asunción's oldest restaurants, Bar San Roque has been a favorite hangout of the city's cultural elite for many decades. The tiled floors, dark wood, marble top bar, and bow tied waiters create an ambience reminiscent of a bygone era. Thick cut *milanesa de surubí* (breaded and fried catfish) is an excellent option. *Tel: 021 446 015, corner of Eligio Ayala and Tacuary, 8am-3pm, 6pm-12am, Gs. 20,000 -60,000*

Burger King A choice for those craving fast food or American-style salads. *Tel: 021 498 368, Palma between 14 de Mayo y 15 de Agosto, Shopping del Sol, and Mall Excelsior (corner of Chile and Manduvira), www.burgerking.com.py, Gs. 10,000-30,000*

Vida Verde A good lunch option for vegetarians, Vida Verde is a small restaurant serving up a medium sized meatless buffet. Offerings include traditional stir-fry dishes made with TVP, breaded eggplant, and Paraguayan-style vegetable casseroles and quiches. They also sell blocks of tofu packed in water and Chinese teas. *Tel: 021 446 611, Palma 634 almost at 15 de Agosto (across the street from Galeria Central and Unicentro), Mon-Fri 7:30am-3pm, Sat 7:30am-2pm, Gs. 15,000-25,000*

Paraguayan Chains

If you're pressed for cash or time, these Paraguayan chains have locations throughout Asunción and are great options for a quick bite, including many traditional Paraguayan dishes, at affordable prices. Plus, all of them deliver!

Ña Eustaquia This popular chain offers traditional home-style Paraguayan snacks for those who don't have time to make them at home. The *mbeju quatro quesos* is a cheese and starch bomb that can't be missed (but may be best shared between two people). The *chipa ryguazu* (chicken filled chipa) has a dry tamale-like consistency that's very good. The main location has a full menu with traditional lunch specials. *Tel: 021 297 480/1, Delivery 021 624 724, Palma and Alberdi (across from Senatur Office) and stands in Shopping Villa Morra and Shopping del Sol (for other locations see website), www.naeustaquia.com, Palma location 9am-12am, Gs 4,000-20,000*

Pancholos Pancholos, with its tereré sipping, straw hat wearing parrot mascot, has all the regular fast food offerings – hamburgers, lomitos, pizzas as well as a wide range of pastas. Pizzas are very tasty, especially the pepperoni and the chicken curry. *Tel: 021 600 660, 021600 408, Palma between 14 de Mayo and 15 de Agosto, Shopping del Sol, Shopping Mariscal López, Mall Excelsior, www.pancholos.com, Gs. 4,000-45,000*

Don Vito Cheap and filling, Don Vito empanadas are round, fried disks of goodness. If you're sick of ground beef or ham and cheese empanadas try their *empanadas de choclo* (corn), *acelga* (kale and cheese), and caprese (tomatoes, mozzarella and basil). *Tel: 021 602 489, Shopping del Sol, Shopping Mariscal López, and various other locations throughout Asunción, www.donvito.com.py, Gs 2,500*

Hermanas Feliciana Fariña Selling every variation of chipa imaginable, the Hermanas are perhaps best known for their bags of *chipa pirú* (also known as "chipitas"). Literally "skinny chipa" in Guaraní, these miniature versions of chipa make great snacks. For those wishing to take a taste of Paraguay back home with them, *chipitas* are your best option – they travel and keep well. *Tel: 021 449 201, 14 de Mayo and Estrella and Shopping Mariscal López (parking lot food court), www.felicianadefarina.com.py, Gs. 4,000-12,000*

La Flor de la Canela Sick of *surubí*? Head to Flor de la Canela for an extensive menu of traditional Peruvian seafood based dishes. A great option at a very reasonable price and the only place in Paraguay you can dine with a large-scale image of Macchu Pichu looming overhead. *Ceviche super especial* and *jalea especial* are two favorites. *Tel 021 498 928, Corner of Eligio Ayala and Tacuary, www.laflordelacanela.com.py, daily 11:30am-3pm, 6:30pm-12am, Gs. 20,000-80,000*

Taberna Española The go-to place in Asunción for traditional Spanish food, this restaurant has a quirky yet homey feel to it. The walls are covered in decorations from the ceiling to the floor. Wise, cheeky, and bizarre sayings are painted all over the walls, and long strands of clam shells hang from the high ceilings. Classic Spanish dishes, good paella, and a delicious onion garlic soup. *Tel: 021 441 743, Ayolas almost at the corner of General Diaz, on Facebook, Mon-Thu 11am-2:30pm, 7pm-11:30pm, Fri-Sat 11am-2:30pm, 7pm-1am, Sun 11am-3pm, 7pm-11pm, Gs. 20,000-80,000*

Chez Bong A great option for those who want to sample Asunción's authentic Korean cuisine without having to venture in to Mercado Cuatro. Cooked in a hot stone pot the *bibimbab* is excellent. There is a vegetarian *bibimbab* (with or without egg) if meat isn't your thing. If it is then go for the *bibimbab con bulgoki*. Traditional *bahn chon* sides are delicious. Sushi is good but expensive. *Tel: 021 222 784, República Francesa 266 between Eligio Ayala and Mariscal Estigarribia, Mon-Sun 11:30am-2:30pm, 5:30pm-11pm, Gs 25,000-50,000*

Il Capo – Peru A long-time favorite among Asunción's Italian food fans, this restaurant serves up freshly made pastas in an intimate and cozy setting. Customer favorites include the soft Gnocchi Il Capo and, although it is not on the menu, the flan dessert is perfect. *Tel: 021 213 022, Corner of Perú and José Berges, www.ilcapo.com.py, Daily 11:30am-12am, Gs. 20,000-60,000*

Confitería Honey Tucked away in a historic residential neighborhood, everything in this coffee shop is delicious from the rich cakes (try the Honey cake) and pastries to the flavorful *empanadas*. Work off the calories afterwards by walking along Mariscal López to view some of Asunción's oldest manors. *Tel: 021 206 200, corner of 25 de Mayo and Vice Presidente Sánchez, www.confiteriahoney.com, Mon-Fri 6:30am-9pm, Sat-Sun 7am-8:30pm, Gs. 6,000-20,000*

La Paraguayita Here you will find traditional Paraguayan food done well. Meats are cooked to perfection and serving sizes are quite large. Meat lovers should try the *asado de costilla* ribs (with plenty of meat on the bone), a juicy *bife de chorizo* or buttery soft *tapa cuadril*. Or go all out and order the *parrilla completa* with more meat than you'll know what to do with. Veggie options include pastas and crepes. Musical accompaniment on many nights. *Tel: 021 204 407, Corner of Brasilia and Siria, Mon-Sat 12pm-3pm, 7pm-2am, Gs. 20,000-80,000*

Michael Bock This German bakery has delicious desserts and a wide variety of freshly baked breads including ricotta bread. They also carry whole grain breads that are hard to come by in Paraguay. Michael Bock provides bread to stores in German communities throughout the country. *Tel: 021 495 847, Presidente Franco 828 between Ayolas and Montevideo, Mon-Fri 6:30am-7pm, Sat 6:30am-1pm, Gs. 8,000-20,000*

Supermarkets Located Downtown

Supermercado Stock In the basement of the Mall Excelsior, this supermarket also has a food court. *Tel: 021 442 640, Corner of Chile and Manduvira, www.stock.com.py, Mon-Sat 7am-9:30pm, Sun 7am-9pm (food court closes half an hour early)*

Supermercado España *Tel: 021 200 902, Avenida España between Brazil and Paí Perez, daily 7:15am-9:30pm*

Villa Morra

See Agroshopping, p129, for options available on Tuesdays in Shopping Mariscal López.

🍴 **Quattro D** Serving up massive cones of soft gelato, 4D is an Asunción institution, frequently drawing crowds regardless of the season. Fruit flavors such as the deliciously tart *mbaracuya* (passion fruit), kiwi, and smooth mango are bright and refreshing while rich piedmont (dark chocolate), nocciola (hazelnut), and tiramisú rival those of any gelateria in Italy. Each serving includes two flavors (three for larger sizes and cones). There is also a full menu of pastas, sandwiches, and meats, if you can resist the temptation to start with dessert. Combine a *lomito 4D* (steak with fries, egg and bacon) with a three scoop cone, and you may never have to eat again. *Tel: 021 600 129, 021 6160-444, corner of Andrade and San Martín, daily 10am-12am, Gs. 10,000-30,000*

🍴 **Churrasquería Acuarela** The best of Asunción's Brazilan-style *churrasquerías*. For a fixed price, take your seat as waiters come to your table non-stop bearing large spears of juicy meats. The buffet also includes salads,pastas, Brazilian pork and black beans (*feijao*). On Sundays, the menu also includes special meats and fish. Dessert and drinks are not included in the fixed price menu. Take a break from eating to get a photo of yourself in front of the enormous grill alongside meat-sword clad waiters. *Tel: 021 609 217, 021 605 183, Avenida Mariscal López 4049, almost at the corner of San Martín, www.acuarela.com.py, daily 11am-1am, Gs. 77,000*

La Creperie Tucked away a couple of blocks from Mariscal López, La Creperie is a charming, slightly quirky restaurant that's perfect for a romantic date or an intimate meal. The bright red walls filled with an eclectic array of posters and paintings, softly lit tables, and baskets of utensils on each table create an atmosphere that is cozy. The menu consists of over thirty different types of savory crepes (including vegetarian), and sweet crepes. The sangria here is also good though on the sweet side. Be sure to sign the wall in one of the side rooms before leaving. Cheese and chocolate fondues are on the menu in the winter. *Tel: 021 607 499, Manuel del Castillo between Monseñor Bogarín and Teniente Zotti, Tue-Sun 6pm-11pm, Gs. 12,000-26,000*

Smuchi This cheerfully decorated sandwich and smoothie shop has been an instant hit with expats and locals alike. Specialty cheeses, and a variety of meats and breads make this sandwich shop a great option if you are sick of *empanadas*. Favorites include *Ni Salado Ni Dulce* (with mango chutney), *Vale* (cured ham, brie, and arugula), and the enormous *Con Todo* (as the name indicates, the works). Smoothie options include a wide assortment of fruits as well as coffee flavored concoctions. Unfortunately, service grinds to a halt when there are more than a handful of customers. *Tel: 021 604 685, Dr Morra 245 almost at the corner of Andrade (two blocks from Quattro D and two blocks from Mariscal López), www.facebook.com/smuchi, Daily 9am-11pm, Gs. 10,000-25,000*

Bellini Pasta Located in the Shopping Mariscal López food court, this pasta bar is a great value with fast and efficient service. As your pasta boils, select a base sauce and up to eight ingredients (from a good variety of cheese, veggies,meats and other ingredients) to be sautéed together, creating a delicious made-to-order dish. Probably the best deal around. *Tel: 021 606 652, Shopping Mariscal López food court (there is a larger more upscale branch in Paseo Carmelitas as well), Sun-Thu 11am-11pm, Fri 11am-12pm, Sat 11am-1am, Gs.20,000-25,000*

O Sole Mío Located in the courtyard of the San Rafael church and community center, O Sole Mío (also known by expats as "Holy Pizza") offers you the opportunity to eat *takakua* (brick oven) baked pizza in the shadow of a mini-medieval palace hidden from street by enormous hedges. The pizza crusts are thin, the sangria is good, and the ambience is like nothing else in Paraguay. Plus you get the "good Samaritan" benefit of helping out a community organization. Be sure to check out the literary cafe and the gift shop with Paraguayan handicrafts, alongside O Sole Mío in

Asunción

the courtyard. The *siciliana* with chunks of salty *pancetta* and sliced onions is especially good. *Tel: 021 609 638, 0982 529 340, Cruz del Chaco 1690, almost at Alfredo Seiferheld (if riding a bus along Argentina towards Eusebio Ayala get off two blocks past the Supermercado Superseis), Sun-Fri 7pm-11pm, Sat 7pm-12am, www.sanrafaelobras.com, Gs. 25,000 -45,000*

Supermarkets in Villa Mora

Real Villa Morra Check out the *productos americanos* aisle for an interesting (and often strange) variety of imported goods – good for comfort food if you are missing home. There is also a food court and an extensive wine cellar. *Tel: 021 600 588, 021 602 030, corner of Avenida Boggiani and República Argentina*

Superseis On the ground floor of Shopping Villa Morra this small supermarket is a good place to stock up on the basics. *Shopping Villa Morra, www.superseis.com.py*

Carmelitas

Un Toro y Siete Vacas This high-end Paraguayan steakhouse serves up an extensive array of tender cuts of beef as well as fish, lamb, and goat. The menu includes international and Paraguayan side dishes and desserts. The *chipa guazú* is exceptionally soft and fluffy. Though upscale, the prices are extremely reasonable given the large portions. Staff is very helpful and friendly. Be very specific about how well you well want the meat cooked,as theytend towards well done. *Tel: 021 600 425, corner of Malutín and Eusebio Lillo, across from Paseo Lillo, www.untoroysietevacas.com.py, Daily 12pm-3pm, 8pm-1am, Gs. 30,000-60,000*

El Café de Acá A cute coffee shop with a Paraguayan twist. The cozy setup in a small house has a relaxing atmosphere with touches of Paraguay throughout, from the patio with a well and a ceramic *kambuchi* water jug to the weathered tiled floors and well-loved cans of Leche Nido over the bar. The menu includes a variety of coffees and teas as well as *tereré* and *mate* service. There are also Paraguayan classics such as a fluffy *sopa paraguaya* and rich *mbeju* as well as *empanadas* and *guayaba* tarts. Fruit infused green tea, *Narciso*, is very refreshing. *Tel: 021 623 583, corner of Teniente. Vera and Dr. Morra (two blocks behind Feria Asunción on San Martín), www.elcafedeaca.com, Tue-Sun 8am-11pm, Gs. 5,000-30,000*

Spaghettoteca Run out of a private home by Italian immigrants, this hidden and unassuming restaurant has some of the freshest pasta in Asunción. Purchase pasta and sauces to go, or eat your meal at tables set up in the family living room, complete with a fireplace and a small bar. Save room for dessert – creamy tiramisú and sabayon with rum spiked figs are real winners. *Tel: 021 604 084, Bruselas 1690, between Avenida San Martín and Viena, heading down San Martín take a right one block before Avenida España – the Spaghettoteca is a house on the right-hand side about half a block away from San Martín with a small, very faded sign in front), Tue-Sat 7pm-11:30pm, Sun 12pm-3pm, Gs. 20,000-50,000*

Romanaccio Pizza & Sangria This excellent pizzeria has such a wide array of thin crusted combinations that you'll definitely want to take advantage of the fact they let you mix and match half pizzas. Grilled eggplant and shrimp-pesto are great choices. Don't forget to order a pitcher of white sangría to wash it all down. Ask for the crust to be baked "*crocante*." *Tel: 021 663 070, Paseo Via Bella, corner of España and Rómulo Feliciángeli (just behind TGIF's), On Facebook, Mon-Wed 7:30pm-12am, Thu 7:30pm-12:30am, Fri 7:30pm-1am, Sat 7:30pm-2am, Sun 7pm-12am, Gs. 35,000-50,000*

TGI Fridays Perfect for those longing for a taste of America – be it American fast food favorites or televised sporting events (American football, golf, tennis). Extensive drink menu. Lunch and happy hour specials. *Tel: 021 623 322, Paseo Via Bella, corner of España and Rómulo Feliciángeli, www.fridays.com.py, daily 12pm-1:30am, Gs. 10,000 to 40,000*

Supermarkets in Carmelitas

Stock Located within Shopping del Sol, this large supermarket also has a food court. *Tel: 021 611 822/7, Shopping del Sol, www.stock.com.py, daily 7am-10pm (food court does not open till 8am)*

Casa Rica Specializing in gourmet foods with an emphasis on German imports, Casa Rica is a great source for specialty foods in Asunción from hard to find spices to imported beers. *Tel: 021 607 937, corner of Aviadores del Chaco and San Martín (at the end of Avenida España), www.facebook.com/casarica.py, Mon-Sat 7:30am-8:30pm, Sun 8am-1pm*

NIGHTLIFE

Asuncenos are a night loving crowd (partially this has to do with the heat since things only start to cool down at night). As with the rest of Latin America, nightlife starts late here. Though some restaurants serve dinner starting at 7pm, most do not begin to fill up until 10pm or later. Cafés and bars will start filling up around 11pm, and showing up at a nightclub before midnight pretty much guarantees you'll have the dance floor to yourself. Attire generally ranges from business casual to semi-formal with men wearing slacks and dress shoes, and women wearing dresses and high heels. Dress codes are more strictly enforced for men; some clubs don't allow people wearing shorts and flip flops to enter. Sneakers are often permissible if paired with slacks and dress shirts. Most nightclubs offer free or reduced entrance to ladies before midnight, however, cover charges may apply across the board during special events. Karaoke is increasingly popular, although Paraguayans tend to favor ballads which can lend a less than upbeat note to karaoke nights.

BARS & NIGHTLIFE

Downtown

Britannia Pub This favorite among expats and locals fills up quickly on week-nights and weekends alike. Well stocked bar includes Britannia's own house beer. Food is affordable and tasty with highlights including fried *mandioca* with garlic and cheese, *picaña* steak platter, and create-your-own salads. The atmosphere is lively and the music is upbeat. During special events and theme nights, part of the terrace is turned into a dance floor and cover charges may apply. *Tel: 021 443 990, Cerro Corá 851 (down the street from the Crowne Plaza Hotel), www.britannia-pub.com, Tue-Thu 6:30pm-2am, Fri 6:30pm-4am, Sat 8pm-4am, Sun 8pm-2am, Gs. 7,000-25,000*

904 Bar Recently opened by the owners of the Crowne Plaza Hotel (directly across the street), this bar is set in a renovated house with nicely decorated rooms and a large interior courtyard. The vibe and crowd are very similar to Brit Pub although the ambience at 904 is more polished. Cover charges apply on special Blues Wednesdays and Rock Thursdays. Check their Facebook page for upcoming events. *Tel: 0985 190 532, 0985 190 539, Cerro Corá 904, between EEUU and Tacuary, on Facebook, Mon-Thu 6:30pm-2am, Fri 6:30pm-4am, Sat 7pm-4am, Gs. 10,000-25,000*

Planta Alta This modern art gallery/bar is a popular hangout for Asunción's artsy crowd. Enjoy drinks on the balcony, live music and film screenings, or just wander around the gallery's ever-changing exhibition rooms soaking in an artistic atmosphere unique to Asunción. Covers sometimes apply during special events. *Corner of Mariscal Estigarribia and Caballero, next to Overall Artesanías, the door has no sign but is marked with the letters "PA" above the doorway and a stairway leading up to the second floor, www.facebook.com/plantaaltagaleria, Wed-Fri 5pm-1am, Sat 9pm-3am, Gs. 10,000-20,000*

Casa Clari Casa Clari benefits from its location within the Manzana de la Riviera cultural center in two ways. The first is the incredible view of the Palacio Presidencial, bright white against a sky blue backdrop by day and nicely illuminated by night. The second is the almost constant breeze from the river. Combined with the relaxed atmosphere and semi secluded location, these make it an excellent spot to take a break while sightseeing in Asunción. Reservations recommended for large groups on Friday and Saturday nights, as it tends to fill up once cultural events downtown let out. Daytime menu is limited to drinks, and a full menu of pizzas and appetizer platters are served after 7pm. *Tel 021 496 476, corner of Ayolas and Paraguayo Independiente, inside the Manzana de la Rivera, www.casaclari.com.py, Mon-Fri 9am-1am, Sat 6pm-1am, Gs. 15,000-45,000*

Café Dalí With karaoke on the ground floor and a dance floor on top, Café Dalí is a good option for those who want to start the night early. Happy hours on Thursdays, Fridays, and Saturdays mean the dance floor is packed while the rest of Asunción has yet to step out for dinner. *Tel: 021 490 890, corner of Estrella and O'Leary, Thu-Fri 5pm-2am, Sat 5pm-4am, Gs. 20,000-40,000*

Orishas This popular dance club plays the latest in salsa and reggaeton. Friday nights are a little quiet – Saturday is the night to go. *Tel: 0983 145 969, Eligio Ayala, between Estados Unidos and Tacuary, Thu-Sat 11:30-7am, Gs 10,000-20,000*

Villa Morra & Carmelitas – Shopping del Sol

The city's best area for bar hopping and going out is on Avenida España from the upscale Paseo Carmelitas (cross street Malutín) on towards Avenida San Martín. This area is full of shopping *galerías* with boutique stores, restaurants, and bars, Paseo Carmelitas being the largest and most popular. Many of the nightclubs in this area allow you to reserve tables or booths for the night in advance. The Manzana T complex one block away from Shopping Mariscal López is your best bet for nightlife in the Villa Morra area with a good selection of bars, restaurants, and one or two nightclubs.

Kilkenny Irish Pub This large high-end Irish pub in upscale Paseo Carmelitas is packed with expats and locals alike. Ample selection of imported beers includes Guinness, naturally, as well as German beers and Argentine microbrews. House band The Kilks are excellent and get everyone dancing with crowd pleasing covers on Wednesdays and Fridays. *Tel: 021 671 421, 021 672 768, Malutin and Avenida España in Paseo Carmelitas, www.kilkenny.com.py, reservations are recommended for large groups, Mon-Tues 6pm-2:15am, Wed-Thurs 6pm-3am, Fri-Sat 5pm-4:30am, Sun 6pm-2am, Gs. 10,000-40,000*

Café Bohemia This small bar and café is known for its themed dance nights ranging from Jazz Mondays to Retro Wednesdays and the especially popular Salsa Thursdays. Though the small dance floor can get cramped, the ambience is good. *Tel: 021 662 191, Senador Long, almost Avenida España, on Facebook, Mon-Wed and Sun 6pm-3am, Thu 6pm-4am, Fri 6pm-5am, Gs. 10,000-30,000*

El Santo Located in the Manzana T complex, El Santo is a good all around bar and dance club playing a wide variety of dance hits from pop, reggaeton, salsa, you name it. Upper balcony is good for people watching and taking a break from the crowded dance floor. *Tel: 021 613 322, corner of Mariscal López and Cruz del Defensor in Manzana T, www.elsanto.com.py, Fri-Sat 8pm-6am, Gs. 10,000-30,000*

Bambuddha Completely covered with bamboo on the outside and decked out with an Asian themed interior, this dance club is a hit with Asunción's elite and the best bet for those staying nearby in Shopping del Sol. Music includes a mix of reggaeton, salsa, top 40's and house. *Tel: 021 621 870, Corner of Avenida Aviadores del Chaco and Profesor Vasconsellos, www.bambuddha.com.py, reservations are recommended for large groups, Fri-Sat 10pm-6am, Gs.20,000-50,000*

Gay-Friendly Nightlife in Asunción

Hollywood Dance Three dance floors with multiple disco balls and good lighting make this club a good bet for a fun night on the town. Music is mostly pop with themed parties on Saturday nights. *Tel: 0982 488 652, 0981 906 494, Independencia Nacional almost at Teniente Fariña, www.facebook.com/hollywooddance, Fri 11pm-5am, Sat 12am-5am, Gs. 20,000-40,000*

Frogus A fun place for karaoke – just remember Paraguayans have a penchant for belting out love ballads. *Tel: 0971 825 676, Estrella 852 between Montevideo and Ayolas, Mon-Sat 8pm-1am, Gs. 10,000-20,000*

La Serafina This small bar and café is run out of the headquarters of Aireana, Asunción's lesbian and women's rights advocacy group. Afternoon snacks and dinner include vegetarian dishes. There is Wi-Fi as well. *Tel: 021 492-835, 447 976, Eligio Ayala 907 almost Tacuary, www.aireana.org.py, Mon-Fri 4pm-9pm, Gs 10,000-20,000*

Trauma Disco Pub One of Asunción's few explicitly gay-friendly nightclubs, Trauma's dance mix is heavy on techno and electronic music. This club is popular with the city's drag queens. *25 de Mayo and Antequera, Fri-Sat 11pm-5am, Gs. 20,000*

CULTURAL ACTIVITIES

Art exhibits, movie screenings, plays, lectures, and musical events are constantly set up by Paraguayan cultural organizations and the cultural centers of several foreign embassies. Most are free or cheap and take place in the center of town near the majority of hotels.

Centro Cultural Juan de Salazar The high caliber Spanish cultural center always has a packed calendar of events with something for everyone. The center has multiple performance spaces where they offer plays, workshops, and musical acts. Art and photography exhibits are very well curated, and there are ongoing film and lectures series as well. There is also an extensive library in the back of the building. A full agenda of events is available on the website. *Tel: 021 449 921, Herrera 834 almost at Tacuary (entrance on Tacuary before 6:30pm and on Herrera afterwards), www.juandesalazar.org.py, Office hours: 8am-2pm, Exhibit hours 8am-9:30pm*

Alliance Francaise The French cultural center is mostly geared towards language lessons (French and Spanish), but there are frequent plays and film series as well. Stop by the Le Bistro café for buttery croissants and piping hot crepes. *Tel: 021 210 382, Estigarribia 1032 almost at EEUU, www.alianzafrancesa.edu.py, Mon-Fri 8am-7:30, Sat 8am-4:30*

Centro Cultural de la Embajada de Brasil A steady stream of musicians and actors draw crowds to the Brazilian cultural center's large and comfortable theater. *Tel: 021 248 4156, Corner of Eligio Ayala and Perú, on Facebook, Mon-Thu 8:30am-6pm, Fri 8:30am-2pm*

Teatro Municipal Ignacio A. Pane Asunción's beautifully restored Municipal Theater offers the public frequent and affordable musical acts, plays, and occasional ballets. Opened in 1889, the theater was shut down in 1995 due to severe deterioration. Four years of restoration work by the Agencia de Cooperación Española, and the Escuela Taller de Asunción brought the theater back to life with beautiful wood floors, original mosaics, and exposed brick walls. The building's bar has a backdrop of a large tiled sheet of marble that is, fittingly, very theatrical. *Tel: 021 448 820, Presidente Franco, between Chile and Alberdi, box office opens at 4:30pm*

Asunción

Going to the Movies

Though Asunción's movie theater offerings are nothing special (mostly mega-blockbusters and horror movies), going to the movies is a cheap way to get a couple hours of air-conditioned relief from the intense heat. Matinee prices are Gs.10,000, weekday tickets are Gs. 20,000, all movies on Wednesdays are half price and weekend tickets (Fri-Sun) are Gs.25,000. There are movie theaters in Shopping Villa Morra (*Tel: 021 610 032, www.villamorra.com.py*), Shopping del Sol (*Tel: 021 611 780, www.shoppingdelsol.com.py/cine.php*) and HiperSeis (*Tel: 021 613 390, www.cinecenter.com.py.*)

SPORTS & EXPLORING ASUNCIÓN'S NATURAL SIDE

Chaco'i

Located across the Bay of Asunción at the southernmost tip of the Paraguayan Chaco, Chaco'i is a small community in a prime bird watching location. The Bay of Asunción is considered an Important Birding Area and is a stopover point for migrating birds. Walking through the community, you will see several large brick towers – these are from old brick factories which produced most of the bricks used in Asunción's buildings during the López era. Guyra Paraguay organizes day trips for bird watching in Chaco'i (see Guided Tours, p65). If you feel like exploring Chaco'i on your own, small covered boats leave from the docks at Playa Montevideo (at the end of Calle Montevideo downtown) every twenty minutes. The fee is Gs. 3,000 each way. Upon arriving at the docks there is a small path to the right that heads upstream – walk down the path or arrange with someone at the dock to take you in a rowboat (negotiate the price first). If you want to stop for lunch, try the humble but tasty *comedor* run by Tía Guille located on the right-hand corner four blocks from the port on the main road (past the soccer field and Ña Vivi's shop). Large portions of typical Paraguayan food cost between Gs. 7,000 to 10,000, and there are also *empanadas*. The last boat back leaves around 5:30pm but it is best to double check times at the docks.

Jardín Botánico

Spread over 670 hectares Asunción's botanical gardens make for a great break from the city's busy streets. Families fill the grounds on Saturday and Sunday, watching pick-up soccer matches, walking along the gardens' tree lined paths and sipping *tereré* in the shade. Asunción's largest park, this is one of the only places in the city that allows camping. The park was originally President Carlos Antonio López's summer home. There is a small zoo and two museums, one dedicated to natural history and Paraguay's history. The natural history museum, known as Casa Baja, contains over 36,000 preserved specimens of Paraguay's flora and fauna. The *Asociación Etnobotánica Paraguaya* (Paraguayan Ethnobotánical Association, *www.etnobotanica.org.py*) has a garden within the botanical gardens where visitors can view the wide variety of medicinal plants that Paraguayans use on a daily basis (especially when preparing *tereré* and *mate*). Over 300 species are featured in the garden, approximately 70 percent of which are native to Paraguay. The medicinal garden can be visited Mon-Fri 8am-12pm but it is best to make reservations by calling the Botanical Garden's main line. *Tel: at 021 290 269, 021 291 255, Avenida Artigas and Prime Presidente, www.mca.gov.py/zoo.htm, from downtown the Linea 44 Artigas can be caught along Olivia/Cerro Corá and pass by the park entrance, daily 7am-5pm, Gs. 2,000, camping Gs. 11,500 per person*

Ykua Bolaños Fire

On Sunday August 1st, 2004 the large Ykuá Bolaños supermarket burned to the ground in what was one of Paraguay's worst modern day tragedies. Around 400 people died in the fire and 500 were injured. Eye witnesses allege the owner of the supermarket (which included a food court and play area) ordered all exits to be locked in order to prevent theft as people ran from the fire. Those deemed responsible were put on trial but the suspiciously short sentences (five years) they received in 2006 provoked massive protests from victim support groups and resulted in a series of appeals and retrials. In 2008 the owners of Ykuá Bolaños were sentenced to ten and twelve years in prison, a ruling which is still considered far too lenient by many.

Parque Ñu Guazú

Sitting on sixty-seven hectares of land on the border between Asunción and Luque, Ñu Guazu ("large field" in Guaraní) is where *Asuncenos* come to get fresh air and exercise. There is a 5.2 kilometer walking path and 1.2 kilometer bike path alongside a small lake, a lily pond, snack shops, play areas for children, small gardens, and patches of eucalyptus trees. Across from the main entrance you will see the Monumento a las Residentas, a large white sculpture of a woman and child dedicated to the female fighters of the Triple Alliance. Ñu Guazú can be crowded on the weekends. Be sure to bring a hat on sunny days as large sections of the track are not shaded. *Avenida Silvio Petrossi, just past the intersection of Aviadores del Chaco and Madame Lynch on your way to the airport. By bus take Linea 28 or 30A (signed "X España"), Summer 5am-9pm, winter 5am-8pm*

Lambaré: Cerro Lambaré

This 136-meter high peak offers a great view of Asunción, Lambaré, and across the river to Argentina. A paved switch-backed road makes its way about eight kilometers to the look-out point at the top of the hill which is topped with a large monument featuring several figures of Paraguay's history. This is a popular spot for families and couples to come drink *mate* and *tereré* together – however it's best to descend before sunset, as after dark, Cerro Lambaré is a popular rendezvous point for the area's couples. *Corner of Juan Domingo Perón and Tomás Pereira, The Linea 23 Zeballos Cue can be caught on Azara, General Díaz or Calle Colón and heads all the way to the turn off to Cerro Lambaré. Linea 41-1 can be caught on Eligio Ayala, Presidente Franco or Calle Colón as well. There is a sign marking the entrance to the right (before the Mormon Church to the left) on Tomás Pereira. From there is it about a half a kilometer walk to the foot of the hill*

Mariano Roque Alonzo: Puente Remanso Fish Shacks

Though a little ramshackle, the riverside restaurants under Puente Remanso are some of the best places to eat freshly caught fish. Relax under the shade and eat breaded and fried fish fillet (*milanesa*) or a fish, tomato, and onion casserole known as "*chupín.*" There are often musicians playing Paraguayan polkas and *guaranias* for tips, and you can watch the fishermen reel in their catch. Next door fish mongers sell fresh fish out of large Styrofoam coolers, often rushing up to potential customers waving enormous fish by the gills. It is a humorous spectacle worth watching. *On the Trans Chaco highway take the last right before crossing over Puente Remanso and then your second left down towards the river (this is about a seven block walk). By Bus: take anything heading down the Trans Chaco such as the Villa Hayes bus. Gs. 10,000-30,000*

Watching a Soccer Game

Asunción's three main soccer stadiums are Estadio Defensores del Chaco and the stadiums for the two most important local soccer clubs – Club Olimpia and Club Cerro Porteño. Tickets can be purchased at each stadium's box office while tickets for national games (such as World Cup qualifiers) can be purchased at Sanri (*Tel: 021 220 940, corner of Mariscal Estigarribia and Brasil*). Tickets for sold out games can easily be purchase through scalpers. Paraguayans rarely buy their tickets ahead of time, therefore scalpers keep quite busy. Since scalping is technically illegal, they will be calling out "*Compro entradas!*" (I'm buying tickets!). You can offset the elevated cost of scalped tickets by buying them just minutes after the game has already started – by then the demand has dropped and so has the asking price.

Cheering on the National Team

The Paraguayan national team is nicknamed "*la Albirroja*" (red and white). During national games the stadium is packed to the brim with energetic fans covered head to toe in red and white cheering for the Albirroja at the top of their lungs. The most popular of the chants, "*Dale dale albirrooooo*," is sung, inexplicably, to the chorus of the 80's pop hit "*Karma Chameleon*" by Culture Club. It is surprisingly catchy!

Estadio Defensores del Chaco The largest and most important stadium in the country, Defensores del Chaco has a capacity of 36,000. It is used for World Cup qualifiers and international tournaments such as the Copa Libertadores. *Corner of Avenida Martinez and Juan Díaz de Solis*

Estadio Olimpia Home to Club Olimpia, this is the easiest stadium to get to as it is on Mariscal López. Club Olimpia has won the Copa Libertadores tournament three times, earning it the nickname "El Rey de Copas" (The King of Cups). Large concerts are often held here as well. *Tel: 021 200 680, Corner of Avenida Mariscal López and Pitiantuta, www.olimpia.com.py*

Gancheros

Throughout the city you will see people rummaging through trash bags placing articles in large wheeled carts (sometimes horse drawn). These people are known as "*gancheros*," and they make their living by collecting recyclables to sell to Asunción's dumps. The first round of collection occurs on the streets where people go through garbage bags and bins collecting metal, cardboard, glass, and plastic. The second round of collection occurs at the dump where all the city's trash is once again picked through by another set of "*gancheros*." Here, smaller items such as paper and plastic bags are also collected. The name comes from "*gancho*," or hook, which is used to pick through the trash.

The majority of *gancheros* sell all their gathered materials to Cateura, Asunción's main dump, which then recycles the materials. The idea of people spending their days digging through trash is not a cheerful one. Though unappealing, this setup does create a steady stream of income for Asunción's marginalized communities. A good day's work can bring in about Gs. 50,000 (approximately US$11), but the daily average hovers more around Gs. 40,000. Attempts at reforming the way recycling is collected in Asunción have been met with protests from the *gancheros*, whose income depends on this informal system. If you want to help out, one thing you can do is pre-sort recyclables before throwing trash out, thus facilitating their collection.

Estadio General Pablo Rojas The stadium for Club Cerro Porteño is located in Asunción's Barrio Obrero. *Corner of Acuña Figueroa and Parapití, www.clubcerro.com*

SHOPPING

Handicrafts

La Recova This building, on the edge of downtown near the port, houses a series of handicraft stores. All types of Paraguayan handicrafts are available, from blankets to thermoses and leather bags. The quality of goods is high. La Recova offers some advantages over the street side stands of Calle Palma, the main one being that you don't have to do your shopping in the sun. El Porteño is a good option for colorful leather bags. *Calle Colón, between Palma and Presidente Franco*

Plaza de la Libertad Artesanía Stands The series of handicraft stands in the Plaza de la Libertad (one of the four plazas that make up the Plaza de los Héroes) specialize mainly in *ñanduti* designs and *ao po'i* clothing and tablecloths. Female backpackers low on space and money should check out the colorful selection of *ñanduti* earrings and floral *dechados* which look great sewn onto a shirt or jeans pocket. *Corner of Estrella and Chile*

Overall Artesanías This store has a nice selection of Paraguayan *artesanías* including pottery by Itá artist Rosa Brítez, hard-to-find appliqué vignettes from Santa María de Fe, and tote bags with drawings by indigenous artist Ogwa (see The Ishir, p318). *Tel: 021 448 657, Mariscal Estigarribia, almost Caballero across the street from Hotel Chaco as well as a store in Shopping del Sol, Mon-Fri 8am-6pm, Sat 8am-12:30pm (8am-6pm in Shopping del Sol)*

Cecilia Fadul Cecilia Fadul is the designer most responsible for making *ao po'i* fashionable among Asunción's elite. Clothes are high-end with great attention to detail. A little out of the way and pricey but worth the splurge if you are looking for beautiful, well tailored pieces with intricate *ao po'i* work. *Tel: 021 607 215, 021 600 419, Corner of Emilio Nudelman and Quesada, Mon-Fri 9am-7:30pm, Sat 9am-1pm*

Pombero Named after the cigar smoking, *caña* (firewater) swigging Paraguayan *mito* or myth (see Meet the Mitos, p44), Pombero is known for its young and modern take on *ao po'i* clothing. Dress shirts for men are pretty standard, but the women's line has

---

La Expo

The enormous fair's full name says it all: *"Expo-feria Internacional de Ganadería, Industria, Agricultura, Comercio, y Servicios."* That would be the "International Cattle Farming, Industry, Agriculture, Commerce and Services Fair." The name just about covers it – you can see anything and everything at La Expo. The first Expo took place in 1975 and was held sporadically until 1988, after which point it has been held yearly. Over the course of two weeks in July, droves of people descend upon the La Rural fairgrounds to see local and international companies showcase their wares and services and partake in several Expo related activities. There is something for everyone: animal showcases, food and games, business lectures, a Miss Expo Pageant, horseback riding competitions and, this being Paraguay, there is even an official celebration of mass.

La Rural is located at kilometer 14 of the Trans Chaco highway in Mariano Roque Alonzo, about twenty minutes by car and forty minutes by bus from the center of Asunción. Buses running down Avenida Artigas are your best bet, and any passing by La Rural should have an *"EXPO"* sign on display. For a calendar of events and more information about La Expo check out the official website: www.expo.org.py.

Asunción

a wider range of styles and sizes (with better tailoring) than what street stands sell. Be sure to ask when they are having their discount sales. *Tel: 021 440 205, www.pombero.com, Estrella 438, almost at Alberdi, daily 8am-7:30pm, Shopping Mariscal López, daily 8am-9pm*

Instituto Paraguayo de Artesanía (IPA) Tent A great option if you don't feel like heading downtown, you can get a little of everything from the stands under the IPA tent. Wood and leatherwork is nice as are *ñanduti* offerings (including cute animal designs still on their wooden frames). ENSY's homemade jams and liqueurs in bamboo cases etched with scenes from the Paraguayan countryside are particularly unique. *Corner of Quesada and Malutín*

Museo Guido Boggiani This museum in San Lorenzo is a great place to buy authentic indigenous crafts (see Museo Arqueológico y Etnográfico Guido Boggiani, p126).

Arana e Hijos Those looking for an extra special *guampa* or *bombilla* will be pleased with the high-end silver offerings of Arana e Hijos. *Tel: 021 662 715, Avenida Mariscal López 3873, almost at O'Higgins (just past Shopping Villa Morra), www.arana.com.py, Mon-Fri 8am-5:45pm, Sat 8am-12pm*

Luque Those looking to buy a serious amount of silver filigree jewelry should head to Luque's main drag, lined with jewelry stores and workshops. The majority are located along General Aquino between the town's two plazas and the church. Though the shops offer a wide variety, almost everything is also available in Asunción's silver stores and *artesanía* stands. Most go to Luque to save on prices, though it isn't worth the travel if you're only buying one or two things. *By bus: Linea 28 (ask to be let off at "la iglesia" and work your way back down the street). By car head out to towards the airport on Aviadores del Chaco (past Ñu Guazú) and take a right just before the old Conmebol building with the soccer ball fountain in front. Take another right (you'll see the snazzy new Conmebol center to left), and at the light take a left. You'll pass the large Los Jardines supermarket to your right before hitting the city center.*

Camping Supplies

Department stores Unicentro and Nueva Americana have decent camping sections with an emphasis on fishing and hunting. Both stores have a better selection in their main branches downtown than in their residential branches.

Unicentro *Tel: 021 445 309/10, Palma and 15 de Agosto and Shopping del Sol, www.unicentro.com.py, Mon-Fri 8:30am-7pm, Sat 8:30am-1pm, Sun 11am-9pm (Shopping del Sol only)*

Nueva Americana *Tel: 021 492 021, Corner of Mariscal. Estigarribia and Independencia Nacional and Shopping Mariscal López, www.nuevaamericana.com.py, Mon-Fri 9am-7pm, Sat-Sun 8:30am-3pm (extended hours at Shopping Mariscal López)*

Camping 44 Camping and hunting supplies. *Tel: 021 297 240/1, Avenida Artigas 2061, www.camping44.com.py*

Electronics

It is not necessary to take a trip to Ciudad del Este in order to take advantage of Paraguay's cheap electronics. In fact, unless you plan to buy several expensive items, it makes more sense to stay in Asunción.

Galería Central Clean and well lit, Galería Central is a good place for cell phones, laptops and digital cameras. The crowd is a mix of Paraguayans and foreigners. Often times, vendors will give you a discount if you don't require an official receipt. Galería Estrella (directly behind Galería Central on Estrella) is another good option. *Palma, between 15 de Agosto and Juan O'leary*

Southern Paraguay
Along Rt 1 with side trips on Rt 4 & Rt 6

Route 1 offers tourists a taste of everything from traditional towns and remote nature to the remnants of Paraguay's rich history. Route 1 cuts south and slightly east across the southern part of eastern Paraguay connecting Asunción to Encarnación. Along the way it passes the satellite cities of Fernando de la Mora and Ñemby before heading further afield to the town of Itá, known for its ceramic artisans.

Next up is Yaguarón, home of the country's most important and impressive Franciscan church. At the town of Paraguarí there is a road connecting to Route 2 past the historic town of Piribebuy (p219). Paraguarí is also the starting point of a newly paved road to Villarica. Along the way this road passes through the town of Sapucai, home to Paraguay's historic steam train workshop. During Paraguay's heyday in the early 1800's a group of engineers and craftsmen were brought over from England to set up a repair shop for the newly created steam train line. The workshop and its many industrial era machines are still standing, including a handful of train cars, in Sapucai. Carapeguá is the turn off point for Parque Nacional Ybycuí. One of the easiest national parks to visit from Asunción, Parque Nacional Ybycuí is popular with Paraguayans and tourists alike. The nearby Salto Cristal is a draw for the more adventurous. Hidden amongst a maze of sugar cane fields in La Colmena the impressive waterfall is harder to reach but certainly worth the trip. Carapeguá is also the main access point for the large and remote Lago Ypoa and surrounding wetlands. Nature lovers will especially enjoy visiting this area as birdlife and aquatic animals abound.

Past Carapeguá the sporadic peaks of the department of Paraguarí give way to the rolling hills that characterize the Misiones department. First up is Villa Florida, the popular riverside town known for its sandy shores and fishing. Next is San Juan, capital of Misiones. The department gets its name from the Jesuit missions which once thrived in this area. The towns of San Ignacio, Santa María, Santiago and Santa Rosa still have structures from the Jesuit's utopian experiment. The large churches were left to decay and were eventually replaced mid-century with modern structures. However, many of the mission's secondary buildings are still in use today. Most tourists overlook these Jesuit towns in favor of the larger and more impressive ruins of the Itapúa province. Yet combining a visit to smaller Jesuit towns with ruins provides a glimpse of what the reductions were like and how they functioned. In addition to the missions, the region is home to new religious traditions as well. The small community of Tañarandy, near San Ignacio, is the site of a dynamic and artistic procession that takes place on Holy Friday of Easter week.

In Santiago, Route 1 connects with Route 4 which leads often overlooked city of Pilar. Cut off from the rest of Paraguay until very recently, this town developed its own identity more akin to that of towns across the border in Argentina. Pilar is the capital of the department of Ñeembucú which is almost entirely made up of wetlands. Further along Route 1 is the turn off to Ayolas, another popular fishing destination and home to Paraguay's second largest hydroelectric dam, Yacyretá, little sister to Ciudad del Este's Itaipú.

Encarnación, capital of the department of Itapúa, is at the end of Route 1. Encarnación is a popular base for people wishing to see the Jesuit ruins. Trinidad, the most popular set of ruins, is north of Encarnación along Route 6 (which leads to Ciudad del Este). Nearby are the ruins of Jesús as well as prosperous agricultural colonies known as the Colonias Unidas. San Cosme y Damián, the third set of ruins, is located west of Encarnación in a town of the same name. Encarnación is not just known for its proximity to the missions though. During the months of February and March the city is flooded with tourists who come to enjoy the glittering spectacle of the *carnavales Encarnacenas*. From Encarnación you can easily cross over to the Argentine border city of Posadas. Encarnación is also a good alternative point of departure for those who wish to visit Iguazú falls but would rather not travel through the heavily transited triple border (known as "*la triple frontera*") between Ciudad del Este, Foz do Iguaçu and Puerto Iguazú.

TRAVELING ALONG ROUTE 1

Travelers will find Route 1 is cheaper, calmer and more picturesque than Route 2. Tourist attractions are evenly spread out, making it a good route to travel on over the course of several days. Itá and Yaguarón are easily accessible by bus and make for quick day trips from Asunción. Day trips to Ybycuí are also doable but can be difficult if traveling by public transportation. The large but remote Salto Cristal (near La Colmena) and the wetlands surrounding Lago Ypoa are very difficult to access without private transport. Tourists will find there is very little infrastructure – restaurants and hotels – along Route 1 until one reaches the department of Missions. From here towns are larger and there is more action. These areas have long been popular with tourists, therefore there is more infrastructure. Misiones, about half way to Encarnación is a good stopping point – either for an afternoon or, if one wants to visit several of the area's Jesuit towns, one or two days. Those who would prefer to head straight to Encarnación can expect the trip to take about five hours by car and six by bus.

> **Recommended bus companies:** La Encarnacena, Nuestra Señora de Asunción. Rysa, and Ciudad de Pilar (turns off in San Ignacio towards Pilar)

> **Major bus stops along Route 1:** Asunción, San Lorenzo, Carapeguá, Villa Florida, San Juan, San Ignacio, Coronel Bogado, Encarnación

Getting to Routes 1 & 2 by Car

Technically both Route 1 and Route 2 begin in San Lorenzo. From Asunción you can get to San Lorenzo via either Mariscal López or Eusebio Ayala/Mariscal Estigarribia (if starting off in the Shopping del Sol area head down España and take a right on Santa Teresa which will connect with Mariscal López). Once in San Lorenzo take a left on to Mariscal Estigarribia (yes, there are two streets named Mariscal Estigarribia in San Lorenzo). Be careful while driving as this heavily transited road cuts through San Lorenzo's main market – many stands spill out onto the street, cars park illegally blocking traffic, and pedestrians cross at will. Once past the market, you will see a highway signs indicating that Route 2 is straight ahead and the turn off to Route 1 is to the right.

Jesuit Towns & Ruins

Paraguay's Jesuit circuit is consists of two types of locations: the Jesuit ruins and Jesuit towns. While most gravitate towards the more impressive ruins, visiting the smaller Jesuit towns is also highly recommended – each has something distinct to offer in helping visitors gain a better appreciation of the Jesuit missions. The ruins are typified by the large red stone remains of the mission churches, photos of which fill tourism pamphlets. These ruins, with their stone sculptures and massive structures provide visitors with a sense of the scale and grandeur of the missions. However, aside from sporadic guided tours, there is very little effort to bring the ruins to life for the visitor. One is left to imagine what the mission might have looked like. Here is where the still-thriving Jesuit towns come in to play. In Jesuit towns, surviving structures such as indigenous dwellings and schools are still in use and woven into the everyday lives of the townspeople. The main churches are gone but their decorative remnants can be found in each town's Jesuit museum and newly constructed churches. Looking at the evocative sculptures and paintings, one is able to better picture the beauty of the Jesuit missions. Combining a trip to the ruins with a stop in one of the Jesuit towns will give you a good sense of Jesuit art, architecture and the legacy of the missions in Paraguay.

What follows is a brief description of the Jesuit towns in order of distance from Asunción.

San Ignacio, km 226 This large town, has several well-preserved buildings which now house the town library, a human rights agency, and the town's two museums (one Jesuit, the other about the Chaco War). The Jesuit museum includes a beautiful collection of large scale sculptures.

Santa María de Fe, km 237 A small quaint town with a beautiful main plaza, Santa María de Fe was once the most important artist workshop of the Jesuit towns. The town museum has an impressive collection of sculptures – the best of all Jesuit towns, hands down.

Santa Rosa, km 250 Santa Rosa offers visitors a true gem – the small Loreto chapel has some of the only remaining frescoes in all of Paraguay's Jesuit missions. Although in need of restoration, seeing the frescoes alongside the museum's sculptures gives a great idea of the decorative beauty in Jesuit buildings. In addition, the town also has a large red stone bell tower from the original mission.

Santiago, km 279 Santiago's museum is set next to the small remains of the original church's adobe walls. The museum has several sculptures but the most interesting display showcases unique tableaus painted onto wooden tablets.

San Cosme and Damián, km 343 San Cosme y Damián has the distinction of being the only Jesuit town where the original church is still in use. The two story building includes some rooms with painted walls and ceilings as well as an extensive attic from which the river beyond can be glimpsed. San Cosme is also home to a new observatory, built in honor of the mission's heritage as one of the most important astronomy centers of South America during the Jesuit era.

The South

Trinidad, km 400 Boasting the largest set of remaining structures from the original mission Trinidad is the most visited of all the Jesuit missions. Highly evocative and intricate designs are carved into the stone ruins of the church. Visitors can also experience the ruins in a different light, literally, with the new Sound and Light show set up by the Ministry of Tourism. Trinidad is a UNESCO World Heritage Site, and rightly so.

Jesús de Tavarangue, km 410 Just down the road from Trinidad, the Jesús de Tavarangue mission is perhaps the most scenic of all the ruins. The imposing remains of the original church include all four high walls with the remains of several columns running through the middle of the interior, now a grassy courtyard, as well as a large bell tower. Like its sister mission Trinidad, Jesús is a UNESCO World Heritage Site.

More Information

The Cámara Paraguaya de Turismo de las Misiones Jesuíticas (Paraguayan Chamber of Tourism of the Jesuit Missions) is a good source for current events along the *Ruta Jesuítica* (Jesuit Route). *Tel: 021 210 550 x 230, Olga Fischer 0985 701 642, www.rutajesuitica.com.py and on Facebook*

Departamento Central

ITÁ

The town of Itá is known for its ceramic production, a tradition that dates back to the colonial era when members of the Franciscan mission used to make ceramic pots. Today the town is best known as the home of Rosa Brítez, famed local ceramist, as well as for the production of ceramic chickens.

"Itá" means stone in Guaraní.

Rosa Brítez's Workshop

A ceramist for over sixty years, Rosa Brítez is one of Paraguay's most renowned artists. This humble but energetic artist is known for her chubby ceramic figures, platters and water jugs with faces of suns and moons, and cheeky Kama Sutra inspired figures, all baked to a deep black hue. Her talent gained her international fame with a long list of clientele that includes the King of Spain and Michael Jackson. Despite her fame Señora Brítez has found herself in dire straits as of late due to deteriorating health and mounting medical bills. Purchasing an authentic Rosa Brítez piece shows your support for Paraguayan handicrafts and artisans. *Tel: 0971 743 526, her home and workshop are on the right-hand side of the entrance to town and hard to miss as they are marked by an enormous sign with her face on it, her workshop and home are one and the same, if the workshop is closed simply ring the doorbell.*

El Centro Artesanal de las Pequeñas Industrias de la Ciudad de Itá (CAPICI)

All manner of handicrafts made by local artisans are on display and available for purchase in this small brick building. Not surprisingly the main emphasis is on ceramics. *Corner of Cerro Corá and Route 1, building is on the right-hand side if coming from Asunción. Mon-Fri 7am-5pm, Sat 7am-12pm*

Lucky Chickens
Itá's most popular items are ceramic chickens with curly clay feathers all over their bodies. Legend has it these *gallinitas de la suerte* bring good luck to their owners.

Parque de la Laguna
One of the most interesting things about Itá (aside from the Kama Sutra ceramics) is the Parque de la Laguna, a four hectare park with a large lagoon in the middle. There are walk ways, a gazebo, and a family of *yacarés* (caiman) that roam freely, swimming in the water, and sunning themselves on the banks. Not to worry though, the local firemen are in charge of chasing them back into the lagoon if they wander too far from the park, something that only tends to happen when it's raining._Presidente Franco and Curupayty – if coming from the CAPICI continue one block along Route 1 (away from Asunción), take a right on Curupayty and the park will be on your left*

Departamento Paraguarí

YAGUARÓN

Iglesia San Buenaventura
If you see just one church in Paraguay (and there many) it should be the Iglesia de San Buenaventura, better known as the Iglesia de Yaguarón. Due to its size and ornate decorations, the church of Yaguarón is one of Paraguay's most important churches. It is impressive on several levels. The building itself is quite large at seventy meters in length supported by thirty-meter high columns of solid *lapacho* wood and two-meter thick adobe walls. The interior is decked out with paintings and wood carvings, decorated with richly hued vegetable dyes of reds, greens and blues, and embellished with gold-leaf. Like artwork in most of the country's Franciscan and Jesuit missions, Yaguaron's sculptures and paintings were done by the mission's indigenous, under the supervision of European artists. In this case Portuguese sculptor José de Souza Cavadas was responsible for the church's beauty.

In 2001 Sr. Antolín Alemán, saved the church from a fire that started when a lightning bolt caused a short circuit which made a fluorescent bulb near the choir balcony catch fire.

The church is dominated by the large resplendent altar, carved out of *pereteby* wood. At the very top is a representation of God holding the world (in the form of a large golden orb) in his hand. Above his head is a triangle representing the Holy Trinity. He is flanked on both sides by archangels Gabriel and Rafael. On both sides of the archangels, stand virgin martyrs with golden palms in their hands which represent peace and justice. Under God is the Holy Spirit in the form of a large dove. To the lower left is St. Buenaventura, the patron saint of Yaguarón and to the lower right is the archangel Michael with a devil under his foot. The Virgin Mary stands at the foot of the stairs to heaven – each stair represents one of the sacraments necessary in order to gain entrance to heaven. St Peter awaits at the top of the stairs accompanied by two angels. The tabernacle, which holds the Eucharist, is decorated with the Lamb of God and surrounded by cherubs.

Although the altar is clearly the most commanding part of the church, the painted ceiling should not be overlooked. Brightly colored panels are decorated with portraits, each slightly different. The beautifully carved pulpit and confessional boxes are also quite lovely. Through the side door next to the altar you can reach a back room with articles that have not yet been restored but are still quite vivid (again, it is worth looking upwards at the painted ceiling).

Tel: 0533 32 229, Located on the corner where Route 1 curves to the right in the center of Yaguarón (only buses heading to Asunción go down this road), daily 6am-11am, 1pm-5pm. Sr. Antolín Alemán who is happy to give tours for a donation to the church. Contact him if the church is closed at 0533 232 321 (his neighbor's land line) or 0982 267 978. He lives at 568 Carmelo Peralta and Mscl Estigarribia (the street the back of the church faces). Tours are also available through COTUR (see Pyporé, p199)

Museo Gaspar Rodriguez de Francia

Childhood home of Paraguay's first president, Dr. Francia, this museum houses many of his personal belongings. There are also paintings of the "Karaí Guazu," as he was known, as well as other objects from the colonial era. The colonial house itself has been recently restored, repairing damages incurred when a tree fell on it during a rainstorm in 2010. *Tel: 0981 912 920 or 0533 232 343, Calle Pirayú 325, Tues-Sun 7am-12pm, Doña Rosa (also known as Ña Chocha) is the museum curator and can open the museum up in the afternoons by request. She lives down the street (towards the main road) at number 502 (gate next to corner house). If she is not around you can also try Antonia, the museum's secretary in her home across the street from the side of the church on Carmelo Peralta*

PARAGUARÍ

Continuing along Route 1 is the town of Paraguarí, capital of the department of the same name. Paraguarí is the turn off for several interesting sites. To the right is the Ruta General Rogelio Benitez which heads north past the historic town of Piribebuy and then connects with Route 2 (see Piribebuy, p219). Next up on the right is the turn off that leads east to Villarica past the town of Sapucai, home to the old steam train workshop. The well-known Frutería Paraguarí, just before the entrance to town, is a good pit stop, whether you are headed down either turn off or continuing south along Route 1.

Monte Aramí

Located 200 meters up on a hill this is a popular destination for religious retreats and offers a great view of the surrounding areas. There are basic dorms for large groups, seven small private rooms and the option to camp. There is no food service – bring your own or head out to the Frutería Paraguarí across the main road. The religious nature of the complex means bringing in liquor is not advised. *Tel: 0531 432 117, 0981 439 444, km 62, 50 meters after Frutería Paraguarí and then 700 meters down a dirt and cobblestone road to the left-hand side (if coming from Asunción), those walking in should note the last 50 meters or so are quite steep, Bungalows Gs. 100,000-120,000, camping Gs. 25,000 per person. Two pools, soccer court, bungalows have A/C.*

Museo Histórico de Artillería

Though just about every museum has a handful of weapons on display, those with a particular interest in military history will find this Army Artillery headquarters' large collection well worth visiting. The old stables have been repurposed to showcase weaponry from every period of Paraguay's history. The cannon collection includes colonial era cannons that were used to surround the Spanish Governor's home before Paraguay declared independence. A cannon made out of bronze church bells from the church of Caacupé can also be seen here. Fittingly, the artillery's chapel has a sculpture of Santa Barbara, patron saint of artillery weapons, complete with a mini-cannon at her feet. *Tel: 0531 32203, just outside town on the road to Piribebuy, permission to visit the museum must be requested at the guard post, Mon-Fri 7am-11am, 2pm-5pm*

Food

Frutería Paraguarí This popular eatery two kilometers before the center of town started off as a small fruit stand and has now expanded into a multi-functional pit-stop. The large restaurant has a decent buffet, mouth watering desserts and fruit salad. Their signature dish, a refreshing fruit salad with papaya, pear, and pineapple can be purchased to-go, as can their fresh juices. *Empanadas, chipa* and sandwiches are also available for purchase. The well-stocked general store next door has a good variety of fruits as well as useful items like thermoses and hats. The other major attraction of the Frutería Paraguarí are the clean bathrooms – the establishment has won the Tourism Ministry's "Cleanest Bathrooms on the Road" prize multiple times. *Tel: 0531 432 406, km 61.5 about two km before the entrance to town (from Asunción). Daily from 6am-12am, Gs. 4,000-20,000*

Chipería El Gordo Located on both sides of Route 1, the Chipería El Gordo stand sells the softest, cheesiest *chipa* in Paraguay. Using the same recipe as their home base in Coronel Bogado (further down Route 1 towards Encarnación) El Gordo's *chipas* are oval shaped and stamped *"El Gordo,"* like a chipa and gold ingot. *Km 61.5 just before the Frutería Paraguarí. Gs 1,000-5,000*

SAPUCAI

Sapucai is intrinsically linked to the history of the steam train – one of the first in Latin America. The name *"sapucai"* means "shout" in Guaraní, a reference to the train's loud whistle. In the 1880's the town became home to the steam train workshop where maintenance was performed on all the trains. The workshop still remains and is a train lover's dream come true. The road to Sapucai is pleasant, winding past the tree covered hills of Paraguarí and through the picturesque town of Escobar. Despite the draw of the train workshop there are no facilities such as restaurants or hotels in Sapucai. However this is sure to change given the recent completion of the paved highway which cuts through the middle of town. Local tour guide Claudio Baez offers a tour of the train station, Villa Inglesa, cemetery and Tapé Bolí for Gs. 70,000 per group with advance notice. *Tel: 0982 847 060*

Train Stations of Yesteryear
The newly constructed road linking Paraguarí to Villarica follows Paraguay's historic train route. Alongside the road you can catch a glimpse of the old stations, recognizable by their yellow and brown paint, and station names written in large white letters on wooden signs. Some stations are in better shape than others but for the most part they have been left to the elements and many of the towns themselves disappeared once the train went out of vogue.

"Taller de Trenes" Train Workshop & Ferrocarril Presidente Carlos Antonio López Museum
From the road the only indication that this tin roofed hangar holds any special value are the rusted train parts outside. But once you step inside the old train workshop it

The South

is clear that this is a historic place. Train cars line the tracks on the right-hand side and to the left are a series of work stations. Like the trains it serviced, the entire workshop is steam-powered. To the left, there are three enormous boilers which drive a giant flywheel. This, in turn, spins an axel that runs the length of the entire building powering all the machines in the workshop. Train enthusiasts and the mechanically inclined will be enthralled by this industrial era gem. The icing on the cake is that everything still functions – if you have the luxury of time it is worth timing your visit to coincide with one of the sporadic special occasions during which the whole thing is set in motion (try the museum itself or the Municipal office for specific dates).

Next door is the small Ferrocarril Presidente Carlos Antonio López Museum which houses objects from the train's history including old schematics used as reference by train technicians until the trains stopped running in the 1990's. Across the way is the *"Villa Inglesa"* where the European train mechanics who serviced the trains lived. These foreigners enjoyed many luxuries such as running water, which, at the time, were unheard of in the countryside. Unfortunately all have fallen into disrepair. *Tel: 0539 263 218, coming from Paraguarí the workshop is on the right-hand side of the road at the entrance to town. To get to the entrance go past the workshop and make a hairpin turn to the right. Mon-Fri 7am-4pm and weekends upon advanced request to the Municipal office at 0539 263 214 or the main central train station in Asunción at 021 447 848.*

Tape Bolí

Those up for a little adventure can make their way up the hill that overlooks Sapucai. The road up the hill is called "Tapé Bolí" after the Bolivian soldiers (prisoners of war from the Chaco War) that constructed it ("*tapé*" is road in Guaraní). The road starts near the town church. As you head higher up the hill you will pass small houses and farms where people continue to live as if neither the train nor the new highway existed.

The turn off to Sapucai is on Bernardino Caballero to the left right before the Paraguarí Hospital (on the left) past town. You will pass a fancy large "Palacio de Justicia" (Palace of Justice) on your right before the road veers right. Sapucai is thirty kilometers from Paraguarí.

If traveling by bus, Empresa Paraguarí (*Tel: 0531 432 479*) has daily buses that run from Asunción's bus terminal for Gs. 12,000.

CARAPEGUÁ

Carapeguá is the center for Paraguay's utilitarian textile industry. Artisans in neighborhoods and villages surrounding Carapeguá dedicate themselves to weaving brightly colored cotton blankets, hammocks, and tablecloths, often dyeing the colorful thread by hand. Aside from stands at the market there are few points of sale in Carapeguá itself – most people sell their goods to salesmen known as "*macateros*" that then distribute them to stores throughout the country. Carapeguá is well known for its traveling salesmen. As a local joke goes, when Neil Armstrong landed on the moon he encountered a guy from Carapeguá selling hammocks.

At the town of Acahay, approximately thirty kilometers from Carapeguá the road forks. The left-hand side road leads thirty kilometers to the Japanese colony of La Colmena The road on the right-hand side leads past the town of Ybycuí (approximately twenty kilometers) to Parque Nacional Ybycuí (approximately thirty kilometers past Ybycuí).

Carapeguá is one of the main access points for the Ypoa wetlands and the location of the access road to Ybycuí (near Parque Nacional Ybycuí) and La Colmena (near Salto Cristal).

The Wetlands of Ypoa

The wetlands, or "*humedales*" of Ypoa (the "y" is really a "u" sound) extend across the southern tip of the Central department through the department of Paraguarí and into the department of Ñeembucú. The Lago Ypoa National

> Ypoa means "water that gives luck" in Guaraní.

Park covers approximately 100,000 hectares of the wetlands. There are four lakes and lagoons in the region – Lago Ypoa, Laguna Cabral, Laguna Paranamí and Laguna Verá. Lago Ypoa is the largest of the three. The park's flora and fauna are largely aquatic – otters, *yacarés* (caiman) and large capybaras swim amongst islands of floating reeds while *ñandu* (rheas), marsh deer and maned wolves roam on land. The few people who inhabit the park's islands live almost completely off the grid – largely cut off from civilization, they survive by hunting, fishing and small scale farming. Due to its importance as a habitat for aquatic flora and fauna this area was declared a RAMSAR site in 1995.

The Water Ghost

According to Guaraní mythology a large "*pira hũ*" (black fish) created the channels linking the wetland's lagoons. This black fish still guards the waterways and is known as "*ypóra*" (water ghost).

The most popular route of access to the wetlands is the road from Carapeguá to Caapucumi. The twenty-kilometer dirt road passes by rural communities before arriving to the edge of the wetlands. One such community is Beni Loma, where a group of artisans weave woolen horse blankets (to be placed under the saddle) known as "*jergas*," as well as rugs and satchels. The artisans process their wool by hand before dyeing and then weaving it on rustic wooden looms to create geometric floral designs. The entire process is quite labor intensive – a small bag can take eighteen hours to make while a *jerga* can take as long as forty hours. In Caacupumí, there is a small visitor's center with an observation tower next to a school house and camp site. From here one can cross to Mosito Isla, a small island in the wetlands reachable only by canoe.

The wetlands are best visited with a guide. Most of the park is on private property and the roads are nearly impossible to navigate using public transportation (even by car, roads are frequently impassable after rains). DTP (see Guided Tours, p65) and Fundación Tierra Nuestra (both based in Asunción) offer tours of the wetlands that include an overland drive to Caapucumi followed by a canoe ride to Mosito Isla. You can also consult Fundación Oñonivepá in Carapeguá itself to hire a local guide (though most will not have private transportation). *Fundación Tierra Nuestra, Tel: 021 220 332, 021 201 106, corner of Cerro Corá and Mayor Fleitas, www.tierranuestra.org.py, Fundación Oñondivepá, Tel: 0532 212 573, Pedro Juan Caballero 947 (two blocks from the main plaza). To get to Caacupumi take the right-hand turn off to Aguai'y 3.5 kilometers past the center of Carapeguá (coming from Asunción). Ask about road conditions if traveling by car.*

The South

LA COLMENA

Founded in 1936, La Colmena was Paraguay's first Japanese agricultural colony. Many of the ancestors of the original one hundred families still dedicate themselves to growing fruit and cultivating honey in this region. Though the town is mostly populated by descendants of these immigrants they have integrated themselves so fully into Paraguayan culture that it is not uncommon to see elderly Japanese couples sitting outside drinking *tereré* and conversing in Guaraní. Despite their integration, many of their homeland traditions are still kept alive. For example, the cooperative store (located on the main plaza near the Municipal Office) sells Japanese goods including fresh tofu. La Colmena offers visitors two unique experiences in the middle of the Paraguayan countryside – an adventure filled trip to the nearby Salto Cristal and an authentic Japanese meal at Hotel Fujimi. In addition, the town's founding coincides with Paraguayan Independence Day and is celebrated with a large festival that includes a *jineteada* (rodeo) attended by the area's *estancia* workers.

Museo Fotográfico Dr. Hideho Tanaka

Located in what was once the agricultural colony's administrative office this museum contains many photos which portray the history of La Colmena as its founding families adjusted to their new tropical home. *Tel: 0537 223 302, one and a half blocks from the town plaza and Municipal office along the main road into town. It may be opened upon request by Ña Tami or Don Tomo who live next door and run the Farmacia La Colmena.*

Lodging

Hotel Fujimi This family run hotel has basic rooms, but the food is the main attraction. For a fixed price the hotel owner will prepare a delicious spread of authentic Japanese food including noodles, soups, fried fish, and vegetarian sushi. The variety is truly surprising given this town's remote location. Meal requests must be made at least one day in advance. The further in advance you can arrange this the better as it gives the owner time to prepare and gather necessary ingredients. *Tel: 0537 223 238, Corner of 15 de Agosto and Colombia, Double shared bathroom Gs.70,000, Double with private bathroom Gs. 90,000*

Food

Hotel Fujimi *See previous listing for details.*

Bar Analía This small diner serves delicious down home Paraguayan cooking including roasted chicken and thick, bright yellow *tallarín* (spaghetti). A good place to pick up sandwiches (try the chicken *milanesa*) for eating at Salto Cristal. Plus the Cardozo Hermanos bus leaving town runs right past along the main road. *Corner of Dr. Hideho Tanaka and Avenida 14 de Mayo one block from the town roundabout/ plaza, daily 9am-6pm, Gs. 8,000-Gs. 15,000*

Getting There

Take the turn off to La Colmena at Carapeguá (km 84) on Route 1, at Acahay follow the fork in the road to the left. The Cardozo Hermanos bus line leaves from the Asunción terminal approximately hourly starting at 4:30am. The last bus leaves La Colmena at 5:30pm. Gs. 15,000

SALTO CRISTAL

Hidden amongst the dense vegetation through a maze of sugarcane fields, the large Salto Cristal waterfall is difficult to access but definitely worth the challenge. Salto Cristal's waterfall is over a forty-two-meter high terraced stone cliff into a pool over thirty meters in diameter and ten meters deep. Running the perimeter of the pool is a rock ledge – usually submerged just deep enough to create a natural wading pool. The vegetation opens up around the pool's edge where one can sit or sunbathe. Daredevils can swim across the pool and dive off the terraced walls. Swimming at the base of this impressive waterfall feels like you've found your own hidden tropical refuge.

Getting to Salto Cristal is part of the adventure. The trailhead is located about twenty kilometers from La Colmena (see instructions below on getting to the trail head). From here it is about 500 meters to the official entrance, manned by the property's caretaker (Salto Cristal is on private property). About 500 meters past this is a small clearing that serves as a camp site. A short trail to the right, perpendicular to the main trail leads through the campsite to the top of the waterfall. The trail then T's out into the stream about two meters wide which winds through the trees and tall grass before plummeting over the edge only a few meters away.

Continuing past the campsite, the main trail ends in a sheer vertical drop-broken by boulders, large rocks and tree roots; this is the hard part. The descent is about forty meters. Take your time going down. Those not wearing adequate shoes may prefer to go barefoot for better grip. If you're in a large group step to the side when possible and let others pass if you need more time negotiating footholds – this is not a good place to fall. Once at the bottom you will see a small stream, runoff from the waterfall. Take a right and head upstream (consider leaving some sort of marking so you can tell where the trail entrance is). The trail along the stream is quite narrow and you may find it is easier in certain sections to simply walk in the water. As you approach the waterfall, the terrain gets rockier and the stream gets wider. Here you will have to climb over a few large boulders after which the vegetation opens up to reveal the Salto Cristal waterfall in all its glory.

It is best to visit Salto Cristal in the morning, allowing ample time for the trip to the trailhead and hike to the waterfall. Camping at the base of the waterfall is nearly impossible and not recommended. Those who plan to camp at the top of the waterfall should be sure to head back to the campsite before dusk as the way back up is only slightly easier than the trip down.

La Colmena has no dedicated taxis, however, those without a car can inquire at Hotel Fujimi or the Municipal office for a local with a truck willing to provide taxi service to and from Salto Cristal (this usually costs about Gs. 100,000). This may require advanced notice so plan to spend the night in La Colmena and head to Salto Cristal the next morning. If you want to camp at Salto Cristal you can arrange to be picked up at a later date. There is usually a Peace Corp Volunteer (*voluntario de Cuerpo de Paz*) in town who can be contacted if you are having trouble with the language barrier. DTP tour operator (see Guided Tours, p65) offers a tour which includes rappelling down Salto Cristal – this can be done as a standalone tour or in conjunction with other area attractions such as Parque Nacional Ybycuí. *Entry fee: Gs. 10,000-15,000, Camping: Gs.20,000 per person per day, transportation to Salto Cristal: Gs. 150,000 – 200,000. A small clearing at the top of the waterfall is used as a camp ground but there are no facilities – you will need to bring and pack out all supplies, food and trash. A first aid kit is essential and, in case of an emergency, travelers should note only Tigo cell phones will get a (weak) signal at the campsite.*

Getting to the Trailhead

From La Colmena, head east on the newly paved road to Villarica. Continue 5.8 kilometers over the Arroyo Rory Mi stream (there is a bridge and a sign). After the bridge there is a bus stop, followed by a right-hand turn off on to a dirt road. There are sometimes signs for "Isla Alta" or "Salto Cristal" at this turn off. This dirt road has pavement and cobblestone on some of its steeper sections. After approximately 5.8 kilometers there will be a school (signed and "Escuela Dr. Moisés") and an Itaipú sign on left that says "Base Chacra Salto Cristal 3 km" and points straight – disregard the sign and take a left. Continue 1.5 kilometers and take a right. To your left you will see a road leading into sugar cane fields and there are woods to the right. After nearly half-a-kilometer, the road divides in to three. Take the middle road which is a slight left and leads you away from the woods. Continue for 1.4 kilometers and you'll see sugar cane fields on both sides of you. Make a left here. About one kilometer later, follow the road as it curves left (ignoring a faint trail to the right) and at 1.6 kilometers you will cross over an earthen bridge. 1.1 kilometers past the bridge you will reach a yellow sign and follow the road to the right. Keep the woods on your right and sugar cane on your left. Continue 1.25 kilometers until the road ends in a clearing which usually has several large piles of fertilizer. The trailhead to Salto Cristal is to the right. Vehicles with high clearance can continue another 500 meters and park at the caretaker's house.

PARQUE NACIONAL YBYCUÍ

Due to its relative proximity to Asunción, Parque Nacional Ybycuí is one of Paraguay's most popular national parks. The park, created in 1973, is approximately 5,000 hectares in size and known for its waterfalls and abundance of butterflies. The park also has much historical significance as it is the home of "La Rosada," Latin America's first iron foundry.

The recreational area begins approximately three kilometers down a dirt and sand road from the park's entrance. To the left is a nice visitor's center and a trail leading to a *mirador* (lookout point). To the right is the camp ground. Flat ground can be hard to come by as the entire area is sloped towards the Salto Mina waterfall which is often erroneously referred to as "Salto Cristal." Past the campground is a trail leading to Salto Guaraní which then backtracks to La Rosada.

> Salto Mina in Parque Nacional Ybycuí is often referred to as Salto Cristal. Do not be fooled! While Salto Mina is nice, it is not nearly as impressive as the real Salto Cristal.

The bathroom facilities include showers, toilets, and ceramic latrines and are in generally nice condition (though not always clean). On the weekends, the park is full of visitors who come to hike the trails, swim at the base of the waterfalls and enjoy the scenery while grilling up some asado and playing volleyball. During the week it is much more tranquil (but the weekends offer more possibilities of hitch hiking the last couple of kilometers not serviced by bus). Campers should be sure to stock up on food (there are a number of small stores in Ybycuí) before heading to the park.

Venturing Further into the Park

Approximately fourteen kilometers past the main recreational area near Salto Mina there is another series of three waterfalls formed by the Arroyo Corrientes creek known as "Mbocaruzú 1," "Mbocaruzú 2," and "Mbocaruzú 3" in the *compañia* of Mbocayá Pucú. These are not accessible by public transportation. Following the road through the park drive about 7.5 kilometers and then turn right for four more kilometers before turning left and continuing for about 2.7 kilometers. The road T's out into the Arroyo Corrientes which forms the waterfalls. From here you can either park your car and continue on foot or ford the river (the water level is usually pretty low) and continue along its path about one kilometer before you reach the first waterfall, Mbokaruzú 1. This waterfall is quite large. The second waterfall, this one smaller with a series of small stepped rocks and a swimming hole, is about one kilometer further downstream. The third waterfall is not easily accessed due to a bifurcation in the Arroyo Corrientes. From Arroyo Corrientes the hike to the first two waterfalls is quite pleasant. Along the way you will pass the occasional person on foot or motorcycle but for the most part it will be just you and the beautiful scenery.

La Rosada

The historic La Rosada iron foundry is located at the entrance to the park just past the end of the paved road. The foundry was the first of its kind in Latin America, created during the rule of Carlos Antonio López when Paraguay was a prosperous and progressive nation. Wood charcoal for the foundry came from the surrounding forest and power was also provided by damning up the Salto Mina. The foundry was destroyed by Brazilian troops during the Triple Alliance war but has been partly reconstructed. The grounds include a nicely curated museum with war artifacts and explanations in both Spanish and English (a rarity). *Daily 8am-4pm*

Getting There

By car, take the turn off from Route 1 at Carapeguá, following signs to Parque Nacional Ybycuí. You will pass through the pretty town of Ybycuí along the way. The pavement ends at the park entrance, thirty kilometers past Ybycuí.

The green Salto Cristal bus travels between Asunción's bus terminal and Ybycuí (*Tel: 0534 226 376*) several times a day. Bus fare is approximately Gs. 15,000. If you are coming from Encarnación you will need to get off at Carapeguá and catch the Salto Cristal bus as it takes the southeast turn off towards Ybycuí (do not be tempted to catch buses headed to La Colmena and Acahay; they will not take you far enough). From Ybycuí there are several buses that head towards the park but most stop about three kilometers away from the main entrance. The walk is nice and hitching a ride is relatively easy on weekends when the park gets lots of visitors. The El Rey David bus and buses headed to Mbokaruzú will sometimes pass by the park entrance but could change their routes depending on the weather – it is always a good idea to reconfirm with the driver. Unfortunately all buses exiting the park leave before 9am so using public transportation only works if you plan to stay the night in the park.

A simpler option is to hire a taxi from Ybycuí. Rates for a one way trip are approximately Gs.60,000. Be sure to specify you want a return trip as well! When pre-arranging for a pickup it is always a good idea to get the taxi driver's contact information just in case.

Lodging

Camping is the only option for those wishing to stay in the park itself. The town of Ybycuí has some simple lodging options and there are one or two options along the road to the park as well. Hotel employees can help arrange for drivers to take you to the park.

Hospedaje Esperanza Your best bet for lodging within the town of Ybycuí itself. Very clean with a kitchen and laundry service as well as a pool in the summer time. The owner Ña Epifania offers meals as well for a very low price. *Tel: 0534 226 320, Bernardino Caballero and Barcelona, Doubles Gs. 40,000 - 50,000 fan, 80,000 A/C, pool, kitchen access, breakfast is not included but can be purchased separately*

Complejo Villa America This large complex has a number of sports facilities including volleyball and soccer courts, swimming pools, as well as options for fishing. Lodging options include bungalows and camping. Staff can help coordinate day-trips to Parque Nacional Ybycuí with local drivers. *Tel: 0534 226 275, 0983 614 065, km 116 (approximately three kilometers before the town of Ybycuí), www.villaamerica.com.py, double Gs. 250,000, camping Gs. 40,000 per person, special packages for New Years and Holy Week (Semana Santa)*

Quindy

The town of Quindy, between Carapeguá and Villa Florida, is best known for soccer ball production. As you enter the town you will see many vendors selling soccer balls along the side of the road.

Departamento Misiones

The defining characteristic of modern-day Misiones is not its Jesuit past but the cattle ranching that occurs on the province's rolling hills. Historically Misiones was always a popular area for ranching – the Jesuit missions engaged in cattle raising and after the Triple Alliance War the provisional government had various settlers from the ranching areas of Uruguay and Argentina move to Misiones along with their heads of cattle and sheep. Today approximately 80 percent of Misiones is used for ranching whereas only 20 percent is destined for agriculture. Visitors can experience the ranching culture first hand at the region's festivals, all of which invariably involve *jineteadas* (rodeos) and the sale of ranching related crafts such as saddles, cowboy boots, wool horse blankets and ponchos. The Emprendimiento Misionero de Turismo (EMITUR), based in Santiago, is a good resource for information about the various festivals and ranches open to visitors in the Misiones department, providing visitors with an up close experience of Paraguay's cowboy culture. *Tel: 0782 20286, Emitur@itacom.com.py, www.emitur.com.py*

Radio Cowboys

For a taste of Paraguay's cowboy culture you can also check out *"Rodeo y Tradición"* and *"Tradición y Cultura."* *"Rodeo y Tradición"* airs Sundays from 10am to 11am on Channel 13. *"Tradición y Cultura"* is run by the Asociación de Jinetes de Paraguay and airs on Saturdays from 2:30pm-3:00pm on Red Guaraní. It is also available in radio format Mondays through Fridays from 10:00am to 12pm on Radio Ysapy FM 90.7 and on the AJP website (*www.ajp.com.py*).

Several towns in Misiones were once prosperous Jesuit missions. After the Jesuits were expelled from Paraguay in the late 1700's their missions passed into the hands of the Franciscans and while several were completely abandoned others eventually evolved into thriving towns. Though the churches (generally the most impressive structures in each mission) have largely deteriorated there still remain vestiges of the area's Jesuit past. Buildings such as school houses and indigenous dwellings (known in Spanish as *"casas de indios"*) are still in use. Remarkably, there are still many religious artifacts from the Jesuit era – locals saved sculptures, altar pieces and other decorative elements from the crumbling mission churches (in some cases sculptures are missing limbs because the churches literally fell down around them). Items that were not sold to private collectors have been donated to the town's Jesuit museums or returned to newly constructed churches. The museums and churches are worth a visit together with a trip the Jesuit ruins of the department of Itapúa.

From Riches to Ruins

Rumors of gold mines, secret tunnels and hidden treasures contributed to the destruction of abandoned Jesuit sites. After the Jesuits were expelled from Paraguay the missions were ransacked by treasure hunters. Many of the missions' stone statues were smashed on the assumption that they were hollow and filled with gold.

VILLA FLORIDA

Located on the white sandy banks of the Tebicuary River, Villa Florida is the gateway to Paraguay's Misiones department and a popular summertime destination. Paraguayans flock to Villa Florida during the months of December and January to enjoy the town's wide white sandy beaches, large shaded plazas and delicious fish dishes served up by the town's restaurants. Fishing in the Tebicuary river is a popular past time year round. During the second week of January the "*Canto a Villa Florida*" festival is held along the riverside Avenida Costanera with many folkloric musical and dance acts. Villa Florida is also a popular destination during Easter vacation (*Semana Santa*). Though the town's residents regularly complain about the excess of partying tourists during *Semana Santa* it is still a pleasant time to visit. There are plenty of wholesome activities such as sports competitions in canoe races, volleyball, and beach football, organized by Villa Florida's municipal office. During the town's anniversary celebration the focus moves towards Misiones' ranching tradition with parades, rodeos, and the typical *asado a la estaca* (see Asado, Misiones Style, p163).

Even at the height of the tourist season Villa Florida manages to maintain a tranquil atmosphere. Unlike San Bernardino, another popular beach destination, there are no nightclubs or bars. Here all the action takes place along the beach with volleyball, horseback rides and boat trips onto the river. Though activities (and many services) grind to a halt, the town is still quite pleasant to visit during the off season. Stroll along Villa Florida's grassy parks and head down to the Avenida Costanera along the river front and you'll understand why the gateway to Misiones is so popular among Paraguayans.

Casa de Turismo Villa Florida – Tourist Information

Located right next to the Parador Touring just past the bridge the Tourism office is well stocked with maps and other information. They can assist you in renting out private housing and organizing fishing trips. Next door there are also stands selling Paraguayan handicrafts. *Tel: 083 240 404*

Beaches

Playa Paraiso Playa Paraiso is the most popular beach in town, and the closest. The beach has spots for camping along the river, a cantina and bathroom facilities. There are motorboat tours along the river that leave regularly. Boats carry about four to five people and charge about Gs. 5,000 for almost an hour-long ride. *Coming from Asunción the access road is on the right-hand side just after the*

The South

bridge after which you take another right towards the river and then a left approximately 3000 meters to the beach, Gs. 5,000 per person, Gs. 10,000 per person for camping

Playa Caracol Though there is no infrastructure, Playa Caracol is another popular spot. *Located across the river from town it is accessed from a sideroad to the left-hand side just before the bridge (if coming from Asunción)*

Playa Yvaga Further away but worthwhile for those with cars. You can also try your luck hitch-hiking – beachgoers may be in a charitable mood. *After the bridge take the second right onto Felicianos Orue (which turns into Curupayty) and continue five kilometers*

Fishing

Villa Florida is a popular destination for fishermen itching to catch a long and spotted *surubí* or a golden *dorado*. During the month of October the *Federación Paraguaya de Pesca Deportiva* (Paraguayan Federation of Sport Fishing) hosts their national fishing contest in Villa Florida. Though the fishing is plentiful, there are no organized tours at the moment. The easiest way to organize an excursion on the river is to find a guide through the Casa de Turismo or one of the hotels. See Fishing, p68, for things to keep in mind when looking to hire a fishing guide or instructor.

Lodging

The majority of visitors to Villa Florida rent houses – many town residents own second homes specifically set aside as rental properties. The tourism office has a list of available houses for rent although it is best to coordinate with them ahead of time if you are going during peak times (Christmas, New Years, Easter week). There are a handful of hotels in Villa Florida, as well. Most have large *familiar* rooms set up for entire families with queen beds and bunk beds. As long as the Tebicuary river's water levels are low camping is a good and popular option. Make sure to bring plenty of insect repellant! Campers looking for peace and quiet are best served by visiting Villa Florida during the week.

Hotel Touring Club Run by the Paraguay's Touring and Automotive Club (TACPy, or *"El Touring"*) this is most established of Villa Florida's tourism facilities. The restaurant is a popular rest stop for long distance buses headed to Encarnación. Rooms were recently added to accommodate overnight guests and there is also the option to camp next to the river. *Tel: 083 240 205, just after the bridge on the left, Gs. 400,000 per room, pool, beach camping, TV, A/C, mini-fridge, kitchenette*

Hotel Nacional de Turismo A bit further from the center, the Hotel Nacional del Turismo is about a four block walk to the river front. The building is built in typical colonial style with high ceilings, cool tile floors and covered corridors. Rooms are spacious and simply furnished. Breakfast is not included though there is a restaurant with meager offerings. Grounds include a *quincho* and nice pool if you don't feel like walking to the river. *Tel: 083 240 207, Rt 1 km 161, Single Gs. 60,000, Double Gs. 90,000, Triple Gs. 135,000, A/C, pool*

Parador Centu Cue This large property is Villa Florida's most scenic option, although it's location on the outskirts of town make it less accessible to those without private vehicles. Guests can enjoy the private beach as well as excursions to fish for dorado. The guest rooms are a little shabby so your best bet is to either camp or rent one of their private waterfront bungalows. *Tel: 083 240 219, 0790 213 537, 0983 435 634, from Asunción take the signed right-hand turn off about 1 km past the bridge and go 7 kilometers down a dirt and gravel path, rooms 120,000 with A/C, cabins Gs. 150,000-180,000, A/C*

Restaurants

Given its prime riverfront location and reputation for good fishing it is no surprise that Villa Florida's gastronomic specialties are fish-based dishes. *Surubí*, *dorado* and *corvina* are the best white fish options, all freshly caught. Popular dishes include *caldo de pescado* (fish soup), *chupín de pescado* (fish casserole with tomatoes and onions), and fish *milanesa* (breaded and fried fillets) napolitano-style topped with cheese or *al caballo* with onions and fried eggs.

Parador Restaurante Tebicuary The most popular restaurant in town. The *caldo de pescado* (fish soup) is delicious and, highly affordable. Menu includes meats and pastas as well as cheaper fast food options for those making a pit stop with a long distance bus. *Tel: 083 240 205, on the left after crossing the bridge (there are often long distance buses stopped in front), daily 6am-11pm, Gs. 10,000-50,000*

San Cayetano This restaurant is more geared towards Villa Florida's locals, and this is reflected in its prices. Good basic Paraguayan food including the ever-present *empanadas* and *lomitos*. Here, all dishes are about ten percent cheaper than touristy restaurants. *Tel: 083 240 318, corner of the main plaza on Feliciano Orue and Villa Florida, daily 7am-11pm, Gs. 10,000-20,000*

La Reja This small family-run restaurant is a highly recommended for its tasty *chupín de pescado*. *Tel: 083 240 326, 0981 515 475, Avenida Tebicuary between Bareiro and Agustín Pío Barrios, daily 8am-3pm, 6pm-10pm, Gs. 15,000-40,000*

Getting There

Villa Florida is approximately 160 kilometers from Asunción on Route 1. Any buses going down Route 1 from Asunción towards Encarnación, Pilar, San Juan Bautista, San Ignacio, and Ayolas pass Villa Florida. The trip takes between two and a half to three hours by bus. Your best options are La Encarnacena and Ciudad de Pilar, both of which leave from Asunción's bus terminal. Nuestra Señora de Asunción and Rysa are also good options. Gs. 20,000.

SAN MIGUEL

San Miguel is known as Paraguay's "Capital of wool." Artisans weave wool from locally raised sheep into everything from blankets to ponchos. Along the road you will see houses with wool creations hanging on the fences and from trees, all for sale. Each June, the town celebrates the *Festival Ovecha Ragué* where local artisans show off their woolen wares and various ranching competitions including a bull run take place.

Cabañas San Francisco

Visitors to this family run *estancia* can kick back and relax in a hammock or get their hands dirty helping with daily chores. Hearty meals are prepared on an old school wood burning oven known as a "*fogón*" – the ranch specialty is *asado de cordero* (barbecued lamb). The mini-zoo includes monkeys, capybaras and *yacarés* (caiman). Owners are energetic and friendly. The ranch is within easy walking distance from Route 1 and only one kilometer outside of town. *Tel: 083 240 328, 0971 216 171, turn off is to the right-hand side (coming from Asunción) at km 173 of Route 1, www.csanfrancisco.com.py, Gs. 120,000-130,000 per person (full room and board), TV, A/C, mini-fridge, pool, fishing pond, mini-zoo*

The South

SAN JUAN BAUTISTA

The capital of the Misiones department, San Juan is a pleasant place to stroll through, especially since the main highway only skirts past the edge of town. San Juan's various large and verdant plazas earn it the nickname "*Ciudad Jardín*" (City of Gardens). San Juan is a university town with several large public and private universities drawing students from the entire Misiones district.

San Juan is also known as the "*Cuna de Mangoré*" (birthplace of Mangoré) – talented composer and guitarist Agustín Pío Barrios, better known for his nickname "*Mangoré*," was born here in 1885. His former house is slowly being restored and is currently a cultural center, adorned with many paintings of the famed artist (but not much else).

San Juan Festival

The Festival of San Juan, held on June 24th, is celebrated throughout Paraguay, though nowhere else as energetically as in San Juan itself. During the festival, the streets of San Juan fill to the brim with cowboys and riders from the area's *estancias* who parade to the Club 24 de junio (known as the "*polideportivo*") There everyone gathers for equestrian showcases while onlookers cheer loudly and purchase meats from an enormous *asado a la estaca*.

One of the highlights of any San Juan celebration are the various games traditionally played. There are sack races (*carrera vosa*), competitions to climb a greased pole for a prize up top (*yvyra syi*), and a Paraguayan take on a piñata using a clay water jug filled with prizes (*kambuchi jejoka*). The most popular games of San Juan are those involving fire. To play *pelota tata* (fire ball) a ball made of rags is soaked in kerosene, set alight and kicked around like a soccer ball. For the *toro candil* someone

---

"San Juan Dice Que Sí" or How to Predict Your Future Love Life

"*San Juan dice que sí, San Juan dice que no*" (San Juan says yes, San Juan says no) is a phrase you'll hear readily during the month of June. This is in reference to a number of San Juan games played by women to fortell their future love lives. Will San Jan will say "yes" or "no" to their desire to find a husband in the coming year? The games are most fun when played with a large group of women and are the rural Paraguayan equivalent of a "Sex and the City" marathon. Some examples:

A chicken is kept without food for a whole day before being spun around in the middle of a circle of women, each with a mound of corn at her feet. The woman whose corn the chicken chooses to peck at first will be the first of the group to get married.

Women take turns picking a fruit from a lemon tree while blindfolded. The degree of ripeness of the fruit will determine the age of their future husband. Green and unripe? She'll be marrying a young guy. Old and mushy? Time to prepare for a geriatric husband.

Scissors, a rosary, keys and a ring are placed on a table or tray and covered with a cloth. Women take turns closing their eyes and reaching for an object, each symbolizing their future. Scissors foretell a career as a seamstress. The key indicates a future housewife (or, in another variation, a property owner). The ring symbolizes marriage and anyone who went for the rosary is headed to the convent (or will simply end up an old maid).

dons a huge headpiece with flaming horns and runs around pretending to be a bull. Usually he prefers to run through the crowd sending groups of teenage girls running in all directions. The dramatic highlight is the *tata ári jehasa* or *tata py-ï ari yejhasa* which means "walking over coals." Hot coals are spread out to create a path about five meters long. As onlookers watch with bated breath the brave walk down the path slowly, all the while calling out *"Viva San Juan!"* sure that their faith in San Juan will protect them. The Festival of San Juan came to Paraguay through Europe where the date falls around the same time as the summer solstice. Some speculate that pagan solstice rituals are the reason for the popularity of fire during San Juan. Of course in Paraguay, San Juan takes place during the cold days of winter so fire is a welcome addition.

Festival del Batiburrillo, Siriki y el Chorizo Misionero

Held in mid-January this festival is the perfect time to try the gastronomic specialties of Misiones. Start off with a cocktail called *"siriki"* made with soda water, *caña* (unaged rum) and *limón sutil*, a lemon whose flavor is subtle, as its name indicates. Then serve yourself some *batiburrillo*, a stew made of onions, green peppers and internal organs (usually of sheep but sometimes cow as well) all simmered in a heavy cast iron pot. Another festival specialty is the *chorizo misionero* (also known as the *"chorizo sanjuanino"*) which is a sausage made of both pork and beef. Both *siriki* and *batiburrillo* are said to have been introduced to the area by a Spanish immigrant named Sebastián Sasiaín. In addition to these dishes the festival features other classics such as *payaguá mascada*, *pastel mandió* (both made out of *mandioca*) and, of course, *sopa paraguaya*.

The South

Asado, Misiones Style

Paraguay is a very carnivorous culture with *asado* (barbeque) being a national past time. Misiones, however, takes their *asado* to a whole new level. Fancy implements such as grills are done away with in favor of large stretches of smoldering coals. Large chunks of meat are skewered on wooden dowels which are staked around the coals and slowly cooked to perfection. For *asados* held at festivals each dowel has a price tag tied around the top. Part of the fun is choosing your piece of meat – fair goers take their time inspecting cuts from every possible angle before making a decision. Once you've made your purchase the tag is marked with your name. There is a thrill that comes with walking away from the mound of coals with a huge cut of meat on a stick – you may never come closer to feeling like Fred Flintstone.

Lodging

Hotel San Juan A small hotel in the center of town with spacious, brightly decorated rooms. *Tel: 081 213 331, Monseñor Bogarín Argaña almost at Waldino Lovera, single Gs. 70,000, doubles Gs. 95,000, TV, A/C*

Hospedaje Ña Nenema This basic *hospedaje* is nothing fancy but does have the advantage of being affordable and well located just at the entrance to town. *Tel: 081 212 667, Monseñor Bogarín and Rosalía Candia, Gs. 50,000 per person*

Restaurants

Waldorf San Juan's nicest restaurant, the Waldorf serves up large portions of tasty Paraguayan classics. The milanesas are particularly good. *Tel: 081 212 209, corner of Monseñor Rojas and Victor Z Romero, 12pm-2:30pm, 7pm-11pm, Gs. 15,000-25,000*

Heladería Crisól More than just an ice cream parlor Crisól has a good per kilo lunch buffet, tasty and hearty *empanadas* and excellent super cheesy *sopa paraguaya*. *Tel: 081 212 703, 021 212 402, Avenida Monseñor Bogarín Argaña between Capitán Martinez and Waldino Lovera across from Plaza Boquerón, daily 7am-10pm, Gs. 5,000-20,000*

Ña Tere A good choice all around, Ña Tere has the best burgers in town as well as large pizzas with thin crusts. Try the *pollo suprema*. *Tel: 081 212 512, Monseñor Rojas and Victor Z Romero Diagonally opposite Waldorf, daily 7am-12pm, Gs. 15,000-25,000*

Getting There

San Juan is located at km 196 of Route 1. The entrance to town is located on the right just as the highway makes a sharp left (this place is aptly nicknamed "*la curva*" or "the curve"). If you see signs for the Kurupí *yerba mate* factory you've gone too far.

All long distance buses headed to Encarnación stop at San Juan (Gs. 25,000). Buses drop off and pick up passengers on either side of "*la curva*" – passengers heading further south towards Encarnación get on at the small triangular plaza while those heading north towards Asunción get on in front of the army barracks across the road. Due to the high volume of university students that commute to San Juan, buses tend to be very crowded in the afternoon and at night.

SAN IGNACIO GUASÚ

The town of San Ignacio was once home to the oldest of the Jesuit missions in the Guaraní territory, founded in 1609 by Fathers Marcial de Lorenzana, Francisco de San Martin and Indian *cacique* (leader) Arapyzandu. Originally this mission was located elsewhere but was forced to move twice due to pressures from *bandeirantes* until finally ending up in its current location (see Mission Under Attack, p168). Modern day San Ignacio still retains remnants of its Jesuit past. The indigenous dwellings along the main plaza are still in

The word "*guazú*" means "large" in Guaraní. The mission was given the name "San Ignacio Guasú" in order to differentiate it from the "San Ignacio Miní" mission (now located in Argentina).

use, as are the original school buildings which now house the Jesuit art museum. Today the town is well known once more thanks to artist Koki Ruiz, the driving force behind many of the town's cultural events including the popular Holy Friday procession in Tañarandy (p167) and several "living portraits" shows in which community members depict classic works of art.

Until the mid 1980's San Ignacio was the capital of the Misiones department and though this distinction passed to San Juan, San Ignacio remains a more commercially active town. There are several banks, stores and a handful of hotels. San Ignacio's large and pleasant main plaza is decorated by a series of large concrete murals with religious themes. The town's entrance is marked by a series of horse heads carved out of stone, in commemoration of the participation of San Ignacio's cavalry in the Chaco War. This is also the turn off for Route 4 which leads west to through the province of Ñeembucú to the city of Pilar. San Ignacio is a good base for visiting various Jesuit towns nearby – doable by car and by bus. Santa María is about eleven kilometers away, Santa Rosa about twenty kilometers, and Santiago is about fifty-five kilometers away.

Museo Diocesano de San Ignacio Guasú

San Ignacio's Jesuit museum is housed in one of Paraguay's oldest remaining Jesuit constructions. Carved into stone out front is a list of the twenty-six Jesuits who served in the missions of Paraguay and died as martyrs. The building, which used to be home to the mission's Jesuit priests, now contains a collection of several large sculptures organized by theme throughout four rooms. Statues are beautifully carved with a sense of movement in robes and expressive faces. Gold leaf still shines off several carvings and extraordinary attention has been paid to the most minute details such as the textures mimicking brocade and lace cutouts along the edges of robes.

The first room, dedicated to the Creation, includes a large pulpit, a sculpture of a child being lead by an angel, and a sculpture of St. Michael fighting with the devil. The second room is dedicated to the Redemption with sculptures featuring the suffering and resurrection of Jesús along with the Virgin Mary. In the third room the history of Christ in the church is depicted with figures of various saints including statues of St. Peter and St. Paul. The fourth room is dedicated to the Jesuit order with several large and evocative statues of Jesuit saints including St. Ignatius, founder of the Jesuit order. This room also has a photograph of the mission's original church which unfortunately fell into a state of disrepair and was demolished in 1920. Though the majority of the church's decorative elements were taken abroad by private collectors, the sculptures which now adorn the museum were safeguarded by members of the community until the museum opened in 1978. *Tel: 082 232 223, Iturbe 870 almost at Marcial de Lorenzana (down the street from the church), Mon-Fri 2pm-5:30pm, Sat-Sun 8am-11am and 2pm-2:30pm, Entry fee: Gs.10,000*

Museo Semblanza de Héroes

This small but interesting museum is divided in two sections. The first contains relics from the Guerra del Chaco and the Triple Alliance war including some interesting paintings depicting key battles as well as portraits of now aging war veterans. The second room contains a large collection of full sized black and white photos from the war. There are also several displaying road constructions throughout Paraguay after the war. *Iturbe almost at Roque Gonzalez across from the church, Mon-Fri 7:30am-11:30, 2pm-4:30pm*

Centro de Documentación "Archivos de la Dictadura Stronista/Casa de las Víctimas"

Located across the street from the church in one of the sections of the *casa de indios* this documentation center is a must-visit for anyone interested in the history of the Stroessner dictatorship and the human rights abuses that took place throughout. In this small office people from the surrounding areas come to have their testimony of past interrogation and torture documented. Many of these victims participated in the *Ligas Agrarias Christianas* (Christian Agrarian Leagues) which worked to organize rural Paraguayans during the 1960's and 1970's. One of the center's most interesting books is a small hand written and illustrated book by the members of a small neighboring community detailing their experience with the Ligas Agrarias and the repression that ensued. Though the book is entirely written in Guaraní the cartoonish illustrations manage to depict the story quite clearly. With testimonies and news clippings posted throughout, the center is quite powerful. This is especially true when you see names of known torturers from the Stroessner era painted on the wall – many of whom are still alive and residing in the area today. *Tel: 082 233 000, Avenida San Roque and Cerro Corá next to the Biblioteca Municipal, Mon-Fri 7am-11am, 1pm-4pm*

Biblioteca Municipal

Next to the Casa de las Victimas the municipal library's walls are covered with photos from Jesuit missions in Paraguay, Brazil and Argentina. If you are headed towards Encarnación and the ruins of Itapúa stop in for a preview of the sights to come. *Avenida San Roque and Cerro Corá, Mon-Sat 7am-12pm, Mon-Fri 1pm-5pm*

Lodging

La Casa de Loli Removed from the center of town, this hotel has a nice atmosphere. Rooms are large and decorated with Paraguayan handicrafts. The hotel's restaurant serves up good Paraguayan home cooking. The outdoor area is nice and includes a pool – much needed if you're walking in from the main road. *Tel: 0782 232 362, Mariscal López 1595, if coming from Asunción take a right on Mariscal López, one block before the main plaza, the hotel will be on your left-hand side approximately one kilometer down the road, www.lacasadeloli.com.py, Single 70,000, Double Gs. 100,000, A/C, pool*

🛏 **Hotel Rural San Ignacio Country Club** Run by a friendly former backpacker from Peru, this pleasant hotel has options at all price levels, from camping and dorm rooms to uniquely decorated private rooms and bungalows. The grounds are extensive, including a soccer field, pool, paddle courts and a walking trail through a large field that leads to a winding creek. Other pluses: pool table, rooms with DVD players, and Wi-Fi. Gustavo and his wife are incredibly friendly and excellent cooks, specializing in dishes baked in the *tatakua* (brick oven). They are happy to accommodate vegetarians as well. *Tel: 0782 232 895, 0975 606 631, five kilometers past town at the turn off to Santa Maria, well signed, www.sanignaciocountryclub.com, on Facebook, Sep-Mar Gs. 75,000-250,000 per person full room and board, Apr-Aug Gs. 75,000-150,000.*

Restaurants

Hotel Rural San Ignacio Country Club Worth the short cab or bus ride for home-cooked country style food in a nice open environment (see previous listing for details).

Rokito's Center Two blocks from the plaza on the main highway. Large portions of Paraguayan style diner food. *Tel: 0782 232 305, Mariscal Estigarribia and Fulgencio Yegros, Tues-Sun, 7am-4pm, 6pm-11pm, Gs. 15,000-20,000*

Getting There

San Ignacio Guasú is located at km 226 of Route 1. All buses to Encarnación and Pilar stop in San Ignacio though the former will get you closer to the center of town (Gs. 28,000).

TAÑARANDY

Tañarandy, a small community about two kilometers from San Ignacio is the site of one of the most dynamic celebrations of Holy Friday in Paraguay. At nightfall on Holy Friday, the entire town (along with thousands of visitors) participates in a candle lit "Vía Crucis" procession. The road running from the town chapel to "La Barraca," property of San Ignacio artist and festival organizer Koki Ruiz, is named the "Yvagá Rape" (pronounced with an emphasis on the last syllable) or "Path to Heaven." The path is lined with candles made out of wax-filled orange halves and bamboo lanterns which community members and visitors alike help to light before the procession. Along the way there are representations of the Stations of the Cross. During the procession religious choir groups known as *estacioneros* sing hymns as they visit each station. Once at La Barraca there are musical acts and the unveiling of "living paintings" in which community members participate in life-sized recreations of famous works of religious art The festive and deeply religious atmosphere combined with the depiction of classical works of art such as Da Vinci's *"The Last Supper"* in a rural setting make Tañarandy an unforgettable experience. For more information on the festivities contact Koki Ruiz's Fundación La Barraca at 082 232 775.

Tañarandy's artsy vibe makes it worth a visit even outside of Holy week. Many houses in the community have quirky painted signs out front depicting each residents' profession. The town chapel, the **Capilla de la Virgen de Caacupé,** is also worth visiting as its interior is beautifully decorated with paintings by Cecilia Ruiz (daughter of Koki Ruiz). The town's name means "land of the irreductibles" in Guaraní and, according to local legend, was given because this is where the indigenous that refused to be part of the San Ignacio mission lived.

Getting There

If coming from Asunción take a left on Cerro Corá (the same street as the church and plaza) and head two kilometers down the dirt road out of town. Along the way you will pass Koki Ruiz's residence to the left-hand side, its entrance marked by owls carved out of stone. On a cool day the walk is quite lovely, cutting through the idyllic Paraguayan countryside. On a hot day it is best to hire a taxi from the corner of the town plaza.

SANTA MARÍA DE FE

This cute little town, removed from Route 1, was the site of one of the most populous Jesuit missions, with over 7,000 indigenous residents. In fact, many of the surrounding missions were founded with the overflow from Santa María. The mission was the site of a large artisan workshop run by Jesuit priests and artists Joseph Brassanelli and Antonio Sepp. The volume and quality of the artwork produced earned the mission the nickname *"Gran Taller de las Antiguas Misiones"* (Great Workshop of the Ancient Missions) and to this day the town museum boasts what is considered by some to be the best collection of art from the Jesuit missions. Today, Santa María de Fe is a small and tranquil town with a beautiful shady plaza where families of monkeys and large flocks of parakeets live. Though there are no large scale ruins, the town does have original adobe buildings from the era around the town plaza. There is also an original cross on Cerro Santa María de Fe. A mere ten kilometers from San Ignacio, a visit to Santa María is an easy day trip, both by car and public transportation. Though for those interested in Jesuit history, it is worth an overnight stay as the town's only hotel is run by an English-speaking theologian and Jesuit scholar with much information on Santa María and the Jesuits in general.

Casa de la Artesanía/Taller de Hermandad

Located opposite the main plaza this women's crafts cooperative creates cloth appliqué collages emblematic of Santa María. These textile works of art are very charming but take as their inspiration one of the sadder chapters of Paraguay's recent history. The appliqués depict the work of the *Ligas Agrarias*, a group which suffered brutal repression at the hands of the Stroessner regime due to their work organizing rural communities. They are available in small amounts in the *artesanía* stores of

---

Missions Under Attack

During the 1600's Sao Paolo, Brazil was the center of a booming slave trade, fueled by the labor needs of Brazil's plantation owners. At the heart of this trade were slave traders known as *"Paulistas"* (also known as *"mamelucos"* and *"bandeirantes"*). Having exhausted the surrounding region's indigenous population the *bandeirantes* set their sights on Paraguay's Jesuit missions during the late 1620's. In the eyes of these bandits the Jesuit Missions, with their concentrations of largely unprotected indigenous, were easy targets. The *bandeirantes* often chose to attack the missions while everyone was gathered for religious services. Once having captured the indigenous they'd sack and destroy the missions, often setting them ablaze.

In the face of the constant raids the Jesuits saw no solution but to relocate their missions, taking with them as many of their flock as possible (for an account of one such move see Saltos de Guaira, the Waterfalls that Made Itaipú Possible p255). Once in areas sheltered from the *bandeirantes'* attacks missions were refounded. Several missions in other areas of Paraguay absorbed the surviving populations of raided missions. Eventually the Jesuits were able to secure permission from the King of Spain for the indigenous to bear arms in self-defense against the *mamelucos*. Many of the Jesuits were ex-soldiers and were able to train indigenous militias. These were repeatedly called upon to serve and protect the colonists at several points. They fought in conflicts with other foreign armies (such as the Portuguese), protected colonists from invasions by indigenous tribes of the Chaco and quelled internal rebellions. Some were armed with guns but most used indigenous weapons such as *bolas*, slings, *lazos*, lances and arrows.

Asunción but if you see something you like in Santa María it is best to purchase them on the spot as this is not something you are likely to see again. *Tel: 0985 277 728, Dr. Francia between Bernardino Caballero and Ciudad de Hayes next to the Santa María Hotel, www.santamariahotel.org, 7am-11am, 1pm-4pm*

Museo Diocesano de Artes Jesuíticas

Santa María's Jesuit museum contains one of the best collections of Jesuit art in Paraguay (and some argue in the entirety of the Jesuit missions). The building, one of the oldest remaining structures in town, dates back to the 1670's and was originally used as indigenous dwellings. It retains several architectural elements from the period including large and sturdy wood beams and hooks for hanging hammocks on the walls. The collection of fifty-six pieces, mostly carved out of cedar wood, is divided by theme and spread out among the six rooms.

The first room contains objects from the old church including a baptismal font, weather vane, and a beautifully carved door, each pane of which is decorated with a passion fruit flower (known as a "*pasionaria*"). The second room, entitled "*De la Companía de Jesús*," displays Jesuit saints. The smaller sculptures were original works of Brassanelli which were then replicated in larger size by the indigenous artisans of the mission. The next room, "*Santos Mártires de la Iglesia*" holds sculptures of martyrs including several versions of the Virgin Mary and the only remaining sculpture of St. Peter as the Pope from the Jesuit missions. In the following room, "*Santos Ángeles y Arcángeles*," there are two representations of St. Michael, of which the Guaraní version includes the Devil.

The fifth room, "*De la Natividad*," features the charming highlight of the museum's collection, the only complete nativity scene from the Jesuit missions. In addition to the usual members of nativity scenes there are also sculptures of local flora and fauna – a bird known as a "*pavo del monte*," a small *kure* (pig) and an *unambú guazú* (quail). All but baby Jesus are original sculptures. In 1983, General Stroessner ordered the original baby Jesus removed from the museum in order to gift it to a friend and a replacement sculpture was made.

The sixth room, "*La Pasión del Señor*," features images of Jesus at various stations of the Cross. Some of these pieces are brought out of retirement for *Semana Santa* activities although there are efforts to make copies in order to better preserve original works of art.

Corner of Mariscal López and Ciudad de Hayes, across from the town plaza, 8:30am-11:30am and 1:30pm-5:00pm. If the museum is closed ask around for Irma Ramirez (0992 697 781) or Isabelino Martinez (0985 788 011) who live across the plaza from the church. They can let you in and give a great tour. Entry fee: Gs. 5,000

English, Spanish and French guided tours are available through the Hotel Santa María across the plaza from the museum.

Santa María Hotel

This small hotel across the plaza from the Museo Santa María is run by Margaret Hebblethwaite an English theologian. Thanks to her strong interest in Jesuit history, the hotel has an excellent library. Margaret is a good resource on the Jesuits and the area's missions. In addition, she works with the community on several projects and runs the Santa María Education fun which helps pay for community members' education. *Tel: 0781 283 311, 0981 861 553, Dr. Francia between Bernardino Caballero and Ciudad de Hayes across from the town plaza, www.santamariahotel.org, Gs. 130,000 per person (half price for Paraguayans), A/C, good library*

Getting There

The turn off to Santa María is located to the right-hand side of Route 1 just six kilometers past San Ignacio (if coming from Asunción). From there it is ten kilometers to the center of town. A taxi from the center of town costs approximately Gs. 30,000.

From Asunción the Mariscal López bus line (tickets sold through Alborada) leaves at 11:45am (approximately five hours) Monday through Saturday (Gs. 30,000). It is also relatively easy to hitch a ride from the turn off along Route 1.

Jesuit Art Workshops

Most of the art produced in the Jesuit missions and on display in the museums was made by indigenous mission residents, under the tutelage of Jesuit artists. Many museum guides will point this out, explaining that the indigenous left their own mark on their works, doting the faces of saints with more indigenous features. However you may find yourself straining to notice any significant difference (aside from size) between the original small scale models created by Jesuit priests and larger copies carved out by their indigenous apprentices. It is perhaps a credit to the talent of the indigenous that the differences are truly minimal.

SANTA ROSA

Founded from the overflow of the Santa María de Fe mission in 1698, at its peak Santa Rosa de Lima was home to over 4,000 inhabitants. Before it burned down in the late 1880's, Santa Rosa's ornately decorated church was renowned as the most impressive in all the Jesuit missions. Fortunately the numerous remaining structures surrounding the main plaza are in remarkably good shape. Among the is a building unique to the Jesuit ruins as a whole – the Chapel of Loreto, beautifully decorated with original frescoes. The church's original bell tower, which survived the fire, still stands, as well. A great number of the original *casa de indios* (indigenous dwellings) surrounding the plaza are in surprisingly good condition. The long exterior corridor running down their length is known by the community as "*La Acera*." Recent additions to Santa Rosa's historic center are the stone sculptures in the main plaza. These include the quirky *Fuente de los Reducidos*, several small sculpted animals, and a fountain featuring a humorous version of the mythical Kurupí (see Meet the *Mitos*, p44), complete with water spouting from his infamously well-endowed nether regions.

Museo Oratorio de Nuestra Señora de Loreto

The town's Jesuit museum is located in the small Capilla de Loreto chapel next to the (new) church. The chapel is unique to all the Jesuit ruins and a beautiful legacy of the artistic sensibilities of the missions as a whole. From the outside the small unassuming chapel appears to be simple colonial house. Closer inspection reveals intricately carved double doors and wooden window frames, hinting at the artistic treasures inside. The frescoes that survive within adorn the entirety of the small chapel, depicting angels moving the Virgin Mary's house in Nazareth to Loreto, the last Judgment, and St. Joseph in his workshop. Dozens of painted bright stars scattered across a deep blue night sky adorn the chapel's wooden ceiling. Also of incredible value is the collection of statues housed in the museum. Among these are what is known as the "Annunciation" collection made up of the statues of the Archangel Gabriel, La Piedad, the Virgin of the Annunciation and the Virgin of

Loreto. This group of statues is considered by art scholars to be an exceptionally beautiful example of the art of the Jesuit missions.

Although the main church is no longer in existence the new church does have an ornately decorated altarpiece that was saved from the fire, as well as replicas of Jesuit statues.

Next to the church is the original eight-meter high bell tower built out of red sandstone. Climb the stairs inside for a nice view of the town plaza and resist the temptation to ring the bells at the top.

Tel: 0858 285 221, Avda. Florida between Presidente Franco and General Díaz (hard to miss as it's right next to the large brick bell tower), across from the main plaza. Entrance to the museum and bell tower is managed by the personnel of the church whose office is located between the church and the museum. Mon-Sat 7:30am-11:30am, 2:30pm-6:00pm – There is no fee although donations to the parish are encouraged

Getting There
Santa Rosa is located two kilometers down a left-hand (if coming from Asunción) turn off at approximately km 246 of Route 1. Local buses to Santa Rosa run throughout the day along Route 1 from San Ignacio and can be caught both in town or at the crossroads to Santa María. The San Juan runs twice daily from Asuncíon for Gs. 28,000.

Departamento Itapúa

The department of Itapúa is home to Paraguay's most visited tourist attractions – the Jesuit ruins. There are three sets of ruins – those of Trinidad, Jesús de Tavarangue, and San Cosme y Damián. Of the three two have been declared UNESCO World Heritage sites. Due to the quantity of remaining structures and quality of their preservation, (as well as proximity to the main road) Trinidad is the most popular set of Jesuit Ruins. Tourists have two choices for lodging – they can stay in the city of Encarnación itself or in one of several hotels along Route 6. The former offers the advantage of multiple options for eating out while the latter provides the opportunity to take in some of Itapúa's natural scenery.

Aside from its rich heritage Itapúa is known primarily for its agricultural production. The area's fertile soil has attracted a wide variety of immigrants – from Brazilians and Germans to Ukrainians and Russians. These groups have set up several agricultural colonies throughout the department farming rice, cotton, and soy, among other crops. The southern section of Ruta 6 (which connects Encarnación with Ciudad del Este to the North) is home to the German towns of Hohenau, Obligado and Bella Vista collectively known as the Colonias Unidas (*www.colonias.com.py*) which produce Colón brand *yerba mate* and Los Colonos brand dairy products. Historically this area was used by the Jesuits to produce *yerba mate*. Today the city of Bella Vista is home to some of Paraguay's largest *yerba mate* factories – of which two are open to the public. To the north, heading into the department of Alto Paraná, Brazilian colonies dominate. Many of Itapúa's agricultural colonies are amongst the country's most prosperous. Unlike the Mennonite colonies of the Chaco and Alto Paraná these communities make full use of their wealth to obtain modern commodities such as satellite dishes and high speed internet.

Unfortunately an exceedingly rapid rate of deforestation has come hand in hand with the surge in large scale agriculture. Within the last thirty to forty years the extensive Atlantic Forest that once covered the department has all but vanished. The San Rafael Reserve encompasses what is left – a small island of forest surrounded by a sea of soy fields. For those interested in admiring the remaining Atlantic Forest's flora and fauna are there are two lodging options – the PROCOSARA lodge and the Kanguery birding station run by Guyra Paraguay. Though somewhat difficult to access both are worth the trip to see one of Paraguay's most biologically rich ecosystems.

Coronel Bogado

Before arriving at Encarnación Route 1 passes through Coronel Bogado, known as the *chipa* capital of Paraguay. Indeed the *chipa* in Coronel Bogado is excellent. Two *chipería* recommendations are the previously lauded Chipería El Gordo (p151) and Chipería Tati, both with stands along Route 1.

ENCARNACIÓN

Known as *"La Perla del Sur"* (the Pearl of the South) Encarnación is Paraguay's southern most city located along the Paraguay River across from the Argentine city of Posadas. The capital of the department of Itapúa, Encarnación is a pleasant city. Most tourists use Encarnación as a base of operations for visiting Posadas or the nearby Jesuit ruins. Though there is not much to see in the city itself it is small and manageable with a handful of good ethnic restaurants. The city's main plaza (*Plaza de Armas*) is very nice and the newly constructed boardwalk (*la costanera*), complete with a Wi-Fi signal, is gaining popularity.

The city is well known throughout Paraguay for its energetic and colorful celebration of Carnaval. Taking place over several weekends preceding Lent, the *Carnavales Encarnacenas* are quite a spectacle. Each night expectant crowds fill the bleachers set up along the city's new boardwalk. One by one teams with parade to the tune of the *batucada* drum line's fast samba beat which inspired the Carnaval route's name: *"El Sambódromo."* Each team or *comparsa* has a minimum of sixty dancers all decked out in tiny bedazzled bikinis and enormous feathered head dresses. All the plumage ends up making the women look like huge exotic birds (albeit partially

---

Flooded Out

The slow and steady flooding of the Zona Baja combined with the construction of a boardwalk (*costanera*) along the river has made displacement a constant issue among Encarnación's marginal population for the past twenty years. A large portion of Encarnación's population made their living working in the Zona Baja's market and few were happy with the prospect of relocating. In addition, distribution of relocation allowances was notoriously uneven – the well connected received large sums early on while the poorer inhabitants of the Zona Baja were not as lucky. Many of the people relocated to neighborhoods created by the EBY (Entidad Binacional Yacyretá) now find themselves stranded in poorly constructed houses far from town in areas serviced infrequently by public transportation. To many, rich and poor, the relocation allowances or *"indemnizaciones"* represented the opportunity for free money. Property owners would often negotiate for payouts from the EBY while at the same time making arrangements for family members or even strangers to move in once they were gone. The new inhabitants could then request their own payouts, providing the former inhabitants with a cut. This scam took place on a large scale as well with ringleaders organizing groups of people to "move" in from all over Paraguay.

naked ones). As they pass by the crowds cheer them on and spray each other with foam. Carnaval is eagerly awaited both by the teams which practice their choreography and decorate costumes and floats for months in advance and spectators who travel from all over the country to enjoy the infectious party atmosphere.

Encarnación's economic activities mostly revolve around commerce with neighboring Argentine city Posadas. Though the commercial activities are not nearly as large in scale (or chaotic) as those of Ciudad del Este a fair amount of people cross the Puente Internacional San Roque González bridge daily to take advantage of the more modern and varied offerings of Posadas and the cheaper imported goods available on the Paraguayan side. The city also has a young feel due to the amount of universities which are attended by many students from the nearby immigrant colonies. An interesting side effect of the city's ethnic diversity is the relatively small amount of Guaraní that is heard on the city streets.

Much of Encarnación's recent history has revolved around Yacyretá, a large hydroelectric power plant managed jointly by Paraguay and Argentina (see Central Hidroeléctric Yacyreta, p186). Though the dam itself is located ninety kilometers downriver in the town of Ayolas, Encarnación is the most populated city upriver from the dam and therefore the most affected by its construction. After years of slowly increasing water levels the entire Zona Baja was completely submerged in 2010. This area was mostly comprised of the market where much of Encarnación's

commercial trade with Argentine neighbor city Posadas took place. The process of relocating the area's residents was long and drawn out, consistently dominating national headlines over the last twenty years. As with the Itaipú Dam, the amount of money generated coupled with very few audits has made the Entidad Binacional Yacyretá (known as "*la Entidad*") which runs the hydroelectric plant a constant source of corruption scandals involving the alleged misdirection of EBY funds and conflicts with inhabitants of the projected flood zone.

Tourists who wish to continue on to Iguazú falls may find Encarnación to be a preferable point of departure over Ciudad del Este to the north. Though further away, Encarnación offers the distinct advantage of a much calmer border crossing. From the Posadas bus station there are several daily buses that make the trip to Puerto Iguazú as well as to the Argentine Jesuit Ruins of San Ignacio Miní.

Carnaval

Carnaval celebrations take place over four consecutive weekends between the end of January and beginning of March (dates vary each year depending on when Easter falls). Tickets are available from the Secretaría de la Comisión de Carnaval (Carnaval Commission) in the ground floor of Encarnación's municipal office as well as in Supermercado España and Stock supermarkets in Asunción. Last minute attendees can also get scalped tickets just outside the *Sambódromo. Tel: 071 200 928, Mariscal Estigarribia and Padre Kreusser, www.carnaval.com.py, Gs. 5,000 – 60,000*

Getting There

Encarnación is located 370 kilometers from Asunción at the southern end of Ruta 1. From the Asunción bus terminal the Encarnacena and Nuestra Señora de Asunción (NSA) are the nicest and fastest options with tickets costing approximately Gs. 65,000. They stop less frequently and are therefore harder to pick up along the way on Route 1 but do tend to stop at Carapeguá and Villa Florida.

Encarnación's bus terminal is very small and crowded – all bus company offices face outwards and there is only a small interior corridor. Most prefer to wait for their buses on the benches surrounding the terminal or in the small restaurants along General Cabañas. Several of the stands across from the terminal offer *mate* and *tereré* services. In the morning hours there is often a small group of women with large baskets full of *yuyos* (medicinal herbs) for *mate* and *tereré* directly behind the stands in the parking lot of the gas station on the corner of Carlos Antonio López and General Cabañas.

Transportation

Encarnación is small city easily manageable on foot. Taxi services are available or you can take a ride in a traditional *karumbé* horse drawn cart – Encarnación is one

---

A Revitalized Waterfront

Encarnación is fast becoming one of Paraguay's hottest summer vacation spots thanks to the "Costanera" project, inaugurated in 2011. Using funds from the Yacyretá hydroelectric dam the city has created eight kilometers of riverside roads and boardwalks, three kilometers of which are sandy beaches. Currently there are three beaches (Playa San José, the most popular, San Isidro and Mbói Ka'é) but the Costanera is projected to be twenty seven kilometers long, so hopefully there will soon be even more places for tourists to enjoy.

of the few cities in Paraguay that keeps up this tradition. These are available at both the bus terminal and the Plaza de Armas (14 de Mayo and Carlos Antonio López). Alternatively, you can rent a car from Localiza.

Localiza *Tel 071 204 097, 071 203 025, Corner of Avenida Irrazabal (Rt 6) and Petronilio Zayas, www.localiza.com.py, Mon-Fri 7am-6:30pm, Sat 8am-12pm*

Tourism Information

Senatur Tourism Information Office *Tel: 0985 794 595, Mariscal Estigarribia between Curupayty and Monseñor Wiessen as well as the Customs building at the border crossing, Daily 7am-5pm*

Koatí Turismo Based out of Bella Vista, Koatí Turismo offers tours of the Jesuit ruins, trips to the area's yerba mate factories, San Rafael and, Iguazú Falls. *Tel: 0767 240 696, 0985 725 530, Corner of Avenida Samaniego and 12 de Octubre as well as a small office in Hotel Papillón, on Facebook, koatiturismo@gmail.com*

🦋 **Fauna Paraguay** Based out of Encarnación, Paul Smith specializes in wildlife and birding tours throughout the country. As the author of several travel guides he has in-depth knowledge of Paraguay's fauna, flora and culture. Tours all over the country with a special emphasis on nature observation. *Tel: 071 207 043, 0985 746 866 but it is better to contact him via email at faunaparaguay@yahoo.com.ar, www.faunaparaguay.com/tours.html,*

Lodging

There are several lodging options in Encarnación, most cater to traveling salesmen who come to Encarnación to do business – as a result most are pretty basic. As a general rule of thumb it is best to avoid hotels close to the university as the streets become cruise spots at night with cars and motorcycles driving noisily back and forth. There are nicer, more scenic options along Route 6 heading north to Ciudad del Este (see Lodging Along Route 6, p178). Their natural surroundings, combined with the proximity to the Jesuit Ruins of Jesús and Trinidad make them more appealing options to those who don't feel like spending much time in Encarnación itself. Note all area hotels fill up quickly during Carnaval season and some may raise their rates.

🛏 **Hotel Germano** This family owned hotel directly across from the bus terminal is the best bet for those on a budget – rooms are very basic but clean. Breakfast is not included. Cheaper options have shared bathrooms and do not include heat or A/C. *Tel: 071 203 346, General Cabañas 488 almost at Carlos Antonio López just across from the bus terminal. Gs. 40,000-60,000 per person.*

🛏 **Hotel Arthur** A very pleasant hotel located at the entrance to town along Route 6. Rooms are large and colorful with comfortable beds. The hotel's nice dining room serves up a good breakfast buffet and there are even DVDs available to rent. Do not be put off by the location – the rooms are set apart from the main road and not noisy. Apartments with kitchens are also available for long term stays. *Tel: 071 205 246, Coronel Luis Irrazabal and Japon, next to the Super Seis supermarket., www.arthurhotel.com.py, Double: Gs: 200,000, Wi-Fi, computers with internet, TV, A/C, mini-fridge, pool, game room*

Hotel Cuarajhy Located two blocks from the terminal – this pleasant hotel is clean with basic rooms and *sommier* style mattresses. The hotel also has a pizzería. There is another branch closer to the center but it is not recommended as the quality of rooms and ambience are not as good. *Tel: 071 206 409, 071 204 922 Sargento Recerchon almost at General Escobar, www.hotelcuarajhypora.com.py, Gs. 80,000 per person, TV, A/C, sauna*

Hotel Cristal Good location one block from the Plaza de Armas, although rooms in the older (and cheaper) section are a bit worn. However the hotel does have a large pool with a good view of Encarnación and the river. Only the rooms in the newer section have real *sommier* mattresses. *Tel: 071 202 371/2, Mariscal Estigarribia 1157 almost at Cerro Corá, Doubles Gs. 175,000 to 200,000, Wi-Fi, TV, A/C, mini-fridge, pool*

Restaurants

🍴 **Hiroshima** Merely flipping through Hiroshima's extensive and colorful menu of authentic Japanese food is likely to make your mouth water. Dishes are delicious and surprisingly affordable. In this landlocked country Hiroshima is your best bet for good sushi and sashimi. If you have a hankering for any authentic dishes (or even green tea) not on the menu, just ask. *Tel: 071 206 288, corner of 25 de Mayo and Lomas Valentinas (entrance is inside parking lot around the corner), Tue-Sun 11:30am-2pm, 7pm-11:30pm, Gs. 10,000-40,000*

🍴 **Mako's Heladería y Confitería** Who can resist the call of an ice cream buffet after a day of walking through the Jesuit ruins in the hot sun? Mako's also serves up juices, coffee and large *empanadas* (including vegetarian options). Plus they have Wi-Fi. *Tel: 071 202 116, Avenida Bernardino Caballero and Lomas Valentinas, www.makos.com.py, daily 7am-12pm, Gs. 6,000-35,000*

Los 2 Chinos Purchase your ice cream at this cute and simple *heladería* and enjoy it in Encarnación's main plaza across the street. The dulce de leche is as rich as can be. *Tomas Romero Pereira and Mariscal Estigarribia. Gs. 5,000*

Karumbé This nice restaurant facing the main plaza offers basic pastas and meats – nothing too fancy but the food is good. Watch the crowds go by from the comfort of their interior dining room or outdoor patio. *Tel: 071 201 147, Mariscal Estigarribia and Tomás R. Pereira, Sun-Thu 11am-1am, Fri-Sat 11am-3am, Gs. 30,000 -50,000*

Media Lunas Calentitas Next to Karumbé and across from Encarnación's main plaza this chain is a good place to enjoy an afternoon coffee and snack, be it a savory *empanada* or sandwich or a sweet dessert. *Tel: 071 201 147, Corner of Mariscal Estigarribia and Tomás R. Pereira, www.medialunascalentitas.com, Thu-Sun 7am-10pm, Gs. 6,000-20,000*

Benndo Pizza Owned by a Mexican-Ukranian couple, this pizzería offers you the option to option to design your own tasty pizza. The quesadillas are good too. *Tel: 0985 818 916, 0975 687 828, 25 de Mayo between Independencia Nacional and Honorio Gonzáles, daily 11am-2pm, 6pm-12pm, Gs 40,000*

Piccola Italia Although a bit removed from the center of town this Italian restaurant has good pizzas and a nice ambience. *Tel: 071 202 344, Pedro Juan Caballero 1894 almost at Rt 1 (Mariscal López), Thu-Tue 5pm-12pm, Gs. 35,000-Gs. 50,000*

🍴 **"Restaurante Oriental" – Mystery Korean place** Finding this hole in the wall restaurant is sort of like going on a treasure hunt – one that ends with a prize of delicious authentic Korean food. The Bulgoki platter, a huge mound of seasoned raw beef cooked on gas burners sunk into the tables, is excellent. *Tel: 071 208 208, General Cabañas between Lomas Valentinas and Independencia Nacional – coming from the bus terminal you will see a white wall on the right-hand side of the street with red Korean symbols and an arrow. Enter and walk through the garden to the restaurant in back. Daily 11am-2pm, 4:30pm-8:30pm, Gs. 20,000-30,000*

Burger King *Tel: 0982 840 057, Superseis Food Court, corner of Avenida Irrazábal and General Cabañas, www.burgerking.com.py, Sun-Thu 10am-11pm, Fri-Sat 10am-12pm, Gs. 10,000-30,000*

Superseis This large supermarket along the main road into town is a good place to stock up on food before heading further afield. There's a cyber cafe as well as Burger King. *Tel: 071 200 009, corner of Avenida Irrazábal and General Cabañas, daily 7am-9:30pm*

Visiting Itapúa's Jesuit Ruins

The ruins have recently received special attention from Paraguay's Ministry of Tourism which developed the *Ruta Jesuítica* (Jesuit Route) project to improve services, activities and information available related to the Jesuit missions. This project lead to the development of the Light and Sound show in Trinidad and construction of an astronomy center at San Cosme y Damián. Perhaps the most useful development has been the introduction of a single ticket (cost: Gs. 25,000 with Paraguayans and residents of Itapúa receiving special discounts) valid for entry to all three sets of ruins. This can be purchased at any of the ruins.

Each set of ruins has one to two guides on staff. If possible it is worth waiting for one to become available for a guided tour. For the most part the ruins are not labeled and visitors are almost entirely dependent on guides to provide historical context and explanations. All the guides work for tips and many are local university students. Very few speak English. If you wish to receive a guided tour of the ruins in English your best bet is to contact the guides listed (this can be hit or miss) or visit the ruins with a tour operator.

Of the ruins Trinidad is the most easily accessed by public transportation, followed by Jesús. Travelers on a budget will want to stay in Encarnación although the lodging along Route 6 is a worthwhile splurge and significantly decreases the travel times to Trinidad and Jesús. San Cosme y Damián can be reached by bus from either Encarnación or Coronel Bogado. Even with a private vehicle those who wish to visit all three ruins should allow for two days – one for Trinidad and Jesús and the other for San Cosme y Damián. The distance and the sights to see are too much for one day – especially since both Trinidad and San Cosme y Damián now offer night time activities as well.

Anatomy of a Jesuit Mission

Each Jesuit mission followed a similar layout, with the main church (*iglesia mayor*) at the epicenter of mission life – both literally and figuratively. At first the churches, along with other buildings were made out of adobe and wood but later there was a shift towards using stone (mostly locally sourced sandstone) as construction materials; only the stone structures have withstood the tests of time. Given its importance it is no surprise that the church was the most ornately decorated of all the mission's buildings. The stones of the church itself were carved – angels and flowers lined the ceilings and there were elaborately framed niches holding stone statues (Trinidad is home to the only intact statue), and in many cases the walls were stuccoed and painted with frescoes. Nature was a popular source of inspiration and decorations often included local flora such as *hoja de guembe*, *guayaba*, and the passion fruit flower. In addition the churches were adorned with beautifully lifelike wooden scultpures (*imágenes*) of saints (these can be seen in Jesuit museums).

In front of the church there extended a large plaza, which, much as in modern day Paraguayan towns, was used for all manner of social and religious activities. A statue of the mission's patron saint (or virgin) was placed in the center of the plaza. Next to the church were a series of buildings which included the residence for the Jesuit priests in charge of the mission along with the schoolrooms, workshops, and food storage rooms (these remain intact in San Cosme y Damián). Behind these buildings lay the cemetery and orchard. The plaza was lined on three sides by indigenous dwellings (*casas de indios*). These long buildings had covered corridors (*corredor yeré*) running along their length and each room belonged to one family. The curved ceramic tiles which lined the roofs of these buildings were shaped upon workers' thighs ("*muslos*" in Spanish) thus earning the name "*musleras*." Many of the buildings included channels for collecting rainwater which was then diverted into the latrines and mission orchard.

Crossing the Border to Posadas

Several buses run between the bus terminal in Posadas to the bus terminal in Encarnación with stops along the way. Buses have signs saying "*Servicio Internacional*" and can be caught on Carlos Antonio López in front of the terminal (the bus does not enter the terminal parking lot). Buses start running at 5am and cost Gs. 5,000 (or 3 Argentine pesos – the buses accept either currency). As citizens of Mercosur countries, Paraguayans and Argentines do not have to disembark for immigration controls at the border – as a result the buses do not automatically stop to let passengers off – you must ask the bus driver to be let off. The bus will not wait for you while you go through immigration but if you save your ticket you can get on the next bus for free. This process is repeated at the immigration controls on the Argentine border as well.

> Immigration control office: 071 206 286, open 24 hours.

Lodging along Route 6

Hotel Tirol Thirteen kilometers from Encarnación the Hotel Tirol is a well established area hotel, receiving guests for over forty years. Only a twenty-five minute bus ride from Encarnación this large complex of stone buildings, multiple pools and walking paths is set into the hillside and feels like it's in a world apart. Hotel facilities are scattered amongst several levels connected by stone stairways. All meals are served buffet style. During Thanksgiving the hotel is deluged with Peace Corps Volunteers from all over the country – a great time for backpackers to make connections and meet travel buddies but a terrible time for those seeking peace and quiet. *Tel: 071 211 054, 071 202 388, Rt 6 km 13, Capitan Miranda, The entrance on the right-hand side of the road (coming from Encarnación) is marked by a large stone archway and sign, all buses that head up Route 6 pass by the hotel – be sure to specify to the driver you wish to get off at El Tirol www.hoteltirol.com.py, Single Gs. 200,000, Double 230,000-400,000, TV, A/C, mini-fridge, pools, tennis courts, pool tables, walking trails*

Parque Manantial The focus on outdoor activities such as swimming and horseback riding makes this park especially popular with vacationing families. Located thirty-five kilometers from Encarnación in the town of Hohenau the extensive grounds (230 hectares) include a rambling creek, several pools and forested areas. A pleasant place for camping, but dorms and bungalows are also available. *Tel: 075 322 250, Route 6, km 35, www.hosteltrail.com/manantial, Day rate Gs. 10,000, camping Gs. 30,000 (does not include pool access which is 15,000), dorms Gs. 55,000 per person, bungalows with A/C Gs. 250,000 per person. Pools, Wi-Fi*

Hotel Papillón A favorite pit stop amongst tourists headed down Route 6 Hotel Papillón is well known for its restaurant's large buffet and classic German dishes. The hotel itself is nice as well and located in a beautiful setting surrounded by trees. From here the *yerba mate* factories of Bella Vista are easily accessed and the Jesuit Ruins are less than twenty kilometers down the road. *Tel: 0767 240 235, Rt 6 km 45, www.papillon.com.py, Single Gs.210,000-260,000, double Gs. 275,000-390,000, TV, A/C, fridge, pools*

Hotel Las Ruinas This small and basic hotel is an option for those who wish to watch the nighttime sound and light show at Trinidad but do not want to deal with catching a bus along Route 6 at night. However the hotel's service is variable and does not compare to that of the area's more established hotels. *Tel: 0985 828 563, next to ruins of Trinidad, www.hotel-a-las-ruinas.hola-paraguay.com, Gs. 70,000-100,000*

SANTÍSIMA TRINIDAD DEL PARANÁ

Founded in 1706 by Juan de Anaya, the mission of Santísima Trinidad del Paraná (usually shortened to Trinidad) was the second to last of the thirty Jesuit missions to be built. Founded with overflow from the mission of San Carlos de Borrome, construction began in 1712. In fact, the mission was still under construction when Jesuits were expelled from Paraguay in 1767. At its peak Trinidad was home to over 4,000 indigenous, all under the supervision of just two to three Jesuit priests.

Of all the missions in Paraguay, Trinidad has the most remaining structures – there are ruins of almost all of the elements that made up a typical Jesuit mission. Visitors to the mission enter onto the exceptionally large main plaza, surrounded on all sides by the indigenous dwellings. The twenty-one stone buildings housed between six and eight families each. The buildings were lined with a long corridor, the arches of which still remain. Visitors to any of the Jesuit towns in Misiones will easily be able to picture these dwellings as they once were – most towns retain a significant portion of their mission's indigenous dwellings. To the right (if facing the main church) is the mission's first church. Unlike most missions there were two churches in Trinidad, the first, referred to as the "*iglesia primitiva*" smaller in size than the second, referred to as the "*iglesia mayor*." Beside this smaller church is the square fort-like watch tower.

> For preservation purposes, thirty percent of the mission has been deconstructed and rebuilt with better mortar.

Trinidad's main, larger church is the mission's most impressive and evocative structure. At eighty-five meters long by forty-three meters wide and fourteen meters high the church is quite large and still retains several examples of the decorative elements that made it one of the most beautiful of all the missions. The exterior wall has a niche with a stone sculpture of St. Paul. This is a rarity as almost all the stone statues in the missions were smashed by looters, who, due to rumors of Jesuit treasure (see From Riches to Ruins, p159), expected them to be filled with gold. Along the walls are large carved stone frames which once displayed elaborate paintings in their interior. The remaining doorways are intricately carved. The church's baptismal font, decorated with *hojas de guembe* (philodendron leaves) is one of the few pieces in the mission to be unearthed almost completely intact. The pulpit, on the other hand was discovered in over 600 pieces and had to be painstakingly reconstructed. The altar, however, was not recovered and has been replaced with an altar created for the Papal visit in 1989. Beneath the spot where the church's original altar once stood are stairs leading below ground to the area where the mission's indigenous leaders or *caciques* were buried.

The highlight of the church is a troupe of musically inclined angels lining the upper walls to either side of what was once the altar. Carved in relief, the robed angels are depicted playing all manner of instruments – the violin, harp, clavichord, trumpet, and maraca among them. These speak to the musical heritage of the Jesuit missions which still lives to this day. There are other angels as well including some shown lighting incense and there is also a depiction of the Virgin Mary the baby Jesus.

Towards the back of the church to the right is a small room functioning as a museum. The entrance is topped by a large stone chalice and framed with elaborately carved Corinthian columns (as is the opposite doorway). Inside the museum are with shelves full of stone pieces including carved angel heads and passion fruit flowers which were found on the premises. Some stones still bear the faint remnants of their original stucco and painted decorations. The tombstone in center display includes use of the Guaraní word "*omano*" which means "die." This room is usually kept locked and only accessible with a guide – it is definitely worth visiting though as it includes a helpful small scale model of the Trinidad mission.

The South

Through the museum is another courtyard, this one surrounded by the remains of the mission's school and workshops. Behind it lays the mission orchard. A covered corridor near the front of the church is home to several more stone pieces including tombstones and two large gargoyles used for water channels.

Once you have walked around all the ruins, admired the elaborate stone carvings and attempted to conjure up an image of what this mission was like at its peak it is easy to see why Trinidad has been declared a UNESCO World Heritage site. *Summer 7am-7pm, winter 7am-5:30pm, Entry fee Gs. 25,000 valid for ruins of Jesús and San Cosme y Damián as well. Guides: Edgar Paredes, Tel: 0985 772 803, Guides: Castorina Obregón 0985 753 997, Kristina Zarza 0985 712 979*

Sound & Light Show

The sound and light show is an interesting opportunity to view the ruins in a different light (literally). Guarani-Baroque music from the Jesuit era is played as floodlights illuminate the *casa de indios* and smaller lights create a twilight effect throughout the ruins. Meanwhile Jesuit themed images are projected onto the walls of the mission's church. The show lasts about an hour and is an interesting way to experience the ruins, though those depending on public transportation may find it is not preferable to a daytime visit. *Thu-Sun, Summer 8:30pm, winter 7pm.*

Getting There

Trinidad is located just off the side of Route 6 at km 30. The turn off is well signed. Coming from Encarnación it is on the right-hand side of the road.

Buses heading past "*las ruinas*" leave from Encarnación's bus terminal every hour. The ride takes between half an hour to an hour so it is best to ask at the terminal which bus will get you there the fastest. Bus fare is approximately Gs. 6,000. If you plan on returning to Encarnación by bus keep in mind that there are significantly less buses on Route 6 past dusk.

JESÚS DE TAVARANGUÉ

Founded in 1685, the Jesús mission moved to current location in 1758, only nine years before the Jesuits were expelled from Paraguay. This was the last of the thirty missions to be built and, in fact, was never completed. It is said to have been home to over 3,000 indigenous.

Though not nearly as complete as the ruins of Trinidad or of San Cosme y Damián, Jesús is impressive in its own right. Built on a high point the mission, with its imposing church set against a beautiful backdrop of palm trees and rolling hills, has a mystical quality. The fact that it receives significantly less visitors than Trinidad only adds to the calm atmosphere.

The church, or *iglesia mayor*, is the mission's principal remaining structure. Most visitors will first glimpse the church from the side before rounding the corner to the main entrance. From this angle the church, a fifty-nine-meter by twenty-four-meter building with eleven-meter high walls (of which only the upper portions were reconstructed) resembles a large fortress.

The Jesús mission used to be linked to the neighboring mission of Trinidad. Together, they were referred to as "*Trinidad y Jesús.*" However, after the expulsion of the Jesuits it became aptly known as Jesús de Tavarangue which in Guaraní means "Jesús, the town that was going to be."

The main entrance to the church is flanked by niches adorned with passion fruit flowers, guavas, and palm and olive branches and topped with a papal insignia.

The church's incomplete interior is the most picturesque part of Jesús. Where brown stone floors were meant to stand grows emerald green grass. Out of the grass jut two rows of seven large, incomplete columns. These were meant to support the roof – which was also never completed. To the right-hand side is a small area meant to hold the baptismal font – the walls are covered in original white stucco which is also visible in some of the decorative columns along the interior church walls.

Exiting the church (to the right) is the original stair case leading to the bell tower. Climb up for an excellent view of the remaining mission structures and landscapes beyond.

Running perpendicular to the back of the church are a series of rooms that were used as the school and workshops. Aside from the church these are the only other large remains of the mission. However vestiges of the indigenous dwellings to the right-hand side of what was once the main plaza in front of the church have been excavated. *Summer 7am-7pm, winter 7am-5:30pm, Entry fee Gs. 25,000 valid for ruins of Trinidad and San Cosme y Damián as well. Guides: Lira Hein 0985 743 340.*

Getting There

The turn off for Jesús is at km 30 of Route 6 just one hundred meters past Trinidad. Coming from Encarnación it is on the left and well signed. Taxis for Jesús can be picked up at the Petrosur gas station on Route 6 at the turn off for approximately Gs.50,000 round trip. Jesús is ten kilometers down this road which, as of 2011 was being paved. The road's landscape and town's colorfully painted clapboard houses make for a picturesque trip. The ruins are just past the main plaza and church.

Those traveling by bus are better off visiting Jesús first and then backtracking to the ruins of Trinidad. Ending the day at Trinidad will provide more bus options for returning to Encarnación or heading further north on Route 6. There are a few buses that run from Encarnación's bus terminal (specify that you want to go to Jesús and not Trinidad) and stop by the Petrosur gas station at the turn off to Jesús throughout the day. The 3pm bus, however, is probably the latest bus one can catch in order to have enough time to return by bus as well (the last bus leaves town at 6pm). *Gs. 4,000-10,000.*

The South

Guaraní Baroque Music

Music was a particular focus of mission life. Jesuit priests with musical backgrounds were recruited from Europe to teach mission residents to both construct and play musical instruments. Each mission had between thirty and forty indigenous musicians who accompanied all the masses. According to historical documents the Guaraní indians were particularly gifted musicians. The Jesuit bands included oboe, lute, harp (from which the modern day Paraguayan harp descended), clarinet, violin, and viola, among other classical instruments. Though the mission choirs and orchestras have long since fallen silent their music has recently been revived. In 1972 over 5,000 musical manuscripts were discovered in a Jesuit mission of Bolivia. These have been studied assiduously by Luis Szaran, the director of Asuncion's symphony orchestra. The music of the Jesuit missions has been a particular passion of his and for over twenty years Szaran has dedicated himself to researching and publishing music played in the Jesuit missions. He even directed a concert of said music in the ruins of Trinidad for the King and Queen of Spain. A four CD collection of Jesuit-era Guarani-Baroque music is avaliable through his website www.luisszaran.org as are various books which include sheet music.

BELLA VISTA

Continuing up Route 6 past the Jesuit missions is the town of Bella Vista. Due to the area's five large *yerba mate* plantations Bella Vista was officially declared the "Capital de la Yerba Mate" in 1992. Every year the *Día Nacional de la Yerba Mate* is celebrated on October 11th. Indeed, *yerba mate* production is the town's main economic engine. Like Hohenau and Obligado, the other towns that make up the Colonias Unidas, Bella Vista is largely populated by Paraguayans of German descent. Most are dedicated to large scale agriculture, not only of *yerba* but also soy, tung and sunflowers (processed into oil), and, most recently, macadamia nuts. The prosperity that has resulted from the combination of fertile soil and farmers with the means and education to work it efficiently is palpable. All three towns have a the feel of a first world suburb (with a Paraguayan twist, of course) that is distinctly different from other, less affluent areas of rural Paraguay.

Mate Roga

The tourism information center, whose name means "mate house" is hard to miss since it is just past the enormous mate gourd sculpture, complete with *bombilla*, on Route 6. In addition to providing information on the *yerba mate* production process the center can help arrange for tours of the *yerba mate* factory, excursions on the Paraná River from the port of Bella Vista, and even a trip to a macadamia nut farm. *Tel: 0767 240 724, Rt 6 km 46 at the Bella Vista roundabout, www.materoga.coloniasunidas.com.py, Mon-Fri 7am-12pm, 1:30-5pm, Sat 8am-11:30pm, 2pm-7pm, Sun 8am-11:30am, 2pm-5pm*

Yerba Selecta Factory

Selecta is one of Paraguay's most popular brands of *yerba mate*. Wearing a typical dress while extending a *tereré guampa*, the Yerba Selecta lady stares out invitingly at Paraguayans from *yerba* packages on the shelves of every grocery store and *almacén*. Visitors to the Selecta factory can witness the entire process that turns the *yerba mate* bush into the loose *yerba* that Paraguayans consume so voraciously as hot *mate* and *cocido* and ice cold *tereré*. *Tel: 0767 240 339, Avenida General Maríal Samaniego km 4.5, from the Bella Vista roundabout take a left (if coming from Encarnación) and the factory grounds will be on the right-hand side about 4.5 kilometers down the road, www.selecta.com.py, Mon-Sat 7am-11am, advanced reservations suggested, entry fee $5USD for foreigners, free for Paraguayans, tours on Saturdays only with prior notice*

RESERVA SAN RAFAEL

Paraguay's 73,000-plus hectare Parque Nacional San Rafael was created in the 1990's in an attempt to protect the region's rapidly disappearing Atlantic Forest ecosystem. The Atlantic Forest is widely regarded as one of Paraguay's most biologically diverse ecosystem and in 1997 San Rafael was declared an Important Birding Area. Visitors to either of the two lodging options within the park may be surprised at the quantity of agriculture taking place around both areas. Protection of the park's flora and fauna is hampered by the fact that much of the park is still in private hands; many large land-owners as well as Mbya Guaraní indigenous communities reside within its borders. Vast tracts of the park are continually razed for cattle grazing and soy farming and clandestine logging operations are so common that park rangers must take extreme caution while on patrol.

👍 Procosara Lodge

The brainchild of Swiss couple Christine and Hanz Hostettler, PROCOSARA is an NGO set up for the protection of San Rafael. Since arriving in San Rafael over twenty years ago the Hostelttler's have witnessed the rapid destruction of the Atlantic Forest surrounding their land – don't miss the chance to talk with them about their experience with the many obstacles that face nature conservation efforts in Paraguay. Visitors can swim in the man-made lake created to generate electricity and walk along three trails leading into the first growth forest where birds, monkeys, and enormous tree ferns abound. Lodging options include two cute and clean wood cabins with private rooms as well as camping facilities. Full room and board is recommended as there are no nearby options and Christine's cooking is excellent. *Tel: 0768 295 046 (Christine Hostettler o Celia Garayo), there is no direct public transportation to the PROCOSARA lodge. Visitors should take a Beato Roque Gonzalez bus to Caronay or Cruce Ynambu from the Encarnación bus terminal (buses leave at 8am and 11:30), having already arranged for PROCOSARA to meet them to go the rest of the way. Expect a long, dusty, bumpy ride. Be sure to ask the bus driver to let you know where to get off (and remind him). You can also coordinate with PROCOSARA to be picked up from further out such as Encarnación. This adds significantly to the cost of the trip out but may be worth it for those who do not want to deal with the bus. Those in private vehicles should note after rain the dirt roads are often only passable with four wheel drive. Gs. 110,000 per person with full board meals; Gs. 20,000 camping per tent, meals separate. Peace Corps Volunteers are often allowed to camp for free. Lake, campgrounds, walking trails.*

Guyra Kanguery Birding Station

The Guyra Retã Nature Reserve offers visitors the chance to see a number of birds both in the grasslands below the Kanguery birding station and the forests to its side. There are nature trails that wind their way through the forest along the edge of a flowing creek and you can even climb up through the hollowed out trunk of an enormous tree to a small observation stand up top. While Procosara is more comfortable, avid birders may prefer Guyra's lodge due to the expertise of their guides. There are no options nearby for purchasing food but those on a budget can consult Guyra about preparing food in the field station kitchen. Reservations must be made through Guyra Paraguay's main office in Asunción (see Guided Tours, p65). *Tel: 021 223 567, 0981 866 383, there is no public transportation to the station. Visitors should take a Beato Roque Gonzalez bus to Potrero from the Encarnación bus terminal (buses leave at 8am and 11:30), having previously arranged for Kanguerý park guards to transport them the rest of the way (Gs. 65,000). Guyra can arrange for private transportation from Encarnación or other points along Route 6, as well as organize an excursion from Asunción. www.guyra.org.py, birding.paraguay@gmail.com, Dorm rooms Gs. 70,000 per person, camping Gs. 30,000, park day pass Gs. 15,000, nature trails*

SANTIAGO

In 1669 the mission of San Ignacio de Caaguazú, located to the north on the edges of the Apa River was forced to relocate (see Missions Under Attack, p168) and chose present day Santiago as its new home. The mission was renamed Santiago and grew to a size of 3,000 inhabitants. Remnants of the town's Jesuit past include many buildings surrounding an enormous shady plaza (the largest in the country) and the

The South

crumbling remains of the walls and foundation of the original church. Santiago's Jesuit museum and church contain a number of large statues and rare examples of "*retablos*," painted wooden tablets that adorned the church. In January the town plays host to two large scale cowboy festivals which draw visitors and participants from ranches in Paraguay, Uruguay, Argentina and Brazil. If you plan to attend it is best to stay in Ayolas as the few lodging options in Santiago (mostly private homes with small rooms for rent) are deluged with festival participants. Santiago is an easy day trip from Ayolas (thirty kilometers away) and San Ignacio (fifty kilometers away).

Museo Jesuítico de Santiago

Santiago's Jesuit museum is located across from the main plaza where the mission's church once stood. The deteriorating church was demolished in the 1920's – to the side of the museum one can still see a few portions that remain of the church's thick adobe walls. The museum has many sculptures, both small and large. The most evocative sculpture is of the Risen Christ wrapped in seemingly wind-swept robes that still shine with gold-leaf. Although they are displayed poorly in a small room to the side of the entrance, the painted *retablos* or wood panels are the museum's most unique pieces. These beautifully decorated panels once stood in the church's main altar and are adorned with angels, stars and even sheep. Next door the town church has a few sculptures as well, including a slightly gruesome statue of Santiago el Matamoro (St. James the Moor-killer) in action – some have suggested that in this case he is chasing after *bandeirantes* rather than Moors. The altar includes decorated panels painted with a baptismal theme. Like the painted panels in the museum these are a rarity amongst the surviving decorations of the missions. *Tel: 0782 20211, Corner of Julia Cuendo de Estigarribia and Fulgencio Yegros, Mon-Sat 8am-11am, 2pm-5pm, Gs. 5,000*

Festival Latinoamericano de la Doma y el Folklore

Held the first week in January this event draws upwards of 10,000 people. The festivities include parades, equestrian shows, horse taming showcases, traditional dances and music as well as massive amounts of asado a la estaca (over 2,300 kilos of meat were consumed in the 2010 festival) and other typical Misiones dishes. The festival is held at Estancia Tacuaty – and organized by Santiago based EMITUR dedicated to tourism in the Misiones department. *www.emitur.com.py*

Fiesta de la Tradición Misionera

Also in January is the Fiesta de la Tradición Misionera held in the main plaza of Santiago and the Lion's Club. The festival is similar to the Festival Latinoamericano de la Doma y el Folklore but has the advantage of being more easily accessible by public transportation.

Lodging

Hotel Estancia Tacuaty Every January this large ranch is filled with cowboys from all over Paraguay coming to participate in the Festival Latinoamericano de la Doma y el Folklore. The rest of the year the *estancia* is a calm place to relax and enjoy the daily activities of large Paraguayan ranch, as well as fishing, horseback riding and swimming. *Tel: 0782 202 86, 0975 626 780, approximately four kilometers from Route 1 along the turn off to San Ignacio and then 1.5 kilometers down a dirt road, www.emitur.com.py, Gs. 160,000 per person (full room and board), TV, A/C, pool*

AYOLAS

Founded in 1899 Ayolas remained a small fishing village until the mid 1970's when Paraguay and Argentina signed a treaty to construct the Yacyretá hydroelectric plant nearby. The resulting influx of over 8,000 engineers and construction workers changed this tiny town forever. Nowadays the sprawling town has a distinctly suburban feel that is very different from most Paraguayan towns (most notably the roads are almost all paved). Ayolas is set on high ground overlooking the Paraná River just as it curves around what remains of the Isla Yacyretá, 90 percent of which was submerged by the dam's reservoir. Though Yacyretá constantly plays second fiddle to the larger, more impressive Itaipú the natural scenery that surrounds the dam makes a visit worthwhile.

> During the Jesuit era Ayolas, then named San José Mi, was the port for the mission of San Ignacio.

Fishing

Ayolas is well known throughout Paraguay as a fishing destination that rivals Villa Florida to the north. In particular tourists (especially Brazilians) flock to Ayolas for the chance to fish a prized dorado out of the waters. There are no organized fishing tours but hotel staff will happily help arrange for a guide. Be careful to negotiate a fixed price ahead of time, especially regarding fuel costs (see Fishing, p68). Though he is based out of Florida, Andrew Esposito of Mission Tours is a good source for connecting with reputable fishing guides in Ayolas. A former Peace Corps volunteer, Andrew is very friendly and well-versed in the ins and outs of organizing fishing tours. Be sure to contact him in advance. *www.Misionesparaguay.com*, *info@Misionesparaguay.com*

Club Social y Deportivo Yacyretá

The nicest area from which to enjoy the view of the river is the Club Social y Deportivo whose grounds are open to the public. From here you can see the river in all its glory, and across from it the vegetation of Isla Yacyretá. This is also a great spot for bird watching – keep your eyes open for burrowing owls that live in earthen nests

---

Jineteadas: Paraguay's Rodeo

Attending a *jineteada* is a great way to see Latin American style of taming wild horses and young colts. See *jinetes* (male riders) and *amazonas* (female riders) strut their stuff during activities that include parades, *doma de potro* (colt taming/ horse breaking), and sometimes a *corrida de toros* (bull race), all to the tune of upbeat music heavy on the percussion and brass. No *jineteada* is complete without the participation of sometimes surprisingly young riders who demonstrate their skills to the delight of the crowds. Many cattle ranches remain family affairs with participants spanning generations from grandmothers and fathers presiding over the events to small children slowly but surely being introduced into the culture starting with *sulky* rides and then working their way up.

   Jineteadas are not specific to Misiones, in fact they are held routinely nationwide. Local radio can be a good place to find out about upcoming *jineteadas*. This is an especially popular past time in rural areas. A good source of information on upcoming *jineteadas* throughout the country is the Asociación de Jinetes del Paraguay. *www.ajp.com.py*

The South

on the hillside. Grab a quick bite or sit down for a full meal before heading down to the club's waterfront – when the levels are low there is a nice sandy beach to sit on.

Lodging

Hotel Nacional de Turismo de Ayolas The Hotel Nacional de Turismo is located on a highpoint above the river. The view is great and there is a walking path down to the river's edge. Like its sister hotel in Villa Florida, the building is built in a colonial style with wraparound corridors, tiled floors, and high ceilings. Breakfast not included. The large fish mounted at the entrance is sure to inspire you to order up ever-popular fish dishes from the hotel's restaurant. *Tel: 072 222 274, 021 222 273, Single Gs. 50,000, Double Gs. 100,000, Triple Gs 120,000, Wi-Fi, A/C, pool, tennis courts*

Hotel Ayolas Located right at the water's edge this hotel has a great view making up for the fact that the rooms are a little worn. The hotel's restaurant is a good option for savoring *surubí* or *dorado* the while admiring the waters where your meal once swam. *Tel: 072 222 381, Double Gs. 140,000-180,000, Wi-Fi, TV, A/C*

Hotel Kadel Located in the center of town, Hotel Kadel is a bit past its prime but worth staying at if hotels on the river are full. Rooms are basic and a bit small. *Tel: 072 222 153, Mariscal López 1292 in the Barrio San Antonio neighborhood, Gs. 50,000 per person, TV, A/C, mini-fridge*

Restaurants

Restaurant Lizza The restaurant's plain and humble exterior belies the quirky ambience that awaits its diners. No surface has been left undecorated – the walls are covered with guitars, harps, and paintings and hammocks and baskets galore hang overhead. Portions are very generous. *Tel: 072 222 1756, at the entrance to town just past the welcome sign, 7am-12pm, Gs.20,000-30,000*

Restaurant del Club Social y Deportivo Yacyretá *See previous listing*

Hotel Ayolas *See previous listing*

Hotel Nacional de Turismo de Ayolas *See previous listing*

CENTRAL HIDROELÉCTRICA YACYRETÁ

The Yacyretá hydroelectric plant's history began in the 1920's when studies were done seeking to improve navigation on the notoriously rapid Paraná River. In the 1950's Paraguay and Argentina began working together to study the possibility of harnessing the power of the river to create electricity and in 1973 the *Tratado de Yacyretá* (Treaty of Yacyretá) was signed between the two countries. With that came the creation of the Entidad Binacional Yacyretá (EBY for short) through which both nations jointly administer the dam.

Yacyretá's construction, which began in 1983, came at a high environmental cost to southern Paraguay. The creation of the 808-meter long dam resulted in the flooding of 90 percent of the Isla Yacyretá (Yacyretá Island) located in the middle of the Paraná River and the complete flooding of Encarnación's lower Zona Baja region (see Flooded Out, p172). Though the EBY created the Reserva Faunístico Atinguy wildlife refuge for animals displaced by the flooding, countless creatures, many of them already endangered, lost their natural habitat. In addition the damming of the river has resulted in the severe depletion of *dorado* fish; the fish elevator constructed within the dam has not been effective enough at aiding the fish to migrate upriver.

Today twenty turbines are in use generating approximately 19,000 kilowatt hours per year – almost a third of what Itaipú generates. Paraguay receives half of the electricity produced, although due to the country's relatively low energy needs, about

80 percent of this is then sold back to Argentina. There are plans to install another series of turbines along the Aña Kua which leads from Ayolas to the dam on the Isla Yacyretá. This is projected to increase the dam's generating capacity to 20,000 kilowatt hours per year.

Much like Itaipú the EBY generates a significant amount of money and as such is a constant source of newspaper headlines decrying corruption. Misuse of EBY funds is rampant and there have been several scandals involving the relocation allowances provided for people who live within the flood zone (see Flooded Out, p172). The construction cost of the dam itself was originally estimated at US $ 2.5 million but to this date totals over US$ 11.5 million. Argentine President Carlos Menem even went on record stating that Yacyretá was a "monument to corruption."

Free tours of the damn are offered daily and last about an hour. The tour begins with a Spanish language video about the dam's construction before visitors are loaded onto a bus which crosses the Aña Kua bridge to the Isla Yacyretá. There the tour passes through the impressive turbine hall before crossing the dam's retaining wall and stopping at the water lock. The

> In Guaraní "yacyreta" has two potential meanings: "land where the moon is born" and "land of difficult waters."

Yacyretá complex also includes a museum with indigenous artifacts found during the construction of the dam and an extensive (but poorly preserved) collection of stuffed birds, mammals and insects from the flood area. Visitors must sign in with their name, nationality and passport number at least half an hour before the tour either by phone or in person (which leaves enough time for a quick visit to the museum before the tour starts). Although transportation is not provided, it is also possible to visit the Reserva Faunístico Atinguy (see following section), and, with special permission, some remaining unflooded areas of Isla Yacyretá. *Tel: 072 222 276, 021 445 055, www.eby.gov.py, tour hours 8:30am, 10am, 2pm, Museum hours 7am-12pm, 1pm-4pm*

RESERVA FAUNÍSTICO ATINGUY

This one hundred hectare park was created to house a representative group of animals displaced by the flooding of Isla Yacyretá. The location was chosen to approximate the animals' original habitat on the Isla Yacyretá. To the left of the main entrance is a wooded area with a walking path to a zoo with cages housing several large felines, anteaters, ducks, *pavo del monte*, macaws and caimans. While following the winding path make sure to look up in the trees to spot monkeys and plenty of birds. Unfortunately the larger animals are confined to excessively (and unnecessarily, it would seem) small cages.

> Atinguy is one of the only places in the world where the maned wolf (known as the "aguara guazu") has been successfully bred in captivity.

The cleared section to the left of the park's main entrance house the animal reproduction area where park experts oversee the breeding in captivity of four endangered species: the *ciervo de los pantanos* (marsh deer), the *pavo del monte* or *mytu* (bare-faced curassow), the *ñandu guazú* (greater rhea), and the *aguara guazu* (maned wolf).

Tel: 0981 413 614 (Dr. Evelio Narvaes, head biologist), Atinguy is only accessible by private vehicle. The turn off for Atinguy is right at the entrance to Ayolas – if coming from Asunción you will have to make a hairpin turn to the left onto the dirt and gravel road and then continue approximately 10 kilometers. 8am-4:30pm

Visiting Reserva Isla Yacyretá

With some advance planning it is possible to visit the Reserva Natural Yacyretá on the island of Yacyretá. The reserve covers over 8,000 hectares, 6,000 of which remain untouched. The remaining 2,000 hectares are home to the reserve's visitor's center as well as approximately one hundred families who survive mostly on assistance from EBY as well as fishing and small scale agriculture. The visit starts off in the small visitor's center – from here you can walk around the island, through the wooded areas, by the lagoons and along the sand dunes, all under the shadow of giant power transmission towers. Be sure to bring binoculars as the birding is quite good and there are also monkeys in the trees. The tour is all done on foot – make sure to take water and pack food. *In order to arrange for a guided visit with a park ranger contact the Sector Medio Ambiente (Environmental sector) of EBY at 072 222 220. Taxis from Ayolas to the island should cost between Gs. 40,000 and 50,000 each way*

Getting There

The turn off to Ayolas is located on Route 1 just past San Patricio at km 258. From there continue about fifty kilometers down the paved road and the signed entrance to Ayolas will be on the right-hand side. Once in Ayolas Taxi Gomez (*Tel: 072 222 817, 0975 649 358, 0985 724 662*) is a good bet for taxi service (he has large vehicles as well for transporting groups).

Ayolas is approximately two hours from Encarnación (tickets cost Gs. 25,000) and six from Asunción by bus (tickets cost Gs. 70,000). The Pilarense and Yacyretá bus lines make the journey from both cities. Since almost all buses to Ayolas pass through Santiago it is possible to stop in Santiago first, visit the Jesuit museum, and then continue on to Ayolas on a later bus.

SAN COSME Y DAMIÁN

Calling the Jesuit mission of San Cosme y Damián "ruins" would be a misnomer as almost all the remaining buildings are still in use by the surrounding community. Perhaps for this reason out of all the ruins San Cosme provides the best feel for what a functioning Jesuit mission was like. Though it is further from Encarnación than both Trinidad and Jesús, San Cosme is a worthwhile day trip, not only for the ruins but also for the beautifully serene natural landscapes that surround them.

Though the mission was founded in Brazil in 1632 it was forced to move several times due to attacks from slave traders (see Missions Under Attack, p168) before settling in its current location at a wide bend in the Paraná River in 1760, only seven years before the order's expulsion from Paraguay. At the time the mission functioned as one of the most important centers for astronomical observation in all of South America (see Father Buenaventura, The Jesuit Astronomer, p190). Today the most distinctive feature of San Cosme y Damián is that it boasts the only original Jesuit church to still be in use.

Originally the entire mission was surrounded by a five-meter high wall, the remains of which can still be seen next to the church. The mission's entrance portal has been reconstructed (the red sandstone portion is original) and features a curious carved bat. Underneath are two chalices, symbols of the medical saints for which the mission is named.

> Saint Cosmas and Saint Damián were twin healers.

At sixty-five by twelve meters with ten-meter high walls the church was meant to be a provisional structure but the Jesuits were expelled before the *iglesia mayor* (main church) could be completed. As a result the church lacks many of the decorative elements still visible in the ruins of Trinidad or Jesús. However, as it remains a fully functional church its interior is adorned with twenty-two wooden sculptures which were carved in the mission's workshops. Many of these conserve their original paint and gold leaf. Highlights include St. Michael battling a hermaphrodite devil and Sts. Cosmas and Damián for which the mission is named. Another prized piece is the gold-leafed wooden chair in used by Pope John Paul II during his visit to Paraguay in 1989. Towards the back of the church are original stone baptismal fonts. The center section of the church floor is original and you can see the decorative etchings creating a geometric tile effect. In 1889 the church was damaged by a fire. The undamaged part remained in use until 1971 when the roof finally collapsed and was not reconstructed until 1991.

> Had the main church been built, this building would have been subdivided into rooms for a school and workshop – this accounts for all the doors.

The corner room behind the church once functioned as a kitchen with an adjacent dining room. In the room to the right (the *lavadero*) you can see an original hand washing station with water coming out of carved faces. Extending to the right are rooms that functioned as the workshops and the school and are still in use today. Restoration of this area took place between 1994 and 1997. All rooms have original decorative elements – painted walls and ceilings, wrought ironwork. The doors of the fourth room (labeled room seven) are original and were used as models for the rest of the mission's reconstructed doors. The second room has a surprisingly sturdy original ladder leading up to the attic, which extends the length of the building. From the second floor you can peer into the mission's courtyard and see the ruins of what was intended to be the main mission church. From the exterior windows the Paraná River is visible in the distance. Be careful when walking around the attic though as all the floorboards are original and there are some areas with gaps.

The last room is believed to have been the observatory where Father Buenaventura studied the night sky. The only vestige of this once famous observatory is the sundial in the building's courtyard. The dial, dating from 1718, marks time from 7am to 5pm in a counter clockwise half circle. Father Buenaventura's legacy has been honored with the creation of a modern astronomy center just across from the mission's main plaza.

> The entrance to the mission cellar was rumored to be the beginning of an underground tunnel leading out to the river.

The now grassy interior courtyard was once covered in stones and designed to funnel rain water towards channels leading to the latrines next to the observatory. Rounding the corner you can walk along the back corridor of the building and enjoy the view.

As with other Jesuit towns, the remaining indigenous dwellings, built along the sides of the main plaza, are currently in use as offices and private homes.

On a cool day the approximately 1.5 km walk down to the river banks is quite enjoyable. If facing the mission walk one block to the right and then take the dirt road to the left which leads all the way down to the water. Another option is to walk to the left along the road that runs behind the mission. Along the way you will pass the traditional clapboard houses of the town's rural residents as well as many oven birds (*alonsitos* or *horneros*) poking their heads out of their circular mud nests in the trees.

The South

Centro de Interpretación Astronómica Buenaventura Suárez

As part of the push for improvements to the *Ruta Jesuítica* (Jesuit Route) Paraguay's tourism ministry inaugurated the Centro de Interpretación Astronómica Buenaventura Suárez astronomy center in early 2010. The center is located in what used to be the *casa de indios* (indigenous dwellings) sector of the San Cosme mission (across the plaza from the church). The planetarium and observatory (equipped with an eleven inch Celestron telescope) allows visitors to place themselves in the shoes of Father Buenaventura Suárez, Jesuit priest and astronomer, observing the night skies of San Cosme y Damián. *Summer 7am-6pm daily, winter 7am-5:30pm daily, Entry fee Gs. 25,000 valid for ruins of Trinidad and Jesús as well. Guides: Rolando Barboza 073 275 286, 0985 732 956, Mariela Cantero 0985 933532, Perla Machuca 0985 732 956*

Ybycuí Sand Dunes

Adding to the allure of San Cosme y Damián are the sand dunes jutting out from the waters of the Yacyretá lake. Exploring the series of small islands, spread across fifty hectares, you may feel you are not in landlocked Paraguay. Some of the dunes are over thirty meters high – unfortunately this is not enough to spare them from becoming completely submerged once the Yacyretá Dam raises the reservoir's waters to the projected eighty-three-meter level. It takes between forty-five minutes and an hour to reach the dunes by boat and, due to the heat, this trip is best done in the early morning. There are several local guides but it is best to contact the tourism commission of San Cosme to see who has upcoming trips scheduled as going with a group will significantly reduce the trip cost (approximate price for a 10-person boat is Gs. 500,000). *Tel: 0985 110 047*

Father Buenaventura: the Jesuit Astronomer

Born in 1678 in present day Santa Fe, Argentina, Father Buenaventura Suarez entered the Jesuit order in 1695. In 1706 he joined the San Cosme y Damián mision and though in 1714 he moved to a different mission he returned to San Cosme several times during his life. Over the course of thirty three years he produced annual comprehensive lunar calendars which were distributed throughout the Jesuit Misiones and include information such as sunrise and sunset times, calendar for lunar phases, solar and lunar eclispses and various other astronomical data as well as information on religious dates and weather predictions. His *"Lunario de un Siglo,"* published in 1740, was an extraordinarily detailed work in which Buenaventura determined lunar activity from 1740 to 1841. The majority of his research for the book was done without advanced astronomical tools which were unavailable in the region. Instead Buenaventura depended on locally sourced materials such as quartz crystals from the Paraná River which he used as lenses.

For those interested in persuing astronomy in Paraguay the Asociación de Aficionados a la Astronomía holds meetings in their headquarters in Asunción the first and third Saturday of every month from 3:00 to 5:00. Their website contains information about constellations visible from Paraguay's night sky as well as information on Guaraní and Jesuit astronomy. The website (*www.astropar.org*) also has Padre Buenaventura's Libro Lunario available in its entirety in PDF format. *Tel: 0982 334 893, Calle Mayor Martinez and Lazaro de Rivera (in Asuncion's Sajonia neighborhood) www.astropar.org*

Lodging

Hospedaje Aguapey This new hotel about eight blocks from the ruins arrange for tours of the mission, sand dunes and surrounding areas including the Yacyretá hydroelectric reserve in Ayolas. *Tel: 073 725 293, 0981 981 729, www.turismoaguapey.jimdo.com, on Facebook, located at the end of the paved road into town across from the police station*

Hospedaje Stella Maris This small humble house has two guest rooms with a shared bathroom. The owners serve up basic but tasty Paraguayan fare including juicy *bife al caballo* (steak smothered in grilled onions and an egg) out of the Stella Marris y Rafael restaurant next door. *Tel: 073 275 207, 0981 474 480, located on the corner directly behind the mission's school building. Gs. 50,000, shared bathroom, A/C*

Getting There

The turn off for San Cosme y Damián is located at km 306 of Route 1 about sixty-five kilometers from Encarnación and eighteen from General Delgado (on the right coming from Asunción). From here it is twenty-seven kilometers down a paved road. Taxis are available from the Coronel Bogado bus terminal for between Gs. 80,000 and Gs. 100,000 round trip.

The La Cosmeña and Perla del Sur bus lines make daily trips between San Cosme and the terminals in Encarnación (approximately a two hour ride) and Coronel Bogado (approximately a one hour ride). The last bus leaves at approximately 4:30pm and bus fare is Gs. 8,000. There are also buses to San Cosme y Damián that leave from Asunción's bus terminal daily. Gs. 55,000.

Departamento Ñeembucú

The department of Ñeembucú is home to some of Paraguay's most extensive wetlands. Over 70 percent of the department is made up of wetlands. Many areas can only be explored with locals who eke out an existence in the wetlands, surviving off fishing, hunting and small scale agriculture. Relatively untouched by development, the area is still home to animals such as *lobos marinos*, nutrias, and any number of birds. The area's sandy soil (there is none of Eastern Paraguay's characteristic red dirt) makes agriculture difficult and most of Ñeembucú's inhabitants live off small scale cattle ranching

The picturesque wetlands of Ñeembucú were the backdrop for some of the most intense battles that took place during the Triple Alliance War. South of Pilar are the historic ruins of Humaitá, almost entirely bombarded by enemy troops, and sleepy fishing towns of General Diaz and Paso de Patria. Birds and fish abound along the banks of the river and in smaller inland lagoons. The area along the country's southern border is quiet and undeveloped, making it ideal for fishing and birding.

PILAR

Pilar, capital of the southern department of Ñeembucú, is also known as the "*Capital de la Cordialidad*" (Capital of Cordiality). With its wide *adoquinado* (cement block) roads and sculptures scattered throughout, Pilar has a different feel than other Paraguayan cities of its size. The picturesque historic center is very walkable and as locals pass you on bicycles you may feel more like you are in a sleepy riverside suburb rather than a city.

As the Paraguay River wraps around Pilar it creates riverfront views in multiple directions. A catastrophic region-wide flood in 1983 prompted the creation of a

The South

retaining wall which also serves as a makeshift boardwalk. Walking along the dirt path you'll see flocks of birds flying amongst the water hyacinths while fishermen slowly make their way up and down the river in colorful wooden boats.

Pilarenses are known for their artistic talents; the city's singers and dancers regularly take first place in national talent competitions. These talents are on display during the *Día de la Juventud* (Sept. 21st) parade complete with decorated floats and the celebration of the founding of Pilar (Oct. 12th) which includes week-long showcases of local talent. For those who can't get enough of ringing in the New Year the *Fiesta Hawaiana* is held during the first week of January. This large party takes place on at the banks of the Arroyo Ñeembucú and draws music acts and revelers from all of Paraguay as well as participants from neighboring Argentina.

Pilar's Larger Than Life Birds

A stroll from Pilar's Plaza Mariscal López to the municipal office along Mariscal López will take you past several colorful statues featuring birds native to the Ñeembucú wetlands. These are the brainchild of local biologist and head of the Asociación Hombre y Naturaleza, Andres Contreras.

Manufactura de Pilar Factory

Established in the early 1930's by an Italian count, Manufacturas Pilar is one of Paraguay's largest cotton processing plants and a major source of employment for Pilar and the surrounding areas. The factory is one of only a handful worldwide to carry out the entire process from raw cotton to finished product (sheets, towels, etc) ready for sale (and export). In addition, various cotton by-products are made on-site including cooking oil, soap and animal feed. The factory operates on steam generated from the company's 27,000 hectares of eucalyptus and is a mishmash of processes from the rudimentary

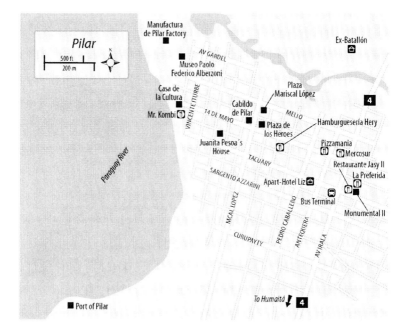

(soaps are cut by hand) to the modern (textiles are printed by laser etching).

Tours are given in the mornings and can be set up by contacting either the Municipality (*www.municipalidaddepilar.com*) or the Public Relations office of Manufacturas Pilar. *Tel: 0786 232 181/6, Mello and the banks of the Paraguay River, www.pilar.com.py*

Museo Paolo Federico Alberzoni

The factory's original founder, Italian count Paolo Federico Alberzoni lived on the factory grounds till his death in 1973. His home has been turned into the Museo Paolo Federico Alberzoni. The museum showcases many of the count's personal belongings from the Old World as well as machines once used in the factory itself. *Tel: 0786 232 386, Corner of Teniente Mendoza and General Díaz, Thurs-Sun 4pm-7pm*

Cabildo de Pilar

Built in the 1820's, this two-story building housed government and military offices before passing into private hands after the Triple Alliance War. In the 1970's it was converted into a museum with displays about the Triple Alliance as well as objects and religious relics from Pilar's history. The museum was recently renovated and many of its artifacts have been restored. *Tel: 0786 232 078, corner of Mariscal López and 14 de Mayo, Mon-Fri 7:30am-11am, 2pm-5pm, Sat 9am-11am*

Plaza Mariscal López & Plaza de los Héroes

This pleasant tree lined plaza is perfect for taking a break. Wander around the large statues representing the department's birds and visit the adjoining Cabildo de Pilar museum.

Casa de la Cultura

Situated where one of Pilar's main streets meets the river, the cultural center has periodic movie screenings, art and photography exhibits. There is also a small coffee shop. *No phone, Gral. Díaz 112 almost at 14 de Mayo, Mon-Sat 8am-1pm*

Juanita Pessoa

Pilar was home to Juanita Pessoa, one time lover of a young Mariscal López. The two met when he was stationed in Ñeembucú as a colonel in his father's army (long before he ascended to the presidency). Mariscal López fathered three sons with Juanita, one of whom was born after Madame Lynch had become Mariscal López's lover. In fact the two women knew each other and Madame Lynch treated Juanita's children well. Her colonial house still stands to this day at (Paolo Alberzoni almost at Teniente Ríos) and some of her belongings are in the Cabildo de Pilar museum.

Lodging

Apart-Hotel Liz The hotel's spacious apartments all have two bedrooms, a bathroom, a living room and kitchen facilities. They are spacious and comfortable. Rooms facing the street also have balconies. *Located about 10 blocks from main plaza and right off main entrance to town; Tel: 0786 232944/5., Tacuary between Antequera and Pedro Juan Caballero, www.lizahotel.com, Singles Gs. 95,000, Doubles Gs 130,000, Triples Gs. 165,000, TV, A/C, kitchen area*

Hotel Monumental II Simple and clean, rooms in this hotel (and its sister hotel down the street Monumental I) do the trick. On the downside it is a little removed from the historic center. However, one positive note is that it's next to the delicious Jasy II restaurant. *Tel: 0786 230 638, Tacuary almost at Ayolas, www.hotelmonumental.com.py Single Gs. 65,000, Double Gs. 100,000, Triple 135,000, computers with internet, TV, A/C, mini-fridge*

Camping

Ex-Batallón Home to the cavalry the *Ex-Batallón* (formally known as the Segunda División de Caballería) will usually allow people to use their camping grounds for free. There are bathrooms and running water and the location along the river makes for great views and good bird watching. *When coming from Route 6 turn right 150 meters before the bridge that leads to downtown Pilar and continue 250 meters to the signed entrance. Talk with the guards at the gate to request permission to camp.*

Food

🍴 **Restaurante Jasy II** Delicious authentic Paraguayan food served in a basic but cheery setting. Jasy II is often recommended by locals for the *surubí* dishes (as well as affordable prices). Try the *surubí a la napolitana* and don't forget to order a dessert such as *kiveve*, a sweet squash puree. *Tel: 0786 231 738, 0975 654 752, Tacuary almost at Ayolas next to Hotel Monumental II, Mon-Sat 6am-3pm, Sun 8am-3pm, Gs. 10,000-25,000*

La Preferida Run by Doña Minu whose cooking features a level of seasoning that is rare in Paraguayan food. Lunch only and they run out quickly. Stop by ahead of time to request special fish based dishes. *Tel: 0786 230 179, Ayolas almost at Tacuary daily 7am-3pm, Gs. 20,000*

Pizzamania Best pizza in Pilar with crunchy thin crust and good variety of flavors including vegetarian (very good) and Mexican pizza. *Tel: 0975 620 992, 14 de Mayo almost at Avenida Irala daily 6pm to 1 am, Gs, 25,000-35,000*

Hamburguesería Hery Burgers are cheap with plenty of toppings to choose from including chilies and hot sauce. *Tel: 0975 614 929, corner of Alberzoni and Dr. Milciades Ortiz, daily 6pm-1am, Gs. 8,000-13,000*

Mr. Kombi This fast food joint may be the only place in Paraguay where you can jump on a trampoline before chowing down on a tasty *lomito*. Vegetarians can get a meatless lomito for half price. *Tel: 0971 173 224, 14 de Mayo 1254, daily 7pm-1am, Gs. 6,000-10,000*

Mercosur A good place to stock up on both basic essentials and imported goodies, Mercosur sells goods from all four Mercosur nations (Brazil, Uruguay, Argentina and Paraguay). They have a good selection of cheeses, hot sauces, and a nice health food section. *14 de Mayo just before Avenida Irala, Mon-Sat 8am-5pm*

Getting There

From Asunción Ciudad de Pilar and La Encarnacena buses makes the six hour journey to Pilar daily, Gs. 60,000. It is best to get tickets ahead of time as buses are often full. These buses can also be caught in San Ignacio at the turn off to Pilar just past Hotel Arapysandu and the horse head monument at the northern edge of town.

The road between San Ignacio and Pilar is particularly good for bird watching. Even from the bus you can see several *garzas blancas* wading around alongside cows in flooded fields and *caracoleros* sitting on fence posts looking down into roadside lagoons for their next meal. Drivers will want to keep their eyes on the road though as Route 4 is infamous for its large potholes.

HUMAITÁ

From Pilar an unpaved stretch of Route 4 extends to the southern tip of the country passing the historic ruins of Humaitá leading all the way to small fishing towns of Paso de Patria and General Díaz at the southernmost tip of Paraguay. The area's location downriver from Asunción made it a strategic battleground during the Triple Alliance and as such, many battles were fought along these shores. Treasure hunters have their pick of war relics, many of which end up on display in the numerous

Triple Alliance museums (both public and private) in towns along the river. The combination of historic ruins, handful of museums and idyllic riverfront scenery make Humaitá a pleasant and worthwhile day trip from Pilar for nature lovers and history buffs alike.

About forty kilometers south of Pilar, the town of Humaitá was witness to much fighting during the Triple Alliance War and as such is of much historic value, though it's location at the far reaches of the country has left it ignored until recently. The *ruinas de Humaitá* are currently the focus of a development project by the Ministry of Tourism which includes the construction of visitors areas and night time illumination of the ruins.

Through the *Turismo Social Sustentable* (Socially Sustainable Tourism) initiative visitors to the department of Ñeembucú can stay with families in Humaitá, Paso de Patria and Isla Umbu for Gs. 75,000 per day (which includes room and board). For more information contact Diógenes Cárdenas at 0975 151 354 or Mabel Franco at 0975 663 636. There are also day tours offered by the Tourism information of Isla Umbú which cost Gs. 250,000 per person and include visits to Pilar, Isla Umbú, Humaitá and Past de Patria as well as meals. Unfortunately the tours do not include transportation – a car is necessary.

Iglesia San Carlos Borromeo

Overlooking the banks of the Paraguay River, the Iglesia San Carlos Borromeo witnessed some of the most intense bombing during the Triple Alliance War. The church was built in 1860 under the orders of Carlos Antonio López and is said to have been one of the most beautiful churches in all of South America. Known by all Paraguayans as the *ruinas de Humaitá*, the church's remains are possibly the nation's most historic monument and an icon of the Triple Alliance War.

> The *Ruinas de Humaitá* are featured on the back of the Gs. 5,000 bill.

Museo Ex Cuartel de López de Humaitá

Serving as military barracks during the Triple Alliance War this building was destroyed in the catastrophic flood of 1983 and later rebuilt using as much of the original materials as possible. *About 150 meters downriver from the Iglesia San Carlos Boromeo (ruinas de Humaitá), Tues-Sun 8am-11am, 2pm-5pm*

Museo Histórico Privado Don Maximo

Privately owned museum with all manner of Triple Alliance War relics from the fancy (French perfume bottles) to the mundane (rusty bullets). Run by the enthusiastic history buff Vincenta Miranda who also acts as a local guide. Vicenta's property was the location of a defensive wall from the Triple Alliance War known as the "*Batería de Londres*," equipped with sixteen canons. Unfortunately what survived of the wall after the war was swept away by a region-wide flood in 1983. *Tel: 0985 270 690, 22 de Septiembre and 18 de Julio, two blocks from ruins in Humiatá, Tues-Sat 8am-11am, 3:30-17:30; Sun 8am-12pm*

Lodging

Hospedaje del Bosque Those who wish to make the most of Humaitá's beautiful scenery can stay in one of the thatched roof bungalows owned by the Candia family. The family also has a small museum with many relics from the war. *Tel: 0786 231 532, corner of Heróica Resistencia and Paso de Patria, Gs. 50,000 per person, fan*

Food

> **La Terraza** Located in Humaitá's plaza "La Terraza" (the terrace) serves down home and delicious cooking daily. Their specialty is *surubí* and it is much cheaper than elsewhere in Paraguay. Take advantage! *Tel: 0786 231 557, main plaza next to the ruins, Tues-Sun 7:30am-2:30pm, 5pm.9pm, Gs. 20,000-30,000*

Getting There

The Empresa Del Sur bus makes the hour and a half trip to and from Humaitá twice daily on weekdays leaving from Pilar's bus terminal (0786 232 755) at 10am and 5pm and returning from Humaitá at 5am and 3pm. Gs. 15,000 to 18,000.

Crossing the Border into Argentina

A ferry operates between the port in Pilar and Puerto Colonia Cano on the Argentine side of the Paraguay River between 7am-1pm for Gs. 25,000. A taxi from the center of town to the ferry costs about Gs. 10,000. From Puerto Colonia Cano there are mini-buses which take passengers to General Mansilla where buses can be caught to Resistencia, Corrientes and Formosa. Be sure to change money in Pilar beforehand as Guaranies are not readily accepted across the river.

Eastern Paraguay

Along Rt 2 & Rt 7 with side trips on Rt 8

Route 2 connects Paraguay's two most important cities – to the west Asunción, capital of the nation, and to the east Ciudad del Este, Paraguay's center of commerce and the gateway to the famed Iguazú Falls. Traveling west to east along Route 2 is a trip through Paraguay's history. Closest to Asunción is a series of towns founded as Franciscan missions during the colonial era. Today, they are well known for maintaining some of Paraguay's most emblematic artisanal traditions – Tobatí specializes in ceramics, Atyrá in leather work, Altos in woodwork, and Itaguá in the spider web like lace creations known as *ñanduti*. The city of Caacupé is the country's spiritual capital, home to the *Virgen de Caacupé* who has been attracting religious pilgrims nationwide since the 1700's. Although most choose make the journey in the days before December 8th (the *Día de la Virgen de Caacupé*) you can always see people walking along Route 2 to Caacupé. Further along the road is the turn off to Piribebuy, a town which saw brutal battles during the Triple Alliance War. Until the 1960's Coronel Oviedo marked the end of the road after which all points east were nothing but jungle. Once the new road, Route 7, pushed eastward, immigrants, both national and foreign, flocked to the region attracted by the prospect of fertile and virgin soil (see The Marcha al Este, p227). Today economic activity in the departments of Caaguazú and Alto Paraná revolves around agriculture with Mennonite colonies leading the way. On Paraguay's eastern border with Brazil and Argentina is the aptly named Ciudad del Este ("City of the East," though it was originally named "Puerto Presidente Stroessner"), a sharp contrast from the idyllic towns at the other end of Route 2. The Paraguayan sector of the *triple frontera* (triple border) is infamous for its frenzied commercial activities, both legal and otherwise. The city is home to Itaipú, one of the world's largest hydroelectric dams, an engineering feat of enormous proportions. Across the border are the magnificent Iguazú Falls a wonder of the natural world. The combined large-scale spectacle of both Iguazú and Itaipú are a great way to start (or end) any trip to Paraguay with a bang.

Route 2 offers travelers many opportunities for side trips. From Asunción one can bypass the chaos of San Lorenzo (where a tangle of traffic mark the start of both Route 1 and Route 2) and arrive at Route 2 via the charming and artistically inclined lakeside town of Areguá. Also along the Lake Ypacaraí is San Bernardino – once a sleepy German village, now the epicenter of summertime activities for Paraguay's elite. Route 8 stretches south from Coronel Oviedo through the province of Guairá before ending in Caazapá. Along the way it passes Yataity, where fine cloth has been woven and embroidered into *ao po'i* clothing and tablecloths since the time of Dr. Francia (Paraguay's first ruler). Guairá is also home to the German colony of Colonia

Independencia, a popular vacation spot nestled at the foot of the Ybytyruzu moun-tain chain. The waterfalls and mountain tops of Ybytyruzu can also be accessed from the university town of Villarrica, capital of the department of Guairá.

TRAVELING ALONG ROUTE 2

Unlike Route 1 which has attractions evenly spread throughout, the main attractions of Route 2 are concentrated on either end and best dealt with separately. Capiatá, Areguá, San Bernardino, Altos, Atyrá, Tobatí, Caacupé and even Piribebuy are easy day trips from Asunción. All are accessible by public transportation, though visiting more than one or two in a day by bus can be challenging as roads are not always accessible to one another. Tourists can tackle the sights of Guairá at a leisurely pace using either Villarrica or Colonia Independencia as a base, the former being more accessible but less relaxing than the later. Those headed to Guairá from Asunción in a private vehicle will find it more convenient to take the new road from Paraguarí to Villarrica (accessible from Route 1). This is much faster than taking Route 2 to Coronel Oviedo and then turning south to Guairá. For the moment, all buses to Guairá from Asunción take the longer route. Ciudad del Este is about four hours from Asunción by car and between five and six by bus (although there are small buses that make express trips in about four hours). TAM airlines (not to be confused with the military transport also called TAM) operates one flight daily between Asunción and Ciudad del Este – this flight then continues onto Sao Paolo, Brazil.

Due to their proximity to Asunción, the departments of Cordillera and Central are popular homes for retired and emigrated foreigners – there is a lot of hotel and restaurant infrastructure, many with German influence. Many establishments can organize excursions to surrounding towns to help you make the most of your visit. The German colony of Colonia Independencia is probably the most pleasant place in Paraguay for those who wish to do a little bit of camping. Camping facilities are clean, well run, and there are options for nature enthusiasts, from horseback riding to hiking. Further towards Ciudad del Este the German influence continues but shifts to a less modern feel as you reach the several Mennonite colonies along Route 7. Though you will find some good restaurants here and there, options for recreation are limited – a hard work ethic is the focus of life in these communities, many of which prefer to remain closed off to outsiders. Ciudad del Este offers visitors a plethora of accommodation options, although prices are much higher than in the rest of the country (excluding Asunción).

Recommended bus companies: Nuestra Señora de Asunción (NSA), Crucero del Este, Rysa, Stel Turismo

Major bus stops along Route 2: San Lorenzo, Caacupé, Coronel Oviedo, Caa-guazú, J. Eulogio Estigarribia (better known as Campo Nueve) and Ciudad del Este.

Getting to Route 2 from Asunción by Car

There are two options for accessing Route 2 from Asunción. The first is similar to the access to Route 1 through San Lorenzo (see Getting to Routes 1 & 2 by Car, p146) and the second is through the road between Luque and Ypacaraí (bypassing the cities of Capiatá and Itaguá). The latter offers the advantage of being less transited and more scenic.

Through Luque

You will pass the large Ñu Guazú park after the intersection with Avenida Madame Lynch. Once past the park, take a right on to Don Atilano Cáceres which runs behind the Confederación Sudamericana de Fútbol (CONMEBOL) building. Take the following right on to Avenida Sudamericana and then turn left at the light on to Avenida General Elizardo Aquino. This road will lead to the center of Luque past the main plazas and church before intersecting with Humaitá, a double avenue. Turn right on to Humaitá. The paved turn off to Areguá is three blocks down on the left (you will pass a mini replica of the ruins of Humaitá on your left). Once you are on this road it is a straight shot to Areguá. Once in Areguá, you must turn left on to the double avenue Mariscal Estigarribia (you will see El Cántaro on the corner) and then take a right at the gas station on to Mariscal Fransisco Solano López which continues through to Ypacaraí. In Ypacaraí turn left at the second traffic light on to General Bernardino Caballero. Once past the toll, the road will curve to the right and lead to Caacupé.

Art Theft

Given the unguarded manner in which much of Paraguay's religious artwork is exhibited, it is easy to assume that these pieces are not particularly valuable. However, carvings from both the Jesuit and Franciscan missions are highly valuable and fetch a good price on the black market. There have been several burglaries in recent years. One of the most high profile robberies occurred at the Museo Mitológico Ramón Elías where twenty-eight pieces including several large Jesuit era statues, all of which were valued at over US$600,000, were stolen. These pieces are now presumably in the hands of private collectors. In some cases, the destination of stolen artifacts is not as lofty. Thieves who stole the church bells of the Iglesia de San Buenaventura in Yaguarón attempted to sell them as scrap metal to an iron foundry; fortunately the bells were spared and eventually returned intact.

The East

Pyporé

La Huella Fransiscana (translated as the "Franciscan footprint") is a recent tourism project developed by the NGO Fundación Tierra Nuestra to improve and increase tourism in Paraguay's Franciscan towns. So far the project has yielded a packaged tour that combines both the religious aspect of the Fransiscan route and the artesanal traditions still maintained in Franciscan towns. The tour starts with a visit to the church of Yaguarón after which the group walks to the nearby Museo Gaspar Rodriguez de Francia, accompanied all the while by a small procession of a traditional indigenous *peteke peteke* band. Next is a visit to a ñandutí workshop in Itaguá where visitors can observe and even partake in the creation of delicate lace designs. The day ends with a meal of traditional Paraguayan foods in Areguá followed by a visit to a ceramic workshop and a stop by the lovely Centro Cultural del Lago. All in all a culturally packed day with an itinerary (and comfort level) that would be impossible to replicate on public transportation. Tours cost US$80 per person with scheduled departure dates approximately two weekends per month. Call or email COTUR for information on upcoming tours and reservations (must be made one week in advance although last minute spots are sometimes avaliable). Other excursions such as visits to patron saint festivals are in the works. *Tel: 021 204 775, 021 204 778, Pypore-lahuellafranciscana@tierranuestra.org.py or info@cotur.com.py*

Departamento Central

Due to their proximity to the capital city the towns of the Central department have largely become satellite cities to Asunción. A significant part of the population of Central commutes daily to Asunción. As a result, buses from Central tend to be packed tight during the mornings and afternoons. The further you get from Asunción, the more pleasant these towns become. Located on the banks of the Lake Ypacaraí, Areguá is particularly nice and often visited by tourists and day trippers from Asunción.

CAPIATÁ

Museo Mitológico Ramón Elías
The creatures of Paraguayan mythology (see Meet the Mitos, p44) come to life in this museum created by local artist Ramón Elías. The statues were created based on interviews Ramón Elías did with Paraguayans throughout the countryside. Some are cartoonish in nature while other creatures are rendered in more frightening fashion. Though interesting the museum may not be worth a visit on its own as many similar sculptures of the *mitos* can be found outside the Folklore store in Asunción (*corner of Mariscal Estigarribia and Iturbe*). The museum also has a number of statues from the Jesuit and Franciscan era, though the collection was greatly reduced following a robbery in 2009 (see Art Theft, p199). Those with a particular interest in religious art should continue on to the town's Franciscan church (open between 4pm-6pm) which has a lovely interior, second only to Paraguay's most important Franciscan church in Yaguarón. *Tel: 0228 634 262, Rt 2 km 19, one km before the entrance to Capiatá on the left-hand side (if coming from Asunción), Mon-Sat 8am-11:30am, 2:30pm-5pm, Sun 7:30am-12pm, Gs. 5,000*

ITAGUÁ

Itaguá is the home of Paraguay's most emblematic artisanal tradition, *ñanduti*. Creating the delicate spiderweb-like designs is a lengthy and laborious process. First a piece of cloth is sewn to a wooden frame or *bastidor* and stretched tight. The general shape of the final design is drawn on to this canvas. Each design is known as a *dechado*. There are over 160 popular *dechados*, though artisans also invent their own. Most *dechados* take their inspiration from the natural world emulating flowers, trees, and animals. Common dechados include those modeled after the passion fruit flower, the guava flower, the fish bone and the machete. These are painstakingly sewn on to the cloth with either sewing thread, for the more delicate *ñanduti de hilo fino* (fine thread) or embroidery thread for *ñanduti de hilo grueso* (thick thread). Traditionally only white thread was used but nowadays *ñandutis* are an explosion of color. Once the *dechados* are complete, the piece is snipped free from the *bastidor*. It is then dampened with a mixture of water and starch and ironed dry to give it a slightly stiff body.

Popular *ñanduti* items include table linens and traditional Paraguayan dance costumes. Prices are shockingly low when you take into consideration the amount of time and labor that goes into making these intricate *ñanduti* pieces. Although the majority of the town's artisans make *ñanduti,* none are able to survive on *ñanduti* production alone. Because *dechado*s can be stitched together to form larger pieces many *ñanduti* articles are made by several artisans, reducing the amount of time it takes to complete a finished piece. A full, ankle length skirt for a dance costume will take one person two months to complete (if working on it exclusively) whereas five artisans working together part-time can finish it in a month. This will sell for approximately Gs. 1,500,000 which must then be distributed amongst the artisans and salesperson. Large and elaborate tablecloths *(manteles)* run about Gs. 750,000 while smaller runners *(camineros)* and doilies *(carpetas)* can cost as little as Gs. 50,000. Individual *dechados* which can be used for appliqués cost as little as Gs. 5,000. *Ñanduti de hilo fino* is very delicate and commands between three and four times as much as the also beautiful but less labor intensive *ñanduti de hilo grueso*. Many artisans also sell *ñanduti* designs still on the *bastidor* which can also serve as a rustic frame.

More Information

For those intrigued by the delicate designs, *"Ñanduti, encaje Paraguayo"* by Annick Sanjurjo is an excellent resource. The book includes interviews with artisans, a history of *ñanduti* and an impressive catalog of *dechados* including many that are no longer made due to their level of difficulty. *www.nandutilace.com* is the accompanying website (in English and Spanish).

Museo San Rafael

Run by the town church parish this small museum has a nice collection of antique *ñanduti* pieces as well as an exhibit displaying the process of making *ñanduti* and several examples of *dechados*. There are displays of religious statues and colonial artifacts but the *ñanduti* is the star. Of particular beauty is a pink and white dress of whisper thin *hilo fino*. *Tel: 0294 220 415, directly behind the Iglesia Nuestra Señora del Rosario, Mon-Fri 7:30am-10:45am, 2pm-5pm, Sat 7:30am-11:30am*

Casa Nidia

Though this store is further from the center, it is worth a visit due to owner Graciela's passion for *ñanduti*. Graciela is a *ñanduti* artisan herself and employs several local women to help make traditional *ñanduti* creations. Graciela is happy to share with her visitors, the art of *ñanduti*, from the technique to the obstacles artisans face and the joys of seeing *ñanduti* sell well at overseas handicraft fairs. If you are in Paraguay for an extended period of time Graciela can make custom pieces as well. However, it is important to check in often and expect delays, especially due to inclement weather (it is harder to stitch the thread when there is lots of humidity). *Tel: 0981 255 062, km 29 on the right-hand side if coming from Asunción about 200 meters past the Bahía gas station, the store has a dark green awning. Daily 7am-6pm though it is best to call ahead of time as Graciela may be out selling her products*

Casa Antonia

Casa Antonia is a nicely organized store with an extremely large selection of *ñanduti*, as well as other handicrafts. Their specialty is crafting custom dresses, and while these may not be practical for the tourist just passing through they make for fun window shopping. *Tel: 0294 220 384, 0982 122 592, 0971 102 911, Rt 2 km 29.5 with a large white sign and tall glass showcase on the right-hand side if coming from Asunción, Mon-Sat 7am-5pm, credit cards accepted*

The East

Instituto Paraguayo de Artesanía – Filial Itaguá

The newly constructed branch of the Paraguayan Institute of Handicrafts has a nice selection of *ñanduti* for sale in the main display room. Upstairs, local artisans participate in three-month long courses on the art of *ñanduti*. Tourists interested in witnessing *ñanduti* making are encouraged to stop by the *ñanduti* workshops held from 1:00pm to 3pm Monday through Saturdays. There are samples of high-end *ñanduti* table linens as well as kitschy items like Barbies in *ñanduti* dresses and shirts with a *ñanduti* Playboy bunny. *Rt 2 (here called Mariscal Estigarribia) almost Palma, the IPA is a multi-story orange, blue and white building on the left-hand side if coming from Asunción. Mon-Fri 7am-5pm, Sat 7am-3pm*

AREGUÁ

It's not every day you can visit a town where the streets are lined with cartoonish ceramic piggy banks and vendors hang out on corners hawking heaping trays of sugar-dusted jelly donuts. An easy day trip from Asunción, Areguá has managed to maintain its tranquil small town feel infused with a unique quirkiness thanks to its artistically inclined population. Areguá, the capital of the Central department, has long been a haven for Paraguay's renowned artists. The town has a number of cultural centers where locally made ceramics are on display and frequent cultural events take place. Stroll past the art galleries and old manors lining the town's cobblestone streets down to the banks of Lake Ypacaraí where canoe rides are available for Gs. 15,000. Or enjoy the landscape from above by heading to the town church whose hilltop location offers one of the best views available of Lake Ypacaraí.

Areguá's Ceramics: from Kitschy to Traditional

Areguá's art scene is an odd mix of high-end art and kitsch, the latter mostly in the form of hokey ceramics. Stalls crammed with soccer jersey clad Porky Pig piggy banks line the street. Lawn ornaments from Snow White and the seven dwarves to herons and swans spill out onto the sidewalk. Particularly popular are frog couples – a grinning male and female frog, their genders made apparent by the female's bright red lips and red and white polka-dot bow. More traditional (and subdued) ceramics can be found in the city's art galleries – the Centro Cultural del Lago and El Cántaro offer the best selection.

Senatur Tourism Information

A good resource for maps of Areguá and more information regarding current events and places of interest. *Tel: 0291 433 500, corner of Nuestra Señora de Candelaria and Mariscal Estigarribia, Mon-Sat 8am-4:30pm*

Guggiari Arte

Guggiari Arte is the exhibition space and workshop of the Guggiari family, well known for their metal sculpting work. Herman Guggiari is the head of the family and is best known for his large scale metal sculptures. His sculptures play with movement and texture and can be seen throughout the streets and galleries of Asunción. His sons have also followed in his footsteps, though their work is a bit more commercial. Large pieces are on display in the gardens while there is a glass walled showroom for smaller works. *Tel: 0291 432 627, Curva Bolaños, on the left-hand side at the entrance to Areguá just as the paved road from Luque makes a sharp left, Tues-Sun 8am-6pm*

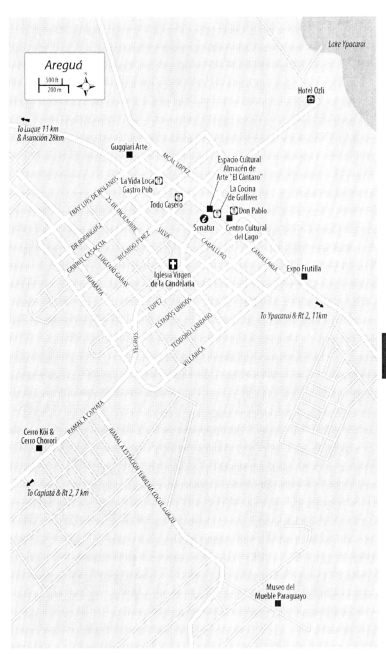

Areguá

500 ft
200 m

Lake Ypacarai

Hotel Ozli

To Luque 11 km
& Asunción 28km

Guggiari Arte

MCAL LOPEZ

Espacio Cultural
Almacén de
Arte "El Cántaro"

FRAY LUIS DE BOLAÑOS

La Vida Loca
Gastro Pub

25 DE DICIEMBRE

La Cocina
de Gulliver

Todo Casero

Don Pablo

Senatur

DR RODRIGUEZ

Centro Cultural
del Lago

GABRIEL CASACCIA

RICARDO PEREZ

SILVA

CABALLERO

CANDELARIA

EUGENIO GARAY

Expo Frutilla

HUMAITA

Iglesia Virgen
de la Candelaria

LOPEZ

ESTADOS UNIDOS

To Ypacarai & Rt 2, 11km

YEGROS

TEODORO LABRANO

VILLARICA

The East

RAMAL A CAPIATA

Cerro Köi &
Cerro Chorori

RAMAL A ESTACION TERRENA COGUE GUAZU

To Capiatá & Rt 2, 7 km

Museo del
Mueble Paraguayo

Espacio Cultural Almacén de Arte "El Cántaro"

Part museum, part gallery, part cultural center, there is always something going on at El Cántaro. Activities range from pottery and woodcarving lessons lead by a group of artisans to film screenings. The *"Almacén de Arte"* features a varied collection of local folk art. A current calendar of events is available on their website. *Tel: 0291 432 954, corner of Mariscal Estigarribia and Nuestra Señora de la Candelaria, www.cantaroaregua.blogspot.com, www.el-cantaro.com, Tues-Sun 9:30am-6pm*

Centro Cultural del Lago

Half a block from Areguá's plaza the Centro Cultural del Lago displays high quality pieces from various artisans. Though the majority of pieces are ceramics, there are some beautiful indigenous works in wood as well. Be sure not to miss the endearing diorama of the town of Areguá celebrating its patron saint festival. There is also a small screening room where national and international movies are shown once a week. The center's founder, Ysanne Gayet (an English woman) is happy to explain the pieces and speaks English. The majority of the items, along with several books on Paraguayan art, are available for purchase. *Tel: 0291 432 293, 0291 432 633, Yegros almost at Avenida Mariscal Francisco Solano López (next to Don Pablo), Summer: Thurs-Sun 10am-7pm, Winter Thurs-Sun 10am-5pm, on Facebook*

Iglesia Virgen de la Candelaria

Glowing white against a bright blue sky, Areguá's main church is located on a highpoint overlooking the town's historic section. Extending in front of the church is a terrace and sloped grassy area with many benches, perfect spots for enjoying the view of Lake Ypacaraí. *Mariscal Estigarribia and Teniente Rojas Silva*

Museo del Mueble Paraguayo

A labor of love by Carlos Colombino, one of Paraguay's pre-eminent artists, this museum features furniture from the 18th and 19th century. About 80 percent of the furniture, from chairs and tables to confessionals come from Colombino's private collection. Everything is well displayed in a uniquely shaped building with multiple levels and an airy interior. Climb to the very top for a nice view of the lush trees and Lake Ypacaraí in the distance. The museum is located on the outskirts of town but well worth the trip. *Tel: 0291 432 833, Calle Palma almost at Estación Terrena, From Areguá's church (corner of Mariscal Estigarribia and Teniente Rojas Silva) continue uphill on Mariscal Estigarriba (at this point known as the "ramal Capiatá Areguá") approximately one kilometer until you see a paved turn off to your left with a taxi stand on the corner ("ramal a Estación Terrena"). Turn left and continue down this road for another one kilometer. When the road curves left, follow the unpaved right-hand fork approximately 150 meters and the museum will be on your left behind a brick wall with a metal entrance gate. If asking for directions use "la casa de Colombino" as a reference point. It is also possible to take a bus from Areguá's main plaza to the turn off along the "ramal Capiatá-Areguá" from which a taxi to the museum should cost between Gs. 5,000 and 10,000. Taxis from town (there is a stand at the corner of Nuestra Señora de la Candelaria and Mariscal Estigarribia) should be about Gs. 15,000, Tues-Sun 2pm to 5pm*

Cerro Kõi & Cerro Chororî

Approximately one kilometer from the center of town are the geological formations of Cerro Kõi and Cerro Chororí. Jutting diagonally out of the hillside, these fine examples of columnar sandstone are quite rare – the only other such formations in the entire world are found in Canada and South Africa. Unfortunately the formations' popularity among tourists along with their relatively unpopulated location have made visitors to the area a favorite target for thieves. It is highly recommended to arrange ahead of time for a local police officer to accompany you in your vehicle. This can be done through Areguá's police station (the *"comisaría de Areguá"*) which is located on the corner of Yegros and Teniente Rojas Silva across from the church (*Tel: 0291 432 206). To reach the formations from Areguá's church (corner of Mariscal Estigarribia and Teniente Rojas Silva) continue uphill on Mariscal Estigarriba (at this point known as the "ramal Capiatá Areguá") approximately two kilometers (you will pass a taxi stand on your left) and take the left-hand turn off on to a dirt road and continue 250 meters, then take a right and continue another 250 meters*

Expo Frutilla

In addition to ceramics, Areguá is known for its abundant strawberry harvest. Each August and September strawberry farmers from the community of Estanzuela hold a strawberry festival along the road between Areguá and Ypacaraí. The roadside stands sell all types of strawberry products from delicious jams, smoothies, liquors and, of course, baskets overflowing with fresh berries. Prices are as low as Gs. 10,000 to Gs.15,000 per kilo. *Ruta Luque-Areguá at km 32.5 just past the center of town. Take the Ypacaraí bus (which can be caught from the Asunción bus terminal or from Avenida Argentina, Avenida San Martin or Avenida Aviadores del Chaco) and ask to be dropped off at the Expo Frutilla (when you start seeing stands on the left-hand side you'll know you're there).*

Lodging

Hotel Ozli This small hotel just fifty meters from Areguá's municipal beach has basic rooms with a homey feel opening out onto a covered corridor. The restaurant serves up Paraguayan basics like roasted chicken and tallarin (thick linguini style noodles with tomato sauce) but guests also have free access to the hotel kitchen. The hotel also has canoes for trips along the lake. *Tel: 0291 432 380, 0982 462 998, 0971 325 179, Avenida Coronel Panchito López just before the lake on the right-hand side (follow Mariscal Estigarribia downhill from the church past the train tracks all the way towards the lake), www.ozlihotel.turismoparaguay.net, Double Gs. 40,000 per person on weekdays, Gs. 50,000 per person on weekends, Wi-Fi, pool*

Restaurants

La Cocina de Gulliver Delicious Spanish food in a nice outdoor setting. Spanish chef Manuel and his friendly wife Justin routinely make paella platters over one-meter in diameter for food expositions in Asunción and their small size paellas are just as show stopping. Other options include fresh baked breads, pork ribs, *tortilla española* and wood fire grilled pizzas. Ask the owners for their recommendations of the day. *Tel: 0291 433 243, 0971 222 618, corner of Mariscal Estigarribia and Nuestra Señora de la Candelaria behind El Cántaro, Wed-Sun 11am-3pm, reservations required for dinner service, Gs. 25,000-50,000*

La Vida Loca Gastro Pub Part restaurant, tapas bar, piercing and tattoo parlor and guest house, this establishment has a little of everything. House specialties are fish and the large 2-person steak platter. It is probably best to decide on a tattoo before ordering a tasty Brazilian *cachasa* based "caipirinha" though. *Tel: 0291 433 426, 0982 917 089, Avenida Candelaria 807 almost at Gaspar Rodriguez de Francia, on Facebook, Tues 6pm-11pm, Wed-Fri 11:30am-3:30pm, 6pm-11pm, Sat 11:30am-11:30pm, Sun 10am-9pm Mon-Fri 6pm-midnight, Sat and Sun 11:30-11pm. Gs. 20,000-50,000*

Todo Casero The name, meaning "everything homemade" says it all. Serving up inexpensive traditional Paraguayan food Todo Casero is an excellent budget option. *Tel: 0291 432 506, 0982 578 515, Ricardo Pérez 80 almost at Nuestra Señora de la Candelaria, daily 7am-9pm in the summer, advanced requests ("por pedido") only during the winter, Gs.10,000-20,000*

🍴 **Don Pablo** Without a doubt Areguá's most popular eatery. Decorated with Paraguayan handicrafts and art the interior of this large house is very nice and intimate. Menu offerings are basic, pizzas and the like, but very tasty. Enjoy your meal and then head next door to the Centro Cultural del Lago or across the street to the community artist cooperative to view works by local artists. *Tel: 0291 432 275, 0291 433 137, Corner of Mariscal López and Yegros, Mon-Fri 7:30am-11pm, Sat 7:30am-12:30p, Sun 7:30am-9:30pm, Gs. 20,000-30,000*

Desserts

For desserts, head down to the corner of Mariscal Estigarribia and Mariscal Fransisco Solano López where most of the town's *bollo* (jelly donut) vendors hang out. You'll have your choice of *dulce de leche, guayaba* jam, and cream filled donuts.

Getting There

Areguá is accessed by a road which links the city of Luque to Ypacaraí (see Through Luque, p199).

Both the Areguá 111 and Cerro Koi buses leave from the Asunción bus terminal, though they can also be caught along Avenida Argentina, Avenida San Martín and Aviadores del Chaco as well. Make sure to specify to the driver that you want to go to the center or church of Areguá (some buses go into surrounding neighborhoods but may not bother to change their signs indicating so).

The historic *Tren del Lago* (steam train) makes the journey out to Areguá every other Sunday (see Tren del Lago, p127).

Departamento Cordillera

Though the towns of the Cordillera department can easily be reached by Asunción, they still retain their small town feel and traditions. Taking a stroll around the town plaza, popping into the historic church, and visiting local artisan workshops, it is easy to understand why these towns are frequented by *Asuncenos* looking for weekend escapes from the city. The department takes its name from the many hills ("*cordillera*" means mountain range in Spanish) in the region.

SAN BERNARDINO

The town of San Bernardino was founded by German immigrants in the late 1800's and named after then President General Bernardino Caballero. This tranquil lakeside community soon became popular as a summer getaway for Asunción's elite. Throughout the high season (December to February as well as Easter week) the cobblestone streets of "San Ber" (as it is often nicknamed) are crowded with people.

Because this town is considered "seasonal" many bars, restaurants and nightclubs are only open during the summer months. However, there are still some famous spots that remain open year round. *Bollos* (jelly donuts) from the Confitería Alemana and a *fruti cream* (part frozen juice part ice cream) from La Casita del Helado are a must-try no matter what time of year it is. During summer weekends, young crowds (some vacationing in San Ber, others driving in from Asunción) hit the nightclubs till the wee hours of the morning.

Recuerdos del Ypacaraí"

"Recuerdos de Ypacaraí" is perhaps the most famous song to come out of Paraguay. Throughout the song a lovelorn man reminisces about a beautiful Guaraní woman he fell in love with at the lake's edge. Written by Demetrio Ortíz and María Teresa Márquez the song has been covered by international stars like Julio Iglesias and Caetano Veloso. This song is particularly beautiful when played on the harp and guitar and is always a good choice to request of Paraguayan musicians.

Even when it's crowded San Bernardino is a very pleasant town to walk around in thanks to its old manors, tree lined cobblestone streets, and, of course, the lake. The lake's highly questionable water quality does not stop people of all ages from taking a dip, jet skiing, and paddle boating around.

Playa la Rotonda

Extending between Mariscal López and Defensores del Chaco this grassy beach is quite popular. There are all types of vendors selling *chipa*, *bollos* and even handicrafts. Two person paddle boats are available for Gs. 20,000 for half an hour and there are also flat bottomed boats that will do a twenty-minute excursion on the lake for Gs. 50,000 per group.

Playa Ciclova

Closer to the entrance to town is the Playa Ciclova. From here it is a pleasant walk to the Plaza Defensores del Chaco where a crafts fair takes place during the summer.

Museum/Centro Cultural Hotel del Lago

See Hotel del Lago in the following Lodging section.

Mirador Bella Vista

Those who really want to earn their *fruti cream* or *bollo* will enjoy the walk up 111 steps to the Mirador Bella Vista lookout point. Up top is a nice sized stone terrace with an enormous white statue of a cartoonish smiling Virgin Mary. You can catch a glimpse of the lake through the tree tops or head to the foot of the Virgin for a perfect panoramic view. *Head uphill from the Hotel del Lago along Teniente Weiler*

Aventura Xtrema

This tour company offers all types of tours from laid back boat trips and walking tours to more adventurous tours such as rock-climbing and scuba diving. Tour details are all available on their website. Reservations are recommended two days prior, however walk -ins are accepted. The Tobatí rock-climbing tour requires a minimum of four people. They can arrange for transportation from Asunción if needed. *Tel: 0981 682 243, 0971 315 709, 0961 639 422, corner of Nuestra Señora de la Asunción and Emilio Hassler (bright red building), www.aventuraxtrema.com.py*

Casa Hassler

Casa Hassler is a museum, art gallery and cultural center, as well as the local office of Senatur (Tourism information). The house originally belonged to Dr. Hassler, a Swiss gentleman who settled here in the late 1800's and dedicated himself to studying Paraguay's flora eventually cataloguing over 80,000 species of plants. *Tel: 0512 232 974, Corner of Luis F. Vaché and Emilio Hassler, www.sanbernardino.gov.py, Mon-Fri 8am-6pm*

The East

Lodging

⌂ **Hotel del Lago** Built in 1888 by some of San Bernardino's first residents, this centrally located historic manor has since been renovated yet has managed to keep its stately charm. Antique furnishings and nicely maintained gardens overlooking Lake Ypacaraí add to the feeling of being in a period piece movie. The museum's cultural center has rotating art and photography exhibits. During the summer, it also showcases various concerts and events. The hotel also offers a variety of cultural immersion tours through the organization Paraguay Hecho A Mano (Hand Made Paraguay). *Tel: 0512 232 201, Corner of Teniente Weiler and Mariscal López across from the main plaza, www.hoteldellago.org, Doubles 320,000-420,000, Triples Gs.350,000, pool, A/C, TV, Wi-Fi*

Pueblo Hotel Just before the entrance into town, you'll find a large hotel that feels a lot like a beach house thanks to its spacious rooms, nice pool and a pleasant sundeck area. The hotel's restaurant is also pretty good and the bar is well stocked. *Tel: 0512 232 195, Calle 8 in between Calle 5 and Avenida Mbocaya, on the right-hand side along the access road into town, Single: Gs. 360,000, double Gs. 390,000, summer time rates are approximately Gs. 100,000 higher per room. Wi-Fi, A/C, TV, pool, tennis courts*

Hotel Los Alpes The San Bernardino Los Alpes is just as nice and welcoming as the branches in Asunción. The hotel is a bit far from town, however buses are easily caught along the main road. *Tel: 0512 232 399 / 232 083, km 46.5 Ruta General Morinigo, www.hotellosalpes.com.py, Singles Gs. 200,000, Doubles Gs. 250,000, Wi-Fi, computer center with free internet, TV, A/C, mini-fridge, pool*

Camping Brisas del Mediterraneo Located about 250 meters from the lake's shore this establishment has something for all budgets – private cabins, dorm rooms and campgrounds. A nice spot to enjoy the natural side of "San Ber." *Tel: 0512 232 459, from the corner Mariscal López and Avenida Kennedy (there is a sign for the campsite opposite the Copaco building) continue 2 kilometers and you will see another sign for the left-hand turn off, buses go as far as the Copaco from which a cab ride costs about Gs. 20,000, www.campingparaguay.org, Camping Gs. 35,000 per person, Doubles Gs. 200,000, Dorm room Gs. 90,000 per person, pool, soccer and volley courts*

Restaurants

⌂ **Confitería Alemana I** No day in San Bernardino is complete without a sugar dusted German style jelly donut, otherwise known as a *bollo*. These are so popular that the Confitería Alemana prepares more than 4,000 per day during the summer time. Bollos filled with *dulce de guayaba* are especially delicious. The bakery specializes in other pastries as well. Meanwhile the restaurant upstairs prepares basic meat and pasta dishes. *Tel: 0512 232 901, Corner of Nuestra Señora de la Asunción and Colonos Alemanes (there is another branch called Confitería Alemana II at the entrance to San Bernardino), Bakery hours: Daily 7:30am-9:30pm, Restaurant hours: Thurs-Sun 9:30am-9:30pm, Gs. 7,000-30,000*

⌂ **La Casita del Helado** This ice cream shop is another San Ber classic known for their *fruti-cream* drinks – part frozen strawberry juice part ice cream served up with both a straw and a spoon. Their increasing popularity has lead to additional flavors including chocolate, peach and berry. It's perfect for a hot summer's day and worth the inevitable brain freeze. *Corner of 14 de Mayo and Nuestra Señora de la Asunción next to the main plaza (as well as another branch in front of Hotel Los Alpes), daily 11am-6pm, Gs 7,000-15,000*

El Rincón de la Vaca Far from the chaos of the city, this restaurant and dairy farm make for a relaxing stop to or from San Bernardino. House specialties include farm fresh dairy products (cheese and yogurt), tasty waffles, and a hearty *bife al caballo* (steak with eggs and onions). It's definitely a good choice for breakfast. After you're done eating, sink into a hammock or saddle up for a scenic horseback ride through the twenty-six hectare farm. You may have to wait for someone to prepare the horses unless you make advanced reservations. *Tel: 0512 232 982, km 43.5 Ruta General Morinigo, Dec-Feb Tues-Thurs 9am-11pm, Fri-Sun 9am-1am, Mar-Nov Fri-Sun 9am-9pm, Gs. 6,000-30,000*

Café Francés This intimate café bills itself as a piece of France in San Ber and, indeed, the menu is packed with a variety of European dishes including cheese, meat, and chocolate fondues, raclette (melted cheese with finger potatoes and other salty goodies) and pierrade (hot stone for cooking small cuts of meat), as well as tarts and other desserts. This is definitely a rare find in Paraguay and a good break from *empanadas*! *Tel: 0512 232 982, Luis F. Vaché almost at Colonos Alemanes (next to Danny's Pizzeria), www.cafefrances.webnode.es, Daily 10am-10pm closed Tuesdays, Gs 20,000-45,000*

Danny's Pizzería The area's best pizza second only to Punto Prima in Altos. New York style pizzas are large with thin crusts. Outdoor seating along the main drag is noisy but good for people watching during the high season. *Tel: 0512 232 446, Corner of Luis F. Vaché and Colonos Alemanes, Daily 5:30-12pm, closed Wednesdays, Gs. 30,000-50,0000*

Getting There

Take either Route 2 through San Lorenzo or the Luque-Ypacaraí road to Ypacaraí (the latter is preferable). After the Ypacaraí toll booth the road will fork – keep straight (the right-hand turn leads down Route 2 to Caacupé). Caution should be taken when driving to San Bernardino on weekend nights during the summer as drinking is a heavy part of the nightlife scene.

The Altos and Loma Grandense buses both head to San Bernardino from Asunción. Loma Grandense buses are nice and frequent and be caught along Avenida Mariscal Estigarribia/Eusebio Ayala (popular stops are across the street from Shopping Multi Plaza in Fernando de la Mora and in front of the Salema Super Centro in San Lorenzo) while the Altos bus can be caught at the Asunción bus terminal. The cost is roughly Gs. 3,500 and it takes about an hour and a half to get there.

ALTOS

Altos' close proximity to San Bernardino has made it an ideal destination for the influx of German immigrants who have been arriving steadily since the late 1800's. As the town's name suggests Altos (Spanish for "heights") is on elevated terrain – some of the best views of Lake Ypacaraí are to be had along the road that leads uphill from San Bernardino to Altos. The town is known for its rustic wood masks, animals and colorfully painted wooden flowers as well as the quirky celebration of patron Sts. Pedro and Pablo (Peter and Paul).

Fiesta de San Pedro Y San Pablo

The nearby *compañía* of Itaguazú holds a three day festival with traditional games and dances in honor of Sts. Peter and Paul from the 28th to the 30th of June. The highlight of the festival is the *rúa* dance which recreates the kidnapping of women by raiding bands of Guaikuru Indians. During the colonial era Guaikuru raids were common throughout the Cordillera region. Ceremonial recreations of the raids were once common during regional festivals. Today, Itaguazú is one of handful of communities that keep this tradition alive. Women dance and sing in a circle with torches lit about. The Guaikurú appear out of the shadows suddenly, entirely camouflaged with wooden masks and enormous costumes made of dried banana leaves (vaguely reminiscent of Cousin It). Also present are the *kambá ra'angá*, (masked men) who play the part of jesters performing comedy skits throughout the festival. This celebration has recently gained the attention of the tourism ministry which makes public transportation to the festival available from Altos for the festival.

The East

For more information it is best to contact the municipal office's tourism secretary, Leonardo Martinez at 0985 893 443.

Lodging

Hotel Punta Prima Enjoy the great view of the lake from either the hotel pool or the restaurant's terrace. Rooms are nice and modern and the restaurant's Italian cook serves up delicious pizza and pasta. The restaurant also features a buffet on Sundays. The chicken pesto pizza is particularly good. The hotel is about two kilometers before the center of town. *Tel: 0982 170 476 for Spanish speakers, 0982 233 770 for English and German speakers, 6 kilometers past San Bernardino on the left-hand side of the road. www.hotel-punta-prima.de, Doubles Gs. 300,000, Restaurant Gs. 25,000-55,000*

Hotel La Grappa The only lodging option in the center of town, Hotel La Grappa is small and pleasant with a nice sized pool. The hotel can arrange for dinner shows (request in advance) including live music as well as rides around town in horse drawn carts and jeep tours of surrounding areas. The restaurant's specialty is *milanesa de surubí* (breaded and fried) but they can also whip up a chupín or caldo de surubí on request. *Tel: 0516 262 436, General Bernardino Caballero and Defensores del Chaco. From the road into town take a right when you reach the church and continue down Mariscal Estigarribia two and a half blocks. The hotel will be on the left-hand side of the road just past the sign for Ña Ñeca, www.paraguay-lagrappa.com (this website also has some good general information on Altos itself), Single Gs. 130,000-150,000, Doubles 180,000-200,000, computer with internet for a fee, A/C, mini-fridge, pool*

Food

Comedor Ña Ñeca A pleasant walk from the main plaza, Ña Ñeca's offers good quality home-style Paraguayan foods such as roasted chicken and pasta. Go early on weekends during the summer as it fills up fast with visitors from San Bernardino. *Tel: 0512 230 059, 0983 227 646, From the church continue down Mariscal Estigarribia two blocks, take a left (you will see a sign for Ña Ñeca) and continue one and a half blocks. The restaurant is on the right-hand side. Daily 12pm-3pm, 9pm-10pm, Gs. 22,000-25,000*

Caipirinha A popular hangout on the edge of town. Play pool, darts and foosball (known here as "*futbolito*") under a thatched roof *quincho* and enjoy the mix of German, American and Paraguayan foods. Don't miss the spicy pork curry with fries. *Tel: 0981 775 339, on the left-hand side entering town about 150 meters past the Puma gas station, www.caipirinha-altos.de, Mon-Fri 6pm-12pm, Sat-Sun 12am-12pm, Gs. 7,000-30,000*

Getting There

Take Route 2 from Asunción and turn on to the road to San Bernardino past Ypacaraí. Drive through the center of town and turn right on to Mariscal López (there is a Copaco building on the corner). From there continue uphill approximately twelve kilometers. The road is paved the whole way.

The Loma Grandense has frequent buses which pass through San Bernardino before heading to Altos (see Getting There, San Bernardino, p209), Gs. 6,200.

CAACUPÉ

Caacupé is known as the "Spiritual Capital of Paraguay." The *Día de la Virgen de Caacupé*, celebrated on December 8th, is one of the most important religious holidays in the nation. Each year over one sixth of the nation makes its way to Caacupé in an impressive display of religious devotion reminiscent of "*The Canterbury Tales.*" However Caacupé draws visitors year round. Many come to visit the basilica which houses the *Virgen de Caacupé* and is much less crowded outside of

> Caacupé's name comes from the guaraní phrase "*Ka'aguy kupe*" which means "behind the forest."

the month of December. The city is a meeting point for the European expats who have moved to the surrounding areas in droves – there are a handful of restaurants and stores that cater to the tastes of this European community. From Caacupé, you will also find the turn offs to Atyrá (thirteen kilometers away) and Tobatí (six kilometers away), both known for their handicrafts and beautiful landscapes. Caacupé is a good place to stop and eat before continuing on to Tobatí which has limited tourism facilities.

Santuario Virgen de los Milagros de Caacupé

Commonly referred to as "*la Basílica*," this imposing church on the main plaza has housed the statue of the *Virgen de Caacupé* since 1980. Given the fervor she inspires, it is surprising to see how small the statue of the virgin actually is. Climb to the *mirador* (lookout point) at the top, and stop along the way to take in the murals depicting the legend of the *Virgen de Caacupé* (see Legend of the *Virgen de Caacupé*, p213). Aside from visiting the Santuario/Basilica, many pilgrims also visit the nearby Pozo de la Virgen or Tupãsy Ykua, a spring whose water is considered holy. *Tel: 0511 244 732, Eligio Ayala between Dr. Pino and Juan E. Oleary, www.santuariovirgendecaacupe.com, Mon-Sat 7am-11:15am, 2pm-4:45pm, Sun 8am-2:45pm*

The Pilgrimage to Caacupé

In this deeply religious country it is common for people to ask particular saints for protection and guidance. A pilgrimage to the hometown of your patron saint, especially on the saint's given feast day (as dictated by the Calendar of Saints), is an offering of gratitude. The *Virgen de Caacupé* inspires a particular devotion in Paraguayans, drawing well over one-million devotees from this nation of six-million to her hometown every year.

Although people can be seen walking to Caacupé throughout the year, the vast majority make the trek in the days leading up to December 8th. At a distance of fifty-four kilometers, the walk from Asunción usually takes a full day and is longer than a marathon. Pilgrims voyaging from further afield often walk for several days. A popular alternative for those short on time or energy is to take a bus, car, or, as used to be common, an ox-cart to a nearby town such as Ypacaraí, seventeen kilometers away, and finish the pilgrimage on foot.

Many Paraguayans walk to Caacupé at least once in their life. Some choose to make a lifelong commitment to the Virgin, returning year after year. Many even make the journey from abroad. Pilgrims of all ages make the trip: from babies in their parents' arms, to the elderly escorted in wheelchairs by family members. People rarely walk alone. Most choose to share the experience with family and friends. As a foreigner, it is easy to find companions for the pilgrimage; every Paraguayan knows at least one person making the trip every year and most are happy to share the experience with foreign visitors.

The journey can demand a fair sacrifice from pilgrims. Some years it seems the Virgin takes pity on her followers by providing cool weather and cloudy skies. More often than not, however, walkers face blazing hot summer days when the asphalt underfoot feels like a miles-long griddle. Although walking is more comfortable at night, extra care must be taken in the dark. The main access road to Caacupé, Route 2, is a heavily transited national highway, too important to shut down for the pilgrimage. Police are on hand to keep traffic from getting too close to the shoulder but even non-believers may find themselves praying to the Virgin as trucks barrel past.

Many of the faithful choose to show their gratitude to the Virgin not by walking but by assisting fellow pilgrims. The road to Caacupé is lined with tents providing all types of services. Religious groups and neighborhood commissions hand out pieces of bread spread with *dulce de guayaba* (guava jam) and serve water or juice. Since most walk in rubber flip flops, tents providing foot and back massages are particularly popular, as are the first aid tents. Those who find their bodies willing but spirits flagging receive encouragement from youth groups who perform songs and cheer them on.

The path to Caacupé is not without temptation. With their by-the-quarter-hour pricing structure, suggestively named motels such as Motel Carpe Diem and Motel Love Toys may tempt even the most devout walkers to stray from the path. There is a saying about couples walking to Caacupé together: "*Fueron entre dos, y volvieron entre tres*" (they went as two and returned as three), so clearly the motels are able to drum up business even in the holiest of times. Tempting other weaknesses, homeowners along the route turn their front lawns into impromptu restaurants, enticing pilgrims with grilled meats and cold beer.

Every pilgrim is a potential customer, and the throngs of people present a golden opportunity for enterprising vendors. Upon arriving in Caacupé one is thrust into a religious street-fair complete with skill games, a Ferris wheel, and stands selling everything from the sacred to the mundane. *Virgen de Caacupé* themed statuettes, jewelry, and t-shirts are hawked alongside sodas, shoes, and cell phones.

As the *Día de la Virgen de Caacupé* approaches, the trickle of pilgrims gives way to a full-scale river of people flowing into the city from all directions. Everyone makes their way to the main square in front of the *Basilica de Caacupé* to stake out a spot. The plaza and surrounding areas are literally carpeted with people. Every surface is occupied by pilgrims, some resting, others talking and praying. In fact, the

---

Tips for Walking to Caacupé

Seeing as the massive countrywide pilgrimage to Caacupé takes place along the side of a highway at the beginning of the Paraguayan summer certain precautions should be taken:

Watch where you're going. The walk takes place on the side of the road – either on uneven footpaths or on the road's shoulder which has raised rumble strips that are easy to trip on, especially at night. Despite police presence some vehicles come too close for comfort so try to keep your distance from the road.

Wear proper shoes: It's a long walk. Don't do it in flip flops (unless you are paying penance).

Bring water or make sure to drink water offered along the way.

Avoid the hottest hours of the day. With the hot sun above and the hot asphalt underfoot walking to Caacupé during the daytime is a brutal affair. Plenty of people walk at night when it is calmer and cooler.

Choose an alternate walking date. Walking to Caacupé still "counts" even if you don't do it on the 7th and 8th. In fact, many choose to walk throughout the week leading up to the 8th. The crowds are smaller and the experience is less intense… that can be a good thing!

term "*función Caacupé*" is Paraguayan slang for a crowded event. Hourly masses are broadcast over loudspeakers throughout the night of December 7th and continue on through the following morning. Paraguay's heart and soul are on display during the pilgrimage. Participating in the *Día de la Virgen de Caacupé* is more than just a religious procession. The bond created between fellow pilgrims in conversation while walking or stopping for food is unforgettable. Walking to Caacupé can be a fun, if at times overwhelming, experience.

Lodging

Lodging in Caacupé can get very crowded during early December in anticipation of the pilgrimage. If you would like to be there for the big day book extra early and consider staying in lodging further from town and arranging for transportation (although streets will be very crowded). Aside from visiting the Basilica there is not much to do in Caacupé itself – people interested in taking advantage the area's natural surroundings will do best to stay in one of the estancias and campgrounds located on the outskirts of Caacupé.

As a result of the combination of Caacupé's natural surroundings and religious importance there are several establishments geared towards hosting religious retreats. Their facilities often include basic dorm rooms, campgrounds, and kitchens. Though they tend to focus on large groups some establishments are able to accommodate campers. Be aware that their religious nature may mean alcohol is not permitted on the premises. In addition expect dorms and kitchens to be minimally stocked as groups usually bring everything from sheets and towels to cook wear.

Zum Thüringer A hotel and restaurant that caters mostly to German immigrants. It is located about four kilometers from Caacupé but as it is on the main road buses in to town can be caught easily. Rooms are simple but clean. Restaurant serves up classic German dishes like bratwurst and "eisbein," has nice ambience and a pool table. Owners can arrange excursions and offers car rentals. *Tel: 0511 242 508, 0981 480 923, Rt 2 km 51.5, www.paraguay-pension.com, Single Gs. 100,000, Double (accommodates up to 4 people) Gs. 200,000, Wi-Fi, TV, A/C, pool. Restaurant hours: Wed-Sun 11:30-4pm, 7pm-12am, Gs. 25,000-35,000*

Hotel Katy María Very centrally located. Rooms have balconies looking out over the Basilica. *Tel: 0511 242 860, Corner of Eligio Ayala and Dr. Pino, Gs. 150,000 per person, TV, A/C, mini-fridge*

The East

Legend of the Virgen of Caacupé

The much revered Virgen de Caacupé originated not from Caacupé but from the neighboring town of Tobatí. According to popular legend in the late 1500's a Guaraní Indian from Tobati's Fransiscan mission was being chased through the forest by raiding Mbaya Indians. A sculptor by trade he had been in the forest looking for wood. Seeking refuge behind a large tree he made a promise to the Virgin Mary – in exchange for her protection he would sculpt her image out of said tree. Once safe he made two statues – a large one for the church of Tobatí and a smaller one which he kept in his home in Caacupé. In 1603 there was a large flood in the area but the statue of the Virgin miraculously resurfaced from the flood waters. From then on she was venerated as the "*Virgen de los Milagros de Caacupé*" (Virgen of the Miracles of Caacupé). Both statues receive much religious devotion although as the patron saint of Paraguay the festivities surrounding the Virgen of Caacupé are unmatched (see The Pilgrimage to Caacupé, p211). Each year the statues of the Virgen de Caacupé and the Virgen de Tobatí are reunited in a special procession.

Asunción Hotel Located behind the Basilica this retro looking mustard yellow and orange hotel is the nicest in town. Rooms are large if a little sparsely decorated. Of the hotels in town this one has the benefit of not being located on the main road (however this doesn't make much of a difference during early December when the entire area is a crazy mess). *Tel: 0511 243 771, Avenida 8 de Diciembre and Juan E'Oleary, www.asuncionhotel.com.py/, Gs. Gs. 100,000 per person, Wi-Fi, TV, A/C, mini-fridge*

Hotel Virgen Serrana A basic hotel across the street from the Basilica. The first floor has a large store selling handicrafts and an enormous variety of religious items – from large statuettes to rosaries and everything in between. Even if you don't stay at the hotel it is worth visiting this *santería* to see the various religious paraphernalia that accompany this town's religious fervor. Rooms on the bottom floor are cheaper while rooms on the top floor are much nicer. *Tel: 0511 24 23 66, www.hotelvirgenserrana.turismoparaguay.net, Ground floor Gs. 70,000 per person, top floor Gs. 150,000 per person, TV, A/C*

Restaurants

El Cucurucho The only place serving up pecan pie in all of Paraguay, *Cucurucho* (Spanish for "ice cream cone") is a must stop for anyone with a sweet tooth traveling down Route 2. Cucurucho specializes in American style desserts including cookies, pies and muffins. There are burgers and fries as well. The *pingüino*, (penguin) a chocolate muffin smothered in soft serve ice cream and chocolate syrup is a glutton's delight. *Tel: 0984 201 545, Route 2 km 44.5 on the left-hand side of the road when coming from Asunción and marked by a five foot tall ice cream cone shaped sign that is visible from the road. Mon-Thu 9am-8:30pm, Fri-Sat 9am-11pm, Sun 9am-8pm, Gs. 5,000-15,000*

Restaurant Chiky One block from the Basilica, this bright yellow restaurant is a popular hangout for the area's expat community. Breakfast spreads include eggs, sausages, juice, fresh bread, and jams. The lunch and dinner menu is ambitious, including curry chicken and steak with cognac sauce. Food presentation is very upscale. *Tel: 0511 244 607, Rt 2 between Iturbe and Independencia Nacional across from the 8 de Diciembre stadium, www.chiky.biz, Sat 10am-12pm, Sun-Fri 10am-10pm, closed Tue, Gs. 15,000-50,000*

Nuevo Super 2 – Patio de Comidas As with all large supermarkets in Paraguay the by the kilo buffet is a dependable source of cheap if not necessarily exciting food. *Tel: 0511 243 651, before the entrance to town on the right-hand side of the highway coming from Asunción, daily 7:30am-4pm, Gs. 5,000-25,000*

Kuña Guapa Aty Stands While the entrance to Caacupé is marked by the American style desserts of Cucurucho, after you leave town the stands of the Kuña Guapa Aty cooperative offer a more traditional Paraguayan way to satisfy your sweet tooth. Approximately one kilometer past the center of town these yellow roadside stands are piled with *dulces caseros* – homemade jams and bars of guava, peanuts and sweet potato as well as *dulce de leche*. The cooperative's name stands for "hard working women." Dulces, most of which are cooked over an open wood fire, require hours of stirring before boiling down to the right consistency (many women have battle wounds inflicted by bubbling jam). For the members of this cooperative, as well as several other families in Caacupé, the labor intensive production of *"dulces"* represents a significant source of income. *Km 57.5*

Paraguayan Tupperware

All along the highway there is evidence of Paraguayans' entrepreneurial spirit. Roadside stands sell cases of produce as well as utilitarian goods like handmade brooms. Also on display is people's inventiveness in the face of limited resources. A surprising variety of containers are given a second life. Nescafe jars are filled with *dulce de guayaba* and soda bottles contain honey and engine oil (sold by the same stand, oddly enough, marked *"Miel y Lubricantes"*).

Getting There

The eastbound section of Route 2 circumvents the center of town and reconnects with the westbound lane approximately 1.6 kilometers later. Drivers coming from Asunción can reach the main plaza by taking a left on to Avenida 8 de Diciembre just after Route 2 forks. If you miss the turn off you can take any of the following left-hand turns and work your way back. There is also a left-hand turn off on to the westbound lane just before both lanes reconnect.

Caacupé is an almost obligatory stop for regional buses on Route 2. These include La Tobateña, Virgen Serrana, Empresa Piribebuy and La Valenzolana (Gs. 4,000). Long distance buses such as those headed to Coronel Oviedo or Ciudad del Este are a pricier but more comfortable option. These generally stop in Caacupé although you should double check before boarding. Coming from Asunción the road curves around the center of town so it is best to get off at the Nuevo Super 2 supermarket at the entrance of town and then walk the rest of the way.

ATYRÁ

Known as *"la ciudad más limpia del Paraguay"* (Paraguay's cleanest city) Atyrá is an attractive hill top town. Wander through the town's two plazas down to the Indio José pedestrian walkway (Peatonal Indio José) where you can admire the leather crafts for which the town is known. Artisans use metal stamps to decorate leather purses, shoes, wallets, and, of course,

> "Atyrá" means "meeting place" in Guaraní and is yet another word in which the "y" is pronounced as if it were a "u."

terere thermoses. For a bit of history pop into the town's church and admire the original carved wooden altarpiece (if the church is not open you can knock on the door of the Casa Parroquial on the left-hand corner from the front of the church). And for the best view from upon high head to the fancy Casa del Monte retreat built into a hillside overlooking town. For a tour of town contact the Municipal office or Gustavo Villalba at 0981 336 420.

Expo-Cuero Atyrá

Every year Atyrá's leather-work artisans gather in stands around the town plaza to showcase their wares. There are occasional leather work demonstrations as well as performances by local bands and dance groups. The event takes place in the town plaza over several days in late September and coincides with celebrations surrounding the town's patron saint, St. Francisco de Asis.

Complejo Marianela Atyrá

Built by Italian priests this impressive religious complex is mostly used for religious retreats but open to visitors who come to enjoy the serene grounds and intricately decorated buildings. Local artisans worked alongside foreign artists to create the complex's murals, oil paintings and wood carvings. Lunch is served on Sundays and goods such as honey, Italian olive oil and very high quality terere thermoses are on sale. *Tel: 0982 101 933, 0972 289 443, if starting at the town church walk behind the church and then take a left for three and a half blocks (you will pass the town cemetery on your left), 7am-12pm, 1pm-5pm*

The East

Lodging

Casa del Monte Located on a hilltop overlooking Atyrá and Lake Ypacaraí in the distance Casa del Monte offers one of the nicest views around. The hotel's restaurant and many rooms are built into the side of the hill and connected by stone paths that wind through the trees (not for the weak kneed). The grounds include a large terrace with a pool, volleyball and soccer courts, a cute duck pond, and a small aviary. Though removed from the town it is worth the journey. The restaurant's service can be hit or miss but the food is generally tasty. *Tel: 0520 20069, 0516 250 050, throughout town you will see signs pointing in the direction of Casa del Monte which is about two kilometers away, once at the outskirts of town you will pass the Complejo Marianela on your left and continue uphill – the road is rocky and uneven at times but a 4x4 is not necessary. Follow the signs which will lead you uphill and to your right, if traveling by public transportation the hotel will pick you up in town for a fee or arrange for a taxi, www.casadelmonte.com.py, food Gs. 20,000-40,000, room rates: doubles Gs. 360,000, triples 430,000, A/C, Wi-Fi, pool and sauna*

Getting There

The turn off to Atyrá is located at km 47 of the westbound lane of Route 2, by the Cruz del Peregrino, a large white cement cross which marks the official entrance to Caacupé. If you are coming from Asunción you will have to overshoot the cross and double back. As the turn off curves right you will pass the Taiwanese Expo Flora on the left. Atyrá can also be reached via dirt road from both Tobatí and Altos.

Both the Atyrá and San Vicente buses leave approximately every half hour from Asunción's bus terminal, Gs. 6,800.

TOBATÍ

Once a Franciscan mission today the small town of Tobatí is well known for its ceramic work. This is both utilitarian and artistic in nature. The town is home to many small scale brick factories known as *olerías*. The majority of these produce bricks by hand. The town's decorative ceramics are mostly produced in the nearby *compañía* of 21 de Julio. One of the main products Tobateños make are water jugs or *kambuchi* in Guaraní (see Kambuchi, p218). However with the advent of running water demand for *kambuchis* has fallen and artisans have had to innovate, creating decorative objects instead. The town's beautiful landscapes make it a great place to go exploring and there are some good places for rock climbing enthusiasts, as well as swimming holes and quaint communities tucked away in the vegetation. Tobatí's church, a legacy of the town's roots as a Franciscan mission, houses the sister statue to the much venerated *Virgen de Caacupé*.

Brick Making

Throughout Tobatí you will see people hard at work making bricks. First the clay is compressed with a mill known as a *trapiche*. Though it is often powered by an ox walking in circles, smaller outfits will simply turn the *trapiche* by hand. Once ready the thick black clay is slapped into wooden molds which hold four bricks each. These are allowed to dry in the sun before the bricks are knocked out. The still damp bricks are then arranged in MC Escher-like zig zag patterns and allowed to dry fully. Once enough dried bricks have been amassed a wood fire is lit in a large oven (itself made of bricks) and the bricks are baked, turning a pale orange in the process. For all this work brick-makers can expect to receive between Gs. 500 and Gs. 700 per brick.

Mirador Tres Caras de Indios

Just before the entrance to town on the right-hand side is a large rock column jutting out of the ground. The base is decorated with three stone sculptures of indigenous faces and steps head to a lookout point up top. From there you can see brick factories of various sizes throughout the area.

Villa Artesanal

Though removed from town, the Villa Artesanal, an activities center for the area's artisans, is worth the visit. Items by local artists are on sale throughout the year, though the best time to go is during the yearly Expo Tobatí (see the following section). The Villa Artesanal is run by Fundación Tobatí, an NGO focused on improving the life of local artisans. Educational workshops are frequently held and housing is provided free of charge for several artisans in the Villa Artesanal and in surrounding neighborhoods. *Tel: 0516 262 162, follow the signed turn off for Fundación Tobatí on the left-hand side of the road into town just after the gas station, the center is on the right-hand side of the road approximately 600 meters away, www.fundaciontobati.org.py, 8am-5pm*

Expo Tobatí

Held every year in late October the Expo Tobatí showcases artisans from Tobatí as well as further afield. As with most town festivals the Expo Tobatí includes performances by local music and dance troupes. Contact Fundación Tobatí for specific dates (see Villa Artesanal).

Don Zenón Páez's Workshop

In addition to ceramic artists Tobatí is home to Don Zenón Páez, a renowned Paraguayan wood carver. Though most of Sr. Páez's work is religious in nature he is also known for his other carvings. The *carreta aza prima* features a peasant in a wagon (*carreta*) pulled by several oxen which is transporting a large felled tree trunk. This scene still takes place throughout the country although in large part the wagons have been replaced by trucks. His most intriguing and labor intensive piece is the Triple Alliance War themed chess set. The darker figures (usually carved from *palo santo*) represent the Brazilian, Argentine and Uruguayan forces of Triple Alliance, complete with sinking battle ships as towers, and the emperors of Brazil as the king and queen. Mariscal López and Madame Lynch play king and queen on the Paraguayan side and the ruins of Humaitá are towers. Paraguay's pawns, all carved out of white *guatambu* wood are represented by the men, women and children soldiers. This quirky chess set takes weeks to complete and sells for several hundred dollars. To see more of Zenón Páez's work ask to visit the recently opened Museo Zenón Paez down the block. *Tel: 0516 22 29, 0516 262020,0516 262 160, Mariscal López and Pedro Juan Caballero 1177, www.zenonpaez.com, the workshop is on the left-hand side of the main road entering town*

Outdoor Activities

The hills of Tobatí offer outdoor enthusiasts a chance to do some rock climbing – a sport which few Paraguayans partake in. The San Bernardino based adventure tourism company Aventura Xtrema (see Aventura Xtrema, p207) offers a full day tour of Tobatí which includes trekking, cave exploration and rappelling (note: this tour requires at least four people and a reservation two days prior is recommended).

The East

American ex-pat Dale Helms has been leading rock climbing groups in the Tobatí area for several years. Dale and other climbing enthusiasts have bolted paths up Tobatí's Itá Porá formation and spent time exploring the area's beautiful landscapes. They usually go every Saturday, often joined by Peace Corps volunteers that make for fun and knowledgeable company. *Tel: 0981 568 570*

Getting There

The turn off to Tobatí is located in downtown Caacupé. If coming from Asunción you will have to follow Route 2 as it veers right and curves around town. To your left there will be a long stretch of grass in a park after which there is a left-hand curve in the road which allows you to double back onto Route 2 in the opposite direction taking you back through Caacupé. Continue about six blocks and take a right on to Juan O'Leary and then take the second right which will lead you all the way to Tobatí. From points east of Caacupé simply look for the right-hand turn off on Juan O'Leary as you begin to enter the center of town (if you pass the plaza and Basilica on your left you've gone too far).

The Villa Serrana bus line (buses say "Tobatí" across the front) leaves from Asunción's bus terminal and the trip takes approximately two hours, Gs. 7,700. You can also take any bus heading down Route 2 past Caacupé (grab a long distance bus headed to Ciudad del Este for the nicest ride), get off at the Nuevo Super 2 supermarket just before Caacupé (a popular bus stop) and then catch the Villa Serrana or Arroyos y Esteros bus from there, Gs. 3,000. There is a man at the bus stop in front of the Nuevo Super 2 who flags down buses for all passengers – simply tell him where you're headed. Another option is to take a bus to Caacupé and then hire a taxi to drive to Tobatí. Specify you will need a ride back and be sure the quoted fare includes wait time.

Kambuchi

Many houses and businesses in the countryside have a large round clay water jug in the corner, usually covered with a plate and a glass. This is known as a "*kambuchi*" in Guaraní and a "*cántaro*" in Spanish. In towns without running water women can still be seen returning purposefully from the river or creek carefully balancing water-filled *kambuchi* atop their heads. Though mostly used for water *kambuchi* are also used to keep *clericó* cool during holiday festivities. Some choose to keep their *kambuchi* on the floor while others have tables with holes cut out specifically to fit the *kambuchi*. Metal *kambuchi* holders are also popular and the more pragmatic choose to keep their *kambuchi* wedged into the nook of a low tree branch or trunk.

SOUTH TO PARAGUARÍ ALONG THE RUTA PARAGUARÍ-PIRIBEBUY

One of the few roads that connects Route 1 and Route 2, the scenic Ruta Paraguarí-Piribebuy (formally named the Ruta General Rogelio Benitez) makes for a beautiful and pleasant drive. From Route 2 the landscape dips down along a series of rolling hills that keep the temperatures cool. Along the way you will see several large farms as well as the factories where *caña* Fortín and local soda Gaseosa Piri are produced. Entering Piribebuy you will pass the San Blas oratory which draws pilgrims from several nearby towns each Feb. 2nd (see Fiesta de San Blas, p220). Past Piribebuy the road climbs slowly but surely through smaller, more rural communities. Children play in fields and cows wander slowly along the side of the road. At the top of a hill to the right is the small Oratorio San Rafael sitting atop an enormous tree covered boulder. The road is dotted with stands selling stone grottos of various sizes for housing statues of saints. A bit further is the right-hand turn off for the Chololó swimming hole. As the road climbs the Cerro Mbatoví it begins to wind through the growing vegetation. Fortunately there are a couple small lookout points to the right from which you can admire the picturesque view and catch a cool breeze. Once descended the road flattens again and leads to Paraguarí where it connects to Route 1. If you are in a private vehicle note there is very little transit on this road so take it slow and enjoy the ride. Unfortunately buses that run the entire road are few and far between. If headed past Chololó in either direction your best bet is to take a taxi from Piribebuy or Paraguarí. Getting from one end to the other on public transportation requires some flexibility and multiple buses. The Empresa Piribebuy has buses that go from Asunción through Piribebuy as far as Chololó. From there a separate Empresa Piribebuy bus heads to Paraguarí. Empresa Piribebuy has one bus that comes from Ciudad del Este between 8:30 and 10am, stops in Piribebuy and connects to route 1 though Paraguarí before heading to Carapeguá. However this bus can be very elusive so it is best to confirm its itinerary with the bus company (*Tel: 0515 212 164*).

PIRIBEBUY

Piribebuy is one of the larger towns tucked away from Route 2 in the Cordillera department. The area's rolling hills and relative proximity to Asunción make it a draw for vacationers, many of whom have summer homes here. An increasingly small number of artisans in town still create the labor intensive *poncho sesenta lista*, said to have been a favorite of Mariscal López. The town is home to two religious festivals which take place during the summer, the *Fiesta de San Blas* which brings in pilgrims from afar and the celebration of *Ñandeyara Guazú*. For those interested in experiencing Paraguay's religious traditions these are lower key alternatives to the neighboring celebration of the *Día de la Virgen de Caacupé*.

Piribebuy is a nice example of a small yet economically prosperous Paraguayan town. There are several large factories in the area including those of Piri Cola sodas and Caña Fortín alcohol as well as a nearby munitions factory. These businesses draw workers from the region and bring money into the town. There are many small businesses in the center of town though fortunately the main plaza and surrounding areas are still quite *tranquilo*. The further you venture down cobblestone roads the more rural life becomes and, due to the area's many hills, the verdant scenery is lovely. As with much of the Cordillera department many *Asuncenos* have vacation homes here and there are many European retirees living here as well (there is even a German gated community, Topachi Ranch). Those who wish to delve into small town life should stay in town while visitors who'd prefer to enjoy the natural scenery will prefer larger, more touristy ranches along the road to Paraguarí.

In terms of history, the town has the dubious distinction of having been one of the only urban areas to see action during the Triple Alliance War. Unfortunately the situation was quite tragic for the town's residents. Four years into the brutal Triple Alliance War the Paraguayan government headquarters was moved to Piribebuy, having previously relocated from Asunción to nearby Luque. In

> Piribebuy means slight chills or goosebumps in Guaraní and is a reference to the area's cool temperatures.

August of 1869 the Battle of Piribebuy was waged between 20,000 Triple Alliance troops and 1,600 Paraguayans, most of whom were women, children and the elderly. Amongst this band of poorly armed patriots was a group of 200 school children from Villarrica, marched to the battle front by their teacher Maestro Fermín López. The battle was short lived and the majority of the survivors executed. To top off the atrocities the hospital was set afire with 600 patients still inside. Only days later a similarly unequipped army made up of mostly children was massacred in nearby Acosta Ñu (see Los Niños Mártires de Acosta Ñu, p225). Months later Marsical López would be fatally wounded to the north in Cerro Corá but by this point the war was already lost. This brutal episode is the reason Piribebuy is also known as the *ciudad heróica* (heroic city).

Fiesta de San Blas

At the entrance to Piribebuy there is a small oratory erected to hold a statue of San Blas. Every year he is honored on February 2nd with pilgrimages from *promeseros* who have promised their devotion in honor of San Blas' protection. Many of the younger *promeseros* don burgundy capes laced with yellow trimmings and crowns in honor of the saint. Though it is a dying tradition there are still several families that journey to Piribebuy in ox drawn carts for the festivities. The intersection of Maestro Fermín López and Pedro Juan Caballero is a traditional campgrounds for these pilgrims. Carts and camping equipment are set up along the sidewalk and ox are allowed to graze up the street in the grounds of the Colorado party headquarters (the *seccional Colorada*) on the corner of Mariscal Estigarribia and Pedro Juan Caballero. During the festival many of Piribebuy's inhabitants prepare a large meal known as a *kaaru guazú* to share with pilgrims. Others may distribute prepared food for free. The festivities include a procession from the oratory to the church on the morning of the 2nd, and a celebratory mass in Piribebuy's main plaza on the morning of the 3rd followed by a procession back to the oratory. The night of the 2nd the town's two social clubs, the Club 12 de Agosto and Club Independiente (both on General Diaz) throw rivaling parties that bring in revelers from all over as well as a fare share of pilgrims. These large dance parties feature big name national musical acts as well as the occasional international band.

> According to lore, San Blas cured a small child with a fish bone stuck in her throat. Because of this he is believed to protect those with throat ailments. In Paraguay it is common for people to exclaim *"Sr. San Blas!"* if someone has a fit of coughing.

Mito Totem Pole

Just before the turn off to Piribebuy, on Route 2, there is a large totem pole depicting the mythical characters said to roam the surrounding countryside (see Meet the Mitos, p44). At the base is the cave dwelling Moñai serpent. His arm extended, the pale Jasy Jateré beckons child victims while the Kurupí stares out vacantly, his enormous phallus wrapped several times around his torso. Up top is Tupá, God. While the *mito* totem pole may be in desperate need of repair its deteriorating state does serve one purpose – it makes the Mitos seem even creepier than usual. *Km 63, Route 2 on the left-hand side of the road approximately one kilometer before the turn off to Piribebuy.*

Balneario & Arroyo Piribebuy

Piribebuy's main creek or *arroyo* is located about two blocks downhill from the town plaza. Though there are some sandy strips but for the most part the shores to either side are grassy and make for a nice picnic spot. When the water level is high enough the small water lock is closed creating the sandy-bottomed municipal pool. During the summer there are often bathers enjoying the cool water and shade from the surrounding eucalyptus trees.

Museo Municipal Capitán Pedro Pablo Caballero

The town museum contains a collection of artifacts pertaining to both the Chaco and Triple Alliance War. The museum's curator, Miguel Angel Romero is very knowledgeable about the town's history and can explain in detail Piribebuy's role during the Triple Alliance War. He is also a sculptor of saints (see Santeros, p35) and usually has several pieces in progress in the back room of the museum. On occasion he will take tourists on a tour of the town church though this depends on the mood of the town priest. Displayed without much fanfare is a traditional *poncho para'i sesenta listas* a local handicraft that is very difficult to make (see the following Poncho Para'i de Sesenta Listas). *Tel: 0515 212 202,0971 179 437 Corner of Mariscal Estigarribia and Yegros with a replica of a cannon out front, Mon-Sat 7am-12pm*

Monumento Batalla de Piribebuy

The battle of Piribebuy is commemorated with a large relief mural located at the site of the Triple Alliance era hospital known as the *Hospital de Sangre*. The mural depicts the women and children of Piribebuy defending their town against Triple Alliance forces. In the lower left-hand corner a fire rages in the *Hospital de Sangre*. In the center is Maestro Fermín López, who led his child pupils into battle. The walk to the mural, past a plaza where children often play soccer, is very picturesque and it can be hard to imagine such atrocities taking place against this peaceful backdrop. *From the Viejo Rincón or the town plaza follow Maestro Fermín López as it crosses Route 2. You will pass over a small creek immediately after crossing the highway and there will be a large plaza on your left-hand side. At the corner take a right – the monument, two blocks away, will already be visible.*

Poncho Para'i de Sesenta Listas

The *poncho para'i de sesenta listas* is a style of poncho that has been made in Piribebuy since the era of Dr. Francia. These beautiful ponchos are hand-woven from fine cotton sewing thread. Working full time four people can complete one poncho in two weeks. Each *poncho sesenta listas* has three components: the main body of the poncho, a strip along the entire edge of the poncho called a *faja* or *randa* and the fringe which hangs along the edge of the poncho. As the name indicates the poncho contains sixty white *listas,* or stripes, the width of which can vary and is up to the personal preference of the weaver. Traditionally the ponchos are black and white although modern tastes have lead to the incorporation of other colors. Due to the length and intricate patterns it incorporates the *faja* is the most complicated section, taking up to ten days to make. Unfortunately, there is no permanent exhibition space in town yet. The best place to see ponchos being made is in the workshop of Rosa Segovia (see the following section). Local artisans also tend to set up stands in the town plaza in the days before the Festival de Poncho Sesenta Listas, a music festival held on the third Friday of every January.

Rosa Segovia's *Poncho Para'i de Sesenta Listas* Workshop

Piribebuy's most renowned *poncho sesenta listas* artisan is Rosa Segovia, an animated women who is happy to receive visitors in her workshop. Each poncho costs around

The East

Gs.1,200,000, of which about 75 percent goes towards material costs. According to Rosa Segovia the weavers continue to make *poncho sesenta listas* for "the love of the art" rather than for a tidy profit. Rosa Segovia has also started making more modern items out of her *sesenta listas* cloth such as handbags and wallets. These are a nice, more affordable alternative to the traditional poncho. *Tel: 0515 212 097, 0972 649 753, to get to Rosa Segovia's house from the town plaza head towards the main road along either Maestro Fermín López or Mariscal Estigarribia. Take a right towards Paraguarí. You will pass a Copetrol station on your right and cross over a small bridge. A block further there is a large highway sign indicating distances to Itacurubi de la Cordillera. At the sign take a left and continue three blocks past a field, hospital (centro de salud) and a soccer court all on the left. Take a left and continue halfway down the block to a brick house marked number 3051 with a small ice cream stand ("Helados San Cayetano") in front.*

Plata Yvygy & Other Ghostly Reminders of the War

The phenomenon of *plata yvygy* is well known throughout Paraguay, but is especially prevalent in ex-battle grounds from the Triple Alliance war. The phrase means "money under the earth" and rumors of buried treasure from the war abound. Specifically, people are on the hunt for several wagons packed with gold coins which were moved to Piribebuy when it was temporarily declared the national capital during the last stages of the war. According to legend the presence of *plata yvygy* is indicated by several supernatural phenomena including strange glittering lights on the horizon and unexplained noises at night. However these treasures can prove elusive – according to legend only certain people possess the ability to unearth them. Many Paraguayans trust their odds though; the classifieds always feature several ads for metal detectors.

Lodging

Hotel Piribebuy The newest hotel in town Hotel Piribebuy lacks the character of El Viejo Rincón but is more comfortable. *Tel: 0515 212 994, 0981 265 153, corner of General Díaz and the Ruta General Rogelio Benitez, Single Gs. 100000, double: Gs. 120,000, TV, A/C*

El Viejo Rincón This old house turned hotel and restaurant is very similar to the majority of houses in town – high ceilings, tiled roofs, a wrap around patio and worn brick floors. Rooms are quite small and basic. The restaurant has excellent *chipa guazú* and *milanesa* and the *bife al caballo* is perfectly cooked every time. *Tel: 0515 212 251, corner of Maestro Fermín López and Horacio Gini two blocks from the town plaza, doubles Gs. 70,000 with fan, 120,000 with A/C, food Gs. 10,000-30,000, daily 7am-3:30pm, 5pm-9pm*

San Francisco Country Club Located right on the road to Piribebuy this complex has cute thatched roof bungalows, a castle shaped restaurant and pools and walking paths for relaxing and enjoying the outdoors. Bungalows are rustic looking on the outside but comfortable on the inside. The Piribebuy bus passes right in front, should you want to head into town. *Tel: 0516 250 301, 0981 802 253, km 66 Ruta General Rogelio Benitez, www.san-francisco-country.com, two person bungalows: Gs. 220,000-270,000 per person with a fee of Gs. 30,000 -40,000 for an additional person. A/C, fan, pool*

Food

El Viejo Rincón The best option in town. *See previous listing for information*

Rikuras A place to satisfy your sweet tooth with homemade desserts and ice creams. Conveniently enough it is just down the street from El Viejo Rincón. *Tel. 0515 212 262, Maestro Fermín López almost Horacio Gini, Daily 8am-6pm, Gs. 8,000-20,000*

El Edén Set up in a private home this dance club offers basic Paraguayan fast food options served at tables in the front yard. There are several hamburger and empanada joints further up the road towards the social clubs. *Tel: 0515 212 252, 0984 145 281, General Díaz almost at Heroínas de Piribebuy www.eledenrestaurante.es.tl, Gs. 10,000-25,000, Saturdays 7pm-12:30am*

Getting There

Driving from Asunción take the signed right-hand turn off at km 64 of Route 2. If you pass the Chipería María Ana on your right then you have gone too far. The center of town is to the right-hand side about nine kilometers from the turn off. If traveling from Asunción along Route 1 there is a large sign for the Eco Reserva Mbatoví along the left-hand side of the road just past the center of town. Follow this road and take a left just after the town church and the next right down a double avenue. The paved road will eventually swing to the left and head away from the center of town towards Piribebuy.

Empresa Piribebuy buses leave Asunción's bus terminal hourly (sometimes as frequently as every half hour) from 5am or so till about 8pm. From the Piribebuy's bus terminal it is about a four block walk to the town plaza. Bus fare is Gs. 7,000.

CONTINUING PAST PIRIBEBUY TOWARDS PARAGUARÍ

Chololó

This series of small waterfalls is a popular swimming spot during the summer months. *Tel: 0515 212 766, 0515 553 965, km 87 Ruta General Rogelio Benitez, coming from Piribebuy and Route 2 the turn off for Chololó is on km 87 on the right-hand side. Follow the dirt road approximately 150 meters; there are hourly Empresa Piribebuy buses that leave from the Piribebuy bus terminal for Gs. 2,300 (these can also be caught on the corner of the main plaza at Heroínas de Piribebuy and Mariscal Estigarribia). These buses stop running at 5pm.*

> "Chololó" is the onamatopeic Guaraní word for waterfall.

La Quinta

Located high on the hillside this upscale farm offers visitors fresh dairy and produce as well as the chance to enjoy an excellent view of the landscapes bellow. Rooms are nicely decorated and comfortable and there are also private bungalows whose balconies provide the best views. Take a stroll around the grounds which include a small grove of pine trees that have been comically bent by the winds that sweep this hilltop and a series of milking stations for the farm's cows. *Tel: 0971 117 444, 0971 117 555, Ruta General Rogelio Benitez km 82.5, from Piribebuy the access road to La Quinta is located on the left-hand side, marked by a small wood sign with a yellow sun between two green hills. From here it is approximately 1 km uphill to the main building. The Empresa Piribebuy bus which heads to Chololó from Piribebuy runs past the entrance (see Chololó) but if coming from Paraguarí it is best to go by taxi, www.laquinta.com.py, day rate Gs. 165,000 or 185,000 w/ lunch and afternoon snack, room rates Gs. 319,000 per person with full board, bungalows Gs. 352,000 per person with full board, Wi-Fi, A/C, TV, pool, sports area, game room*

Eco Reserva Mbatoví

Perched at the top of Cerro Mbatoví the Eco Reserva Mbatoví offers visitors a series of outdoor activities from trekking to a small ropes course, a zip line and rappelling.

Safety equipment is included and in good condition. Outdoor activities start at 9am and 2pm and run for 3.5 hours. People should arrive at least thirty to forty-five minutes ahead of the start times. Many of Asunción's tour operators offer a day trip to Mbatoví in conjunction with lunch at the nearby La Quinta. *Tel: 021 444 844, 0981 387 007, 0971 299 250, Ruta General Rogelio Benitez km 72, taxis from Paraguarí are between Gs. 25,000 to 30,000 and about Gs. 30,000 to Gs. 35,000 from Piribebuy. Reservations must be made at least two days in advance (and prepaid if for a party of more than three people), www.mbatovi.com.py, Gs. 130,000 per person*

CONTINUING ALONG ROUTE 2

Eusebio Ayala

Eusebio Ayala is well known throughout Paraguay for its *chipa* production, over-shadowed only by the official "Chipa Capital," Coronel Bogado. Eusebio Ayala's popular *chiperías* make great pit stops. Here Paraguayans' love of *chipa* is on display – it is not uncommon for the parking lots *chiperías* to be jam packed with all manner of buses, cars, vans, and motorcycles.

⌂ Chipería María Ana

Started by single mother María Ana López, this roadside *chipa* stand has burgeoned into a bustling business with piping hot *chipa* served almost round the clock. As you pull up *chiperas* (all single mothers) race to your car, each more eager than the next to sell her *chipa*. They also sell steaming cups of sweet *cocido*. There is a small cantina where you can pick up other snacks and drinks and the bathrooms are kept clean. The store itself is on the right-hand side of the road leading towards Ciudad del Este but those going the other way need not despair – María Ana has *chiperas* stationed on that side as well. This *chipa* stand is so popular there is even a song written about it ("*Chipería María Ana*" by Quemil Yambay). *Tel: 0514 215 457, Rt 2 km 68.5, daily 3am – 11pm, Gs. 2,000-5,000*

The Life of a Chipera

Making and selling *chipa* is one of Paraguay's most prevalent cottage industries. Some people work for road side *chipa* stands while others are "freelance" *chiperas* that walk around town, baskets of *chipa* perched atop their heads. Many *chiperas* have a fixed route, stopping by hair salons, mini-markets and government offices daily to sell to their clientele. Most *chiperas* mix the dough by hand – only larger commercial ventures use electric mixers to make their dough. During holidays such as Easter week *chiperías* big and small receive large orders. Although the majority of *chiperas* are women you can also see men selling *chipa* on the street. Many choose to sell both *chipa* and *cocido* which certainly requires excellent balance.

Throughout the country (with the exception of the Chaco) there are stands along the roadside selling *chipa* to passers by. *Chiperas* working roadside stands work on commission receiving between 10% and 30% of the sales from each basket. You will often see them trying to outrun each other to get to potential customers. Most stands have negotiated exclusive deals with bus companies that travel along their road and *chiperas* hop on buses constantly to sell to passengers. Watching a *chipera* squeeze all the way to the back of a crowded bus without dropping any *chipa* is an impressive sight.

La Casa del Maní
This nice roadside store sells all manner of peanut products as well as honey cake. *Tel: 0981 886 800, 0981 953 635, Rt 2 km 69, daily 7:30am-6pm, Gs. 5,000-12,000*

Chipería Leticia
A better option for those who want to eat something in addition to *chipa*, Chipería Leticia has a by the kilo buffet. The specialty is fried pork, and of course the *chipas* made on the premises. There is also a minimarket. *Tel: 0514 215 509, Rt 2, km. 74.5, open daily 24 hrs, Gs, 2,000-35,000*

Chipería Barrero
Chipería Barrero is the best known *chipería* in all of Cordillera. However, you don't need to go to Eusebio Ayala to try their chipa as they have trucks constantly winding through the streets of Asunción blaring *"Chipa Barreeeero!"* through loudspeakers. They often park outside of popular nightclubs in the wee hours of the morning and sell to exiting revelers. While the *chipería* itself sells normal Gs. 2,000 *chipa* the trucks are usually only stocked with enormous Gs. 5,000 rings about half a foot in diameter. *Tel: 0981 559 858, Rt 2, km 79, www.chipabarrero.com, open daily 24 hrs Gs. 2,000-5,000*

Los Ñinos Mártires de Acosta Ñu
The Battle of Acosta Ñu, fought almost entirely by children on the Paraguayan side, is one of the most tragic events of the disastrous Triple Alliance War. This battle came only days after the neighboring town of Piribebuy was the site of massive casualties. According to witnesses the child soldiers were attacked viciously and the battlefield set ablaze. The anniversary of this horrific event was declared *Día del Niño* (Children's Day) as a tribute to all the child martyrs of the war. Every year the *Día del Niño* is celebrated on August 16th with festivals in schools and parties that include a *chocolatada* (hot chocolate and cake) and plenty of gifts all around.

Departamento Caaguazú

At the city of Coronel Oviedo, where Route 2 turns into Route 7, the landscapes become flatter and there is a significant drop in population density and a shift in focus towards large scale agriculture. While many of the Paraguayan inhabitants of the departments of Caaguazú and Alto Paraná still survive on small scale farming the majority large scale farming is done by foreigners – Brazilians and European and American Mennonites who have the financial capacity to expand to mechanized agriculture. Tourists will find that, until Ciudad del Este (which belongs to the department of Alto Paraná), there is not much in the way of attractions along Route 7. Coronel Oviedo marks the start of the start of Route 8 leading south to the department of Guairá which has much to offer tourists (see Route 8, p228). Both Coronel Oviedo and Caaguazú are mostly commercial hubs. The series of small towns that follow are almost all Mennonite colonies where the focus is on labor rather than recreation.

CORONEL OVIEDO
Located roughly in the middle of Eastern Paraguay the city of Coronel Oviedo (often simply called "Oviedo") is a major transportation hub. Here Route 2, which starts in Asunción, becomes Route 7, which ends in Ciudad del Este. Route 8 runs South

from Coronel Oviedo past Villarrica all the way to Caazapá and North to San Estanislao where it connects with both Route 3 (which continues North connecting with Pedro Juan Caballero and Concepción) and Route 10 (which heads East to Salto de Guairá and the border with Brazil). Though Coronel Oviedo is the largest in the area those wishing to visit towns in the neighboring department of Guairá will be better off using the city of Villarrica as a home base.

Lodging

Hotels in Oviedo are pretty evenly priced so you are better off deciding where to stay based on your travel needs. For those whose plans involve visiting the city it is best to choose a hotel in town. If you are just passing through and do not plan to do anything in Oviedo itself there are several decent options at the entrance to town along Route 2. For those who want get some fresh air before continuing on there are two nice ranches (*estancias*) that can be visited in the outskirts of Oviedo – Granja Alto Liebe right off Route 8 and Estancia Don Emilio about eight kilometers off Route 8.

Hotel San Ser Though this is the furthest from the center of Coronel Oviedo this hotel has the nicest grounds. The hotel's five hectares of woods including plenty of citrus trees provide a natural ambience which contrasts sharply with the rest of Coronel Oviedo. Enjoy the view from the hotel terrace. *Tel: 0521 200 826, Rt 2 km 129.5 at Mariscal Estigarribia and Humaitá on the left-hand side of the road if coming from Asunción. If you pass the crossroads leading into town you've gone too far, www.sanserhotel.com, Singles: Gs. 60,000-90,000, doubles 90,000-110,000, TV, A/C, pool*

Hotel Bertea The *nivel básico* (basic) rooms are nothing fancy but all have TV and A/C and are the cheapest lodging in Coronel Oviedo (there are also higher priced *nivel superior* and *premium* rooms). The location is good if you are just passing through. Next door is the popular restaurant Parador La Nona and there is also a bus ticketing agency within the same building. *Tel: 0521 202 019, Rt 2 km130 (on the left-hand side if coming from Asunción), Single Gs. 40,000-60,000 and Gs. 100,000-150,000, Doubles Gs. 60,000-80,000 and Gs. 120,000-180,000, TV, A/C*

Granja Alte Liebe Easily accessible from Coronel Oviedo, Granja Alte Liebe's well maintained grounds are perfect for a day trip or escape from the city. Stroll along the walking paths that lead past the farm's citrus groves, man-made fish pond, and unique rock faced pool. Those who want to feel as far removed from the city as

---

Peanuts

Known as "*maní*" in Spanish and "*manduvi*" in Guaraní, peanuts are a typical crop consumed by Paraguayans in many forms. *Dulce de maní*, a chewy version of peanut brittle made with sugar cane honey (*miel de caña*), is one of the most popular peanut based foods. Home made *dulce de maní* is sold on buses and roadside stands throughout the country, usually costing from Gs.500 to Gs.1000. They are also referred to as *kaí ladrillo*, or "monkey bricks," presumably because monkeys love the sweet, nutty treat as much as humans do. Another sweet peanut snack is candy-coated peanuts called *maní garrapiñado*. Ground peanuts, called m*anduví kui* are often added to *cocido* and also consumed as a dessert along with sugar cane honey. This dish, caked "*manduví kuí con miel*," is often referred to jokingly as "*viagra paraguaya*." A less traditional but still popular form of consuming peanuts is as peanut butter which is produced for the most part by Mennonite cooperatives. This peanut butter or *manteca de maní* (literally "butter from peanuts") is excellent, made only with ground peanuts and salt (though some cooperatives also add in chocolate or sesame seeds).

possible can request to stay in one of the two cabins towards the back of the property alongside a small man made creek. *Tel: 0521 200447, 0991 554 818, Route 8 km 147, thirteen kilometers south of Coronel Oviedo on the left-hand side of Route 8, On Facebook, restaurant open summers only, Bungalows Gs. 60,000 per person, camping Gs. 30,000 per person, A/C, pool, fishing*

Lodging in Town

Hotel Center A very nice hotel in the downtown area close to Oviedo's large main plaza. Rooms are big and halls are nicely decorated with unique metal work incorporating ñanduti designs. Laundry service is a nice perk. *Tel: 0521 204 610, 204 611, 0972 534 766, Defensores del Chaco and Vice Presidente. Sánches between the Stock and El Machetazo supermarkets, Single Gs. 60,000-70,000, double Gs. 90,000-100,000, Wi-Fi, computers with internet, TV, A/C*

La Estancia de Don Emilio A taste of rural Paraguay with the comforts of an upscale ranch, La Estancia de Don Emilio sits in the middle of a 4000 plus hectare private estate, 1,300 of which remain untouched. Owned and operated by descendants of French immigrants along with a friendly Paraguayan staff. Relax in the pool, enjoy horseback riding or take part in daily farm tasks, if you want to get your hands dirty and really earn the four meals provided per day. Rooms combine the best features of traditional Paraguayan architecture along with elegant furniture brought over from the Old World. *Tel: 021 660 791, 021 603 994, 0981507 105 ask to speak to Señora Magabí. If in a private vehicle drive approximately six kilometers south from Oviedo and turn left at the sign for the airport, drive eight kilometers on this dirt road which will dead end at the estancia's large white main gate. If traveling by bus you can take a taxi from Oviedo or inquire with Señora Magabí about the possibility of being picked up either in Oviedo or from the entrance on Route 8. www.donemilioestancia.com, US 60$ per day although there is a slightly lesser rate for Paraguayans and those holding a Paraguayan ID card, Pool, horseback riding*

The *"Marcha al Este"*

Although now considered a major transportation hub within Eastern Paraguay Coronel Oviedo was not always so. Before the 1960's Route 2 stretched east from Asunción only as far as Coronel Oviedo and only the first half was paved. In 1955 the *"Marcha al Este"* (March to the East) road construction project was undertaken to give Paraguay access to the Atlantic Ocean by way of Brazil. Thus Route 7 was created, extending from Coronel Oviedo all the way to the Paraná River and border with Brazil. According to General Pereira Ruiz Díaz, placed in charge of the project "Paraguay pretty much ended at Coronel Oviedo" with miles and miles of wilderness separating it from Brazil.

The *Marcha al Este* is undoubtedly one of Paraguay's most important road construction projects. The road opened up the easternmost section of the country to a land rush. Drawn to the prospect of virgin land and new opportunities, enterprising people from all over the country moved to the wilderness to make new lives for themselves. These colonists weathered many hardships in the wild and had to wait many years for basic services such as running water. With the completion of the road in 1957 came the founding of Puerto Presidente Stroessner, now named Ciudad del Este. The Puente de la Amistad connecting Ciudad del Este to Brazil's Foz do Iguaçu was inaugurated in 1965 and construction of the Itaipú Hydroelectric Dam began in 1975.

The *Marcha al Este* project's resulting population boom brought progress to the eastern departments of Caaguazú and Alto Paraná (which today still has the country's fastest growing population) but this progress had a severe impact on the area's natural resources. In Guaraní Caaguazú means "large forest," in reference to what used to be the region's primary natural resource. The region's new inhabitants dedicated themselves in large part to logging, resulting in a rapid rate of deforestation which continues today as the remaining forests are felled to make way for farmland.

Food

Parador La Nona A popular pit stop, the Parador La Nona has a decent sized buffet with pastas, salads and a wide variety of grilled meats. *Tel: 0521 202019, Rt 2 km 130 next door to Hotel Bertea just before the entrance to town, Gs. 10,000-20,000, daily 6am-11:30pm*

Sudamericana Located relatively close to the entrance to town Sudamericana is a Brazilian style *churrasquería* where a fixed price brings round after round of meats right off the grill. As with all churrasquerías it is best to go when there are lots of diners. *Tel: 0521 205 101, Mariscal Estigarribia and Las Residentas on the left-hand side of the road entering town across the street from a Puma gas station, Gs. 20,000, Mon-Thu 8am-3pm, Fri-Sat 8am-3pm, 6pm-12am*

Charlot A pleasant little restaurant with nice ambience tucked away from the main road into town. The international menu (pastas, chicken and meats) is somewhat limited but delicious and well priced. Service is very good as well. *Tel: 0521 203 790, 0971 428 273, Eulogio Estigarribia and Dr. Jara, Gs. 10,000-25,000, Tues-Sat 11:30am-2:30pm, 7pm-12pm, Mon 7pm-12pm*

Getting There

To get to the center of Coronel Oviedo from Route 2 (coming from Asunción) one turns North (left) at the crossroad with Route 8 known as the "*cruce*" just past the Parador La Nona and Hotel Bertea on the left. The center of town is about ten blocks away. If you pass the bus terminal on your right you've gone too far.

In addition to the recommended bus lines for Route 2 the Yvytyruzu bus is a good option for travel between Asunción and Coronel Oviedo (this bus often continues to Villarrica). Note there are actually two terminals in Coronel Oviedo. The larger terminal along Route 2 just before the crossroads with Route 8 is serviced by national and international long distance buses heading to and from Ciudad del Este. From here you can catch buses heading south on Route 8 to Yataity, Colonial Independencia, and Villarrica or north to Santaní (officially labeled on maps as "San Estanislao"). There are also several buses which head to the second bus terminal in town on the corner of Argaña and Primero de Marzo. This smaller bus terminal is serviced by local buses from the surrounding rural communities. Local buses headed to the larger terminal and crossroads are usually labeled "*Cruce*."

Route 8

GUAIRÁ & CAAZAPÁ

From Coronel Oviedo, Route 8 extends south through the department of Guairá which offers tourists several interesting attractions. First up is the quaint town of Yataity where the majority of the country's finely woven and embroidered *ao po'i* textiles are made. Nearby is the German colony of Colonia Independencia. This is an excellent place to enjoy the natural beauty of the Ybytyruzu mountain range, from afar or up close and personal, depending on how much outdoor activity you are up for. Villarrica is the capital of the department but still manages to maintain a small town feel. During February and March (depending on the year) the streets are full of music and dancing as the annual *Carnaval Guaireño* (holding its own against larger *Carnavales Encarnacenas*) takes hold of the city. All three locations are easily accessible by car and bus from both Asunción and nearby Coronel Oviedo. The newly paved road connecting Paraguarí to Villarrica makes the sights of Guairá a doable day trip from Asunción, although you should plan to spend at least one night in order to have time to really take in the relaxing environment. Travelers connecting in Coronel Oviedo via bus should note that both Yataity and Colonia Independencia are approximately two kilometers removed from Route 8 so it is best to verify whether the bus goes into town ("*entra al pueblo*") or just lets passengers off at the entrance to town. At the southern end of Route 8 is the department of Caazapá, which, while picturesque, is rarely visited by tourists.

Gua'i

A common nickname for a native of Guairá is "*guaireño*" or "*gua'i*." Villarrica is often referred to jokingly as the "*República Independiente de Villarrica*" and the department itself as the "*República del Guairá*." Guaireños have a reputation amongst Paraguayans for swimming against the current. At any rate they definitely have a distinct pride in their department and capital city which gives the area a particular charm.

YATAITY DEL GUAIRÁ

The idyllic town of Yataity is synonymous with the production of finely embroidered cotton known as "*ao po'i*." In households throughout Yataity women, men and children work to create all manner of elaborately embroidered clothing and linens out of this finely woven cloth. There are various small storefronts in town where one can peruse different *ao po'i* options, all surprisingly affordable, especially when you take into account the lengthy production process.

"*Ao*" (pronounced "ow") means cloth or clothing in Guaraní and "*po'i*" (pronounced "poe-e") means fine or thin. *Ao po'i* developed as a result of the isolationist policies of Paraguay's first post-colonial leader Dr. Gaspar Rodriguez de Francia. Without access to imported cloth Paraguayan women had to make their own fabric starting with raw cotton which was spun into thread, woven into cloth and later decorated with embroidery. Nowadays much *ao po'i* cloth is made by machine at the Textiles Pilar cotton factory in Southern Paraguay but still hand sewn and embroidered. However the Narvaja sisters of Yataity, Ña Digna, Ña Paula and Ña Sara, still maintain this tradition, selling delicately woven items out of their homes and the *Tejedora del Poyvi* stand at the yearly Expoferia del Ao po'i. Originally all of Guairá was dedicated to this but now only Yataity maintains the town-wide tradition.

When visiting Yataity keep in mind that most stores close for siesta time. Plan to arrive early in the morning or afternoon in order to not get caught during downtime. If you end up in Yataity during siesta you could do worse than hang out under the shady trees of the town's main plaza or walk down to the local pond where there are plenty of birds (watch out for loose cows though). There is no lodging within the town of Yataity itself, although Granja Ñemity is located right at the entrance to town. Most visitors choose to stay in nearby Villarrica.

Instituto Paraguayo de Artesanía – Filial Yataity

If you are interested in learning more about the process of making *ao po'i* visit the Yataity office of the Paraguayan Handicrafts Institute. Try your hand at turning raw cotton into thread and test your hand-eye coordination on the working loom (expert cloth makers can make up to two meters per day). It is best to call ahead of time as IPA employees are often out in the community leading classes. *Tel: 0549 200 96, Coronel Bogado almost at Paí Hadra, Mon-Fri, 7am-3pm*

The East

Expoferia del Ao po'i

During this yearly event the area's *ao po'i* artisans gather in the town plaza to sell their wares. The Expoferia usually takes place between the end of November and early December and includes dance and music performances and a fashion show where artisans can show off the latest *ao po'i* fashions, as well as the crowning of Miss Expoferia Ao po'i. Although *ao po'i* is sold in Yataity's stores year round the Expoferia is a good time to visit as it saves you the time of going from store to store.

Taking Cues From Nature

Many *ao po'i* stitches are inspired by Paraguay's natural surroundings. Popular stitches include: *jupirupi'a* (frog eggs), *ju'i retyma* (frog legs), *abejita* (little bees), *panal de abeja* (honeycomb), *ysyry* (stream) and *ysyry'i* (little stream).

Lodging

Granja Ñemity Enjoy the view of Yataity and the surrounding areas from the hotel's fourth floor observation deck and stroll along the grounds which include a small pool and a soccer field and lots of shady trees. There is also a small store and restaurant serving empanadas and other Paraguayan basics. *Tel: 0549 200 950 971, 228 901, 021 512 028, located at the crossroads between Rt 8 and the northernmost entrance to Yataity, approximately one km from Yataity itself and twenty-six kilometers from Coronel Oviedo, Gs. 80,000 per person, Gs, 150,000 for full room and board, Camping Gs. 30,000 per person. AC, pool*

Food

Pukurui Ña Rosa runs this small unassuming (and unsigned) restaurant. It is best to stop by ahead of time and put in a request for milanesas, empanadas or other basic Paraguayan dishes. *Located on the left-hand side just before the paved road turns left at Avenida de las Artesanas, Gs. 5,000-10,000*

Purchasing Ao po'i

Cooperativa Yataity Ao po'i Ltda. The cooperative is the biggest store in Yataity and employs many area women. Prices are a little bit higher than in neighboring stores but it is a good place to get an idea of the wide variety of *ao po'i* products available. The cooperative also has a nice bathroom. *Tel: 0549 200 18, on the corner of the town plaza facing the front of the church (there are no street signs but the Cooperativa itself is well signed), cooperativaaopoiyataity.blogspot.com/, Mon-Sat 8am-12pm, 1:30pm-5pm, Sun 8am-1pm*

Oga Guazu Though the store is small friendly shop owners Marina and Olga have a good variety of tablecloths, men's shirts, adorable little girl dresses and interesting blankets, runners and floor rugs made of *ao po'i* scraps. *Tel: 0549 20082, corner of Avenida de las Artesanas and Francisco Velázquez just where the paved road into town turns, Mon-Sat 7am-8pm*

Guadalupe Artesanía A large selection of men's and women's clothing with many original designs and different items you might not see in other stores. The fit on women's clothing is good. *Tel: 0549 20005, first store across the street from the Cooperativa Yataity, daily 8am-5pm*

Confecciones Dany This small workshop specializes in men's shirts – if they don't have one you like it can be made within the hour. *Tel: 0549 20040, Corner of Buenos Aires and Coronel Bogado, daily 7am-9pm*

Modernizing Ao po'i

Although *ao po'i* is a traditional Paraguayan handicraft in existence since the start of the nation it has only recently come into vogue among the upper classes in Asunción. Three Asunción-based brands are responsible for *ao po'i's* return to the spotlight. Designer Cecilia Fadul has been a pioneer in popularizing the use of *ao po'i* in women's fashions from blouses to wedding dresses. Shopping Británico is largely responsible for popularizing (and export-ing) men's dress shirts made out of *ao po'i* (they look similar to *guayaberas*). More recently trendy clothing line Pombero has come on the scene offering modern, youth-oriented designs including strapless dresses and tunics. Though all three employ artisans from Yataity they do not have storefronts in town (see Shopping, Handicrafts, p143, for store listings).

Getting There

Yataity is located at km 164 of Route 8. There are two entrances to town from Route 8, approximately one kilometer each other. Route 8 can be accessed by either Route 2 or by the road which connects Paraguarí on Route 1 to Villarrica on Route 8.

The Guaireña bus line has several direct buses that run daily to Yataity from Asunción for Gs. 25,000. Yataity (also known as Yataity del Guairá) should not be confused with Yataity del Norte. There are also buses that head to Yataity from the bus terminals in both Villarrica and Coronel Oviedo, however it is best to verify that the bus enters town and does not just drop passengers off at the entrance to town.

COLONIA INDEPENDENCIA

Nestled at the base of the Ybytyruzu mountains the town of Colonia Independencia, known as *"La Tierra del Vino y del Sol"* (the land of wine and sun) was founded by German immigrants after World War II. Unlike the majority of Paraguay's German-influenced towns Colonia Independencia is not populated by Mennonites. Rather than religious freedom, the town's German inhabitants are mostly drawn by a sense of adventure and the chance to stretch their retirement pensions abroad in an already established German community. Though Colonia Independencia also has Paraguayan inhabitants there is a decidedly German feel to the town. Street signs are mostly in German and the stores carry a wide variety of German products. As you enter Colonia Independencia (right after the welcome sign) you will spot your first sign that, despite the setting deep in the countryside, Colonia Independencia is no ordinary rural Paraguayan town. Perched high on the hilltop is the privately owned Castillo Echauri, fashioned to look like a medieval castle, complete with turrets and arrow slits. The town has a small center which is very pleasant to walk around, but for the most part everything in Colonia Independencia is spread out. From here you are within day trip distance of several waterfalls and peaks in the Ybytyruzu moun-tains (see The Cordillera de Ybytyruzu, p232).

Overall the quality of lodging in Colonia Independencia is very high as most establishments cater to foreign vacationers. There are special rates for campers as well as for those on extended stays. Most lodging options specialize in providing full room and board which perhaps explains the lack of restaurants in town itself. Many also have transfer services (for a fee) or pickups from Asunción and can arrange for excursions to surrounding areas and points further afield (even as far as Iguazú Falls). All are located at some distance from the town itself but most are on the main road from which catching a bus into town is simple.

The East

Oktoberfest

Being a town heavily populated by Germans it is logical that Colonia Independencia celebrate Oktoberfest. The festival is celebrated in October (or sometimes the beginning of November) every year at the Club Deportivo Aleman with an all-night beer bathed party. Traditional German foods are served and many people choose to come dressed up in lederhosen. For more information contact the Club Deportivo Aleman. *Tel: 0548 26522, www.clubaleman.com.py*

Parque Municipal de Independencia

Should you decide to venture into town the municipal park is a short walk from the main plaza and church. With a wide creek winding its way through the park this can be a good place to whet your appetite for nature if you can't make it out to the nearby waterfalls. The park is a nice spot for picnic. Right before the entrance to the park is a bakery/ice cream/pizza store (closed on Wednesdays and Thursdays). *From the town's main plaza on Avenida Mariscal Francisco Solano López follow the road running alongside the town church and then turn left before going over the small wood bridge.*

Salto Suizo

Salto Suizo (Spanish for "Swiss Waterfall") is the tallest and most visited of the area's several waterfalls. A relatively small amount of water cascades over the sixty-two-meter high cliff top and is often nothing more than a fine mist by the time it reaches the swimming hole below. Just behind the waterfall is a cave which cuts into the rock face providing cool shade on a hot day. The main trail leads to the bottom of the waterfall but you can also hike through the woods and large patches of bamboo to the top where the view is stunning. For those who wish to stay the night there is a small campsite about a kilometer and a half away. *From the road to Colonia Independencia take a right-hand turn at the roundabout and head into town. This*

The Cordillera de Ybytyruzu

The Cordillera de Ybytyruzu mountain range is a rarity in mostly flat Paraguay. The range is home to peaks and waterfalls that exert their pull on Paraguay's nature lovers. At 842 meters above sea level the Cerro Tres Kandú is the highest peak in all of Paraguay. Other popular peaks are Cerro Akatí, Cerrito and Cerro de la Cruz. At sixty meters Salto Suizo is the tallest and most visited of the area's several waterfalls. From the rotary on the road between Mbocayaty and Colonia Independencia take a right and head to the center of Colonia Independencia. This road will T out into the double avenue Avenida Mariscal Fransisco Solano López. Here take a right and continue about three blocks (the road will turn to cobblestone). Here you will find the signed left-hand turn off down a dirt road leading to Cerro Acati (seventeen kilometers), Salto Paí (five kilometers), Salto San Vincente (seven kilometers), Salto Mbyyui (four kilometers), and Ita Letra (twenty kilometers, although this last one is more easily accessed from Villarrica).

If you'd rather not venture out on your own Asunción based DTP (*www.dtp.com.py*), Paraguay Natural Ecotourism (*www.paraguaynatural.com.py*) and Villarrica based Karumbé Xtreme (p238) offer guided tours of Ybyturuzu's sights including rappelling down the Salto Suizo waterfall. In addition, Colonia Independencia's Municipal Tourism Secretary (*Tel: 0548 265 277 or Marcelo Rejiu, 0981 367 208*) can help coordinate for transportation to the Salto Suizo, by truck as well as by horse (though riders are completely responsible for all safety and handling of horses).

road will end in the town's double avenue Avenida Mariscal Francisco Solano López. Take a left past the town's main plaza and church. The road will soon turn to cobblestone and you'll pass a Petrosur gas station. Just before the Plaza de la Independencia there is a signed right-hand turn for Salto Suizo (along with a sign for the Reiterhof horse ranch). Continue two kilometers and then take a right and continue five kilometers to the Salto Suizo trailhead. The last kilometer must be done on foot.

Salto Cantera

Surrounded by dense vegetation the Salto Cantera (also known as the Chorro Cantera) is about twelve meters high. From here the Itá creek continues to flow over another series of small waterfalls. *The trail is located along the road to Colonia Independencia just opposite the entrance to the Hotel Sport Camping. It is about fifteen minutes by foot though you can also arrange to visit on horseback or with a guide at the Hotel Sport Camping.*

Salto Pa'i

More of a natural waterslide than a waterfall, Salto Pa'i is very popular among families with children. The swimming hole is deep enough to jump into from the surrounding boulders. *From Avenida Mariscal Fransisco Solano López (see Salto Suizo) take a right and follow the road until it becomes cobblestone. Take the signed left-hand turn down a dirt road which leads to Salto Pa'i, about five kilometers away.*

Itá Letra

A curious series of over fifty petro glyphs etched into a cliff face about twenty kilometers from Villarrica. The figures consist of curved zigzags, spirals and crossed lines and strange curvy shapes. The site's name literally means "rock with letter" and much has been made of the inscriptions' mysterious origins. Many believe them to have been made by Viking explorers (though this theory has been officially investigated and discredited). Another theory is that they are evidence of the Tapé Avirú, a series of pre-colonial roads stretching from the Atlantic to the Pacific coast. Be careful as there are many wasps in the area. *Itá Letra is located twenty-two kilometers from Villarrica in the small community of Tororó. As it is on private property it is best to visit with a tour guide (see Karumbé Xtreme, p238).*

Lodging

Hotel Sport Camping One of the first hotels coming into town the Hotel Sport Camping has regular rooms as well as cute circular bungalows. Grounds include two pools and a small stream as well as a mini soccer space. Spacious bungalows are divided into two sections and you can reserve one or both depending on the size of your party. A tour of the nearby Salto Cantera is free for all guests. The owners can arrange for tours of the surrounding areas as well as horseback riding and mountain bike rentals. There is also a restaurant and during the high season the cook prepares delicious wood oven fired pizzas. *Tel: 0981 885 198, on the left-hand side of the road just after the town's welcome sign, www.hotel-sportcamping.de, Bungalows Gs. 130,000-180,000 per couple, Singles: Gs. 110,000, Doubles: 130,000, Camping Gs. 25,000, Wi-Fi, TV, A/C, pools*

Hotel Independencia This large hotel's grounds include two pools and a restaurant with a great view of the Ybytyruzu mountains. The restaurant serves up German specialties (though only on nights and weekends during the low season). Rooms in the main hotel are very spacious. *Tel: 0981 308 588, 0971 302 931, on the left-hand side approximately four kilometers before town, the two story hotel's large patio make it hard to miss, www.hotel-independencia.com, Single: Gs, 140,000, Double: Gs. 160,000, Triple: Gs. 190,000, Wi-Fi, TV, A/C, pools*

The East

Hotel El Indio Removed from the main road and with only three rooms this small hotel has an intimate, peaceful feel that sets it apart from Colonia Independencia's larger establishments. Rooms are very nice and fully screened leading on to a wraparound porch with a nice view of neighboring fields and the hills beyond. The hotel's restaurant serves up good German food, though breakfast is not included in the room rates. *Tel: 0984 355 922 (German and English speakers), 0984 355 993 (Spanish speakers), take the signed left-hand turn after Hotel Independencia down a dirt road approximately 1km and then take a signed right-hand turn for another 500 meters, www.el-indio.de, Single: Gs. 115,000, Double: 140,000, Gs. 25,000 per additional person, Wi-Fi, A/C, mini-fridge, pool*

Hotel Tilinski One of Colonia Independencia's first tourist establishments, Hotel Tilinski is well known for its pretty grounds and delicious food. Rooms are starting to show their age. Due to the distance from town it is best to opt for full room and board. Among the restaurant's highlights is the fluffy ricotta cheesecake. *Tel: 0548 265 240, past town on the right-hand side down a 700-meter gravel road, Gs. 190,000 per person (full board), 130,000 (just breakfast), Gs. 300,000 per couple (full board), 170,000 (just breakfast), camping Gs. 10,000 (pool access is extra), TV, A/C, pool*

Restaurants

El Mangal One of the few establishments in town. Indoor and outdoor dining under the shade of enormous mango trees make for a nice ambience. Menu includes a wide variety of beef, pork, chicken and fish dishes. Crispy French fries with mushroom sauce make for an oddly satisfying snack. *Tel: 0548 265 449, 0981 302 108, Panchito López and Boquerón, daily 11am-10pm, Gs. 15,000-50,000*

Deutsche Bäckerie Michael Bock This specialty bakery has fresh baked goods including whole wheat breads, ricotta bread and all manner of delicious treats. *Tel: 0981 611 289, five kms past town after the right-hand bend in the road just past the Shell station (this is past the entrance to Hotel Tilinkski), Gs. 10,000-25,000, Fri 2pm-5pm*

Super Almacén 50 This well-stocked general goods store has a wide selection of baked goods including fresh breads and cakes. Their chocolate-nut bars are particularly delicious. A surprisingly large liquor and *yerba mate* selection. *Five kms past town a little bit further from Michael Bock next to the Esso station. Mon-Sat 7am-12pm, 2pm-6pm*

Getting There

The turn off to Colonia Independencia is located on Route 8 in the town of Mbocayaty, approximately six kilometers north of Villarrica. Coming from Villarrica the turn off is on the right-hand side, about three blocks before the road curves sharply to the left. With the exception of Hotel Tilinksi all lodging options are before the right-hand entrance to the center of town itself (approximately seventeen kilometers from Mbocayaty). The road into town ends in a small roundabout and double avenue. To the right are access roads for various waterfalls (see Cordillera de Ybytyruzu, p232) and to the left are the town plaza, church, access to the municipal park and access to the Salto Suizo (see Cordillera Ybytyruzu). If you continue down the road to the left it eventually reconnects with the main road, winds past the entrance to Hotel Tilinski and swings right leading to communities deeper in the countryside.

The Ybytyruzu bus line has daily buses from Asunción to Colonia Independencia, Gs. 30,000. Independencia and Sudetia buses can also be caught at the Villarrica terminal (*Tel: 0541 42979*).

VILLARICA

Known as the *"Ciudad Culta"* (cultured city), Villarrica has been home to many of Paraguay's artists, from musicians Felix Perez Cardozo to poets Natalicio Talavera, Manuel Ortiz Guerrero, and award winning authors Agusto Roa Bastos and Helio Vera. Villarrica's cultural streak continues today with the presence of several large universities. The students lend the city a youthful energy which reaches its apex during the *Carnavales Guaireños*, when costumed performers in glitter and feathers parade down the *carnaval* circuit to the energetic samba drum beats and applause from visiting crowds.

Thanks to its various plazas and parks, and nearby rural areas Villarrica is one of Paraguay's most pleasant mid-sized cities. It has the amenities of an urban area – various restaurants and hotels – as well as the charms of more rural areas – neighborhoods laid out along red dirt roads on the outskirts of town and the proximity of natural attractions such as waterfalls.

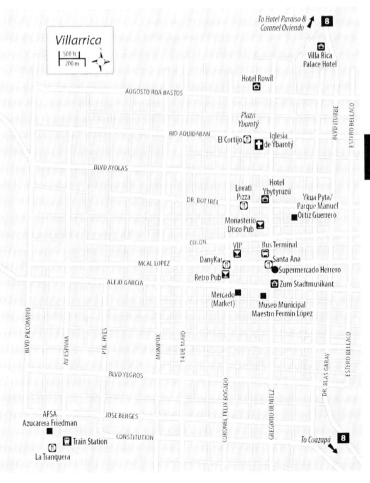

Take a walk or ride a traditional horse drawn *karumbé* around town enjoying the city's many nicely maintained colonial style houses, as well as the old train station (now defunct) and large sugar factory just where the town gets more rural. Stroll through the town plaza to the museum, one of the best in the countryside, and then head to the charming Ykua Pyta park, whose lagoon is home to a friendly family of capybaras. And stick around as night falls to see the modern and young side of Villarrica as the streets and bars fill with university students. From Villarrica the towns of Yataity and Colonia Independencia, as well as the attractions of the Cordillera de Ybyturuzu (see Cordillera Ybyturuzu, p232) are easily accessed, both by car and bus. Its status as capital of the department of Guairá and large student population mean Villarrica has several lodging and eating options for every budget, as well as several bars and nightclubs.

The Wandering City
The city of Villarrica (officially "*Villarrica del Espíritu Santo*") was founded in 1570. Due to constant threats from Brazilian slave traders (see Missions Under Attack, p168) the city was forced to move a total of seven times until it came to its present location in 1690. This nomadic history earned Villarrica the nickname "*la andariega*" (the wanderer), fact which is commemorated by the monument with seven plaques in the city's Plaza Libertad.

Riding a *Karumbé*
Villarrica is one of two towns in Paraguay known for its *karumbé* or horse drawn taxis (the other being Encarnación). *Karumbé's* seat two people comfortably (with a bit of space for backpacks) and taking a ride in a colorful *karumbé* is a fun way to tour the city. Most of the *karumbés* are located in front of the bus station. Some will even approach you offering tours – pick someone charismatic you feel you will be able to communicate well with to make the most of your tour. *Karumbés* run about Gs. 15,000 per hour but you can also agree on a fixed price ahead of time for a tour – make sure it includes the park, old train station and the sugar factory.

Ykua Pyta/Parque Manuel Ortiz Guerrero
One of the highlights of Villarrica is a visit to the Ykua Pyta park. A mere three blocks from the main avenue this park takes up two full blocks. There is a nice walking path that winds around the large artificial lake, home to a family of capybaras ("*carpinchos*" in Spanish). These tame and mild mannered creatures are so used to people that they will waddle right up to you (most likely expecting to be fed). Get close and sit still to hear their strange chattering noises. The park has many benches from which to enjoy the view as well as a municipal pool and tennis courts for those who want to be more active. The park is formally named the "Parque Manuel Ortiz Guerrero" in honor of the *guaireño* poet and musician. Alongside the lake there is a pretty sculpture and fountain inspired by his poem "*Panambí Vera*" (Brilliant Butterfly).

Manuel Ortiz Guerrero
Born in Villarrica on the 16th of July of 1897, poet, musician and playwright Manuel Ortiz Guerrero is one of the city's most celebrated artists. His name may be unfamiliar to most foreigners but stick around long enough and you are sure to hear his influence on Paraguay's cultural scene. Guerrero was friends with well-known Paraguayan musician and composer José Asunción Flores who set many of Guerrero's poems to music. Today the result of their collaboration is several songs which are now part of the canon of Paraguayan folkloric music including "*India*," "*Panambí Verá*," and "*Paraguaype*."

AFSA-Azucarera Friedman
Founded in 1910 Azucarera Friedman is one of Paraguay's oldest sugar factories. As you approach you'll see large trucks piled high with sugar cane from nearby fields (in smaller outfits the sugar cane is transported by ox-cart). Tours of the factory can be requested at the front office. Though they are not always granted it is worthwhile for people interested in agriculture and manufacturing. *Tel: 0541 42305, Corner of General Duarte and Constitución, www.afsa.com.py*

Train Station
Historically Villarrica played an important role as a transportation hub for logging and *yerba mate* industries. The train station was key for transporting goods both east towards Asunción and south west to Encarnación. Sadly, there are few remnants of the trains and tracks, most having been pillaged for sale as scrap metal. Although there is no longer much going on at the old train station the scenery is quite nice and the ride out is a reminder that even in Paraguay's larger towns a people are living a rural lifestyle only a few blocks from the center of town.

Museo Municipal Maestro Fermín López
The Museo Municipal Maestro Fermín López is one of the country's nicest museums outside of Asunción. The museum's exhibits cover all aspects of Villarrica's history, with artifacts from the original indigenous inhabitants including a canoe carved from an enormous tree trunk, to those of the city's founding fathers. As with all Paraguayan museums there are relics from both the Chaco and Triple Alliance War as well. Displays are well-done with lots of explanatory text (unfortunately only in Spanish, but still a rarity amongst most museums). The final room is dedicated to the life of local poet Manuel Ortiz Guerrero (also honored with a sculpture in the Ykua Pyta park). The building dates from 1842 and played a significant role throughout Villarrica's history as the area's main school. It is named after Triple Alliance War hero Maestro Fermín López who trained his students to fight as soldiers in the tragic battles of Piribebuy and Acosta Ñu (see Los Niños Mártires de Acosta Ñu, p225). *Tel: 0541 41521, corner of Natalicio Talavera and Juan Pablo II behind the cathedral. Mon-Fri 7am-5pm (guided tours in Spanish till noon), Sat 8am-12pm*

Iglesia de Ybarotý
Of the two churches in town this is the most interesting due to its unusual red stone façade construction. Worth peaking in if it's open but the view from the outside is the most interesting. *Anasagasti between Aquidaban and Manuel Ortiz Guerrero, one block from the Plaza Ybarotý towards the entrance to town*

Itá Letra
Of the Cordillera Ybytyruzu's attractions this is the closest to Villarrica (see The Cordillera de Ybytyruzu, p232).

Carnaval Guaireño
Villarrica is well known for its traditional *Carnaval Guaireño* held over the course of several weekends each February and March. While not quite as big as Encarnación's *carnaval* it is still a big production and lots of fun drawing revelers from all over the country. Usually the *carnaval* route is set up on General Díaz which passes by the church, main plaza and Gobernación building. The whole city becomes a party but for a good view of the costume clad samba dancers it is worth buying a seat in the stands. Prices vary depending where along the route you want to sit as well as what

The East

day you are buying tickets for. There are some general sections (*gradería*) that are cheaper but seats are on a first come first serve basis. To buy tickets contact the Municipal Office (see Quick Referece, p8, for listings).

Curious to see what the *Carnaval Guaireño* looks like? The website www.gua-i.com.py has several year's worth of *Carnaval Guaireño* photos posted.

Festival de la Raza
This yearly music festival draws musicians from all over the country to Villarrica to show off their talents in the packed indoor Estadio Ykua Pyta (next to the Ykua Pyta park). Generally held the second week of October.

Primera Ciudad Digital
In 2010 Villarrica became the first city in Paraguay to offer free 24 hour Wi-Fi service in public spaces. The move to offer Wi-Fi in plazas and boardwalks has been copied by other cities such as Ciudad del Este and Encarnación. Villarrica's Wi-Fi hotspots are in the Plaza de los Heroes and the Plaza Libertad.

Tours

Karumbé Xtreme Karumbé Xtreme is an association of guides specialized in the department of Guairá. They are your best option for seeing Guairá's natural beauty if you don't have a car or do not want to pay the extra expense to take a tour from Asunción. The association offers guided tours of Villarrica and trips to the waterfalls of Colonia Independencia, Itá Letra, the peaks of the Cordillera Ybytyruzu. They also specialize in extreme sports and many of these trips can include an element of trekking and rappelling. Though some guides may be available on the spot it is best to try to coordinate with them a day in advance (see Guided Tours, p65, for more advice on hiring independent guides). *Tel: 0983 453 821, www.karumbe-xtreme.es.tl, www.activeb.es/karumbe-xtreme*

Lodging

Hotel Ybytyruzu Villarrica's oldest and most established hotel the Hotel Ybytyruzu is located in the middle of the action just blocks from the bus terminal, main plaza and Ykua Pyta park. Rooms are clean and neat though a tad small and the hotel's restaurant has an extensive menu and high quality food. *Tel: 0541 42390, 054140844, 0541 41507, corner of Carlos A. López and Dr. Bottrel, www.hotelybytyruzu.com, Single Gs. 120,000, Double Gs. 200,000, Triple Gs. 260,000. Wi-Fi, TV, A/C*

🏠 **Hotel Restaurant Zum Stadtmusikant** A little off beat (starting with their quirky logo) this centrally located hotel has a homey feel and a lot of personality. Rooms are cute and spacious and open out onto a nice covered corridor. In lieu of a guestbook they allow you to sign on the wall. Staff is very friendly and the German owners can help organize tours of Villarrica and surrounding areas as well as Iguazú Falls and can even arrange for a transfer by private taxi from the Asunción airport. The hotel restaurant has lunchtime buffet of German and Paraguayan food from 11:30-3:00, pastries and sweets from 3:00 on and then serves food a la carte from 8pm on. Often have internationally themed weeks such as "Indian week" or "Italian week" and there is outdoor seating so you can watch the city buzz by. *Tel: 0541 41444, Gregorio Benitez 767 and Mariscal Estigarribia just past the Supermercado Herrero supermarket, www.zum-stadtmusikant.de, Gs. 65,000 per person (does not include breakfast which costs Gs. 15,000), TV, A/C, Wi-Fi, pool. Restaurant Tue-Thu 11am-1am, Fri-Sat 11am-2am, Sun 11am-6pm, Gs. 15,000-30,000*

Hotel Rowil A cheap and basic option at the entrance to town, Hotel Rowil caters mostly to students. Rooms are colorful but kind of haphazard looking. In the same 2-story white and blue building as Rowil Music store. *Tel: 0541 42852, Pai Anagasti and José Asunción Flores, Single Gs. 50,000 with fan, Gs. 60-70,000 with A/C, Double Gs. 60,000 with fan, Gs. 70,000 with A/C*

Villarrica Palace Hotel This surprisingly large hotel is Villarrica's fanciest lodging option, though lacking a little in the cleanliness and personality departments. Rooms are nice and spacious. Its location on the outskirts of towns means it is not the best option for those without private transportation. Adjoining restaurant Adelia has decent meals. *Tel: 0541 43048, 0541 42832, 021 595 541, corner of Route 8 and Río Apa at the entrance to town, www.sosahoteles.com, Single Gs. 135,000, Double Gs. 220,000-275,000, Triple 330,000. Wi-Fi, TV, A/C, pool*

Hotel Paraíso A quiet option on the outskirts of town this small German-run hotel has a lot of character and nice grounds. Rooms are spacious and nicely decorated. The owners offer guided tours as well as car rentals (which, handily, include a cell phone to take along) for those who want to explore on their own. Breakfast does not come included although the restaurant offers a wide variety of options including oatmeal and omelets (a rarity in Paraguay). The extensive menu's lunch and dinner offerings including burgers, salads and German dishes. Great ambience with every possible surface occupied by what must be the largest collection of functioning cuckoo clocks in Paraguay. *Tel: 0541 40262, 0982 797 158, 0981 243 805, Rt 8 km 168 about five kilometers before the entrance to Villarrica if coming from Coronel Oviedo, www.hotel-paraiso.de, Single Gs. 80,000, Double Gs. 120,000, Triple Gs. 160,000, TV, AC, mini-fridge, Wi-Fi, pool. Mon-Thu 12pm-10pm, Fri-Sat 12pm-12am, Sun 12pm-6pm, Gs. 20,000-35,000*

Restaurants

La Tranquera A well established restaurant specializing in meats served on personal table top mini-grills. Take a break from chowing down to get your photo taken with the large sculptures of Paraguayan Indians. Nice ambience and good service. *Tel: 0541 42185, down Avenida España just across the tracks from the old train station, Tue-Sat 7:30pm-12am, Sun 11am-3pm. Gs. 40,000-60,000*

Lovati Pizza Even in Paraguay college students go hand in hand with pizzerias. Lovati Pizza has delicious pizzas cooked *a la piedra* on a pizza stone. The key when ordering is to stick to the thin crust (*masa fina*) and ask for it to be cooked "*crocante*" (otherwise it tends to be undercooked). The menu also includes burgers and fries *Tel: 0541 43682, General Díaz almost at Dr. Botrell, daily 7pm-12pm, Gs. 18,000-35,000*

DanyKar One of Villarrica's most popular fast food options, Danykar's patrons regularly spill out onto the sidewalk across from the Plaza de los Héroes. Villarrica's top spot for people-watching. If they're too full head next door to Pizzería El Maná. *Tel: 0541 41648, Coronel Bogado between Mariscal López and Mariscal Estigarribia across from the Plaza de los Héroes, daily 11am-3pm, 6pm-1am, Gs. 10,000-20,000*

Supermercado Herrero Your basic supermarket buffet options with the added benefit of a cyber café. *Tel: 0541 42 587, corner of Gregorio Benitez and Mariscal Estigarribia, Mon-Sat 6:30am-9pm, Sun 6:30am-12pm, Gs. 5,000-20,000*

El Cortijo An unassuming restaurant with surprisingly good meals. The menu consists of mostly pastas and meat dishes. After your meal take a stroll around the Plaza de los Comuneros and check out the unique looking Iglesia de Ybarotý just down the street. *Tel: 0541 42542, 0981 867 745, corner of Paí Carlos Anasagasti and Aquidaban (underneath the Hotel Asunción), daily 11am-3pm, 6pm-10pm, Gs. 20,000-30,000*

Santa Ana This small restaurant near the bustling Villarrica bus terminal has the town's cheapest good eats. Rotisserie chickens (*pollo al espiedo*) with rice are a favorite and there are other Paraguayan diner food classics as well. *G. Benitez between the bus terminal and Supermercado Herrero, 8am-5pm, Gs. 7,000-12,000*

Mercado Villarrica On Friday mornings local farmers set up stands with their produce in front of the Plaza Libertad. Stop by to have some freshly made *mbeju* and fresh brewed *cocido*. *General Diaz between Juan Pablo II and Alejo García, Fri 5am-12pm*

The East

Bars & Clubs

VIP (Villarrica International Pub) This swanky bar's mint green exterior gives way to all wood interiors filled with the sounds of karaoke and live music. Frequented by both students and older folks alike, Villarrica International Pub has the comfortable feel of an American bar. Sangría pitchers are good if you need a break from Brahma or Pilsen. *Tel: 0541 44029, 513 General Diaz almost at Ruiz Diaz De Melgarejo, on Facebook as VIP Pub Karaoke, Wed-Sat 7pm-6am, Gs. 10,000-30,000*

Retro Pub Another American-style bar, this one with an emphasis on classic rock (though you may be unfamiliar with some of the classic hits played here). Frequent live music. *Mariscal Estigarribia and Coronel Bogado by the Plaza de los Héroes, Tue-Sun 8pm-12am, Gs. 10,000-30,000*

Monasterio Disco Pub A fun place to dance the night away to the latest *reggaeton* hits. As with Asunción's night clubs the action doesn't start till 1am and dress codes are enforced for men (aka: no flip flops or shorts). *Tel: 0541 43797, Natalicio Talavera and Curuapty, Thu-Sat 11pm-6am, cover ranges from Gs. 10,000-30,000 depending on the night's theme and whether there is an open bar*

Getting There

Villarrica can be accessed by both Route 1 and Route 2. Via Route 2 you turn south onto Route 8 at Coronel Oviedo and continue approximately forty kilometers. Via Route 1 you turn northeast at the town of Paraguarí and take a road that leads past the town of Sapucai along the old train route which meets Route 8 at Villarrica. The latter is a much faster and more pleasant option since the road from Paraguarí to Villarrica is almost devoid of any traffic whereas Route 2 is heavily transited.

Both the Guaireña (*Tel: 0541 42678*) and Ybytyruzu (*Tel: 0541 41221*) bus lines have several daily buses that go to Villarrica from Asunción by way of Coronel Oviedo for Gs. 28,000. Villarrica's bus terminal (*Tel: 0541 42979*) is located smack in the middle of the city's market which can make for a chaotic but colorful experience as vendors hawk all manner of goods to travelers and taxis, moto-taxis, and karumbés all vie for what street space is not taken up by market stalls. Keep in mind that buses leaving Villarrica for surrounding areas at night tend to be very crowded with commuting students.

Departamento Caazapá

CAAZAPÁ

Caazapá was originally a Franciscan mission town, founded by the famed Franciscan Fray Luis de Bolaños in 1607. The name is short for "*Caaguy jehasapa*" which means "past the forest." The town is home to the Ykua Bolaños spring, famed for never running dry even during times of drought. Deep in the Paraguayan countryside, Caazapá is rarely visited by tourists. However, should you find yourself in this remote and rural area of Paraguay take the time to soak in the relaxed attitude of a town so *tranquilo* that many restaurants won't even bother to charge you for *mandioca*. Stroll down the town's surprisingly nice palm tree lined main avenue, peak into the church to admire the original altar and then head to the Ykua Bolaños to soak in a little local history.

The Traveling Barber

One of Caazapá's most inventive entrepreneurs, *El Pingüino* is a traveling barber who rides his bicycle through the city, lawn chair and barber tools in tow. Flag him down if you need a haircut and he will set up shop and get to work.

Iglesia de San Pablo & Capilla de San Roque

This bright white church is modern on the outside but houses some very nice examples of wood carvings from the colonial era on the inside. In front of the church just behind the museum are remnants of the mission's indigenous dwellings, known as Acera Pucú. If you are interested in seeing more relics from the original mission be sure to head down three blocks Mariscal Estigarribia (towards the entrance to town) and take a left for four blocks along Coronel Bogado to visit the town's secondary church, the Capilla de San Roque. Though in some disrepair the small chapel has much original woodwork from the Franciscan mission.

Museo Fray Juan Bernardo

A small but nicely organized museum with religious objects from the colonial era. *Tel: 0981 335 006, General Genes between Mariscal Estigarribia and Presidente Hayes across from the town church. Hours are ostensibly 7am-noon but you are likely to have to ask someone at the Municipal Office to open the museum for you (two blocks away on Teniente Rojas between Dr. Paiva and Luis. A de Herrera)*

Ykua Bolaños

A very pleasant park and *poli-deportivo* (sports complex) this is home to the Ykua Bolaños spring as well as a number of sports facilities. The spring itself is surrounded by stones and marked with a large white relief sculpture depicting the moment Fray Luis de Bolaños struck his staff against the rocks. Provided the sun is not strong, Ykua Bolaños is a pleasant walk from the center of town. *From the main plaza continue one block down Mariscal Estigarribia and take a left on to Fray Luis de Bolaños. This road continues a bit past town to the park.*

The Legend of Ykuá Bolaños

According to legend when Fray Luis de Bolaños arrived in Caazapá to establish a new mission he was met with resistance from local Guaraní indigenous leaders. Having suffered through a seven year drought they were understandably hostile and doubting, demanding proof of the existence of Bolaños' God. The father tapped his staff against the stones and from that spot a spring burst forth and has not stopped flowing to this day. As with many of Paraguay's springs, rumor has it that the waters are enchanted; once you bathe in or drink from the spring you are destined to fall in love with someone from Caazapá. The irony of the situation is that, while the spring never runs dry, the town of Caazapá itself has regular water shortages due to a low water table and lack of wells.

Festival del Ykua Bolaños

Every year Caazapá's Ykua Bolaños park is filled to capacity with revelers who come to enjoy the musical performances of the Festival Ykua Bolaños. Local acts get going around dusk on the 25th of January and the festival culminates the next morning with performances from well-known national (and sometimes international) acts. In the days preceding the festival there are a number of activities in town including artesanía fairs and horse shows. For more information contact the Municipal Office (see Quick Reference, p8, for listings).

The East

Getting There

From Villarrica continue about sixty kilometers south on Route 8. Caazapá is the last town on Route 8 before it switches from asphalt to dirt. This dirt road continues south, eventually connecting with Route 1 in Coronel Bogado – however the going is slow and road conditions can be questionable past Caazapá.

From Asunción the La Yuteña (*Tel: 0542 232258, 021 558 774*) bus line has several buses per day, Gs. 30,000. However if you are headed to Caazapá it is worthwhile to stop by Villarrica first. La Yuteña stops in Villarrica but La Guaireña (*Tel: 0541 42678*) is a much more comfortable ride. From Villarrica the Tebicuary (*Tel: 021 555 991*) bus line makes daily trips to Caazapá.

Lodging

Hotel Las Palmas The nicest hotel in Caazapá, just at the entrance to town with a pretty exterior. Rooms are basic and minimally decorated, opening out in to the interior garden. There is a small restaurant adjoining as well. *Tel: 0542 232 264/5, www.laspalmashotelpy.com, Single Gs. 60,000, double Gs. 120,000, TV, A/C, pool, computers with internet*

Hotel Junior A small hotel with decent rooms. Interestingly the majority of the hotel's recent renovations were funded by a uranium mining company that was operating in the area but has since gone out of business. *Tel: 0542 232 060, Corner of Presidente Hayes and Dr. Paiva, www.hoteljuniorpy.com, Single Gs. 60,000, double Gs. 80,000, sporadic Wi-Fi, TV, A/C*

Estancia Loma Linda Estancia Loma Linda is a good place to kick back, relax and enjoy Caazapá's countryside. The natural setting is ideal for horseback riding, bicycling, fishing, partridge hunting, accompanying ranch hands on rural activities, and taking a break from the heat in the shade of the colonial style corridors or the refreshing pool. Meals include homemade jams, cheeses, baked goods and produce from the ranch itself. *Tel: 021 683 003, 0981 402 713, continue southwest on Route 8 past Caazapá to the town of Maciel and then continue approximately seventeen kilometers and you will see the entrance on the right-hand side), www.estancialomalinda.com, advanced reservations are required and can be made through APATUR at www.turismorural.org.py or 021 210 550 x126/127 Mon-Fri 8am-5pm, Gs. 300,000 per person includes full room and board, A/C, pool*

Food

Casa Rica This bar's *chipa* is the area's best – buttery and cheesy. *Dulce de leche* filled *alfajores* make for a good dessert. *Tel: 0542 232 480, 0981 321 015, Mariscal Estigarribia between Dr. Paiva and General Genes, Daily 9am-6pm, Gs. 5,000-15,000*

La Florida *Empanada*s are La Florida's specialty and there are even vegetarian *choclo* (corn) *empanadas* – a rarity this far from Asunción. Cold drinks, sandwiches and packaged snacks are also on sale. *Tel: 0542, 232 209, corner of Mariscal Estigarribia and Silvio Chamorro, Mon-Fri 8am-10pm, Sun 5pm-10pm, Gs. 5,000-25,000*

CAAGUAZÚ

"*Caaguazú*" stands for "large forest" and it is due to these once-vast natural resources that the city of Caaguazú is known as the "*Capital de la Madera*" (wood capital). The stretch of Route 7 that runs through is crammed with all manner of wooden furniture for sale – from children's playhouses to bedroom sets. Similar to Coronel Oviedo, Caaguazú is a commercial hub for the department (also named Caaguazú). Although the city's main drag is a jumble of commercial signs and billboards, the atmosphere is pleasant and *tranquilo* just blocks away as paved streets give way to cobblestone roads. There is not much for tourists here, but, should you be in the area, the small Ykua la Patria park is worth visiting as are the town church and plaza with their large murals. There are lodging options along Route 7 and in town itself. The latter are preferable as they are less noisy and closer to eating options.

Ykua La Patria

During the mid 1800's Caaguazú's first inhabitants settled at the edges of the Ykua la Patria spring. Today the spring winds through a small terraced park with a playground and mini amphitheater. *Corner of Capitan Troche and Silvio Petirossi*

Church of Inmaculada Concepción

Built in the 1960's Caaguazú's main church is surprisingly striking thanks to a recent renovation that included the addition of three large murals to the façade. The central mural is a copy of the painting *"Virgen de la Inmaculada Concepción"* by Spanish Baroque painter Bartolomé Murillo. To the left is a mural depicting St. Francis of Asis and to the right one showing a shining cross. The plaza across the street has a large mural by the same artist, Argentine Jorge Aguirre, depicting the history of Caaguazú. *General Garay and Mariscal López*

Lodging

Cesar Palace Hotel Centrally located and down the street from a large shaded plaza, the Cesar Palace is definitely the nicest hotel in town. It is run by the same company that owns Hotel Tajy Internacional on Route 7 but is a quieter option. *Tel: 0522 43096, Avenida Manuel Godoy and Roberto L. Petit, across the street from the large Stock Supermarket, www.sosahoteles.com, Single: Gs. 80,000, double Gs. 100,000, triple Gs. 150,000, TV, A/C*

Hotel Tajy Center A small and unassuming hotel, Tajy Center is a clean option with a friendly staff. Breakfast is decent. Just around the corner from the town's church and adjoining plaza and a nice walk from Ykua la Patria. *Tel: 0522 41801, Avenida. General. Bernardino Caballero and Yegros, Single Gs. 77,000, Double Gs. 100,000, triple Gs. 130,000, TV, A/C*

Hotel Tajy Internacional Similar to Cesar Palace Hotel but with the benefit of an outdoor area in the back with a quincho and a pool. *Tel. 0522 40118, Rt 7 km 177 on the left-hand side if coming from Asunción, before the (right-hand) road to the center of town, www.sosahoteles.com, Gs. Single 90,000, Double Gs. 125,000, TV, A/C, pool*

Food

Bamboo A nice juice and *empanada* joint just opposite the plaza on Caaguazú's main drag. Basic *empanada* offerings are expanded to include sweet options – *dulce de leche*, *maní con leche* (peanuts and milk) and *dulce de batata* (sweet potato) on weekends and Friday nights. Interior courtyard has nice wooden furniture, although the street traffic can get a little noisy. *General Bernardino Caballero between Juan O'Leary and Roberto L Petite across from the plaza, daily 7am-12am, Gs. 1,500-3000*

Rústico's Fare is about the same as Bamboo's, minus the sweet *empanadas*. There are burgers and lomitos as well. Outdoor area is nice and quieter. *Tel. 0982 942 927, San Lorenzo almost at Godoy, daily 7am-12am, Gs. 1,500-3000*

Supermercado Stock The per kilo buffet is a dependably cheap option. *Tel: 0522 41470, Avenida Manuel Godoy and Roberto L. Petit, Mon-Sat 6:30AM-9pm, Sun 6:30am-8:30pm, Gs. 10,000-20,000*

CAMPO NUEVE / J. EULOGIO ESTIGARRIBIA

This is a curious corner of Paraguay. Campo Nueve (literally "Field Nine") is made up of a number of Mennonite settlements from a variety of countries including Germany, Canada, and the United States. The town is somewhat informally segregated, with the Mennonites living on the south side of Route 7 and Paraguayans on the north side. This may seem weird but people seem to take it in stride. There is a marked difference between the two sides. The Paraguayan side is similar to other midsized communities abutting the main road. A jumble of small houses extends away from the asphalt quickly giving way to dirt roads and a more rural setting. On the Mennonite side nice cobblestone streets lead to communities removed from the main road. Houses have a distinct foreign feel with modern construction, sprawling front lawns and painted picket fences.

Agro-business is the name of the game here. Campo Nueve is home to the Lactolanda dairy factory, at the moment the largest in Paraguay. Past this factory the landscape is dotted with many grain silos and in town there are several banks and farm machinery distributors. Even in this fertile area of Paraguay farming is risky business. In order to increase their income many of the area's male Mennonites leave Paraguay and their families for long stretches during winter in order to pick up seasonal farming jobs in the northern hemisphere.

Changing Names along Ruta 7

Many communities between Caaguazú and Ciudad del Este have two names: the official name and the name more commonly used by the general public. J. Eulogio Estigarribia is better known as Campo Nueve and Juan Manuel Frutos as Pastoreo. During the Stroessner era these settlements were given new names honoring members of the Colorado party. Though these official names still appear on documents such as maps, you will find that many people have reverted back to using the town's original names. If you plan on spending much time in this area it is best to know both names, just in case. In addition to the aforementioned towns Juan Emilio O'Leary is also known as Paraje Cheiro Kue and Juan León Mallorquín as Ka'arendy.

Lodging

Hotel Alff Though a bit small, this hotel's rooms are well appointed. All are on a second story opening out to a small outdoor corridor. The hotel's nearby restaurant (two buildings away) serves up grilled meats *rodizio* style (all you can eat) but also has a la carte options including pizzas. Plus it is likely the only restaurant in Paraguay whose exterior has a large painting of 80's TV puppet alien Alf. *Tel: 0528 222 336, 0528 222 427, Rt 7 km 213.5 on the left-hand side of the road in the center of town, Single Gs. 80,000, double Gs. 140,000, TV, AC. Restaurant daily 6am-11:30pm, Gs. 20,000-40,000*

Hotel Germania This hotel's rooms are larger and brighter than Hotel Alff's and there is also a small pool. No restaurant but it just across the road from Churrasquería Alff. *Tel: 0528 222 800, 0973 556 306, Rt 7 km 213.5 on the right-hand side of the road if coming from Asunción, www.hotellagermania.com, Single Gs. 75,000-95,000, Double Gs. 110,000-140,000, computers with internet, TV, A/C, pool*

Restaurants

Sul de América A large, high ceilinged restaurant known for its wide selection of grilled meats. The large buffet includes a pasta bar on Sundays. The *pizza salamín* is excellent, topped with homemade salami. This is also available for sale along with sausages, breads, cakes and sandwiches. Another excellent product is honey produced by the Eirete Ñuaîi cooperative located down the road in Juan Manuel Frutos/Pastoreo. Harvested under strict quality controls the honey is excellent and purchasing a bottle is a great way to support local beekeepers. *Tel: 0524 225 203, 0971 415 671, km 200 of Rt 7, thirteen kilometers before Campo Nueve at the entrance to Pastoreo/JM Frutos, Mon-Sun 6am-11:30pm, Gs. 15,000-35,000*

Hildebrand Hildebrand's main selling point is that their buffet includes fish (although not on Thursday night). The caldo de pescado (fish soup) is quite tasty and the *mandioca* fish sticks are certainly an innovative use of *mandioca* you're unlikely to see elsewhere in Paraguay. They also have the nicest roadside bathroom along Rt 2/7 so it's worth a pit stop. *Tel: 0528 222 232, km 209 Route 7, Mon-Sat 9am-2pm, 6pm-11pm, Gs. 30,000-40,000*

Lactolanda Factory The Lactolanda Factory is a popular stop with travelers along Route 7 who stop in to cool off with Paraguay's best soft serve ice cream. Run by the La Holanda Cooperative (named for both the country and the type of dairy cow they use – Holland), this is the largest dairy factory in Paraguay. Over 300,000 liters of milk is produced per day and the factory is capable of producing up to twenty-five tons of powdered milk daily. Other dairy products include cheese and yogurt. These are all sold in the factory's storefront but the star is the soft-serve. Flavors include chocolate, strawberry, *dulce de leche* and peach. Servings are generous and inexpensive – if you can resist getting a large tub then go for the waffle cone. Fortunately the soft serve is also available at the Super Campo 9 supermarket in town, although flavor selection is more limited (this is also a good place to stock up on other Mennonite specialties: oatmeal, peanut butter and sauerkraut). *Tel: 0522 42860, approximately one kilometer past the eastern edge of town on the left-hand side if coming from Asunción, Mon-Sat 6:30am-12pm, 2pm-5:30pm, Gs. 5,000-15,000*

Frankonia Another good place to stretch your legs and grab a bite to eat. This cute German-run café serves up good sandwiches ham and pork sandwiches and tasty desserts. The nice bathroom is another plus. *Tel: 0674 20065, km. 246 Ruta 7, www.frankonia.com.py, Tue-Fri 7:30am-7pm, Sat 7:30am-4:30pm, Gs. 10,000-15,000*

Getting There
Campo Nueve is located at km 213 of Route 7. Approximately ten kilometers before town (at the turn off to Juan Manuel Frutos/Pastoreo) there is a toll booth that charges Gs. 9,000 (charged in both directions, unlike most tolls in Paraguay). Discounted prepaid toll cards are available for those who will make this trip often.

All buses going to Ciudad del Este will stop in Campo Nueve. The fastest is Expreso Guaraní, Gs. 45,000.

Tajy Stroessner
Kilometer 258 of Route 7 is marked by an enormous *lapacho* tree. It is in this spot that General Alfredo Stroessner officially inaugurated this stretch of highway, event which was commemorated by a small cement mural entitled "Tajy Stroessner." Today you can see the spot in the upper corner where the ex-dictator's name has been chiseled out of the mural. A look at the enormous tree gives you a sense of the magnitude of the old growth forests that once covered this region.

Ciudad del Este

Ciudad del Este is Paraguay's largest city, located on at the edges of the Paraná River which forms a triple border with Brazil (home to sister city Foz do Iguaçu) and Argentina (home to the smaller Puerto Iguazú). This is a city of extremes, from the bustling commercial sector to the large scale wonders of the Itaipú Hydroelectric Dam and the nearby Iguazú Falls. Many tourists find Ciudad del Este overwhelming and are scared off by the city's shady reputation. However those who delve deeper will find Ciudad del Este has its own particular charms. The city boasts an active nightlife which draws partygoers from neighboring Foz de Iguaçu. As Paraguay's most ethnically diverse city there are many restaurants serving food not found elsewhere in the country such as authentic Middle Eastern cuisine. And while all pale in comparison to Iguazú Falls, the nearby Salto Monday and Monumento

Moisés Bertoni are good ways to enjoy Ciudad del Este's natural side. If Ciudad del Este (often abbreviated to CDE) is your first entry into Paraguay rest assured that chaos surrounding the Friendship Bridge is the antithesis of the laid back *tranquilo* atmosphere in the rest of the country.

Ciudad Puerto Presidente Stroessner was officially founded in 1957 as part of the Marcha al Este (see The Marcha al Este, p227) road construction project intended to create a route for Paraguayan goods to reach the Atlantic by way of Brazil. Shortly thereafter the Puente de Amistad (Friendship Bridge) was built stretching over the Paraná River and linking the new city to Foz do Iguaçu. But it was the construction of the Itaipú Hydroelectric power plant (then the largest in the world) that really prompted the rapid expansion of the city. Construction began in 1975 and continued for almost twenty years during which time the population of Ciudad Puerto Presidente Stroessner ballooned. In

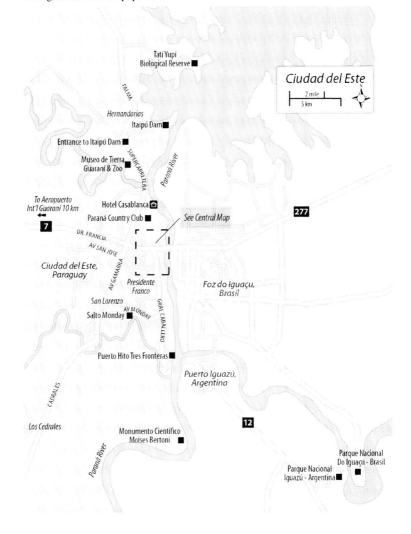

1989 just days after a coup ousted General Stroessner from power the city was aptly renamed Ciudad del Este, meaning City of the East. Today, in combination with the Itaipú Hydroelectric power plant Ciudad del Este is known for its high level of commerce. Forbes Magazine declared it the third largest commercial city in the world after Miami and Hong Kong in 1996. Though the action has died down since then Ciudad del Este still pulsates with commerce, both legal and otherwise.

A number of factors combine to make Ciudad del Este the commercial hub that it is. This tax-free zone is a major draw for foreign shoppers who take advantage of the low prices, favorable exchange rates, and astonishing variety of products available. Between the street stalls selling handicrafts and cheap designer knockoffs to the fancy shopping *galerías* selling electronics and high end goods there is something for every taste and every budget in Ciudad del Este. The Brazilian government allows its citizens to bring up to US $ 300 worth of merchandise into Brazil without having to pay an import tax. Many people make big business from this exemption. Every day thousands of Brazilians journey over the Friendship Bridge by car, motorcycle and foot to buy goods in Ciudad del Este for re-sale across the border in Foz de Iguaçu. These professional shoppers have earned the nickname "*sacoleiros*" derived from "*saco*," the Portuguese word for bag. Indeed the commercial sector, which starts literally inches

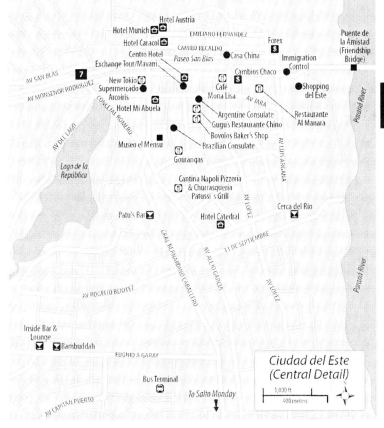

Ciudad del Este
(Central Detail)

from the border, is jammed with people carrying bags and boxes stuffed to the brim with electronics, designers knock offs and all manner of other goods. However, the value of these goods is rarely less than US$300; Ciudad del Este's vendors are more than happy to provide *sacoleiros* (as well as tourists) with false receipts to present customs officials. After sundown larger scale smugglers head for makeshift drop off points up and down the Paraná's rarely patrolled riverbanks, unloading boxes from rickety boats and picking up parcels thrown off the bridge. While Ciudad del Este is notorious for drugs and weapons trafficking the majority of the goods smuggled into Paraguay are foodstuffs such as onions, tomatoes, chicken and beer.

Trash in CDE's Commercial Area

In order to pass over the border more efficiently *sacoleiros* generally dispose of as much product packaging as possible before packing up their purchases. Sadly all these materials end up littered all over the streets of Ciudad del Este. In fact, locals can tell if the day's sales have been good based on the amount of trash strewn around at night.

SAFETY

Though Ciudad del Este is infamous for all manner of trafficking these unsavory aspects of the city are unlikely to affect your visit, unless you go looking for trouble. Vendors in the commercial sector have a vested interest in keeping crime against tourists and shoppers to a minimum. Still, you should keep your guard up, as you would in any crowded marketplace. Do not wear flashy clothing or jewelry and keep valuables such as cameras and cell phones well hidden. Using common sense should keep you from being the victim of petty crime. Because of the cramped conditions the commercial sector can pose certain physical safety concerns. Be sure to duck out of the flow of traffic to look at maps or consider purchases. *Sacoleiros* are moving fast, often with large quantities of merchandise and limited visibility. Avoid carrying large bags which will hinder your flow through the narrow maze of people.

The Softer Side of Ciudad del Este

Ciudad del Este is known for its commercial sector, packed to the brim with vendors and shoppers alike. Only a few blocks away though the atmosphere quiets down, and stall-lined streets give way to green plazas and pretty houses. Many of the city's neighborhoods were originally built for Itaipú employees. With larger properties and nicer houses the Area Uno (all Itaipú neighborhoods are numbered "*Areas*") was reserved for higher ups in Itaipú, although current owners no longer have to be affiliated with the hydroelectric plant. Just opposite the man-made Lago de la República from the center of town the Barrio Boquerón neighborhood has become the focal point of the city's nightlife with several upscale bars, restaurants, and nightclubs.

Some of the area's wealthiest families live fourteen kilometers away in the exclusive Paraná Country Club. Taking a stroll through this gated community you could easily imagine yourself in an upscale neighborhood of Southern California. Large mansions abound (and are not surrounded by walls as in most of the country's wealthy areas) and there are several sports fields. From here the view of the Paraná River and the lush vegetation growing on its shores is unparalleled. Rather than walk the club's teens ride around in golf carts or ATVs. At the entrance to the country club are a supermarket, school, restaurants and a hospital, ensuring that many residents need not venture into Ciudad del Este's city center at all.

TOURISM INFORMATION

There are two tourism information offices, one at the border and another downtown. The border office (located next to the Immigration office) has plenty of maps and pamphlets but the staff can be hit or miss. The downtown office, named Turista Roga is new and modern and includes a cyber café. *Tel: 061 511 626, 061 508810, 061 508 811, Border office: Puente de la Amistad in the median across from Shopping del Este, Turista Roga: Avenida Adrián Jara and Mariscal Estigarribia in front of the Parque Verde plaza. Mon-Sun 7am-7pm*

Brazilian Consulate Americans who wish to visit the Brazilian side of Iguazú Falls or continue travel in Brazil will need to obtain a visa from the consulate if they don't already have one. Keep in mind there is a processing time of one to two days though it is possible to do it in one if you show up early with all the necessary paperwork. *Tel: 061 500 984/6, Corner of Calle Pampliega and Pai Perez #205, www.consbrascde.org.py, Mon-Fri 8am-12pm, 2pm-4pm*

Argentine Consulate *Tel: 061 500 945, 061 500 960, 061 500 638, seventh floor of the Edificio China building on Boquerón and Adrián Jara, www.embajada-argentina.org.py/V2/consulados/consulado-gral-en-cde, Mon-Fri 8am-1pm*

Car Rental

Localiza *Tel: 021 683 895, Aeropuerto Internacional Guaraní, Mon-Sat 9am-1pm, 2pm-4pm*

Avis Rent a Car *Tel: 061 504 770, Avenida San Blás 1294, www.avis.com.py. There is also an office in the airport (Tel: 0983 602 825) but they only deal with advanced reservations, Mon-Sat 8am-6pm*

CHANGING MONEY

Many larger businesses are willing to accept dollars, euros, and Brazilian reals and Argentine pesos without any problem. However smaller purchases made on the street should be made in Guaranies. If headed to Iguazú Falls change money beforehand as park entrance fees cannot be paid in Guaranies.

Cambios Chaco *Tel: 061 514 221, 336 Monseñor Rodriguez almost at Regimiento. Piribebuy, Tel: 061 509 500, 860 Adrian Jara almost at Curupayty, www.cambioschaco.com.py, Mon-Fri 6:15am-3:30pm, Sat 6:15am-1pm*

Maxi Cambios *Tel: 061 509511/3, Corner of Avenida Adrian Jara and Curupayty, www.maxicambios.com.py*

Forex *Tel: 061 501 075, Shopping King Fong, office number 115, Avenida San Blas almost Regimiento Sauce, www.forexparaguay.com.py*

TRAVEL AGENCIES

Most travel agencies offer three basic packages: The Itaipú Hydroelectric Dam combined with the Itaipú zoo and museum, Salto Monday combined with the Monumento Moisés Bertoni, and of course Iguazú Falls. Some also offer Ciudad del Este city tours but the "highlights" are rather mundane. It is unnecessary to hire a tour guide for the Itaipú reserve – if you do not want to ride the bus hiring a taxi for the day is sufficient although a guide can take the legwork out of requesting special permissions for the Itaipú engineer's tour or to visit the Tati Yupi reserve. Guided tours are recommended for Moisés Bertoni because of the need for special vehicles. If you plan to stay in Ciudad del Este but want to visit both the Brazilian and Argentine side of the falls in one day a guide can be useful for border

> Several scenes from the movie *"Miami Vice"* were shot in Ciudad del Este in 2006.

The East

crossings although hiring a private taxi may be cheaper and serve the same purpose. In addition to the agencies listed below all Asunción based travel agencies have Ciudad del Este/ Iguazú Falls packages available. Agencies are accustomed to working with citizens of Mercosur countries who do not need entry and exit stamps. Be sure to specify you will need to go through immigration controls at all borders in order to avoid future problems with passport controls.

Exchange Tour *Tel: 061 500 766, 061 50067, Edificio Saba, Avenida Nanawa 90, www.exchangetour.com.py*

Mavani *Tel: 061 514 386, Edificio Saba, Avenida Nanawa 90, www.mavani.com.py*

GETTING THERE

Ciudad del Este is about a five hour drive from Asunción along Route 2 which turns into Route 7 at Coronel Oviedo. Navigating the crowded commercial sector of Ciudad del Este in a car is only for extremely patient and careful drivers. It is best to park in a guarded parking lot or hotel and explore this area on foot.

By Bus

There are several companies with buses between Asunción and Ciudad del Este. As with all long distance bus travel in Paraguay double floor (*doble piso*) buses are a nicer option. The best company is Nuestra Señora de la Asunción (*www.nsa.com.py*) with tickets costing between Gs. 50,000 and Gs.70,000. There are also several buses that run between Ciudad del Este and Encarnación along Route 6 with prices between Gs. 45,000 and 60,000.

By Air

Ciudad del Este's Aeropuerto Internacional Guarani is located approximately thirteen kilometers away in Minga Guazú on Route 7. TAM (the Brazilian airline, not the Paraguayan military one) has flights to Asunción and Sao Paolo, Brazil, on a regular basis. The flight takes less than an hour. Taxis to the center of town run around Gs. 120,000. *Tel: 0644 20884, 0644 20842*

GETTING AROUND

Downtown Ciudad del Este is very easy to get around on foot. In fact, in the commercial center, traveling by car is quite difficult and by motorcycle can be dangerous. During the day walking around is safe as long as you use common sense. Though they are relatively expensive (minimum fare is Gs. 20,000) taxis are your best bet after sundown. Points of interest outside the city such as the Itaipú Hydroelectric dam, Salto Monday waterfalls and Iguazú Falls are reachable by bus and taxi.

When navigating in Ciudad del Este there are a few key reference points to be aware of.

The Friendship Bridge (Puente de Amistad): This marks the border with Brazil and the end of Route 7.

Rotonda Oasis roundabout: This roundabout at the intersection of Route 7 and Avenida Pioneros del Este marks the end of the commercial sector. This is a major bus stop for local buses entering the city along Route 7 and buses coming from the bus terminal along Avenida Pioneros del Este.

Kilómetro Siete: The intersection of Route 7 and the "*Supercarretera*" highway which leads north past the city of Hernandarias and the Itaipú Hydroelectric power plant all the way to the city of Saltos de Guairá. All long distance buses turn off Route 7 here to head to Ciudad del Este's bus terminal.

Getting to the border by bus can be frustrating as traffic is often at a standstill in the commercial sector. Many find it is faster to walk from Rotonda Oasis down Avenida San Blas to the foot of the bridge than to go by bus. If you are arriving to Ciudad del Este by bus but wish to walk to the border you will need to get off your bus at Kilómetro Siete just as it turns right towards the terminal. From here you can take any bus continuing on Route 7 towards downtown. Ask to be let off at Rotonda Oasis (there is a small bus terminal and an Esso Shop on the right-hand corner) and continue on foot from here. You may find it is faster to walk on the street than between the stalls but be on the lookout for motorcyclists and men with push carts. Once past immigration you can climb aboard buses headed to Puerto Iguazú or Foz do Iguaçu (see Iguazú Falls, p261).

Bus Terminal

From Ciudad del Este's bus terminal the Linea 4 bus heads into town and towards the commercial district. The bus can be caught on the corner of Agustín Barboza and Antonio Garcete diagonally opposite the entrance to the bus station. The bus will run the length of General Bernardino Caballero (which turns into Avenida Pioneros del Este) until it intersects with Route 7 at Rotonda Oasis. *Tel: 061 510 424, corner of Agustín Barboza and Antonio Garcete, Open 24 hours*

ACTIVITIES

The *Zona Franca* Commercial Sector

The commercial heart of the city begins just inches from the border at the base of the Friendship Bridge (*Puente de la Amistad*) and continues uphill along the parallel streets Avenida San Blas and Avenida Monseñor Rodriguez until they intersect with Pioneros del Este. Action is at its heaviest closest to the bridge. There are two main shopping options to choose from: street side stalls and multi-story shopping malls known as *galerías*. Goods sold on the street tend to be cheaper in both quality and price and vendors are open to bargaining. *Galerías* are by far a more comfortable, if less adventurous, option. Some are labyrinthine buildings with many small store-fronts selling electronics and other goods while others are luxury affairs with specialty goods, food courts and central A/C.

Paseo San Blas

Though the majority of streets in the commercial sector are lined with stalls Paseo San Blas offers the most pleasant street shopping. The pedestrian walkway has the air of a middle-eastern bazaar with innumerable stalls selling traditional Paraguayan handicrafts as well as cheap clothes from China and Brazil. There are several large cement sculpted murals depicting Guaraní culture on Paseo San Blas. Those with a knack for bargaining will enjoy shopping here but linger too long you'll be swarmed with vendors and jostled by *sacoleiros* trying to squeeze past.

Mona Lisa

One of Ciudad del Este's oldest and most established shopping galleries, Mona Lisa is worth a visit even if you aren't shopping. This gallery specializes in luxury goods. They have everything from high end wines sold out of a dimly lit, temperature controlled wine cellar, to authentic Persian rugs. There is also a nice café and fancy restaurant. If you visit one shopping gallery in Ciudad del Este it should be this one for the sheer spectacle of it all. *Tel: 061 500 645, large blue building on the corner of Monseñor Rodriguez and Carlos Antonio. López, www.monalisa.com.py, Mon-Sat 7:30am-4:30pm*

Shopping del Este

You can't shop any closer to the border than this new complex. From here you can also get a good view of Ciudad del Este's shoreline and the maze of commerce heading uphill from the border. *Tel: 061 503499. Across the street from Paraguayan immigration controls at the Friendship bridge, Mon-Sat 8am-10pm, Sun 8am-12pm*

Casa China

A nice *galería* with a little of everything. Hard to miss with its enormous, almost cartoonish, red pagoda over the mirrored glass entrance. *Tel: 061 500 335, Avenida San Blas 26 almost at Toledo, www.casachina.net, Mon-Sat 7:30am-5pm, Sun 8am-12pm*

Lago de la República

Need a break from the commercial sector? Take a walk down to the man-made *Lago de la República* lake just southwest from the center of downtown's residential district. A nice walking path surrounds the lake and there are several places to stop and watch the birdlife. In addition there are a number of restaurants located near the southernmost tip of the lake. *From the intersection of Adriana Jara and Pioneros del Este continue downhill past the Supermercado Arcoiris and the local bus terminal on your right. The road will fork and the left-hand side continues downhill to the lake.*

Tips for shopping in Ciudad del Este

– Get an early start. Most stores operate on Brazilian time and close up shop around 3pm when the last of the *sacoleiros* start heading for the border.

– Do your research beforehand. Salespeople are not necessarily knowledgeable about their electronics and language barriers can also prove to be an issue.

– Many stores keep specialty and larger items in a separate stock room. Often you will have to follow someone to this second location to pick up your purchase, receipt in hand. Given the amount of negative press Ciudad del Este gets this can seem very sketchy but it is standard operating procedure.

– Be sure to test out items before leaving the store. Again, you may have to accompany someone to a second location where store technicians will test it for you.

– Check all packages before leaving the store.

– Don't buy large ticket items on the street. There is a lot of risk of buying fake (or "*mau*" in Portuguese) goods. Smaller stores are hit or miss and almost everything on the street is a knockoff. Stick to better established galleries in order to increase your chances of getting legitimate goods (although there is never a 100% guarantee).

– Interested in purchasing a new camera or cell phone but don't want to head to Ciudad del Este? Asunción also has a number of smaller *galerías* dedicated to the sale of electronics. While their selection does not come close to Ciudad del Este's the experience is much more pleasant and calm and the price difference is minimal (see Shopping, p143).

Museo El Mensu

Within the municipal grounds on the eastern side of Avenida Pioneros del Este this small museum is set up in one the city's first houses. There are a couple of historic items from Ciudad del Este's founding, along with some indigenous artifacts. Not worth a visit on its own but you can pop in while waiting for a bus to Itaipú along the road out front. *Tel: 061 501 706/10, Avenida Pioneros del Este almost at Avenida Dr. Eusebio Ayala, Mon-Fri 7am-1pm*

ATTRACTIONS OUTSIDE OF CIUDAD DEL ESTE

Itaipú Dam

The Itaipú Hydroelectric power plant is considered one of the Seven Wonders of the Modern World. One of the world's largest hydroelectric dams, Itaipú was only recently surpassed in production capacity by China's Three Gorges dam. In 2008, a record breaking year, Itaipú produced 94.7 billion kilowatt hours worth of energy. The hydroelectric dam is managed by the Entidad Binacional Itaipú, an organization that is part governmental organization part private company and is jointly run by Brazil and Paraguay. The energy produced by the hydroelectric reserve is split evenly between the two countries with ten turbines under Brazilian ownership and the other 10 under Paraguayan ownership. Energy from two turbines is used to cover approximately 71 percent of Paraguay's national energy needs (though one hundred percent could be covered if Paraguay's energy transmission infrastructure were improved). Paraguay sells energy from the remaining turbines to Brazil at a controversially low price (see The Divisive Dam, p254). Through Itaipú, Brazil is able to cover approximately 16 percent of its national energy needs.

Initial planning for the dam began in 1966, though the official Itaipú Treaty between Brazil and Paraguay was not signed until 1973. In order to allow for construction of the dam a two km long channel was excavated to reroute the Paraná River. The detour channel was completed in 1978 and construction of the dam itself took place between 1978 and 1982. The sheer manpower needed was responsible for the rapid growth of both Foz do Iguaçu and Ciudad del Este. At one point Itaipú employed over 40,000 people, almost as many people as were forced to relocate from the projected flood zone. In late 1982 the Paraná River was dammed and the ensuing flooding filled what was from then on known as the Itaipú Reservoir. Construction was completed in 1991 with a final bill of US$ 18 billion. The resulting monolithic structure is eight kilometers long, 196 meters tall and comprised of over 12 million cubic meters of concrete. Touring the dam can be fascinating, though even at Paraguay's most popular tourist destination English speaking guides are hard to come by.

> The name Itaipú comes from Guaraní and means "singing stone" in reference to the sound of water hitting a small island located near the original construction site. "Itá" means stone, "y" means water or river, and "Pu" means sound or noise.

In addition to the dam itself the Itaipú complex includes an Environmental Center made up of the Museo de Tierra Guaraní, a zoo, six nature reserves, an aquiculture station, forestry project, and a hydraulic lab. Visits to all Itaipú facilities are free of charge although the nature reserves, aquiculture station, and hydraulic lab, require advanced reservations and special permissions. For reservations and more information contact the Visitors Center (*Centro de Recepción de Visitas* or CRV). *Tel: 061 599-8040, www.Itaipú.gov.py, rpmd@Itaipú.gov.py*

The East

Touring the Dam
The only way to see the dam is by joining an official guided tour. Visitors are required to bring ID (such as a passport) and register at the visitor's center before the tour. Tours include an introductory video about the construction of the dam, a tour of the inside of the dam including the machine room, and a bus ride through the complex which includes an elevated view of the dam and spillways. If you are lucky one of the fourteen 483-meter long spillways will be open. This impressive sight is rare as spillways are only opened when there has been a true excess of rain and flooding upriver (visiting during an El Niño year ups your chances). *Tour hours: Mon-Fri 8am, 9:30am, 2pm, 3pm, Sat 8am, 9:30am, 10:30am, 2pm, 3pm, Sun 8am, 9:30am, 10:30am*

Technical Tours
Technical tours of the dam are available for professionals in the sciences (such as engineers). These tours must be solicited in writing at least one week prior to the visit with the *Centro de Recepción de Visitantes* (if you are visiting with a tour operator they can make these arrangements for you). The tour is about 2.5 hours and

---

The Divisive Dam

From its inception Itaipú has been a lightning rod for conflict. Environmentalists protested the negative impact of the flooding while those opposed to the Stroessner dictatorship wondered about illicit deals between the Paraguayan and Brazilian government (at the time both countries were governed by military dictatorships). Today Itaipú is often the subject of controversy. Politically appointed Itaipú directors are constantly being switched out like a game of musical chairs. Hydroelectric energy payments (known as "*royalties*") represent one of Paraguay's main sources of income – as a result Itaipú officials are constantly being accused of misappropriating funds for everything from personal profit to covering political campaign costs. Aiding to the corruption, there is no mechanism set up for internal audits. Jobs at Itaipú are among the highest paying employment opportunities in the country with salaries that are orders of magnitude higher than those available in the public or private sector. As such accusations of nepotism are common.

One of the most controversial aspects of the dam's operation is the sale of excess energy to Brazil. The fixed price for this energy stipulated in the original 1973 Itaipú treaty is only a fraction of the current market value for electricity. Thus Paraguay looses a significant amount of money in the transaction while Brazil, which resells the energy internally at market rates, makes a tidy profit. The terms for resale of energy to Brazil are decried by the majority of Paraguayans as unfair and are a constant sticking point in bilateral relations. In 2009 President Lugo managed what was then considered to be a major political accomplishment – an early renegotiation of the Itaipú treaty scheduled to expire in 2023. At the end of a lengthy negotiation process Brazil agreed to increase the price paid for Paraguay's excess electricity (more than tripling the income generated) and to allow Paraguay to sell energy directly to the Brazilian market in the future and to other markets starting in 2023. Brazil has also agreed to fully finance the construction of a 500 KV electricity substation running from Itaipú to Villa Hayes, the cost of which represents about a fifth of Paraguay's outstanding debt for the construction of Itaipú. This substation is badly needed to bolster the country's overloaded electrical grid and is an essential part of the infrastructure needed to sell energy to neighboring Argentina in the future.

includes a walk deep into the dam itself where you can stand at the very foot of the dam with 273 meters of cement separating you from the 1,350-square-kilometer reservoir filled with 29 billion cubic meters of water.

Luces de Itaipú Light Show

Itaipú also offers a brief night time show that consists of a movie about the dam and a five minute light show, set to music, during which the length of the dam is slowly illuminated. As with the regular Itaipú tours this show is free of charge. However it is necessary to reserve a space (leaving ID or passport number) by Thursday afternoons. Plan to take private transportation (cab or tour company) as buses are unreliable at this hour. *Fri-Sat 7:30pm-10pm (winter hours may vary).*

Getting to the Dam

The dam is located fourteen kilometers North of Ciudad del Este in the city of Hernandarias along the side of the *"supercarretera."* Entrance to the *Centro de Recepción de Visitas* (Visitors Center) is on the right-hand side of the road (if coming from Ciudad del Este) and hard to miss. The entrance to the Museum and Zoo is located just before the CRV on the left-hand side of the road.

Taxi ride is about Gs.50,000 from Ciudad del Este's bus terminal – coordinate with the driver for a rate if you want him to wait for you to finish the tour of the dam.

Buses marked "Hernandarias" will go past the entrance to the dam. In Ciudad del Este these head north down Avenida Pioneros del Este, turn west (left) on the Ruta Internacional, and then North (right) at km 4. Specify you want to get off at

---

Saltos de Guaira: The Waterfalls that made Itaipú Possible

From an environmental conservation perspective one of the most lamentable collateral damages of the construction of Itaipú was the flooding of Paraguay's largest waterfalls known as Saltos del Guairá or Salto Grande de las Siete Caídas. It is hard to imagine, but Iguazú Falls paled in comparison to this series of enormous waterfalls which were described by Captain Azara in 1788 as follows:

"Above the falls the Paraná is 4,600 yards wide, when suddenly it becomes contracted to a narrow channel of 60 yards, containing almost as much water as all the rivers of Eurpoe collectively, and rushing downward with indescribable fury. The fall is not vertical, but a plane with an incline of 50 degrees, equal to a perpendicular fall of 56 feet. The noise is heard 20 miles off, and the spray rises in columns visible several miles away. The very earth seems to vibrate at the shock."

These massive waterfalls played an important role in Paraguay's early history. In the 1630's the Jesuit missions of the department of Guayra upriver from the falls were constantly falling prey to slave traders from Sao Paolo, Brazil. In an attempt to save the remains of the missions Father Antonio Ruiz Montoya decided to relocate all remaining members of the Guayra missions (approximately 12,000 indigenous) to the south of the falls, effectively using the Saltos de Guairá as a shield from further attacks. Movie buffs will recognize this event from the Oscar award winning film *"The Mission,"* which was filmed mostly in Colombia, rather than Paraguay.

Curious to see what the Saltos de Guairá looked like? Until the creation of the Itaipú Reservoir (also known as Lago Itaipú) visitors were able to admire the magnificent falls from from a series of rope bridges. As the demise of Saltos del Guaira became imminent more and more tourists flocked to visit the falls. There are several online forums with photos of the falls as well as videos on Youtube.

Itaipú or at the *Centro de Recepcion de Visitas*. This bus can take a while so your other option is to take any bus going from the commercial area along Avenida Pioneros del Este or the Ruta Internacional to km 4 and then take any bus heading north towards Hernandarias. However you should confirm with the driver that the bus will pass Itaipú/Centro de Recepción de Visitas as some of the buses heading North only go as far as the Paraná Country Club (and many buses are poorly signed). Bus fare is approximately Gs. 2,700.

Museo de la Tierra Guaraní & Zoológico Regional

The museum and adjoining zoo are the most visited sectors of the Environmental Center. The museum is well designed with displays showcasing the region's original inhabitants, indigenous as well as fauna. There is a large collection of taxidermied animals representing the fauna native to the dam's flood zone. Interactive displays bring visitors closer to the indigenous Guaraní culture in the second section of the museum. Archeological artifacts found in Alto Paraná and Canindeyú before the flood are also on display.

In order to mitigate environmental damage resulting in the dam's construction Itaipú undertook "*Operación Mymba Kuera*" (Guaraní for "animal catching") which, according to Itaipú's press materials, saved over 36,000 animals from the flood zone. A walk around the zoo's grounds will bring you in close contact with a number of the flood zone's natural fauna. Capybaras, tapirs, peccaries and maned wolves have relatively large living areas and can be seen bathing and roaming about. Unfortunately the rarer felines such as jaguars and pumas are confined to extremely small cages which serve to underscore the negative environmental impacts of the hydroelectric plant's construction. *Tel: 061 599 8040, located two kilometers before the Itaipú Dam on the left-hand side of the road (coming from Ciudad del Este), Mon 2:30pm-5:pm (museum only) Tue-Sat 8am-11:30am, 2:30pm-5pm, Sun 8am – 11:30am*

Nature Reserves

Itaipú's six nature reserves, totaling 38,000 hectares, are used for scientific research and nature conservation. All are located upriver from the dam along the Paraná River. They include: Tatí Yupi Biological Reserve (seventeen kilometers to the north of Ciudad del Este), Pikyry Biological Reserve (thirty-three kilometers north), Itabo Biological Reserve (ninety-four kilometers north), Limoy Biological Reserve (174 kilometers north), Carapá Biological Refuge (264 kilometers north), and Mbaracayú Binational Biological Reserve (next to Salto del Guairá, not to be confused with the Rerserva Natural del Bosque Mbaracayú to the east, managed by Fundación Moisés Bertoni). Permission to visit any of the reserves is obtained through the *Centro de Recepcion de Visitas*. Though all include visitors facilities Tati Yupi is the most readily accessible and geared towards visitors (see the following section). Most are accessible from side roads off the road connecting Ciudad del Este (Route 7) to Salto del Guairá (Route 10). You will need private transportation to get to these reserves. It is best to consult with Itaipú as to the state of access roads as well as facilities for the remaining five reserves as they are rarely visited by tourists.

Refugio Biológico Tati Yupi

Located on a small peninsula jutting out into the Itaipú Reservoir (Lago Itaipú) the Tati Yupi reserve is a world away from the hustle and bustle of Ciudad del Este. The park protects 2,245 hectares of natural habitat. Visitors wishing to enjoy the area's natural side will be happy exploring the park's streams and small waterfalls. Walk or bike along several trails or take in the scenery at the edge of the lake. Visitor's facilities include two dorms rooms with thirty beds each, A/C, a camping area and kitchen facilities. Rangers can arrange for sulky and tractor rides and can lend out bicycles (though these may be in questionable shape). There is a snack bar but it is best to bring your own food. There is no bus that runs to Tati Yupi – expect a taxi from Ciudad del Este to cost about Gs. 100,000 one way.

Salto Monday

Approximately ten kilometers from Ciudad del Este in the neighboring town of Presidente Franco this small park makes for a nice excursion (and respite) from the city. The series of three, forty-meter high waterfalls dropping from the dense vegetation are impressive in their own right even though they suffer a bit of "younger sibling syndrome" due to their proximity to Iguazú Falls. In fact it is probably best to visit them first, before Iguazú Falls. The grounds include a tranquil park and a walkway that takes you to the edge of the waterfalls. Plans are underway to revamp the park in time for the Copa América soccer tournament scheduled to be held in Brazil in 2015. *Mon-Sun 7:30am-6pm (though camping is permitted). Entrance is Gs. 3,000*

Getting There

By bus: Catch the Tres Fronteras buses on Avenida Pioneros del Este heading south (towards the bus terminal). Fare: Gs. 2,200. The bus should drop you off about five blocks from the park. This bus does not run on Sundays.

By car: From the Arco Iris head south on Avenida Pioneros del Este (this will turn into General Bernardino Caballero) towards Presidente Franco. After approximately 5.5 kilometers take a right on to Avenida Monday. Approximately two kilometers down Avenida Monday there is a fork in the road. Follow the left-hand fork and continue approximately 1.3 kilometers. The park entrance will be on the left-hand side.

Monumento Científico Moisés Bertoni

Located on the banks of the Paraná River the Monumento Científico Moisés Bertoni was formerly owned by Swiss scientist Moisés Bertoni who spent over 35 years in the late 1800's and early 1900's studying Paraguay's flora, fauna, and indigenous culture. From this tranquil spot in the Paraguayan wilderness he made several valuable contributions in the realm of the natural sciences. The reserve, known as a "scientific monument," is comprised of 199 of the original 10,000 hectares given to Bertoni by the Paraguayan government in 1989 for the formation of an agricultural colony. The land was donated by Bertoni's descendants in 1955. His large two story former house, situated at a bend in the Paraná River, has been turned into a museum with many personal items as well as pieces from his scientific collection (which at one point contained upwards of 40,000 specimens of flora and fauna). From here there is a nice view of the Paraná River and you can walk down to the banks of the river. Unfortunately swimming is not permitted due to the strong current. Birds and monkeys can be spotted ducking behind enormous jackfruit (*jaká*) hanging in the trees along the reserve's nature trails. The reserve's natural beauty and lush forest stand in stark contrast to the surrounding soy fields and point to the alarming deforestation suffered in the region. The Monumento Científico Moisés Bertoni is located in Puerto Bertoni, forty kilometers from Ciudad del Este. It is best to go with a tour or private guide as the access road is unmarked and in poor condition requiring a 4x4 vehicle. *Tues-Sun 7:30am-3pm*

LODGING

Visitors will find Ciudad del Este to be more expensive than the rest of Paraguay, even when compared to Asunción. There are many lodging options though decent budget hotels are few and far between. If you are uninterested in the commercial sector there is little reason to stay close to the Friendship Bridge (you can always take a quick stroll during the day). Hotels near Avenida Pioneros del Este offer easy access to buses which can take you to nearby sites such as Salto Monday and the Itaipú Hydroelectric plant.

Hotel Austria A favorite among regular visitors to Ciudad del Este. Though rooms are average the hotel is best known for its culinary offerings. The hotel breakfast is extensive by Paraguayan standards and the restaurant specializes in German cuisine. The hotel's wraparound balcony offers a great view of the river – from up high the area looks quite peaceful. *Tel: 061 504 213/4, Calle Emiliano R Fernandez 165 almost at Capitan Emeterio Miranda, www.hotelaustriarestaurante.com, Single Gs. 150,000, Double Gs. 170,000, Triple Gs. 220,000, Wi-Fi, computers with internet, TV, AC, mini-fridge. Restaurant hours Mon-Sat 11am-10pm*

Hotel Munich Comparable to Hotel Austria but without the food or views. *Tel: 061 500 347, Corner of Emiliano R. Fernandez and Capitan Emeterio Miranda, Single Gs. 150,000, Double Gs. 180,000-190,000, Triple Gs. 220,000, TV, A/C, mini-fridge*

Hotel Catedral A bit removed from the commercial sector, Hotel Catedral is one of the cheaper options in Ciudad del Este. Rooms are somewhat depressing though and mattresses can be a little saggy. *Tel: 061 502 770, Corner of Pampliega and Avenida Oscar Ortellado, Single Gs. 55,000 -80,000, Double Gs. 80,000, Triple Gs. 100,000, TV, A/C*

Hotel Caracol A cheap option around the corner from the more popular and well established hotels Munich and Austria. Rooms are basic but the lobby is nice and has internet access. *Tel: 061 504 618, Camilo Recalde 6012 almost at Capitan Miranda, Single Gs. 100,000, Double Gs. 150,000, Triple Gs. 210,000, TV, A/C, mini-fridge*

Moisés Bertoni

Dr. Moisés Santiago Bertoni (1857 – 1929) is a well known figure in Paraguay. Often refered to as "el sabio Moisés Bertoni" (the wise Moisés Bertoni) he is cherished as a foreigner who dedicated much of his life to the study of Paraguay's natural environment. This avid environmentalist moved his family from his native Switzerland to Misiones, Argentina in 1884 and in the early 1890's was given the land that is now Puerto Bertoni by the Paraguayan government to start the Guillermo Tell Colony. He subsequently dedicated the remainder of his life to exhaustive studies of the area's flora and fauna as well as indigenous inhabitants, making significant contributions to the scientific community. He was called upon by the Paraguayan government to establish the National School of Agriculture and also served as head of the national Department of Agriculture. His extensive study of the Guaraní Indians led to the publication of multiple volume work entitled "La Civilización Guaraní" (the Guaraní Civilization). He disseminated information about his discoveries through aptly named Ex-Sylvis (latin for "From the forrest") printing press.

Bertoni is best known for the discovery of *ka'a he'ê* (see *Ka'a he'ê*, Paraguay's Sweet Spot,p35), the sweet plant used by local indigenous He named the plant "Stevia rebaudiana bertoni" in honor of his wife, whose maiden name was Rebaud.

Hotel Mi Abuela Set up in an old house this hotel is cute and has a much more homey feeling than the city's other hotels. The location, right off Avenida Pioneros del Este is within walking distance of the commercial sector. Rooms are basic but large, many with the building's original high ceilings. The small interior courtyard includes a few caged monkeys. The cute café decorated with old photos serves up affordable daily lunch specials and fast food. *Tel: 061 500 333, Avenida Adrián Jara almost at Pioneros del Este (across from Hotel Convair), Single Gs. 120,000, double Gs. 160,000, triple Gs. 200,000, Wi-Fi, TV, AIC*

Centro Hotel Despite its location on the outer edges of the commercial sector the ambience in this minimalist and modern hotel is calm. Rooms are on the small side but clean and nicely decorated. *Tel: 061 514949, Corner of Avenida Nanawa and Monseñor Rodriguez, www.centrohotel.com.py, Single US$50, double: US$60-70, triple: US$100, Wi-Fi, computers with internet, TV, A/C,*

Casablanca Located in the exclusive Paraná Country Club (technically in neighboring Hernandarias) this is the most luxurious option around and perhaps the nicest hotel in the whole country. Each room in this large Spanish mission style building is plushly decorated and appointed with high end amenities. The views from the terrace and pool are breathtaking and it is easy to forget you are near one of the largest commercial sectors in the region. Those planning to splurge should remember to include transportation costs to and from Ciudad del Este in their budgets. *Tel: 061 572 121, Avenida Botero Norte 69, Paraná Country Club, Hernandarias, www.casablancahotel.net, Single US$70 -85, double US$85- 100, triple US$100 - 115, Wi-Fi, TV, A/C, mini-fridge, pool*

RESTAURANTS

Ciudad del Este has variety of dining options that can't be found in other parts of the country. For those that have already spent significant amount of time in Paraguay the city's ethnic restaurants are a welcome break from *empanadas* and *lomitos*. Some of the best food can be found at hole-in-the-wall restaurants. As with lodging food prices are higher than in the rest of the country.

Restaurante Al Manara A great place to sample Ciudad del Este's middle-eastern fare. Select your dish using the picture menu on the wall but remember that it is easy to over order. Two dishes can easily feed up to three or four people. Hummus, pita, and garlic sauce are musts. Brazilian-style food is also available as are hookahs with a selection of flavored shisha tobacco. *Tel: 061 514 038, 061 510 149, Shopping Continental, 2nd floor, Rubio Ñu between Monseñor Rodriguez and Adrian Jara. 2nd floor Shopping Continental, Mon-Sat 7am-2pm, Gs. 20,000-40,000*

Gugu's Restaurante Chino Gugu's has the best Chinese food in town and the locals know it, as proven by the lunch crowds. Show up early to beat the rush. A fun photo menu takes the guess work out of ordering. Frosty shaved ice drinks are delicious as beverages to accompany your meal (try the passion fruit or *mbaracuyá*) or as desserts (try the peanut chocolate). *Tel: 061 512 494, Boquerón 266 about half a block from Adrian Jara, Mon-Sat 10:30am-9:30pm, US$2.50 -15*

New Tokio One of the few places in landlocked Paraguay offering high quality Japanese food. Lunch service includes a buffet and a la carte options but sushi lovers will prefer the all you can eat sushi and sashimi specials at dinner. *Tel: 061 5503 840, Corner of Avenida Pioneros del Este and Avenida Adrian Jara in the same building as the Arco Iris supermarket (walk up the stairs to the right of the supermarket entrance), Mon-Sat 11am-2pm, 5pm-10pm, Gs. 15,000-60,000, sushi dinner special Gs. 66,000, sashimi dinner special Gs. 81,000*

Churrasquería Patussi's Grill One of Ciudad del Este's most popular Brazilian style *churrasquerías* located a short distance from the commercial sector. The meat just keeps on coming so make sure to go with an empty stomach. They usually have or are willing to make some sort of pasta dish for vegetarians. *Tel: 061 502 293,* *located on the second floor of a mini mall on Avenida Monseñor Cedizch and Alejo García (above Cantina Napoli Pizzería), www.patussigrill.com, Mon-Sat 11am-3pm, 6pm-12am, Sun 11am-3pm, Gs. 80,000 per person*

Cantina Napoli Pizzería This pizzeria's wide variety of pizzas includes stuffed crust pizzas and dessert pizzas. They also deliver. *Tel: 061 513 204, 0973 589 144, 0983 106 974, Avenida Monseñor Cedizch y Alejo García (underneath Patussi Grill), www.cantinanapoli.com.py, Mon-Sat 11am-3pm, 6pm-12am, Sun 5pm-12am, Gs. 20,000-50,000*

Bovolos Baker's Shop A simple cafeteria tucked away in the commercial sector. Savory options include pastas and sandwiches and baked goods include brownies, muffins, macaroons and cakes. Cappuccinos are good as well. *Tel: 061 510 486, Boquerón 148 across from the CCPA, Mon-Sat 7am-6pm, Gs. 3,000-20,000*

Café Mona Lisa Take a break from shopping for electronics to enjoy something from the Mona Lisa café's extensive drink menu which includes iced coffees, hot coffees and cocktails. They also serve sandwiches and desserts. For a more extensive (but also more expensive) menu head to the Mona Lisa restaurant. *Tel: 061 500 645, Monseñor Rodriguez and C.A. López # 525, www.monalisa.com.py, Mon-Sat 8am-4pm, Gs. 10,000-25,000*

Gourangas This Hare Krishna run restaurant is one of the few restaurants in Paraguay catering to vegetarians. Daily menus include curries and soups as well as fresh fruit juices. *Tel: 061 510 362, Pampliega almost at Eusebio Ayala behind the Municipal office, Mon-Sat 7:30am-2:30pm, Gs. 15,000*

NIGHTLIFE

Tourists will find Ciudad del Este has a very active nightlife featuring a slew of upscale clubs and bars. Expect prices to be significantly higher than those of comparable Asunción locales. While many people choose to cross over to Foz do Iguaçu, Ciudad del Este is becoming popular with Brazilians who make the trek in reverse to take advantage of favorable exchange rates. Most of the best options are located about ten minutes by cab from the center of town in the residential neighborhood of Barrio Boquerón although there are some options in the city center. It is best to take a taxi at night to avoid walking through the mayhem of downtown afterhours (when cleanup crews are dealing with the debris left by the day's economic activity).

Cerca del Río (CRK) A bit removed from the center, this pub has a modern ambience bathed in multi-colored lights, numerous flat screen TVs and a great view of the Friendship bridge. Music is mostly rock with frequent classic and Latin rock tribute acts as well. *Tel: 0983 565 005, Avenida 11 de Septiembre almost at Río Paraná across the street from the Hotel Casino Acaray, on Facebook, Fri-Sat 8pm-5am, Gs. 25,000-40,000*

Inside Bar and Lounge Take a seat at this cool lounge's luminescent bar or head outside to people watch. Ambience is pretty relaxed during the week while dance events heat things up on weekends. *Tel: 061 503 110, www.insidebar.com.py and on Facebook, corner of Avenida General Garay and Aca Caraya, Wed-Sat 6pm-3am, Gs. 20,000-40,000*

Bambuddah A popular nightclub among Asunción's elite, Bambuddah's Ciudad del Este location has become popular with the city's young and hip crowd. Most nights include a cover fee though there are promotional prices before midnight. *Tel: 0973 539-889, Lomas Valentina y Garay, www.bambuddah.com.py and on Facebook, Gs. 40,000-60,000, Fri-Sat 10pm-6am*

Patu's Bar Though there is less emphasis on décor and atmosphere Patu's is a popular nightlife option in the center of town. Menu includes pizzas and burgers. *Tel: 061 506 508/9, Avenida Bernardino Caballero 480, www.patusbar.com, Tue-Sun 5pm-1am, Gs. 20,000-35,000*

Iguazú Falls

Discovered in 1542 by Spanish explorer Álvar Núñez Cabeza de Vaca the Iguazú Falls are one of the seven wonders of the natural world and rightly so. These majestic waterfalls are a site to be seen. Fortunately this can be accomplished from a myriad of angles. There are paths leading through the forest alongside the falls, boat trips that take visitors as close as safely possible to their base, elevated walkways that lead over the river to the very mouth of the falls, and even helicopter tours allowing visitors to admire them from fair above. There are several ways to visit the falls and which is most convenient depends largely on your budget, timeframe and visa status.

The falls are located smack on the border between Argentina and Brazil. While the Brazilian side is quite popular, the Argentine side is cheaper and offers more value for your money – the grounds are more extensive and there is a wider range of activities available. It is possible to visit both sides in one day, although logistically this usually requires private transportation.

Together, the Argentine and Brazilian parks total over 252,000 hectares of protected semi-deciduous Atlantic Forest that are a safe haven for over 450 species of birds, eighty species of mammals and 2000 plant species as well as innumerable reptiles, amphibians and insects. Despite the influx of visitors, you will still be able to see a variety of animals by the waterfalls (especially towards the beginning and end of the day) – butterflies abound, toucans and other birds are in the trees. You may even spot caimans sunning themselves on the rocks by the water. By far the most visible are the *coati* which roam freely, instantly recognizable by their long pointy snouts and striped tails. Though they are cute, resist the urge to get too close – they have become accustomed to receiving food from park visitors (though this is strictly forbidden) and will put to use their surprisingly sharp claws if tempted with food.

> Make sure to change money into local currency before entering the park as neither side accepts Paraguayan money (though they do take dollars and euros).

Border Control Issues

Because Brazil requires visas for American tourists many choose to visit the Argentine side of the falls. Although in order to reach the Argentine side of the falls from Ciudad del Este one must pass through Brazil, there are options for tourists without Brazilian visas. The first is to take the El Práctico bus which runs between the Ciudad del Este and Puerto Iguazú, Argentina bus terminals without stopping for Brazilian immigration controls (see following section). The other is to take the ferry which runs between the ports of Presidente Franco and Puerto Iguazú.

Those joining private tours may find their drivers are able to breeze past immigration controls in Brazil and Paraguay altogether. Be aware that it is your responsibility to make sure you are properly stamped into and out of each country. A failure to do so could result in a fine the when exiting Paraguay or Brazil later on. Insist that your driver or guide allow you to be stamped in and out of each country. Most are used to dealing with Mercosur members who do not need stamps.

Parque Nacional Iguazú – Argentina

At 67,620 hectares in size this park encompasses about two thirds of the falls themselves. Declared a World Heritage site in 1984 the park offers visitors numerous trails for enjoying a variety of views of the falls and coming into close contact with the region's flora and fauna. A short walk from the park entrance is a small train named the "*Tren Ecológico de la Selva*" (ecological train of the jungle) which leads from the visitor's center to various trailheads. Some trails are more physically demanding than others and handicapped accessible trails are clearly marked. If the water levels are low enough you can take a free boat ride across to Isla San Martín which offers additional trails, views of the waterfalls and swimming on a small beach near the foot of the falls. For most the highlight of the Argentine side is the *Garganta del Diablo* (Devil's Throat) path – an elevated pathway that crosses wide stretches of the (deceptively tranquil looking) Iguazú River before leading out to the very mouth of the *Garganta del Diablo* waterfall. The massive amounts of water continuously spilling over the 700-meter long edge of this 82-meter high shoehorn shaped precipice are mesmerizing. For additional fees you can rappel, take a motor boat ride to the foot of the falls, or go on a moonlight tour of the falls (this option is available only five nights per month with advanced reservations). Shoes with good traction are recommended as walkways can get slippery and you should expect to get moderately soaked by the waterfall spray. *Tel: From Paraguay: +54 3757491469, from Argentina: 0800 266 IGUAZU (4482), www.iguazuargentina.com, Entrance fee for non-Mercosur foreigners is 85 Argentine pesos with special discounts available for two day visits (note you can only pay for the park entrance with Argentine pesos); hours: 6am to 6pm*

Getting There

Taxis from the Ciudad del Este bus terminal to Puerto Iguazú are about Gs. 130,000 and to the Argentine falls are approximately Gs. 180,000.

By Bus

In order to visit the falls by bus you must first make your way to the Puerto Iguazú bus terminal from which there are regular buses to the falls.

The bright yellow El Práctico bus runs from 6am to 6pm between the Ciudad del Este and Puerto Iguazú bus terminals bypassing Brazilian immigration completely (an good option for those without Brazilian visas). Buses depart every forty minutes until about 3:30pm after which there are no buses until 6:00pm. Service is not as frequent on Sundays so it is best to get an early start. If you catch the bus at the bus terminal you will need to stop at Paraguayan immigration to get stamped out (be sure to ask the driver to let you off as most riders do not need to stop here). Hold on to your ticket – once you have obtained your stamp you can use your ticket to hop on the next El Práctico (if you are already downtown it is unnecessary to double back to the bus terminal – simply walk to the bridge and catch the bus after getting stamped out). Tickets cost Gs. 8,000 (which can also be paid in Argentine pesos). Another option is the Crucero del Norte bus (also yellow) with "Puerto Iguazú/Argentina" on the front which can also be boarded just past immigration controls. Tickets cost Gs. 10,000 (can be paid in Argentine pesos). The first bus leaves the Ciudad del Este bus terminal at 8:20am (arriving at the border between fifteen and forty minutes later depending on traffic) and continue to run hourly throughout the day with the last bus departing from Puerto Iguazú at 5:45pm and from Ciudad del Este at 7pm.

From the Puerto Iguazú bus terminal, yellow buses marked "Cataratas/Waterfalls" will drop you off at the entrance to the park. The seventeen-kilometer trip takes approximately twenty minutes. Buses leave from the terminal every half hour starting at 7:10am till 7:40pm and return from the park every half hour starting at 7:45am and ending at 8:15pm.

By Ferry
Another option is to reach the falls by ferry, which is ideal for those who are skittish about crossing through Brazil due to visa issues. The ferry departs hourly from the Puerto Hito Tres Fronteras in Presidente Franco on the Paraguayan side of the Paraná River and docks at the port of Puerto Iguazú. The journey along the triple border between Argentina, Paraguay and Brazil formed by the meeting point of the Iguazú and Paraná Rivers (twenty-three kilometers downriver from Iguazú Falls) is very enjoyable and takes about fifteen minutes. Depending on the day, the ferry includes several minivans packed to capacity with contraband goods such as beer and produce from Argentina. *Tel: +54 3757 – 422845 (in Argentina), the fee is Gs. 5,000 per person and Gs. 20,000 per vehicle, departures every 45 minutes Mon-Fri 8:30am-5:15pm from Presidente Franco and 8am-5:30pm from Puerto Iguazú. Future plans for bus service between Ciudad del Este and Puerto Iguazú using the ferry are in the works. Immigration officials can help arrange for taxis in to town on either side. Taxis to Puerto Hito Tres Fronteras should run about Gs. 50,000 from the Ciudad del Este bus terminal. The "Matiuaud Directo Franco" bus can be caught along Avenida Pioneros del Este and will drop you off about ten blocks from the dock (ask to go to "el hito"). However, the latter option is not recommended as the area is very desolate and not safe for walking.*

PARQUE NACIONAL DO IGUAÇU – BRAZIL

Created in 1939 Parque Nacional do Iguaçu covers an area of 185,262 hectares and was declared a UNESCO World Heritage site in 1986. The Brazilian side of the falls offers visitors a spectacular panoramic view of the falls. The section of the park open to visitors mainly consists of one walking path that runs upriver past a series of smaller sections of the falls before arriving at the foot of the longest section of the waterfalls. An elevated walkway takes you to the foot of the falls where everyone crowds for photos (be prepared to protect both yourself and your camera from the spray). Here, the waters of the Iguazú River empty themselves along the seventy-two-meter precipice in a watery spectacle that can be hypnotizing. There are also options available for boat rides and rappelling though due to the exchange rate these activities are less expensive on the Argentine side. *Tel: +45 35218383 (in Brazil), www.cataratasdoiguacu.com.br, Winter hours 9am-5pm, Summer hours 9am-6pm. Entrance fee: 37 Brazilian reals*

Getting There
In order to reach the Brazilian side of the falls by bus you must first make your way to the Foz do Iguaçu bus terminal. There are several buses that make the trip between Ciudad del Este and Foz do Iguaçu leaving approximately every twenty minutes during the day. However, keep in mind you will need to get off the bus at the border to be stamped out of Paraguay – make sure the driver will be willing to wait

for you to pass immigration controls. Some may prefer to simply catch one of the many buses to Foz do Iguaçu once past immigration. From the Foz do Iguaçu bus terminal city bus number 120 Parque Nacional runs to the Brazilian park every twenty minutes and takes about forty minutes.

Taxis from the Ciudad del Este bus terminal to the Foz do Iguaçu bus terminal are about Gs. 70,000 and to the Brazilian falls are Gs. 150,000.

Northeastern Paraguay

Along Routes 3, 5, & 10

Few visitors venture into the sparsely populated northern half of eastern Paraguay. This area, consisting of the departments of San Pedro, Amambay, Canindeyú and Concepción is less developed, with fewer roads and less infrastructure than their southern counterparts. While safety concerns have lately kept the flow of tourists to a minimum, each department has sites worth visiting.

Heading northeast from Asunción, Route 3 passes through the satellite cities of Mariano Roque Alonzo (where the Trans Chaco Highway begins) and Limpio before arriving at the small town of Emboscada. The town is known mainly for two things: its sandstone mining tradition and the quirky patron saint festival during which participants don costumes made of feathers and dried banana leaves. Further east is the town of Arroyos y Esteros. The town's name, which means "Creeks and Marshes," aptly describes the landscapes in this part of Paraguay. Route 3 then enters the department of San Pedro. It is here that Fernando Lugo built his reputation as a left leaning arch bishop and advocate of farmer's rights before eventually winning the presidency in 2008. San Pedro is one of the poorest departments in Paraguay, a situation that has given rise to frequent protests and calls for land reform.

The small town of San Estanislao (more commonly known as Santaní) marks the crossroads with Route 10, which continues east to the department of Canindeyú, and the road south to Coronel Oviedo. It is a good place to stock up on supplies or stop for lunch, if you are in a private vehicle. Continuing north about halfway between Santaní and Yby Yaú is Santa Rosa del Aguaray which is the turn off for one of Paraguay's most unique tourist attractions, Rancho Laguna Blanca. A white sandy beach at the edge of a pristine lake, Rancho Laguna Blanca is as close to a private beach vacation as you can get in this landlocked country. The beach attracts all manner of visitors from city folk from Asunción to families from nearby Mennonite colonies.

Yby Yaú marks the cross roads with Route 5 which runs East-West. To the East is the Parque Nacional Cerro Corá national park. The park is easily accessible from the main road and has many trails leading through the lush vegetation. Cerro Corá is historically significant as a former Triple Alliance War battleground and the site where Mariscal López met his death at the hands of Brazilian troops. Many use the nearby city of Pedro Juan Caballero as a base for visiting Parque Nacional Cerro Corá. Though the city has a reputation for being haven to drug traffickers and other unfriendly elements it is very pleasant and surprisingly modern. Pedro Juan Caballero and neighboring Brazilian city Ponta Porã blend together seamlessly, divided only by a double wide avenue that extends the length of both cities.

The Northeast

To the west along Route 5 is the port city of Concepción at the banks of the Paraguay River. Known as *"la Perla del Norte"* (the pearl of the north) Concepción has always been a major shipping hub for goods coming from the Paraguayan Chaco as well as Brazil, via Pedro Juan Caballero. A handful of passenger ships dock in Concepción, making the city a popular departure point for adventurous backpackers heading north on the river to Vallemí, Fuerte Olimpo and Bahía Negra or south to Asunción (see Traveling Along the Paraguay River, p305). Backpackers also enjoy staying at Granja El Roble, a small farm in the nearby town of Belén. This cute family run farm is an excellent place to relax while planning your next Paraguayan adventure with German owner Peter Dirk. Vallemí, the northernmost city of the department of Concepción, is home to a series of limestone caves as well as the country's largest cement factory.

With the exception of Brazilians who flock to Salto del Guairá to buy cheap electronics, the department of Canindeyú is rarely visited by tourists. However, as one of the last remaining reserves of Atlantic Forest, the Reserva Natural Mbaracayú is well worth a visit. A small community of Aché Indians live in the forest, which is also the habitat of the rare *guyra campana* (bell bird).

TRAVELING ALONG ROUTES 3, 5, & 10

Extreme poverty and porous borders have lead to a series of safety advisories for tourists traveling to this area of Paraguay. Foreigners are advised by the US State Department to steer clear of the departments of Amambay and Canindeyú due to the prevalence of marijuana plantations and trafficking, especially along the border with Brazil. In addition the departments of San Pedro and Concepción have recently seen the rise of the Ejercito del Pueblo Paraguayo (EPP) members. This small left wing group has been labeled a terrorist organization by some but characterized as merely small group of bandits by others. The EPP has been linked to a handful of high profile kidnappings over the past decade and throughout 2010 there were several violent confrontations between the police and alleged EPP members. For the most part common sense should be enough to keep foreigners out of trouble as they have not been specifically targeted by drug traffickers or EPP members. It is best to refrain from camping or straying too far off the beaten path and to steer clear of potentially controversial topics of conversation (such as drugs and politics). Travel along paved roads is generally safe and may include police or military checkpoints but tourists should refrain from driving along smaller roads in Canindeyú and Amambay.

Recommended bus companies: NASA, La Santaniana (though bus quality may vary so be sure to ask for a *doble piso*).

Departamento Cordillera

EMBOSCADA

Emboscada is a cute Paraguayan town known for its artisanal mining industry. Sandstone from Emboscada is used all over Paraguay to create cream colored facades for buildings. Emboscada is also well known as the location of Tacumbú, Paraguay's primary prison. During the Stroessner dictatorship many political prisoners were kept here. The best time to visit Emboscada is on July 24th to catch the patron saint festival held in the community of Minas de Emboscada, notable due to feathered costumes worn by its participants.

Fiesta Patronal San Fransisco Solano

Every July 24th the small community of Minas holds festivities in honor of their patron saint, St. Fransisco Solano. Festival goers known as the *"guaicurú"* wear masks and elaborate costumes covered head to toe with all manner of feathers. These costumes, which are mostly made of chicken and guinea hen feathers, can take months to create. Some people wear traditional masks while others sport rubber Halloween masks. The day's events include an early morning mass followed by traditional dancing by the feathered *guaicurú*. The *guaicurú* also make an appearance during a special mass held on the night of the 22nd. *Minas Cue is located five kilometers from the center of Emboscada. For a festival itinerary contact Emboscada's municipal office.*

> Emboscada is home to Paraguay's largest afro-american population, descended from Uruguayan slaves who came to Paraguay in the 1820's.

Departamento San Pedro

The department of San Pedro is one of Paraguay's poorest, with the majority of its population dependant on small scale and subsistence agriculture for survival. The province is known for *"sin tierras"* (those without land) whose frequent land invasions are highly politicized. President Lugo began his presence in the national political scene as the Bishop of San Pedro, preaching in favor of the rights of rural farmers, known as *"campesinos."*

⚓ RANCHO LAGUNA BLANCA

In landlocked Paraguay any body of water is a potential vacation spot with families crowding river banks and creek beds to enjoy respite from the heat. Secluded within San Pedro, Laguna Blanca is one of the country's most picturesque and pristine waterfront getaways. The 147 hectare lake is crystal clear with white sandy shores surrounded by dense vegetation. The lake's waters are very shallow, creating a natural wading pool perfect for small children (and sunbathing adults). Aside from the natural beauty, what sets Laguna Blanca apart from other bathing areas in Paraguay are the strictly enforced environmental regulations. Beach goers and campers must keep music at a low level and are prohibited from littering or entering the water with beverages. Advance reservations are necessary as there is a one hundred person cap on visitors per day to keep environmental damage to a minimum. Kayaks, snorkels, a rowboat and even horses are available for a fee or you can just pass the time floating amongst the lake's tall reeds (bring your own floats or use your ground pad in a pinch). Those in private vehicles can also inquire for directions to a series of large sand dunes located approximately two hours away by car. The ranch offers both beach camping and basic rooms, though the latter fill up fast. Meals are only available during the high season (December-April) but campers are free to prepare their own food (though there is nowhere nearby to purchase food, so you must bring in everything including beverages). During the week this secluded ranch has the feel of a private beach. On the weekends and over holidays it fills up with vacationers including large families from nearby Mennonite colonies (try not to stare as conservative Mennonite women take a dip into the lake fully clothed).

The Northeast

As of 2010 Laguna Blanca was officially declared a protected area. The lake's sandy shores and the scrub like savannah that grows from it are typical of the Cerrado ecosystem. This bio-diverse nature reserve is home to a number of important bird species including the White-winged Nightjar which is known to breed in only two other areas in the world. In fact the conservation NGO Para la Tierra (*www.paralatierra.org*) runs a field station in Laguna Blanca (about 250 meters round the left-hand side of the lake). English speaking Karina Atkinson can provide excellent information about the area's flora and fauna. Nature lovers and photographers with time on their hands can also volunteer or intern with Para La Tierra (an excellent way to enjoy Paraguay's natural side with the added benefit of having the lake at your fingertips). *Tel: 021 424 760, the turn off to Laguna Blanca is located at a medium sized crossroads called Cruce Santa Rosa in the town of Santa Rosa de Aguaray on km 330 of Route 3. To the left is a road heading to Nueva Germania and Puerto Antequera and to the right is a dirt road heading to Laguna Blanca (there are often several taxis parked here). From here it is approximately twenty-three kilometers to the main entrance. There are signs but these are frequently removed. By car following the dirt road you will cross over two bridges after which the road forks. Take the left-hand fork and continue till you see an elevated water tank on the right-hand side of the road. Take a right here and cross over another bridge after which you take a left towards Colonia Santa Barbara. The large signed entrance is on the left-hand side of the road. Once at the gate you may need to call the main number or talk to the people living across the road in order to be let in. A three-kilometer long dirt and sand road leads from the main entrance to the visitor's area by the lakeshore. Buses from Asunción to Concepción and San Pedro pass by Santa Rosa de Aguaray, however you must make sure they are going via 25 de Diciembre (signed "por 25" or "x 25"). Buses going along the Trans Chaco highway to Concepción will bypass Route 3 entirely and buses going via Coronel Oviedo will add at least two hours to the trip. Two buses headed to the Colonia Santa Barbara and Carapaí run from the Cruce Santa Rosa past the main entrance to Laguna Blanca. The Galaxia passes by at 12:30pm daily (returning past the entrance at between 7:30 and 8am) and La Paraguaya passes by at 2:30pm (returning between 10:30 and 11am). Only La Paraguaya runs on Sundays leaving at 2pm and returning at 11am. Show up early for all buses, just in case. www.lagunablanca.com.py, Camping Gs. 30,000 per person (bathroom facilities are generally well maintained), There is also a rustic cabin with simple rooms (bunk beds) for 80,000 per person including breakfast (some people choose to stay in Santa Rosa del Aguaray but due to the bus schedule this is only feasible in a private vehicle), meals (only December-April) Gs. 20,000 per person, horseback riding, kayaking, snorkeling. Advanced reservations required.*

Departamento Concepción

The department of Concepción extends north from the department capital of the same name to the northern border with Brazil, marked by the Apa River. While Concepción is a department of beautiful rivers and dramatic landscapes, lack of paved roads makes areas to the north especially hard to reach. However, attractions close to the Paraguay River such as the limestone caves in Vallemí and San Lázaro are accessible by boat and bus. Parque Nacional Paso Bravo and Parque Nacional Serranía de San Luis are national parks with abundant flora and fauna but no infrastructure for visitors.

CONCEPCIÓN

The city of Concepción was founded in 1773 to protect territories to the south from attacks by indigenous tribes and the neighboring Portuguese. This area saw much action towards the end of the Triple Alliance War. Mariscal López met his demise in Cerro Corá

> Concepción is known as "*La Perla del Norte*" (the pearl of the north).

(now a national park) to the east and his wake was held in Concepción. With its strategic location on the Paraguay River, Concepción became an important shipping hub during the late 1800's and early 1900's. *Yerba mate* and wood arrived from Paraguayan provinces to the east as well as the Brazilian province of Matto Grosso. These goods were then transported downriver to Argentina. During this period Concepción received a large influx of Italian, Spanish, and Arab immigrants who left their mark on the city in the form of beautifully decorated manors. Many of these buildings are still standing and, though some have been left to crumble, others have been nicely restored.

Though its prominence faded somewhat Concepción continues to be an important national transportation hub. Boats departing from Concepción serve as a lifeline for the people in the departments of Alto Paraguay (on the western side of the river) and the department of Concepción (on the eastern side of the river) where the roads are frequently impassable. Adventurous backpackers are increasingly traveling to Concepción in order to board passenger boats which make their way north to Vallemí, Fuerte Olimpo and Bahía Negra as well as south to Asunción. During the weekends Concepción fills with youth from nearby towns who arrived in droves on motorcycles. The city also draws crowds from Pedro Juan Caballero who comes to enjoy nightlife without the risks inherent in Pedro Juan's after hours.

The city is home to three museums, each representative of a different era of Paraguay's history. The Museo Villa Real is a testament to the city's role during the Triple Alliance War when it was used by Mariscal López as a headquarters for his troops. The Museo Cívico has on display several paintings from Concepción's heyday as a trading post. And the small Museo de Arte Contemporáneo has examples of Paraguayan contemporary art including works by renowned artist and Concepción native Carlos Colombino.

The Northeast

Restoring Concepción's Historic Buildings

A handful of the city's important historic buildings have recently been restored by students of the Escuela Taller de Concepción. This school offers two-year programs in trades such as construction and electrical wiring with students putting their education to practice by working on restoration projects throughout the city's historic district. Restored buildings include the Palacete Municipal (Municipal building), the Obispado de Concepción, and the Palacio Otaño (now home to the Contemporary Art Museum).

Tourism Information

Concepción's lively director of tourism, Celso Ruiz Diaz, can be found in the Municipal office (see Palacete Municipal) or in his house directly across the street. *Tel: 0331 242 710, 0981 292 179*

Immigration Office Though Concepción is not technically a border town, the immigration office is equipped to provide exit stamps for those venturing northwards to Bolivia or Brazil along the Paraguay River (see Traveling Along the Paraguay River, p305). If you plan to continue from Bahia Negra to Bolivia it is imperative to get your exit stamp in Concepción before boarding any passenger boat headed north. If you are planning to cross over in to Puerto Murtinho, Brazil, you can get an exit stamp at Isla Margarita (see Obtaining Exit-Stamps Before Continuing to Bolivia and Brazil, p310), however it may be easier to obtain it in Concepción. *Tel: 0972 193 143, Corner of Presidente. Franco and Pedro Juan Caballero (inside past the office of the Registro Civil), Mon-Fri 7am-1pm, 2pm-4pm, the Director of Immigration, Hever Centurión is happy to coordinate with tourists who are unable to pass by during office hours. It is best to call ahead either way as the office sometimes does not re-open in the afternoons.*

Chaco'i

Across the river from Concepción is the island of Chaco'i, home to a handful of families. Most cross the river every day by row boat or motor boat to work in Concepción. Walking along the island's dirt roads you will see the quaint scenes of rural lifestyle typical throughout Paraguay-farm animals, crops, and small churches. The island is a good side trip should you tire of Concepción's motorcycle clogged streets. *Water taxis cross between Chaco'i and the port of Concepción at the end of Presidente Franco throughout the day (if going late in the day be sure to arrange for your water taxi to take you back). Gs. 5,000*

Museo Cívico (Museo Histórico y Teatro Municipal)

A quirky museum exhibiting the belongings of one of Concepción's many Italian immigrants. The Museum's highlight is a series of paintings depicting many of the architectural gems of Concepción's heyday, a number of which are still recognizable today. There is also a painting depicting the old port of Concepción from 1890. The museum's director, Sr. Teófilo Medina, is passionate about the city's history and is willing to provide a guided walking tour of Concepción's historic buildings if his schedule permits. *Tel: 0971 803 951, Corner of Cerro Corá and Mariscal López diagonally opposite the back entrance of the Palacete Municipal, Mon-Sat 6:30am-12:30pm, 1pm-5pm*

Museo de Arte Contemporáneo

This small museum houses a surprisingly good collection of Paraguayan contemporary art including works by Ricardo Migliorisi, Carlos Colombino and Ofelia Olmedo. There is also a small collection of drawings by well known indigenous artists Ogwa and Pitoé. The quality of the collection is perhaps due to the fact that the museum was founded by renowned Paraguayan artist and Concepción native Carlos Colombino. The museum has several of his pieces, unique works of art created by painting, engraving and sculpting large panels of wood almost as if they were a canvas. This technique, invented by Colombino, is known as "*xilopintura.*" The building itself, known as Mansión Otaño, was renovated by Concepción's Escuela Taller. *Tel: 0971 803 951, corner of Mariscal Estigarribia and Cerro Corá across the street from the Palacete Municipal, Thurs – Sat 7am-11am, 2pm-5pm*

Museo Municipal del Cuartel de la Villa Real

This museum is housed in what was the command post for the Paraguayan Army during the Triple Alliance War (though the building itself was built during the colonial era). Fittingly the museum's collection is mostly made up of Triple Alliance War relics including the chassis of a wagon which belonged to Eliza Lynch. *Tel: 0971 803 951, Corner of Mariscal Estigarribia and Carlos Antonio López. Mon-Sat 7am-11am, 1pm-5pm*

The Northeast

Palacete Municipal

Built in 1898 the Palacete Municipal now houses the city's municipal office. It sits in the center of the block, surrounded on all sides by pretty gardens. Peak inside to see the two large scale relief murals depicting the founding of the city and the battle of Nanawa fought during the Chaco War. *Tel: 0331 42212, corner of Mariscal. Estigarribia and Cerro Corá, Mon-Sat 7am – 1pm*

Monumento a la Madre

Looming over the city's main avenue, this twenty-four-meter high monument to the Virgin Mary (specifically the *Virgen María Auxiliadora*) was erected in 2002. The monument includes a small lookout point at the base of the virgin's feet. At night the cream colored statue is nicely illuminated. *Corner of Avenida Pinedo and Mayor Julio Otaño*

Puerto de Concepción

Stop by on Sundays and Tuesdays to watch all manner of cargo, from mattresses to motorcycles and tomatoes, get loaded and unloaded from boats heading upriver to Vallemí and Bahía Negra. *The port is located at the end of Presidente Franco*

Expo Norte

These days Concepción's economy is fueled by cattle ranching. There is no better time to see the influence of the area's cattle ranches than at the yearly Expo Norte fair held every September. There are rodeo shows, food and games, and of course, a beauty pageant. *www.exponorte.org*

Granja El Roble

Owned and operated by charismatic nature enthusiast Peter Dirk and his friendly Paraguayan wife Andresa, Granja El Roble is a real gem. Stay in rustic cabins built by Peter himself and stuff yourself with Andresa's deliciously hearty meals including fried fish, home-

> The small town of Belén is bisected by the Tropic of Capricorn.

made pâté, fresh baked breads, and possibly the best fish soup in all of Paraguay. Catch *pacú* in the fish ponds, take a dip in the swimming hole, or relax in a hammock while adorable pet capybara Mimi angles for a pat on the head. Adventure seekers will find their match in Peter. He can help arrange for a variety of trips throughout Paraguay including boat trips along the Paraguay River (he speaks Spanish, German and English) and birding excursions to the Chaco. Do not miss the opportunity to go tubing with him along the nearby Ypane River. A great place to relax or kick-start a Paraguayan adventure, Granja El Roble should not be missed. *Tel: 0985 898 466, a taxi from Concepción costs about Gs. 70,000 but Peter is able to provide a ride most mornings with prior notice, there are also hourly buses from Concepción for Gs. 5,000 (tell the driver to let you off at El Roble and follow the signs from the main road), if driving from Concepción head to the roundabout at the entrance to town and take the unpaved road that heads east to Belén (you will pass the quirky Monumento al Indio that looks like a tall skinny pyramid with holes in it) continue sixteen kilometers and take a left at the signed turn off and continue seven kilometers where the entrance will be on your right. If coming from Asunción head west along Route 5 until the paved right-hand turn off to Belén (approximately eighteen kilometers past the town of Horqueta by the Parador Trópico 21), at the town of Belén take a right and continue two kilometers down a cobblestone road until you see the* *signed right-hand turn off to Granja El Roble, www.paraguay.ch, all prices include full room and board, camping US$10 per person, cabins range between US$20 and $40 with one to two rooms and a variety of amenities (check website for more details on each option).*

Lodging

✌ **Hotel Francés** Housed in one of the city's characteristic old manors Hotel Frances is a very nice hotel with a lot of charm. Rooms are decorated with Paraguayan handicrafts and there is a large outdoor garden with a jacuzzi and pool. The hotel's restaurant has a good breakfast buffet (available to non-guests for Gs. 12,000), lunch buffet (Gs. 30,000) and excellent fish dishes. Try the *surubí a la teja. Tel: 0331 42750, 0331 42600, Corner of Presidente Franco and Carlos Antonio López, www.hotelfrancesconcepcion.com, Singles Gs. 125,000, Double Gs. 190,000, Triple Gs. 220,000, Wi-Fi, computers with internet, TV, A/C, mini-fridge. Restaurant hours 11:30am-2:30pm, 6:30pm-11:30pm, Gs. 20,000-50,000*

Hotel Victoria Another hotel housed in an old manor, this is step down from Hotel Frances but still a comfortable option. Rooms open out on to a street facing courtyard which can be a little noisy. *Tel: 0331 42256, 0331 42826, Corner of Presidente Franco and Pedro Juan Caballero, Single Gs. 90,000 with A/C, Gs. 50,000 with fan, Double Gs. 120,000 with A/C, Gs. 90,000 with fan*

✌ **Hotel Center** A good bargain in the middle of downtown Concepción. Rooms are very basic as are bathrooms. Street facing rooms are very noisy and interior rooms are dark and gloomy. However the location, price, and late checkout time are convenient and there is a karaoke bar downstairs. Rooms on the third floor are accessed by a steep and narrow staircase. *Tel: 0331 242 360, Presidente Franco between 14 de Mayo and Fulgencio Yegros, Gs. 30,000 per person with fan, Gs. 45,000 per person with A/C, TV*

Food

✌ **Restaurant Toninho y Jandira** This Brazilian owned restaurant offers delicious meat and fish dishes, accompanied by various fresh vegetable sides and Brazilian style rice and beans. The food is plentiful, ambience lively and wait staff friendly. *Tel: 0331 241 415, Mariscal Estigarribia between Iturbe and Cerro Corá across the street from the Palacete Municipal (Municipal Office), daily 11am-3pm, 7pm-10pm, Gs. 35,000-50,000*

Restaurant Valens Burger A large restaurant with a laid back feel, Valens offers a wide variety of Paraguayan comfort food as well as fast food options. Ambience is a bit lacking. Pizzas are good and mashed potatoes are very buttery and satisfying. *Tel: 0331 240 234, Corner of Avenida Pineda and Brasil, daily 7am-2pm, 5pm-12am, Gs. 12,000-40,000*

✌ **Comedor Ña Benita** This small restaurant located in Concepción's market is well known for its owner Ña Benita's *caldo de pescado* (fish soup) though other Paraguayan staples such as *tallarín* and *estofado* are also good options. A cheap and fun option for those not put off by eating in the market. *Schreibert and Mayor Lorenzo Medina across the street from the La Paraguaya hardware store, Mon-Sun 5am-3pm, Gs. 10,000-15,000*

Habib's Owned by Concepción's tourism secretary, Habib's is a cheap and tasty place for hamburgers and *lomito árabe* (shawarma). *Tel: 0981 292 179, Corner of Presidente Franco and General Díaz, daily 6pm-12am, Gs. 8,000-15,000*

Heladería Amistad A cute ice cream parlor that also serves fast food. Pizzas are a good option and there is also an affordable daily lunch special. *Tel: 0331 241 184, Corner of Presidente Franco and Nuestra Señora de Concepción (their sign also says Anahi), daily 7am-11pm, Gs. 15,000-30,000*

✌ **El Heladero** Coffees, ice cream and desserts make this small store a good retreat from Concepción's heat and humidity. Try the *cappuccino helado* made with ice cream. *Tel: 0331 242 350, Brazil and General Garay, daily 11am-10pm, Gs. 5,000-15,000*

The Northeast

Getting There

From Asunción drivers can either head north along Route 3 and then west at Yby Yaú on Route 5 or head north along the Trans Chaco Highway to Pozo Colorado and then east to Concepción over the Puente Nanawa bridge. While Route 3 takes longer, the road conditions are preferable as the road between Pozo Colorado and Concepción is notorious for its large potholes.

Both NASA and La Concepcionera buses run from Asunción along the Trans Chaco highway and then take the turn off east to Concepción at Pozo Colorado (NASA is preferable), costing Gs.60,000 and taking six to seven hours. Catching buses in Pozo Colorado is also an option for tourists coming from the Chaco. La Santaniana also runs from Asunción but heads north through San Pedro and then turns West along Route 5 at Yby Yau – the cost is the same as heading through the Chaco but the trip can run about two hours longer. There are several buses that run between Concepción and Pedro Juan Caballero – the trip takes four to five hours and costs about Gs. 40,000. Turismo García also operates a bus from Ciudad del Este to Concepción for Gs. 80,000 which takes about ten hours.

The Concepción bus terminal is about 7 blocks north from the center of town – taxis to the city center or port from the terminal run between Gs. 20,000 and Gs. 30,000. Unless making a connection at the bus terminal you can easily get off at the "la Avenida" stop along Concepción's main avenue, Avenida Pinedo, a couple of blocks from Calle Presidente Franco (most hotels are on this street which dead ends at the port). When leaving Concepción you can board buses at the terminal (which will ensure a seat) or by the plaza (known as the "Parque Infantil" or "Plaza Infantil") on the corner of Avenida Pinedo and Marsical López.

Concepción is serviced by two passenger boats. The Cacique II travels between Asunción and Vallemí while the Aquidaban travels between Concepción and Bahía Negra. Both travel weekly. For those who only want to take the boat one way it will be preferable to take the leg heading downriver as boats are generally faster and less crowded. For more information on either boat see The Cacique II and The Aquidaban, p305. Taxis from the terminal to docks should be about Gs. 20,000.

VALLEMÍ

Vallemí is one of the northern most cities in Eastern Paraguay. This curious and remote city is home to a series of recently discovered limestone caverns. The area's inhabitants live mostly off the mining industry. Paraguay's largest cement factory, the Industria Nacional de Cemento (INC), is located on the riverbanks just south of the city center. The factory's large quarry is clearly visible on the left-hand side of the road when arriving in Vallemí. Those not employed by the INC work in small scale quarries mining dolomite, marble, and limestone or in lime manufacturing factories. This work is backbreaking as almost everything is done manually, from breaking rocks with sledgehammers to loading them on to cargo ships one wheelbarrow at a time over rickety planks. Vallemí is a very surprising town which at times can contrast greatly with its remote surroundings. Due to the presence of the INC the entire town is paved with cement. There are several nice plazas around town decorated with sculptures by local artist and INC worker Sebastian Amarilla. North past Vallemí the Paraguay River begins a series of twists and turns winding its way up through the Paraguayan Pantanal towards the northern triple border with Brazil and Bolivia (see Traveling Along the Paraguay River, p305).

While Vallemí may not merit a side trip all on its own it is a good way to break up a trip along the Paraguay River. Those returning from Bahía Negra can save themselves a full day on the passenger boat by stopping in Vallemí and continuing to Concepción by bus. The same is true of the trip from Concepción to Bahía Negra, however you may have to make previous arrangements with the boat captain if you want to reserve a cabin. Due to the town's remote location expect to pay a premium for food and fuel.

Making Art out of Cement

Local artist and INC cement factory mechanic Sebastian Amarilla is responsible for the dynamic and expressive monuments in Vallemí's many plazas. At the entrance to the INC is "*Gratitud al Supremo Dios*" depicting a muscular man holding a loaf of bread and rocks aloft. According to the artist this symbolizes the way in which the residents of Vallemí have turned the area's natural resources into their daily bread. In the middle of the *Plaza de los Mártires* (Plaza of the Martyrs) along Calle Río Paraguay is a highly evocative monument entitled "*Niños mártires de Acosta Ñu*" depicting the surviving children of the Triple Alliance era battle of Acosta Ñu (see Los Ñinos Mártires de Acosta Ñu, p225) working together to raise a tattered Paraguayan flag and rebuild the nation. Near the port of Vallemí is the new Plaza Flora y Fauna with a large multi piece sculpture in honor of the flora and fauna of the region. In the center is a fountain with a large *dorado* fish splashing out of the water. The surrounding sculptures depict birds and large animals of the region.

Lodging

Hotel El Prado Very clean and spotless, this is the nicest hotel in town, located along the river near Vallemí's port. *Tel: 0351 230 324, 230 545, Avenida General Bernardino Caballero about 500 meters from the port along the river. Gs. 56,000 per person. TV, AC*

Hospedaje La Brazilera While not as nice as Hotel El Prado this family run hotel certainly has more character. Rooms are cheerfully decorated with murals and paintings of Pantanal landscapes as is the hotel's restaurant. Owners are extremely friendly and can regale you with wild tales of fishing for sting rays in the Apa River. Very good Brazilian and Paraguayan food is available in the hotel's restaurant (ask in advance if you would like to eat fish). *Tel: 0351 230 636, Avenida Mariscal López 125, hotelmeson.tripod.com, Double Gs. 90,000 with private bathroom, Gs. 70,000 with shared bathroom, A/C. Restaurant hours 7am-9pm, Gs. 15,000-20,000*

Food

El Triángulo A well stocked supermarket across from the large plaza by the main docks. A good place to stock up on supplies before boarding the Aquidaban or Cacique II. *Tel: 0351 230 203, 0351 230232, Corner of Avenida Río Paraguay and Primero de Mayo, daily 7am-12pm, 2pm-7pm*

Caves of Vallemí & San Lázaro

There are several limestone caves in Vallemí and the nearby district of San Lázaro, most of which were discovered by adventurous employees of the INC cement factory. With stalactites of up to six meters in length the Santa Caverna is the most impressive cave, though for conservation purposes tours are generally limited to scientific expeditions. Discovered in 2006 the cave gets its name from a large stalagmite which is said to be shaped like the Virgin Mary (you will have to use your imagination to see the resemblance). Nearby is the Tres Cerros cave, which was the first to be discovered. Unfortunately many of its stalactites have been cut down by vandals. The Caverna San Lázaro, also known as Cantera 54 is easily accessed and has over fifteen large caves. The Calera Risso is a seventy-meter deep open roofed cave which is popular for rappelling. In addition to limestone formations all the caves have impressive tree roots penetrating through their ceilings and extending into the floor. Perhaps the easiest cave to visit is the Cambá Hópo cave which is only 300 meters from the INC factory and accessed via a fifteen minute boat ride from Vallemí's port. The caves, most of which are on private property, must be visited with private guides who can provide safety equipment such as helmets and headlamps. Depending on your budget and how many people there are in your group you can choose to go by motorcycle or car. Be sure to bring plenty of mosquito repellant. Expect to pay between Gs. 250,000 to 300,000 per person if riding motorcycles and Gs. 400,000 per person if making the trip in a car. While making arrangements it is important to confirm which caves will be visited. With the exception of Cambá Hópo caves are all accessed via dirt roads which can become impassable after rains. Adventurous tourists can also inquire with guides about the possibility of rappelling in Calera Risso, Caverna San Lázaro, or along the cliffs above Cambá Hópo. For tours contact Francisco Narvaez (*Tel: 0985 192510*) who works for the INC and is credited with the discovery of the Santa Caverna, or Hugo Soilan (*Tel: 0351 230 764*) or Pedro Benitez (*Tel: 0985 158 637, 0351 230 664*), both of whom work for the tourism department of the Municipal Office. They can also arrange for tours of the INC cement factory.

Industria Nacional de Cemento
This cement processing plant, the county's largest, produces most of the cement used in Paraguay. Visiting the factory you can see every stage of cement production. Limestone is first mined from the factory's large quarry after which it is transported via conveyor belt to a large mill where it is crushed into a fine powder. The powder is mixed with additives before entering enormous cylindrical rotating kilns. Within the kilns, which are fired at 1000 degrees Celsius, the powder undergoes a multi-step process which causes it to fuse together into small pellets known as clinker. The final product is Portland Cement, which is the main ingredient in concrete. The tour's highlight is getting a chance to peer through a window into the rotating kiln and see the clinker bouncing around inside. The clinker inside is white hot, so much so that you must wear a welder's mask to protect your eyesight when looking in. *The INC factory is located about 1.7 kilometers downriver from Vallemí's port. Follow Avenida General Bernardino Caballero as it turns left, away from the river. You will pass the large "Gratitud al Supremo Dios" sculpture on your left before reaching a traffic circle where the right-hand road leads to the factory entrance (picture ID is needed), www.inc.gov.py, for a tour of the cement factory contact the guides listed above.*

Playa Dorada
Just to the north of Vallemí is the confluence of the large Paraguay River running north-south and the smaller, fast running Apa River running east-west. The banks of the Apa River are wide, sandy, and at most times desolate. The only sign of life across the river in Brazil is a small military base. Sitting on this beach it can feel like you are the only person for miles and miles. Take care when swimming in the river as the current is strong and there are many sting rays. *Inquire at your hotel for a ride to the Apa River (this will most likely be via motorcycle as there are few cars in Vallemí) and about the possibility of fishing in the river.*

Getting There

Vallemí is located 200 kilometers to the north of Concepción along a dirt road which is in the process of being paved. From the center of Concepción head north on Teniente Avalos which is two blocks parallel (away from the river) to Avenida Pinedo. Along the way you'll pass Loreto, Paso Horqueta, and the Tatigaty and Aquidaban creeks which are popular swimming spots among locals. After the town of San Alfredo the road is more sparsely populated and there are no gas stations until Vallemí. Unpaved sections can become temporarily washed out after rains so it is best to inquire with bus companies about current road conditions.

Both Concepcionera (*Tel: 0351 230 446, 0331 240 813, offices on Jóvenes por la Democracia three blocks from the river*) and TTL Libertador (Tel: *0351 230 613, 0331 42320, 0331 43414 offices across from Hotel El Prado*) run daily buses from the Concepción bus terminal at 6am and 5am respectively. Tickets are Gs. 60,000. The ride is bumpy and dusty and takes between five and seven hours (not accounting for delays due to road conditions). Buses make one bathroom stop in the small town of San Alfredo.

Vallemí is serviced by two passenger boats – the Cacique II, which travels between Asunción and Vallemí, and the Aquidaban, which travels between Concepción and Bahía Negra. Both travel weekly. For those who only want to take the boat one way it will be preferable to take the leg heading downriver as boats are generally faster and less crowded (see The Cacique II and the Aquidaban, p305).

Departamento Amambay

Once you cross from San Pedro north into Amambay, the flat scenery gives way to the bizarre looking rock formations that make up the Cordillera Amambay. The combination of strangely shaped reddish sandstone formations jutting out amongst lush green tropical vegetation give the Amambay department one of Paraguay's most unique landscapes. The department is home to the Parque Nacional Cerro Corá and a unique natural water formation known as Ojo de Mar. Many caves in the area have petro glyphs which bear witness to the area's original indigenous inhabitants. There are also unsubstantiated rumors that the inscriptions were made by Viking explorers. Stranger things have happened in Amambay.

PEDRO JUAN CABALLERO

Active commerce with neighboring Brazil gives this town a surprisingly modern feel with several commercial buildings and wide roads paved with cement bricks known as "*adoquín.*" Most of the town's larger businesses line the Avenida Internacional (also named Avenida Dr. Francia) which separates Pedro Juan from the Brazilian city of Ponta Porã. As the major border town in the province of Amambay, known for drug trafficking, caution should be taken in Pedro Juan, especially at night. During the daytime, the city is calm but it is best to respect the informal nighttime curfew and steer clear of any potential trouble.

> Pedro Juan Caballero is nicknamed "*la terraza del país*" (the country's terrace).

Tour operators and tourists often choose to access the Pantanal by crossing over the border in Pedro Juan Caballero and taking advantage of Brazil's superior highway system to get to Porto Murtinho on the banks of the Paraguay river. Buses

The Northeast

to popular tourist destinations within Brazil such as Porto Murtinho and Bonito leave regularly from the bus terminal in Ponta Porã.

Laguna Punta Porã

It is around this small lake that the city's first inhabitants lived. The plaza surrounding the lake includes a monument in honor of the settlers as well as a traditional wooden wagon. Visitors can enjoy the park's tranquil atmosphere and paddle around the lake in paddle boats. *The park is located between the streets of Mariscal López, Natalicio Talavera, Alberdi and Julia Miranda Cueto Estigarribia.*

Motorcycle Rally

Each November the city's streets are flooded with motorcycle enthusiasts who come to participate in the motorcycle convention hosted in Ponta Porã. The event regularly draws more than 10,000 participants and fill both cities' hotels. *www.ppmotorcycle.com*

Food

Pizza's House A large, modern pizzeria whose back section opens out on to the Laguna Ponta Porã park. A pizza, beer tower and view of the park make for a relaxed evening in Pedro Juan. *Tel: 0336 273 497, corner of Mariscal López and José Martinez, daily 6pm-11:30pm, Gs. 30,000-50,000*

Shopping China Importados This massive big box store is a good place to stock up on items that are hard to find in Paraguay. You can find everything from food to electronics and beauty products. The food court has several options including Quattro D gelato and a Burger King. *Tel: 0336 743 433, Route 5 and Callejón Internacional (at the intersection between Route 5 and the border), www.shoppingchina.com.br, Mon-Sun 8am-7pm, Gs. 10,000-20,000*

Supermercado Stock The Stock supermarket food court is a cheap and dependable option with a per-kilo buffet. *Tel: 0336 73026, 033674145, corner of Teniente Herreros and Iturbe (across from Plaza Teniente Valdez), www.stock.com.py, daily 8am-8:30pm, Gs. 10,000-20,000*

Lodging

Eiruzú Hotel A large option in the center of the city with a funky 70's vibe. Grounds are nice and include a small pool. *Tel: 0336 272 435, Corner of Avenida Mariscal López and Mariscal Estigarribia, www.hoteleiruzu.blogspot.com, Singles: Gs. 165,00, Doubles Gs. 300,000, Triples: 400,000, Wi-Fi, TV, A/C, pool*

Money Exchange

Multi Cambios *Tel: 0336 73 888, Mariscal López 1460 almost at 14 de Mayo, www.multicambiossa.com, Mon-Fri 8am-5pm, Sat 8am-12pm*

Getting There

Pedro Juan can be reached from Asunción one of three ways. The fastest is to drive north along Route 3 and then head east on Route 5 at Yby Yaú. Both roads are completely paved and in very good condition. Another option is to head east on Route 2 and then north at Coronel Oviedo, connecting to Route 3 in San Estanislao (though there is no particular benefit to this route). If you want to pass by Concepción you can drive north along the Trans Chaco highway and then head east at Pozo Colorado.

The bus ride between Pedro Juan Caballero and Asunción takes between six and seven hours. Nasa (*Tel: 0336 273 835*), La Santaniana (*Tel: 0336 272 152, 0336 272 708*), and Cometa del Amambay (*Tel: 0336 273 555, 0336 273 247*) run daily buses from Asunción's terminal for Gs. 70,000. Nasa and Cometa del Amambay also run daily buses from Concepción, a journey which takes about four to five hours and costs Gs. 30,000. The bus terminal is located opposite the Laguna Ponta Porã at the corner of Avenida Teniente Herero and José Martinez.

NEARBY ATTRACTIONS

Parque Nacional Cerro Corá

This 12,000 hectare park is one of Paraguay's most visited national parks. The park is important both for its conservation of the Cerrado ecosystem as well as its historical significance. On March 1st 1870 Mariscal López met his death at the hands of the Brazilian Army, which effectively brought the disastrous Triple Alliance War to an end. The country's fallen leader is commemorated throughout the park with monuments, statues and an enormous white cross. Visitors can learn more about the park's history as well as its flora and fauna through displays in the small visitor's center museum. Walking paths lead down to the edges of the Aquidaban Nigui River as well as to the Cerro Muralla, a natural terrace. From this lookout point you can see Amambay's characteristic rock formations jutting up all around. Many of these formations, known as *"cerros,"* have ancient petro glyphs etched into the walls, rumored by locals to have been left by Vikings. Cerro Corá is an easy day trip from both Concepción and Pedro Juan Caballero (the former being a cheaper base of operations). Those who wish to stay overnight can sleep in a small guest house or camp. *Parque Nacional Cerro Corá is located about forty kilometers and an hour's ride from Pedro Juan Caballero. Buses that run between Concepción and Pedro Juan Caballero (as well as Asunción and Pedro Juan Caballero) will drop passengers off at the turn off to the park. From the turn off, which is on the right-hand side if coming from Pedro Juan Caballero, it is about one kilometer to the park entrance.*

Ojo del Mar

A hundred-meter wide lagoon in the middle of dense tropical vegetation, this curious site is said to be the result of an ancient volcanic eruption. The source of the formation's water is unknown as is its depth. Adding to the mystery is the remote location (120 kilometers north of Pedro Juan Caballero) and rumors of a monster hiding in the depths of the greenish waters. Due to the poor roads and security risks of traveling unaccompanied in Amambay, it is best to visit Ojo de Mar with a tour operator. The site is approximately fifty kilometers to the west of the city of Bella Vista del Norte which is an official border crossing with Brazil's Bela Vista.

Crossing into Brazil

It is very easy to cross the border between Pedro Juan Caballero and Ponta Porã. All you have to do is simply walk across the Avenida Dr. Francia. However getting official immigration stamps for either country at this border is notoriously inconvenient as the Paraguayan and Brazilian immigration check points are located on opposite ends of Pedro Juan Caballero and Ponta Porã respectively and have different office hours. The easiest way to get both stamps is to hire a taxi to take you to both immigration offices. Some tourists who plan to enter Brazil but return to Paraguay simply choose not to bother getting stamps from either country. Though this is simpler in the short run, you do run the risk of being fined should irregularities be noticed by immigration agents at a later border crossing. The key to pulling this off is to avoid getting stamps as you cross into Brazil as well as when you cross back to Paraguay.

The Northeast

Immigration Pedro Juan Caballero *Tel: 0343 16312, Naciones Unidas 144, Mon-Fri 7am-12pm, 1:30pm-9pm, Sat 8am-12pm, 1:30pm-9pm, Sun 7pm-9pm*

Immigration Ponta Porã The immigration office is located within the federal police station one block past the border near the Paraguayan consulate. *Tel: 3431 1428, Avenida Presidente Vargas, Mon-Fri 9am-12pm, 1pm-4pm*

Departamento Canindeyú

With the exception of its capital, Salto del Guairá, the department of Canindeyú is rarely visited by tourists. The department is home to the mountain ranges of Mbaracayú, Amambay and San Joaquín, all of which are habitats for the much threatened Atlantic Forest ecosystem. Salto del Guairá is often visited by Brazilian tourists looking to shop for inexpensive goods. However, Salto del Guairá has a reputation for being more family friendly than the chaotic Ciudad del Este.

RESERVA DE LA BIOSFERA DEL BOSQUE MBARACAYÚ (MBARACAYÚ RESERVE)

Covering approximately 64,500 hectares the Reserva de la Biósfera del Bosque de Mbaracayú (Mbaracayú Biosphere Reserve) protects both the Cerrado ecosystem as well as the one of the few existing remnants of Atlantic Forest (Bosque Atlántico del Alto Paraná) in Paraguay. The park's varied landscapes are home to several endangered species including jaguars, tapirs, and giant ant-eaters. This is also one of the few remaining habitats of Paraguay's national bird, the *pájaro Campana* (bare throated Bell bird), whose exotic song inspired the famous harp composition of the same name. Members of the Aché indigenous community live within the park and are allowed to carry out traditional hunting and gathering rituals. The park is administered by Fundación Moisés Bertoni which also runs the Centro Educativo Mbaracayú, an educational center for girls living within the park, in conjunction with Fundación Paraguay. Visitors can walk, bike or canoe around the park alone or with a park guide. There are also guided tours to the forty-meter tall Salto Carapá and to communities within the park. Visitors can camp or stay at the park's hotel which provides meals at a reasonable price. Given the park's rich biodiversity and varied terrain it is an excellent option for nature enthusiasts. *Tel: 021 608 740, 0347 20147, to arrive by car head east from San Estanislao/Santaní on Route 10 approximately ninety-one kilometers to the town of San Isidro de Curuguaty there take the left-hand turn off heading north continuing approximately forty-five kilometers to the town of Villa Ygatimí. From here the reserve entrance is twenty kilometers to the east. While most visitors to the park arrive in private transportation with guided tours it is possible take public transportation from Asunción. Empresa Canindeyú (021 555 991) has an 11am and 11:30pm buses to Villa Ygatimí. However the ride is rough and you will have to arrange a pick-up from Villa Ygatimí, www.mbertoni.org.py, Single: Gs. 75,000 shared bath, Gs. 85,000 private bath, Double: Gs. 100,000 shared bath, Gs. 120,000 private bath, Triple: Gs. 130,000, camping Gs. 30,000, Advanced reservations are recommended.*

The Paraguayan Chaco
Along Rt 9: the Trans Chaco Highway

The Paraguayan Chaco, one of South America's last vast wildernesses, exercises a particular pull on intrepid travelers drawn by the region's curious history and its many wild animals. Stretching from the city of Mariano Roque Alonso to the northwestern border with Bolivia, the Trans Chaco Highway traverses the entire length of the Paraguayan Chaco, one of the country's most inhospitable regions. As the Trans Chaco Highway leads north, it passes through the Chaco's two ecoregions – the humid Chaco and the dry Chaco. The humid Chaco (also known as the "*bajo Chaco*," "*Chaco húmedo*," or "*Chaco Austral*") encompasses the southern half of the department of Presidente Hayes. This region is characterized by flooded savannahs filled with *mbocayá* palm trees. Further north, is the transition zone between the humid and dry Chaco, commonly known as the Chaco Central. This area encompasses the northern section of the department of Presidente Hayes and southern sections of the departments of Boquerón and Alto Paraguay. It is here that the majority of the region's fresh water reserves and population are concentrated in the Mennonite cities of Filadelfia, Loma Plata, and Neuland. The dry Chaco (also known as the "*alto Chaco*," "*Chaco Boreal*," or "*Chaco seco*") continues from here, stretching past the northwestern border with Bolivia and northeastern border with Brazil. Past the small town of Mariscal Estigarribia, the region is a true no-man's land with settlements few and far between. The dry Chaco is overgrown with semi desert scrub brush, and seemingly all plants in the region are covered in thorns.

Although it makes up approximately 60 percent of the national territory, the Chaco is home to barely three percent of Paraguay's population. While Eastern Paraguay was being colonized beginning in the 1500's, the Chaco proved too hostile for European newcomers. Throughout the colonial era, the region's disparate indigenous tribes rebuffed attempts at evangelization and colonization with vicious attacks. The Chaco remained relatively untouched by outsiders until the late 1800's when the region's vast natural resources began to interest both Paraguayans and foreigners. Their involvement in the Chaco changed the region forever. Throughout the late 1800's and early 1900's, factories popped up along the edges of the Paraguay River to extract tannins for curing leather from the massive *quebracho* trees that grew in the region (see **Carlos Casado and the Tannin Industry**, p314). This era was also marked by persistent rumors of vast deposits of natural gas in the Chaco region. This eventually resulted in the Chaco War between Bolivia and Paraguay. Waged between 1932 and 1935, the war saw massive casualties, partly due to the extremely hostile terrain on which it was fought. In fact, by some estimates, more soldiers died

The Chaco

of dehydration than from active combat. Though in the decades since the war rumors of gas and oil deposits have persisted, exploration companies have yet to find anything substantial in the Paraguayan Chaco.

In the 1920's, faced with the looming border dispute with Bolivia, the Paraguayan government attempted to populate the still desolate area by allowing a series of Mennonite communities to emigrate to the Chaco. Though the first generation struggled to survive in the remote and harsh wilderness, the colonists' hard work and perseverance has created some of Paraguay's most prosperous communities. Throughout their history, the Mennonite colonies have been a focal point for progress in the region with infrastructure projects such as the Trans Chaco Highway, a power transmission line from Itaipú, and plans for the construction of an aqueduct. However, the Mennonites do generate controversy amongst Paraguayans due to various tax and other exemptions provided by the national government and their alleged poor treatment of local indigenous peoples.

> For excellent photos of the Chaco's wildlife check out www.chaco-wildlife.org

Armed conflict, religious evangelization, and industry have significantly impacted the lives of the Chaco's indigenous inhabitants. While some of the Chaco's indigenous communities maintain a traditional lifestyle, many have been forced to integrate with the modern world in order to survive. Indigenous men flock to the Mennonite colonies and area cattle ranches in search of low wage jobs while others choose to migrate to larger cities such as Concepción or even Asunción. Though the majority are of non-Guaraní ethnicities, many have learned Guaraní, Spanish, and even German in order to improve work opportunities. Several indigenous communities have been relocated from other areas of Paraguay to the Chaco by the government, often in order to make way for agricultural ventures.

The Chaco is marked by an astonishing biodiversity of flora and fauna including over 500 species of birds and 150 species of mammals. The Chaco is home to several of Paraguay's most endangered species including large mammals such as jaguars, pumas, and tapirs. These are elusive, but with patience and the aide of an experienced guide determined nature enthusiasts may find their efforts well rewarded. The region's birdlife is most easily spotted, especially in the salt water lagoons. Here jaibirú storks and flamingoes, coscoroba swans and a number of migratory birds can be found.

TRAVELING ALONG THE TRANS CHACO HIGHWAY

The Trans Chaco Highway begins in Eastern Paraguay in the city of Mariano Roque Alonzo, fifteen kilometers to the northeast of Asunción. The highway then crosses the Paraguay River by way of the Puente Remanso. From here, the nearest city is Villa Hayes, named, as is the entire department, after American President Rutherford B. Hayes. There is not much for tourists in this riverside city, though the nearby San Fransisco agricultural school is worth the visit. Continuing north is Pozo Colorado, a dusty town noteworthy only for being at the crossroads with Route 5 which leads east over Puente Nanawa across the Paraguay River to the city of Concepción.

The cities of Filadelfia, Loma Plata, and Neuland are clustered together approximately 170 kilometers to the north of Pozo Colorado and function as the administrative centers for the Fernheim, Menno, and Neuland Mennonite colonies respectively. Of the Chaco's major cities, Filadelfia has the most tourism infrastructure, followed by Loma Plata. The largest of the Mennonite colonies, Filadelfia is a good base for those interested in seeing the region's flora and fauna as well as historic sites. Standard tours include a visit to the Mennonite themed museums of each city (Filadelfia's museum being the largest and most popular), combined with a trip to Chaco War battle grounds of Fortín Boquerón and nature observation in one of a handful of nearby salt water lagoons such as Campo María, Chaco Lodge, or Laguna Capitán.

The Palo Borracho

In keeping with the Chaco's inhospitable nature almost all the region's flora seems to be covered in thorns. Perhaps the most visible example of this phenomenon is the spike covered trunk of the *palo borracho* (drunken stick) tree. These bizarrely bulbous and spiky trees dot the landscape of the Chaco Central and Alto Chaco, each one stranger looking than the next. The trees have adapted to the dry climate. The sponge-like interior of their trunks puff up with water absorbed during the rainy season. During the Chaco War, many sharp-shooters sought cover in hollowed out *palo borracho*, carving out a small hole in the tree through which to point their guns. Despite their aggressive-looking exteriors *palo borrachos* do have a softer side, quite literally. Throughout the winter large oval pods hanging from the branches explode into large cotton-like tufts which drift away in the wind, carrying the tree's seeds with them. And during the fall the trees are blanketed with large pink and white flowers. The grounds of the Hospital Eirene in Filadelfia (*Tel: 0491 32194, about one kilometer down Calle Trébol*) and Neuland's main plaza offer excellent and quirky looking examples of *palo borracho* trees.

As you pass Filadelfia, the conditions of the Trans Chaco Highway deteriorate as the road reaches the city of Mariscal Estigarribia. Every year the nearby community of Santa Teresita holds their Arete Guazú festival in celebration of the harvest. Though Paraguay has a significant indigenous population, this festival is one of the few indigenous ceremonies that can be relatively easily witnessed by tourists. Mariscal Estigarribia is home to a major military base and the immigration and customs check point for those continuing on to (or entering Paraguay from) Bolivia.

Rutherford B. Hayes: Paraguay's Favorite American President

Many Americans are bemused when they learn that one of Paraguay's largest departments is named after American president, Rutherford B. Hayes. The 19th president of the United States played an extremely important role in Paraguayan history. In the aftermath of the disastrous Triple Alliance War, there remained several disputes over territory between Paraguay and the victors of war (primarily Brazil and Argentina). One such case was a large part of the Chaco to which Argentina laid claim. The region was to be divided into three sections. The territory between the Bermejo River and the Pilcomayo River was to pass into Argentine hands. The territory between the Verde River (just north of current day Pozo Colorado in the Central Chaco) and Bahía Negra (the northernmost border of Paraguay) would remain in Paraguayan hands, and the territory between the Pilcomayo River and the Verde River was to be submitted to international arbitrage by President Rutherford B. Hayes. In 1878 the American president ruled in favor of Paraguay, a decision which allowed Paraguay to retain a significant portion of the Chaco. Thus the department was named after the American president who is probably more revered and well-known in Paraguay than in his homeland.

Past Mariscal Estigarriba the Chaco is a veritable no-man's land where few Paraguayans and even fewer tourists venture. Buses to Santa Cruz, Bolivia continue north and then turn off the Trans Chaco highway, heading west towards Mayor Infante Rivarola, the last stop before the border. A dirt road turns off towards the wilderness north of Mariscal Estigarriba to the remote Defensores del Chaco national park. Adventurous nature observers head here in the hopes of spotting jaguars and other endangered animals. Continuing north from Mariscal Estigarriba along the Trans Chaco highway one arrives at the smaller and often overlooked Teniente Enciso national park. Past this point, the road is traveled only by infrequent trucks transporting livestock from remote northern ranches and cargo trucks bringing in merchandise (both legal and otherwise) from neighboring Bolivia and Brazil.

> Although there are a handful of ATM machines in the Mennonite colonies, it is best to travel with enough cash to cover expected and unexpected expenses, especially if driving.

A land of extremes, the Chaco takes its toll on visitors – those who wish to brave the wild on their own must be extremely careful, while the comforts of a private tour come with a steep price tag. Although expensive, hiring a private guide is a worthwhile option for those interested in nature observation. With the exception of birds and armadillos, animals are rarely spotted along the main road. Traveling with an experienced guide will increase your likelihood of seeing wild animals. Private guides can facilitate visits to parks and reserves as well as private properties (such as ranches and private nature reserves) where fauna is known to be abundant. In addition, reputable guides will be adequately prepared for any eventualities along the

Driving in the Chaco

The Chaco presents drivers with a series of challenges. The Trans Chaco Highway is a two lane road (one in either direction) stretching straight into the horizon without a bend in sight making it very difficult to judge the distance of oncoming vehicles. At night the road is illuminated only sporadically. The condition of the road itself is fairly decent until Filadelfia but begins to deteriorate thereafter (especially once past Mariscal Estigarriba). In the Northern (*Alto*/Dry) Chaco, the dusty clay ground leads to a phenomenon known as "*talcal*," in which the road is covered with slippery dust. Military officers at Mariscal Estigarriba's base jokingly refer to a nearby *talcal*-covered road as the "*tunel del tiempo*" (the time tunnel) because once you start on it you never know when you will make it to the end. In addition to slowing down driving, the fine *talcal* can also obscure serious potholes. Approximately 120 kilometers north of Mariscal Estigarriba, the pavement ends and the *talcal* begins, giving way to sandy ground as one travels further north. It is generally unwise to veer off the asphalted road (even in and around the Mennonite communities) without a 4-wheel drive vehicle.

Adequate supplies, especially water and fuel should be packed. A good rule of thumb is to take at least one gallon (four liters) of water per person per day plus extra for the car radiator in case of overheating. Most Chaco experts recommend traveling with two spare tires. Between the potholes on the Trans Chaco Highway and plants with massive thorns (some up to a couple inches in length and thicker around than a ball point pen) along the side roads, it is better to be safe than sorry. Should you need them, spare parts for popular model vehicles can be obtained in the Mennonite colonies.

way. Fauna Paraguay, Guyra Paraguay, Hans Fast, and Gran Chaco Tours, the last two based out of Filadelfia, are good options (see Chaco Tour Guides, p288). Striking out on your own in the Chaco can be prohibitive both in terms of scheduling and expenses. Of the sites mentioned above, only the Mennonite museums are accessible by reliable and frequent public transportation. Public transportation to national parks is sporadic, especially during the summer when both climate and road conditions are grueling. Whether traveling by private vehicle or relying on buses, proper precautions must be taken when going off the main road (see Driving in the Chaco, p284). The Chaco is sparsely populated with few places to stock up on provisions beyond the Mennonite colonies (Mariscal Estigarribia is the last dependable source for fuel), so it is absolutely essential to pack a surplus of supplies.

Many backpackers mistakenly believe they will be able to catch a glimpse of the Paraguayan Chaco while traveling via bus to Santa Cruz, Bolivia. Unfortunately these buses depart from Asunción in the afternoon, reaching the Chaco once the sun has gone down. If you wish to continue on to Bolivia after exploring the Chaco, buses headed to Santa Cruz pick up passengers in Mariscal Estigarribia.

Recommended bus companies: Both Nasa-Golondrina and Stel Turismo have buses that service the Chaco's most populated towns. Buses tend to be either sweltering or freezing depending on whether the A/C is working.

Major bus stops along the Trans Chaco Highway: Villa Hayes, Pozo Colorado (turn off to Concepción), Filadelfia, Mariscal Estigarribia.

The Chaco's Lifeline

Construction on the Trans Chaco highway began in 1956. The road proved essential for the economic development of the area, especially for the Mennonite colonies. Much of the assistance for the road's construction came from the Mennonites themselves in the form of the "Pax Boys," participants in the Mennonite Central Committee's conscientious objector program (known as PAX). Over fifty "Pax Boys" came to Paraguay to help build the Trans Chaco Highway. Until the highway reached the Mennonite colonies in 1961, goods were transported to Asunción by way of the Paraguay River, a journey which took days to complete. Today, the Trans Chaco Highway remains the only major paved road in the Paraguayan Chaco and is a lifeline for the region's inhabitants. Mennonites and ranchers transport their dairy products (over 50 percent of Paraguay's dairy production), crops, and cattle to Asunción on enormous trucks while the region's indigenous inhabitants travel along the road as they emigrate from remote villages to the city in search of employment. In addition, the road is a key transportation route for goods entering and exiting Bolivia.

Departamento Presidente Hayes

CHACO'I

Chaco'i is an excellent choice for a quick and easy taste of the humid (*bajo*) Chaco. Though technically in the Chaco, this small community is easier accessed by boat from the port of Asunción (see Sports and Exploring Asuncion's Natural Side, p140).

Old Lady Tree
The Guaigui Piré (Ruprechtia triflora) tree's name means "old lady skin" in Guaraní in reference to the tight curls of bark that peel off the tree's trunk.

ESCUELA AGRICOLA SAN FRANCISCO

Run by the Paraguayan NGO, Fundación Paraguay, the Escuela Agrícola San Fransisco is a boarding school and model farm where high school students from all over the country learn sustainable farming techniques. All of the farm's products are organic, and environmental conservation techniques such as solar cooking and heating are practiced. In addition, the school has recently started a tourism training program, and guests are able to stay overnight in the hotel run by students and faculty. As you stroll the grounds be sure to look upwards to catch a glimpse of monkeys in the trees. The farm is an easy day trip from Asunción by car or bus. It is best to visit during the week since most students return home on the weekends. There is also a small indigenous community next to the turn off to the school along the Trans Chaco that sells handicrafts. If you can't make the trip, you can still support the school by visiting their stand in Asunción's Agroshopping farmer's market (see Agroshopping, p129). One of the most popular items is the farm's deliciously rich Cerrito brand dulce de leche. *Tel: 0271 272 223, Ruta Transchaco km 46.5 on the left-hand side (if coming from Asunción), you will see the school's yellow roadside stand (sign reads Parador Cerrito) after which you turn left and follow a dirt road approximately one mile until you reach the school campus, by bus catch the "La Chaqueña" bus along Calle Brazil in Asunción and ride it to the end of the line (approximately two hours), www.fundacionparaguaya.org.py, guided tours Gs. 20,000 per person, Double Gs. 60,000 per person, Wi-Fi*

ESCUELA PAÍ PUKU

After hours of driving along the Trans Chaco Highway, the Escuela Paí Puku is an interesting and heartwarming stop. This boarding school was created by a Belgian priest in 1965 (presumably he was tall, as Paí Puku means "tall priest" in Guaraní) to

---

Water in the Chaco: A Precious Resource

Fresh drinking water is fundamental for both humans' and animals' survival in the Chaco. During the Chaco War, major battles were fought in order to maintain access to fresh water lagoons, and dehydration was one of the main causes of death among soldiers. It is no coincidence that today the Chaco's main population centers are near fresh water sources. During the dry season, droughts are often so severe that cattle ranchers are unable to keep their livestock from dying of thirst. For indigenous communities relocated to remote areas, survival is highly dependent on motorized water pumps installed by the government.

Given the scarcity of this resource a variety of water collection methods are employed. Many people dig artificial ponds known as "*tajamares*." Buildings are often fitted with rooftop gutters which channel water into above ground tanks. Another option is a system known as a "*tanque Australiano*," whereby windmills are used to pump water into a raised pond. When traditional water sources run dry, indigenous peoples still living in the wild often find themselves forced to leave the forest in search of water and end up drinking from water collection ponds in nearby cattle ranches.

With the Chaco's population reaching unsustainable levels, water collection is only one piece of the puzzle. As of 2010 there were a number of desalinization plants operating in the region, and there are plans to create an aqueduct to transport water from the Paraguay River to the Mennonite colonies.

educate children of the region whose parents mostly live and work in the surrounding cattle ranches (*estancias*). For nine months out of the year, students learn skills such as carpentry, dressmaking, nursing, plumbing, and electrical work. The school's wood work shop is well known throughout Paraguay as a source of unique and well-made furniture. In typical Chaco fashion, the school's buildings themselves are constructed almost entirely out of *karanda'y* (palm) logs which look a lot like toy Lincoln Logs. While visiting, be sure to check out the kitchen where an enormous cauldron hangs over a roaring fire as teachers prepare food for their 500 plus students. Donations in the form of school supplies are a nice way to repay the school for an informal tour. *Tel: 0971 369 890, 0971 293 739, Ruta Trans Chaco km 157, www.paipuku.org*

PARADOR PIRAHU

An obligatory stop, Parador Pirahu has developed an almost religious following amongst Trans Chaco Highway regulars who enjoy the pit stop's delicious food and unique diner-style ambience. The extensive menu includes a wide variety of *empanadas* and garlic sticks that pack a punch. Reliably clean bathrooms are an additional (and important) bonus. There is also an adjacent hotel which mostly caters to long haul truck drivers. *Tel: 0991 700 683, Asunción office 021 228 859, Ruta Trans Chaco km 249 (about twenty kilometers before Pozo Colorado), daily 6:30am – 8:30pm, Gs. 3,000-30,000, room rates: Triple Gs. 160,000, TV, A/C*

POZO COLORADO

Pozo Colorado marks the crossroads with Route 5 which heads east crossing over the Paraguay River to the city of Concepción. Unless you are stopping for gas or to catch a bus to Concepción, there is little reason to stop here. Most Trans Chaco buses make pit stops in Pozo Colorado. If you travel on one of these buses, don't dawdle as they have been known to leave passengers behind.

Departamento Boquerón

FILADELFIA

As the capital of the Boquerón Department, Filadelfia is the epicenter of activity in the Central Chaco. It is the administrative center of the Fernheim colony which was founded by Russian Mennonites in 1930. Today, with its banks, supermarkets, gas stations, hotels, and restaurants, Filadelfia is an oasis of modernity just off the desolate Trans Chaco Highway. Though most Paraguayans associate Filadelfia with the Mennonites, there are a number of non-Mennonite residents as well. Walking down the wide, dusty streets you are as likely to see blonde farmers in overalls, as modern looking Paraguayans speaking on cell phones, and indigenous women wearing long skirts decorated with bright cartoonish prints. Indigenous and *mestizo* Paraguayans as well as Brazilians have been attracted to the area by the prospect of job opportunities. As with most Mennonite communities in Paraguay, Filadelfia is highly segregated with the majority of non-Mennonites living in the Barrio Amistad neighborhood and the city's indigenous residents living in Barrio Villa Guaraní. Here, houses are rudimentary, made of brick and corrugated tin roofs. Across town in the Mennonite neighborhoods, there are large German style houses with picket

The Chaco

fences and well tended gardens. The Emerald City of the Paraguayan Chaco, Filadelfia is a strange but interesting place.

Of the Mennonite colonies, Filadelfia is the most frequented by tourists. Aside from the museum, however, there is little to see. Filadelfia is best used as a base of operations for nature visits. Though pricier than Asunción, this is a good place to stock up on supplies before heading into the wilderness. Those particularly interested in Mennonite history can take public or private transportation to visit the museums of neighboring Loma Plata and Neuland (though for the average tourist, Filadelfia's nicely organized museum will suffice). If your visit coincides with carnival (usually held between late January and early March), be sure to head over to the indigenous neighborhood to participate in the Arete Guazú (see The Arete Guazú, p295). This is one of the few times when it is easy to interact with the local indigenous communities (for an even more unique experience, head to the Arete Guazú in Santa Teresita, just south of Mariscal Estigarribia).

Almost all of Filadelfia's businesses are located along Avenida Hindenburg, one of the town's few paved roads. This main drag is flanked by two large monuments. The first monument at the entrance to town is named "Living and Growing Together" and was built in celebration of the Fernheim colony's seventy-fifth anniversary. It features stylized forms representing the various ethnic groups that live in the area, all facing a large cross. Towards the other end of town is a similarly abstract monument to the fiftieth anniversary of the colony's founding.

Chaco Tour Guides

Hans Fast A gregarious middle-aged gentleman, Hans Fast is one of the region's leading guides with several decades of experience. If he is unable to take you himself, Hans will be able to connect you with the right people to make the most of your Chaco experience. *Tel: 0492 52422, 0981 203 375, hfast@tigo.com.py (Though he is listed here, technically Hans Fast lives in Loma Plata)*

Cattle Ranching in the Chaco

Despite the many obstacles it presents, the Paraguayan Chaco has become increasingly exploited by large scale cattle ranchers. What makes the land in this remote corner of South America so attractive is its comparatively low cost. A tract of land in the Paraguayan Chaco can cost as little as half the price of comparable land in neighboring Argentina and Brazil. In addition, soil conditions are such that grass grows readily (especially popular varieties such as Gatton Panic and Tanzania which are ideally suited to hot climates), providing abundant food for cattle. In fact, the grass can sometimes grow high enough for the cows to get lost in it and die of thirst. In many regions of the world, grass-fed cattle may require up to twenty hectares per head. However, in the Paraguayan Chaco, cattle ranchers are generally able to allocate about one hectare per head of cattle. Given the region's intense heat, it is no surprise that most cattle ranchers favor breeds of cattle able to survive in high temperatures such as Nelore or Brahma (both originally from India). The heat does have its benefits though, most notably the lack of parasites. Unlike cows raised in Eastern Paraguay, which reach market weight in three years, Chaco cattle are often ready for slaughter in two years.

Though land prices are cheap in the Chaco, the upfront costs for setting up a cattle ranch in this region are very high. Roads must be created, landing strips cleared, fences erected, and wells dug. With the exception of a small number of wealthy Paraguayans, the cattle industry in this region is largely dominated by Mennonites and Brazilian *estancieros*.

Gran Chaco Turismo The only full scale tourism operator in the region, Gran Chaco Turismo offers reasonably priced day trips to nearby attractions as well as longer tours to points further afield. English, German, and Spanish are spoken. This is your best bet for arranging tours on short notice. Owner Norbert Epp can help coordinate small groups and single travelers with flexible schedules into a joint tour for price savings. *Tel: 0491 432 944, 0981 223 974, Avenida Hindenburg 247-S between Unruh and Industrial, www.granchacoturismo.net*

Fernheim Cooperative Tourism Office A good resource for information about the Mennonite colonies themselves, the Fernheim Cooperative's tourism office has plenty of reference materials on hand. Office manager, Agate Harder (nicknamed "Gati"), can arrange tours within Filadelfia and speaks English, German, and Spanish. *Tel: 0491 417 380, 0985 820 746, Avenida Hindenburg between Calle Trebol and Calle Unruh, behind the Jakob Unger Museum, turismo@fernheim.com.py, Mon-Fri 7am-11am*

Museo Jakob Unger

A very good museum spread over two buildings. The main building, constructed in 1933, is one of the few remaining original administrative houses from the Fernheim cooperative. Out front stands a large saw, the first machine in the community saw mill. Inside there are many artifacts from the original colonists including the first printing press used to print the Mennonite newspaper "Mennoblatt," still in existence. The second floor houses objects from the Chaco War, a collection of photos documenting the immigration of Mennonites to the Chaco, and photos from the construction of the Trans Chaco Highway. There is also an enormous excavated glyptodon, an ancient mammal that resembles an armadillo on steroids. Exiting the main building and walking through the park, you will find the second building dedicated to the Chaco's natural history. The museum houses an impressive collection of stuffed animals from the Chaco, all set against picturesque Chaco landscapes. Animals are well-labeled, so visiting the museum is an excellent way to learn about the region's fauna. The back room is dedicated to the various indigenous groups (Ayoreo, Enlet, and Aché) that predated the Mennonite's arrival to the Chaco and includes utilitarian objects, textiles, feathered headdresses, handicrafts, weapons, and ceramics. The park surrounding the museums is nice as well, with several large examples of the quirky palo borracho tree (see The Palo Borracho, p283). *Tel: 0491 417000, Corner of Hindenburg and Unruh, turismo@fernheim.com.py, Mon-Sat 7am-11:30am (consult with the tourism office or the reception desk at Hotel Florida ahead of time if you'd like to visit the museum after hours).*

Centro Chaqueño para la Conservación e Investigación

Formerly known as the Proyecto Taguá, this research center is dedicated to the conservation of the Chacoan peccary (known as "*taguá*" in Spanish and Guaraní.) The pens at Proyecto Taguá allow you to see three different species of peccaries up close. Signs by the pens provide a decent amount of information about the peccaries, so it is worth visiting even if the center's director Juan Campos is not able to guide you himself. There is a newly built guest house with two dorm rooms and kitchen for visitors. The center's location makes this an ideal place for nature enthusiasts who cannot afford guided trips into the Chaco (be sure to bring food supplies as the nearest stores are in Filadelfia). The center is also an excellent option for those interested in the Chaco War but without the time or money to visit Fortín Boquerón. Just to the left of the center's main gate is Fortín Toledo, a series of trenches from the Chaco War. Follow the path as it leads above and into the trenches and past a military cemetery. *Tel: 0971 107 200 or Sr. Victor Robles at 0981 263 078 for reservations, at km 475 of the Trans Chaco highway turn left (if coming from Asunción) and continue approximately nine kilometers following the signs to the center. If coming from the center of Filadelfia you can reach the Trans Chaco Highway by taking a left at the intersection of Avenida Hindenburg and Calle Trebol, continuing down Calle Trebol past the Sanatorio Eirene about twenty-five kilometers. From here cross the Trans Chaco and continue as indicated above, Gs. 100,000 per person, fan, kitchen access*

Lodging

Hotel Florida The nicest and most centrally located of Filadelfia's lodging options, the Hotel Filadelfia is popular with tourists and other visitors to the area. Taking a refreshing dip in the pool and grabbing a bite to eat in the courtyard under the shade of a large guava tree are excellent ways to take the edge off a hot and dusty day of sightseeing in the Chaco. Rooms on the high end are fancy, while basic rooms with shared bathrooms and fans instead of A/C are a good deal for those on a budget (reserve these early as they fill up fast). *Tel 0491 432 151/5, Avda. Hindenburg Nr. 165-S across the street from the Fernheim Cooperative offices and the Jakob Unger Museum, www.hotelfloridachaco.com, Single Gs. 145,000-200,000, Double Gs. 190,000-280,000, Triple Gs. 240,000-300,000, budget rooms Gs. 50,000-70,000 per person, breakfast not included with cheaper rooms but available for Gs. 23,000, TV, A/C, mini-fridge, fan, pool, Wi-Fi*

Hotel Golondrina Centro Though lacking the ambience (and pool) of Hotel Florida, Hotel Golondrina Centro is a good second choice. Rooms are comfortable, and there are also cheaper options for those who want to forgo the comforts of a TV, mini-fridge or A/C (a money saver recommended for winter months only). *Tel: 0491 432 218, Calle Industrial 149-E, www.hotelgolondrina.com, Single Gs. 90,000-120,000 w A/C, Double Gs. 145,000-195,000, Budget rooms with fan, shared bath and no breakfast: Single Gs. 55,000, Double Gs. 100,000, computer with internet, TV, A/C*

Hotel Golondrina Avenida Located a few blocks from the center of town along the main drag, this hotel gets the job done with basic rooms at a low cost. *Tel: 0491 432 643, 0491 433 111, Avenida Hindenburg 635-S, www.hotelgolondrina.com, Single Gs. 90,000-105,000 w A/C, Double Gs. 145,000-170,000, Budget rooms with fan, shared bath and no breakfast: Single Gs. 55,000, Double Gs. 100,000, computer with internet, TV, A/C*

Hospedaje Los Delfines A run down budget option popular with area truckers and laborers. While rooms are inexpensive, you get what you pay for. However, this is the one place where you are more likely to meet average non-Mennonite *Chaqueños*. Some travelers may be willing to give up comforts for this unique cultural experience. Not recommended for solo female travelers. *Tel: 0491 432 376, Corner of Unruh and Miller, Double Gs.35,000 shared bath and fan, Gs. 50,000 private bath and A/C*

Hotel Touring Club Run by the Touring and Automobile Club this hotel is very modern and airy. Facilities include a restaurant, large pool, and covered grilling area (known as a "*quincho*"). Rooms are comfortable and well appointed. As this hotel is located along the Trans Chaco Highway before the entrance to Filadelfia, it is only a practical option for those in private vehicles. As with all area hotels, expect it to be packed to capacity during the Trans Chaco Rally. *Tel: 0493 240 611, hoteltouringclub@hotmail.com, km 443 Ruta Trans Chaco by the turn off to Filadelfia. Single Gs. 120,000, Double Gs. 160,000, Triple Gs. 240,000, TV, A/C, pool*

Food

Girasol Churrasquería Filadelfia's most popular (and most expensive) restaurant. There is a buffet, and the meat options flow freely. *Tel: 0491 32078, Unruh between Hindenburg and O Miller, daily_ 11am-1:30pm 6pm-11pm, Gs. 40,000-60,000*

El Rincon Under the same management as Girasol, El Rincón is a similarly good restaurant tucked away in the Portal del Chaco mini mall. Menu includes pastas, pizzas, and fast food. The house specialty is the all you can eat *picaña corrido* meat platter. *Tel: 0491 432 496, 0981 876 935, corner of Avenida Hindenburg and Calle Amistad, daily 11am-2pm, 6pm-12am, Gs. 45,000-60,000*

Restaurant Hotel Florida The hotel's restaurant is quite good and popular with guests and non-guests alike. Pizzas are a tasty and affordable option. During the cooler hours of the night, dining in the hotel's courtyard can be pleasant. *Tel 0491 432 151/5, Avda. Hindenburg Nr. 165-S across the street from the Fernheim Cooperative offices and the Jakob Unger Museum, www.hotelfloridachaco.com, restaurant hours daily 6am-10pm, Gs. 30,000-60,000*

Supermercado Cooperativa Fernheim The storefront for the Fernheim Cooperative is worth visiting to see the wide variety of goods produced in this Mennonite colony as well as the various items imported from Europe. There are also a number of reference materials on the Chaco and the Mennonite colonies in both English and German. *Tel: 0491 417 000, corner of Avenida Hindenburg and Calle Unruh, Mon-Sat 6am-11: 30, 2pm-6pm*

Supermercado Boquerón A surprisingly large supermarket with a variety and selection rivaling that of supermarkets in Asunción. The adjoining food court has a buffet as well as a la carte options. Of Filadelfia's restaurants, this is the most affordable. *Tel: 0491 432 128, Corner of Boquerón and O Miller, daily 7am-12pm, 2:30pm-8pm, Gs. 45,000-60,000*

Getting There

The turn off to Filadelfia is located at km 443 of the Trans Chaco Highway. From here, take a right and continue for approximately fourteen kilometers. The entrance to town is marked by a large cement sculpture commemorating the seventy-fifth anniversary of Filadelfia's founding.

Both Nasa-Golondrina (*Tel: 021 551 731*) and Stel Turismo (*Tel: 021 551 647*) operate daily buses from Asunción to Filadelfia. Tickets cost between Gs. 65,000 and 70,000. Most buses leave Asunción in the late evening or night, arriving in Filadelfia in the wee hours (the bus ride takes six to seven hours). Buses run along Avenida Hindenburg past both Hotel Golondrina Avenida and Hotel Florida. Travelers continuing on to Bolivia can take a Nasa-Golondrina bus to Mariscal Estigarribia and catch buses to Bolivia at the Immigration and Customs checkpoint. The Nasa-Golondrina bus terminal (*Tel: 0491 432 492*) is located on Chaco Boreal and O'Miller.

LOMA PLATA

This remote region of Paraguay was first scouted out by a group of Canadian Mennonites as a possible location for a new colony in 1921. Six years later, the colony of Menno was established. Yet the colony's journey to their new home was anything but easy. Financed by American and Canadian Mennonites, the small group of immigrants voyaged from Canada to Buenos Aires, Argentina, by ship. They then travelled by ship up the Paraguay River to the town of Puerto Casado in the Paraguayan Chaco. At the time, Puerto Casado was the epicenter of the Chaco's tannin industry (see Carlos Casado and the Tannin Industry, p314). The settlers were forced to remain in Puerto Casado for a full year while the Paraguayan government prepared the official land grant. During this time, the settlers suffered many hardships including a massive typhoid outbreak which killed ten percent of the community and caused many more to despair and abandon the mission. The final trek to their new home was another odyssey. The first 145 kilometers were done on the Carlos Casado company railroad, normally used to transport enormous *quebracho* tree trunks to the riverside tannin

The Chaco

factory. The Mennonites had to travel the remaining one hundred kilometers through the wilderness by horse drawn carts and on foot.

Despite the many hardships they faced, the colonists managed to turn Loma Plata into a thriving town. The city functions as the administrative center for Chortitzer Cooperative (*www.chortitzer.com.py*) which distributes the popular Trebol brand of dairy products. The journey of the original scouting team and first group of settlers is depicted in the cooperative's museum in the center of town. Tours of the Trebol factory can be arranged through the cooperative's tourism office. The citizens of Loma Plata make regular trips to Canada which means you are more likely to run into more English speaking Mennonites here than in the other colonies. However, of the three colonies, Loma Plata also has the reputation for being the most traditional and closed off to foreigners.

Coopertiva Chortitzer Komitee Tourism Office Walter Raltzalf can help arrange for tours of the town's free museum, the Trebol dairy factory (approximately Gs. 150,000) and the Isla Po'i experimental farm. *Tel: 0492 52301/401/501, Avenida Central next to the museum, turismo@lp.chortitzer.com.py*

The Mennonites

It is hard to find a greater testament to the value of perseverance, sacrifice, and team work than the successful Mennonite colonies in the Chaco region. Arriving in a remote and foreign land with few resources to their name, the Mennonites fought against the odds and within a few generations were at the head of some of Paraguay's most important industries.

The Mennonites branched off from the Catholic faith in the 16th century. Lead by the Dutchman, Menno Simons (a former Catholic priest), the Mennonites believe in separation of church and state, pacifism, and reject infant baptism in favor of adult baptisms. These controversial stances made the Mennonites targets of religious persecution in Holland and Germany and forced them into a nomadic existence. At first they sought refuge in Prussia and later Russia, from which they then immigrated in waves between the 1870's and 1930's to several countries in North and South America, including Canada, the United States, Mexico, Argentina, Brazil, Uruguay, and Paraguay.

During the late 1920's Mennonites from Canada began to explore the possibility of setting up a new colony in Paraguay. Given the looming territory dispute with Bolivia, Paraguay was eager to accept the new settlers, hoping that their presence would establish a foothold in the Paraguayan Chaco (at the time populated only by a small handful of indigenous tribes). The government promised the Mennonites exemption from military service, freedom of religion, and the freedom to run their own education system. The colony of Loma Plata was established in 1927, and in 1930 a second group of immigrants, this time directly from Russia, settled in Filadelfia. Though they were in one of the most remote corners of the country, the Mennonites did not remain isolated for long. In 1932, war was declared with Bolivia and troops descended upon the region. Ironically, having spent their lives preaching pacifism, the Mennonites now found themselves in an active combat zone. The war proved providential for the Mennonite colonies though. Previously unable to get their goods to market in Asunción, the Mennonites were now able to sell all manner of provisions to the Paraguayan army. Mennonite assistance in the form of food, water, and roads, proved essential to the Paraguayan army during the war.

Museo Histórico de la Colonia Menno

Though small, this museum has a very nice selection of photos documenting the history of the Menno colony. The journey of the original scouting team from 1921 receives special attention with vivid descriptions, photos, and even the original map presented to the potential colonists. There is also a map detailing the route taken through the Paraguayan Chaco to arrive at Loma Plata. Other photos depict many different aspects of life in the Mennonite colonies from education to farming. *Tel: 0492 52301, Avenida Central next to the Chortitzer Cooperative, Mon-Fri 7am-11am, 2pm-6pm (to visit on weekends contact Walter Ratzalff at the cooperative's tourism office)*

Salt Water Lagoons of Riacho Yakaré Sur

The basin of Riacho Yakaré Sur is a system of interconnected lagoons in the Central Chaco. These lagoons are excellent for nature observation, especially for spotting birds. From April to September, flocks of Chilean flamingoes can be found and from August to November many migratory birds can be spotted. The most visited reserve is Campo María, owned by Loma Plata's Chortizer Komitee. Campo María possesses a large wooden observation tower from which one can appreciate the extent of the

---

Menonites continued…

One of the keys to their success was the cooperative system, whereby everyone works together in an organized fashion towards common goals. In addition to the influx of income generated by the Chaco War, the colonies also received assistance from more established Mennonite communities abroad. Donated farming and well digging machinery allowed for large steps forward, as did technical assistance from foreign-educated agronomists. Even the Trans Chaco Highway, vital lifeline to Asunción, was built with the help of foreign Mennonites (see The Trans Chaco Highway, p282). In 1947, a third colony was established in Neuland. The 1960's brought access to credit which allowed for the adoption of mechanized farming.

Today supermarkets countrywide are stocked with products from the Mennonite cooperatives, such as Co-op and Trebol dairy products and Oschi meats. Crops such as peanuts, sorgum, cotton, and sesame are grown for national and international consumption. The cooperatives' dairy factories produce over two-thirds of the milk products consumed in Paraguay. Cattle ranching has recently become popular and profitable with over 80 percent of local beef exported to foreign markets.

Although they are of European descent and maintain their cultural heritage, many Mennonites do in fact consider themselves to be Paraguayan. Many have taken on Paraguayan traditions such as speaking Guaraní, eating *asado*, drinking *tereré*, and retiring for a midday *siesta*. With new generations the rigid traditions and boundaries of the original colonists have become more flexible. Many Mennonite youth go to Asunción or even abroad to study in a university before returning to the Chaco. The advent of cell phones, television, and motorcycles has further weakened the grip of the old guard. However, in many respects the Mennonites remain a traditional bunch, closed off from the rest of Paraguayan society. Intermarriage with non-Mennonite Paraguayans is rare and relations with indigenous workers are strained. In fact, most visitors to the colonies will be surprised at the cool reception they are given by locals.

Perhaps due to its status as the department capital, tourists will find Filadelfia the most welcoming and worth visiting of the colonies. Those with a particular interest in the history of the Mennonites may be interested in visiting Neuland or Loma Plata as well, each with its own small museum. Visitors should keep in mind that due to their religious nature, life comes to a complete halt on Sunday in all three Mennonite colonies.

The Chaco

lagoon. Laguna Chaco Lodge is the largest of the Chaco's lagoons and has been designated as a Ramsar site. During the dry season these lagoons can dry up completely leaving behind large expanses of salt covered soil. These sights are best visited with guides as they are on private property and can be difficult to access. In addition, local guides will be knowledgeable about which lagoon is currently sporting more wildlife.

Isla Po'i

Isla Po'i is the Chortitzer Cooperative's experimental farm. A variety of tests are performed here to determine the best conditions for the cooperative's current crops. Potential new crops are also grown on the farm and studied extensively before being approved for planting by cooperative members. The sixty-two hectare experimental farm has fields of fruit trees, pasture, ornamental trees, and crops such as cotton, peanuts, and sesame. The farm is an excellent example of the high value Mennonite farmers place on education and research. As guided tours are not readily offered to the public, Isla Po'i is best visited with a tour guide.

Lodging

Hotel Loma Plata Inn Without a doubt the nicest hotel in Loma Plata. Rooms are large with comfortable beds, and there is a wide breakfast selection as well as free internet use. There are future plans for a pool. Despite being on the far end of town, this hotel is the most centrally located and closest to the Nasa-Golondrina bus office. *Tel 0492 253 235, 0492 60983, Corner of Eligio Ayala and Manuel Gondra (behind the Chaco's Grill restaurant), Single Gs. 130,000-150,000, Double Gs. 180,000-200,000, Wi-Fi, TV, A/C*

Hotel Mora A large facility, Hotel Mora is a good option for those who want to enjoy the outdoors (there's plenty of shade). Rooms are spacious and spotless. Owner's Spanish is very limited. This hotel is a ways outside of town and is therefore not convenient for those relying on public transportation (though they have a taxi service). *Tel: 0492 52255, Calle Sandstrasse 803, follow signs from main rotary, Single Gs. 85,000, Double Gs. 120,000-170,000, TV, A/C, mini-fridge*

Eating

Churrasquería Chaco's Grill A great place to kick back and relax while pigging out on plate after plate of juicy, locally raised beef. Compliment your all-you-can-eat meat with the salad bar and an ice-cold beer. *Tel 0492 252 166, Eligio Ayala and Manuel Gondra in front of the Hotel Loma Plata Inn, Tue-Sun 11:30am-2pm, 7pm-11pm,Gs. 62,000*

Getting There

The turn off to Loma Plata is located at km 423 of the Trans Chaco Highway and is marked with a large highway sign. From here Loma Plata is twenty-two kilometers down a paved road to the right (if coming from the south). There is also a road connecting Filadelfia to Loma Plata. From the center of Filadelfia, drive to the intersection of Avenida Hindenburg and Calle Trebol and take a right continuing approximately twenty kilometers (the road will quickly revert from paved to dirt) until the right-hand turn off that leads approximately five kilometers to the center of town.

Nasa-Golondrina (*Tel: 0492 52521 in Loma Plata*) runs a daily service from Asunción (Gs. 70,000) as well as a couple of daily buses from Filadelfia.

Mennonite & Indigenous Relations

When the Mennonites first arrived, the Enlet and Nivacle tribes frequented the area. Since the establishment of the Mennonite colonies, the region's indigenous population has grown; most are drawn to the area in search of employment opportunities. The Mennonites have encouraged the indigenous to settle and adopt Christianity, although notably they have been encouraged to set up parallel towns rather than mix with the Mennonites themselves. The ASCIM or *Asociación de Servicios de Cooperación Indígena Mennonita* (www.ascim.org) was created to foster Mennonite-indigenous relations and provide indigenous with their own land and assistance in matters of health, education, and agriculture. However, many are quick to point out that the benefits of such organizations only reach indigenous groups willing to give up their traditional beliefs and practices. In general, Mennonite-indigenous relations are a touchy subject and therefore best not to be brought up in conversation with area tour guides.

NEULAND

The newest of the Chaco's Mennonite colonies, Neuland was founded in 1947 by Mennonites escaping religious persecution in the Soviet Union. At 2,474 people, Neuland was the largest of the area's colonies. The majority of Neuland's original settlers were women, the Mennonite men having been sentenced to Siberian work camps. These women fled from the Soviet Union to Germany, from where they were then allowed to immigrate to Paraguay. Today Neuland is home to the Cooperativa Multiactiva Neuland (*www.neuland.com.py*) which produces Co-op dairy products, as well as beef, fish, and crops such as peanuts and sesame. The town's plaza and museum are nicely done, though only those truly intrigued by the Mennonites will find this to be enough of a reason to visit Neuland. For most a better reason is its proximity to the Chaco's most well known battle ground, Fortín Boquerón. Travelers on a budget can save money by taking a bus to Neuland and travel by taxi to Fortín Boquerón, twenty-seven kilometers away.

Cooperativa Neuland Tourism Office Manned by the charismatic and enthusiastic Heinz Weibe. He is more than happy to lead visitors on a tour of the cooperative offices, museum, and town plaza. Be sure to call ahead to make sure Mr. Weibe is available, as his vivid descriptions of life in Neuland are what make the tour worthwhile. *Tel: 0493 240 201/4, 0971 701 634, Office is located within the cooperative headquarters, hweibe@neuland.com.py*

Parque Chaco Boreal

This small, nicely maintained plaza next to the cooperative is the site of three commemorative statues. The first statue is of a Mennonite woman working the land and is located in the main plaza. The statue is an homage to the widowed women who came to Paraguay seeking a new future. The second and third are memorials for the twenty-fifth and fiftieth anniversary of the colony's founding. On the far end of the plaza, there is a well-digging machine donated to the colony by Dutch Mennonites in 1967. This machine was used to dig more than 1000 wells in the area, a key improvement for the colonists (who were hand digging wells at that time). Nearby is Freundschaft Park which has been left in a natural state in order for visitors to have an idea of what the area looked like when the Mennonites arrived.

Museo Histórico de la Colonia Neuland

Of the three Mennonite museums in the Chaco, Neuland's gives the best idea of life as one of the region's original settlers. The museum has been set up to resemble a typical Mennonite dwelling with a main house, a covered barn for farming equipment, and a separate building for the kitchen. Inside you will find various items used by the Mennonites upon their arrival including butter churns, sausage fillers, and many handmade objects and inventions that are a testament to their "make it work" attitude. Particularly interesting are the large egg incubators used to transport eggs during the week-long journey to the market in Asunción and a strange machine created to make ceramic bricks and tiles (including those used to build the museum). *Tel: 0493 240 201/4, 0971 701 634, tours must be arranged with the Cooperativa Multiactiva Neuland's tourism office*

Getting There

The turn off to Neuland is on km 450 of the Trans Chaco Highway. From here turn left (if coming from Asunción) and continue for about twenty-five kilometers down the paved road that leads to the center of town.

Stel Turismo (*Tel: 021 558 196*) runs daily buses from Asunción, Gs. 80,000, and Nasa-Golondrina (*Tel: 0491 432 492*) runs daily buses from Filadelfia.

Lodging

Hotel Boquerón Located across the street from the cooperative, Hotel Boquerón is pretty much the only game in town. Although it is your only option, it is not a bad one. Rooms are nicely done and the restaurant serves up a decent meal and has a small lunch buffet as well. *Tel 0493 240 311/669, 0971 401 063, Located directly across from the cooperative supermarket, www.neuland.com.py/servicios/hotel-restaurante-boqueron, Single Gs. 60,000 shared bath, Gs. 75,000 private bath, Double Gs. 110,000 shared bath, Gs. 120,000 private bath*

FORTÍN BOQUERÓN

Founded in 1928 to stop the advance of Bolivian troops, Fortín Boquerón is one of the Chaco War's most significant historic landmarks. Strategically located near fresh water reserves, Fortín Boquerón played a key role in the hostilities between Paraguay and Bolivia both before and during the Chaco War. Today, it is the site of a large

---

A Historic Site

In December of 1928, Fortín Boquerón was overtaken by Bolivians troops; this was in retribution for a surprise attack by Paraguayan forces on Fortín Vanguardia to the north near Bahía Negra. These incidents almost set off the already practically inevitable war between Paraguay and Bolivia. However, both sides reached an agreement, mostly because neither was yet prepared for war. Paraguay agreed to rebuild Fortín Vanguardia while Bolivia ceded control of Fortín Boquerón.

After war was officially declared in 1932, Fortín Boquerón was once again overtaken by Bolivian troops eager to gain access to the area's water reserves. On September 9th, 1932, Lieutenant Coronel José Félix Estigarribia launched an attack on Fortín Boquerón in an attempt to regain control of the region. Thus began the Battle of Boquerón (*Batalla de Boquerón*). An estimated 7,000 Paraguayan troops fought against the 500 Bolivians within Fortín Boquerón as well as the 3,500 Bolivian reinforcements troops that later came to their aid (these estimates, as well as casualties, vary depending on the source). Fortín Boquerón remained under siege for twenty days after which the Bolivians surrendered unconditionally. The victory at Boquerón was key, allowing Paraguayan troops to advance into Bolivian territory and September 29th is celebrated as a national holiday (*Victoria del la Batalla de Boquerón*).

museum dedicated to the Chaco War, boasting an extensive collection of Chaco War photos and weaponry. The museum is run by the friendly Carlos Aguero, a walking Chaco War encyclopedia. The premises also retain many of the original 3,800 meters of trenches, most about 1.5 meters deep. Although they are no longer fortified with barbed wire and snipers, the thorny vegetation surrounding the trenches and the intense heat is enough to make you pity the Chaco War soldiers. The trail follows along the old trenches and leads to two small cemeteries for Bolivian and Paraguayan soldiers. Along the way, there are *palo borracho* trees whose trunks were hollowed out to create hiding places for snipers. The area along the trenches is overgrown, but at the site of the Paraguayan cemetery you will see the savanna-like cleared lands with wild grass similar to what the battle field looked like. Presiding over the Paraguayan cemetery is a large, original cross. The clearing in front of the museum features an evocative statue of a Paraguayan soldier created by famed Paraguayan artist Herman Guggiari. *Tel: 0981 242420, Fortín Boquerón is located fifteen kilometers from Neuland and 30 kilometers from Filadelfia and is best visited with a guide (Heinz Weibe of the Neuland Cooperative's tourism office or Gran Chaco Turismo in Filadelfia are good local options). Another option is to hire a taxi for a round trip from either Filadelfia or Neuland (the cheaper of the two). However this will cost almost as much as a tour. The road which leads from Neuland to Fortín Boquerón is unmarked, therefore those driving in private vehicles should consider taking along a guide or getting specific directions in town, museum hours Wed-Sun 8am-5pm (it is best to call ahead and ensure Sr. Aguero will be there to open the museum).*

SANTA TERESITA

Santa Teresita is a small indigenous community located about three kilometers from the center of Mariscal Estigarribia along the Trans Chaco Highway. The community is home to Guaraní Occidental, Guaraní Ñandeva, Nivacle, and Manjui ethnic groups, although due to cultural differences there is very little mixing amongst the groups. The community's church is completely circular with a round altar, an adaptation to suit indigenous religious traditions. It is in this church that Pope John Paul II held a mass during his 1988 visit to Paraguay. Every year during carnival season, the Guaraní community hosts a three day indigenous carnival or festival named "*Arete Guazú*" (meaning large celebration). While the *Arete Guazú* is celebrated in Guaraní communities throughout the region (including those in Argentina and Bolivia), Santa Teresita's is considered to be one of the more authentic celebrations in Paraguay. The festival has yet to draw many tourists, but the people of Santa Teresita are very welcoming to foreign visitors. Expect to be asked to participate in dancing and, on the third day, be covered in mud along with everyone else. This is a highly sacred festival, so be respectful at all times, especially in regards to photography. As there is no lodging in Santa Teresita itself, the best thing to do is to stay in Mariscal Estigarribia and walk or hitch to Santa Teresita. *Arete Guazú* dates vary each year (ranging from the end of January to the beginning of March) and are decided upon by community leaders. The best way to find out when the *Arete Guazú* will be held is to contact the Municipal Office in Mariscal Estigarribia (*Tel: 0494 247 201*).

The Chaco

MARISCAL ESTIGARRIBIA

Mariscal Estigarriba, named after Chaco War hero José Felix Estigarribia (featured on the Gs. 50 coin), is the last dependable source of fuel and food along the Trans Chaco Highway as it heads north towards Bolivia. This is also the last place to get an official exit stamp before the border with Bolivia. The sprawling town is home to the Chaco's largest military base, the Base Aereo Militar Mariscal Estigarribia. The town is mostly populated by various indigenous groups, members of the military who live

---

The Arete Guazú

The *Arete Guazú* is one of the most important celebrations of the year for the Guaraní indigenous community. The festival, traditionally held over the course of three days, is all about celebrating the community spirit. People who have emigrated for work return in droves to rejoice with the community and honor those members who have passed away. The unbreakable bond with the community's ancestors is emphasized throughout the *Arete Guazú* through a variety of rituals and traditions.

The first two days of the *Areté Guazu* consist largely of dance circles. A group of musicians playing drums and flutes provide a slow and steady beat while people hold hands and shuffle fairly slowly in circles, changing directions when the drumbeats reach a crescendo. As they dance, people focus on the memories of their deceased loved ones; many are moved to tears. When the musicians take a break, the crowds disperse to the shade of nearby trees and buildings to chat with each other and drink. The beverages of choice are homemade *chicha,* made from fermented fruit, and beer (less traditional but more easily obtained). Rain is considered to be a special blessing from God, and even if there is thunder and lightning dancing continues unabated. The atmosphere is festive, relaxed, and charged with emotion.

Costumes are yet another way that people connect with their ancestors during the festival. Men and young boys don costumes and channel the spirit of their ancestors, sometimes going as far as adopting altered mannerisms. Despite the heat, they wear long pants, long sleeved shirts and sweaters, close-toed shoes, gloves, masks, and even sunglasses over the masks. All of the clothing is painted and embellished with bright fabric scraps cut into fringes. A mask made of *palo borracho* might symbolize a grandfather dedicated to agriculture, while one with feathers could represent a hunter. Some people take a less traditional route using rubber Halloween masks. A select group of young men dresses in white pants, long-sleeve white shirts, and long pointy white hats with ribbons flowing from the tops. In an interesting mix of tradition and modernity, the outfits are painted from top to bottom with all manner of figures from skulls, ying yangs, to anarchy symbols and even Metallica logos.

The third day of the *Arete Guazú* is the most action packed. It is on this day that a group of men known as the *kuré* (meaning pig in Guaraní) emerge. Covered in mud from head to toe, these "pigs" run through the crowds leaving in their wake a trail of laughing, muddy victims. The *kuré* especially like to target female festival goers, taking great delight in dumping mud on their heads. Older women may fight back by trying to pull down the *kure's* shorts. Later in the day the *toro-toro* takes place. A mock battle in the mud between men acting as a bull and a jaguar, this is said to symbolize the struggle between European colonists and the Guaraní. Throughout the day the music and dancing continues. The Arete Guazú comes to a close with a visit to the cemetery, the most literal form of honoring the community's ancestors. It is here that costumes are removed and discarded, thus allowing the ancestors to return to the spirit world.

on the base, and a handful ranch owners (*estancieros*). The town is also a popular rest stop for truckers on their way to cattle ranches to the north or transporting goods to and from Bolivia. There is not much for tourists in Mariscal Estigarribia. However, the nearby indigenous community of Santa Teresita holds a yearly festival known as the *"Arete Guazú"* which can be a unique cultural experience. The land further north along the Trans Chaco Highway is home to several cattle ranches, small military outposts, a handful of indigenous communities, and three national parks (Parque Nacional Teniente Enciso, Parque Nacional Médanos del Chaco, and Parque Nacional Defensores del Chaco).

Base Aéreo Militar Mariscal Estigarribia

The military base in Mariscal Estigarribia is the largest in the Chaco and serves as a home base for the smaller more remote outposts of the region. Visiting the base is an interesting way to kill time while waiting for the next bus to Bolivia. On most days, picture ID, a friendly attitude, and willingness to chit chat with the military officers are all that is needed to enter. The military base is home to a large lake which can provide a welcome break from the intense heat. Across the lake is a small island where caimans and capybaras live (as well as a fair amount of dogs and roosters). To get to the lake, walk all the way to the end of the military base's main road (approximately 1.7 kilometers) past a row of *palo borracho* trees, and then take a left. You will come to a fenced in area, and the lake will be visible beyond. There is a small covered barbeque pit and several trees for shade but the mosquitoes might force you to head straight for the water. On the way to the lake you will pass the Dr. Luis María Argaña Airport, home to a 3.8-kilometer long landing strip that is quite out of place, given the area's infrequent air traffic. This large runway has generated a lot of controversy with many claiming it is part of a U.S. plan to build a permanent military base in the Chaco. In fact, American tourists may find locals to be suspicious of them as rumors that the U.S. intends to steal both the gas deposits in the Chaco and fresh water from the Guaraní Aquifer have been circulating for several years. *The entrance to the military base is on the left-hand side of the road approximately one kilometer past the immigration office.*

Lodging

Hotel La Laguna Also known as Hotel Francés, this is the only decent option in town (there are bare bones *hospedajes* used by local truckers, but these are not recommended). The hotel is nearby the immigration and customs control point where all buses continuing to Bolivia are obliged to stop. In addition, Hotel Laguna functions as an agent for the Yacyretá bus line. If you purchase your ticket to Santa Cruz, Bolivia ahead of time, the administration will arrange for you to be picked up at the hotel. This is convenient, as most buses to Bolivia pass Mariscal Estigarribia in the wee hours of the morning. However, in order to catch the bus at the hotel, you must get your passport stamped earlier in the day as the bus will stop at Hotel Laguna having already passed by the immigration office. If you board the bus at Hotel Laguna without having previously been stamped out, you risk being turned away at the Bolivia border, an inconvenience that is not worth chancing. *Tel: 0494 247 250, 0983 100 060, Seven blocks (approximately 1.3 km) past the immigration and customs building on the same side of the road just behind a medium sized roadside lagoon. Singles Gs. 60,000 with fan, Gs. 90,000 with A/C, Doubles Gs. 80,000 with fan, Gs. 140,000 with A/C*

Food

In addition to the restaurants listed here, there are several surprisingly well-stocked convenience stores along the Trans Chaco Highway. Including in the towns of Chaco Soft (closest to the Hotel La Laguna and with internet access at Gs. 6,000 per hour), Ibañez (next to Hotel La Laguna), 4 Hermanas, and Kuarahy (which, though further away, sometimes accepts credit cards, *Tel: 0494 247 205/276*).

Restaurante Venecia / Heladería Rosario Though it is a ways from the immigration office and Hotel La Laguna, this small but cute restaurant is worth the walk (although, as always, you should avoid doing so during the hottest part of the day). Menu includes a variety of meats, pizzas, chicken, and salads. The A/C is a welcome respite from the heat, as are the many ice cream dishes (try the *copa capuchino*). There are also computers with internet access for Gs. 8,000 per hour. *Tel: 0494 247 248, Avenida General E.A. Garay and Algarrobo just down the street from the large town plaza, Tue-Fri 7pm-12am, Sat-Sun 5pm-12am, Gs. 15,000-50,000*

Restaurante Italiano Most tourists will find this the easiest option to reach as it is next to the immigration office. However it is only open sporadically. Serves pastas, pizzas, and fast food. *Tel: 0494 247 231, Between the immigration and customs offices and the neighboring Petrobras gas station, Gs. 20,000-35,000*

Getting There

Mariscal Estigarribia is located at km 530 of the Trans Chaco Highway. Take caution while driving as the condition of the Trans Chaco Highway deteriorates noticeably past Filadelfia with many potholes along the way.

Nasa-Golondrina has two daily buses from Asunción and one bus from Filadelfia. The ride from Asunción takes about eight hours and bus fare is Gs. 80,000.

CROSSING INTO BOLIVIA

Yacyretá (*Tel: 021 551 725*), Stel Turismo (*Tel: 021 551 647*), Río Paraguay (*Tel: 021 555 958*), and Pycasu (*Tel: 021 551 735*) have buses that run between Asunción and Santa Cruz, Bolivia. The long, dusty ride takes between twenty-two and twenty-four hours and costs about US $50. Unfortunately, the ticket price is often the same whether you board the bus in Asunción or catch it Mariscal Estigarribia. It is a good idea to bring your own water and snacks. All buses make an obligatory stop at Mariscal Estigarribia's well-lit 24 hour customs (*aduana*) checkpoint. While the bus is waiting at customs, passengers must visit the immigration office to be stamped into or out of Paraguay.

Those wishing to board the bus in Mariscal Estigarribia should note most buses from Asunción arrive at the check point between 2am and 4am. Tickets to Santa Cruz, Bolivia can be purchased directly from the bus drivers, however to be safe, it is better to purchase them beforehand. The simplest way to handle this is to book your ticket through the Yacyretá office at the Hotel La Laguna as they can also arrange for the bus to pick you up at the hotel which makes for a more comfortable wait (see Hotel La Laguna under Lodging in this section). Whether you are boarding the bus at the customs check point or the Hotel La Laguna be sure to pass through Immigration beforehand.

By Car

After passing through immigration controls in Mariscal Estigarribia, continue north on the Trans Chaco Highway approximately 110 kilometers until the crossroads with Picada 108 (should you need extra fuel you can continue ten kilometers past

Mariscal Estigarribia to La Patria where there is a gas station). Here take a left and follow the road another 110 kilometers to the small town of Mayor Infante Rivarola. Continue another five kilometers or so to the border with Bolivia.

Immigration Office

Whether you are continuing to Bolivia by bus or private vehicle you must be officially stamped out at the immigration office in Mariscal Estigarribia. There are no immigration agents at the border itself (230 kilometers away in Mayor Infante Rivarola). From the main road the small immigration office is slightly to the right of the customs building. If it appears closed you might have to bang on the door loudly – there is a back room immigration officials stay in during downtime. *Tel: 0494 247 315), At the entrance to town on the right-hand side if coming from Asunción, open 24 hours a day*

PARQUE NACIONAL TENIENTE ENCISO

Located alongside the Trans Chaco Highway, Parque Nacional Teniente Enciso is the most easily accessible of the Chaco's national parks. At 40,000 hectares, the park is on the small side, but is charming and an excellent example of the dry Chaco habitat. This park is a good option for those who are interested in the Chaco's flora and fauna but do not have the time or resources to visit the larger, more remote Parque Nacional Defensores del Chaco. The park has only one official marked trail of about two kilometers. The trail makes a loop through the park's characteristic vegetation including the *palo borracho*, spindly and bluish *palo santo, quebracho blanco*, covered in craggy pale bark, and, of course, thorny cacti galore. In addition, there are several Chaco War era trenches along the trail. The vegetation is thin enough that you can go off trail in some parts, but make sure to check yourself for ticks afterwards. If you are visiting without a tour guide, it is possible to see other areas of the park with the park ranger (provided you donate gas money). The park is home to peccaries, deer, armadillos, and jaguars, though spotting the latter takes luck and patience. As with the rest of the Chaco, you are more likely to see wildlife if you visit with an experienced tour guide.

Teniente Enciso also operates as the administrative headquarters for the sand dune covered Parque Nacional Médanos del Chaco ninety-five kilometers to the north along the Trans Chaco (unfortunately this park is difficult to access due to the sandy nature of the road and the lack of visitor's facilities).

Teniente Enciso was once a military post, and the old headquarters have been transformed into a well appointed visitor's center. There are several dorm rooms, some of which even have A/C. Out front there is an impressively large *palo borracho* tree, home to many birds. Should you choose to do so, there is plenty of space to camp – just make sure to find a shaded area. The center has a kitchen (though you may have to provide the park guard with money to purchase cooking fuel) and barbeque facilities. If you are short on food, there is a small store about 800 meters from the park headquarters at Cruce San Miguel, but you pay a hefty premium.

Getting There

Parque Nacional Teniente Enciso is located at km 700 of the Trans Chaco Highway. From Mariscal Estigarribia continue north on the Trans Chaco Highway to the tiny town of La Patria (this is a good place to stock up on gas and food if you haven't done so already). Past La Patria, the Trans Chaco Highway is no longer paved. The park entrance is twenty kilometers past La Patria on the right-hand side of the road about twenty meters past the large welcome billboard. A 4-wheel drive vehicle is not needed for this trip during the dry season as only the last twenty kilometers are on unpaved road.

Nasa-Golondrina (Tel: 0494 247 282) runs a weekly mini-bus (nicknamed the "Nasa'i" meaning "little Nasa" in Guaraní) from Mariscal Estigarribia on Tuesdays. However, this schedule is subject to change, so it is important to reconfirm it by phone or, better yet, at the Nasa-Golondrina bus terminal in Mariscal Estigarribia. Bus fare is Gs. 50,000.

Tatus of the Chaco

Scurrying across the road at all hours of the day armadillos are one of the most commonly spotted animals of the Chaco. The Chaco is home to several armadillo species which are usually referred to by their Guaraní names such as the *tatú carreta* (giant armadillo), *tatú bolita* (three banded armadillo), *tatú poju'i* (lesser hairy armadillo), and the *tatú hu* (nine banded armadillo). While the word *"tatú"* means armadillo in Guaraní it is also Paraguayan slang for female genitals. So don't be surprised if the discussion of *"tatús"* elicits a few chortles or off color jokes from Paraguayan travel companions.

PARQUE NACIONAL DEFENSORES DEL CHACO

At 780,000 hectares, Parque Nacional Defensores del Chaco is Paraguay's largest national park. The park's size is particularly important as it provides enough protected land for several species of large felines such as jaguars and pumas to survive. The park is also home to members of the Ayoreo indigenous tribe, many of whom remain voluntarily isolated from the modern world. The park's main visitor's center is located at Madrejón and includes dorm rooms and a kitchen as well as a small campsite. Plan to bring all supplies including food, water, and fuel for the center's generators. There is a lake by the visitor's center that attracts the area's wildlife. One of the most distinct features of the park is Cerro León. At over 600 meters above sea level Cerro, León is the second highest peak in Paraguay and a rare geological formation in the flat plain that is the Chaco. Cerro León is not one mountain but a series of small ones grouped together over an area about forty kilometers in diameter. This area of the park is ideal for nature observation and includes a campsite. It is accessed by a road that leads west from the park's main entrance at Madrejón. Park rangers can take you to Cerro León, although you will have to cover fuel expenses.

Getting There

Traveling by private vehicle (only 4-wheel drive will do) should only be attempted during the dry season with the accompaniment of a trained guide. Road conditions are difficult and help can be very difficult to come by in an emergency. From Filadelfia head north along Avenida Hindenburg approximately forty kilometers to the crossroads with Teniente Montanía. Continue north approximately 165 kilometers past Fortín Teniente Martinez to Fortín Madrejón and the entrance to the park. From Mariscal Estigarribia there is a road that leads east to Teniente Montanía. The turn off from the Trans Chaco Highway is approximately one kilometer before the Mariscal Estigarribia immigration office.

Nasa-Golondrina (*Tel: 0491 432 492*) runs a weekly bus from Filadelfia. However, due to road conditions and lack of passengers, this bus does not run frequently. Be sure to double check with Nasa-Golondrina before making any travel plans. The best person to talk to is Sr. Silvio Espinola (*Tel: 0971 700 352*) who works at both the Nasa-Golondrina office in Filadelfia and the Technomundo store next door. Bus fare is Gs. 50,000.

The Trans Chaco Rally

With the exception of cattle ranchers, avid hunters, and occasional environmental conservationists, few Paraguayans visit the Chaco. The one exception is during the yearly Trans Chaco Rally, organized by the Paraguayan Touring and Automotive Club (TACPY). This grueling three stage rally usually draws between fifty and ninety national and international rally teams. The rally was the brainchild of Phillip Bell, an American consultant, who approached the TACPY in 1970 with the idea for a rally in the Chaco similar to rallies he had witnessed in Kenya. The first Trans Chaco Rally took place in September of 1971, along the then unpaved Trans Chaco Highway. The rally has grown in popularity each subsequent year (though it was suspended by presidential decree from 1984 to 1986) and is now one of the most important sporting events in the country, drawing thousands of enthusiastic fans to the region and bringing lucrative sponsorships for rally drivers. Normally desolate towns fill to the brim with visitors during the rally, and local hotels, restaurants, and watering holes see their profits soar.

Every year the Trans Chaco Rally (also known as the *Rally del Chaco*) begins with a festive send off, complete with fireworks, from Asunción's Mariscal López Shopping. Rally enthusiasts then descend upon towns along the rally route to cheer on their teams, while those who can't make the trek stay informed with up to the minute coverage by national media and fan filmed videos uploaded to YouTube. Over the course of three days, rally drivers and their cars are subjected to the Chaco's grueling conditions including heat, dust, and, of course, difficult terrain. Breakdowns are frequent, and less than half of the teams are able to overcome the obstacles and finish the race.

Although it has many fans and brings a lot of economic activity to the region, the Trans Chaco Rally is not without its detractors. Every year, environmentalists raise concerns about the damaging effect rally cars have as they tear through already fragile ecosystems (often running over animals in the process). In addition, some of the rally stages take place along main roads putting pedestrians at risk. The general spring break style debauchery of the rally's followers is also of concern both for environmental and social reasons. Revelers leave mounds of litter, and the incidence of prostitution among the Chaco's indigenous women spikes conspicuously during the rally. Despite these concerns it seems unlikely that the Trans Chaco Rally will be suspended any time soon. In fact, the Paraguayan Chaco may soon become home to a new rally. There are rumors that the Paraguayan Chaco will be incorporated into the Rally París-Dakar route which shifted from Africa to South America in 2009. For more information on the Trans Chaco Rally visit www.transchacorally.com.py

The Chaco

The Paraguay River

The Paraguay River flows north to south extending 1,260 kilometers down the length of Paraguay, bisecting the country into Eastern Paraguay and the Chaco. The river's navigability and strategic location between Brazil and Argentina make it a large thoroughfare for commercial transportation, both national and international. Due to poor road infrastructure, the river also serves as the main source of transportation for communities in the departments of Concepción and Alto Paraguay

At its northernmost point (in Paraguay) is the culturally and biologically diverse department of Alto Paraguay. As part of the Pantanal ecosystem, this is one of the best places in Paraguay for nature observation (see Departamento Alto Paraguay – The Pantanal, p311). The area is also home to several indigenous tribes living in small communities along the riverbanks. Near the border with Bolivia and Brazil is the small town of Bahía Negra. Although remote, it is still serviced by boat, bus, and airplane, making it an ideal place from which to venture into the practically uninhabited wilderness of the Pantanal. The Los Tres Gigantes birding station to the north along the banks of the Negro River is an ideal spot for nature observation. Neighboring Bahía Negra is the Ishir community of Puerto Diana where the indigenous still maintain their ancestral traditions.

Flowing 160 kilometers south in a series of large looping twists and turns, the Paraguay River passes Fuerte Olimpo. Located at the base of The Cerro Tres Hermanos mountains, it is considered the gateway to the Paraguayan Pantanal. As capital of the Department of Alto Paraguay, Fuerte Olimpo has more infrastructure and services than ports further upriver. Another 150 kilometers to the south is Colonia Carmelo Peralta where travelers can pass through Paraguayan Immigration before entering the Brazilian tourist town of Porto Murtinho on the other side of the river.

Further downriver are the port towns of Puerto Casado and Puerto Pinasco. During the tannin boom in late 1800's and early 1900's these towns were home to foreign owned tannin processing plants (see Carlos Casado and the Tannin Industry, p314). When this industry collapsed, many found jobs in the quarries of Vallemí on the opposite bank of the river. Located on the northwestern-most tip of Eastern Paraguay, Vallemí is the site of Paraguay's National Cement Factory and home to many small scale quarries. There are also a handful of limestone caverns that can be visited with guides (see Caves of Vallemí and San Lázaro, p275). Just past Vallemí is the Apa River, a fast-changing river that marks Paraguay's northern boundary with Brazil. This also marks the southernmost limits of the Paraguayan Pantanal.

About 140 kilometers to the south of Vallemí is the city of Concepción, one of the largest ports along the Paraguay River. Goods, from the Chaco to the west and Pedro Juan Caballero and Brazilian state of Matto Grosso to the east, have traditionally been transported here before being shipped downriver to Asunción and Buenos Aires. As the port of call for passenger ships making their way north to Bahía Negra and south to Asunción, Concepción is an increasingly popular stop among adventurous backpackers. Approximately 110 kilometers south is the small port of Puerto Antequera. This port is used mostly to transport agricultural products from the Department of San Pedro, whose capital, the city of San Pedro del Ycuamandiyú, is fourteen kilometers to the east. Villa Hayes is the last major port before the city of Asunción. Originally the failed Nueva Burdeos (New Bordeaux) colony, this is the site of one of Eliza Lynch's most infamous tantrums (see The Infamous Eliza Lynch, p31).

Asunción, capital of Paraguay, is located 872 kilometers to the south of the border with Bolivia and Brazil. The city's port is located in the bay of Asunción, which is also internationally recognized as an Important Birding Area. There are no passenger ships that travel south of Asunción to Pilar, although it is possible to hitch a ride on a cargo ship to the city of Pilar. Before meeting up with the Paraná River and flowing across the international border with Argentina, the Paraguay River passes the historic site of Humaitá where picturesque ruins from the Triple Alliance War remain on the riverbanks to this day.

TRAVELING ALONG THE PARAGUAY RIVER

Traveling along the river is one of Paraguay's great adventures. There are three passenger boats that make weekly trips up the Paraguay River. The Aquidaban sails between Concepción and Bahía Negra, while the Cacique II sails between Asunción and Concepción, and the Crucero Paraguay sails between Asunción and Fuerte Olimpo. Of these, only the Crucero Paraguay is exclusively for tourism purposes. Which boat you choose depends greatly on your budget and timeframe. Another option for those who wish to tailor trips more to their specific desires is to rent a boat (some are available without a crew, others with a crew and captain). And for those without a restrictive schedule who are willing to go with the flow (literally), there is the possibility of hitching a ride on one of several cargo boats transiting the river.

The Cacique II & the Aquidaban

Traveling on one of these two passenger boats is an interesting, if not particularly comfortable, experience. The boats offer a unique opportunity to see not only the region's diverse flora and fauna, but also to interact firsthand with the region's culturally diverse population. Boat crews are made up mostly of working class Paraguayan *mestizo*s. The crew and passengers are mostly male, however many of the *almaceneras* (shopkeepers) aboard are women, and some crew members bring their wives and children along when possible. Passengers include members from Maskoi, Chamacoco/Ishir, Tomaharo, and Ayoreo indigenous communities along the river. You will also see many Brazilians onboard migrating to work on large cattle ranches (*estancias*); many have been given permission to bring their nuclear families along.

The boats offer budget conscious tourists a chance to do some nature tourism on the cheap. As you travel up the river, wildlife will become more abundant, especially once past Fuerte Olimpo. Those with a keen eye (or knowledgeable travel companion) will be able to spot *yacaraé* (caiman) and other aquatic animals, such as capybaras, lounging on the sandy banks of the river. Although you are unlikely to see elusive animals such as large felines, taking a riverboat ride can be an inexpensive way to catch a glimpse of the region's more visible fauna, especially birds. Be sure to bring binoculars, and prepare to spend a lot of time on deck.

While the experience is a unique one for any foreigner, it is important to keep in mind these are not boats aimed at tourists. The boats are not built for comfort and come equipped with only basic amenities. Space is at a premium; decks are crammed with cargo, hammocks strung close together, and cabins are tiny. The most comfortable way to travel on either boat is to travel downriver during the dry season. During the rainy season, the region's silt and clay roads are frequently impassable, making the riverboats the only reliable mode of transportation. Boats become much more crowded, both with passengers and cargo (which can include animals). Combined with the intense summer heat, it can make for an unpleasant journey. If you cannot avoid traveling along the river in the summer and rainy season, it is best to sleep with your cabin door open for maximum airflow and to ensure access to the bathrooms (passengers may fall asleep on the floor blocking your closed cabin door). Regardless of the season, the journey upriver is longer and more crowded than the return trip. In addition to being loaded down with cargo and passengers, boats are fighting the current when chugging northward. The journey downriver can be more pleasant with less cargo (this time mostly raw materials) and passengers, and a shorter travel time. It is sometimes possible to fly Bahía Negra (p319), and then take the boat back down. Another option for shortening the boat ride is to take a bus to Vallemí or Fuerte Olimpo, and then catch the boat (either heading up or down river) from there.

Arrival & Departure

Starting points for trips upriver (Asunción for the Cacique II and Concepción for the Aquidaban) are the only fixed departure times for either boat. Arrival and departure times from there on out are subject to conditions on the river and the time spent loading and unloading merchandise in each port.

Basic meals are available at a cheap price from the boat's kitchen (put in an order ahead of time), but be aware that river water is used to wash dishes and prepare meals. If you are concerned about hygiene you can bring your own food or purchase cookies, crackers, and produce available from the boat's many vendors. Due to the amount of food on board, bugs are common even in cabins. Boats have a communal sink near the bathrooms that is used by passengers for hand washing and by vendors for washing dishes. Some bathrooms have toilet bowls and others just ceramic latrine style drains. Interestingly, the bathrooms can be on the cleaner side of the Paraguay public bathroom spectrum thanks to hoses and/or shower heads that can be used to wash away anything icky. Everything is washed into the river, but water for the sink and bathrooms is also pumped from the river. Unless you are up to drinking river water it is best to bring water purification tablets or lots of bottled water along. If you have to use water from the sink for drinking, avoid doing so when the boat is docked.

What to Bring

- ✓ Cash – costs for excursions from Vallemí, Bahía Negra, and Fuerte Olimpo are high due to their remote nature and fuel costs, and there are no reliable ATMS past Concepción.
- ✓ Ziplocs or containers for food – to keep critters at bay.
- ✓ Sunscreen and a hat – you will not be able to resist going on deck when there is a cool breeze.
- ✓ Hammock – if you are not renting a cabin, then bring your own hammock just in case (nylon/parachute hammocks pack down smallest).
- ✓ First aid kit.
- ✓ Soap, flip flops, toilet paper, towel – for the bathroom.
- ✓ Cards or games to pass the time. Ones that are easy to share with fellow passengers are the best.
- ✓ Twine or rope for jerry rigging cabin doors shut or semi shut (for airflow).
- ✓ Binoculars.
- ✓ Warm clothes for cool nights, especially during the winter.
- ✓ Sleeping bag or sheets. Beds come with no linens.
- ✓ Luggage or pack lock.
- ✓ Headlamp or flashlight.

A Floating Market

The majority of Alto Paraguay's population lives in riverside communities serviced by the boats. The Aquidaban serves as a floating market, and is, in many cases, the only reliable source of produce and commercial goods for communities along the river. Several small scale vendors operate open stalls selling everything from clothing to eggs, bread, and canned foods. Many of the passengers themselves are also vendors shopping their wares from port to port. Mere moments after docking, the boat will fill with locals making their way up rickety planks to do their shopping and pick up deliveries. Meanwhile, the boat's crew unloads deliveries for the town's merchants from the deck and hold – commercial shipments include everything from cooking gas canisters, to packs upon packs of soda bottles and beer cans. Merchants aren't the only ones who use the boats as delivery services; many of the region's cattle ranches place orders to have construction materials and other goods delivered either to directly to private docks or to the nearest port. Fishermen from indigenous communities frequently load large plastic barrels full of baitfish to sell to Brazilian tourist fishing boats in towns like Porto Murtinho. While the movement of goods on and off the boat is interesting to watch, unless you want to be woken up every time goods are loaded or unloaded it is best to forgo hammocks and sleeping on deck for a private cabin.

Lancha Aquidaban (Concepción to Bahía Negra)

Tel: 0331 242 435 Agencia Cohelo (Concepción office) or 0972 678 695 (Pedro Coelho), located across the street from Concepción's docks at the end of Presidente Franco, Mon-Fri 7:30am-12pm, Sat 8am-11am (but is often open earlier when the Aquidaban and Cacique II are docked)

Upriver Schedule: The Aquidaban makes weekly departures from Concepción Tuesday mornings between 9am and 11am. It arrives in Vallemí on Wednesdays between noon and 6pm and Fuerte Olimpo between noon and 6pm. It docks in Bahía Negra between 6am and 4pm on Fridays.

Downriver schedule: Departs Bahía Negra on Friday afternoon (two to three hours after arrival). Arrives Fuerte Olimpo ten to twelve hours later, usually between 1am and 2am, and arrives in Concepción Sundays between 11am and midnight.

Cost: The trip from Concepción to Bahia Negra costs Gs. 100,000.

Accommodations and food: Small cabins with one to two bunk beds are available. Cabin reservations must be made over the phone or in person. These must be reconfirmed in person before 7am the day of departure. A four person cabin runs about Gs. 80,000. Note that there is no guarantee that you'll have a cabin to yourself. Reservations for cabins on the return trip are made with Pitin, the boat's cook. There is limited hammock space in the hallways between cabins. Some people stake out a spot on benches along the boat hallways. Food and beverages are available from the boat's kitchen, but you must put in an order ahead of time as it goes fast. Typical Paraguayan food is served; it is quite tasty but don't brave it if you haven't already developed an iron stomach.

Things to keep in mind while on the Cacique II & Aquidaban:

– Respect fellow passengers and crew: For many people on board, the boat is their place of business. Vendors and crew members use downtime between ports to rest. Be respectful of the crew, especially if you are making the return ride back.

– Leave your cabin: Take advantage of the opportunity to interact with Paraguayans of varied backgrounds. Making friends along the way will increase your knowledge of the area. No matter where you disembark you are likely to run into fellow passengers from the boat around town that will be happy to help you figure out where to go and what to see. Children will be happy to point out animals on the riverbanks when they spot them, and adults have a plethora of knowledge regarding the ports and private ranches you'll pass along the way.

– Interact with children: There are several children on board traveling with their families – they will express the most interest in you and can be your link to increased interaction with other passengers. If you like children, then bring some loose sheets of paper and colored pencils to hand out. Be sure to set limits on children entering your cabin or using your belongings though. If you need privacy send them back to their families.

– Watch your stuff: Cabin doors do not lock or sometimes even fully close. Keep an eye on your belongings, especially while at port when several people will be getting on and off the boat.

– Guard your space: Hammocks and available deck space are on a first come first serve basis. If you are not getting a cabin make sure you stake out your space early. Once you leave your spot it will be up for grabs unless someone stays behind to guard it for you.

– Don't stray at port: With the exception of larger ports such as Concepción, Puerto Guaraní, Vallemí, and Bahía Negra, the boats do not linger. Once all cargo is loaded or offloaded, the boat takes off. Do not wander far, and ask for an estimated departure time before getting off.

– Crew and passengers are predominantly males. Female travelers should travel with a travel buddy or a group, or if that is not possible befriend female vendors.

Barco Cacique II (From Asunción to Vallemí)

Tel: 021 492 829 (Asunción), 0981 402 324, (Sr. Segovia) and Agencia Cohelo (see Aquidaban contact information above) in Concepción. For travel from Asunción, arrangements must be made boat side at Playa Montevideo on Monday or Tuesday.

Upriver schedule: Departs from Playa Montevideo (at the end of Calle Montevideo downtown) in Asunción at 7pm on Tuesday. Stops in Concepción on Thursday at 6am and arrives in Vallemí on Friday at 3pm.

Downriver: Departs Vallemí Friday evening arriving in Concepción on Sunday morning and in Asunción on Monday morning.

Cost: Asunción to Concepción is Gs. 80,000 and to Vallemí is an additional Gs. 40,000.

Accommodations and food: Small two bunk cabins are available for Gs. 50,000. Floor fans are available during the summer. There are spots for hanging hammocks, though you must bring your own. Food is available for purchase, though it is best to bring your own just in case, along with bottled water.

River Traffic

The Paraguay River begins in Matto Grosso, Brazil, flowing through the length of Paraguay into Argentina's Río de la Plata and finally emptying into the Atlantic Ocean. This makes it ideal for transporting cargo – shipments along the river range from commercial goods to raw natural resources such as minerals and stones. Along the river you will see a wide variety of boats, from rickety old push boats to enormous container ships. Smaller, non-push boats employ a complex system of ropes and knots to latch containers to their sides and transport them downriver. The importance of the Paraguay River as a means for shipping also creates potential hazards for the region's delicate ecosystem. The proposed Paraguay-Paraná Hidrovía Project contemplates drastic changes to the river in order to improve transportation infrastructure from neighboring countries through Paraguay and into the Atlantic Ocean. Environmentalists are concerned as dredging would increase the speed of water flow and accelerate draining of the surrounding wetlands.

Cargo Boats

There are several cargo boats that make their way up and down the river delivering goods. If you are able to catch a cargo boat at port, it is possible to hitch a ride. This is an especially good option when roads are washed out and you don't want to wait for crowded passenger boats to arrive. Speak to whoever looks like they are in charge (it is best to wait until the crew takes a break from loading or unloading cargo). As crews are mostly male, with the possible exception of a cook or girlfriend, it is best not to make this trip as a single female. Before boarding, stock up on food (bringing extra to share or exchange with crew and other passengers) and make absolutely sure there is a planned stop at your final destination. Keep in mind you will be at the mercy of the boat's schedule – this could mean spending several hours or even a full day picking up merchandise at ports along the river. Cabins are reserved for crew members – you will have to sleep on the floor, benches, or in an unoccupied hammock (here is where bringing your own can come in handy). There are likely to be a handful of other passengers to interact with along the way. Be sure to ask for permission before entering any area of the boat. When looking for a boat to hitch on, keep in mind that one with open sides will offer an incredible view of the Pantanal's scenery. The Guaraní, which makes regular trips between Fuerte Olimpo and Asunción, can be a good option.

Crucero Paraguay

For those who prefer packaged tours, the Crucero Paraguay is the only available option short of hiring a private guide and boat. This luxury cruise boat offers a three day tour from Asunción to the Lower Chaco and a six day tour departing from Asunción and Concepción to Fuerte Olimpo. Both include daily side trips led by professional nature guides, excursions on the river in smaller boats, and visits to sites on land. All cabins have queen-sized beds, air conditioning, and private bathrooms. The boat includes a dining room, conference room (that doubles as a dance floor), and rooftop deck complete with a pool and bar. This is definitely the most comfortable way to enjoy the Paraguay River, however excursion dates are few and far between. *Tel: 021 232 051/2,0981 520 277, www.cruceroparaguay.com, Prices range between US$550 and US$1,600 per person (including all meals and excursions). Discounts are available for passengers traveling in groups or with small children as well as passengers with Paraguayan ID cards. Contact for detailed itineraries and reservations. Be sure to specify a need for English speaking guides. The Crucero Paraguay also offers nighttime cruises around the Bay of Asunción.*

Fishing Boats for Hire

There are several private boats available for hire, if you choose to make your own trip on the river. Peter Dirk of Granja El Roble (*Tel: 985898446, www.paraguay.ch*) in Belén (see Granja El Roble, p272) is a good on the ground source of information on small boats available for hire from Concepción and is often available to act as a knowledgeable guide. Contact Rosa Fernández at Agencia Aventura (*Tel: 0971 819 822, 0982 391 018, agenciaaventura@gmail.com*) to reserve larger boats in Concepción. These boats, generally used for fishing expeditions, can accommodate eight to

---

Obtaining Exit-Stamps Before Continuing to Bolivia & Brazil

There are two official Paraguayan immigration offices along the river, one in Concepción and the other in Carmelo Peralta. If you plan to continue upriver from Bahía Negra to Bolivia, it is essential to get your exit stamp in Concepción before boarding the Aquidaban. As Concepción's immigration office's hours can be sporadic, it is best to contact the Director of the Immigration office, Hever Centurión (*Tel: 0972 193 143 or hevercenturión@hotmail.com*) and arrange to have your passport stamped the day before departure (see Departamento Concepción, Immigration Office, p269). American travelers should note it is essential to obtain your Bolivian visa in Asunción before heading up river.

Those exiting Paraguay vía Puerto Murtino must visit the immigration office in Carmelo Peralta. The Aquidaban makes a stop at Isla Margarita, an island in the middle of the river with Carmelo Peralta on the Paraguayan bank and Brazilian tourist hub Puerto Murtinho on the other. On its way upriver, the Aquidaban arrives at Isla Margarita in the middle of the night. There are small water taxis that can take you to either bank. If you choose to spend the night in Puerto Murtinho, make sure to return to Carmelo Peralta in the morning for your exit stamp. Or simply get your exit stamp ahead of time in Concepción. There are plans for the construction of a bridge uniting the two cities, but such large infrastructure improvements are notoriously slow to come to fruition.

twelve passengers in rooms with A/C and include smaller motor boats for side trips on the river. The Barco Hotel Sueño del Pantanal is similar but based out of Carmelo Peralta further upriver (*Tel: 0984 152682, Luis Penayo*).

When hiring a boat for a day-trip (or longer), make sure to specifically ask whether you are expected to bring your own food and beverages and if the price includes fuel.

Barco Ten Caten A two story fishing boat with four smaller motor boats. Room can accommodate up to twelve passengers and have A/C. Based in Concepción. *Tel: 0336 274 200, 0971 801 234, (Sergio Ten Caten or Rosa Fernández), www.tencaten.net, agenciaaventura@gmail.com*

Barco Siete Cabrillas *Tel: 0971 800 907, www.sietecabrillas.com*

Barco Santa Filomena *Tel: 0971 819 822, 0982 391 018, Rosa Fernández*

Traveling by Land & Air

Road conditions in the departments of Alto Paraguay and Concepción make boats the most dependable way to reach ports along the river. However a handful of ports are also intermittently accessible by bus and airplane. Paraguay's military air service, TAM (Transporte Aereo Militar, not to be confused with the commercial airline TAM) has weekly flights to Bahía Negra which occasionally stop in both Vallemí and Fuerte Olimpo. Although this is the fastest way to get to the Pantanal, it is also the least dependable. The plane has a minimum quota of passengers that must be met for any flight to depart in order to cover fuel costs. As the runways in Alto Paraguay are not paved, the plane can be delayed several days due to weather conditions. If you would rather fly than take the boat or bus, you will need a very flexible travel schedule. There are weekly bus services to both Fuerte Olimpo and Bahía Negra in the dry season and daily buses between Concepción and Vallemí. Rain and mechanical problems have been known to cause delays along the way. Although buses make short stops, it is best to bring your own food and water. Road conditions make regular ground transportation impossible during the rainy season.

Languages on the Riverboats

Most of the crew members speak a mixture of Guaraní and Spanish (*Jopará*), but as you make your way further upriver you will hear several other languages. At Puerto Leda and Puerto Casado you are likely to catch snippets of Korean from members of the Moon sect who have established colonies in the area. Many Brazilians ride the boats to get to cattle ranches upriver and speak more Portuguese than Spanish. As you pass indigenous communities such as Puerto Guaraní, Puerto Esperanza, and 14 de Mayo, the balance of indigenous languages will shift from Guaraní to Ishir. The difference between the sounds of the two languages is striking and indicative of the difference between the two indigenous cultures.

Departamento Alto Paraguay – The Pantanal

Located in the very heart of South America, the Pantanal is the largest freshwater wetland in the world. Extending over a large portion of Brazil, as well as Bolivia and Paraguay, the Pantanal is over 140,000 square kilometers in size. The southernmost extension of the Pantanal is located within the Upper Paraguay River Basin which empties into the Paraguay River. Encompassing most of the department of Alto Paraguay, this is the country's least populated and most biologically rich area, home to hundreds of species of flora and fauna. The best towns along the river from which to experience the beauty of the Paraguayan Pantanal are Fuerte Olimpo (capital of the department of Alto Paraguay) and Bahia Negra, the country's northernmost town. Both are accessible by riverboat, bus, and airplane although the last two are highly subject to weather conditions during the rainy season (October to March). The Aquidaban boat (see Lancha Aquidaban, p307) is the most dependable mode of transportation, but also slowest.

Alto Paraguay is one of Paraguay's poorest and most remote regions with very little in the way of tourism infrastructure. Expect to be roughing it unless you pay for a private guided tour and transportation. Despite these setbacks, the incredible concentration of flora and fauna, coupled with the scarcity of commercialized tour operations makes a trip to the Paraguayan Pantanal a rewarding adventure and a must for any nature lover (especially bird watchers).

Lying at a lower elevation than surrounding areas, the Pantanal is a large alluvial plane throughout which a wide variety of ecological sub-regions are found. During rainy season up to 80 percent of the region is flooded. The Pantanal functions as a huge sponge soaking up rain water. This absorbing action causes an important buffering effect that protects the southern regions of both the Paraguay and Paraná Rivers from flooding. The rainy season's elevated water levels in the north can take up to six months to arrive downriver. The name Pantanal comes from "*pántano*," the Spanish and Portuguese word for swamp, though during the dry season the water recedes and the marshlands turn into grass-covered savannahs.

The Pantanal is home to hundreds of birds species and is a popular stopover for migrating flocks. With its distinctive black head, red collar, and enormous white

Fishing in the Paraguay River

Subsistence Fishing

Indigenous communities have survived for hundreds of years along the banks of the Paraguay River, and fishing is an integral part of their culture and tradition. You will see many people, including small children, fishing from the river banks, often using nothing more than a line with a hook. Others fish in the river itself, silently weaving through the water hyacinths in small wooden canoes and row boats. Many prefer to improve their odds with large nets stretched across the water. In theory there is a fishing ban in place from November to December, although for many respecting the *veda* is problematic as it means giving up a significant source of food and income.

Sport Fishing

Paraguay has yet to exploit the river's plentiful fish for sport fishing purposes. Most sport fishing boats along the river depart from Brazilian town of Porto Murtinho (opposite Carmelo Peralta). A number of Porto Murtinho based tour operators offer multi-day fishing trips on the river that include daily fishing excursions in motorboats accompanied by private fishing guides and cabins with amenities such as air conditioning and television.

Eating Fish

Given the prevalence of fish, it can be surprisingly hard to find restaurants serving fish based dishes. Savoring the river's bounty takes advanced planning. Ask around for suggestions on the best place to eat fish and then notify them of your desire to eat a fish based meal (a couple of hours advanced notice should do). Make sure to pre-arrange a price and find out just how much you will be getting – a plate or a pan-full. *Chupín de pescado* is a casserole made with tomatoes and onions, topped with melted cheese. It is almost always a good choice, especially when made with *surubí*.

body, the jaibirú is the world's largest stork and the easiest bird to spot. The enormous flocks of jaibirú that gather along the river and inland lagoons are truly an amazing sight to see, but even the sight of a single jaibirú, is likely to make your day. The jaibirú (or "*tuyuyu*" in Guaraní meaning "swollen neck") is endearingly awkward on land but graceful once it is in the air.

Caimans, or *yacarés*, are the most prevalent aquatic animals, present in the thousands (see How to Spot a Yacaré, p319). Capybaras, the world's largest rodents, can also be seen swimming in the river, ducking back and forth along the *camalotes* making use of their large webbed feet. Rarer still are giant river otters which make their nests along the river banks. The river is home to over 263 fish species, the most well-known include *surubí*, *pacú*, *pintado*, *dorado*, and piranha (see Fishing in the Paraguay River, p312).

The area's larger animals, including the marsh deer (*ciervo de los pántanos*), giant anteater and tapirs, are harder, but not impossible, to spot. A combination of experienced guides, patience, and a little luck will increase your chances of seeing them. Most elusive (and prized by poachers) are the jaguars and pumas.

Along with the more enjoyable and welcome animals, there are plenty of insects. Mosquitoes are particularly abundant during the rainy season, and turning a headlamp on at night will inevitably result in being swarmed by flying insects of all sorts. Repellant and protective clothing will allow you to concentrate more on sightseeing than bug swatting.

Lilac flowered water hyacinths (known as "*camalotes*" in Spanish, "*aguapé*" or "*aguapey*" in Guaraní), float along the river providing protection for birds and other animals. Massing together into *camalotales* these plants create an ever shifting labyrinth that is fascinating to watch but presents a real navigation challenge for smaller boats. They can sometimes block the entrance to narrow tributaries entirely – anyone journeying past Bahía Negra to the shallow Negro River needs to make sure their motorboat is properly equipped to handle this possible complication.

From high points it seems the Pantanal is an ocean of palm trees, called *karanday*. These trees are used to their maximum potential by the area's inhabitants. Most houses are constructed from *karanday*, and the indigenous use the palm's leaves to weave baskets, hats, and other goods, some for utilitarian purposes and others for sale to tourists.

Although greatly reduced by exploitation from the tannin industry (see Carlos Casado and the Tannin Industry, p314), there are still significant *quebracho* forests in the region.

For more information on the Paraguayan Pantanal check out "Gran Pantanal Paraguay" written and photographed by wildlife photographer (and former Peace Corps Volunteer) Emily Horton.

The dry season (April to September) is the best time to visit the Pantanal; roads are more reliable and the temperatures less sweltering, making for a more comfortable and accessible experience. The end of the dry season is particularly good for birding as this is when birds are nesting. During the rainy season, travel to the Pantanal is very difficult due to road conditions. The intense heat and increased presence of mosquitoes are also contributing factors for making the rainy season less than ideal. Should you visit the Pantanal between October and March, expect most of your travel to be done by boat.

Carlos Casado & the Tannin Industry

Saddled with debt in the aftermath of the disastrous Triple Alliance War in the late 1800's, the Paraguayan government sold vast quantities of national territory at rock bottom prices to foreigners. In 1886, the Argentine company, "Empresa Carlos Casado," purchased over five and a half million hectares of land in the Paraguayan Chaco (representing about 15 percent of the total land in this region). The company exploited the Chaco's vast *quebracho* forests for the production of tannin, at the time the most widely used chemical for curing leather.

The wood of the Schinopsis Balansae is a deep red color and extremely dense and hard, thus earning the name "red axe breaker" or *Quebracho Colorado*. This tree is native to the eastern Paraguayan Chaco, found mostly in the northern areas of the Presidente Hayes department and across the entirety of the department of Alto Paraguay. *Quebracho* extract, obtained by cooking *quebracho* chips, is about 65 percent pure tannin, making it an ideal source of tannin for the leather tanning industry.

At its peak, the Casado Company's *quebracho* extraction plant established in Puerto Casado was producing up to 2,400 tons of tannin monthly. Other companies got in on the game establishing tannin production factories in nearby Puerto Pinasco, Puerto Sastre, and Puerto Guaraní. All made use of the existing indigenous populations, subjecting them to extreme work conditions for little pay. In order to reach *quebracho* forests further inland, the Carlos Casado company built a railway extending 145 kilometers westward to a point called Punto Riel (the rails themselves were made from *quebracho*, owing to the wood's extreme hardness and durability). The first wave of Mennonite immigrants arrived by boat to Puerto Casado in the late 1920's to colonize land purchased from the Casado company itself. In order to reach their final destination deep in the Central Chaco, they traveled by train to Punto Riel, and then continued on in horse-drawn carts (see The Mennonites, p292). During the Chaco War, the railway was used to transport everything from soldiers to tanks and supplies to the frontlines. Puerto Casado's key role during the war earned the new name "La Victoria" (the Victory).

At its height, the Carlos Casado company fueled a booming economy in Alto Paraguay, but once the tannin industry declined, the company's dealings left a bitter aftertaste still present to this day. Although land was donated for the creation of a municipality, the majority of the town's infrastructure remained in company hands. In the year 2000, the entire town of Puerto Casado and much of the surrounding area was sold off to the Unification Church of Reverend Sun Moon (better known as "the Moonies.") The result has been an ongoing land dispute involving the company, the Moon sect, the Paraguayan government, and the town's 6,000 plus residents, as well as the region's Maskoi Indians who demand legal ownership of their ancestral lands.

Paraguayan composer Rubén Domínguez Alvarenga describes Puerto Casado's history in his song *"Puerto Casado"*:

"Little town of mine where I was born, you were left alone, your sons emigrated because all is finished. The *quebracho* is gone, the factory closed down. There is no more work. And the land, although Paraguayan, has another owner. My father fought during the war, my little town, defending the Chaco's soil in '32. But it was all in vain, the enemy was not Bolivian, but that fellow countryman that gave the Chaco's land to an usurper."

Puerto Casado remains a historic example of exploitation of Paraguay's natural resources and people by foreign companies, an issue still present today in much of the Chaco with the presence of large scale Brazilian soy and cattle farms.

Guided Tours to the Pantanal

If taking a guided tour to the Pantanal, be sure to inquire whether visas to Brazil are necessary. Some companies prefer to access the Pantanal through Brazil by crossing over the border in Pedro Juan and traveling to Porto Murtinho, making use of the country's superior highway system. Others may simply include stops in the Brazilian Pantanal on their itinerary. Some tourists find it is worthwhile to pay the premium for more comfortable travel conditions as well as guides experienced in both the region's wildlife and possible travel hazards. Be sure to specify a need for English speaking guides if necessary.

FUERTE OLIMPO

Fuerte Olimpo offers visitors an interesting cross of Pantanal experiences from the historic to the natural. Fuerte Borbón, a semi-abandoned fort dates back to the colonial era when the Spanish and Portuguese were busy carving up the region. The small indigenous museum is a testament to the region's original inhabitants, still surviving to this day in the nearby community of Virgen Santísima. Fuerte Olimpo is the last large town along the river, after which the region's communities become fewer and further between. For this reason, Fuerte Olimpo is known as the "*puerta de entrada*," or gateway, to the Pantanal. Nestled between the Cerros Tres Hermanos (Three Brothers Mountains), Fuerte Olimpo's hilly territory makes for amazing views of the surrounding Pantanal. The town's church plaza and bell tower offer great views in exchange for minimal exertion. More of a hike but worth the payoff, is the 500 plus stair walkway leading to a lookout point at the top of the middle of the three mountains. There is also the possibility of venturing out in private boat or vehicles to get a closer look at the region's wildlife along the river and in inland lagoons.

Fuerte Olimpo is a good choice for travelers who want a taste of the Pantanal without going all the way to Bahía Negra. As the official capital of the Alto Paraguay province, it is a bit more accessible and populated. It is still, however, remote, and facilities for tourists are limited.

Tourism Information Office Inquire here about guided trips along the river for both sightseeing and fishing as well as visits to the Virgen Santísima Ishir community. If the office is closed, look for tourism secretary, Alcides Gallagher, in the Municipal office across the street or Hotel AA (he is the owner). *Tel: 0497 281 155, located in a small building in the Plaza Municipal, Mon-Fri 7am-3pm*

Puerto Pinasco: Birthplace of Paraguay's "Friendship Day"

July 30th is celebrated as the *Día de la Amistad*, or Friendship Day, in Paraguay. This celebration was created in 1958 in Puerto Pinasco by Dr. Ramón Artemio Bracho. Along with a small group of friends, Dr. Bracho founded the *"Cruzada Mundial de la Amistad"* (World Friendship Crusade). Their call for a celebration of friendship with an official *"Día de la Amistad"* quickly gained traction and is now celebrated (on different dates) throughout Latin America.

On the *Día de la Amistad* people gather with friends to share a meal or drinks and exchange small gifts. Co-workers might go out to lunch together to celebrate. Gift giving is informal, although some groups like to organize white elephant exchanges called "*amigo invisible*" (invisible friend). Gifts need not be large or fancy, in fact they are almost always a little cheesy. Should you be in Paraguay during the *Día del Amigo*, take the opportunity to thank anyone who has been friendly or helpful to you by wishing them a "*feliz día del amigo*" via phone call or text message, or give them a small present. It will be greatly appreciated.

The Paraguay River

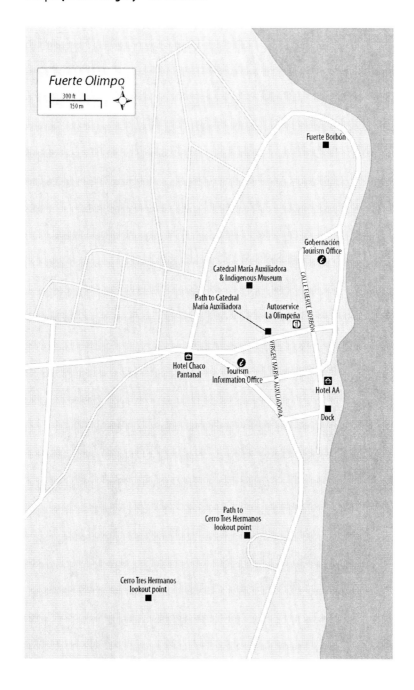

Fuerte Olimpo

300 ft
150 m

N

Fuerte Borbón

Gobernación
Tourism Office

Catedral María Auxiliadora
& Indigenous Museum

Path to Catedral
María Auxiliadora

Autoservice
La Olimpeña

CALLE FUERTE BORBÓN

Hotel Chaco
Pantanal

Tourism
Information Office

VIRGEN MARÍA AUXILIADORA

Hotel AA

Dock

Path to
Cerro Tres Hermanos
lookout point

Cerro Tres Hermanos
lookout point

Gobernación Tourism Office Another tourism information office, this one is located within the Gobernación building. They can also help plan outings around Fuerte Olimpo and to the Virgen Santísima community. See or call Juan Batista de León. *Tel: 0497 281 005, the large two story brick Gobernación building is located three and a half blocks upriver from the docks on the right-hand side of the pretty Calle Fuerte Borbón double avenue, Mon-Fri 7am-3pm*

Catedral María Auxiliadora & Indigenous Museum

Fuerte Olimpo's main church is impressive in both its construction and surroundings. The large, stone church features two bell towers housing Italian church bells and a large German clock. The spacious stone plaza in front of the Catedral de María Auxiliadora acts as a terrace overlooking the river. For a view from even higher up, you can walk up the bell tower, stopping to visit the small Indigenous Museum located on the second floor. The museum features artifacts and photographs of the daily life and traditions of nearby indigenous communities. *To get to the church walk upriver along Virgen María Auxiliadora street (the main paved road running parallel to the river) to the pretty stone walkway leading a short distance uphill. If the entrance to the museum is locked, inquire in the church or with the priest whose office and living quarters are located along the right-hand side of the church.*

Fuerte Borbón

Fuerte Borbón was constructed by the Spanish in 1792 in order to protect this remote area from incursions by Portuguese *bandeirantes*. The Spanish also found themselves fighting local Mbya indigenous tribes understandably resistant to their presence. After independence Paraguay's first leader, Dr. Francia, renamed the fort and surrounding areas Fuerte Olimpo as a symbol of Paraguay's severed ties with Spain. Wariness of neighbors to the east continued past Paraguay's declaration of independence, and in 1817, the fort was rebuilt and fortified. Remnants of the stone fort include the outer walls and a small lookout tower. The fort offers a nice view of a sheltered bay where you can see wildlife as well as local families fishing. Unfortunately, there is no sign explaining the fort's historical significance. *To get there head upriver from the docks along the paved double avenue Calle Fuerte Borbón or the retaining wall. The steps up to Fuerte Borbón are located just after passing the Gobernación building and the local hospital.*

Dealing with the "Tuju"

Mud, or *"tuju"* as it is called in Guaraní, is a major factor of life for people in the Paraguayan Chaco. Alto Paraguay's clay and silt ground quickly turns to mush during a rainfall. This can spell disaster for anyone planning on traveling through Alto Paraguay in a vehicle. Don't risk it during the rainy season, or you may end up stuck. Even walking short distances can be complicated – remember, there's no sturdy sidewalk to provide stable ground. Make sure to wear shoes with traction, walk slowly, and realize that at some point you will probably end up flat on your rear end in the mud. Just chalk it up to a Chaco merit badge and move on.

Cerro Tres Hermanos Look Out Point

The best view of the area is undoubtedly obtained by ascending the 500 plus step walkway on the middle of the three hills or *cerros*. From the lookout point on top you can see the Pantanal as it stretches for miles and miles across Paraguay to the east and Brazil to the west. The lack of infrastructure in sight gives you a good idea of how remote and lush the province of Alto Paraguay can be. Bring lots of mosquito repellant and water and avoid the mid-day heat. *To get to the path walk inland one block from the docks and then head about 300 meters downriver before taking your first left and head to the end of the block. The entrance to the walking path is not clearly marked so it is best to ask someone for directions to "el mirador" or "la antenna de COPACO."*

Nature Trips

There are small boats and local guides available to lead day trips along the river entering into smaller tributaries to observe flora and fauna. Expect to pay between Gs. 300,000 to 600,000 depending on the size of your group and boat. Make sure to double check whether you'll need to bring own food, and if you want to fish, ask about supplies. Inquire with Alcides Gallagher at the Tourism Information Office or Hotel AA or with Juan Batista de León at the Gobernación's tourism office.

Lodging

Hotel Chaco Pantanal Located about four blocks from the docks at the base of one of the three *cerros*, Hotel Chaco Pantanal has clean and comfortable accommodations. There is a choice of rooms with a fan or air conditioning. Owner, Asuncena Gallagher, is very friendly. *Tel: 0497 281 021, 0981 267 457, from the docks head towards the Municipal Office, and continue one block past the end of the triangular Plaza Municipal. The hotel is on the right-hand side of the road. Gs. 35,000 per person for rooms with fan, Single Gs. 80,000 with A/C, Double Gs. 120,000 with A/C. A/C, fan*

Hotel AA Overlooking the river, Hotel AA is the most scenic option in town, although not the most comfortable. Rooms are a little cramped with an assortment of bunk beds and queens. Each has a private bathroom, fan, screened in windows, and a screen door. All open out on to the nice wraparound deck with a great view. Hotel AA is well known for its locally caught fish dishes (other meals can be requested as well), though the kitchen's cleanliness leaves much to be desired. *Tel: 0497 281 017, The hotel is visible from the dock, but the entrance is around the bend. Leaving the dock take a right past the large oil drums, and continue till the end of the block. Take another right, and walk to the side entrance down a small walkway between two buildings, Gs. 40,000 per person, fan*

The Ishir

Throughout their history, the Ishir tribe (also known as the Chamacoco) has lived along the banks of the Paraguay river. With deep cocoa complexions, the Ishir have a look that is very distinctive from the majority of Paraguay's indigenous groups. The Ishir tribe is known by outsiders for their large ceremonial feather head and neck pieces, body painting, as well as decorative bags made of caraguatá plant fibers. Ogwa, an Ishir shaman born in Bahía Negra, is perhaps the most well-known indigenous artist in Paraguay. His line drawings and paintings depict the natural world in which the Ishir survive as well as Ishir myths and legends. His works are on display in the Museo del Barro and silkscreened onto tote bags and t-shirts in Overall Artesanías, both in Asunción. This tribe has been studied extensively by anthropologist Ticio Escobar (*www.ticioescobar.com/*) whose works include *"The Curse of Nemur In Search of the Art, Myth, and Ritual of the Ishir"* and by musicologist and anthropologist Guillermo "Mito" Sequera whose works include *"Tomáráho: La Resistencia Anticipada."* The Museo Andrés Barbero and Museo del Barro in Asunción and the Museo Guido Boggiani in San Lorenzo have good displays about the Ishir tribe.

Food

Autoservice La Olimpeña This decent sized store is a good choice for stocking up on basics. The owners are very friendly and interesting to talk to as they used to operate a market river boat which sunk a number of years ago (there is a painting of it on the wall above the cash register). The house diagonally opposite the double avenue sometimes sells meat *empanadas* and cake. *Tel: 0497 281 059, Aviadores del Chaco and General Caballero, Mon-Sun 7am-12pm, 3pm-9pm*

Getting There

The road to Fuerte Olimpo is accessed via a turn off on the Trans Chaco Highway at km 415, known as *Cruce de Los Pioneros* (from here it is 360 kilometers away) or from Loma Plata (330 kilometers away). A dirt road leads north from here to Toro Pampa, where it turns east to Fuerte Olimpo. The final stretch between Toro Pampa and Fuerte Olimpo is well known for being rich in bird life, especially flocks of large jaibirú storks. However this should only be attempted in a 4-wheel drive vehicle during the dry season with proper supplies (see Driving in the Chaco, p284) and a guide as it is easy to get lost and there are few people on the road to provide help if needed.

Stel Turismo operates a twice-weekly bus services along the 770 kilometers from Asunción to Fuerte Olimpo. Buses depart on Mondays and Fridays at 7pm arriving around the afternoon the following day, Gs. 165,000. They leave Fuerte Olimpo on Monday and Thursdays around midday arriving in the following morning in Asunción. This schedule is subject to change due to weather and road conditions. During the rainy season the eighteen hour bus ride is likely to take much longer due to delays along the way.

The Aquidaban arrives from Concepción on Thursdays between noon and 5pm. On its return from Bahía Negra, it arrives in Fuerte Olimpo between midnight and 3am. If you are traveling by boat from Bahía Negra, it is best to make your accommodation reservations ahead of time (see Lancha Aquidaban, p307).

TAM military airlines will sometimes stop in Fuerte Olimpo during their Asunción-Bahía Negra trips. However, this is not a particularly reliable option. Contact Sonia Suarez 0983 454 486 to confirm if a stop in Fuerte Olimpo is planned.

How to Spot a Yacaré

Yacaré, or caiman, can be easily spotted sunning themselves along the river banks, their mouths open in wide grins. They are a bit harder to pick out once submerged in the water, but not impossible. Look for small black protrusions in the water – usually only their two eyes will come up, but you can sometimes also spot bumps on their tails. It is also possible to both see and hear female *yacarés* when they are in heat as they make loud pig-like grunts and snorts and raise their heads and tails high out of the water.

BAHÍA NEGRA

Bahía is the last settlement along the Paraguay River before the border with Bolivia. This is a very remote area with no significant populations nearby in neighboring Brazil or Bolivia. The town's location makes it an ideal departure point for trips further upriver to see undisturbed wildlife. The river's flora and fauna seem to increase exponentially just north of Bahía Negra (you are not very likely to see animal life within Bahía Negra itself). From Bahía Negra you can take day trips out onto the river, head inland, or visit the Guyra Field Station further upriver in order to truly immerse yourself in nature (see Venturing Farther into the Wild, p323).

The Paraguay River

Bahía Negra exhibits the Paraguayan Pantanal's raw beauty as well as the harsh realities faced by of one of the country's most removed communities. The town was of strategic military importance during the Chaco War and housed a large military presence during the Stroessner dictatorship but has since declined in size and importance. Until recently, electricity for the entire town was provided by a generator that only ran from 6am to midnight. The town's first cell phone tower (Tigo) was installed in 2008 providing Bahía Negra with a significant link to the outside world. As with most other riverside communities of Alto Paraguay, area cattle ranches are the main source of employment. Most of the town relies on fishing both as a business and for personal consumption. Daily you can see people in small boats out on the river as well as young children casting fishing lines from the shore. There is very little small scale agriculture and most rely on the Aquidaban boat for produce.

There is not much to see in the town itself, however *Bahía negrenses*, as they are called, are a friendly bunch. You can easily spend a couple of hours walking around town talking with folks, especially if you are willing to partake in *tereré* or buy a couple of beers. The guys from the Naval base, most of whom are in Bahía Negra on assignment, tend to be especially talkative. If you arrive on the Aquidaban you are likely to be greeted by fellow passengers around town throughout the length of your stay.

The Municipal office can often provide basic tourist information and help arrange for lodging with area families. They will most likely send you to the Eco Club for tour information. *Tel: 021 490 237 (however this number is not particularly useful as it rings in Asunción), the office is a two-story yellow and red building on the right-hand side of JJ Sanchez about one block downriver from the docks.*

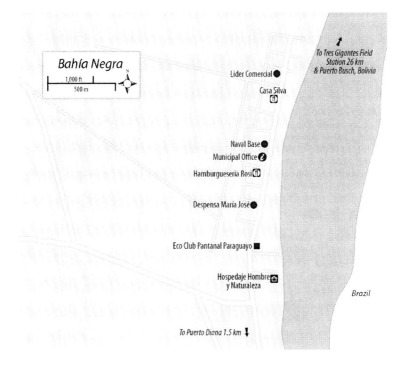

Eco Club Pantanal Paraguayo

A community organization of local youth dedicated to conservation efforts in the area. They operate the town's radio station Bahía Negra Poty and also have a small cultural center. Members are enthusiastic and can provide walking tours of Bahía Negra and Puerto Diana. Most are still in school though, so expect to work around their schedules. *Tel: 0982 559 789 (Nilza Frutos) or 0982 814 022 (Saul Arias), a small log building with a radio tower out front about six blocks from the docks on the left-hand side*

Puerto Diana

Puerto Diana is one of the largest Ishir communities in Alto Paraguay, located about a three kilometers from Bahía Negra. Walk or drive there with a local guide to see how the Ishir make use of the area's palm trees for housing, view the production of indigenous handicrafts, and meet community members. It is also possible to arrange fishing trips with community members. Though you can also venture off on your own, it is best to go accompanied by someone from Bahía Negra that knows the community well. Contact Cesar (*Tel: 0981875651*) the chief of Puerto Diana to arrange for a walking tour that includes nature trails for Gs. 40,000. Be sure to avoid the mid-day sun and take plenty of water.

River Guides

Don Aliche (*Tel: 0984 155 339*) is an extremely knowledgeable local guide, available to lead motorboat trips along the river. He knows a lot about the area's wildlife and will make a concrete effort to help you spot as many animals as possible. Should he not be available, contact Guyra or Hombre y Naturaleza. They will be able to recommend knowledgeable guides with proper equipment (and language skills, if necessary). As always, when hiring a guide, make sure to be very specific about whether prices include fuel. Those who are interested in doing so can inquire about fishing excursions in a traditional dugout canoe instead of a motorboat.

Lodging

Hospedaje Hombre y Naturaleza (Centro Ecológico "Onota") Elevated cabin built out of *karanday* logs. Enjoy a beautiful view of the river from the protection/comfort of a screened in porch. Rooms have bunk beds and private bathrooms. Camping facilities are also available and kitchen access is permitted. The lodge serves as a headquarters for Hombre y Naturaleza's Centro Ecológico "Onota." They can arrange for fishing and sightseeing excursions upriver as well as a visit to the Ishir community in Puerto 14 de Mayo. Hombre y Naturaleza also operates lodges in Bolivia. If you wish to continue upriver, they can arrange for transportation to Puerto Suarez (280 kilometers upriver) to visit the "El Tumbador" center next to Laguna Cáceres. *Tel: 0982 898 589 (Mario Bobadilla), 0982 862 543 (Sra Dionisia), located seven blocks from the docks on the left-hand side, Gs. 50,000 per person, camping Gs. 30,000 per person, fan*

Don Aliche's Hospedaje At the time of publishing, Don Aliche, the town's charismatic river guide, is putting the finishing touches on a basic guest house with three small rooms as well as an area for hammocks. *Tel: 0984 155 339. Although since Don Aliche is often on the river and out of cell phone range it is best to ask around for his "hospedaje" once you arrive in Bahía Negra or inquire with his family who run Despensa María José.*

Food & Supplies

There are a several small stores located along JJ Sanchez, the main street running parallel to the river. In addition to the stores listed, there are several families that are able to provide hamburgers, *empanadas*, or other food upon request (most have signs noting "*Empanadas*"). During *siesta* time, most will appear closed but you can still try your luck by clapping and asking if they have prepared food to sell.

Hamburguesería Rosi An open-air fast food joint with a nice, rustic ambience. Enjoy a burger while basking in the cool night breeze. *About one block downriver past the municipal office on JJ Sanchez. Open daily 7pm-11pm, Gs. 7,000-12,000*

Lider Comercial A very nice and tidy grocery store with all the basics as well as cooked meals. Owner Gloria Payá also runs a leather goods and indigenous handi- crafts store next door. Woven baskets and wood carvings from nearby Puerto Diana are well made and well priced. *Tel: 0984 302 309, about three blocks upriver from the docks on the left- hand side of JJ Sanchez, Gloria lives on the premises and is always willing to help visitors, so just clap or knock if the store appears to be closed*

Casa Silva Run by Don Silvia, this small restaurant can prepare *empanadas* on re- quest. *Tel: 0982 329 297, Avenida Coronel Sanchez and Silvio Pettirosi, open upon request, Gs. 2,000-7,000*

Getting There

Given its remote location, it is no surprise that visiting Bahía Negra requires a fair amount of time and a flexible schedule. Those who are pressed for time can fly there and take the boat or bus back – however this is only works if the weekly flight leaves as scheduled.

The Aquidaban is the most reliable method of transportation to Bahía Negra, although unfortunately it is also the slowest. Departing from Concepción on Tuesday mornings it arrives in Bahía Negra around midday Friday. (If you are not thrilled about spending three days on the boat you can knock a day off by taking the bus from Concepción to Vallemí on Tuesday and boarding the boat in Vallemí on Wednesday afternoon. However if the road between Concepción and Vallemí is washed out, the bus ride could take longer than expected.) The Aquidaban departs Bahía Negra on Friday afternoons (about three hours after its arrival) and gets into Concepción around Sunday afternoon. One way fare is Gs. 100,000 and is pro-rated if you are getting off along the way (see Lancha Aquidaban, p307).

Due to time and budget constraints, some travelers may not be able to spend a week in Bahía Negra waiting for the Aquidaban to return. If you are making a roundtrip on the Aquidaban, consider using the time spent docked in Bahía Negra to take a short journey by motorboat further upriver for nature observation. The boat is docked for a couple of hours while merchandise is loaded and unloaded. Call ahead and reserve a river guide to meet you at the port and take you upriver. Make sure to double check the Aquidaban's approximate departure time and request that your guide get you back in time. Should you arrive after the Aquidaban has left, your guide should be able to catch up to the boat – the boat's crew are used to having people board in the middle of the river via motorboat.

Transporte Aero Militar operates a twenty passenger cargo plane that usually departs on Wednesday mornings from Asunción, sometimes making stops in Vallemí and/or Fuerte Olimpo along the way. This is the fastest way to get to Bahía Negra, although the plane's departure can be pushed back to Thursday or Friday or cancelled entirely depending on weather conditions and passenger volume. This should be taken into consideration if you plan to fly to Bahía Negra on Wednesday and take the Aquidaban back on Friday. Flying both ways is ideal but is not often possible. Airfare is Gs. 350,000 one way, but you may also have to pay a per kilo surcharge for luggage. Reservations must be made in advance with Sonia Suarez in Asunción at 0983 454486.

Stel Turismo (*Tel: 021 558 196*) has a weekly bus service during the dry season departing from Asunción Tuesday evenings and arriving in Bahía Negra Wednesday afternoons. The bus departs Bahía Negra on Friday mornings although it will often wait for arriving Aquidaban passengers. The schedule is highly dependent on road conditions so be sure to double check with Stel Turismo before making plans. Poor road conditions and bus maintenance mean the bus can get stuck along the way for several hours and, in some cases, days. Bring food and water just in case. One way tickets cost Gs. 180,000.

By car one heads towards Fuerte Olimpo but continues north past Toro Pampa (instead of heading east) approximately 115 kilometers to Bahía Negra. As with Fuerte Olimpo, this journey should not be attempted outside of the dry season and without the aid of a guide. A 4-wheel drive vehicle loaded with proper supplies is essential (see Driving in the Chaco, p284).

Threats to the Pantanal

The Pantanal is a delicate ecosystem which serves as home to an astonishing amount of animals. It also acts as a regulatory system for the Paraguay River, guarding communities to the south from flooding. Unfortunately, this pristine wilderness is under constant threat by large industries such as mining and agriculture, as well as smaller but equally dangerous enterprises such as poaching. Agriculture in particular is very damaging to the fragile balance of the Pantanal. Clear cutting makes room for grazing cattle while robbing native animals of their habitats. Without trees to hold it in place, soil erodes quicker depositing sediment into the rivers. These may end up re-routed, causing flooding in other areas. Large felines such as jaguars and pumas are seen as nuisances by ranch hands and regularly killed to protect livestock. Both agriculture and mining are responsible for toxins entering the water system. Poachers disrupt the balance of the animal chain by eliminating prized predators such as jaguars and *yacarés*, in turn allowing their respective prey to flourish unchecked. Most of the Brazilian Pantanal is under private ownership and the areas of Bolivia and Paraguay covered by the Pantanal are among the most remote and least populated of both countries. This makes it difficult to enforce existing laws designed to protect the area. Although on the books Paraguay's environmental protection laws are quite good, in reality there are very few resources and little political will to make significant enforcement efforts.

VENTURING FARTHER INTO THE WILD

Los Tres Gigantes Field Station

Run by nature conservation NGO Guyra Paraguay, Los Tres Gigantes is a nature reserve along the banks of the Río Negro which safeguards 15,000 hectares of the beautiful Pantanal ecosystem. The station is named after the three large endangered species that can be found in the region: the Giant Anteater, Giant River Otter and Giant Armadillo. Visiting Los Tres Gigantes is an extraordinary experience bringing you face to face with the Pantanal's rich biodiversity without any tourists. The station has two dorm-style bedrooms and one large double, each with their own bathroom. The kitchen is available to prepare food, but be prepared to bring supplies. Upstairs includes a screened in porch and downstairs there are hammocks and a nice dining room with reading materials. Although the station is screened, expect to deal with a fair number of insects. The station includes three walking trails that follow the river and then head inland. Be sure to bring lots of repellant. Park guards are a wealth of information, but you need to be proactive if you want guided tours. Do not miss the opportunity to take advantage of their expertise, as they are happy to accompany you both on land and in kayaks along the river. *Tel: 021 229 097, the station is located twenty-six kilometers upriver from Bahía Negra, approximately thirteen kilometers past the confluence of the Negro River and Paraguay River, and is accessible only by motorboat. Reservations must be made ahead of time with Guyra headquarters in Asunción. They can arrange for guided tours around Bahía Negra and Puerto Diana as well as for transportation via motorboat to the station (about US$60 per round trip), though you can shop around Bahía Negra for a better price. US$25 per person without food, US$35 per person full board, Gs. 70,000 per person for day trips, Gs. 30,000 per person for camping.*

Fortín Galpón

In 1908, the ruling Liberal party created Fortín Galpón, a penal colony for Colorado Party political prisoners, along the Verde River. Trapped in a kind of Paraguayan Devil's Island, the prisoners were subjected to the region's many hazards (from pesky insects to dangerous felines), and to innumerable cruelties at the hands of their captors.

CONTINUING NORTH UPRIVER TO BOLIVIA

It is becoming increasingly popular for backpackers to make their way to Bahía Negra, and on to Bolivia by motorboat. The boat ride to Puerto Busch takes about forty minutes, during which time you are likely to see a fair amount of wildlife along the river. The border crossing at Puerto Busch is nothing more than a small military outpost. Though they will take down your information, tourists must officially pass through immigration in Puerto Quijarro (from which you can take the train to Santa Cruz or cross over to Corumbá in Brazil). From Puerto Busch it is about 180 kilometers to Puerto Suarez which, in turn, is about ten kilometers from Puerto Quijarro. A taxi from Puerto Busch to Puerto Suarez costs about US$100 and can be arranged through the military outpost. Don Aliche (see River Guides, p321) has made the trip to Puerto Busch with tourists several times, and Hombre y Naturaleza can help coordinate to get you as far as Puerto Suarez. In order to avoid trouble in Puerto Busch, it is best to have obtained a Bolivian visa ahead of time.

Language Reference

Spanish (in bold text) and Guaraní phrases are provided if both are used commonly. There are many words that even predominantly Guaraní speaking people only use in Spanish. In these cases only the Spanish translation is provided as using the Guaraní translation would not prove useful. Many of the phrases below are a mix of Guaraní and Spanish.

NOTES ON GUARANÍ PRONUNCIATION

Almost all Guaraní words are pronounced with an emphasis on the last syllable, whether or not the word is written with an accent.

Y: pronounced as a "u"

J: pronounced as a "y"

Ch: pronounced as "sh"

Nd: the n is mostly silent

Mb: the b is mostly silent

> An useful, tongue in cheek, online resource for learning Guaraní is the *"Lets talk Guaranime"* blog at www.guaranime.blogspot.com written by RPCV Paulette Perhach

Guaraní has a number of nasal sounds indicated with a ~ above the vowel. Mastering the differences between a normal vowel and a nasal one can be quite tricky and is probably not worth worrying about unless you have an extended stay in Paraguay and are working closely with predominantly Guaraní speaking communities.

That Tricky Y

The Guaraní "y" is a difficult sound to describe. The sound comes from the back of the throat rather that the front of the mouth. When pronouncing it can be helpful to press your teeth together and stick your jaw out slightly.

GREETINGS

¿Qué tal? / *¿Mba'eichapa?:* How are you?

¿Cómo te va? / *¿Mba'e la porte? ¿Mba'eteko pio?:* How's it going?

¿Ha upei?: And then? (literal translation); What's up? (colloquial translation)

Buenos días: Good morning.

Buenas tardes: Good afternoon.

Buenas noches: Good night.

Common responses:

¿Bien, y vos? / *¿Iporã, ha nde?*: Good, and you?

Más o menos / *omarchá*: So-so.

Adios: Goodbye (often used as an informal greeting)

Nos vemos / *Jajotopata:* See you later.

Ahata aju: I'm leaving and then I'll return (literal translation); goodbye with an understanding that you probably won't be returning (colloquial translation).

Vení un poco / *Ejumina:* Come here.

Sientate / *eguapy:* Sit down.

Gracias / *graciamante*: Thank you.

De nada: You're welcome.

No hay porqué: There is no reason (literal translation); You're welcome (colloquial translation).

FOOD & BEVERAGE

Tengo hambre / *che vare'a:* I'm hungry.

Estoy satisfecho / *che ryvatã:* I'm full.

Bien frío / *ho'ysã porã:* Nice and cold.

Muy rico, muy delicioso / *heterei:* Very delicious.

Jaha jakaru: Let's eat.

MISCELANEOUS

¿Te gusta Paraguay? / *¿Nde gustá Paraguay?*: Do you like Paraguay?

Me gusta Paraguay / *Che gustá Paraguay*: I like Paraguay.

¿Te hallas (por acá)?: Are you comfortable here?(literal translation); Are you happy? (colloquial translation).

Estoy feliz en Paraguay / *Che avy'a Paraguay pe:* I am happy in Paraguay.

¿De dónde sos? / *Mo'o gua pa nde?*: Where (specifically what country) are you from?

Soy de___ / *Che ___gua:* I'm from ___.

Te digo no más: I'm just saying (literal translation); Just kidding (colloquial translation).

Yo se / *Che aikua'a:* I know.

Yo no sé / *che ndaikua'ai:* I don't know.

Me olvidé / *Che resarai*: I forgot.

Puedo / *Ikatu:* I can.

No puedo / *Ndikatui*: I can't.

Estoy cansado / *Che kane'o*: I'm tired.

Estoy pila'i / *Che pila'i*: I have little battery (literal translation); I have no energy (colloquial translation).

Así no más / *Peichante*: it's fine as is, indicating there is no need for further action.

Sí o sí: Yes or yes (literal translation); no matter what (colloquial translation).

Quiero ver / *Ahechase*: I want to see.

¿Quieres ver? / *¿Rehechase?*: Do you want to see?

Difícil / *Hasy*: Difficult.

Fácil / *Ndahasyi*: Easy.

Falso / *Gua'u*: Fake.

Caro / *Hepy*: Expensive.

Barato / *Ndahepyi*: Cheap.

Grande / *Guazu* / *Tuicha*: Big.

Hace calor / *Hakú*: It's hot (see Haku etere'i, p53).

Pequeño / *Michi*: Small.

Supermercado *(masc)*: Supermarket.

Mercado (masc): Market.

Almacén (masc), *despensa (fem)*: Small (usually family run) store.

Ferretería (fem): Hardware store.

Farmacia (fem): Pharmacy.

Banco (masc): Bank.

Casa de cambio (fem): Money exchange house.

Pasaje (masc): Ticket and ticket fee.

Baño (masc): Bathroom.

Baño moderno (masc): Bathroom with running water.

Letrina (fem): Latrine.

Pozo (masc)/ Ykua (masc): Well.

LANGUAGE COMPREHENSION

¿Qué significa ___? / *¿Mba'epa he'ise ___?*: What does ___ mean?

¿Cómo se dice ___? / *¿Mba'eichapa oje'e ___?*: How do you say?

Che añeha'a añe'e Guaraní: I'm trying to speak Guaraní.

COMMON SUFFIXES

These Guaraní suffixes are routinely added to Spanish words.

Hina: equivalent to "ing," i.e.: *"Estamos trabajando hina"* (We are working)

Pá/ pi'o/ piko: used to indicate a question, i.e.: *"¿A dónde pi'o te vas?"* (Where are you going?) or *"¿Por qué, piko?"* (Why?)

Kuera: indicating plural, i.e.: *Turista kuera* (tourists)

SUPERLATIVES

'i: small, either in size or amount.

Ete/ eterei: Very, i.e.: *Haku eterei* (very hot)

ASKING FOR DIRECTIONS

¿Dónde queda? / *¿Mo'o opyta?:* Where is ___? ____

¿Qué colectivo va a ___? / *¿Mba'e colectivo oho ____pe?:* What bus goes to ___?

¿Está lindo el camino? / *¿Iporã la tapé?:* Is the road in nice?

¿Está feo el camino? / *¿Ivaí la tapé?:* Is the road ugly (meaning in bad shape)?

¿Queda lejos? / *¿Opytá mombury?:* Is it far?

¿Queda cerca? / *¿Opytá agui?:* Is it close?

Quiero ir a ___ / *Ahase ___ pe:* I want to go to ___.___

¿Cuántos kilómetros? / *¿Mboy kilómetros?:* How many kilometers?

Allá / *amoité:* Over there.

Aquí / *ko'a pe:* Here.

Ahora / *ko'anga:* Now.

Ruta (fem): Literally "route" in Spanish this refers to the main highway.

Asfaltado (masc) / *ruta hu (fem):* Paved road – the Guaraní translation is "black road." Directions often involve *"Sigue el asfalto/asfaltado"* meaning follow the paved road.

Camino de tierra (masc) / *tapé pyta (pronounced "putá") (masc):* dirt road – the Guaraní translation is "red road."

Empedrado (masc): Cobblestone road.

Tapé po'i (fem): Foot path, in Guaraní "fine or thin road."

Doble avenida (fem): Double avenue, a street with a median in the middle.

Picada (fem): Trail – new roads cut into the jungle or wilderness.

Rotonda (fem): Roundabout.

Ramal: Turn off/branch road.

Pueblo (masc) / *tava (fem):* Town.

Compañía (fem): Small, remote, community, usually deep in the countryside.

Chacra (*fem*) / *kokue (masc)*: Agricultural fields.

Monte (*masc*): Though **"monte"** technically means woods it is used to refer to any area of wilderness.

LANGUAGE CLASSES

Idiomas en Paraguay (IDIPAR) This established language institute offers foreigners a variety of options for learning Spanish or Guaraní, from intensive courses to private lessons. Can also arrange for home stays. *Tel: 021 447 896, Manduvirá 963 between Colón and Montevideo, www.elmercadoazul.com/idipar.edu.py*

Alliance Française The French cultural center offers Spanish lessons, in addition to French. *Tel: 021 210 382, Estigarribia 1032 almost at EEUU, www.alianzafrancesa.edu.py, see listings under "Cursos" on website for class schedules.*

Mariela Gonzalez A long time Spanish and Guaraní language trainer for the Peace Corps, Mariela is sometimes available to provide private lessons between training cycles. If she is not available she will be able to recommend other skilled language trainers. *Tel: 0981 777 436. Author recommended*

OTHER LANGUAGE RESOURCES

"Guarani-English/English-Guarani Concise Dictionary" by A. Scott Britton is currently the best Guaraní-English dictionary available. Guaraní-Spanish dictionaries, however, are available at most local book stores.

Contact us at
www.otherplacespublishing.com
info@otherplacespublishing.com